W9-BMV-343

First Ladies

1 00

2 of 2
Set 2 00

Also by Carl Sferrazza Anthony

*First Ladies: The Saga of the Presidents' Wives
and Their Power, 1789–1961*

First Ladies

VOLUME II

THE SAGA OF THE PRESIDENTS' WIVES AND THEIR POWER

1961–1990

≈

CARL SFERRAZZA ANTHONY

WILLIAM MORROW AND COMPANY, INC.
NEW YORK

Copyright © 1991 by Carl Sferrazza Anthony

All rights reserved. No part of this book may be reproduced or utilized in any form or by any means, electronic or mechanical, including photocopying, recording or by any information storage and retrieval system, without permission in writing from the Publisher. Inquiries should be addressed to Permissions Department, William Morrow and Company, Inc., 1350 Avenue of the Americas, New York, N.Y. 10019.

Recognizing the importance of preserving what has been written, it is the policy of William Morrow and Company, Inc., and its imprints and affiliates to have the books it publishes printed on acid-free paper, and we exert our best efforts to that end.

Library of Congress Cataloging-in-Publication Data

Anthony, Carl Sferrazza.
   First ladies (vol. 2): the saga of the presidents' wives and their power, 1961-1990
   Includes bibliographical references and index.
   Contents: [1] 1789-1961—[2] 1961-1990.
   1. Presidents—United States—Wives—History.
   2. Presidents—United States—Wives—Biography.
   I. Title.
E176.2.A58   1990   973'.0992   [B]   90-5858
                                                CIP
ISBN 0-688-07704-8 (v. 1)
ISBN 0-688-10562-9 (v. 2)

Printed in the United States of America

First Edition

1 2 3 4 5 6 7 8 9 10

BOOK DESIGN BY JAYE ZIMET

To the happiest time:
autumn auction rights, carriage house cider,
Friday reunions, Mabel Sundays,
old records and Empire, the hearth of home,
the brilliant blue hope of the mid-August skies and shore.
And to thee who gave it.

Acknowledgments

THE MOST SPECIAL thanks to friends and colleagues, Byron Kennard, Meredith Burch, Donnie Radcliffe, Edward and Rita Purcell, and Hilla Del Re for their longtime interest, support, inspiration, and suggestions. Agent Michael Hamilburg took enthusiastic interest in the project, and editor Lisa Drew had monumental patience and thorough commitment. She, along with David Means and Bob Shuman, put up with incessant requests.

For understanding through the difficult years of researching and writing of the book, and scouting material, I am grateful to Glenn Pinder, Jim Elder, Carrie and Sue Scott, Duke Zeller, Bill Hitchcock, Amy La Guardia, Michael Del Villar, Eric Michael, Louise Lang, Robert Sierralta, Alan Cohen, Louise Cayne, Barbara Zacharek, Donna Smith, Arlene Alligood, Kevin DiLallo, Josephine Cerone, Richard and Connie Brousell, Deenie Howett, Don Fraher, Brian Latker, Jerry Haft, Virginia Blodgett, Peter Easley, Dean Hara, Peter Klein, Jacqueline Dubois, John Fitzgerald, John Harper, Lyndon Booser, Sy Loewen, Camlyn Craig, Chris Edwards, Sarah Smith, V. V. Harrison, Lester Hyman, Robin Roosevelt, Sally Blue, Wesley O'Brien, and Michael Privitera.

Professional colleagues provided support, most especially Margaret Brown Klapthor, curator emeritus of the Division of Political History at the Smithsonian. Roger Kennedy, director of the National Museum of American History, curators Karen Mittelman, Edie Mayo, Kate Henderson, Faith Ruffins, and Herb Collins, and staff member Marilyn Higgins gave helpful suggestions. Rex Scouten, former White House chief usher, now curator, Betty Monkman, and Bill Allman of the Curator's Office put up with frequent questions, always giving an answer. Charles Kelly and Mary Wolfskill of the Manucript Division of the Library of Congress both went beyond and above in pulling items which would be helpful, and lent dimes for the copy machine. Bernard Myer and Gloria Hunter of the White House Historical Association kept an open door to "talk shop." With academic perspective, Betty Caroli, author of a study on aspects of the role, shared insights, and Lewis Gould, author of the eminent study on Beautification, took time to discuss our mutual interest at a conference.

"J. B." West, former White House chief usher, granted a delightful interview in the spring of 1980, on Eleanor Roosevelt, and we subsequently talked of the other First Ladies with whom he worked, illuminating stories he touched on in his book. Thanks also to his hospitable wife, Zella.

Regarding Mamie Eisenhower's post-White House years: Barbara Eisenhower Foltz is the personification of kindness. Her honest observations, wit, and gentle way of correcting misconceptions were impressive. Her son, David, spent a Sunday afternoon answering questions about Mamie's political perspective in her last years, over the telephone. The late Milton Eisenhower gave me a full afternoon in March 1984 full of humorous and warm but also pertinent stories about his sister-in-law, and clarified rumor by providing fact. Mary Jane McCaffree Monroe, Mrs. Eisenhower's staff director, provided tender and funny vignettes of her boss in retirement.

Tish Baldridge gave new insight on Mrs. Kennedy's arts program, as Arthur Schlesinger did on her political instincts. Dave Powers recalled Mrs. Kennedy's role in campaigns as well as November 22. Nancy Tuckerman not only provided her own reminscences as social secretary but facilitated the most minute of questions. Since I was young, she has given warm support. The first White House curator, Jim Ketchum, offered new perspectives on Mrs. Kennedy and her restoration. The late Molly Thayer was frank in her helpful responses. My interview with Liz Carpenter was one of the most helpful for the entire book, a rousing perspective of a reporter who covered First Ladies and worked with one. Katie Louchheim gave permission to use her papers. Sharon Francis gave texture to the personal side of beautification. Bess Abell provided glimpses into the era, and Scooter Miller into the personality of her friend Lady Bird Johnson. Lynda Robb provided an honest and engaging portrait of her mother, as well as her own personal thoughts on the role with an impressive sense of history. Sunny Betty Tilson of Mrs. Johnson's office calmly handled my frantic inquiries—and always took my call.

Helen Smith gave countless hours discussing Mrs. Nixon, Vietnam, and Watergate, and provided press, scheduling, and project resources. Connie Stuart provided lively glimpses of the East Wing. Julie Eisenhower is intelligent, honest, and objective in considering her mother's public role, and fact-checked the most minute details. Her warmth and character shine through. She is an impressive person. Former president Nixon responded to questions about Mamie Eisenhower through his assistant John Taylor, and I thank them both. From the Ford years, I must give special thanks to Jack Ford, who gave well-considered insights into his mother's political instincts. Susan Rose and Patti Matson, who also worked for both Mrs. Nixon and Mrs. Ford, gave time generously out of their schedules. An especial thanks to Ann Cullen, Mrs. Ford's assistant, the first to listen to me. After reading only drafts of early chapters, she provided confidence and opened doors.

One Sunday afternoon, Mary Hoyt gave me almost two hours on the phone, answering every question with thoroughness. Gretchen Poston took time to answer questions volleyed at her from a phone booth in New York. Madeline Edwards and Crystal Williams were patient and attentive to all questions, and friendly in the process. Joel Odlum offered new insights into Mrs. Carter's sense of justice. Many who worked in the Reagan White House provided insights and clarification. I am most grateful to James S. Rosebush, who gave me the chance to work briefly in the East Wing as speechwriter. Elaine Crispen took time to consider my questions and discuss issues. Wendy Toller, Mary Gordon, and Betsy Koons of the Press Office treated me not as a routine writer, but as one recording history. Dodie Kazanjian provided insights early on. In many ways, the project was given a leap by Nancy Reynolds, another example of those who listened to a history and journalism student's idea. Thanks also to Lisa Cavelier, who now runs Mrs. Reagan's office. Ann Grimes shared her perspectives on Mrs. Bush. Press Secretary Anna Perez, Deputy Press Secretary Sondra Haley, and Press Assistant Jay Suchan were incredible in patience and immediate facilitation of questions to Mrs. Bush.

I also want to especially thank the dedicated staffs of the presidential libraries. The FDR Library was patient with my many requests via telephone, as were the Ford and Truman libraries. The Kennedy Library was able to guide me directly to the multitude of their sources. At the Johnson Library, Linda Hanson, Claudia Anderson, and Nancy Smith assisted during my short trip to Austin. At the Eisenhower Library, Thomas Braniger provided expert assistance on resources. The audiovisual staff of the Nixon Archival Project provided material. Mary Closer at the National Archives helped get the Reagan era photos. At the Martin Luther King Library, Mary Ternes guided me through their vast picture archives. I'd like to thank some journalists who've covered the East Wing: Helen Thomas, Nancy Dickerson, Betty Beale, Sarah McClendon, Anne Cottrell Free.

Special thanks to the audiovisual staffs of the presidential libraries and National Archives: Donna Kotterell, James Hill, Phil Scott, Mary Young, Kenneth Hafeli, David Stanhope, and Mary Kloser.

Without the assistance and support of Jay Dutton, this project could never have been completed. Warmest thanks to him.

And finally, I'd like to very much thank Jacqueline Kennedy Onassis, Lady Bird Johnson, Pat Nixon, Betty Ford, Rosalynn Carter, Nancy Reagan, and Barbara Bush. Each answered all my questions, never requested to see the manuscript, and not only complied with follow-up, but several often offered further information. In the late seventies, Mamie Eisenhower answered several questions by handwritten letters. Without the generous cooperation of these First Ladies, the complete story of our own times could not be fully told.

Contents

List of Illustrations

Preview

PRECEDING THIS WORK was a first volume that chronicled the First Ladyship from its inception, in May of 1789, to the January 1961 Inaugural. The opening scene had *Martha Washington* (1789–1797), wife of the first president, making the journey by coach from her home in Virginia, to New York City, then the nation's capital. Through the various eras, other prominent women made their mark on the Ladyship. *Abigail Adams* (1797–1801) was a political partner to her husband, *Dolley Madison* (1801–1817) forged the role of First Lady—for her husband as well as President Jefferson—through her political influence, interactions with the press and public, and undertaking of a special project—to name just her most obvious aspects. Not only was she the first to appear on a magazine cover but, according to tradition, the term "First Lady" was first used in eulogizing her. *Julia Tyler* (1844–1845) was a beguiling and savvy New York debutante who eloped with the incumbent president and scandalized the nation with her audacious coquetry, hedonistic lifestyle, and a joie de vivre that she infused skillfully in the more political aspects of her role. She was the first incumbent to be photographed. *Sarah Polk* (1845–1849), her successor, was an intelligent, albeit judgmental, woman, pious, hardworking, and her president's primary political adviser. *Mary Lincoln* (1861–1865) was perhaps the most vilified—her political power and predilections for material comforts during wartime being the two primary complaints. *Julia Grant* (1869–1877) possessed qualities similar to Mrs. Lincoln's but wholly escaped censure. *Lucy Hayes* (1877–1881) became renowned for banning liquor.

Frances Cleveland (1886–1889, 1893–1896) was quite unlike her predecessors, the most obvious difference being that she entered the role by marrying the president in the White House. Subjected to press and public interest and exploitation as none other before her had been, at twenty-one years old "Frankie" proved to be so much the unwitting celebrity that only forcibly could she maintain her privacy. In the new century, women like *Nellie Taft* (1909–1913) proved that the First Lady could be both traditional hostess and thorough political power. The first publicly to support suffrage, she had tremendous influence over the president. *Ellen Wilson* (1913–1914), continuing in this tradition, is best remembered for her project work to help clear the capital's slum dwellings, though she died before seeing it finished. She was succeeded as wife and First Lady by *Edith Wilson* (1915–1921) who became legendary, accused of being "the first woman President." It was undeniable that she'd held far more personal power over her president during his crippling stroke than any of her peers. As of the opening of Volume Two, Edith is still alive, in Washington, having attended the 1961 Inaugural and admiring Mrs. Kennedy. *Florence Harding* (1921–1923) was part of the line of politically powerful First Ladies, exercising open, public influence in government, sometimes managed with her reliance upon the zodiac readings of her White House astrologer.

Unlike the first volume of this work, the size of which permitted in-depth study of only selected women, in this sequel I've followed each First Lady's entire life, focusing even more on their tenures because of new material made available to me, and the desire to correct misconceptions. There is quite literally a proliferation of material beginning with 1961. The tone of the second text may be slightly different from that of the previous volume. Since books by other authors have overemphasized the speculative and invented or exaggerated material on some of the living former First Ladies, I purposefully strove to emphasize balance. There was no attempt to ban valid critical commentary, for that only reinforces balance. If there was a tendency to accentuate their accomplishments, it was because the women's shortcomings and rivalries are well-known. Their social and political achievements and friendships with each other are less known. In telling an institutional history that involves political, diplomatic, social, and economic events in American history, and in terms of political viewpoint, I strove to tell history from their personal perspective. And, to present political motivation, I've discovered that one must at least attempt to understand human motivation.

I disbelieve the attempts to "rate" them in a "job," categorizing them as "great," or "near-great," a "hostess," or "helpmate." They're all individuals in a role subject to press sophistication and public demands that change from era to era. How can one compare a Mary Lincoln, whose mental health was affected by a physical state that very likely included an illness—diabetes—of which the technology of the day was unaware, to, for example, a Betty Ford, who lived in a time when science permitted cancer to be operable, and psychology was a profession? How fair is it to judge the education of a Lady Bird Johnson, who was able to study at a university, with that of a Julia Tyler, whose possibilities for education were limited by what society deemed improper for a "female" to study? Mrs. Reagan had seen Europe and Asia before becoming First Lady. Mrs. Madison never left America. The only comparisons I found valid were when a shaping of the role was clearly based on a predecessor's view, usually a contemporary one. There is occasionally a First Lady of one era who clearly manages her role, or has the same character traits as one of her long-past predecessors, and its manifestation transcends time. Pat Nixon and Grace Coolidge had the same positive philosophy. Frances Cleveland and Jacqueline Kennedy were treated the same way by the press and reacted similarly.

First Ladies	Term of Incumbency
Martha Washington	1789–1797
Abigail Adams	1797–1801
Martha Jefferson	(died before husband's presidency)
Dolley Madison	1801–1809 (hostess for Jefferson)
	1809–1817
Elizabeth Monroe	1817–1825
Louisa Adams	1825–1829
Rachel Jackson	(died before husband's presidency)
Emily Donelson	1829–1837 (hostesses for Jackson)
Sarah Yorke Jackson	
Hannah Van Buren	(died before husband's presidency)
Angelica Van Buren	1838–1841 (hostess for Van Buren)
Anna Harrison	(husband died before her arrival)
Jane Harrison	1841 (hostess for Harrison)
Letitia Tyler	1841–1842
Priscilla Tyler	1842–1844 (hostesses for Tyler)
Letitia Semple	
Julia Tyler	1844–1845
Sarah Polk	1845–1849
Margaret Taylor	1849–1850
Betty Bliss	(assisted as Taylor hostess)
Abigail Fillmore	1850–1853
Mary Fillmore	(assisted as Fillmore hostess)
Jane Pierce	1853–1857
Abby Means	(assisted as Pierce hostess)
Harriet Lane	1857–1861 (hostess for Buchanan)
Mary Lincoln	1861–1865
Eliza Johnson	1865–1869
Martha Patterson	(assisted as Johnson hostess)
Julia Grant	1869–1877
Lucy Hayes	1877–1881
Lucretia Garfield	1881
Ellen Arthur	(died before husband's presidency)

First Ladies	Term of Incumbency (cont.)
Mary McElroy	1881–1885 (hostess for Arthur)
Rose Cleveland	1885–1885 (hostess for Cleveland)
Frances Cleveland	1885–1889, 1893–1897
Caroline Harrison	1889–1892
Mary McKee	1892–1893 (hostess for Harrison)
Ida McKinley	1897–1901
Edith Roosevelt	1901–1909
Nellie Taft	1909–1913
Ellen Wilson	1913–1914
Edith Wilson	1915–1921
Florence Harding	1921–1923
Grace Coolidge	1923–1929
Lou Hoover	1929–1933
Eleanor Roosevelt	1933–1945
Bess Truman	1945–1953
Mamie Eisenhower	1953–1961
Jacqueline Kennedy	1961–1963
Lady Bird Johnson	1963–1969
Pat Nixon	1969–1974
Betty Ford	1974–1977
Rosalynn Carter	1977–1981
Nancy Reagan	1981–1989
Barbara Bush	1989–present

As Volume Two opens, *Jacqueline Kennedy* has just become First Lady, and although she is thirty-one years old and the press and public focus on her "style," her substance is quite formidable as well, albeit largely unreported. As Volume One chronicles, her creative talents and interests, including poetry, photography, theater, ballet, illustrating, painting, and writing, ripen and take shape. Weeks before the Inaugural, she had set in motion her private goal to not redecorate but restore the White House by commencing a personal in-depth architectural and decorative study of the mansion's history. In the long run, she hopes to write a guidebook. It is a childhood dream. She is also far more her husband's political partner than she lets on: as a Senate wife, she drafted his '56 endorsement of Adlai Stevenson, provided literary quotes for his speeches, and heatedly participated in private political debates with JFK and a circle of their mutual friends, interested particularly in foreign affairs. As a Senate wife, she'd also translated French political and socioeconomic studies for Kennedy's crucial stance on the American involvement in Vietnam.

Lady Bird Johnson is now Second Lady, and though she had striven to try to help Lyndon be nominated as president, during the 1960 campaign she worked the South particularly well, especially on the issue of civil rights. Since childhood, this Texan woman had an acute sensitivity to the natural settings around her, but it was urban blight that she first became aware of as a young Congressional wife who literally followed in the footsteps of Eleanor Roosevelt. Mrs. Johnson is also an old hand at Capitol Hill politics, and not only knows congressional wives Pat Nixon, Betty Ford, and Jacqueline Kennedy, but the more senior women like Mamie Eisenhower, Bess Truman, Eleanor Roosevelt, and Edith Wilson.

Pat Nixon has just "lost" the "election" to the Ladyship to Mrs. Kennedy. After having served eight full years as Second Lady, Pat Nixon has not only become a friend to Mamie Eisenhower but an international goodwill ambassador, creating the first full public role of the vice president's wife's position. Although there are many difficult aspects to political life that she is all too pleased to relinquish, she has developed into a politically savvy adviser to her husband. She has met Mrs. Wilson and Mrs. Truman and attended a speech given by Mrs. Roosevelt.

Betty Ford is the wife of a Michigan congressman, and though living what appears to be a thoroughly conventional life of housewife and mother in suburban Virginia, a sense of feminism and feminist issues had stirred in her for personal reasons, stemming back to the thirties. A Republican, she openly admits to considering Eleanor Roosevelt a role model, maintains her longtime friendships with Pat Nixon and Lady Bird Johnson, and has had an acquaintance-apprenticeship with Bess Truman and Mamie Eisenhower.

Rosalynn Carter is a Georgia housewife whose marital relationship increasingly becomes also a business partnership—from peanut farming to a growing interest in civic affairs. In the segregationist South, Rosalynn is an open integrationist.

Nancy Reagan has been married to Ronald Reagan for several years and is in fact still working as an actress, doing General Electric commercials and television episodes with her husband, who increasingly becomes not only politically conservative but outspoken as such in his role as GE spokesman. Through her parents, Nancy Reagan knows Mamie Eisenhower, and has been in the presence of Grace Coolidge, Eleanor Roosevelt, and Edith Wilson.

Barbara Bush is a Republican housewife and mother in Texas whose husband has political ambitions, and whose father-in-law is the U.S. senator from Connecticut. Her son's reading difficulties sparked an interest in literacy, and bigotry against a black family maid stirs her sensitivity to civil rights. In the fifties, Barbara Bush has already met Jacqueline Kennedy, Pat Nixon, and Eleanor Roosevelt.

And so, now, the chronicle continues, in January 1961.

Someday, I hope that someone will take the time to consider the role of First Lady and assess the many burdens she has to bear and the many contributions that she makes.
—Harry S. Truman
President, 1945–1953

PART I

Camelot and the Turbulent Sixties 1961–1969

What they want is an equality of opportunity, a full partnership with men. . . .
Today feminist and feminine are regarded as contradictory terms: one cannot, it seems, be both, as the suffragettes
once were. By the same token political
and feminine are mutually exclusive.
Politicians by definition are aggressive.
A woman seeking political office must
therefore behave like a woman and not
like a politician since aggressive women
are of course not feminine.

Peggy Lamson
*Few Are Chosen: American Woman in
Political Life Today*, 1969

Cherchez la Femme

IN CONSIDERING THE ENTITY of First Lady, Jacqueline Kennedy thought, "[T]here's so much she can do. Things she cares about that she can help. . . ."

While Jacqueline, who had lived in Washington since she was thirteen, had long had an interest in the history of the White House, she had "never thought much about the role of the President's wife" until JFK won the election, and in the pre-Inaugural period she "developed convictions about what the White House should represent to the country and to the world . . . American excellence."[1]

On her initial working day as First Lady, Mrs. Kennedy asked to meet with David Finley, chairman of the Fine Arts Commission, an old family friend, to broach the idea she had been evolving during the transition. She asked his advice about forming her *own* Fine Arts Committee, to restore the White House, and hoped that he would approve and serve on it. He would, and gave the White House its first gift, his own magnificent highboy.

Her step-uncle, Wilmarth S. Lewis, book collector and Horace Walpole authority, had told the young Jacqueline, "There were three geniuses of the 18th century and two of them were American—Jefferson, Franklin and Diderot." She wondered, rhetorically, "Why shouldn't the White House represent that tradition to the nation and to foreign visitors of state? Why should it not inspire people, make them proud of their country's heritage, not just function as a hotel where official entertainment took place?" To her, "what needed to be done seemed obvious."

She explained simply, "Presidents' wives have an obligation to contribute something. People who visit the White House see practically nothing that dates before 1900 . . . . people should see things that develop their sense of history. . . . I'd feel badly [sic] if I had lived here for four years and hadn't done anything for the house. . . . Like every President's wife, I'm here for only a brief time. I want to do this. . . . Everything in the White House must have a reason for being there. It would be a sacrilege merely to redecorate—a word I hate. It must be restored and that has nothing to do with decoration. It is a question of scholarship. It wasn't a matter of wanting to restore it or not, it was something that had to be done." It was a hard sell. West Wing Press Secretary Pierre Salinger said, "[A] number of people in the government," including JFK, were "largely unenthusiastic at first . . ." Jackie admitted, "I was warned, begged and practically threatened" not to undertake a restoration." But she did.

Her friend Jayne Wrightsman's husband, Charles, suggested that Jackie form a committee under the nation's most distinguished expert on Americana, Henry Francis Du Pont, creator of the famous Winterthur Museum rooms. Later, she stated that "Persuading Henry Du-Pont . . . a Republican, to head this committee was very important, as his reputation would deflect criticism . . . [and] would show that the restoration was for historical, not political, purposes . . ." Mr. Du Pont, she said, "worked tirelessly to help."

The president arranged a lunch with his wife, legal counsel Clark Clifford, and himself. Apprehensive, yet sympathetic to his wife's goals, he wanted the guidance of Clifford, whom he greatly esteemed. Clifford warned her that Americans considered the White House "a sacred cow," and that no request could possibly be made for public funds to be spent on the project. He agreed to help her and to serve on her Fine Arts Commission. He also came up with the idea of establishing a White House Historical Association.

Jacqueline was delighted. She had long understood the value of such associations. Her step-aunt, Annie Burr Auchincloss Lewis, had been the Rhode Island member of the Mount Vernon Ladies Association, and her mother was associated with historic Stratford Hall, the birthplace of Robert E. Lee. She had grown up "seeing the good work" of the Newport Preservation Society.

Clark Clifford drew up the necessary legal documents, and the White House Historical Association was chartered as a nonprofit organization, and established as "a legal entity that would continue to function in future administrations . . . obliged by law to provide a curator . . . and it was expected to do the things other historical associations do." This meant that it could publish books that would bring in revenues. Jacqueline was determined to eventually publish a White House guidebook.

On February 23, 1961, the first step in the restoration process was taken. The White House Fine Arts Committee of fourteen was officially established. At their first meeting, Jacqueline delivered a short speech and cited some of the objects she hoped they could soon acquire. Clifford followed, emphasizing that donations would be tax-deductible. A "Special Advisory Group" was formed, consisting of museum directors, and a Paintings Committee and Library Committee were subsequently established to concentrate efforts on those fronts. In the meantime, Jackie had been exploring.

A century and a half of White House furnishings not sold at auctions in the past had been accumulating in a nearby warehouse. Mrs. Kennedy "spelunked" through it, and immediately recognized some furniture from old books she had been studying. More and more furniture was dusted off, identified, repaired, and brought to the White House. In the mansion itself, she toured every corner, storage space, and closet, "discovering" forgotten treasures. In the Broadcast Room, where the finds were gathered, Jacqueline, in slacks and sweater, became caked in grime, lifting Jackson's chairs to look for identification marks, wiping Lincoln's china, unroping T.R.'s Aubusson rugs. When Irish linen sheets ordered by Lou Hoover were discovered unwrapped, even they were used, in the Queen's Room bed. When photographs of two Monroe chairs appeared in newspapers, Charles Francis Adams, a member of her committee, donated the one he owned and had copies made to complete the original set of twelve. The nationwide response encouraged Jacqueline.

The First Lady distinctly defined her project for the public: ". . . the White House does and must continue to represent the living, evolving character of the Executive Branch of the National Government." She said the restoration's first duty was not to a partisan administration, nor her personal tastes. Her goal was to have at least one object from every presidential family. She sought routine items that were used by presidents and First Ladies, though they weren't readily available for purchase at any price. Those would have to come from the American people—descendants, memorabilia collectors, history buffs, the average citizen.[2]

The acceptance of public gifts raised legal questions that the First Lady asked Clifford to explore. Congressional action was necessary. So, like so many of her predecessors, Jacqueline Kennedy lobbied Congress, and her social secretary said she was "adept at helping along the legislation . . ." Maintenance of the White House technically fell under the Department of Interior, so Jacqueline focused her attention on New Mexico senator Clinton P. Anderson, chairman of the Senate Interior and Insular Affairs Committee.

Senator Anderson was extremely reluctant to accept the First Lady's invitation to afternoon tea, having long avoided becoming "mixed up"—as reporter, and friend of Jacqueline, Molly Thayer wrote—"with women in cultural matters, in which he, as senator, was involved." But he came.

Jacqueline launched into her cause, explaining how she had discovered Lincoln china that nobody had seemed to know about. She pressed her case for some sort of federal legislation that would forever protect such treasures, enable the White House to accept other gifts, and give the mansion museum status. After the meeting, the senator found the arm-twisting painless, and said the "enthusiastic" First Lady "would do a good job!" More important, he said, "I can't let this gal down . . . sometimes in politics one agrees to do something—and never does it—but *this* was different."

On August 15, Senator Anderson introduced "Jackie's bill," number 2422. Shortly after, Texas congressman J. T. Rutherford did the same in the House. Neither bill, in its initial form, passed, but their intents were incorporated into Public Law 87286, reading in part: "Be it enacted by the Senate and House . . . primary attention shall be given to the preservation and interpretation of the museum character of the principal corridor of the ground floor and the principal public rooms on the first floor of the White House . . . Sec. 2. Articles of furniture, fixtures, and decorative objects as are acquired by the White House in the future when similarly so declared, shall thereafter be considered inalienable and property of the White House . . ."[3]

Jacqueline hammered out guidelines on gift acceptance, to avoid conflict of interest from donors who might be involved with government, or those who inflated value for tax deductions. In the end, it was the First Lady who made all decisions on what to accept. To those donors wanting to make cash donations, she would first suggest specific items that were needed, making their gift more relevant. She was no figurehead, but directed and coordinated everything personally with her "capability for detail." Meanwhile, items needed to be identified and repaired before they could be displayed. That called for an expert who was also a historian. "The White House belongs to the American people," she said, "A curator would take care that it is preserved for them." And so, Jacqueline Kennedy met with Dr. Leonard Carmichael, secretary of the Smithsonian, and asked for his guidance. He suggested a Smithsonian employee, Lorraine Pearce, to be succeeded by William Elder, and finally James Ketchum.

Ketchum recalled the day a truck from New Jersey returned White House possessions lent for an exhibition. A door was propped open, and the unpacking slowly began. A woman appeared from nowhere and started removing the items from the back of the truck. When they finished, one of the movers asked Jim Ketchum who she was. Ketchum told him, The First Lady. "The mover's jaw slacked," he recalled. "She was dressed in a pullover sweater and jeans . . . she could carry the heaviest mirrors!" The sight of the soignée First Lady moving furniture and setting candelabras became a common one around the metamorphosing rooms.

Curator Ketchum recalled, "She was an amazing person not just for the times, but for all of White House history. She lavished love and reverence on the house . . . She reminded us that 'our obligation goes from Abigail Adams up to the present.' By virtue of the fact that she put herself in so prominent a position, it was obvious that she was the

moving force . . . But she didn't like to get the credit she deserved . . . She strove . . . to not put herself in the spotlight, [but] to give credit to donors, or the committee."[4]

But her guidance prevailed. When Henry Du Pont suggested that a fine period mantelpiece be placed in the Queen's Room, she held out for the "ugly charm" of the last one actually carved in the White House carpentry shop, under FDR. To Mr. Du Pont, Jacqueline gently asserted, "We always have to make concessions to history . . ." At Mrs. Wrightsman's suggestion she asked the venerable French decorator Stephane Boudin specifically to plan a proper setting to evoke the French Empire style favored by President Monroe. The White House state rooms were of monumental proportions, and she soon realized that the decorator she had been using had little experience on such a scale.

When *Life* magazine wanted to do a full-color story on the restoration, the First Lady knew it would boost the magazine's sales. She agreed to give an interview—if *Life* made a contribution. She believed the White House should be given a decorator's discount, and when a dealer inflated his price for a needed rug, she was "ENRAGED at everyone trying to gyp the White House. Tell him if he gives it [to the White House] he can get a tax donation and photo in our book—if not—goodbye!"[5]

Discreetly, the First Lady personally beguiled some of America's wealthiest citizens and institutions. When she learned that an heiress had willed some valuable Cézannes to the White House, she went down to inspect them, long displayed at the National Gallery. The gallery director had instinctively downplayed the two greatest paintings, but she spotted them, in dim light on the gallery wall, partially blocked by two guards. Soon after, they hung in the White House. When Jackie discovered that millionaire publisher Walter Annenberg owned the only life portrait of Benjamin Franklin, she employed flattery: "President Kennedy and I thought it would be wonderful if you, as a great Philadelphia editor, would give the White House the portrait of Philadelphia's greatest editor." Annenberg later joked that Jackie's call was "the most astute arm-twisting I've ever been up against in my life." He donated the portrait.[6]

Possessions of former residents returned: Van Buren's Empire chairs, Washington's armchair used in the first Presidential Mansion, Julia Grant's writing desk, china of Lucy Hayes, Carrie Harrison, and Sarah Polk. Taylor's fireplace fender, Tyler's "astral lamp," Arthur's gold whistle, Jefferson's inkwell—even Pierce's handkerchief. First Ladies' images included a Martha Washington counterpane, Dolley Madison miniature, and an engraving of Mary Lincoln greeting Julia Grant.

Donors were as diverse as the gifts. Richard Rodgers gave an eight-day clock, Mayor Dan Pasquale of Nerano, Italy, presented an oval photograph brooch of U.S. Grant set in gold, with sixteen diamonds and sixteen pearls on behalf of the citizens of Massa Lubrense. Few knew the presidential association of the "children of Winthrop Rutherford" who gave a suite of Duncan Phyfe furniture. Their stepmother had been Lucy Mercer, FDR's mistress. The National Association of Colored Women's Clubs presented an engraved porthole portrait in memory of Frederick Douglass. Not all were helpful. Harry Truman did not wish to part with the Theodore Roosevelt–Stanford White mantelpiece with carved buffalo heads, original to the State Dining Room, which he had incorporated into his library. So Jacqueline had a copy made by the original firm, and invited Alice Roosevelt Longworth to assist at its unveiling.

Jacqueline's sense of history drifted upstairs as well, to the private rooms. A sitting room that had been the president's office until the West Wing was built in the Theodore Roosevelt administration she made into the Treaty Room, with dark green baize walls, Grant furniture, and framed facsimiles of all the treaties that had been signed in it. The second-floor Oval Room received Louis XVI furniture in the bright yellow style favored by Dolley Madison. Nor did she overlook reproductions that were themselves historic. In the East Hall a Lou Hoover nook was created with the furniture she had had copied from Monroe pieces.[7]

The White House Library, a small paneled ground-floor room, had few books in it. Jacqueline believed it "should contain the most significant works of American history and literature and that the list should be made public." There was space for only fifteen hundred volumes. Yale Library's James Babb headed the committee of scholars who would choose the books.

As her assistant in this project, Jacqueline called upon historian and administration adviser Arthur Schlesinger, who kept an office in the East Wing. She called his "American Classics Project" for the Library a "brilliant idea" and got the president to support it. She wrote Arthur that she didn't want to use the name "reference library" because it might drive off donors, though she felt "a library is dead if not used." Yet she worried that if an announcement was made that it was open, all staff members would come in and books "will all start disappearing . . . so let's just keep it a tacit understanding that the library is for whoever wants to use it—we will have a watchdog there somehow . . . & we will word the press release so no one knows whether or not it can be used. You can dress up in 18th century costume & sit there all day tomorrow reading Civil Disobedience."

Schlesinger also kept the First Lady busy with books relevant to her role. She was "enthralled" with Henry Adams's *Democracy*, which parodied Julia Grant in a satirical view of social maneuvering in Gilded

Age Washington. "I wouldn't have loved it [earlier]," she thanked him, "as much as I do now!" When he sent Jackie a copy of the nineteenth-century *Ladies of the White House*, a series of biographies of her predecessors with a note reading, "For the lovely culmination," she responded, "I won't show it to any other First Lady, I promise!"[8]

In the family quarters, Jacqueline had a kitchen and dining room installed for family use. In her bedroom, Mamie Pink was replaced by blue and white, with framed drawings and her Georgetown furniture. Her most cherished possession was the little Empire desk from which she conducted her work. It had belonged to her father.

Tish Baldrige considered the vast changes a "metamorphosis of the White House itself into a museum of American Presidential history." Jackie's project was having a ripple effect all across the country. Slowly, disarmingly, she educated the general public in American history. Tish recalled, "In every release or statement about some new item or development . . . she insisted on including historical background. She always devised a way of providing 'news' on the particular era and decorative style, what region of the country it was crafted in—who was the historical figure that might have owned it—what did he do in history." Jackie's subtlety cleverly made the past relevant to the present.

From his perspective, Jim Ketchum also noticed another flowering —"historic preservation." He said, "More and more, we heard about Governors' Mansions and State Houses which were doing research, and restoring the old structures accurately." Jacqueline received an increasing number of letters from community leaders interested in historic preservation, seeking landmark status or advice on how to save a historic home or structure. She was ecstatic over the reactions. "I have worked harder on this project than I ever have on anything," she said, "and so it has been especially gratifying."[9]

In several hundred notes, letters, and memos, Jackie provided instructions on any and every subject that related to the house. The instructions might be as short as a paragraph or as long as twelve pages. "That tremendous concentration and attention to detail," commented a stupefied Jim Ketchum. "The smallest details [which] she knew all would add up to the big picture. . . . Later . . . she [sent] verbal instructions by using the dictabelts used by the Signal Corps . . . from wherever she was . . ."[10]

Congress provided the Kennedys, as it did all families, $100,000 to refurbish the private quarters. Jackie felt "it would not be right" to ask for more, but the restoration project would always need ongoing funds, aside from donations. She unwrapped her solution—a guidebook.

The woman who had penned poems and stories as a child, written and illustrated a self-satirical book with her sister, and enjoyed a brief journalism career made perhaps her most enduring decision. Jackie

Kennedy would finally produce her White House history book, illustrated in color with old prints and modern photographs of newly acquired furnishings and artwork. The proceeds of *The White House: An Historic Guide* would go directly to the purchasing fund. During her first week as First Lady, she had raised the idea of her book with director of the National Gallery of Art John Walker, and later wrote that "this must be scholarly—and not talk down to the public—then they will learn from it—and I have never seen a case, in politics or books, when talking down did any good—it just bores people. . . ." He agreed to help, but there was a problem. For the book to earn money, it had to be owned as a legal copyright. Government publications were public domain. Jacqueline didn't want to go to a commercial publishing company. So, following Clark Clifford's guidelines, she technically orchestrated her own.

On November 3, 1961, it was announced by the East Wing that the White House Historical Association's "purpose is primarily educational. Income from the sale of this booklet will be used to publish other materials about the White House, as well as for the acquisition of historic furnishings and other objects for the Executive Mansion." It was acknowledged that the book had all been Jackie's idea.[11]

Now, there was an association to publish the book to raise funds to buy furnishings to restore the White House, *but* there was no seed money to print it. Walker made a delicate inquiry to Melville Bell Grosvenor of the National Geographic Society, asking if they would take the color photographs of the rooms and possessions, and print them for the book. All along Jacqueline had envisioned her book in the *National Geographic* size and format. Grosvenor not only said yes, but agreed to print the entire book gratis, "as a public gesture." The First Lady considered it an "incredibly generous offer." Over the months, she would quietly read and edit Lorraine Pearce's draft, emphasizing a compact text "so as to not lose the attention of young readers," because "education and particularly arousing the intellectual curiosity of children at an early age had always been of passionate interest" to her. The book would be done in a year.[12]

Some administration officials still feared the restoration as a political liability. Much was made of the fact that the Blue Room was now white with blue accents, and a clarification was made by no less a person than the president. After Jacqueline released a statement, "It should be obvious by now that the aim of the Fine Arts Committee is to restore not change the White House," JFK added, "the room will remain blue." Technically, it did not.

Still others criticized that French was replacing American furnishings, ignoring the fact that Thomas Jefferson had had French furniture and that it was President Monroe who had first outfitted the entire house with French furnishings. Tish said the First Lady was "livid when criticism was so obviously motivated by politics." The restoration was above politics. That was clear in the administrative papers that first outlined the formation of the committees—created to outlast the Kennedys for administrations to follow—including Republicans. The president stood by his wife against critics. "The restoration had been a more formidable operation than anyone realized," he later said, "Mrs. Kennedy displayed more executive ability for organization than I had imagined she had."[13]

Mrs. Kennedy recreated the aesthetic ambiance of a grand manor house in the traditions of the late eighteenth and nineteenth centuries. That went beyond furniture and into entertaining, capturing the spirit of the early presidents. Again, managing behind the scenes, Mrs. Kennedy orchestrated every minute detail, the cumulative visual effect of which was an intangible "feel" that was nevertheless discernibly different. Good food was served. Previous administrations back to FDR had endured private and official meals turned out by a Filipino cook in the navy mess, which had been by all accounts inedible. Informal Jeffersonian round tables were introduced to stimulate conversation, and the finest American and foreign wines were drawn from lists compiled by expert Frederick Wildman.

She also "set up a system, as in France," where the state greenhouses grew the seasonal flowers to be used in the official residences.

This effort was both suggested and guided by her friend horticulturist and landscape gardener Rachel Lambert Mellon. Mrs. Mellon also helped with flower arrangements for the White House. Flowers had previously been bought wholesale at exorbitant prices from Washington florists "and ran heavily to purple orchids." The White House gardener was replaced by Irwin Williams, a talented Park Service gardener found by Mrs. Mellon. Appropriate containers were chosen for each room, some of them vermeil pieces from the Biddle collection that had not been cleaned for years. Mrs. Mellon created arrangements for each room at each season of the year, and all were photographed and put into an album, so "no President's wife would ever again have to start from scratch."

At the request of the president, Mrs. Mellon redesigned the Rose Garden, then a patch of lawn crisscrossed by narrow beds. She created a magnificent space anchored by four giant magnolias where the president could honor distinguished citizens. Mrs. Mellon also created a garden by the East Wing, where future First Families could find privacy in the afternoon when the tourists were gone. It contained topiary, herbs for the kitchen, and a grape arbor for shade.

Now the flowers were beautiful, fireplaces lighted, lights dimmed to the level of candlelight, drinks offered before dinner for the first time, and the Kennedys circulated among the guests after receiving them in a formal line. It all proved a proper setting for Jacqueline's shining evenings of the arts.

On her second working day as First Lady, Jackie had invited New York City Ballet impresario George Balanchine for tea, asking, "What can I do for the arts?" She was determined to have them accorded the same esteem in America that European arts were accorded in their countries. Looking pale, still not recovered from John's emergency birth and the Inauguration, she had offered him tea. "You don't have anything stronger?" Balanchine asked. He was charmed by her.

In April he took part in a Washington panel on the subject "If I were president . . ." He said he would only want to be president if he could have Jacqueline Kennedy as First Lady, and then, with her help, do what should be done to bring beauty into people's lives. Subsequently, he wrote her a letter, urging her to take on the role of "spiritual savior" of America.

"I don't mean in a religious sense," he wrote, "but I mean to distinguish between material things and things of the spirit—art, beauty. No one else can take care of these things. You alone can—if you will.

"Your husband is necessarily busy with serious international problems and cannot be expected to worry too much about the nation's art and culture. But woman is always the inspiration. Man takes care of the material things and woman takes care of the soul."

It would be seen how she would carry out his exhortation.

Her immediate and most visible technique was to present the performing arts in the White House, and she even had an easily assembled stage built and placed in the East Room. Jacqueline was adamant that only "the best of the performing arts in America should be represented at the White House, and that American artists should be invited to State Dinners." Jerome Robbins staged a ballet performance. The American Shakespeare Festival performed. Ernest Hemingway's unpublished novel was read in excerpts by Fredric March. Cellist Pablo Casals performed. Since America had recognized Spain's Franco, he had refused to play in the United States. For President Kennedy, he made an exception.

Both Kennedys "shared the conviction that the artist should be honored by society," and "[a]ll of this," Mrs. Kennedy would later point out, "had to do with calling attention to what was finest in America, what should be esteemed and honored."[14]

She was very much a symbol of the liberation from the notion that America had to be bourgeois. "Thank you," wrote writer Lincoln Kirstein to JFK, "for restoring to the United States the pleasures and powers of the mind." John Steinbeck rhapsodized, "What a joy that literacy is no longer prima facie evidence of treason." Mary Day, the director of the Washington Ballet, said, "With the new Administration, we have hope for survival."[15]

Jacqueline later stated her reason and her role in trying to establish an American branch of government headed perhaps someday by a secretary of arts and humanities:

". . . the arts had been treated as a stepchild in the U.S. When the government had supported the arts, as in many WPA projects, artists were given a hand and some wonderful things emerged. It had seen in Europe how proud those countries were of their arts and artists. Of course, they had a longer tradition of patronage, going back to kings, Popes, and princes, but modern governments continued this support. Our great museums and great performing companies should of course be supported, but the experimental and the unknown should also be thrown a line. Our contemporary artists—in all the media—have excited the world. It was so sad that we couldn't help them more."

In terms of the role of government in the arts, and the role of an arts secretary, Jacqueline said that "of course, she and the President talked of these things." She amplified:

"It was something the President responded to and cared about for his country. What other president had had a poet read at his Inauguration and so many great writers invited to it? The public had to feel the need for support of the arts; you couldn't just jump in and name a Czar."

Having a Department of the Arts became her long-range, and for the moment unstated, goal, but reporters Ralph Martin and Marianne Means both confirmed that it was the First Lady who "persuaded" the president to make the appointment of a special White House arts consultant.[16]

It was Arthur Schlesinger who recommended August Heckscher of the Twentieth Century Fund for the short-term temporary role of "special consultant to the president on the arts." Heckscher's main objective was to determine how to best implement government aid to the arts, and establish an advisory council on the arts. Mrs. Kennedy's goal was to have his role made permanent and at the Cabinet level. Heckscher said that in the summer of '61 when he began his work, Jacqueline had not yet been "prominently identified" with the arts. He knew the administration was not only breaking into a new arena, but one that could be easily criticized, and he applauded what he called Jacqueline's "somewhat ambivalent" feelings about involving herself in public debate on government funding of the arts. Though he felt the press thought she was constantly working in this area, "Mrs. Kennedy herself was much too wise to be busy every moment promoting the arts. She would do one thing with superb taste and it would have a tremendous impact."[17]

Jacqueline outlined her goals in a frank letter to Congressman Carroll Deane, less than two weeks after her husband's Inauguration: "I share your desire to make Washington a world cultural center, and I hope to contribute in every way I can myself to the elevation of the arts in our country. But . . . I have always felt that one should not go on committees if one is not prepared to be a working member . . . at present . . . I can help our joint cause best by doing the things I can do as . . . mistress of the White House."[18]

One cultural-political issue that Jacqueline Kennedy adopted early was the dream of a Washington National Cultural Center, to resemble New York's new Lincoln Center. There was only one large theater in Washington (the National) and Constitution Hall, where the symphony played. Touring and local ballet, opera, and symphony companies had to perform in makeshift spaces from high school auditoriums to movie theaters. President Eisenhower had signed the legislation for it, but Congress only provided the land for the center. The $30 million needed to build it had to be raised from private donations. Some claimed it was Jacqueline who persuaded the president to support the plan for one centralized center with theater, concert, and opera hall all under one roof, instead of scattered throughout the capital. Over the months, she would turn increasing attention to the center.[19]

August Heckscher said he purposely kept his distance from the First Lady, because he was concentrating on establishing a firm relationship with the president and didn't want his role to be associated with the restoration. He saw her frequently, but had only one "long talk" with her. "She told me then how much the President did care about the Cultural Center . . . and she said that he had recently said to her, 'All right, Jackie, I guess now we've got to call in all the fat cats that I've been saving for the [1964] campaign.' She said, 'Mr. Heckscher, I will do anything for the arts you want . . . Except road bills.' I told Mrs. Kennedy 'Don't worry about . . . the legislative bills.' . . . Then, with sort of a smile, she said, 'After all, I'm *not* Mrs. Roosevelt.'"

Doing that "one thing with superb taste" became Jacqueline's specialty as unofficial arts ambassador. Whenever the First Lady made one of her rare public appearances, it was almost exclusively on behalf of the arts. Her policy proved effective.[20]

When Jackie opened a National Gallery of Art exhibit of the treasures of Egyptian King Tut's tomb, she told the press, "I remember as a child reading about the discovery of the tomb. This was one of the things I hoped most in the world to see some day." United Arab Republic ambassador Mostafa Kamel said the exhibit was done to rally interest in saving the ancient temples of the Nile Valley, in danger of being flooded by the Aswan Dam. Publicly, Jackie remained Sphinx-like. Privately, she got to work on it.

Her powerful presence the night she attended the opening of the new Lincoln Center's Philharmonic Hall was witnessed by one young musician on stage, Mark Crosby. He recalled the air of anticipation about "her" in the vast hall, and the moment when suddenly a white spotlight was flashed on the First Lady. Again, the event focused on arts funding: former schoolmates endowed a seat there in Jacqueline's name, and when next in New York to receive a Fine Arts Institute award, she herself endowed a seat, in memory of her father.

Nowhere did Jackie's élan pervade more indelibly than in the capital. Her knowledge of contemporary art was kept refreshed through old friend Bill Walton, who discussed it with her, and also showed her his own current canvases. Before he left for the South Pole to paint, the First Lady ordered aerial photos of Antarctica's landscape for him. In her press secretary's office were two massive modern canvases. An abstract painting hung in the office of the Federal Aviation Agency chief. The Pan American Union gallery featured the contemporary Polsello of Argentina. Jane Wheeler, a Washington hostess, stopped collecting Delft pottery for abstract sculpture, and chaired a committee that brought modern art into new airports. Art historian Sue Scott pointed out that it was largely because of Jackie's interest, support, and visits that the Washington Gallery of Modern Art managed to flourish—a first in the conservative capital city.

In Kennedy Washington, Edith Wilson was too old and Eleanor Roosevelt too busy to be Queen Mothers, but like a Queen Stepmother Alice Longworth savored the revived arts of conversation. Jackie said Alice was a person she "knew well and saw often." When asked how Jacqueline was able to make so many changes so quickly, Alice would twinkle, "Cherchez la femme."[21]

If there was one sphere where Jacqueline had great influence— much to her annoyance—it was fashion. Her designer Cassini admitted that she "played a very active role" in the design and simple cut of her clothes, and choice of monochromatics. He said she "almost single-handedly created a revolution in good taste. . . . It was the first time in history that a look had originated in America and overtaken the world." Her dressmaker said Jacqueline usually ignored advice, since she knew how she wanted to look. Jackie acknowledged her impact to Cassini: "I know that I am so much more of fashion interest than other First Ladies [but] refuse to have Jack's administration plagued by fashion stories of a sensational nature—& to be the Marie Antoinette or Josephine of the 1960's. . . ."

Fashion was no minor industry, and Jackie no minor influence. The serious economic fact was that $11 million a year was spent on the women's clothing industry, $4 million on accessories. Before the First Lady made her first London appearance, Reuters reported that English milliners worked through the night to fill orders for pillboxes "just like Jackie." Even JFK protested when she was hatless, "What would Alec Rose [milliners' union president] do to us in an election!"

When a pregnant Jackie had managed to still wear flattering clothes, the Lane Bryant chain marketed "First Lady Maternity Fashions." After photographs showed Mrs. Kennedy in a particular style of her trademark sunglasses, cheaper copies exploded onto the market. Strapless and single-shoulder evening sheaths, Pucci pants, and English jodhpurs were copied and sold at cheaper prices. Belt-makers were ecstatic that the First Lady's suits used big belts, reviving their industry. Fashion writer Marilyn Bender said the First Lady "set an example" for other young Catholic women when she appeared in a mantilla veil instead of a hat. Store mannequins appeared in windows with bouffant hairdos. Even the Communists fell prey as the Leningrad fashion magazine Mody published ads for clothes replicating Jackie's. The "Jackie Look" quite literally swept the globe. It was not just her chic that provoked the avalanche. By the third month of her husband's term, Jackie Kennedy had become a modern-day Cleopatra conquering nations.[22]

The first hint came during a Canadian visit with JFK. She was in the Canadian Senate listening in the visitors' gallery when Senate speaker Mark Drouin told the House of Commons that Mrs. Kennedy's "charm, beauty, vivacity and grace of mind have captured our hearts," and turned to JFK to tell him, ". . . many Canadians searched the civil registers to see if she was a Canadian." Jacqueline became the first incumbent First Lady in tenure honored with mention on the floor of a foreign legislature. But, just fourteen days later, her French ancestry and grasp of the language would prove a catalyst for diplomacy.

On May 31, Jacqueline Bouvier was going to return to Paris. She asked if she might meet André Malraux, the minister of culture in the de Gaulle Cabinet. Malraux was delighted and took it upon himself to plan her itinerary. The State Department was uncertain just how the Parisians would respond to the First Lady. Before her arrival, Jacqueline taped a television interview, speaking flawless French. The response was good. But no one, including the president, anticipated the greeting of Air Force One at the Paris airport.

Jack emerged first, and there were cheers. But when Jackie, a vision in powder blue, descended the steps, the gathered crowds broke into deafening applause. The de Gaulles waited below. When presented with a bouquet by two little girls, Jacqueline spoke her first words in France: "Merci beaucoup." Quickly, the thunder changed into a hypnotic chant. The French, so often wary of Americans, were saying something, at first inaudible. Then it became clear.

"Vive Jacqui! Vive Jacqui!"

As the motorcade moved along the avenues of Paris, nearly a quarter of a million more inhabitants continued the chanting.

"*Vive Jacqui! Vive Jacqui!*"

Gathered in front of the Quai d'Orsay where the Kennedys were staying, at the Child Welfare Clinic, which she visited that afternoon, at the Elysée Palace where the de Gaulles hosted their lunch for the Americans—everywhere Jackie appeared was heard the deafening chant of thousands who crushed police barricades.

It may have been Jack's trip, but it was Jackie's Moment.

The next morning Mrs. Kennedy adorned the first page of French— and some American—newspapers. A cartoon in France's *Liberation* showed the de Gaulles in bed, with Madame saying in surprise to her embarrassed husband, "*Mon Dieu, Charles!*" Encircled in his thought cloud above was Jackie's picture. News commentators in Austria and England, where she was going next, made the Paris reaction their lead story, further enhancing "*le fièvre de Jacqueline.*"

So many French Bouviers were demanding to meet her that when the First Lady's *real* cousins, Miche and Kathleen Bouvier, were announced at the Elysée Palace, de Gaulle, assuming they were imposters, whispered to a guard to expel them. "Despite the tight fit of her stunning formal evening gown," wrote Kathleen, "Jackie somehow managed to leap across the floor, cut off the official bouncer in his tracks, embrace us both, and lead us to the welcoming line."

De Gaulle's Versailles dinner was an almost surreal event. Amid the acres of sculptured gardens, statuary, and fountains stood the palace, and within the Hall of Mirrors, where Edith Wilson had once been forced to hide behind a curtain to watch Woodrow speak on the treaty, Jacqueline dined beside de Gaulle. She amazed him with her knowledge of French history, her ability to hold deep conversations about French theater and literature, and her role as personal interpreter for the two presidents. "I now have more confidence," de Gaulle told JFK, "in your country." None questioned Jacqueline's contribution to diplomacy. As Jack wryly admitted, "My wife speaks good French. I understand only one out of every five words . . . but always de Gaulle." After dinner a ballet performance was held in the aquamarine theater of Louis XV.

Few stopped to realize that Versailles, the ballet, even, in some degree, the couture industry, were all institutions backed by the French government. Art, architecture, music, poetry, history, performance, and literature were all fostered under the auspices of le Ministère de la Culture, headed by Malraux. André Malraux spent a morning showing her through the Jeu de Paume museum. Malraux's two sons had been killed just days before in a car accident, and Jacqueline was moved that he would still accompany her. Schlesinger said "an enduring friendship began. His was no mere agency, but an entire department, and Jacqueline knew precisely how important its impact had been on France."[23]

At the next stop, Vienna, Kennedy and Khrushchev did not achieve their goal of amicable relations between the two superpowers, but even the chairman was charmed by Jacqueline. When photographers asked him to shake hands with the president, Nikita piped up, "I'd like to shake her hand first."

During the formal dinner, the mischievous side of Jacqueline emerged as she engaged Khrushchev in what Schlesinger compared to an Abbott and Costello routine. She had just read Lesley Blanch's *Sabres of Paradise,* and asked the premier about the Ukraine of the 1800's. His reply was the specific number of teachers per capita that the Soviet Ukraine had over the czarist Ukraine. Jacqueline bantered back, "Oh, Mr. Chairman, don't bore me with statistics." Khrushchev broke into loud laughter, moved his chair closer to Jackie's and became cozy. Jacqueline, noting the fact that one of the dogs put into space by the Soviets had recently had pups, teased him, "Why don't you send me one?" Two months later, when a terrified puppy was brought to the White House in the arms of Khrushchev's son-in-law, the president asked, "How did that dog get here?" Sheepishly, Jacqueline admitted, "I'm afraid I asked Khrushchev for it . . ." Khrushchev also sent her liqueurs, a picture album of Moscow, a gold tea set in a red leather case, phonograph records. And nine bottles of perfume. CBS even broadcast a *News Special Report* entitled "Gala in Vienna."

From Vienna, Jackie went to London, privately to attend the christening of her sister Lee Radziwill's daughter, and publicly, to be honored with Jack at a dinner hosted by the queen, becoming the first First Lady since Eleanor to dine at Buckingham Palace. Then she and the Radziwills headed for Greece. On Hydra, at a taverna, Jackie joined in the Bouzouki folk dance "Kalamatianes." On thyme-scented Epidaurus, she watched the Greek National Theater rehearse Sophocles' *Electra* in the ancient amphitheater. At one point she told reporters of Greece, "One day I will have a home here." A cartoon parodied the fact that patrol boats protected her from photographers as she water-skied, Jackie responding, "Maybe I should wear a veil."

Her social role had political impact. From behind the Iron Curtain, the Polish magazine *Swait* concluded, "Jackie has entered the group of a few women in the world who, today, as in times past, set the style and tone of their epoch . . . but never before has her influence been so farflung or so quickly disseminated. The face and silhouette of Jackie are known to all people all over the whole civilized world." The *New York Mirror* said Mrs. Kennedy established "a new mass response" to America.[24]

Just before her return, the American press rushed to claim her as their own, but not *just* as a First Lady. A new dimension unfolded. With Jacqueline Kennedy, the First Lady role alarmingly magnified from public persona into an exaggerated, larger-than-life image. The image was consciously concocted and cultivated by the press, not the principal. For her, it was an extremely difficult burden, an unreal exemplar.

Her image had little to do with her work. Few gave attention to the person who had goals to accomplish, regardless of whether or not she was popular. In fact, the adulation was often insulting to her intelligence. Her celebrity intruded on her privacy, and consequently her ironclad limitations on her role began to serve as refuge from the intensity of global fame.

Magazines continually asked who the "real" Jackie was, but few cared to focus in on the spirit of the woman, which was key to her rather unique interpretation of her role. Her own mother spoke of her daughter's "marvelous self-control and discipline, which conceals a certain inner tension. She feels very strongly, very intensely about things." There was the Charmer. *New York Times* editor Cifton Daniel thought that Jackie had "expensive taste . . . was a romantic, a bit naughty, and beguiling." There was the Conversationalist. Commerce Secretary Luther Hodges said that she spoke to one "as if you're the most important person she has ever met." And, importantly, there was the Loner. Old friend Martha Bartlett described the First Lady as a "sweet-natured person and interested in many people, but she also has another side, of needing to be alone and reflective."

Privacy actually nurtured Jacqueline's role, for without it she felt trapped, unable to do her best. She found physical activity helpful, explaining, "I could work better at my desk after I had some exercise." She walked, rode horses, played tennis, swam, and water-skied. Her schedule included at least half an hour of morning exercise. But exercise didn't lend itself to privacy. Almost always, everywhere, there were the Secret Service agents, or the press, or the public. Even when she rode to hounds, security agents and often photographers were present. When a Secret Serviceman trailed her lone beach walks, Jackie quipped, "You keep doing that, and you'll drive the First Lady into an asylum."[25]

Mr. West said Jacqueline was the most complex of the First Ladies he'd served. At any given moment, she was impishly irreverent or regally aloof. "She had a will of iron, with more determination than anyone I have ever met . . . so deft and subtle, that she could impose that will upon people without their even knowing it." While she liked things scheduled, she herself was spontaneous. She took advice, but only when she solicited it. She wasn't ever goaded into anything she personally didn't want to do.

And, though she knew precisely what she wanted, and how and when she wanted it done, there was also a soft side to her, one the public never knew. After meeting about two dozen members of the domestic staff, she could immediately recall each of their names and duties, without notes nor assistance, and to each of them, as Mr. West recalled, "She was quick to show gratitude, as well as concern about their getting adequate days off and raises in salary. And, I observed, she held them very high in her affection." When painter Joseph Karitas was asked to work late in completing a project at the First Lady's request while a snowstorm raged, Jackie had him stay overnight, served dinner and breakfast, and then the next morning had the floral shop create a double corsage for his wife.[26]

Jim Ketchum said, "With every single member of the staff, she always showed a kindness, a consideration for them as human beings. She was the least selfish person I've known. When you dealt with her, it was an honest one-to-one relationship . . . she liked to be the victim of her own sense of humor. She took her role and her work seriously, but she didn't take *herself* seriously." Stories of her arch satire were legion. Once, she eyed Mr. West with his arm in a sling and purred, "You look so glamorous—just like Zachary Taylor!"[27]

She was also intensely serious. Part of the motivation behind the restoration was her grasp of the past's relevance to the present. "Before everything slips away, before every link with the past is gone, I want to do this," she explained to Hugh Sidey about the restoration. "When the last Civil War veteran died a year or so ago, that was a break with the past. I want to find and go to all these people who are still here, who know about the White House . . . ." When Alice Longworth or FDR, Jr., visited, Jackie explained to Caroline that they, too, had lived in her house.

Even for Jacqueline, in her First Lady role, the notion that she was now part of history was unreal. "I wondered 'What are we doing here?' and 'What are we going to be doing in a year or so?'" I would go and sit in the Lincoln Room . . . To touch something I knew he had touched was a real link with him. . . . I could really feel his strength. I would sort of be talking with him." She said that Jefferson inspired her, but that Lincoln was the most human to her.[28]

Few considered that this First Lady was only thirty-one years old in a role filled for decades by women old enough to be her mother. (At thirty-one, Eleanor Roosevelt had been the insecure wife of the assistant navy secretary preoccupied with social calls.) And yet her schedule reflected her balance as mother and First Lady. Her day began with breakfast in bed, on a tray, awaking as early as eight, as late as noon. After toast and honey, juice and coffee, she went immediately to her children for about an hour, and later spent time in the afternoon with them. In between she worked upstairs in her unofficial "office," the Treaty Room.

"Jackie," said one of the Kennedys, "wants to be as great a First Lady . . . as Jack is a President." But it would be on her terms. As she explained to an English journalist, "I will never be a committee woman or a club woman. I am not a joiner."

Of the First Lady role, Jackie admitted, "[O]f course, she can't expect to be a completely private person. She will have an official role which she must play and accept with grace . . ." She had no doubts that she could. Jacqueline Bouvier had been reared in the Puritan ethic of doing one's duty to the fullest, and had confidence in her social, administrative, and intellectual abilities.

In the same spirit that Eleanor and Bess had defied criticism to interpret the role as best suited them, so, too, did Jackie. Arthur Krock described her as a "Victorian wife." In the sense that her family was a priority, Jacqueline Kennedy was as traditional as Mamie Eisenhower. Bess Truman was the First Lady whom Jackie admired most, because Mrs. Truman had always been there for her husband and daughter, who had remained unspoiled. "If you bungle raising your children," Jackie said, "I don't think whatever else you do well matters very much. And why shouldn't that be an example too?"

She made few afternoon appearances because of her postlunch time slot with Caroline and John. "If I were to add political duties," she explained, "I would have practically no time with my children." She put her foot down when Tish, who tended to overload her schedule, said she "just *had* to" do a particular thing. Mrs. Kennedy retorted to Mr. West, "I don't *have* to do anything."

When later, on her doctor's orders, she canceled her attendance at official engagements involving receiving lines, she left town for Margot Fonteyn and the newly defected Rudolf Nureyev's first U.S. appearance with the London Royal Ballet, leaving an embarrassed JFK to appear in her stead at the annual Congressional Wives Reception in the White House. It was the first time in history that a president attended an event as *the First Lady's* representative.

But when she did appear, she stole the show. "Does it matter if I can't come?" the president told one event organizer. "After all, Jackie will be there."[29]

The president discussed her role with reporter Marianne Means: "It is up to each First Lady to do what best fits her temperament and personal inclinations . . . First Ladies are not public officials . . . It is up to her to do what she can, within her own limitations . . . Her first duty is to her husband and her children—when her husband is also the President, that duty is considerably expanded. . . ." Jackie's popularity was often the butt of his witticisms as well. He told a group of visiting students that one of them might someday return as president, "or better yet, as a President's wife."[30]

Criticism didn't deter Mrs. Kennedy. Like Grace Coolidge, Eleanor Roosevelt, and even Mamie Eisenhower, Jackie was able to draw the line between private person and public persona. As she explained, "In this job there's always going to be a flare-up about something. And you must somehow get so it doesn't upset you. I think I was always fairly good at it. I can drop down this curtain in my mind."[31]

Jacqueline Kennedy was literally besieged by the press. It became immediately evident to the Kennedys and their staffs that they had a problem on their hands. There was no way—legally or otherwise—to control what the press reported about Jackie.

She had not been uncomfortable with the press during the campaign, but now the situation was quite different. *Good Housekeeping* magazine wanted Jacqueline to write a monthly column, but like Mamie, she refrained. During the campaign, she had granted print and television interviews, and held several press conferences. Now, she no longer did so. It took enormous manpower and time just to handle inquiries spurred by outside sources, let alone those that the East Wing released.[32]

As a former reporter, the First Lady kept tabs on which journalists were working for what publications. She was aware of her own press. When *Newsweek* reported that three French wines had been served at a presidential luncheon, the First Lady immediately had it clarified: "There was only one, and it was domestic."

Jackie was distressed when she felt that her publicity eclipsed her projects, but when the press employed invasive news-gathering methods for stories about her private life and children, she became angry and unresponsive. As one observer later wrote, "What so many have interpreted as coldness or aloofness might more accurately be read as self-protection." Whenever she made an appearance, the women's press corps, kept at a distance, were out in full force. While some claimed that she contemptuously isolated women reporters as "the harpies," the actual guest lists to White House functions showed that she invited at least one member of the women's press corps and escort to state dinners. She didn't resent them personally; she resented their techniques.[33]

As UPI reporter Helen Thomas wrote, Jackie "was news twenty-four hours a day." The public responded to her, editors responded to their public, and reporters to the demands of their editors. They were instructed to cover Jackie—any way they could, even intruding on her privacy. It was a difficult position for both reporter and First Lady. Jackie fully understood how the media worked. She was cooperative in providing information on her work, but private time was to be exactly that. It was a perspective the reporters generally ignored. Helen Thomas said, "In all fairness to Mrs. Kennedy, I'll admit we were insatiable. . . ." They used spyglasses, coaxed quotes out of maids, and tried to discover and infiltrate the places she might slip into.[34]

The youth, physical resemblance, and family life of Jacqueline Kennedy replicated the circumstances of seventy-five years earlier, when Frances Cleveland was avidly pursued by the press. Only very elderly Americans could have remembered how doggedly reporters had many times ruined *her* privacy. Whereas that era had marked the maturity of photography, the "Jet Age" was the turning point for television. Now, if Jackie water-skied with astronaut John Glenn, or was thrown from her horse, the world saw it on the evening news. Mrs. Kennedy's temper was tested. Once, a journalist asked what her German shepherd liked to eat.

Jackie scribbled back a one-word response. "Reporters."

– 2 –

"Madam President"

FOR THE FIRST time in history, a First Lady required her own press secretary.

Because of Jackie's media deluge, she asked Pamela Turnure, formerly a member of Senator Kennedy's staff, to take that position. Turnure had her own secretary, Frenchwoman Pierrette Spiegler, who was also charged with answering the overwhelming mail from France.

At that moment, besides the development of television networks' news departments and documentary programming, "living color" technology had advanced. Few ever saw Mamie's pink, but now a tanned Jackie in cobalt blue and lemon yellow could be scrutinized on the TV set. Turnure became the first East Winger who had to deal with networks and their complaints. In one memo to the president, she informed him that "NBC's feeling now is that . . . we have overprotected Mrs. Kennedy . . ."[1]

Pam admitted, "I always look at my job as one to help preserve Mrs. Kennedy's privacy and not create publicity." In a long memo, Jacqueline outlined this new job of First Lady press secretary, calling it a "buffer . . . to shield our privacy—not get us into the papers . . . publicity in this era has gotten so completely out of hand—& you must really protect the privacy of me & my children—but not offend them all . . . Pierre [Salinger] will be your boss (I will be really—as you & I will decide everything together) but all releases & things will come from him—But you must work in my offices." She warned Pam to watch her comments even in private, since people took it as the word of the First Lady. Jacqueline summarized her policy on ideal press as a "minimum of information given with maximum politeness."[2]

Jackie herself worked every day from large folders sent up by her staff, dealing with restoration work, public statements, correspondence, and scheduling. When Jack once suggested she take an East Wing office, she toured through, and found secretaries running about, and phones ringing incessantly. She compared it to "an old Rosalind Russell movie." She kept her Treaty Room office. Still, as Mr. West recalled, as her own staff director, she had an "ingenious way of getting things accomplished."[3]

Like Eleanor, Jacqueline knew how to find experts, whether East or West Wing staff, antique, horticulture, arts, or publishing advisers. "You can't do it all by yourself," she explained, "so you must pick the people you know are qualified for each field and tell them what [it is] you wish—and supervise it all, as nothing is ever any good without [the] overall unified supervision of the person who is putting all this in motion."[4]

After her press staff, the First Lady's correspondence division served as the most prominent contact with the general public. Hortense Burton, affectionately nicknamed "Mother," was chief of public correspondence, an enormous task considering the hundreds of thousands of letters Jacqueline ultimately received. In her first year there was an average of 250 letters a day, some addressed to "Your Majesty," and "Madam President." About 40 percent was fan mail. One of Mrs. Kennedy's work folders was marked "Comprehensive Sampling," and included a cross section of the mail. On political issues, she most frequently wanted to see letters that dealt with child welfare and education, and if some were pleas for assistance, she had them forwarded to the Department of Health, Education and Welfare. The most poignant were often answered by the First Lady. There were many letters of gratitude from writers, artists, musicians, and performers, some of whom offered to entertain at the White House. More than in past administrations, there was a high volume of foreign mail.

Heading operations and answering directly to the First Lady was Social Secretary Letitia Baldrige. Witty but tough, Tish staked her claim the first day—literally. While male co-workers attended the Inaugural, she had run about their offices replacing their new typewriters with the inferior ones left in the East Wing. She had consulted both her predecessors, Mary Jane McCaffree and Edith Helm, about running the East Wing. The staff consisted of a full total of forty, a number that included typists and messengers.

Tish often checked with Salinger or the president before making final decisions on the First Lady's statements. The great volume of political mail—one addressed the "intelligent wife . . . who understands the problems of the day, and one who can gain her hunband's ear"—was sent to executive departments for response. Many teenagers also wrote Jackie asking advice on romance, skin trouble, and makeup. The standard response was: "Mrs. Kennedy is not at liberty to comment on personal matters of this nature. . . ."

With this comparatively large and independent East Wing, there were inevitable frictions with the West Wing. Tish wrote that it was a simmering "civil war . . . based on nothing less than sex . . . our male colleagues would walk all over us unless we fought back. The presidential assistants tried to force decisions affecting Mrs. Kennedy on our office without consulting us." Sometimes the East and West Wings were out of synch. Moments after Pamela Turnure denied a rumor that the Kennedys were building a Virginia home as "absolutely untrue," Salinger confirmed it. Pam made it clear, however, that any news released from the West Wing that related to the mansion had to be cleared by the East Wing.[5]

Publicity for Jackie's projects raised no protest from the West Wing, but the one press matter on which the Kennedys disagreed was the amount of public exposure appropriate for their children. Jackie realized that Jack enjoyed having them photographed, and that it served as a positive form of public relations. But she strove always to keep them out of the public eye.

Early in every trip away, Jacqueline wrote out foreign postcards, put foreign stamps on them, and sent the batch to Mr. West. Caroline and John got their daily cards, and no postal clerks had read the messages. Ketchum recalled her "natural give-and-take with them . . . a normal life." The foursome of Jack, Jackie, "Buttons," and John cloistered themselves for long weekends together. Friends might drop by for part of a day, but it was really just the four of them.

After deciding not to renew their lease on a Virginia hunt country home "Glen Ora," Jackie planned to build their own nearby. She sketched out the room layout herself, but the house, Wexford, would not be ready for some time. They spent summer holidays at Jacqueline's family's Newport home, and the Kennedys' Hyannis compound. Later, they would rent a more private home on Squaw Island, a peninsula right next to Hyannis Port.[6]

The Kennedy marriage was both teasing and tempestuous, attached and independent, but always private. During the day, Jackie would sometimes surprise Jack by popping into his office. Once, she sent him a large basket of freshly cut grass with a note attached, poking fun at her earnest self: "From the White House Historical Association—Genuine Antique Grass from the Antique Rose Garden." The president's eyes brightened when his wife appeared in her beaded, strapless gowns with long white gloves for state dinners. Schlesinger said that JFK was "even entertained by her occasional bursts of undiplomatic candor." "Imagine," the president joked, "when I thought I heard Jackie telling Malraux that [German Chancellor] Adenauer was 'un peu gaga'!"

They loved needling each other. The president told a group of adoring nuns with a straight-faced expression that "Jackie here always wanted to be a nun . . . she really planned to take the order." Jackie once presented him with a rather abstract canvas, saying that it was a painting of Bill Walton's for which she had paid six hundred dollars. She waited a moment, and then confessed that it was one of Caroline's finger paintings.

On another occasion, chatting with him and Ben Bradlee and Bradlee's first wife, Toni, about the psychological battle between the sexes, Jackie piped up, "Oh, Jack, you know you always say that Toni is your ideal." Suddenly serious, Jack responded to her with the name he'd first known her by.

"You're my ideal, Jacqueline."[7]

Tish thought that one of the most important things the First Lady did for the president was to relax him and divert him from the worries of office, in the evenings, "by inviting fascinating journalists, artists, writers together for these cozy dinners."[8]

One evening, the world's most elusive woman arranged for her Hollywood counterpart, Greta Garbo, to dine with her and Jack.

The dinner was lively, Garbo illustrating a dry wit. JFK's longtime friend Lem Billings had bragged about meeting Garbo earlier, intimating they were friends. Jackie mischievously asked the actress to act as if she had never met Billings, and the Swede gamely went along. When later asked what impressed her most on an after-dinner tour of the mansion, Garbo replied, "The President's teeth." She meant his scrimshaw. Jackie also hosted a series of private dance parties, at which "The Twist" and cha-cha were played, and guests included American and European friends and national journalists. The First Lady, a devotee of jazz, was said to be a wicked Twister. It was quite a startling change. As Molly Thayer cracked, "Can you imagine Mrs. Truman or Mrs. Eisenhower doing the Twist!"[9]

Of the Kennedy relationship, Hugh Sidey insightfully pointed out at the time, "Their nomadic lives, their separateness—a phenomenon of great wealth—was not fully understood by the public, which clung to its older ideas of married life. . . . There was a stratum of whispered cocktail conversation that insisted the Kennedy marriage was in trouble, but those stories had been around since the day they were married in 1953, as similar reports had plagued previous presidents. Both Kennedys would confess early adjustment difficulties in their marriage, as in most marriages, and there were still obvious tests of will, as in most marriages. But the fact was that as time went on the marriage grew stronger."

John and Jacqueline Kennedy had a bond that temperament, old habits, and idiosyncrasies could not break.

Only a very few people knew that the president spent about three hours, nearly every day, upstairs, behind closed doors, with one particular woman. His wife. Just before lunch, when he was in the White House, he'd swim in the enclosed pool, following which he proceeded upstairs to the private quarters. There, he and Jackie lunched from trays. Mr. West recalled, "He closed the door, firmly. Mrs. Kennedy dropped everything, no matter how important, to join her husband . . . During these hours . . . No telephone calls were allowed, no folders sent up, no interruptions from the staff. Nobody went upstairs, for any reason."

At that quiet time, Mr. West said he could vaguely hear the strains of music drifting from the room, where Mrs. Kennedy occasionally played records on her hi-fi set. Mr. West affirmed that only the domestic staff "was attuned to the intimacy that actually existed between the young couple. . . ." Though, like all couples since the Hoovers, they each had their own bedroom, West recorded that on most mornings, JFK's valet George Thomas "would find him absent from his bedroom . . . tiptoe into the room next door, and gently shake the President— so as to not awaken the President's wife."[10]

It remained one of the most publicly speculated upon, and yet intensely private, presidential marriages. Even their public pronouncements about each other were guarded. Discussing mutual emotions embarrassed them, and instead they focused on their independent lifestyles and their projects. Jacqueline was quoted in England's *Sunday Dispatch* as saying, "Jack has some interests that are purely his and I have, also." Yet Massachusetts political figure Edward Berube recalled how, in discussing Jack, she told him, "I'm the luckiest girl in the world."

"My wife is a very strong woman," the president said in describing Jackie, "romantic by temperament, sensitive, intuitive, [with a] fantastically retentive memory."[11]

Besides keeping their private life private, they didn't discourage the fallacy that Jackie was devoid of political influence. That she was in fact avidly interested in JFK's goals, programs, and speeches remained a well-kept secret. While working with her, Arthur Schlesinger perceived that the First Lady was curious about politics, but that she tactfully refrained from discussing issues. He later commented that "she carried her self-defense to inordinate extremes, as when she would pretend a total ignorance about politics or impose a social ban on politicians." A *Boston Globe* story, however, revealed that the First Lady had expanded some of the political roles she played during the Senate years into the presidency, claiming that critiquing JFK's speeches was her forte and, "She, more than he, insists on the short sentences that have lent an additional brilliance to his language . . . more quietly—more importantly, he has come to rely on her judgment in gauging public interest and public response."

Few realized just how intent a warrior Jackie was for the New Frontier. As one friend revealed, "She follows every roll-call in the Congressional Record. She is intensely loyal to Jack and resents votes against his program[s]." She considered his Space Program initiatives important and particularly expressed her disapproval of opponents to the president's School Bill. When she spotted a bachelor Republican senator who had dated Tish, but voted against the School Bill, the First Lady asked her driver to pull up to the curb. She rolled down the window and called out gaily to him, "I thought you were going to be nice to us. Because if you're not, I won't let you take out Tish Balridge anymore."[12]

The days following April 17, 1961, proved to be the most devastating to the president's prestige, when he assumed total responsibility for the Bay of Pigs debacle. The CIA had trained and armed nearly fourteen hundred Cuban exiles fighting that island's Communist leader, Fidel Castro. They landed on Cuba's west beaches in the Bahia de Cochinos (Bay of Pigs), attempting to overthrow the Castro government. The invasion completely failed, and over twelve hundred of the men were captured. In the weeks following, Jacqueline would attempt to divert discussion away from the Bay of Pigs into more upbeat subjects because it still depressed the president. She chastised his friend Red Fay one night, "I had hoped we were going to have a pleasant dinner, instead of having Jack go through one of those sessions on the Bay of Pigs." Later that year, she expressed her admiration for the Cuban exiles of the failed invasion.

At the Miami Orange Bowl, using her son as a subject, the First Lady delivered a speech in Spanish, praising the gathered Brigade 2506, the Cubans who had been captured, but returned in exchange for American food and medicine: "He is still too young to realize what has happened here, but I will make it my business to tell him the story of your courage as he grows up. It is my wish and my hope that some day he may be a man at least half as brave as the members of Brigade 2506."[13]

Jackie was keenly aware of all Jack's public appearances, speeches, and press. Sometimes, said Dave Powers, "she'd tag items like newspaper articles and editorials and ask the president for his response on issues . . . She always had his ear and his attention." Jackie scrutinized publications concerning her husband, once dictating a note to Schlesinger that "there is a mistake in the President's address in the Inaugural book . . . page 269 paragraph 9 should be changed to 'call to service *surrounds* the globe.'"[14]

She stayed informed of the true nature of domestic crises largely through her husband. After U.S. Steel and seven other steel companies went ahead with their threatened price increase after the president urged them specifically not to, he made an angry quip that some newspapers did not print. It was Jacqueline, impressed with the importance of it being recorded exactly as stated, who wrote it down in her own handwriting for the president's files: "My father told me what sons of bitches big businessmen were, but I never believed it." Once, as JFK was conferring with David McDonald, president of the United Steel Workers, he asked McDonald what he thought about a statement made by Roger Blough, chairman of U.S. Steel. McDonald started, "Well that . . ." Suddenly, the First Lady walked in, and the conversation stopped. Later, Jacqueline cornered him. "Dave, when you were talking to Jack and you said, 'That . . .' did you mean Mr. Blough?'" He said yes. She said, "I thought so," and broke into laughter. Rarely did she let on how aware she was.[15]

Deputy Defense Secretary Roswell Gilpatric, who said she had a "core of steel," attested to her interest: "She was always asking me all kinds of questions about the Pentagon, about the flow of power. She had heard her husband mention all kinds of names of people at the Pentagon and she wanted to know what kind of power they had, whether they were motivated mostly by ambition or by their loyalty to the President. She was deeply concerned about how much they could be trusted."

Bill Walton asserted of his friend, "This is a very strong dame. She'll discuss topics with the President, and beat him down." Jacqueline was personally close to Gilpatric, Commerce Undersecretary Franklin Roosevelt, Jr., and Defense Secretary Robert McNamara, but it was Attorney General Robert Kennedy who most frequently served as political conduit and confidant for his sister-in-law. Writer Ralph Martin recalled that at one political briefing held at Bobby's house, she "asked hard, searching questions and got deeply involved in the discussions." When she once told Bobby that she wanted to shock Jack with a complicated political question, he prepped her. After Jackie asked Jack if it was true that "confirming Albert Beeson to membership on the National Labor Relations Board has the effect of wrecking the Bonwit Teller clause of the National Labor Relations Act," the president "almost choked with laughter."[16]

Arthur Schlesinger stated, "From time to time, of course, she did [ask political questions], as one crisis or another dominated the headlines, and he would tell [McGeorge] Bundy to show her the cables." Jackie confidentially told a reporter that Bobby had called the Kremlin to reach Soviet diplomat Georgi N. Bolshakov, "in a rage about something." The White House had repeatedly denied that the phone call had been made, but the First Lady knew it was true and had remained publicly mute about it, understating her knowledge of such things, maintaining the administration stance.

Schlesinger wrote that "while she had strong, intelligent and quite liberal political views, she did not press them . . . She felt, I believe, that the President was immersed in public policy all day and deserved a respite in the evening. She had been told that Mrs. Roosevelt harassed FDR about public matters, and she was determined not to make that mistake . . . she rather downplayed her own views during the White House years."[17]

Only rarely did the First Lady's political role become public knowledge. When a labor dispute arose with the Metropolitan Opera's musicians' union, Labor Secretary Arthur J. Goldberg entered talks attempting to resolve it. Assistant Labor Secretary Reynolds admitted to *The Washington Post* that Goldberg entered the case "at the request of the White House," but that "it was Jackie Kennedy and not John F. that got us into it."[18]

Uninterested in becoming an activist, Jacqueline effectively used the hostess role as political statement. When a gift of a Steuben glass crystal set was offered to the White House, she opted instead for glass manufactured in depressed West Virginia. When some tried to convince her to buy finer glassware, the First Lady retorted, "[T]he whole problem is still West Virginia—it [the answer] is still NO—and will be until they aren't poor any more. . . . I would practically break all the glasses & order new ones each week—it's the only way I have to help them. . . ." When the company advertised their famous client and renamed the glassware design "President's House Crystal," selling them out at ten dollars a dozen, Jacqueline said, "I didn't mind at all, as I thought it was nice to help West Virginia. . . ." It was the one commercial venture in which she hoped a manufacturer *would* use her as advertisement.[19]

As hostess, she also contributed to America's alliance with Pakistan's president, Ayub Khan. On March 23, JFK had warned the Communist Vietnamese that the United States would not tolerate a conquest of Laos. Few nations supported him, but Pakistan offered troops, and it was politically important that relations with Pakistan remain not only stable but friendly. It was the First Lady who personally created an enchanting evening for Ayub Khan's state visit.

Emulating the Versailles dinner, Jacqueline planned a historic state dinner at Mount Vernon, the first such affair ever held outside of the White House. She had guests driven in limousines to a Washington pier, then transported in four vessels, with live music on each. Guests approached the house through a flank of marines in blue, and dined by candlelight on French specialties transported by army trucks from the White House. The *New York Herald Tribune* asked, "What would Martha have said?" One guest, a Congressional wife, long recalled the night.

Betty Ford was frequently at White House events, as the wife of a Republican from whom the administration was trying to get legislative support. Betty recalled with excitement the magical evening at Mount Vernon, the balmy air, mint juleps on the portico, the dinner tents that looked like garden living rooms. She was amazed that Mrs. Kennedy had persuaded the Mount Vernon Ladies' Association to permit use of the home. During dinner Lady Bird and Lyndon invited Betty and Jerry to join them on the ride back to Washington on their host yacht. However, word came from the Kennedys that they wanted the Fords on *their* boat, so Betty and Jackie sailed back together. Mrs. Ford, like other Washington women, "copied" the Jackie Look. "It was epidemic, that wardrobe."[20]

Jacqueline was always interested in foreign affairs and leaders in the news. Before Morocco's King Hassan was to meet with JFK, she wrote Hassan a five-page personal letter, and on learning that he had appeared on *Meet the Press*, discussing problems of the Middle East, she asked for a transcript to review. Tish felt that Mrs. Kennedy "was most fascinated by international politics [and] knew . . . details . . . I'm sure she discussed things with President Kennedy. She is like a sponge—she absorbs everything—everything she hears. She may not say anything, but she always listens very intently. And she was well-informed by being a presence . . ."[21]

Jacqueline was thoroughly American, and yet international. Besides French, she spoke Spanish and a little Italian, but the Latin culture held a special appeal for her, and South Americans responded emotionally to her understanding of them. *El Alianza para el Progreso*, the president's ten-year plan to raise the housing, education, medical, and employment standards for Latin America, was close to her heart. Just as Julia Tyler had been a spiritual foster parent for Texas annexation, so was Jacqueline to the Alliance for Progress. As Julia's Texas association was the subject of a political cartoon, Jackie's goodwill was also subject to a cartoon, showing her leading JFK, who was carrying a document marked "Alliance for Progress," walking down the side of a sombrero, the rim filled with cheering Latins screaming "Jaqui!"

In her first weeks, Jacqueline had joined officials for the president's speech outlining his opinions and plans for Latin American affairs. "I get all my views from him," she said at the ceremony. Her rare noon outings with JFK were often associated with Latin America, like attending Pan American Day at the OAS, her trips south of the border served as superb public relations for the Alliance.

At the end of her first year, Jackie joined the president on his South American trip, focusing on Alliance projects, and enchanting the natives, from Venezuelan president Betancourt to the street crowds in Caracas—estimated to be the largest turnout for any foreign visitor. In Bogotá, Colombia, she was cheered and swamped again, making a vivid impression in yellow suit and hat as she gave a speech in Spanish. Crowds varied the familiar "Jaqui!" chant with "Heh, Miss America!"

On a manure-covered Venezuelan farm, Jacqueline, in an apricot suit, stepped vivaciously into the field before a gathering of several thousand peasants. JFK introduced a "Kennedy who does not need an interpreter," and Jacqueline delivered her first speech on behalf of the Alliance, putting political goals into a family context: "No fathers or mothers can be happy until they have the possibility of jobs and education for their children. This must be for all and not just a few." The crowds wildly applauded and whistled. CBS said she "stole the show." On a later trip with Jack to Mexico, she gave a five-minute Spanish speech to residents of a rural housing project. Crowds rained colored confetti on her, and one Mexican wrote a song about her. When President Lopez Mateos spoke in Spanish about the United States, she visibly frowned at his anti-American comments. When she spoke in Spanish, however, Mateos broke into a torrent of praise for Jackie's linguistics and beauty.[22]

Dave Powers said that in South American countries, Jackie "took interest in subsidized housing improvements that could be made by the Alliance. . . ." Some of her administration allies were directly involved in Latin aid programs, namely Schlesinger, who assisted in UN and Latin American affairs, and brother-in-law Sargent Shriver, director of the Peace Corps. But it was Ted Moscoso, U.S. coordinator for the Alliance for Progress, with whom she said she worked most closely. She was "devoted to him." Tish thought that of all the administration's international changes Jackie was most vitally interested in the Alliance. "With the Latins . . . she felt education was so vital to every other phase of life—economics and so forth. She'd often ask about the children's health and education programs initiated there. . . ."[23]

To the administration, there was no question that she had a beneficial impact on South American relations. Ambassador to Brazil Lincoln Gordon said Jacqueline had become "a folk heroine" in that country, her face adorning the covers of its magazines. The USIA soon requested that the First Lady tape a Spanish greeting for the opening of their new Bogotá, Colombia, station, because it could prove "politically

valuable." Many Latin American leaders felt it indispensable to their standing back home just to meet her.[24]

Just before the first group of Peace Corps volunteers were to begin work in Honduras, Honduran First Lady Alejandrina Morales came to America to watch their training, and asked to see Jackie informally. Ambassador Charles Burrows claimed none too tactfully that since she "was not here officially, Mrs. Kennedy was not interested in seeing her." Soon after, as the Moraleses planned an *official* U.S. visit, Jackie, at Hyannis Port with her children during the summer, was not at a working lunch for Colombia's president, and the press reported the next day that she'd been waterskiing. Burrows said that news "went around the world." Even though the lunch was just for the two presidents, a nervous Mrs. Morales took it as an omen that Jackie wouldn't be present for their welcome, and Burrows got a call saying that if that was the case, Mrs. Morales wouldn't even get off the plane. He wrote a "tough" letter to the White House saying that "if she's not going to receive . . . let's call the whole thing off . . . it'll cause more damage than good will."

Not only did Jackie receive Señora Morales upstairs at the White House, but she welcomed her at the airport, even bringing a rose bouquet.[25]

Jacqueline was often present at meetings of UN American ambassador Adlai Stevenson and JFK, later confiding to FDR, Jr., that "Jack can't bear to be in the same room with him [Adlai]." Roosevelt related the story to his mother. Mrs. Roosevelt and Mrs. Kennedy had a bond in their friendship with Adlai. Eleanor sat right behind Jackie at the UN on September 25 when the president spoke to the General Assembly. They had not seen each other since sharing a campaign platform in October 1960, in Harlem. Eleanor was honored as "special adviser," to America's delegation for the UN's sixteenth session, but for the first time, she was mainly a figurehead. Her strength was ebbing from a rare blood disease that taxed her energy. But it didn't stop her. She continued to travel extensively, alone, carrying her own bag.

In 1961, Eleanor decided to write Jackie with the sort of encouraging advice only one of the sorority could pass on to another: "I know there will be difficulties in store for you in the White House life but

perhaps also you will find some compensations. Most things are made easier, though I think on the whole life is rather difficult for both the children and their parents in the 'fish bowl' that lies before you." The two First Ladies began a warm correspondence, Jackie even sending Eleanor one of Caroline's drawings, and writing that she'd just read a story to her about Fala. Mrs. Roosevelt said publicly that it was a thrill to have "so young, intelligent and attractive" a First Lady. She praised Jackie's Paris and Austria conquests, saying that smiling through weariness and looking interested "at all times is a remarkable feat, especially when it is considered that we do not have the long training given to royalty. . . ." She thought the White House restoration showed a great sense of history.

When Eleanor visited the White House, JFK paused to let her enter the front door first. "No, Mr. President, you go first. It's protocol." For a woman who had so vigorously eschewed convention, the slight gesture was remarkable. Eleanor toured the restored rooms and proclaimed, "I loved it. It's light and bright and beautiful." Lawrence Fuchs, Philippines Peace Corps director, recalled Eleanor's reaction: "She was so impressed and delighted . . . She said . . . Franklin . . . would turn over in his grave. He would never let her do things like this." She thought it "marvelous" that the young couple "had terrific courage and zest for living," and she "was interested in them personally." Mrs. Roosevelt and her friends David and Edna Gurewitsch were in Switzerland when she received a several-page handwritten letter from Mrs. Kennedy. The president had originally asked Eleanor to write Jackie with advice on what institutions she might visit in South America, and this was a warm, effusive response to that.

Eleanor remained outspoken, urging an agreement with the Soviets to keep space demilitarized, and joining a group calling for the government to bring the Vietnam question to the United Nations. She was appointed by Kennedy to chair his Commission on the Status of Women, and pressed him to hire "able women" from her list. She said, "[J]udge a candidate . . . on fitness for office. I would like to see us get away from considering a man or woman from the point of view of religion, color or sex." She supported an Equal Rights Amendment, but refused to see public problems "through the unique lens of gender."

One observer said Eleanor Roosevelt was generations ahead of her time because "she felt deeper."[26]

Before one of her commission meetings, Eleanor received a telegram from Texas: "Please extend to the members of your hard working commission our best wishes for a fruitful and pleasant meeting at Hyde Park which has been the setting for so much worthwile thoughts and doings for their country." It was signed "Lady Bird and Lyndon Johnson."[27]

Jacqueline developed a close relationship with the Johnsons, who donated a gift of Lincoln's appointments book for the restoration. LBJ also arranged to have a White House chandelier first installed by Ulysses S. Grant returned, from its later placement at the Capitol. Lady Bird always dropped her own plans if Mrs. Kennedy needed a substitute. At their first Congressional ball, after Jack and Jackie and Lyndon and Lady Bird switched dancing partners, the First Lady quipped to LBJ, "Oh, I'm getting a much better dancer." She believed that the Johnsons deserved greater respect than was usually accorded vice presidents and Second Ladies, and changed protocol by having their names announced at "*every* occasion" because it embarrassed her to have them "just disappear like maids" at receptions.

During the campaign, Lyndon had asked native Texan reporter Liz Carpenter to serve on his staff, and she increasingly found herself also handling the Second Lady's press. Lady Bird took an avid interest in Lyndon's role as chairman of a Committee on Equal Employment Opportunity, and relished traveling with him on foreign trips. She combined traditional wifery with progressive values, and comparisons were drawn between her and Eleanor.[28]

If Mrs. Roosevelt had rhapsodized that Jacqueline was "full of life," it was the senior member of the sorority who fell most deeply under her spell. Edith Wilson managed to host a grand luncheon for the First Lady on March 27, serving crab soup and asparagus, inviting "[a]ll Democrats . . ." She thanked Jacqueline for her and the president's "charming attentions" on Inauguration Day, and wrote to "[p]lease tell your indefatigable husband how proud of him we are." The public was again reminded of Edith when a retired black White House seamstress, Lillian Rogers Parks, published her memoirs. Edith read it, and age hadn't dimmed her bigotry. When discussing it with some friends, she told her own maid to "[g]o upstairs and get that nigger book."

Edith endured. She broke her arm. Her hair was falling out. When her sister died, Jacqueline wrote her offering "deepest sympathy," and telling her "you are very much in our thoughts." Through the crisp leaves of October, Mrs. Wilson grandly sailed up the steps of the White House to witness the president's commissioning of a Wilson memorial. In the Oval Office, the young president and old First Lady sat together. A once curvaceous icon who'd danced the cakewalk and wore beaded Worth gowns was now withered in her pearls and purple suit in this age of the twist. JFK handed the imperious "Mrs. President" the pen after signing the bill. "I didn't dare ask you for it," she joked. Everyone laughed. She had rarely been submissive.

A week later, Edith celebrated her eighty-ninth birthday at an annual Virginia lunch with friends, where discussion came around to a new biography of her, written by Alden Hatch. After reading the inferences that her regency had indeed been full of political power, she

dropped a note to Hatch: "You made me a perfect virago!" She also revealed that she hadn't burned her love letters from Woodrow, but would leave them with her papers. For the New Frontier, she agreed to serve as a trustee of the Freedom from Hunger Committee. The president's director of Food for Peace, George McGovern, wrote her that he was "delighted" that she would join the group on December 14.

But after Thanksgiving, Edith became housebound with respiratory trouble. On the day she was scheduled to dedicate Washington's new Wilson Bridge, Edith died peacefully in her sleep. Her funeral and burial took place at the National Cathedral. The Trumans, Eisenhowers, and Kennedys did not attend, but the latter sent Alan Shepard and Arthur Schlesinger as representatives. Eleanor sent a telegram to the "Wilson Family," with "regret that I cannot be with you for the services. . . ."

Edith's large oval portrait, showing her in shades of violet, would be donated to the White House, but her papers proved most revealing. Among them was a sad little poem from her first husband upon the death of their child. As Mrs. Woodrow Wilson, she had never mentioned the child, and barely mentioned Norman. A file revealed her kind fostering of "your little Filipino friend," who became a renowned artist—a warm correspondence that existed from 1920 to just days before her death. Hers was an amazing story: a poor girl from the Virginia mountains to a jewelry store counter to the seat of power. She had been in the presence of women from Julia Grant to Betty Ford. The very papers she chose to leave would prove that she had indeed exerted some of the power that she had spent fifty years denying. Few remembered that there had been an equally influential first Mrs. Wilson, but after Edith's death, at the opening of the Smithsonian's Museum of History and Technology, it was revealed that one of Ellen Wilson's daughters specifically stated that she didn't want the mannequin representing Edith placed in the same display case as that of her own mother.[29]

A month before Edith's death, another sorority elder came to see Jackie. Harry and Bess Truman came for an overnight stay, and for both women the visit was happily private. Bess remained mute. When asked in her one and only television interview if she would like to say anything about politics, specifically or generally, she harrumphed, "No, not in either category thank you." She offered that her Missouri retirement meant "occasional dullness," and that she missed Washington. Of the restoration changes, Bess said, "I wish I had thought of them." After dinner, when JFK asked Truman to play the piano, all they could find was a song about Mrs. Eisenhower: "Once in Love with Mamie."

In June, Mamie Eisenhower had also returned to the White House, ostensibly to attend a luncheon for the Japanese premier, but also to look over the new rooms with Jackie before lunch. Mamie told reporters, "It looks lovely . . . some changes have been made, but it's basically the same." It was not exactly praise. When she saw that a silver chandelier had been gilded, Mamie gave out an audible moan. To most, she politely said that Jackie was "awfully young," but told her doctor that she was "brazen and frivolous," and thought she should be spending more time at the White House, managing the budget as she had. Of her successor, Mamie flatly said, "[S]he has no respect for money at all." Barbara Eisenhower, however, thought that Mamie actually admired the way Jacqueline had managed the restoration, and "probably wished she had thought of it. Especially saving government money. I'm certain she'd have admired that."

Certainly the former First Lady could be none too happy about the buttons circulating through Washington just before she left: MAMIE START PACKING—THE KENNEDYS ARE COMING. But if she was hesitant about her successor, Mamie was still an old hand at influencing Ike and the new Administration. When former Eisenhower Chief of Staff Sherman Adams was under investigation for income-tax evasion, and on the verge of being indicted by a federal grand jury, Mrs. Eisenhower interceded, fearing that "Mr. Jones [a pseudonym used for Adams] might commit suicide"—a fact corroborated by a Justice Department official, who thought the anxious Adams was "ready to jump out a window." Ike approached Senator Dirksen to approach President Kennedy and intervene "as a personal favor to me, to put the Jones indictment in the deep freeze. . . . He'll have a blank check in my bank if he will grant

me this favor." And that is how, albeit unwittingly, Mamie Eisenhower influenced the endorsement of Kennedy's test-ban treaty by the two leading Republicans, Senator Dirksen and her husband.

If Middle American Mamie had her doubts about Jackie, she was not alone. As the Nevada, Missouri, *Daily Mail* reported, "[A] good many conservative American ladies shuddered at the thought of 'that girl' in the White House." The visual contrast between Jackie and the average American "lady" was glaringly, almost humorously apparent. One reception line photo showed an amused First Lady in a simple hot-pink dress, gloveless, hatless, and without jewelry, greeting a bespectacled grande dame in flowered cartwheel hat, with gloves and oversized handbag. But if any still had doubts about the young, rich, and thin "girl," who danced The Twist, rode to hounds, and spoke softly, they were about to change their tune as they tuned in, through "the miracle of television."[30]

". . . *Goddess of Power*"

As 1962 BEGAN, Jacqueline Kennedy undertook still *more* projects.

When Bill Walton told her about an imminent plan to demolish Lafayette Square's historic row houses, across from the White House, a shocked First Lady determined to stop it. She asked David Finley, chairman of the Fine Arts Commission, to stroll with her through the park, examining the buildings slated for destruction. The second-oldest structure was the town house from which America's first "Queen Mother" figure, widow Dolley Madison, had reigned. "I want to preserve these wonderful old houses," Jackie told the expert. Then, in her understated way, she dropped a seemingly calm request. "How can I do it?"

Finley directed her to Bernard Boutin, chief administrator of the General Services Administration. That night, she privately conferred with the president over the matter. The next morning she was on the phone with Boutin. To him, she would state frankly how to best preserve the square in a private memorandum, illustrating again her discipline in learning details, this time in architecture:

> Because of our interest in history and preservation, it really does matter a great deal to the President and to myself that this is done well; we have received so much mail on this subject . . . at least I can spare him some minor problems . . .
>
> (1)—*The East Side of Lafayette Square:* They are now planning to put up a hideous white modern court building. All architects are innovators, and would rather do something new than in the spirit of old buildings. I think they are totally wrong in this case, as the important thing is to preserve the 19th century feeling of Lafayette Square . . . write to the architects and tell them to submit to you a design which is more in keeping with the 19th century bank on the corner. It should be the same color, same size, etc. When they have sent you these designs, would you be good enough to show them to me on my return from India?
>
> (2)—*The West Side of Lafayette Square:* Again, the architects came up with the most unsuitable, violently modern building which would be such a jarring note on the Square even though it might be good architec-

ture all by itself. As we cannot save the facades of all the houses on that side of the Square, I think it is of vital importance that, again, the new building be in the same style as Decatur House on the North and the other old houses on the South. However, in the photograph I am enclosing, the architect sketched a design for two buildings, and I think this is perfect—and so does the President. So, would you please have the architect submit you plans for this and just tell them they have to do it. I am sure you can figure out an efficient way of allocating different departments to each building. Again, could I see these plans on my return from India?

(3)—*The Old Court of Claims Building:* This is on the corner of Pennsylvania Avenue and 17th Street. It may look like a Victorian horror, but it is really quite lovely and a precious example of the period of architecture which is fast disappearing. I so strongly feel that the White House should give the example in preserving our nation's past. Now we think of saving old buildings like Mt. Vernon and tear down everything in the 19th century—but, in the next hundred years, the 19th century will be of great interest and there will be none of it left; just plain glass skyscrapers. The Fine Arts Commission and the architects want to tear this down and put a Park in its place because they think it makes the block more symmetrical.

I hope you will use all your influence to see that this building is preserved and not replaced with a few trees. We also have received a great deal of mail on the subject of this building. This building . . . could either again be used by the Corcoran or by the Modern Museum of Art, which people are trying to start in this city . . . I am sure that you can find a use for it—either renting it out so that the government gets the money or putting a government department in it . . .

I cannot tell you how much I am counting on you for your help in this matter. It is so discouraging; for months now these plans have gone back and forth; no one seems to know who has the final say—and, before you know it, everything is ripped down and horrible things put up in their place. I simply panic at the thought of this and decided to make a last-ditch appeal.[1]

To a pessimistic president and Bill Walton, Jackie cracked, "You white-livered characters need some help and I'm going to get involved. The wreckers haven't started yet, and until they do, it can be saved." Because of her, the contracted architectural plans for the modern buildings were postponed, and GSA made the decision to make no decision for a short period, hoping some suitable alternative would arise. Jackie's halting the bulldozers came at a crucial moment. Within several weeks, JFK ran into architect John Warnecke, who immediately drafted his ideas. The First Lady continued looking into alternatives to the monolithic structures. On September 24, Arthur Schlesinger sent Jacqueline government reports from the FDR administration on their planned square redesign.[2]

Meanwhile, Warnecke had come up with a solution of building new but unprepossessing red-brick offices to rise behind the town houses. Bernard Boutin recalled Jacqueline's "delight when I told her that we were moving ahead and were about to award a contract." Two days later, the First Lady went over to Boutin's GSA office to view the preliminary blueprint plans. Boutin said the plans were "so voluminous that . . . we'd spread them on the floor and would go on hands and knees from one plan to another. . . . She always had comments to make on whether she liked something or whether she didn't, and would make recommendations or suggestions." Jackie approved, and on October 17 attended the unveiling of the Lafayette Square model. Bill Walton said that without the First Lady, "we never would have saved the square."[3]

She was already laying plans for further involvement in historic preservation. With the president, she took personal interest in a long-range plan to have Pennsylvania Avenue redeveloped. She assumed the chairmanship of the Committee to Save Blair House, conducted under GSA's auspices, and Boutin said, "We worked very closely with Mrs. Kennedy . . ." Jackie's support was enlisted to block a plan to demolish

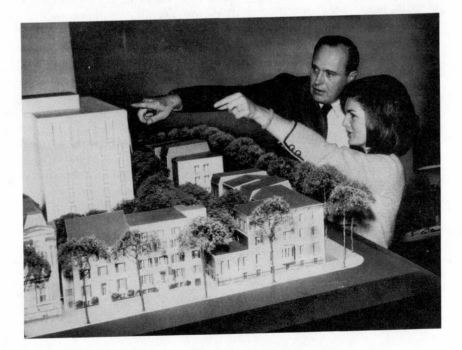

the Grant era Executive Office Building, as well as the Victorian Court of Claims building directly across the street. Though the latter "took precedence over the EOB because Bill Walton informed her it was in more immediate danger of being destroyed," both were saved.[4]

Mrs. Kennedy's efforts dovetailed at a time when an urban movement was just beginning to revitalize decrepit downtown areas. Efforts were made to restore old buildings and make them viable spaces for modern office use. In time, the federal and state governments would provide tax incentives to those conducting restorations. By the visibility of her interests, Jacqueline Kennedy was viewed as a "pioneer of the historical preservation movement" emerging in the early sixties.

The First Lady was now ready to begin the first phase of her determined goal to create an American Department of the Arts.

André Malraux was coming to dinner.

Malraux was considerably more than an officeholder, and his life intrigued Jacqueline. She read his novels *La Condition Humaine* and *L'Espoir* in college. She knew of his career as a French Resistance leader during World War II, and as a Spanish Civil War pilot. Malraux would later dedicate his book *Anti-Memoirs* to Jacqueline Kennedy. .

As she later wrote, Jacqueline "hoped one day to have a Minister for the Arts in the Cabinet, but much groundwork would have to be done before that would be possible." After their Paris trip, she had "persuaded" the president to formally invite the minister of culture to the United States. Jacqueline "hoped his visit would call attention to the importance of the arts, which received little government support in the United States, whereas in other countries they were subsidized by the government." President Kennedy received Malraux with the highest honors, usually accorded only to a chief of state. Whether or not it might result in a Cabinet position or agency for the arts, Jacqueline felt the Malraux dinner "would be a wonderful way to focus attention" on the need for *some* form of government assistance to the arts.

For several months before the visit, she planned all the details herself. When she learned that Malraux would be speaking in New York, *she* chose the administration's representative and wrote him a convincing letter:

> I know that the French Ambassador has written to ask if you would speak in answer to André Malraux at the great Franco-American dinner in New York May 15. It is such an important occasion and you are the only person who could properly respond to Malraux. If you could just make as moving a speech as you did about Mr. Sam at the Democratic dinner—As you know Malraux is the Minister of Cultural Affairs in France—this visit here is such an important one—for all the cultural side of our country—the dinner we will give for him at the White House

May 10 will be like the Casals dinner—in that all the great American writers & poets will be there—His speech in New York will be a major one—and it is so vital that the most important & the most eloquent person—you—be there. I know how busy you are—and I wouldn't write if I didn't think that he and his visit are so significant. My best wishes to you always, Jackie.[5]

Lyndon Johnson accepted.

Jacqueline later wrote that she "worked carefully on the guest list for the State dinner, wanting to include artists admired abroad, not only the traditional, establishment ones" it was suggested she invite. She recalled that Tennessee Williams "was too shy to come," but she called him, and he accepted. She had the fathers of modern abstract painting—Mark Rothko and Franz Kline—and playwrights—S. N. Behrman and Arthur Miller—to the dinner. She chose leading artists in all the different disciplines: ballet's Balanchine, poets St. John Perse and Robert Lowell, painter Andrew Wyeth, theatrical director Elia Kazan, French author Henri Bernstein, actress Geraldine Page.[6]

Jacqueline recalled that one immediate result was Malraux's whispering to her after dinner, "'Je vais vous envoyer La Joconde.' [I will

send you the Gioconda—the Mona Lisa], and he came back with her the next year." The loan of the famous painting was made officially not to the American government, but personally to Jacqueline Kennedy. She attended its gala exhibit opening at the National Gallery, a tanned vision in pink sheath, escorted by Malraux and JFK. With complete innocence, she wrote about the mad crush of humanity at the opening, fighting just to catch a glimpse of the enigmatically smiling dark woman of "magic" who cast a "spell." She was, of course, referring to the Mona Lisa.[7]

In the midst of arts lobbying and historic preservation, the First Lady raised eyebrows when it was announced that she had accepted CBS's suggestions that she give the nation a television tour of the restored White House rooms.

Jackie appeared slightly nervous, with normal makeup and ubiquitous bouffant. Each room she entered and described was a separate "scene." She and anchorman Charles Collingswood rehearsed just once, and with the producer discussed her movement and narration in conjunction with camera angles. During the taping, she spoke entirely from memory, often adding spontaneous remarks, a tiny microphone hidden in her red suit jacket. During the full seven-hour taping, she successfully ignored the conspicuous lights and cameras, and men in the control truck, watching on monitors, told Collingswood, "It's a good set and a good star." The production cost $130,000 (the average of a weekly variety-show program), paid for by CBS. Immediately after, Jackie watched tapes of the endeavor, scribbling notes for changes that were later made. The next week she read narrations for still pictures that were to be used in the final production. Under the white blaze of TV lights, it was Jackie at her best.[8]

Aired on February 14, 1962, A Tour of the White House with Mrs. John F. Kennedy was carried by the three networks, viewed in 28.3 million homes. The Nielsen television-rating system conservatively estimated the audience at 56 million. Another estimate ran 80 million. About three out of four Americans watched. The tour proceeded from the ground floor to the state rooms, but Mrs. Kennedy also insisted on showing the half-completed Treaty Room to visually illustrate the process.

Jacqueline mentioned that Caroline Harrison "complained that she had no privacy," Grace Coolidge added third-floor rooms, and Mary Lincoln "made her husband rather cross because he thought she spent too much money." She spoke of Julia Grant's desk, and Dolley Madison's sofa. She added that she was glad the executive offices no longer shared the family floor, but judiciously avoided partisan politics. Still, some read politics into her narrative. She did give Latins a plug by praising Colombia's restored President's Palace, and mentioned her

West Virginia glassware, one television commentator later claiming that she had been politically inspired to make the comment. When asked about the role government might play in the arts, she avoided the overture: "That's so complicated. I don't know. I just think that everything in the White House should be the best. . . ." She wasn't ready to go public with her arts-government plan.

The response was immediate. Two million dollars, in mostly small amounts, flooded in for the restoration. The First Lady received ten thousand laudatory letters, one child writing that his "dad was going to watch *Maverick,*" but that Jackie prevailed. A member of the "loyal opposition" wrote her that her tour "compels the abandonment of all political bias . . ." It was Barbara Bush. The Academy of Television and Sciences trustees even presented "the star of the program" a special Emmy Award for the show's contribution to furthering American history education, but the public had watched with equal curiosity about her. One Texas housewife seemed to say it all as she recalled "watching and listening to Mrs. Kennedy more than thinking about the White House." Fourteen foreign nations immediately requested copies of *Tour*, and she suggested that she dub narration in Spanish and French herself. The State Department realized what they had caught an inkling of in Paris. The government had a bona fide movie star on their hands.

The United States Information Agency arranged to have *Tour* telecast on European television, made reel copies and distributed it to 106 other countries, including six Iron Curtain nations.[9]

The reaction produced nothing short of worship.

In England, 8.75 million citizens watched. The London *Sunday Times* said she was "obviously absorbed in the scholarship," the *Observer* called her voice a "phantom intimacy," and a Birmingham editorial said she "influenced people." In Sweden, the liberal *Expressen* said it was "effective public relations."

In non-European and Communist countries, the film was shown by direct projection to auditorium audiences. Iran's empress wanted to see it "as soon as possible," and the shah asked to see it the next night. In Tel Aviv, the only criticism of journalists was that it wasn't in color. A liberal party paper ran a forty-column-inch story about it, resulting in a "run" on the film. It was booked weeks in advance. In Karachi, Pakistan, twenty-seven thousand people saw it in forty-four showings. In Bombay, the Indo-American Society auditorium was filled to saturation, and upon demand, the Working Women's Guild was given a special showing. In New Delhi, seventy-three hundred people from journalists to leading educators to embassy personnel watched in twenty-one separate showings. Helsinki's USIS reported the "film is valuable." In Moscow the American embassy's cultural attaché invited 150 guests to view it, after which he was "besieged with requests for information materials on the U.S." Japan, Korea, Africa, and Latin America all received copies, and showed *Tour* to their demanding crowds.[10]

It was on the crest of this fame that Jackie left in March for a solo journey to India and Pakistan, billed as a "goodwill" trip. Few, however, realized that Jacqueline played an important political role. Diplomatic relations had been strained several months before when India planned a military action against Portugal, which still held a colony on its west coast in Goa Province. The United States indicated that it favored eventual Portuguese pullout, which insulted the Indian government. In careful consideration of India's bête noir, Jackie and traveling companion, sister Lee, would also proceed to Pakistan.

Before she arrived in India, Jacqueline stopped off in Rome and became the first incumbent First Lady to be received by a pope. Four of her predecessors had been presented to popes before or after their husbands were in office, but Jackie was the first Catholic, and her meeting with John XXIII, conducted entirely in French, received tremendous press. She also accepted the invitation to meet with Italian president Giovanni Gronchi for a private talk. It was the first time an American president's wife met alone with the democratically elected president of a European nation.[11]

In India she was a hit the moment she greeted the crowds. The First Lady clasped her hands, and slightly bowed. It was India's traditional form of salutation.

Jackie acquiesced in all customs. She wore the traditional Indian "Tilak" paint applied to women's foreheads. She slipped out of her shoes and into the traditional cloth covers on her feet when visiting a temple. Against the Secret Service wishes, she participated in the ritual of *holi*, the throwing of powdered chalk at one another, symbolic of

good's triumph over evil. She laid roses at the cremation spot of Mahatma Gandhi. For a Caucasian woman to show such a respect to a third world people was rare, and it won unanimous praise in India.

The number of journalists covering her India trip was the second largest for any visiting dignitary—President Eisenhower's had been the greatest. It was India's second most covered event after its 1947 independence, and its Overseas Communications Service increased its radio-photo facilities threefold. After Jackie attended a sari fashion show, bought several bolts of the material, and later wore one, the costume became the latest rage. Her celebrity spread like fire through the country, and more Indians turned out to see her than to see Queen Elizabeth. A mesmerized old lady who walked nearly twenty miles to see Jackie pronounced, "She is Durga, the goddess of power." When she was presented with a pearl necklace, a special song was written to commemorate *that*. A royal bamboo arch was made for her to pass under. She sailed down the Ganges on a ceremonial raft. Jacqueline became so idolized in India that the domestic staff who served her there placed her photograph on a wall next to a Hindu god and the Virgin Mary. In America, a cartoon pictured an Indian lying on a bed of nails beaming at rows and rows of pictures of Jackie, captioned "Feeling No Pain!" Mrs. Kennedy wasn't called "Jackie," or "Jacqueline," or "President's wife" or "First Lady." She was titled "Amerika Maharani" (American Queen).12

Premier Nehru was mesmerized with Mrs. Kennedy, and even taught her the yoga exercise of standing on her head. So taken was he that he chose not to lobby about Goa and other internal troubles with Kashmir and Pakistan. And yet, though Schlesinger wrote that Nehru "scrupulously avoided politics," the trip helped remove "the lingering pique about Goa." The First Lady remained acutely aware of partisanship in India; to keep all factions happy, she decided to accept the invitation to be the overnight guest of the liberal governor of Rajastan as well as the conservative maharajah of Jaipur.

In Pakistan it was more of the same.

She went down to the Khyber Pass on the West Pakistan–Afghanistan border, feted by tribal chieftains, and along her return route to Peshawar, natives spread luxurious Afghan carpets for her motorcade to pass over. In Afghan hat, she even winked back at a border guard.13

Throughout, Jackie sent Jack affectionate "reports of trip's progress," and in one letter he wrote her, "The stories and pictures of your trip have been wonderful. The reports and pictures seem to confirm that you are well and happy. Galbraith is looking a little tired. Caroline and John came home yesterday and are very well and brown. We all miss you very much. All love. Jack."14

Pakistani president Ayub Khan not only gave Jacqueline a bay gelding, but matched Nehru in treating her as an American queen, which was easier than attempting to comprehend what a democracy's First Lady traditionally meant. It helped make the "unofficial" role further recognized as official.

When told that some American bigots criticized the idea of a white woman fully interacting with peoples of different, often scorned, races, the First Lady permitted Pakistani newspapers to quote her that "reactionary influences and spokesmen in the United States were best ignored." JFK remained loyal to Jackie's mission. Just as she defended his programs, the president never let a critic of his wife's public work go unchastised, even if it was his friend Ben Bradlee of Newsweek, which editorialized that her trip avoided poverty-stricken sites. When Bradlee called to discuss a Supreme Court vacancy, the president expressed anger at Newsweek's coverage of Jackie's trip: "That wasn't one of your better efforts, was it? . . . I don't get all this crap about how she should have been rubbing her nose in the grinding poverty of India. When the French invite you to Paris, they don't show you the sewers; they take you to Versailles." Two days later, Jack was still defending Jackie. "Ken Galbraith told me Jackie took all the bitterness out of our relations with India. If I had gone there, we would have talked about Kashmir and Goa, but Jackie did a helluva job."[15]

There was grumbling about the trip's forty-five-thousand-dollar cost from New York Senator Javits, who sent a letter "loaded from every angle." LBJ defended the First Lady in a letter to Senate Majority Leader Mansfield, saying it was "a semi-official trip in that Mrs. Kennedy was the President's Representative." To critics who said, "Who needs a young woman in the latest fashions visiting these underdeveloped countries where there are so many poor?," Alex Drier of ABC responded, ". . . when 1964 rolls around . . . They are going to have to beat Jackie Kennedy." The president thanked Drier after hearing the comments about Jackie's "effect on my political life," saying, "[I]t was heartwarming to know that the public image she creates in your mind reflects such a credit to her country."[16]

Throughout the trip, the USIA filmed Jackie's every move. It was edited gratis by United Artists, and made into a full-length "movie," for commercial distribution, to be shown free in over eight thousand American movie theaters during the Christmas season with a Tony Curtis and Yul Brynner film, Taras Bulba. Jackie Kennedy, in the fullest sense of the word, had become the "movie star" of the American government. Republican congressman Glenard Lipscomb ordered an investigation into the legality of showing a free movie, and later announced a Comptroller General ruling that USIA had no legal right to give the film to any other film distribution company.[17]

Though some grumbled that Jacqueline's pleasurable travels weren't part of her "job," it was her four-week summer vacation that provoked severe criticism. Her choice of Italy seemed the bone of contention. To internationalist Jacqueline, there was no difference between a respite in Italy or New England, so in the summer of '62 she took a "private" vacation to Ravello with Caroline, the Radziwill family, but *not* the president. It proved her first experience with the persistent European photographers dubbed "paparazzi" (bugs) in the Fellini film *La Dolce Vita.*

The paparazzi went to great lengths to capture Jackie in sandals, headkerchiefs, Pucci pants, and sunglasses. On her first day there, fifty paparazzi gathered in an offshore launch, snapping away. At night, she walked through the café-filled streets, listening to Italian mandolins, mixing with the natives. One day she shopped through the narrow Capri streets. Jackie was made an honorary citizen of Ravello and made an acceptance speech in Italian, with Caroline and Anthony Radziwill beside her in tarantella costumes. But when the First Lady took the children to the local beach, the paparazzi had their field day. Jackie, wearing her bathing suit, was flattered by the enthusiastic Italian crowd and began smiling and waving. Photos of her were speedily rushed into print in global newspapers and magazines. Never had Americans seen their First Lady so scantily clad, and some women dashed off condemnations to the press. The unspoken fact was also clear. Unlike most of her matronly predecessors, she was attractive in a bathing suit.[18]

The day Jackie returned home, one hundred women of the "Concerned Citizens of America" picketed the airport with their messages: "America has a severe balance of payment problem. President Kennedy has exhorted the Nation to restrict spending abroad. . . . WHY ARE YOU EXEMPT FROM THE SACRIFICES. . . ? The first lady occupies a place of unusual dignity . . . Yet night after night you have been seen dancing in public bars until dawn with men unescorted by their wives. DOES THIS SET A PROPER EXAMPLE FOR THE YOUNG WOMEN OF AMERICA? At this period your husband is facing overwhelming problems . . . in full view of the world, you have indulged . . . in an excess of hedonism . . . WOULD YOU NOT BETTER HAVE SERVED THE NATION . . . BY REMAINING HERE AT HOME BY HIS SIDE?"[19]

A right wing Baptist "Reverend Ray" excoriated the First Lady from his pulpit as having worn indecent clothing, and outlined his indignation in a letter to Oregon senator Wayne Morse, which soon after was widely reprinted in Bible Belt newspapers. At that very moment something else happened. The commercial press, like the USIA, realized they had a star. To them, the First Lady was a public figure who could be used to make money. The minister's letter was shortly turned into cash when *Photoplay* magazine offered readers the chance to give their opinion. If they bought the magazine, they could clip a coupon for a mail-in poll that asked, "Has Jackie gone too far—or has Reverend Ray? Be the Judge!"[20]

At first cover stories on the First Lady in magazines like *Modern Screen* were benign. Then they twisted quotes into teaser banners. But during the '62 peak, they began suggesting to readers that they could affect Jackie's life by giving their opinions to her in polls. *Movie TV Secrets* published a false story claiming that a Hollywood producer had offered the First Lady a $10 million movie contract, and then turned it around, asking readers, "How do you feel about the issue? Should Jackie Kennedy accept? . . . Send your opinion. . . ." *Photoplay* defensively stated that "Stardom transcends professions. . . . Mrs. Kennedy is in every sense a beautiful, glamorous, exciting star. . . ." *Modern Screen* said she was "living a role that few actresses could play. . . ."[21]

The "Jackie factories" grossly violated the unwritten rules of the private lives of First Ladies to a degree not seen since Frances Cleveland. Past First Ladies had had admirers, but Jackie had frenzied fans. Print and broadcast coverage visibly hyped Jackie's Asian trip, and she returned the most famous woman in the world. A Japanese girl practiced posture and an Indonesian girl studied English because they both emulated Jackie. She won the Dutch magazine *Margriet's* "Woman of the Year" contest. The Australian ambassador admitted, "I fell in love with her . . . great company, bubbly and just nicely irreverent."[22]

At home, Jackie's image seeped into pop culture. NBC news did an entire special, *The World of Jacqueline Kennedy*, for fans. A Jimmy Durante-like one-liner made the national circuit, "Good night, Mrs. Kennedy, wherever you are." The newly crowned Miss America wistfully told audiences, "If only I looked like Jackie." A cartoon pictured an irate wife berating her husband, "I'll bet Jack wouldn't yell at Jacqueline if she were overdrawn!" San Francisco's "Jackie" Home for homeless children got dozens of phone calls every time Mrs. Kennedy was in the news because people thought she was associated with the fourteen-year-old establishment. A Gallup poll said 7 percent of America's women got a bouffant hairdo because of Jackie.

Jackie even had the dubious distinction of being the first First Lady to be a subject in a television cartoon series. In one of their episodes, Hanna-Barbera's "Flintstone" housewives Wilma Flintstone and Betty Rubble went shopping, stopping in amazement at a slim mannequin in pillbox and bouffant. Wilma shrieked to Betty, "It's the Jackie Kennelrock Look!"

Reaching its zenith in 1962, "the Jackie Look" hit Hollywood, which had been largely responsible for marketing the fifties "dumb blonde" with Marilyn Monroe, Judy Holliday, and Jayne Mansfield. Now, with Jackie Kennedy, the "brainy brunette" came into vogue, with television characters like Laura Petrie on the *Dick Van Dyke Show*, who wore Capri pants and flat shoes and had a flip-curl bouffant. The '62 season opening *Jack Benny Show* featured yet another Jackie look-alike, spoofing the real woman. "Mrs. Kennedy with her many interests and travels, voice and individual coiffure," wrote Jack Gould of the *New York Times*, "is a celebrity in her own right." Hollywood designer Edith Head said Jackie was fashion's "greatest single influence in history." Like Mrs. Roosevelt's, Jackie's recognizable voice was immediately satirized, but this time on record albums, the most popular being the first presidential satire, *The First Family*. The most famous parody was *The Tour of the White House*. At the beginning of the tour, "the First Lady" asks cameramen to come through "the oak panel doors," followed immediately by the sound of splintered wood. "I can't help but wish," says the calm voice, "that your cameramen had opened the doors before coming through."23

Tish pointed out that hostesses and caterers copied Jackie's round tables, flower arrangements, and dinner menus. After her Mount Vernon state dinner, tourist attendance there boomed. But just like the craze over "Frankie" Cleveland, "Jackie Fever" began to manifest damaging repercussions. Gradually, even the legitimate press exaggerated stories about Mrs. Kennedy on the most dubious tips. In December 1961, an Associated Press story reprinted in most of the nation's newspapers, including the *Washington Star*, reported that Jackie had danced The Twist until midnight at the Golden Falcon nightclub in Fort Lauderdale with Kenny Miller of New York's Peppermint Lounge, where the dance had originated. The wire story told the nation that Miller had taught the First Lady "to twist" the year before, at a private New York party hosted by Senator Javits. That was at least true. And it was true that she was in Palm Beach for Christmas. But she had never left there. And at the moment she was said to be dancing, her father-in-law had suffered a stroke.

JFK was livid about the story, woven out of a mere report that a woman (Stephanie Javits) resembling Jackie had been at the nightclub. He contacted Salinger, who, after some effort, was sent an apology by the AP, but trying to deny every untrue story became nearly impossible by '62. The press staffs could make only vain attempts to handle the Jackie phenomenon.24

The first wave of Jackie's fame was felt at the White House. Tish informed Pierre Salinger that "Mrs. Kennedy has been asked to receive about 300 awards in the last 14 months . . . most . . . ghastly." Among the thousands of gifts Jackie received was a "ceramic beer wagon full of plants, drawn by horses. . . ." There were petty letters. One woman chastised Jackie for missing church, another warned that riding to the hounds was dangerous. A gentleman accused her of "being used to pro-

mote Paris styling," a sentiment echoed by Clare Luce, who said Fran-
cophilism was unpatriotic.[25]

When *Photoplay* used Jackie's picture on their June 1962 cover, it
launched an avalanche of indignant letters. White House aide Ted
Sorensen wrote to the Better Business Bureau, hoping that they would
"enforce" standards regarding the "name and likeness of the First
Lady." Jackie had herself determined that "commercializing on the
Presidency" was "something I will fight against," but once it was realized that there was no law to limit what should have been censored by
taste alone, the floodgates broke. House of Lords whiskey used a Jackie
lookalike, smoking cigarettes in their ads, while a Florida marine shop
did the same to sell waterskis. A Jackie voice parody sold The Rambler
American station wagon on TV commercials. Ray-Ban sunglasses made
no attempt to veil its ad. There "she" was, in riding habit, on a horse,
with vast oversized sunglasses.[26]

Whenever it was known that she even *might* be appearing somewhere, crowds began accumulating several hours before her possible arrival. If she was there, the Secret Service was out in force, and police
sent in dozens of extra men. In Venezuela, for example, twenty thousand troops had been ordered out to ensure that people didn't get too
close. When she appeared, the surging masses verged on hysteria,
screaming "Jackie! Jackie! Jackie!" If she didn't come, the event would
still be sold out. Charity chairmen knew that just dangling the possibility of her appearing boosted ticket sales. Ben Bradlee recalled the
"physical discomfort" that Mrs. Kennedy showed "as she walked slowly
into this crowded hall to get stared at—not talked to—just simply
stared at. Her reaction, later to become so familiar, was simply to pull
some invisible shade down across her face, and cut out spiritually."[27]

Given the explosive potential of the situation, Jacqueline's public
appearances and statements had to be handled with even greater care.
Even innocuous remarks could be twisted. When Concern, a parents'
group "protesting the barnyard morals" of the movie *Cleopatra*, asked
the First Lady to fight "pornography," she asked Schlesinger to draft a
careful message. She approved it in final form, but it was decided to
leave it in the third person, signed by a staff member. It said that
though Mrs. Kennedy "shares your concern about these matters . . .
books and films of genuine artistic merit have often been denounced as
pornographic; and for this reason it is necessary to proceed with care,
responsibility and full respect for an artist's right to explore a variety of
segments and experience. After all, not too long ago some people were
protesting *Huckleberry Finn* as an indecent book, not fit for family reading. Attacks on such books as Salinger's *Catcher in the Rye* will look
equally absurd in years to come. Here, as in many other matters of
morality, Mrs. Kennedy feels that the basic responsibility lies in the

home and the family. Sometimes there is danger in looking to laws to do the job that fathers and mothers should be doing."28

While one star kept rising, another was slowly burning out.

In late, muggy August, Eleanor Roosevelt gamely went campaigning for New York Democrats, climbing atop a sound truck throughout the boroughs. She had a 102° fever. In the deepest pocket of Harlem's urban poverty, she stood on a box to speak, and a crowd gathered. A small black girl came up to her with an armful of flowers. "You see, I had to come," Eleanor smiled to a friend. "I was expected."29

On August 26, Eleanor appeared on ABC's Issues and Answers, discussing her Status of Women Commission work, with producer Peggy Whedon interviewing. In the studio, Eleanor refused to wear makeup or take off her hat, sinking silently into her chair. But when the red light flashed, indicating the cameras were on, "the old pro took over," recalled Whedon.

Eleanor said that the time for legislation guaranteeing equal rights for women was coming. She swiped at business for being unprogressive, and said the nation must "realize that we live in a revoluntionary period . . ." She praised JFK's civil- rights and liberties efforts and attempt to "enlighten the American people . . ." Whedon watched Eleanor carefully, and wrote that "her face was luminous, her mind was so facile . . ." Mrs. Roosevelt warned against "fear of change." It was her last media appearance.30

Mrs. Roosevelt was in excruciating pain, slowly dying, of incurable bone-marrow tuberculosis. The world responded with an outpouring of emotion. Edna Gurewitsch recalled that "there wasn't any corner of the earth that didn't send her a prayer, a letter. Every religious sect in the entire world was represented. They were all praying for her, every different culture . . ." One letter arrived that well expressed the sentiments: "Along with millions of other people in the world who admire and love you, we are thinking of you and wishing you a rapid recovery." It was from Lady Bird and Lyndon Johnson.31

Suddenly, just five days after Eleanor's birthday, the world faced its gravest danger. President Kennedy was informed that the Soviets were preparing offensive missile bases in Cuba. Two days later, he was told by the Soviet foreign minister that it was not an offensive buildup—a flat lie. JFK canceled an appearance due to a "cold," and immediately phoned Jackie to return to the White House from Glen Ora with the children.

At four o'clock that afternoon, The New York Times reported that the president and his wife took a private walk through the Rose Garden. That is when Jacqueline learned what only a few in the world knew: There was a real possibility of worldwide nuclear annihilation. With one of the most top-secret crises in history, the president trusted the discretion of his wife and confided in her. She was one of the first nonofficials informed of the situation, and was one of the few nonmilitary personnel to be allocated one of the pink tickets permitting entry to a secret CIA shelter, in case an emergency evacuation was called. Days later, as the crisis remained unresolved, JFK suggested to Jackie that she leave the White House and go back to the country, so that she would be nearer the shelter site. She refused to leave him.

On Monday evening, the world discovered what Jackie already knew. As Kennedy said in his television address to the nation, "The purpose of these bases can be none other than to provide a nuclear strike capability against the Western Hemisphere."[32]

The president had told the Kremlin that America would attack first, and the situation remained unchanged for a week. The First Lady's entire agenda was immediately canceled. August Heckscher had persuaded Mrs. Kennedy to receive a large contingency of poets who were in Washington, but the event "fell just at the time of the Cuban Crisis and she cancelled it." Calm returned only when Khrushchev announced the Soviet withdrawal of the missiles.[33]

Mrs. Kennedy had been closer than any previous First Lady to the threat of global destruction. Lord Harlech recalled an intensely serious conference on nuclear war with the president. The only other person there was Jackie. She was taking notes on the conversation. Afterward, JFK designed a small silver October calendar with that historic week deeply engraved. Only two women received calendars. One was the president's secretary. The other was Jacqueline. Schlesinger recalled her "calling me after the conclusion of the Cuban missile crisis and saying, 'Jack has been so much involved in Cuba; he needs diversion. I want to have a dinner of sheer entertainment. Whom should we have?'" With her persistence, she helped put the crisis behind him.[34]

Meanwhile, in a New York hospital, Mrs. Roosevelt railed against the needles in her arms and the oxygen tanks keeping her alive. "Utter nonsense," she said. She clenched her mouth to pills, or hid them in the back of her cheek. "I am a tough old bird," she quipped. Trude Lash wrote that Eleanor had "helpless anger at the . . . world who tried to keep her alive. . . . She was not afraid of death at all. She welcomed it. She was so weary and infinitely exhausted, it seemed as though she had to suffer every human indignity, every weakness, every failure that she had resisted and conquered so daringly during her whole life—as though she were being punished for being too strong and powerful and disciplined and almost immune to human frailty."[35]

Eleanor was granted her wish to be taken home, to "rejoin the human race." But, she said, "All I want . . . is to be turned over." On November 6, she signed a shaky "A.E. Roosevelt" to a ten-dollar check. It was a tradition begun during the Depression when a First Lady picked up a hitchhiker, and helped him get a job. The grateful man said if he had a daughter he'd name her Eleanor. Mrs. Roosevelt said no, just make her a godmother. Every year since the child's birth, she mailed her the little gift. To the end, Eleanor remembered her hitch-hiker's daughter.[36]

Mrs. Roosevelt died the next day.

She had once told Edward R. Murrow that she was "pretty much a fatalist," that one must accept all that came one's way, concluding about life *and* death that "the only important thing is that you meet it with courage and with the best that you have to give . . ." She be-lieved the spirit passed into another world: ". . . there must be some 'going on . . .' There is a future—that I'm sure of . . ." She thought there had to be "some reason" for "all that you go through here."

At the UN, Adlai Stevenson eulogized her best: "What we have lost, what we wish to recall for ourselves, to remember, is what she was herself. And who can name it? . . . We pray that she has found . . . a glimpse of the sunset. But today we weep for ourselves. We are lonelier; someone has gone from one's own life . . ." To the goal of "a better life" she had dedicated "her tireless energy and the strange strength of her extraordinary personality."

On November 11, friends, family, and First Ladies gathered at Hyde Park for Eleanor's funeral. Jackie, Lady Bird, and Bess were there, join-ing their husbands. Even Ike came. But someone seemed to be missing. After the funeral, Edna Gurewitsch recalled, "Everyone was waiting. Waiting for her to come. Of course, you realized at the same time that she wouldn't. She would never walk into a room again and brighten it . . ." The most moving tribute was one of those Eleanor cartoons. Openmouthed, eye-popping angels peeked behind billowy clouds. "It's Her," read the caption.[37]

At the height of "Jackie Fever," Eleanor had written in her column about the changing First Lady role. Of her experience, she said the Depression and war had required "background and understanding of so-cial justice and social needs . . ." Even more was now needed. Obliquely referring to nuclear war, she said that a First Lady and her husband couldn't "give way to apprehension," though more aware of real dangers and threats, they must always be confident, they must not be politically resentful of any enemies when it was possible to make them allies. All this demanded from a First Lady "a high order of intel-ligence, of self-discipline, and a dedication to the public good. We are extremely fortunate to find these qualifications in the White House at the present time."[38]

With Eleanor's death, many were comparing Jacqueline with her most famous predecessors. Robert Frost said, "There have been some great wives in the White House—like Abigail Adams and Dolley

Madison—so great that you can't think of their husbands, presidents, without thinking of them. It looks as though we are having another one now." Other women, however, were being compared to Mrs. Kennedy.[39]

Look magazine was to dub this brunette "a Republican version of Jacqueline Kennedy," with her "same spare figure . . . same air of immaculate chic." Indeed, photographs showed Nancy Reagan in the "Jackie Look." It was to Amelia Gray at her tony Beverly Hills dress shop that Nancy "talked often about Jackie and the style and grace" she brought to the White House. Nancy was no longer a fifties housewife. Now, the Reagans were part of an exclusive crowd of politically concerned, self-made multimillionaires.

Ronnie was still acting, but politics had become a priority. "Not a day goes by," wrote Nancy to a friend in 1962, "when someone doesn't come to the house and ask Ronnie to run for senator or governor or even President of the United States. It boggles the mind but maybe it'll get me out of the carpool." Reagan publicly decried Kennedy's Medicaid Program, and the Supreme Court decision to stop school prayers. Nancy mirrored her husband's politics and agreed with his views. They often dropped in at Palm Springs, bastion of conservative Republicans, where Ike and Mamie wintered annually. Pat Nixon and her family also called on the Eisenhowers in January 1962, and Julie recalled Mamie's tour of the town, and suggestion they stop for ice cream. In "hot pink" dress and sweater, "slightly tottering on her two-inch spike-heeled pink pumps" she led Pat and her daughters to the counter of a shocked soda jerk.[40]

Pat Nixon loved California life, and her path occasionally crossed Nancy's. The Nixons entertained the Reagans, who lived just a short drive down the coast, at their Beverly Hills home on at least one occasion, and Pat recalled fondly "an absolutely beautiful 10th wedding anniversary the Reagans gave for themselves at the Beverly Wilshire Hotel. There was lots of dancing, lots of toasting." Nancy recalled first meeting Pat during the '60 campaign, when Ronnie had campaigned for Dick.

Part of the reason Mrs. Nixon was so happy was that she was out of politics, and her daughters were finally enjoying a normal life. That joy was short-lived. In '62, Nixon was running for governor. Pat only half-joked that if he really went through with it, "she was going to take her shoe to him." Maintaining a private family life wasn't the only basis for her opposition: The party was split, with Nixon in the moderate camp bitterly opposed by archconservative John Birchers. Pat firmly told Dick, "I've thought about it some more, and I am more convinced than ever that if you run it will be a terrible mistake." She acquiesced with reluctance only after both daughters supported his wish.

Pat maintained an independent campaign schedule, and it was she who decided to appeal also to Democrats and independents, and have her appearances called "community receptions." She was less in touch with the main headquarters, and therefore did not come to know well a man who smoothly moved into the machinery, H. R. Haldeman. She was, however, sensitive to the lingering press that was hateful toward Nixon, but she applied her philosophy: "If you know in your heart that you are right and you believe in the power of truth, you cannot be eternally upset by the things you hear every day. You just get on with the business at hand." But, when Dick lost, Pat's daughters, for the first time, saw her cry.

Six months later, life changed again when they moved to New York's Fifth Avenue. A relieved Pat told a friend, "We're out of the rat race."[41]

Meanwhile, Mamie had made a second return to Washington.

Mrs. Eisenhower had agreed to serve with Mrs. Kennedy as honorary co-chair of the National Cultural Center fund-raising drive, and on June 22 she came to lunch with Jackie to talk about it. Afterward, the two women stepped out onto the North Portico for the gathered press, who treated it like a treaty signing. A smiling Mamie in blue-white print fifties dress and matching turban happily posed for photographs, effusively chatting with reporters about how nice the lunch had been, and how beautiful the house looked. She barely hid her pride in Jackie, who stood back and listened with hands clasped and a thoughtful grin that kept growing. When Jackie spoke, Mamie beamed, eyeing the First Lady's blue dress. Even Mamie had momentarily caught a little Jackie fever. "Might even get me one of those bouffants," she joked that afternoon to Mr. West. The sorority endured, again cutting across politics and generations. Both agreed to appear on a television special for the cultural center. As a symbol of her new support for Jackie, Mamie parted with the cherished personal possession of a large 1890 mahogany oval table, her donation to the restoration, in memory of her father.[42]

The November closed-circuit TV special had live coverage of the Kennedys at a Washington dinner commencing the fund-raising of $30 million needed to build the cultural center. On a special linkup, Mamie beamed by satellite from Augusta, as Jackie outlined her goals:

Tonight seems to be at long last the beginning of what for so long has really been just a hope . . . An encouragement for all of us to keep working on . . . It's important for many reasons . . . a living symbol for our national appreciation and pride in the arts . . . a needed setting for artists from abroad . . . It's no secret how Washington has needed something like this . . ."[43]

Jackie seemed comfortable in her second television address to the nation, but her personal handiwork emerged even more with the publication of her book, *The White House: An Historic Guide.*

Just before the final draft was approved, she wrote Schlesinger a "frantic" note. "I really am very pleased with it—though I think it may be a bit confusing as it throws so much information at one. However layout will be simplified. Text is not earth shaking—but I think it is OK—do you? Please tell me the truth—as this guidebook is desperately important . . . JFK says I should write short introduction—then I don't have to be mentioned in text—which I find offensive. . . ." Jacqueline emphasized, "Something about effort to bring back historical things—without making one sound conceited" should be added, as well as a "Marvelous closing sentence worthy of Euripides."

The first edition of 250,000 went on sale the Fourth of July, but on June 28, copies were presented to the Kennedys. Dr. Grosvenor spoke, looking at Jackie: "Every line, every picture represents your own particular attention." David Finley added, "Mrs. Kennedy has been the inspiration for its publication—her knowledge of history, her good judgment and her impeccable taste are evident in every page." Finally, JFK congratulated "my wife." In the foreword, Jackie said she hoped that both the public and "scholars" would profit from the book.

Overruling advisers, Jackie wanted the book sold right at the tourist entrance to the mansion, explaining, "Just let me try it for a little while. If there are protests—we will sell it in book stores or somewhere else." Then she went back to her drawing pad and designed display and sales tables. There were no protests. In fact, Jackie's book was bought by one in five tourists. Within eighteen months, it would reap nearly sixty thousand dollars, and the entire first edition sold out in less than ninety days. Eventually, it was also sold at museums and art galleries.

Meanwhile, by the last month of 1962, Jackie was planning a *second* book, this one collective biographies of the presidents. Again, the concept was entirely hers. In a long instructional memo to Arthur, she said it should be the size of the *National Geographic*, but with "not so much about each Pres. & nothing about the job (unless a moving forward in some Pres. words)." She wanted something so "someone like me can get a vague but interesting idea of each Pres. (for instance I haven't a clue what party Pierce or Buchanan were of or what they did—except fail)—It must be short enough so people will read it all—in other words all on one page." She wanted Washington's portrait "covering whole cover," and the first page to be a chronological listing. "Then a double page for each Pres.—I would hope they wouldn't have more (except I guess in some cases you'll have to) as that detracts from the concision I want. So many people and children are lazy—if they can learn something in a glance at a page—they will do it—rather than thumb through a history book—Also this book must be witty." She wanted the left page to be the full-color White House portrait of each president "up till modern times—then photos."

For text, she wanted a "lively, even controversial big sketch (not just born, married, wrote Monroe Doctrine, died) with some description of their character." At the bottom of the page, she wanted a quotation from each man, "surrounded by a red line," and on the back cover, the Great Seal. She concluded that "if you can do all this I will carve your name on the Blue Room mantelpiece. It[']s your penance for not coming to India when we were there." Jackie also drew a cartoon of herself in an ethereal gown with arms outstretched, wandering down a hall past busts marked Lincoln and Washington. Beneath it, she scribbled, "Last yr. in the W. House I was looking for Arthur Schlesinger—where is he—behind what door—down the long corridors past the statues—is he writing the guidebook or is it only a dream?"[44]

The new book would be published, the restoration continued, the cultural center, Lafayette Square, a secretary of the arts—Jacqueline

Kennedy's projects were soaring. And shortly after 1963 began, she was to follow in Frances Cleveland's steps with another surprise. The First Lady of the United States was pregnant.

— 4 —

1963

MANY NOTICED A relaxed attitude in Jacqueline as 1963 began. Earlier, she had said that her title "always reminded me of a saddlehorse." Now, she told Mr. West, "But, I am *the* First Lady."[1]

Pregnancy didn't stop her from persisting with her projects. When she learned that a state visitor, the grand duchess of Luxembourg, was a Shakespeare devotee, she conceived of an evening program entitled "Poetry and Music of Elizabethan Times," personally selecting the poetry excerpts to be read and ordering from the Library of Congress a large quantity of taped music, choosing the final pieces to match the poetry.[2]

Through the urging of sister-in-law Eunice, Jackie became interested in having the first mentally retarded employee at the White House. Though a Civil Service Commission directive later recommended this, its chairman, John Macy, said that "the President and Mrs. Kennedy had sought to place somebody there even before our program was under way."[3]

Mrs. Kennedy also focused her interest in youth education into tangible gestures. In her travels, she chose to visit public welfare institutions for children, and her official gifts were useful presents to such institutions. She began a White House "Children's Concerts" series, intended "to be . . . culturally stimulating." Jackie had young composers perform "to give them recognition early in their careers," as well as Paul Winter playing jazz and the Black Watch bagpipers. She also asked the president "if it might not be possible to invite all the foreign students in the United States to receptions" because having herself been a foreign student in France, she believed "understanding a foreign culture [was] invaluable for international understanding . . ." Large contingents were invited; almost every foreign student in the United States came to Jackie's White House.[4]

Raising money for the National Cultural Center preoccupied her, and she used her personal talent to help, drawing and painting Christmas cards. A press release revealed that it was her "own idea," and that the two ink-and-watercolor designs, that she titled "Good Tidings," (a trumpeting angel) and "Journey of the Magi," (the three Wise Men), would be printed and ready for distribution throughout the country by Hallmark for the yuletide season. Hallmark's president thought Jackie's talent "displays an unusual amount of craftsmanship."[5]

Mrs. Kennedy was also lobbying for the plan that called for saving the Nile temples by moving them. Though UNESCO and Egyptologists managed to raise about $50 million, they still lacked needed funds. She concentrated on the "financial and technical problems" of UNESCO, which, Schelsinger wrote, "leaves the political problems with . . . the President."

But behind the scenes, she emeshed herself in politics as well, later admitting that she "convinced" President Kennedy "to ask Congress to give money to save the tombs at Abu Simbel which would have been inundated by the building of the Aswan Dam." Congress had previously treated it as a nonissue. The president said he would support her, only on condition that she "could convince [Congressman] John Rooney of the Appropriations Committee (who was always against giving money to foreigners)." West Wing aide Richard Goodwin began compiling a report of cost estimates and techniques to move the temples, so that Congress would have an accountable basis upon which they could formally donate matching funds of about $10 million. Proudly, Jackie recalled how she and Goodwin invited Congressman Rooney to the White House "and convinced him." Goodwin said funding was due to Jackie's power. In gratitude, Egyptian president Nasser would give the Temple of Dendur to America.[6]

The First Lady remained avidly interested in the president's programs, now focusing more on domestic issues. Space exploration became as important to her as it was to him, but in a more personal way she enjoyed the astronauts Shepard, Cooper, Schirra, Carpenter, and Glenn as individuals. She equally admired their wives for banding together "so often out of necessity." Upstairs, before a White House reception in their honor, Jackie broke the ice: "You're all doing what I did for the first two years in this place . . . you're whispering."[7]

Increasingly, the Kennedys spent time together and shared ideas. They jointly designed a new American Medal of Freedom. Disappointed in the caliber of official gifts for foreign dignitaries, Mrs. Kennedy visited the Hall of Native Minerals in the Smithsonian with Leonard Carmichael. She then asked jeweler David Webb if he would donate his services to design presentation paperweights, incorporating some of the most beautiful native minerals. Webb accepted and produced a series of ravishing objects. JFK told a friend in confidence,

"You have no idea what a help Jackie is to me, and what she has meant to me." In public, the couple still kidded each other. Even at a formal state dinner for the shah and empress of Iran, Jack, looking at the empress's staggering jewels, jested to Jackie, "She's outdone you! She's really outdone you!"[8]

With Kennedy's shift toward domestic affairs came his focus on the divisive and consequential struggle for civil rights. Though she didn't make public statements on racial segregation, in her own quietly defiant way, the First Lady stood her ground against bigots. Through Belford Lawson, the president's adviser on civil rights, Jackie met John Johnson, publisher of important minority magazines *Jet* and *Ebony*, and campaigned in black sections of Buffalo and Dayton. G. Mennen Williams, later assistant secretary of state for African affairs, recalled Jacqueline's presence at an important strategy meeting on civil rights that national black leaders were having with Jack and that she was "natural, friendly, and hospitable . . . interested in all that went on."[9]

For the most part, Jackie's civil rights views were subtly amplified. When the National Council of Negro Women was raising funds for a memorial to Mary Bethune, she wrote a support letter. She went into the most poverty-stricken section of Washington to visit "Junior Village," a notorious overcrowded halfway house of nearly nine hundred mostly black children who were abandoned, orphaned, or of parents unable to support them. Not since Eleanor had a First Lady made such a visit. Journalist Peter Lisagor said that Tish "had an assignment from Mrs. Kennedy to find unsung artists" for the White House, and after a tip that there was a superb American black opera singer, renowned in Europe, Jackie wanted her to perform, and the singer accepted. It was Grace Bumbry, and Lisagor added that "she became a name in her own country for this one appearance."

Her most public act came as a mother, supporting school integration. Jackie warmly welcomed the little son of black assistant presidential press secretary Andrew Hatcher into the White House nursery school that she established for Caroline and other administration children. The First Lady's invitation could have provoked a negative backlash. Instead, it used the White House as an example of her integration stance.[10]

Opposition in the South remained firm. Outside a Georgia peanut warehouse office someone put a sign: COONS AND CARTERS GO TOGETHER. It was Rosalynn Carter who tore it down, and hid it in a closet where it stayed for years. By 1963, Jimmy Carter had been elected to the state legislature. It had been Rosalynn's first campaign for her husband, and she called it "sheer drudgery." Carter won only after contesting a fraudulent loss, and a disillusioned Rosalynn realized politics wasn't always honest. Though she stayed home and continued running the business while Jimmy was in Atlanta, she said she liked being a political wife. Criticism, however, hurt and angered her.[11]

Jackie remained informed of the details of the civil-rights struggle, and in a book she was preparing as a surprise gift for the president, she chose his ordering of the National Guard to enforce desegregation at the University of Mississippi as one of the political events to highlight. What "enraged" her more than any single event of the movement was the use of police dogs against marchers and other violent attacks in the Deep South.

When the all-male Metropolitan Club refused to desegregate its membership, Robert Kennedy and other administration men resigned. With the First Lady's encouragement, they decided to form their own, integrated club. Jackie was with RFK upstairs in the mansion, as the plan was discussed, and broke in to suggest, "You might use the third floor of the White House." Largely through him, she kept informed of civil rights. Dave Powers recalled that "she was very close to Bobby because Jack was close to him . . . She would listen to Bobby with that compassion for people who are suffering the most." Mr. West said that one servant claimed that Jackie had expressed concern about how bail could be raised for the "Freedom Riders," jailed for their participation in Martin Luther King's desegregation march.[12]

JFK freely discussed civil-rights legislation with his wife. He once told her in detail about the refusal of Alabama police to employ and train blacks, and his frustration with New York Congressman Emmanuel Celler, chairman of the House Judiciary Committee, then considering the Civil Rights Bill.

Jackie's stand against bigotry sometimes found its way into the press. As a sign of support for the UN International Children's Emergency Fund, the First Lady bought ten boxes of their Christmas cards—its one major fund-raiser. The DAR quickly charged that UNICEF's nonsectarian themes were "part of a communist plot to destroy all religious beliefs and customs," but the public reacted by immediately buying out all the cards of the same design Jackie had purchased. Even the Polish *Swait* magazine praised her "lack of racial prejudice."[13]

If she didn't acknowledge racism, neither did she sexism. Close friends of hers had carved out independent professional careers for themselves, and she never questioned their choices or capabilities. It remained glaringly obvious that she was no average housewife. In one memo, Tish wrote that Jackie "reads everything* . . . on the woman's page . . . *except the recipes." With women, Jackie emphasized internationalism. As she wrote to the editor of *Women's Weekly* of Japan, "The women of Japan and the United States have played an important part in creating the friendly ties which now exist between the two countries, and I know that by working together we can do much more to increase international understanding." Her power over her sex was evident from her public mail and the stories written about her in women's publications. Even the Democratic National Committee asked her to "do [radio] spots aimed at women and particularly the Spanish-speaking element" for "Operation Knowhow."[14]

Although pregnancy confined her as summer approached, Mrs. Kennedy still kept abreast of Jack's policy speeches. She considered his June 10 American University "peace speech" perhaps his best, and felt the press hadn't given it enough attention. She had strong emotions about the threat of nuclear war.[15]

In June, Tish left her job as Social Secretary and was replaced by Nancy Tuckerman. Jackie's friendship with "Tucky" extended back to early school days, and she now headed the East Wing at a crucial turning point in the First Lady's role. With the election campaign less than a year away, and the birth of her child about ten weeks away, Jackie would be retreating for a few months, mapping out objectives for the next five years. The restoration was established and almost running itself. Her private role would change too, as her children matured. Nancy knew Jackie's personality and preferences so well that the First Lady turned over much of the detail work and management to her. "Tucky" was to Jackie as "Tommy" had been to Eleanor—a discreet, supportive friend who was always an equal.

Nancy found Jackie "wonderful to work for . . . extremely creative and imaginative in all areas of her role . . . [her] marvelous sense of humor and sense of the ridiculous made working for her great fun." Nancy's presence also provided the confidante the First Lady had lacked for her first two years.

Nancy recalled one occasion when the Goodyear Blimp company invited Jackie and the children to take an impromptu ride. The Secret Service, never happy about spontaneous events, only knew they were going to a designated spot in Virginia. Goodyear said there was room for only three guests. So, Nancy said, "Mrs. Kennedy, Caroline, and John vanished into the blimp and slowly the aircraft headed upward, and cross-country. The Secret Service agents were frantic! They ran to their cars and desperately tried to follow the blimp by land."[16]

For Jackie, an easier atmosphere now pervaded. As soon as she departed in June, the White House buzzed with the preparations for the new baby. A nursery was being readied. She celebrated her July birthday with her family at their rented Squaw Island home, resting privately, awaiting her baby's September birth.

On August 7 she was suddenly rushed to Otis Air Force Base hospital. Just after noon, Pierre Salinger announced that she had given birth to a son, Patrick Bouvier. The president flew up from Washington. In the hospital, he wheeled Patrick to Jackie's room, and placed him in her arms. Six weeks premature, and suffering from a respiratory syndrome, Patrick was taken by his father to the intensive-care unit at Boston's Children's Hospital. The child was the first born to White House incumbents since the Clevelands' daughter Esther who, now, as an older woman, offered her prayers for the infant's recovery. The White House bond stretched nearly a century.

Worried about Jackie, Jack left the hospital for a few hours to be with her. When Patrick died two days later, the president returned to his wife, and cried in her arms.

Letters provided some comfort. One read, "You give so much happiness—you deserve more. We think of you—pray for you and grieve with you. Would say more but you would have to read it—and I fear want to answer it—don't." It was from Lady Bird and Lyndon. In thanking the Schlesingers for their note, Jackie wrote, "Some letters really do help—and I just wanted to tell you that—from Jack & me."[17]

It was the president who penned little notes to all five medical officers at Otis, not just for trying to save Patrick, but also in appreciation for their care of Jackie. He thanked Dr. Jablonski for "ease and comfort in her illness." To Dr. Sanislow, Jack wrote, "Your attention and concern for Mrs. Kennedy's welfare . . . was very helpful and comforting and both of us are deeply grateful to you."[18]

Jack told Red Fay, "It is so hard on Jackie. She wanted to have another child. Then after all the difficulties she has in bearing a child, to lose him is doubly hard." Bill Walton spoke of how Jackie "hung onto him," and how Jack "held her in his arms." When he came to Otis to take her home, photographers witnessed a flash of open affection between the couple. Jack was holding Jackie's hand, leading her to the car. At the funeral, Jack took off a Saint Christopher's medal that he wore around his neck and placed it in the small white casket. Jackie had given him that medal on their wedding day.[19]

The president had to return to Washington. August 28 was a landmark in the civil-rights movement. That day, Martin Luther King was leading a "March on Washington," of 250,000 whites and blacks. It was less than three weeks after Patrick's death, but Nancy Tuckerman later said that Jackie, "wanted to be there for the March on Washington [when JFK met with the leaders]. It was her doctors who told her she just couldn't go. She regretted very much not being there, but watched with interest on television."[20]

September 12 in Newport, two weeks later, was also a landmark, one not covered by the press. As the golden dusk of a New England late summer eve glowed over the emerald lawn of Hammersmith Farm, the president's helicopter landed. As Jack stepped out, Jackie impulsively ran to him, here where precisely ten years ago she had made her very first appearance as a public person, at their wedding. Ben Bradlee said it was "the most affectionate embrace we had ever seen them give each other. They are not normally demonstrative . . ." A party of toasts and reminiscences was held. Then Jackie presented her gift to Jack.

They were three elaborate books that she had created, showing her changes in the White House and its grounds. Mr. West said they qualified as fine-arts books, with photographs and explanatory text. The last book was a red leather, gold-lettered album chronicling the administration in detail by tracing the evolution of the Rose Garden. Jackie had obtained a printed copy of his daily schedule, alongside which was placed a photograph of the developing garden as it looked that day. Then, at the top of each page, the First Lady handwrote a quote from newspaper articles as they related to administration politics, programs, crises, or special events. She had been working on the book for two-and-a-half years, always aware of his political activity.

She also gave him a private, and significant, token. It was another medal depicting Saint Christopher, who traditionally was to protect the wearer, away from home, wherever he might travel. Then Jack presented his gift, a letter listing the unusual antiquities of a New York dealer from which she could choose. She selected a simple bracelet from Egypt with a coiled serpent design. She would wear that bracelet forever.

After dinner, Jackie had tears in her eyes when she told the Bradlees how much their friendship meant to her and Jack, and how their sympathy letter upon Patrick's death had deeply affected them. "They are the most remote and independent people we know most of the time," Bradlee recalled, "and so when their emotions do surface it is especially moving."[21]

Red Fay recalled, "With all her sophistication, she couldn't conceal her love for Jack." And, he thought, "[s]ince their roles complemented each other in so many ways, Jack did a poor job of trying to conceal his pride in Jacqueline's accomplishments as First Lady. He was not a demonstrative husband in public, and was rarely seen by others kissing or embracing his wife. But the pride and love were so obvious to anyone who saw them together, particularly during the Presidential years."

Fay was amazed when Jackie was able to identify several of the Greek and Roman antiquities Jack had brought back for her from Italy, during his past spring trip to Europe. "Ask Jackie any question you can think of dealing with Greek or Roman history and she will give you the answers," Jack told Red. Then the boasting husband began quizzing his wife, using a Greek history volume as his reference source. Fay said she answered rapid-fire: "It was an amazing performance. She obviously had had no opportunity to prepare herself ahead of time. . . ." Later, in private, Jack revealed, "I'd known a lot of attractive women in my lifetime before I got married, but of them all there was only one I could have married—and I married her."[22]

It wasn't just sentimental friends who saw the change. White House policeman Kenneth Burke couldn't help noticing how JFK was "proud of the great changes Mrs. Kennedy had made and so anxious actually for important people to see [them] first hand . . ."[23]

Meanwhile, in Athens, Lee and Stas Radziwill were dining with Aristotle Onassis, previously under scrutiny by the American government for alleged illegalities in his shipping business. Onassis had met and liked both Kennedys in the fifties, had introduced Kennedy to Winston Churchill in the south of France, and impulsively suggested that Lee invite her sister to Greece to cheer her up, and use his yacht *Christina* for an Aegean cruise. JFK, concerned by his wife's continuing depression after the death of their son, urged her to accept, anticipating some criticism but feeling his wife's recuperation was vital. She accepted, and was accompanied by the Radziwills and Franklin D. Roosevelt, Jr., and his wife Susan. Because he wanted the trip to be a rest, Onassis decided to absent himself, so there would be no conflict of interest, but the sisters insisted that he join them. After briefly returning to Washington and greeting Ethiopian emperor Haile Selassie, the First Lady left for Greece.

Sometimes the ship's communications system broke down, and Jackie was unable to make her nightly call to Jack. So, from her sumptuous stateroom, she wrote long, detailed ten-page letters to him. In one she wrote, "I miss you very much—which is nice though . . . also a bit sad. I know that I always exaggerate—but . . . I realize here that I am having something you can never have, the absence of tension—I wish so much that I could give you that . . ."

Onassis invited Alexis Minotis, head of the Greek National Theater, along on the voyage, and he provided the sisters with the detailed legends of each island and Greek mythology as they visited ruins and inspected antiquities. With the Radziwills she took tea with King Paul and Queen Frederika.

The sisters then went on to Morocco where the First Lady was feted by King Hassan. It was the time of the Berber tribesmen's annual pilgrimage to Marrakech to pay homage to their king. She watched their fearless displays of horsemanship and firearms from the king's magnificent black-and-silver tent, with members of his family.

Back home there was some mild criticism. The *Philadelphia Bulletin* published a picture of the sisters in bathing suits with "two unidentified men," while Ohio Republican congressman Oliver Bolton delivered a speech saying the First Lady showed "impropriety" by accepting "the lavish hospitality . . ."[24]

On her way home, Jackie stopped in Paris, buying neckties for Jack and meeting with de Gaulle, who presented her with a bouquet. Upon her return, the Kennedys grew even closer, dining alone more frequently. One day, when she broke into a smile, he told a friend, "See

that smile on her face? I put it there." When told that Cuba's Che
Guevara had said that Jackie was the one Yankee he hoped to meet,
JFK cracked, "He'll have to wait in line."[25]

Happy, Jacqueline was animated. She talked of the Greek dancing,
and of eating with her fingers in Morocco. She donned a caftan that
Hassan had given her, put on Moroccan music she'd bought in Marrakech. She was ready even for campaigning. During her husband's
term, she'd seen the world but not America. Now, the Kennedys
planned a summer vacation for '64 in the Montana mountains. Jackie
took an avid interest in whether LBJ would be on the ticket again.
When Jack asked her to come on a scheduled swing through Texas, she
impulsively piped up, "Sure I will, Jack. We'll just campaign. I'll campaign with you anywhere you want." She flipped her red appointment
book open, and marked across the dates of November 21 to 23.
"Texas."[26]

The family spent the weekend of November 10 at their newly built
home "Wexford," their intended retreat for a possible second term.
Jackie looked forward to more restoration work, and cataloging the entire White House collection. As Jim Ketchum recalled, "She wasn't
pleased with loans, because donors could always take them back and
sell them for high prices as 'White House' items. She wanted to get
permanent items . . . She wanted art that went beyond portraits . . .
she had a lot more goals to accomplish in the second term."[27]

Jackie would step up her efforts for the arts: Some of Heckscher's
suggestions were to be enacted. She planned on having Margot Fonteyn
and Rudolph Nureyev dance at the White House. As far as publications
went, she said she "assumed there would be more books eventually,
perhaps on Presidents' wives, and on other special items from the
White House collections." Her historic preservation lobbying might go
public with national legislation protecting landmarks. The cultural center would consume her creativity in private and public efforts.[28]

On a personal level, she would be spending more public time with
the president now, too, with more foreign visits on the horizon. Both
looked forward to their Far East trip, including Japan and the Philippines and what would be her triumphant return to India and Pakistan.
They were even thinking of moving the date up, leaving right after
New Year's. De Gaulle was coming in February. The president realized
that relations with China would eventually have to be reestablished,
and was considering a trip there in his second term.

They mused about the future, beyond the White House. She teased,
"What are you going to do, Jack? I don't want to be the wife of a
headmaster of a girls' school." JFK told friend Charles Bartlett that he'd
like the ambassadorship to Italy because "Jackie would like it."[29] And,
so their future together lay before them, to joke about, to think about.
To dream about.

November 22

In Texas, reporters immediately noted Jackie's popularity, one writing that she might "turn out to be the President's secret weapon in the 1964 campaign." She wanted details now, asking Dave Powers exactly which elements of each town were Democratic, and how they'd gone in 1960, precisely which politicians she was going to be meeting at each event. With the Kennedys were the proud Texans Lyndon and Lady Bird. Jackie later asserted that they would have been on the '64 ticket.[1]

On Thursday the twenty-first, after a stop at San Antonio, they arrived at Houston's Rice Hotel. The manager ignored JFK and happily blurted, "Good evening, Mrs. President!" Dave Powers only half-teased JFK when he reported that "a hundred thousand more people came out to cheer for Jackie." That night, at a League of United Latin-American Citizens, the president turned the microphone over to his wife, "in order that my words may be even clearer." She gave a rousing speech in Spanish. Jack's eyes met hers with pride. After talking to one guest, he admiringly told her, "The man said you were wonderful."[2]

Late that night they flew to Fort Worth. The next morning, outside the hotel, JFK greeted a crowd of several hundred, and answered their calls of "Where's Jackie?!" by deadpanning, "Mrs. Kennedy is organizing herself. It takes longer. But of course she looks better than we do after she does it." In fact, she was getting dressed, and Bill Walton recalled that Jack had "picked out that suit she had on." It was pink, with a matching hat.[3]

Downstairs, the chamber of commerce breakfast started. When Jackie appeared, the crowd of two thousand broke into mad applause. JFK quipped, "Two years ago I . . . was the man who had accompanied Mrs. Kennedy to Paris. I am getting somewhat that same sensation as I travel around Texas . . . Nobody wonders what Lyndon and I wear. . . ." Back upstairs, he asked if she'd campaign in California in two weeks. "I'll be there," she replied. Then they flew to Dallas, headed to an airport called Love Field.[4]

At the airport, Jackie impulsively did what reporter Tom Wicker said he never saw her do at "any other time." Amid shouts of "Jackie, baby!" she and JFK "exchanged quick glances and, like naughty children, stole off towards the fence . . ." She was given a bouquet of deep

red roses. She climbed into the left side of a sleek navy-blue car. Jack
sat at her right. They proceeded through the hazy white sun into the
heart of noontime Dallas.[5]

Two cars behind, the Johnsons were noticing the smiles, the confetti, the placards being happily waved from windows. Tonight, after all
the public appearances, Jackie and Jack were to travel with them to
their LBJ Ranch for the weekend.

The motorcade continued, through a cool underpass, then down a
hill. Abruptly, Lady Bird heard a sharp crack, over her shoulder, followed by two more. Firecrackers, she thought.

Jackie would recall, "And just as I turned and looked at him . . . I
remember thinking he just looked as if he had a slight headache . . .
then, he . . . put his hand to his forehead, and fell into my lap." She
lunged toward the back of the car and screamed, "My God, they've
killed Jack! They've killed my husband!"

Lady Bird remembered a Hospital sign. She was hustled into the
building, and passing the presidential limousine, she saw the Kennedys.
Only then did she comprehend what had happened.[6]

In Missouri, Bess Truman heard about it while in bed recuperating
from a serious bout of influenza. In New York, Ike and Mamie were
attending to some business. Ike was out, and when Mamie first heard
the news, she tried in vain to get word to him by telephone. Ike rushed
to Washington the next day. Mamie went first to Gettysburg and would
join him on Sunday, packing a black outfit for Monday. Also in New
York, Pat Nixon was watching TV. The program was interrupted with a
news flash.

In Alexandria, Virginia, Betty Ford was at home, in her kitchen,
when the wall telephone rang. It was Jerry, who had taken their son
Jack to George Washington University, where he heard the news. He
rushed to his Capitol Hill office, and called Betty. In Georgia,
Rosalynn Carter was at the hairdresser's when she got a call from Jimmy
about the assassination. She immediately sprang up, hair half-undone,
to join him at home and watch the news. In California, Nancy Reagan
heard it on the radio, "driving my car along San Vincente Boulevard in
Los Angeles." Barbara Bush would recall, "George and I were campaigning in Tyler, Texas, and we flew back to Houston to be with our
children."[7]

Jackie instinctively knew. At the emergency entrance, just before
Jack was taken out of her arms, Dave Powers came up, somehow hoping
JFK would be fine. Jackie looked up at him from her seat. "Dave, he's
dead."[8]

She was asked to stay outside the emergency surgery room, and sat
by herself on a metal folding chair in the hallway. Lady Bird went to
see her. She had always considered Jackie "insulated." Now, Mrs.
Johnson thought she seemed "quite alone." She put her arms around

Jackie, and mumbled some comfort. Jackie was called in. She leaned down and kissed Jack. She held his hand. The Catholic Church's last rites were spoken. She slipped her wedding ring off and onto his hand, because she said she "wanted to give him something." It was an Irish custom of "together in life, together in death." It would later be retrieved.[9]

The sudden horror, not just of death, but also the manner in which it had so brutally occurred, had naturally put her in shock. But somehow through the devastation of it, she managed to almost step out of herself, to shore herself with a reservoir of strength.

She boarded Air Force One, took off her white gloves, now stiffened red, and unconsciously set them on top of a newspaper headline, DALLAS WELCOMES JFK.[10]

Lyndon and Lady Bird entered. Judge Sarah Hughes arrived.

Now, once again, a First Lady sublimated her private person for the public persona. She joined the Johnsons in the front cabin, just before he was to be sworn in, explaining simply, "I think I ought to. In the light of history, it would be better if I was there." History guided her now.[11]

Lyndon put his arm around Lady Bird, and kissed Jackie lightly on

the cheek. Bird slipped her hand into Jackie's and whispered, "The whole nation mourns your husband."[12]

Few stopped to think that Jacqueline Kennedy had herself come within inches of being murdered. Not since Mary Lincoln had a First Lady's own life been so threatened.

The vice president raised his hand to take the oath of office, on this plane carrying his predecessor. Mrs. Kennedy, in her stained pink suit, stood on his left side. And, Lady Bird, in the bright yellow of Texas, was on his right.

It was an appropriate place for her to stand. She was always at Lyndon's right hand, ready for anything.

Even the presidency.

– 6 –

Symbol

"OH, LADY BIRD, we've liked you two so much," Jackie told her successor. "Oh, what if I had not been there. I'm so glad I was there." Mrs. Johnson was struck by the sight of "that immaculate woman exquisitely dressed, and caked in blood." She asked if Jackie wanted to change.

Then the woman Lady Bird always considered "gentle" also showed "fierceness."

"I want them to see what they have done to Jack."

Lady Bird was overcome. ". . . you know we never even wanted to be Vice President and now, dear God, it's come to this."[1]

Dave Powers was amazed when Jackie asked him, "'Your whole life you were involved with him. Now what are you going to do?' She said this with the casket right there. Her immediate concern was for others. She put away all her own grief . . . she was worried about all of us. She's tough. Very tough. Not just courage. You don't have to be tough to have courage. But she's tough." On the long trip back East, she was also thinking of the nation and the world. Nobody knew if this had been a plot to overthrow the government or, like Lincoln's murder, likewise to kill other officials. There was hysteria and uncertainty. When the assassin was identified, Jackie's first thought of Jack was, "He didn't even have the satisfaction of being killed for civil rights . . ."[2]

She was determined not to break down: Her family and the nation would get through this together.

On the plane, she remembered how impressed Jack had been with a group of military cadets in Dublin; she remembered his speech about lost causes when the Black Watch bagpipers had played on the White House lawn a few short days ago. The cadets and bagpipers would be part of the funeral.[3]

The plane landed at Andrews Air Force Base where a limousine waited, but she rode with Jack, and Robert Kennedy, in the back of a navy ambulance to Bethesda Naval Hospital where the autopsy was performed. There, she gave some instructions, guided by history. Word went from Bill Walton to Mr. West to Jim Ketchum that Jacqueline wished the East Room to replicate Abraham Lincoln's lying in state. An old engraving was found, and within hours the East Room was hung with bunting of black netting over chandeliers and windows, and urns were filled with magnolia leaves. Before JFK's flag-draped casket arrived, the Lincoln catafalque, kept at the Capitol, was ready.

The sun was almost up when Jacqueline Kennedy accompanied her husband's coffin back into the White House, still dressed in her pink suit. "We must just get through this," she told everyone, "be strong for two or three days." Persuaded finally to sleep, Jackie had been up for nearly twenty-four hours. Few stopped to realize that she was part of a continuum, but whereas Margaret Taylor and Mary Lincoln had been too distraught even to enter the East Room, and Florence Harding had eerily spoken to her late husband, Jacqueline, like Lucretia Garfield, Ida McKinley, and Eleanor Roosevelt, lost no composure as she walked into the room at 10:00 A.M. Saturday morning to be alone one last time with her husband. She placed a letter that she wrote him by his side. A few minutes later, she returned with her children. A brief service was held.[4]

Others came to the East Room. Betty and Gerald Ford knelt and prayed at the casket, and called on Jackie. Mrs. Ford recalled that the whole situation seemed unreal as she moved "through a haze of pomp." Ike arrived and prayed. Mamie would be there tomorrow. Harry Truman came alone; Bess had been advised to recuperate at home. After the Johnsons prayed in the East Room, they went to a service at St. John's on Lafayette Square, where Dolley Madison had been baptized, and where Eleanor had gone hours before becoming First Lady. To Lady Bird, the rest of the day was a blur. She had to sell their house and relinquish management of her radio-television station. By night, she just collapsed.

Together with Bobby Kennedy, her children, and the Johnsons, Jackie rode to the Capitol for the memorial service the next day. Mrs. Johnson looked out at the thousands of silent faces, sad but not openly sobbing. Everyone refrained from crying, she thought, because Mrs. Kennedy did. The widow was a symbol. Lady Bird couldn't help feeling that she was part of a Greek tragedy. At the Capitol, she joined the world in watching Jackie kneel in prayer and kiss the flag-draped coffin, under the cavernous Rotunda. Mrs. Johnson thought that Jackie had now developed a "love" and "rapport" with the American people. At the Capitol, Betty Ford was "too deep in shock to cry."[5]

JFK had planned to return from Texas to go with Jackie to "Wexford" in Virginia, for a secret meeting with Ambassador Henry Cabot Lodge, who had been summoned from Saigon. Lodge's hawkishness was of increasing concern to the president. He was searching for a way to relieve the ambassador of his duties and to gradually diminish the U.S. presence in Vietnam.

JFK had scheduled a White House meeting on this subject for Monday morning, November 25.

The meeting was advanced a day, with LBJ presiding. On Sunday the twenty-fourth, Defense Secretary Robert McNamara, Secretary of State Dean Rusk, Special Assistant McGeorge Bundy, General Maxwell Taylor, and others conferred at the White House to consider an important question. The answer was that President Lyndon Baines Johnson would "continue John Kennedy's policy" in Southeast Asia. The "assistance," to prevent communism from spreading into South Vietnam, was acknowledged as a state of war, though not declared.[6]

Jackie, over security objections, decided that she and Jack's brothers would walk the eight blocks from the White House to the Monday funeral at St. Matthew's Cathedral, a ritual few Americans had experienced. She said that the entire official group, including world leaders, could ride in limousines, but that she was going to walk. When Chief of Protocol Angier Biddle Duke tried to dissuade her by saying the others would no doubt also walk if she did, and asking what they would do if it rained, Jackie responded, "Then we'll march under umbrellas." The Secret Service gave in on the condition that LBJ ride in a closed car.[7]

Meanwhile, Mrs. Eisenhower had come down Sunday morning from Gettysburg, and joined Ike. Because of their age, they would drive to the church. To brother-in-law Milton, her voice became sad when she later recalled "those little children without a father." She also felt it was time to heal an old breach. Impulsively, Mamie invited Harry Truman, staying at Blair House, to share their limousine and ride to St. Matthew's. He accepted. In church, they sat near each other.[8]

Mrs. Kennedy remembered everyone. She invited Belford Lawson, JFK's civil-rights adviser, and his wife to the funeral service, seating them next to President de Gaulle and Emperor Haile Selassie. Lawson recalled that it "was a little thing, but it showed that Mrs. Kennedy had not forgotten civil rights." The entire household staff—dozens of people who were not royalty or advisers or millionaire art experts—were all included by Jacqueline. Maid Cordenia Thaxton recalled how "Mrs. Kennedy . . . sent us all the little invitations to the funeral."[9]

Betty Ford decided instead of joining Jerry at the church to go directly to Arlington National Cemetery. She stood waiting near the raw ground of the burial plot. At about that moment, the funeral mass was ending. Besides Jackie, Lady Bird, and Mamie, Pat Nixon was there, with her husband.

Dick had written movingly to "Dear Jackie," telling her, "I want you to know that the nation will also be forever grateful for your service as First Lady. You brought to the White House charm, beauty, and elegance . . . and the mystique of the young in heart which was uniquely yours made an indelible impression on the American consciousness." Jackie responded to him, but addressed a subject that was obviously for Pat as well:

"You two young men—colleagues in Congress—adversaries in 1960—and now look what happened—Whoever thought such a hideous thing could happen in this country—I know how you must feel— so closely missing the greatest prize—and now for you . . . the question comes up again—and you must commit all you and your family's hopes and efforts again—Just one thing I would say to you—if it does not work out as you have hoped for so long—please be consoled by what you already have—your life and your family—We never value life enough when we have it—and I would not have had Jack live his life any other way—though I know his death could have been prevented and I will never cease to torture myself with that—But if you do not win—please think of all that you have—With my appreciation and my regards to your family . . ."[10]

Everyone came out of the church after Mrs. Kennedy. On the steps, as the coffin was carried out, she whispered to her son. He saluted. It was the most famous picture of the whole funeral, but another bespoke emotions of what the day had done. A photographer snapped a single picture of Ike, Mamie, and Harry. Mamie looked somber. And she was holding Harry Truman's hand. When Truman's daughter had learned that Ike and Mamie were planning on heading back to Gettysburg in the late afternoon, she invited them for sandwiches and coffee first, at Blair House. The Truman-Eisenhower "feud" had healed.[11]

The Nixons also attended the burial service, and so they headed out of the church, joining hundreds of other official cars, through the human sea blanketing the streets. In a strange way, it was like the 1961 Inaugural. Many of these women had been gathered together there. Now, Lady Bird was thrust into it all. Pat would glimpse her, and Jackie, at Arlington, where Betty Ford watched as everyone "came pouring over the slope . . ."[12]

Again, it was Jackie who made the immediate decision that the president was to be buried in Arlington—not Massachusetts. Against more disagreement, she prevailed with her decision to have an eternal flame lighted at the gravesite, a flame to burn for a life cut short. The burial complete, Mrs. Kennedy was handed the flag which had draped the coffin. As everyone began retreating, Betty Ford decided to pay respects at the site. There was only one other person there. He pressed a button, and the casket was lowered into the ground. Now suddenly, to Betty, "he was really dead." She began to shake, and turned to leave.[13]

Mrs. Kennedy's job was not finished. For several hours, she represented the United States government. By her own motivation, after the funeral, she received the visiting state leaders in the Red Room. She received separately de Gaulle, Haile Selassie, and Ireland's de Valera in the Yellow Oval Room. De Gaulle said, "She gave an example to the whole world of how to behave." When she met with Colombia's former president Alberto Lleras Camargo, she thanked him profusely for his support of the Alliance For Progress, and wept in recalling the visit she had made to Colombia, where she first inspected the work of the Alliance. Aristotle Onassis was one of the few private citizens to be received during the day.[14]

One cousin observed that she was "the *real* President of the United States," and illustrated the seriousness of that as "she made a brief attempt to patch up the enmity and tension that had developed of late between England, France, and the United States. She was functioning now on a wholly new level."[15]

Meanwhile, Jackie began the self-imposed task of composing hundreds of handwritten letters to people whom she remembered as being special to Jack. She responded brightly to a sympathy letter from the oldest of the former presidents, nonagenarian Herbert Hoover, admitting to falling into "hero worship" of him. "You were always wonderful to my husband," Jackie wrote, "and he admired you so much."[16]

After the state leaders left, Jackie gathered with intimates, reminiscing about JFK's life while a nearby television replayed the day's images. As Ben Bradlee wrote, "Sometimes she seemed completely detached, as if she were someone else watching the ceremony of that other person's grief. Sometimes she was silent, obviously torn." One staff member said that Jackie "carried us through . . . She kept so many of us from falling apart."[17]

The next day, Mrs. Kennedy invited Mrs. Johnson to tea, just the two of them, providing details on the household to assist her successor's transition. The chief usher and the curator were both called up. Lady Bird observed Jackie alive, warm, steely, full of stamina. Mrs. Kennedy offered advice, and a revelation: "Don't be frightened of this house— some of the happiest years of my marriage have been spent here . . ."[18]

Superficially, they seemed dissimilar, but in some ways they were

alike. Both had pursued journalism careers, both put their families before other roles, and both revered and were always aware of history—
history past, and the history they were living.

And both did well as public personae as long as their private persons
were nurtured. For like Jackie, Lady Bird Johnson shielded herself. Mrs.
Johnson needed time alone, away from family, staff, and role. She realized this just days after the assassination. She also made "a dare" for
herself, a self-imposed discipline, and began a White House diary.

After their meeting, Jackie and Lady Bird went downstairs to hear
the new president speak to members of the Alliance for Progress. Only
after the funeral did Jackie learn that LBJ and Lady Bird had defied the
Secret Service and walked through the street, too. "I almost felt sorry
for him because I knew he felt sorry for me," Jacqueline later recalled.
"I was really touched by that generosity of spirit. I always felt that about
him."[19]

The Johnsons felt many things. They'd come to know and appreciate Jackie as a person. Because they understood how large a role she'd
played in JFK's administration, privately as well as publicly, they offered
to fulfill her every request. As a result, Jacqueline Kennedy was for a
fleeting period not only the most famous but the most powerful woman
in the world, indirectly helping get more legislation passed than any of
her predecessors. There was unfinished political business that had been
important not only to Jack, but to herself as well.

Jacqueline later recalled that "JFK was going to sign a paper naming
Richard Goodwin to the first Cabinet Post for the Arts on November
22." Now, there was to be no arts secretary. But her efforts would not
go for naught. Lyndon Johnson would sign into legislation the National
Endowment for the Arts and the National Endowment for the Humanities, embodying aspects of the Cabinet role Jackie had envisioned, as
well as the funding she had hoped such a department might accomplish
on behalf of artists. "In a way," she would later write, "the NEA and
the NEH have achieved all this."[20]

Mrs. Kennedy told LBJ that the National Cultural Center was "the
cause closest to my heart." Just sixty-one days after the assassination, a
joint resolution of Congress decided to rename the National Cultural
Center "the John F. Kennedy Center for the Performing Arts." Jacqueline wrote LBJ that "It is so important to me that we build the finest
memorial—so no one will ever forget him—& I shall always remember
that you have helped . . ." LBJ later wrote her, "I find it a selfish
motive, but one over which my disciplines have no power: I enjoy
reading a letter from you just for the sheer pleasure of hearing you speak
on paper." She was asking the president if he might appoint a friend of
hers as trustee of the cultural center. He responded, "Your request will,
of course, be instantly granted."

President Johnson knew that the Kennedy administration's focus on the arts was due most of all to Jackie, and he credited her directly for the development of the center: "I know how much the Center means to the extension of the arts in Washington, D.C. And I also know how deep within you goes your own affection and interest in this enterprise. So much of your handiwork and so much of your own being is in it." There would not be even so much as a Jacqueline Kennedy plaque at the center, yet some of the quotes from JFK's speeches on the arts that would be engraved on the building reflected Jacqueline Kennedy's influence.

Jackie would also ask LBJ to foster the Pennsylvania Avenue re-development, because "I thought it might come to an end." When she learned of his "strong endorsement," she was particularly "grateful that you are carrying it on." Fearing that the world would forget that it was John F. Kennedy who had committed America to the space program, to landing a man on the moon, she requested of the new president that he rename the Cape Canaveral Space Center after JFK, though later, she felt ". . . that was so wrong, and if I'd known it was the name from the time of Columbus, it would be the last thing that Jack would have wanted."

President Johnson, immediately caught up in the growing Vietnam question, poverty, illiteracy, civil rights, and the early calls for some sort of attention to the environment, touched a sentimental note in recalling an era that was already receding into history. "Time goes by too swiftly, my dear Jackie," he wrote. "But the day never goes by without some tremor of a memory or some edge of a feeling that reminds me of all that you and I went through together."[21]

Meanwhile, Nancy Tuckerman oversaw a staff answering eight hundred thousand sympathy letters sent to Jackie, just as Dorothy Dow had done for Eleanor. Congress voted Jackie fifty thousand dollars for staff and office space for one year to handle the mail, the annual ten-thousand-dollar presidential widow's pension, and Secret Service protection for her and the children. She would be guarded for life, unless she remarried. LBJ also ordered agents for the Trumans and the Eisenhowers.

Jackie had taken it upon herself to clean out JFK's desk, and when she opened the drawer, she found two newspaper clippings. One, from the *Washington Daily News*, said that in India, she "has even outdone President Eisenhower as a drawing card." The other was written while she was in Pakistan, and it quoted her as saying that she was sad that Jack was not there with her.[22]

On her last night in the lonely house, Mrs. Kennedy stayed up until dawn writing personal thank-you notes to every single member of the domestic staff. She composed the citation for the Secret Service agent who she felt had saved her own life. She wrote a condolence letter to the widow of the policeman who had also been shot by the same assassin. She went to sleep at four-thirty in the morning.[23]

On her last *day* there, Jacqueline Kennedy wisely used the symbolism of White House stationery on which to pen her thoughts in a remarkable and most important letter. The so-called "apolitical" First Lady addressed the most serious question facing the world—nuclear war. What made it all the more astounding was that the addressee was Nikita Khrushchev:

> The danger which worried my husband was that war might be started not so much by the big men as by the little ones. While big men know the needs for self-control and restraint—little men are sometimes moved more by fear and pride. If only in the future the big men can continue to make the little ones sit down and talk, before they start to fight.[24]

Jackie bid farewell to every single member of the household staff, and even walked over to the telephone operators' room because they couldn't leave their post. Then, she proceeded downstairs to watch, partially hidden behind a screen, the first presentation of the new Presidential Medals of Freedom. One was awarded to Jack posthumously. Finally, as guests left, Jacqueline Kennedy slipped out of the White House. When Mrs. Johnson walked in, she found a little bouquet and note for her, from Jackie.

"I wish you a happy arrival in your new house, Lady Bird . . ."

And then she added, innocently enough, a last phrase.

"Remember—you will be happy here."[25]

A Can Do-er

LADY BIRD JOHNSON'S reverence for First Ladies was the most graceful honor one of the sorority could bestow on her often-forgotten predecessors. One cartoon even pictured a wife at Mount Rushmore snapping to her husband, "I bet if Mrs. Johnson had any say about it, their wives would be up there."

She would note that she stayed in a building that had once been Edith Wilson's school and a hotel room once occupied by Eleanor Roosevelt. She'd enjoy Alice Longworth's wickedly perfect Nellie Taft impersonation. At Hearst Castle, she'd sleep in the same bed that Grace Coolidge had. She owned Julia Tyler's autographed calling card, drank from an Abigail Adams glass, and viewed the room where Rachel Jackson died. Mrs. Johnson believed that Eleanor Roosevelt "was driven by very strong spiritual determination," and remarked of Dolley Madison, "I've always liked her very much because she seemed like she enjoyed her role. To be there, and not enjoy it is a great sadness. Of course, there are triumphs, and tragedies."[1] Though she felt she'd had "zero preparation" for the role, the new First Lady felt she must be a "showman and a salesman, a clothes horse and a publicity sounding board, with a good heart, and a real interest in the folks," determining to "go more, do more, learn more . . ."[2]

She thought of the public role's constraints as "the harness of hairdo and gloves," and refused to "live in a cage." She said a First Lady should ideally be bilingual, and able to shift emotional gears as she went from appointment to appointment. All in all, she relished the "rat-a-tat of . . . duties . . . a cram course in the history and people and scenery . . ."[3]

With "experience," as "businesswoman and politician," she consciously interpreted her role. "Each person makes her own path, as I've said lots of time, she is only chosen by one man. She's not elected. There are no requirements of the job . . . you do what makes your heart sing . . . he is elected, and they are there as a team. And it's much more appropriate for her to work on projects that are a part of his Administration, a part of his aims and hopes for America. Time will pass, and she'll get around to hers later on!"[4]

Immediately, she affirmed that her role must "emerge in deeds not words," because "in this space age, passive citizenship is a luxury nobody can afford." Lady Bird Johnson viewed the Ladyship as "[a] daily working job." Her staff sent out a statement of her "duties" and though "hostess," was first, it listed a primary one as "advancement of the President's programs." In fact, she immediately made trips to poverty-stricken parts of Pennsylvania, to Alabama's Marshall Space Flight Center, and Georgia and Ohio government health and housing programs. "I just try to pull the curtain back a little bit wider on human problems," she explained, "so people may see, think, and act."[5]

Although she approved memos with "CTJ" (for Claudia Taylor Johnson), to the world she was always "Lady Bird." The name caused confusion for some British subjects who assumed that "Lady Bird" was married to a "Lord Lyndon." In one nation, there was even a WELCOME BLUE BIRD sign.

Her sunniness rarely displayed dark spots either publicly or privately. Mr. West called her "earnest" but "protected," as if she had an invisible emotional shield. Longtime friend Scooter Miller described the First Lady as "guarded and careful. She keeps her own counsel, and doesn't get very close to too many people . . . She can be hard to know . . . Doesn't pull pranks. She's always been serious. She likes Faulkner and O'Neill . . ." Daughter Lynda said her mother "is always on an even keel. And, if she wasn't we didn't know it. Every so often she needed to withdraw, alone by herself, and her favorite White House room was the little blue-white Queen's Sitting Room at the end of the hall, because, 'It only has one door.'" Lady Bird said she was happy to be "a controlled person."[6]

After Mrs. Johnson once revealed, "I could have made a good architect," a staff member thought, "That's very rare for her to make a claim, but . . . her mind, her operation, is with the senses. We were in Mexico and she said 'I want to know [what] that bird is there . . . I want to know if that tree is a so-and-so. I want to know the seasons . . . the senses of sound and smell.'" As Lynda recalled, she applied that inquisitiveness to a grueling work schedule. "Mother is a workaholic. She strictly follows the old Puritan work ethic. 'I must be doing good works all the time.' Whenever I would pull her out to go to lunch or to a museum I had to convince her it was good for her . . . All of her trips to supposedly enjoy herself had a purpose." The only leisure Mrs. Johnson took were snippets of bowling, bridge, swimming, sunbathing on the roof, and watching *Gunsmoke*.[7]

She maintained her pace even in comically trying moments. One night, she locked herself outside of the family quarters. Holding herself erect, in her bathrobe, she walked down the grand staircase—running into several musicians and staff—through the hallway to the elevator, and went back upstairs. When LBJ spontaneously suggested sending some visiting astronauts' wives to Paris as representatives, Lady Bird came to the rescue by taking them to her closet and lending them her gowns. All she could give John Dewey—a sudden overnight guest of LBJ's—however, were Lyndon's oversized pajamas. Lynda said her mother was like one of *Candide*'s characters, with a "best of all possible worlds" attitude toward life's unpredictability.[8]

Scooter Miller elaborated on how Lady Bird's personality affected her approach to the role. "She is not vain. She never hesitated to slip on her eyeglasses. Everything about her is honest. She has a direct response to questions. She never lies. She might just avoid an issue but Bird has always told the truth." There was a finespun texture to her role. Barbara Howar, close to the Johnsons for a period, observed that "it did not take long to see that she was in charge . . . for all her obvious contributions, [she] was best behind the scenes . . ."[9]

Above all, there was always a power that cast itself as calm. When the president shouted at her, Mr. West thought it "almost abusive," yet noted that rather than wrathful, she became withdrawn, her face "beatific." When faced with a trauma that entered her sphere, West said she "tuned it all out." He found her sometimes "remote." Always, she could compartmentalize her thoughts with a tremendous skill of concentration. As she worked, Mrs. Johnson often softly hummed.

The Johnsons breakfasted in bed together around seven-thirty, then she dressed and sat at her office desk, dictating, reviewing schedules, speeches, and correspondence. There were intermittent conferences with her staff, and if she wanted to work alone, she'd use the Queen's Sitting Room or her office–dressing room, managing the buzzing LBJ White House like a corporate board chairman. If she didn't have a working lunch, she had her soup and salad alone. Afternoons were filled with meetings, ceremonies, and welcomes. Nearly every day she took an hour alone to dictate into her recorder, assiduously maintaining her diary. On the rare evenings without guests, she read.[10]

Unlike most of her predecessors, Lady Bird kept in daily, often hourly, touch with her staff, and for the first time an East Wing employee definitively helped shape and further institutionalize the role. It was all run by the whirlwind whom the First Lady affectionately and familiarly called "Miss Liz," longtime friend Elizabeth Carpenter. Though Carpenter was in fact both chief of staff and press secretary, her ocean of responsibilities defied pigeonholing. She assumed the dual role because "I had more more experience. And I wanted to." Paraphrasing her boss, she breezily summarized her role: "I help her help him."

Liz had access to the president and even helped write his jokes. The First Lady's hesitation in reading her own press "slightly annoyed" Liz, but if Lady Bird delivered a speech or issued a release that failed to

spark interest, she'd meet with her to discuss why. Scooter Miller called Carpenter a "formidable woman with a willing subject." For Mrs. Johnson's goals, the tricks of Carpenter's trades—journalism and public relations—matched perfectly. Liz understood how newspapers worked, what reporters wanted as news, and how to maintain good PR for her "client." For reporters pondering coverage of a Lady Bird event, Liz would lure with press packets, yet solicit their advice and suggestions.[11]

As staff director, she and the First Lady hammered out a modern Ladyship, incorporating and developing the best of Mrs. Roosevelt's and Mrs. Kennedy's innovations. If the sixties was a tumultuous decade where dicta were broken, and new rules became a permanent part of "Establishment" institutions, the Ladyship was no different. The East Wing throbbed with ideas or crises, and in her busy office Liz kept ballgowns and a framed St. Francis of Assisi prayer—"the one where you are big about everything . . ." One of the military men who shared the space with the East Wing grumbled, "We're an Army in a goddam boutique."

Mr. West said that Liz was just one of the "generals." The other was Social Secretary Bess Abell, daughter of a former Kentucky governor, whom Carpenter called a "Cecil B. DeMille . . . [with] an easy Lauren Bacall air . . . ," always attending National Security Council meetings for state-visit briefings.[12]

Communications was a priority. Mrs. Johnson's distinctively folksy cadence made her public speeches seem easy, but according to Carpenter—also the main speechwriter—they weren't. Particularly for West Wing writers. "We had to confiscate . . . Presidential speechwriters but they were always too stilted. They would have some good phrases but we'd have to run them through and put it in Lady Bird's language. She didn't want to sound pontifical. Speeches were a good form for her . . . more poetry than policy." Mrs. Johnson said she was "dragged by duty or shoved by Liz" into making speeches. "I had to brace myself to speak of my husband and myself. I had to steel myself to . . . voice beliefs. Later I came to realize that the people I talked to were like me and I didn't need to be scared of them." Scooter Miller said that Mrs. Johnson "loved words . . . [and] always thought before she spoke." She even tried to anticipate reporters' questions with the right response. Lady Bird credited a schoolteacher for instructing her to avoid being trite and to use strong verbs. When she spoke of moving into the White House, for example, Mrs. Johnson recorded, "History thunders down the corridor at you."

Words were the focus, too, of her correspondence. Lady Bird frequently told the letter writers to "go to the dictionary . . . Let's make these letters glow. I see them framed in hotels—from First Ladies and Presidents, and I want mine not to have any grammatical errors. I want them to be ones I'm proud of."[13]

Overall, East and West Wings had smooth relations because of the president's own respect for the distaff. Still, there were difficulties. Minutes before LBJ made a national speech on a social program, Liz learned of it and managed to have a single line inserted, pointing out that Mrs. Johnson was the program's chairman. To the president's press secretary, Liz fired off a memo: "What goes on over there in the West Wing that is [so] worthwhile that you can't tend to these little details?" When West Wing adviser Marvin Watson stopped the East Wing's daily national newspapers, Liz had to fight to reinstate them. She succeeded.[14]

As a reporter, Liz had scrutinized Bess and Mamie, but openly admired Mrs. Roosevelt. In one press release just months after LBJ became president, she affirmatively wrote that "Mrs. Lyndon B. Johnson has shown a blend of natural political instinct and amazing energy that may produce one of the most active First Ladies in America's history." Helen Thomas was one of several reporters who saw that Carpenter invited comparison to Eleanor.

At the Eleanor Roosevelt Memorial Foundation Dinner in the spring of 1964, Mrs. Johnson said her predecessor's "conscience was her counselor . . ." She added, "I met her first in print and admired her. I met her later in person and loved her." Lady Bird handled her schedule just as Eleanor had, using White House rooms and gardens to meet group after group, one after the other. As Eleanor had become friends with the "Green Room Girls," Lady Bird spent more time with the women's press corps than any other group, and liked them. But there were distinct differences. Mrs. Johnson purposefully avoided alienating those who might disagree with her. Her speeches and goals were less strident. She kept a lower profile.[15]

Other comparisons were obvious. On a trip to Kentucky, Mrs. Johnson was given a country quilt by local women, and expressed the desire that such crafts could be widely sold as a way of alleviating poverty—almost verbatim as had Ellen Wilson a half-century before her. In what would prove the most curious—and unknown—link of all, Mrs. Johnson had first learned of the urban blight of Washington as she toured the slums with Mrs. Roosevelt, who had learned of the same circumstances by trailing behind Mrs. Wilson on her crusade. It was only in this third generation of the sorority that substantial results would emerge.[16] Lady Bird shared another similarity with both women. She was her president's political partner. She called LBJ "a good man in a crisis . . . exciting . . . exhausting." He bragged that "Bird is the only person who has never disappointed me." She sweepingly described her partnership with him as "balm, sustainer and sometimes critic . . ." Liz called her the "eyes, ears, reporter and supporter" of the president.[17]

Academic Eric Goldman, hired to advise and observe the administration by LBJ, worked closely with the East Wing. He believed that LBJ had "a thoroughgoing respect for the judgment of his wife in all matters. He talked with her about everything, and he paid close attention to her reactions. She rarely took a rigid position or argued; as she once said in a phrase that was only half-joking, 'I infiltrate.'" Goldman claimed that they "talked politics, all aspects of it, on a basis of equality. . . ." Mrs. Johnson admitted that "Lyndon believes that anything can be solved, and quickly." She was more pragmatic, a balance to his exuberant, and tyrannical, style.[18]

Initially, Lady Bird hoped that Lyndon's being closer to home would mean a more normal schedule. But LBJ held meetings and briefings frequently into sleeping hours—often regardless of where he was or what he was doing. Consequently, whether it was one o'clock in the afternoon or the morning, Lady Bird was frequently there for talks on the economy, racial strife, international treaties, or Vietnam.

In her first months, after waiting several hours for Lyndon to return from the office for dinner, she ate alone and was lonely. She determined to be "even mean" if necessary to get him to eat and sleep at regulated hours. An alternative she developed was to momentarily interrupt meetings with sandwiches. His spontaneity sometimes annoyed her, like the time he had different-sized ten-gallon hats brought out as gifts for the prime minister and foreign minister of Japan. In her bathing suit after a swim, she routinely walked into the presidential bedroom where suddenly she confronted LBJ having a rubdown and conferring with a dozen or so men. She shrieked and darted out. She said it was a lesson to her that in this house she should always have her hair coiffed and donate her ancient bathrobe to charity. "It is no secret that her husband was a difficult man to live with," said Scooter Miller, "but she understood him completely."[19]

She did become irritated with the press coverage of LBJ's idiosyncracies—like picking up their beagle by the ears, and ordering the White House lights shut off—deeming it "foolishness." She frequently criticized his speeches as too long, and passed notes to him to that effect. When once she scribbled, "That's enough," he kept going. Another time he read her "Close soon" note out loud, getting an audience laugh. But Bird got her one-liners in, too. When reporters asked her opinion of the orders of the president's doctors that he not speak after minor throat surgery, the First Lady retorted, "We're going to make the most of it."[20]

If she felt strongly enough about something to raise objections, LBJ would listen, because—as most people discerned—he valued her judgment. As Lynda stated, "He looked upon his own wife as someone who was capable of doing anything. He held her up for us. He would always say, 'Be like your mother.' And she was smart. She wouldn't show him her own failings. He'd always say, 'She never gossips!' Well, of course she did. Mother is human."

One reason they worked in sync was that, though gentle, Lady Bird savored the challenge of national politics as much as LBJ did. She kept close tabs on how congressmen and senators stood on all issues—especially LBJ's. She still kept her notepad and pencil handy and passed along all her frank observations to the president. Once, while entertaining the wives of legislators, she admitted that she'd rather be with their husbands and LBJ discussing his policies. Another evening, she attended a Senate briefing, keeping pace with the intricate details of a tax bill. The exact degree of power she had over him, however, often remained secret. "She should talk it over with her husband straightforwardly," Lady Bird explained of the ideal First Lady who argued issues with her president, "but then she should be quiet in public." She admitted to making him "do a few things," her best tactic being to pin memos to his pillow. "We were better together than we were apart," she said. "He made me grow, he flattered me, shoved me, ridiculed me, loved me into doing things I never thought I was big enough to do."[21]

According to reporter Ishbel Ross, Mrs. Johnson "reviewed drafts of his [LBJ's] speeches and at times helped him give cadence to his words. He took criticism from his wife better than from any of his advisers, and she gave it to him without hesitation. . . . Her method was to listen to what he had to say on a controversial question, give it careful thought, and then comment, 'This is what I think about it, and why.'" Bird wanted to be kept informed on serious issues, from nuclear policy to wiretapping. She felt the administration's forte was communications, but though her relationship with LBJ's series of press secretaries was friendly, she dismissed the notion that one, Bill Moyers, was the single "liberal and bright" West Winger. Early on she realized that no Cabinet member was indispensable, and when LBJ was making later changes, she had decided opinions on who would work, and be loyal. As Congresswoman Lindy Boggs would recall, the First Lady was often in the "session with the boys."[22]

Special Assistant and Counselor Harry McPherson stated that the president "trusted her advice" so much that he didn't even blink when she'd walk right into a meeting he might be having with the Joint Chiefs of Staff and secretary of state. McPherson said LBJ "depended on" her. Vice President Humphrey bluntly said that the First Lady not only "had an effect" on LBJ, but "made him come to heel . . . I watched that many times." Merle Miller, who wrote a study of LBJ, observed that ". . . she knew the ins and outs of all the legislation Lyndon sent up to the Hill and could discuss it intelligently."

Liz thought that although loyal, Lady Bird "always retained the sense of self within her that made her able to remain a strong person, and even though he was very much the catalyst, and she was the amalgamist . . . she generally ended up doing what she wanted to. . . ." Lynda asserted, "My mother never felt she was denied anything by my father, and she always knew she was capable of accomplishing anything she wanted to."[23]

Mrs. Johnson intently focused on foreign affairs through her contact with world leaders. Her first solo trip was as the official representative of the president to the state funeral of the king of Greece. When the Italian president came to the White House, she asked for a briefing on Italy's economy and politics. Liz recalled, "She had a big world map on the private floor, and would pull it down and study what other countries surrounded that country, what are their pressures. She read all of those extensive books of background papers prepared by State. . . ."[24]

"As a public figure," Mrs. Johnson explained, "my job is to help my husband do his job." Goldman said she "accepted or rejected an activity according to the criterion of how much it helped the President's broad purposes, specific programs or political position . . . [her] support

[was] . . . given in a supplementary, low-key manner . . . without 'creating controversy.'" Liz offered, "She's perceptive, but she doesn't push. That is an innate being-born-under-the-magnolia-blossoms refinement. She won't [credit herself], but that's also good politics."[25]

When Lady Bird once recommended a specific individual for a job at HEW, LBJ "bawled holy hell" to Secretary Wilbur Cohen that "[y]ou put Mrs. Johnson up to it." He hadn't, but it illustrated how protective LBJ was when he thought someone might be taking advantage of his wife's role. Still, journalist William White thought that while Bird "never frontally challenged" LBJ, "she often had her way . . . [and] managed it by indirection. . . ."

Lady Bird refused to adopt LBJ's mercurial attitude toward aides who disagreed with him, and worked on patching up the animosity if she could. National security adviser McGeorge Bundy thought she might have often successfully done this as Mamie had, by working through the aide's wife on the "old girl" circuit. Mrs. Johnson's alliances with political wives served administration purposes as she could gently cajole Senate and Congressional wives into working on their husbands to support her husband's programs. She recalled how during political briefings for Congress, "The spouses—most generally wives, in a few cases men of course—were invited by me to come upstairs and see the family quarters. Sometimes we had our own little program." These friendships often transcended political differences, like her relationship with Betty Ford. Just seven days after the Johnsons moved into the White House, Betty Ford was dining at Lady Bird's side, along with other Congressional leaders and their wives all discussing whether the United States should recognize the new Dominican Republic government.[26]

Esther Peterson, LBJ's special assistant on consumer affairs, credited the First Lady as an influence over the president in his attention to the advancement of women. Lynda pointed out that her mother's influence may indirectly have affected the careers of perhaps thousands of women working in government. "Father was well aware that we were not allowing people to live up to what God had given them. . . . On women, when he learned that the government would permit them only to reach a certain G-S level, he had a meeting about it, and it was raised overnight. He felt there was a great amount of potential we were losing."[27]

Upon receiving an honorary doctorate of law from Texas Women's University in March 1964, the First Lady pronounced, "In almost every sphere, the influence of women is constantly growing . . ." At an Alabama college, she noted that women were still a separate student body, but proudly observed how they and women leaders of the state were especially invited to hear her speak. Lady Bird said one reason she went to a space center was to highlight the increased role women had in space technology. About one in five employees there were women.[28]

During her tenure a perceivable change occurred that questioned the postwar return of the woman to domesticity. From Mamie Eisenhower to Jacqueline Kennedy that tradition had continued, but with the publication of Betty Friedan's *The Feminine Mystique* in 1963, and the founding of the National Organization for Women, the issue of a woman's role in America was beginning to be publicly examined. The long debated ERA was not yet approved by the Senate, and Lady Bird was never swept into the issue, but she affirmed women's power: "Women can do much in their civic life. They can alert citizens to be interested in the affairs of their city. They can push and prod legislators. They can raise sights and set standards. . . ." She also called for women to assume an increased role in public issues: "For me," she re-vealed, "and probably for most women, the attempt to become an in-volved, practicing citizen has been a matter of evolution rather than choice . . . But 25 years [after] the invention of the nuclear bomb has left us no choice."[29]

On her own desk, the First Lady kept a little sign, "Can Do." To the American Home Association, the First Lady altered an Edmund Burke quote to say, "The only thing necessary for the triumph of evil is for good men—*and good women*—to do nothing." Some even credited her with trying to have a clause inserted on women's equality in what was shaping up as the Civil Rights Act.

Mrs. Johnson's first major speech, to the 1964 graduating class at Radcliffe, was perhaps her most eloquent: "I urge you to enter outlets, not as the super woman, but as the total woman, a natural woman, a happy woman. If you achieve the precious balance between a woman's domestic and civic life, you can do more for zest and sanity in our society than by any other achievement . . . [with] the right to partici-pate fully—whether in jobs, professions, or the political life of the com-munity. A remarkable young woman is appearing . . . she rejects a number of overtones of the emancipation movement as clearly un-workable. She does not want to be the long-striding feminist . . . en-gaged in a conscious war with men. She wants to be—while equally involved—preeminently a woman, a wife, a mother, a thinking cit-izen." She also made a pitch for more women to vote: Though there were more women voters, more men actually used that right.[30]

Paralleling administration efforts on behalf of women, Mrs. Johnson hosted "Women Do-er Luncheons," an idea of Liz's—expanded by the First Lady and inspired by Eleanor Roosevelt's press conferences at which she invited women experts on various issues to speak. A timely issue was chosen as the luncheon's focus, a leader on the issue spoke, and "other women of achievement in different fields are invited to lis-ten and discuss." They featured women from Dr. Mary Bunting, the first woman appointed to the Atomic Energy Commission, to Judge Marjorie Lawson of the D.C. Juvenile Court. There would be a total of sixteen luncheons held in a four-year period, and at one of the first, the First Lady declared, "The longer I live—and the more I travel, the more impressed I am with the remarkable things that remarkable women are doing." Carpenter emphasized that Mrs. Johnson "always insisted—and this was the strength of it—on including some that she said were 'ordinary women, average women' . . . she didn't want every-body in there as an achiever. She wanted the true test, the 'average' test."[31]

Though she didn't have an art background, Mrs. Johnson also dili-gently continued Mrs. Kennedy's work. Lyndon Johnson passed many of JFK's programs, but at the same time, he didn't forget Jackie's achievements. On March 7, 1964, LBJ signed Executive Order 11145, which provided permanent federal funds for the office of White House curator and established the Committee for the Preservation of the White House. Of the restoration, the curator said, "It took two strong individuals to make it work, and both must be given credit. Mrs. Kennedy for establishing it, and Mrs. Johnson for continuing it at a crucial moment."

When Mrs. Johnson made several visits to Mrs. Kennedy in Georgetown, gently trying to coax her back to the White House for committee meetings Jackie told her, "I cannot return . . ." Mrs. Johnson understood. Jackie later described herself as living "in my own shell of grief," and explained, "Even driving around Washington I'd try to drive in a way where I wouldn't see the White House. They'd ask me to every state dinner . . . I think she [Lady Bird] understood, but out of courtesy they just kept sending me the invitations. It was just too painful for me to go back to that place."[32]

Sympathy for Mrs. Kennedy hadn't abated. On January 14, 1964, she became the first former First Lady to formally address the nation on television, giving her thanks for "the hundreds of thousands of messages" sent her, and discussing the future Kennedy Library. In the spring, Mrs. Johnson decided to officially rename the landscaped East Garden as the "Jacqueline Kennedy Garden." When she brought this news to Jackie, Mrs. Kennedy said no, that First Ladies shouldn't be recognized, just the presidents. Then she acquiesced jokingly that perhaps her initials could be scratched into a tree, or her name put under a bench. Uncertain of how she'd react to being back at the White House, Mrs. Kennedy sent her mother to the dedication in her stead, and newspapers characterized it as a snub. Jackie explained, "I suppose again that's where the press makes things difficult. That was so generous of Mrs. Johnson to name the garden after me. . . . So I suppose they were saying how awful of me not to come, I can see that was an uncomfortable position for her." She hoped the Johnsons understood, but added, "I wouldn't blame them at all if they thought sometimes 'Listen, couldn't this girl just—' . . . the press did blow it up an awful lot."[33]

In Georgetown, Lady Bird noticed that tourist buses parked right in front of Jackie's house. There was speculation that she'd move to Europe. Instead, she returned to the city of her youth, as had Julia Tyler almost exactly a century before. That summer, Pam Turnure issued a press statement: "Mrs. Kennedy feels that the change in environment to New York from Georgetown, and its many memories, will be beneficial to her and her children." And there was anonymity there. Both Pam and Nancy Tuckerman moved with her, to run the former First Lady's office.[34]

At thirty-four, she was a single parent, and, as such, was determined to guide the education of her children until they were mature. She concentrated on developing their understanding of the world, and during school vacations encouraged their exploration of different cultures. She would open all doors to them—her own interests in journalism, photography, the performing arts, museums—and their father's world—public service, politics, law. The world saw them as Kennedys, but they were very much their Bouvier mother's children.

Contrary to all public speculation, Jackie was devoted to the Johnsons, and began a warm correspondence with both. Rumors persisted that LBJ would soon name her to a political post, either as an ambassador, or as special consultant to the arts, and CBS wanted her to give a television tour of the Vatican restoration. However, except for her work with the Kennedy Library, the JFK Center for the Performing Arts, and historic preservation efforts, Mrs. Kennedy withdrew as a public person.

If Jackie avoided public life, Lady Bird gingerly stepped into it. It was when LBJ declared "unconditional war on poverty," during his first State of the Union address that she was moved to involve herself in such an effort. She believed that federal spending on the poor could be done without damaging "self-reliance," but retained a pragmatic perspective. In accepting the national chair of Head Start, which provided preschool education and medical care to underprivileged children, under the Office of Economic Development headed by Sargent Shriver, she declared that she had "great hopes that this program will be the big breakthrough we have been seeking in education—the insurance against school dropouts—the insurance for a smaller welfare roll . . . [but] such an ambitious program is filled with pitfalls and disappointments. And there will be doubters who are quick to point them out. But we are not working with people who live neat and tidy and secure lives. We are trying to . . . throw a lifeline to families . . . lost in a sea of too little of everything—jobs, education, and most of all perhaps—hope."

Mrs. Johnson visited Head Start and other welfare programs, "summarizing and evaluating comments on the Administration's conduct and policies," for LBJ. Before making her first trip, to Pennsylvania coal-mine regions, the First Lady consulted with the director of the Area Redevelopment Administration. Along with forty newswomen, Lady Bird toured the depressed area. In a textile mill, she noted that most workers were mothers and—assuming that unemployed husbands were taking care of the domestic chores—wondered about its sociological impact in two decades. She had no illusions of what was accomplishable by a First Lady's trips except attracting public attention, but she would continue to hold substantive meetings with Shriver to explore how she might continue to help Head Start and track its progress.[35]

But it was a June day that would change her life, and in turn the nation's. As she recalled, "Lyndon was in Michigan . . . at a college campus and talked about the environment and I thought 'That's for me!' Of course that's a very broad subject . . . from cleaning up the dirty rivers . . . to saving wilderness areas to supporting the national park system . . . to opening up some areas of inner city to beauty and recreation. So, from then on that became the theme of my years. . . ." In April, after she'd toured some western sites and spoken enthusiastically of the land with Interior Secretary Stewart Udall, he realized that she had more than a polite interest in the environment. One of Liz's press releases at the time described Mrs. Johnson as "America's Green Thumb." Soon everyone would know why.[36]

For the moment, however, her plans were on hold because his were. LBJ remained uncertain about running for the presidency. In the wee hours of the morning of Saturday, June 6, 1964, he got a phone call from McGeorge Bundy. The call was about, as she called it, "the mounting anxieties from Southeast Asia." It was a trickle, but ominous nonetheless.

Mrs. Johnson drafted a nine-page analysis, on whether LBJ should run, of which she sent copies to his doctors and a West Wing assistant for review. "I dread seeing you semi-idle, frustrated, looking back at what you left . . . You may look around for a scapegoat. I do not want to be it. You may drink too much—for lack of a higher calling." She would amplify that he might find "achievement amidst all the pain," but added, "I can't carry any of the burdens . . . I know it's only *your* choice." Her analysis was "To step out now would be wrong for your country . . ." Marking it, "Personal, please," she didn't want him to quote her.[37]

LBJ carried the Kennedy legacy to reality on July 2, when he signed the Civil Rights Act. Lady Bird, the only woman in the front row, wondered how many years it might be before the words became full reality. Civil rights would remain of utmost importance to her, and when some proponents staged a White House sit-in, she considered going down to see them. Lady Bird knew the Act would also provoke anti-LBJ sentiment in the South, but believed that many whites there also wanted the change. She was right. When she later went to speak in Alabama, the Ku Klux Klan's imperial wizard called it "Pinko tripe," but there was a placard, DRAFT LADY BIRD FOR GOVERNOR.

To some it seemed odd that such a traditional southern woman would be so liberal on civil rights. Few knew that her mother had been an open integrationalist in a time and place where it provoked scorn. Liz believed that Lady Bird's mother was her role model, but she'd also had childhood friendship with a black playmate, "Doodlebug." The first time she was conscious "of the difference" was when "Doodlebug's Christmas presents all seemed to be serviceable things . . . not toys . . . she never had any built-in prejudices. . . . She wasn't *pushing* it, but she never had to reverse herself. . . . Civil rights came naturally to her."[38]

Reporter Helen Thomas asked the First Lady for her reaction to the news that Secretary of State Dean Rusk had offered to resign because his daughter was marrying a black. Liz recalled that Lady Bird was caught off guard, but "perfectly" replied, "I do hope things go well for those two young people." The *Chicago Defender*, a national black daily, heralded the news that the wife of Congressman Augustus Hawkins and Mrs. Johnson "were arm-in-arm as she and the Congressional wives were shown the First Family living quarters. . . ." It was a small act of great symbolism.[39]

Mrs. Johnson kept politically balanced. At one point, when the president criticized Alabama governor George Wallace, Lady Bird warned that his statement sounded as if he were "questioning his integrity." She invited the DAR to the White House because she believed that their work in educating mountain children had been ignored, and that their being dismissed as bigots had gone on for too long.[40] If the Democrats attempted to maintain balance in '64, the Republicans opted for nominee Senator Barry Goldwater's "extremism." Some of the party's women attending the Convention weren't pleased about it.

Mamie Eisenhower acquiesced to head the national women's committee of Goldwater for President, but during the primaries she'd supported moderate Pennsylvania Governor Bill Scranton. At the convention, Nancy and Ronald Reagan were staunch Goldwater conservatives, and he'd been stumping the country hawking a standardized speech. Nancy Reagan still emulated Jacqueline Kennedy's style, but not her substance: Nancy supported George Murphy in his run for U.S. Senate from California, while Jackie supported his opponent, Pierre Salinger, telling a reporter that JFK had "valued his advice and counsel on all major matters." Pat Nixon was not happy about Goldwater, and hadn't wanted to attend the convention. When Goldwater defended extreme conservatism, her husband said that "almost automatically she began to stand up. . . . I reached over and put my hand on her arm and we both sat there, not applauding." Betty Ford attended the convention as well, after which she and Jerry were planning a family beach vacation. Two days before they were to leave, Betty awoke with sharp pains in her neck. It was a pinched nerve, and after several weeks in traction, she began physical therapy, along with dosages of painkillers prescribed by doctors.[41]

Between conventions, on August 4, Lady Bird was reminded of the increasing burdens on LBJ. That day he went on television with the news that America had retaliated to a North Vietnamese attack on two American destroyers saying, "We still seek no wider war . . . [but] firmness . . . is indispensable . . . for peace. . . ." She felt "proud," and thought the response "excellent." Every Tuesday now, LBJ met with the secretaries of defense and state. Vietnam increasingly dominated their talks.[42]

Though it was Lady Bird's proud moment, the media at the Atlantic City Democratic Convention focused on her predecessor. As had once been suggested for Mrs. Wilson and Mrs. Roosevelt, some thought Mrs. Kennedy should be nominated as vice president. While Jackie didn't appear in the convention hall, she did attend a reception in her honor, thanking "all of you who helped President Kennedy in 1960," and standing in the reception line with Lady Bird. Mrs. Johnson watched the moving film on JFK with "tightly controlled composure," following which Bobby Kennedy told her that she was "doing a wonderful job as first lady." In fact, unknown to most, she had played a role in forestalling a potentially explosive situation at the convention.[43]

Just before it commenced, Mississippi blacks declared thay they'd been purposely barred from that state's all-white delegation, and in retaliation formed the Mississippi Freedom Democratic party, demanding to be recognized and seated. Martin Luther King, Jr., among other civil-rights leaders, pressed LBJ publicly to support them. It was the First Lady whom the president asked to draft a statement on their stance. Lady Bird wrote, "I believe the legal delegation ought to be seated. I am not going to bend to emotionalism. I don't want this convention to do so either. The election is not worth that. I am proud of the steady progress that has been made in the area of human and equal rights. . . . I would not change a line of what has been passed or written. So long as I am President I will continue to lead the way within the guidelines of the law and within the framework of justice." A compromise was achieved, and Mrs. Johnson's statement was not used, but it illustrated her similarity to and difference from Eleanor who—on civil rights particularly—tended to be more radical. Lady Bird also believed in civil rights, but wouldn't abruptly upset the status quo to serve that purpose.[44]

It was in support of civil rights and with a determination to help keep the South Democratic that Lady Bird Johnson undertook the most active public campaigning assumed by a First Lady. For four days, starting from Alexandria, Virginia, and proceeding through North Carolina, South Carolina, Georgia, Florida, Alabama, Mississippi, and ending up in New Orleans, the First Lady would make forty-seven prepared speeches at sixty-seven stops, through 1,682 miles from the back of the "Lady Bird Special" train. Both Liz Carpenter and Bess Abell travelled with their boss.

It was the first "selling of the First Lady." There would be "Lady Bird Special" hostesses with blue shirtwaist dresses, white gloves, and sixties roller-brim hats. Liz put together a public-relations packet, with one sheet almost like a theatrical review, headed "What the Writers Say About Mrs. Lyndon B. Johnson." Columnist Richard Wilson was quoted as calling Lady Bird an "executive type." Ruth Montgomery predicted that Mrs. Johnson "will combine sociability with social conscience." And it was Helen Thomas who compared Lady Bird Johnson to Eleanor Roosevelt.[45]

What most impressed Carpenter was Mrs. Johnson's handling of politicians through whose territory she would be passing: "[S]he did not want it to come as a surprise to the Senators . . . so she got on the phone with as many as she could get . . . and suddenly she [became] . . . more Southern . . . and she says 'Senator, this is Lady Bird

Johnson. I'm thinking about coming down your way to campaign . . . I want to get some advice.' I mean we already knew what we were going to do. . . ."

In her first speech, Lady Bird explained, "I know that many of you don't agree with the Civil Rights Bill, or the President's support of it, but I do know the South respects candor and courage and I believe he has shown both. It would be a bottomless tragedy for our country to be racially divided. . . . It is a national challenge—in the . . . North . . . in the South." She kept raising the Civil Rights Act: "The law to assure equal rights passed by Congress last July with 3/4s of the Republicans joining 2/3rds of the Democrats, has been received in the South for the most part in a way that is a great credit to . . . white merchants and Negro leaders . . ."

Democratic politicians who didn't support LBJ on civil rights couldn't unchivalrously ignore the First Lady. Even segregationalist Dan Moore, gubernatorial candidate in North Carolina, popped up after his wife warned him of the consequences of ignoring Mrs. Johnson. When Lady Bird spoke of the "New South," of "glistening skylines," and "prosperity . . . in the factory and on the farm," she added smilingly, "I would be remiss if I didn't point out that these years of growth were Democratic years."

There would occasionally be protesters catcalling, and signs like FLY AWAY BLACK BIRD, but only in South Carolina did it become rude. At a rally, the infirm wife of a state senator somewhat shocked Mrs. Johnson when she snapped into a mike at protesters, calling them "white trash" and shaming them to "Shut your mouths and listen to a First Lady." At one point there was even a threat of a bomb being placed under a bridge over which her train would pass. The FBI also investigated whether there would be Klan contingents at the stops. Nothing materialized. To those who screamed her down from the back of the train, Mrs. Johnson calmly but tersely replied, "In this country, we have many viewpoints. You are entitled to yours. Right now, I am entitled to mine."[46]

One who witnessed the often-violent resistance to civil rights in the South was Rosalynn Carter. Jimmy, again a successful candidate for state senate, would only occasionally be joined by her in Atlanta. In Plains, Rosalynn continued running the peanut business. Her mother-in-law opened and ran the local LBJ campaign headquarters, and often found her car vandalized at a day's end. When son Chip wore an LBJ button, he was so bullied in school that Rosalynn found him crying. Vicious rumors spread about the Carters because of their LBJ support, yet Rosalynn persisted in defending the family's stance. And her role was growing. In the evenings, she worked on State Senator Carter's correspondence.[47]

Mrs. Johnson did not escape personal attacks as a result of the Civil Rights Act. Perhaps the most slanderous was a little book, *A Texan Looks at Lyndon,* discreetly printed and sold for one dollar in Birch Society bookstores, and whose author, J. Evetts Haley, told readers to "read and circulate . . ." Because she was a woman, Lady Bird's professional skills were warped into a "cold and calculating business mind— perhaps 'the real mind behind the President.' . . . Is Claudia Taylor Johnson . . . more interested in power such as Macbeth's wife wielded? . . . Women journalists eulogize her as another Eleanor Roosevelt . . ." The worst attack, however, was several publications' attempt to make it appear that the First Lady was a slumlord of black tenant-farm families who lived in shacks on property she'd inherited. She'd been unaware of the real condition, and rather than having the poor families dispossessed, she directed that people not be forced from their long-held homes and charged no rent.[48]

Just weeks before the election, Lady Bird involved herself in an incident that had the potential for causing a major political setback. One of the Johnsons' closest friends, and an administration official, Walter Jenkins, was arrested in a YMCA men's room near the White House, charged with soliciting another man. LBJ was in New York, preparing to address an annual dinner, when he was phoned with the news. He immediately made some calls. One was to Lady Bird.

Jenkins submitted his resignation. In New York, the president ignored the crisis. In Washington, the First Lady did not. She summoned *Washington Post* owner Katherine Graham and editor J. Russell Wiggins to the White House. Wiggins recalled the First Lady ". . . issued a statement declaring full loyalty to Walter Jenkins . . . It was a great statement, and we did print it, of course. . . . I am practically certain that it was her own statement and she issued it without talking to Lyndon." It read: "My heart is aching today for someone who has reached the end point of exhaustion in dedicated service to his country." She remained nonjudgmental.[49]

As Barbara Howar noted, Lady Bird Johnson was "tolerant and sympathetic of human failings, an undisputed lady when it came to giving the benefit of the doubt—impressive generosity, considering her own exemplary conduct." No First Lady had dealt with homosexuality as a public issue, but Lady Bird's gentle manner helped divert the scandal from dominating the last weeks of the campaign. By election day, it had dissipated. LBJ won.[50]

One woman who supported LBJ but did not vote for him was Jackie Kennedy. She later explained, "I know, at least I heard, that he [LBJ] was hurt that I didn't vote in 1964. . . . This is very emotional but . . . I'd never voted until I was married to Jack . . . I thought: 'I'm not going to vote for any [other person] because this vote would have been his.' Of course I would have voted for President Johnson. It wasn't that at all . . . it was something a widow would do."[51]

As her one-year official mourning neared its end, she maintained an interest in global issues. She was the only woman present at a luncheon meeting of United Nations ambassadors hosted by Secretary-General U Thant, in honor of former French premier Edgar Faure. She met privately with the Irish president and West Berlin mayor. A New Jersey Democratic group proposed her as a candidate for the U.S. Senate, and some urged LBJ to appoint her ambassador to France or Mexico.

The letters between Jackie and the Johnsons began to extend beyond the official mourning period, into the new administration, and she signed her letters to them with "love." Their friendship remained secret. There was no political motivation or agenda behind it, and while the press and many Johnson staffers believed the rumor that there was a strain between Mrs. Kennedy and the LBJs, the letters prove that nothing was further from the truth. Jackie decided not to attend the 1965 Inaugural because she did not want to distract from the Johnsons' moment. A new era was clearly evident. The Inaugural Gala was a showpiece of mid-sixties stars, with Carol Channing, Barbra Streisand, Harry Belafonte, Carol Burnett, Julie Andrews, Margot Fonteyn, Rudolf Nureyev—Lady Bird thought he looked like one of the Beatles—and Woody Allen—who sent her into "gales of laughter." During the Inaugural Parade, there was even a "Lady Bird Special" float, but at the actual swearing-in her role was startlingly evident to millions watching on TV. As Mrs. Taft had broken precedent by publicly riding beside her husband back from his Inaugural ceremony, so, too, did this First Lady start a tradition. As Lyndon Johnson repeated the presidential oath, Lady Bird Johnson was holding the Bible on which his hand rested.[52]

– 8 –

The Yellow Rose

AT ONE RECEPTION, Fritos sat beside éclairs on the buffet, and nothing seemed amiss. It was the LBJ style.

So was dancing. Mrs. Henry Ford so energetically "hully gullied" that her breasts popped out of her strapless dress. First Daughter "Watusi Luci" even danced the "frug" with the president, but the First

Lady refrained. There were the ubiquitous barbecues at the LBJ Ranch. For her friend Carol Channing who'd sung "Hello Lyndon" in the campaign, Mrs. Johnson hosted an evening showcase performance of *Hello Dolly!* with Betty Ford and her husband in attendance.

Lady Bird sponsored the first White House fashion show, but the seemingly innocuous affair had a subtle political agenda: hand-painted "Discover America" scarves (created in honor of LBJ's program by the same name) were showcased against the backdrop of slides of scenic America. Other events had political overtones. When Bill Cosby told jokes at the White House, he was the first comedian—and the first black—to do so. After Sarah Vaughan sang, she broke down in tears, explaining that just a few years before she'd been unable to get a hotel room. Now, she was singing in the home of the president of the United States.[1]

But the CTJ style would soon be distinctively marked by a simple symbol: the flower. Trowel in white-gloved fist, the Yellow Rose of Texas, the First Lady of the Land, blazed the land, leaving her mark.

On February 3, 1965, she began exploring the multifaceted issue of the environment with Laurance Rockefeller, who was chairing LBJ's Conference on Natural Beauty that spring. Later that day, she met with philanthropist Mary Lasker about flower planting and held sway with five Cabinet members discussing the War on Poverty. The next day, she was conferring with an expert on urban renewal. On the third day, she launched "beautification," at a Women Do-ers Luncheon. Nobody— least of all the First Lady—was satisfied with the term, but it best coalesced ecology, gardening, landscaping, environmental protection and urban renewal. She had foresight without being a Pollyanna. As she simply explained, "We have misused our resources, but we haven't destroyed them. It is late. It is fortunately not too late . . ."[2]

Liz recalled that Stewart Udall, Mary Lasker, Laurance Rockefeller, and Brooke Astor encouraged Lady Bird to form a national committee. "But it's very Lady Bird-like that she said 'first, we'll do it our own city.'" As chair, she formed her Committee for a More Beautiful Capital, with landscape experts, philanthropists, public officials, and civic leaders, meeting monthly. The group's diversity represented their goals. The only black member, Walter Washington of the National Capital Housing Authority—later appointed the first mayor of Washington— wanted efforts focused on neighborhoods. Philanthropist Mary Lasker wanted flowers planted near the monuments. Projects were done in conjunction with the Interior Department, and a subsequent Society for a More Beautiful National Capital served as a complement with private monies put to use for Lasker's goals.

Six days later, Lady Bird's committee had its first meeting. With Udall at her side, the First Lady outlined her general goals, the first priority being to "beautify" the tourist areas, with plantings, re-landscaping, and general cleanup. The motto was "Plant masses of flow-ers where the masses pass."[3]

Two million bulbs were planted, 83,000 flowering plants, 50,000 shrubs, 137,000 annuals and 25,000 trees. Ten thousand azaleas lined Pennsylvania Avenue. The Park Service stated that the largest daffodil planting in the history of civilization occurred as 2 million were spread throughout the capital. The city's circles and triangles were trimmed with hedges. Laurance Rockefeller donated twenty-five thousand dollars to clean oxidized statues, although the First Lady was disappointed that her least favorite Yankee—General Sherman—was the first to be scrubbed off.

With the Japanese ambassador's wife, Lady Bird planted a new grouping of cherry-blossom trees, almost fifty-three years to the day after Nellie Taft had done so with Viscountess Chinda. She literally helped change the "Mall," the sweeping greensward from the Capitol Building to the Washington Monument. Modern art collector Joseph Hirshhorn was scouting cities for an appropriate museum to house his collection, and over a period of several years Lady Bird gently arm-twisted him into giving it to the Smithsonian, to be housed in a new museum bearing his name. He said that she "completely charmed me."[4]

Noticing scruffy patches near National Airport, she told the Federal Aviation Agency administrator that shrubs would help. She thought landscaping was a skill missing from Jobs Corps workers, and wondered if it might be added to their training program. She supported and aided the legislative push for Pennsylvania Avenue redevelopment. When she, Udall, and Nathaniel Owings squatted over Avenue blueprints, LBJ walked in and asked, "What in hell, Udall, are you doing down there on the floor with my wife?"[5]

During the committee's second meeting, they headed into a low-income-housing area, a stop made at the insistence of the First Lady. She told the interior secretary, among others, that all efforts would flop if they failed to consider the deprived neighborhoods where urban ugliness intensified psychological depression. It was at Walter Washing-ton's suggestion that Mrs. Johnson toured Greenleaf Gardens, a low-income black housing development. He firmly believed—along with civic leader Polly Shackleton and Katie Louchheim—that focus should be on the inner city. Through his subcommittee, efforts on different fronts began: landscape improvements, maintenance and cleanup of three city schools; the installation of recreation areas; massive neigh-borhood trash cleanups; a summer "Project Pride," which employed black college and high school students in a program of tree con-servation, pest control, sanitation sweeps of a crumbling neighborhood, and the summer "Project Trail Blazers," which put over a hundred de-prived teenagers into restoration and crafts projects.[6]

Mrs. Johnson never thought that planting flowers would solve ghetto poverty, but she applied her general philosophy that doing something inspirational was better than just debating the issue. Her example in the poorer communities spurred people to help themselves, and she even supported an ambitious plan to rehabilitate the decayed areas surrounding the Capitol, though it ultimately failed for lack of financing. Unknown to the press, she frequently rode around the inner-city alleys "to check on the progress of the beautification effort and to see what else needs to be done." Without regular funding or adequate staffing, Lady Bird Johnson became the single greatest influence on the visual impression of the federal city in her era. In the spiritual chain from Ellen Wilson to Eleanor Roosevelt to Lady Bird Johnson, something was finally being done.[7]

On May 24, 1965, the First Lady made more news by addressing the

White House Conference on Natural Beauty. Her speech contained no specific policy, but it set the personal tone of what legislation meant: "Our peace of mind, our emotions, our spirit—even our souls—are conditioned by what our eyes see. . . . Ugliness is bitterness. . . . During these two days you will discuss and originate plans and projects both great and small . . . The vaster scope of it will call for much coordination on the highest levels . . . there is much that government can and should do, but it is the individual who not only benefits, but must protect a heritage. . . . I firmly believe this national will can be given energy and force, and produce a more beautiful America." She stated that most great cities and landscapes were the result of "autocratic societies," and asked, "Can a great democratic society generate the concerted drive to plan, and having planned, to execute great projects of beauty?"[8]

Mrs. Johnson took notes as she later moved among the 115 panelists from business, labor, public service, community organizing, botany, and other related professions and she kept abreast of the work of the federal National Council on Natural Beauty and a private Citizens' Advisory Committee, attempting always to have a representative at meetings of the latter, and even recommending appointees to it.[9]

Her lobbying was polite but firm. After receiving a citizen's report that the worst local eyesore was an air-force base near the highway, she spoke with Defense Secretary McNamara. Within days, McNamara had it cleared. She encouraged ordinances regulating air-pollution control, and when Mrs. Johnson held a "substantive meeting" with the U.S. Conference of Mayors, she recommended that they lobby Congress for more local beautification funding. Deftly, she avoided becoming embroiled in conflicts between the federal government and conservation groups over the planned construction of dams at the Grand Canyon and the dimensions of the National Redwood Forest park, but permitted herself to be a venue between the government and the opposition.[10]

She was somewhat successful involving the private sector: The National Coal Association supported her opposition to strip-mining; Shell Oil found financial value in maintaining clean stations. Stressing that beautification was good business, she encouraged utility companies to replace overhead electric wires underground.[11] The First Lady remained tactful with industry. In Milwaukee she omitted mentioning the litter of beer cans.

To her, beautification was a "cram course" on disciplines as diverse as city planning, land usage, safe waste-disposal, and mass sanitation management. Walter Reuther of the United Auto Workers reported to her that most factory workers were unable to afford to vacation in the scenic parts of the world, and suggested, "We need to bring the beautiful places close to home." To her, it was a common denominator:

"The environment is where we all meet; where we all have a mutual interest; it is one thing that all of us share. . . ."[12]

Civic groups long advocating similar themes hitched themselves to her work. Lady Bird was pitted against "Litter Bug" when—as a tribute to her—Keep America Beautiful, Inc., sent out one thousand informational packages to state and local officials suggesting community programs and role models. In its cover letter, Mrs. Johnson said that "it is always time to fight litter . . ."[13]

There were humorous, and unexpected, repercussions. Some thought that beautification meant Mrs. Johnson was worried about makeup and hairdos. Keep America Beautiful asked people not to be "pigs," and the pork industry protested to Congress. When yellow tulips were planted at a war memorial, a veteran's group angrily wrote the First Lady that yellow indicated cowardice. They were replaced with red ones.[14]

The overwhelming reaction was positive. Liz Carpenter recalled that suddenly they were "getting this following . . . . every time she mentioned it . . . there'd be this burst of mail, and from the unlikeliest people, like neon-sign makers—who wanted to do something more creative . . . so we began studying signs that are used in Europe—like a coffeecup for a coffee shop . . ." The result was the first official East Wing employees hired to work specifically on a First Lady's project. Sharon Francis, originally of Udall's office, handled beautification; Cynthia Wilson oversaw its correspondence.[15]

Other movements were stirring. By March 1965, Vietnam had become a thorn. LBJ confided to Lady Bird, "I can't get out. I can't finish it with what I have got. So what the Hell can I do?" She sensed the "start" of new strategies like stronger military action, and attempts at "convincing people" that LBJ was doing the right thing. If old friends fell by the wayside on the issue, she hoped they would someday return.[16]

It was during the White House Festival of the Arts in June that Vietnam first confronted the First Lady. The trouble began when Robert Lowell reneged on his agreement to read his poetry, in a public letter to LBJ protesting the war. *The New York Times* put the Lowell controversy on the front page. Then came a letter against LBJ's Vietnam policy signed by leading writers. Of those scheduled to read, one withdrew and three publicly excoriated the administration, Then novelist John Hersey let it be known that he'd read his poem "Hiroshima." Lady Bird requested a copy of it from Eric Goldman, who'd organized the festival. The next day she met with Goldman and her staff to discuss Hersey.

The First Lady read a passage that referred to Truman's use of the atomic bomb, then quietly placed it down, explaining, "The President

. . . can't have people coming to the White House and talking about President Truman's brandishing atomic bombs." Goldman tried to justify the reading, but she made it clear: "The President is being criticized as a bloody warmonger. He can't have writers coming here and denouncing him . . ." Again, Goldman justified. Mrs. Johnson directly stated, "The President and I do not want this man to come here and read this." Goldman said that would be "White House censorship." Lady Bird flushed; "Censorship is a harsh word." Goldman said she repeated herself, adding, "The question is how to best handle the situation."

Mrs. Johnson opened the festival with a gracious speech, with no reference to the turmoil. Hersey read "Hiroshima," sometimes glancing directly at the First Lady. After he finished, Mrs. Johnson, who'd applauded the other readings, "sat motionless." The day after the festival, she nevertheless called Goldman to "congratulate" him, only obliquely referring to the "difficulties created for the President."[17]

Meanwhile, the East Wing had to form a speaker's bureau of Cabinet and Senate wives to handle the flood of requests for talks on beautification, but most groups wanted only Lady Bird. So, Liz began organizing national trips.

Mrs. Johnson would travel over one hundred thousand miles on about forty beautification journeys. In one 3-week period alone, she made seven of them. Touring national parks and forest lands had the double advantage of promoting LBJ's "Discover America" program. She recalled that America was "beginning to have a little balance of payment problem . . . Lyndon . . . wanted American money to be spent in America . . . he said, 'Go and see your own land . . . these great national parks.' Particularly the ones that are not heavily visited." She proved effective. At Big Bend Park, for example, tourist numbers tripled after Lady Bird's ballyhooed trip there.[18]

To paraphrase a song of the era, Lady Bird was a day-tripper. She'd go mountain climbing in Georgia, and poking through old houses in New England. On her first trip, Mrs. Johnson traveled comfortably with a contingent of reporters, including representatives of all three networks and several legislators, deep into Virginia. Along the way was the best—wildflowers in highway meridians—and worst—billboards— proof of her message.

On another trip, Liz arranged for shrimp boats to come close to shore for the perfect photo opportunity as Lady Bird slipped out of her shoes for a picturesque walk along a beachfront. In Texas, the First Lady led a group across the Comanche Indian Trail, with a vista of mountains, tumbleweed, cactus, and bluebonnets, resting for a lunch from the Odessa Chuck Wagon, with Mariachi music. As they climbed a mesa, they could see Mexico. At night, it was dinner on red-checkered tablecloths, sitting on Navaho rugs around a campfire and listening to old tales of Indians, white men, conquistadores, and Pancho Villa. There was an all-day white-water rapids raft excursion down the Rio Grande, with Lady Bird at the helm like a western Cleopatra in sunglasses and cowboy hat, a gleeful flotilla of press bubbling in her wake. Although she once thought that the use of an old schoolhouse as the setting for the signing of the Education Bill was "corny," the First Lady recognized the value of staging.[19]

When they had a large press contingent, Liz chartered an airplane. Otherwise, she, Mrs. Johnson, and Secret Service agents traveled Eleanor style. Tourist class on commerical flights, the train, even an eleven-hour car ride from Cleveland. At one stop, one reverential restaurant waitress thought she was serving *the* Mrs. Johnson, as in Mrs. Howard.[20]

The trips weren't covered exclusively by women reporters—Art Buchwald went on one, and upon seeing a vista of snowcapped mountains sighed, "What a lovely place for a lot of billboards." Only Julia Tyler, Florence Harding, and Eleanor Roosevelt had courted the press

persistently as Lady Bird Johnson. She would later admit, "Yes, I used them the best I could. We all used each other . . ."[21]

There was even a compliment from Republican Clare Luce, often a critic of Democratic First Ladies: "If Mrs. Johnson persists in her crusade for America the beautiful, I venture to suggest she will be doing more for her country than any President's wife has ever done." Doris Fleeson, a friend of Jackie's who had also covered Eleanor, felt Lady Bird "hasn't an enemy in the world and [has] a public all her own." *National Wildlife* magazine called the First Lady the "secretary of the exterior."[22]

Lady Bird, having "lived openly and unafraid and quite candidly with people all my life," was unintimidated by the press. Television didn't always flatter her. After her first TV interview, the First Lady vowed never to be unprepared again. She doubted her skill to do an ABC special on Washington beautification, but pushed herself because it might inspire others to form local committees. So many technical problems plagued the taping, she admitted "every one of us was ready to swear. . . ." At one point the boat transporting her died in the mucky Potomac. "A Visit to Washington with Mrs. Lyndon Johnson" aired November 25, 1965. By then Mrs. Johnson had helped accomplish the most tangible result of her public work. It was called "Lady Bird's Bill."[23]

"It is helpful," she said with understatement, ". . . for a First Lady with a cause to have a husband who believes in it, too." Just after the election, LBJ had told Commerce Secretary Luther Hodges that "Lady Bird wants to know what you're going to do about all those junkyards [along highways]." It was estimated that sixteen thousand existed, 10 percent of which were in Texas. The result was a bill focused on junkyard cleanup, scenic landscaping, and removal of billboards from America's highways. Under the Act, 20 percent of federal highway grants would be refused to states whose interstate and major highways ignored the bill. A committed LBJ scribbled a note to Hodges that, with the First Lady's inspiration, garden clubs and other interested groups could organize into lobbying Congress.

Liz recalled that Mrs. Johnson was ". . . not . . . an arm-twister, but she'd try to touch base in the most effective way. They [Congress] had such respect for her." For the bill, the First Lady lobbied not only Congressional wives but members of Congress. Liz remembered, "We happened to be in Chicago and she got a phone call from him [LBJ] and he'd say 'Now, I'd call [Rep.] Rostenkowski . . . tell him what you want to do and I bet he'll listen to you . . .' And so she'd get them on the phone with that leading-by-the-hand . . . presented in her own way, and of course, charmed the hell out of 'em. . . ." The problem was that many congressmen who represented small towns were being begged and threatened by small businessmen in their districts whose most vital advertising was on highway billboards.[24]

One administration aide believed Mrs. Johnson would relinquish parts of the bill, but that LBJ didn't want anyone to "be able to write a headline saying that Congress administers defeat to Lady Bird!'" It was "a matter of personal honor" to his wife, and as he told his staff and Cabinet, ". . . I love that woman and she wants that Highway Beautification Act. . . . By God, we're going to get it for her." Representative Bob Dole sarcastically suggested that "Lady Bird" be substituted every time "secretary of commerce" appeared in the bill. The bill passed the Senate, but stalled in the House, and a Florida congressman complained, "Never, never has this body known such arm-twisting." The Johnsons had already acquiesced to a diluted version with heavy axing to specific appropriations, but after a late-night session on October 7, the House passed the "Lady Bird Bill."

The president signed the bill with one pen, and handed it to his First Lady. To enforce the new law, Lady Bird's personal choice, Fred Farr, was made coordinator in the Bureau of Public Roads. Funds for enforcement were denied by Congress, but an undaunted Lady Bird began appealing to the private sector for better highway planning and landscaping.[25]

There was a minor backlash. A Montana billboard proposed: IMPEACH LADY BIRD. The First Lady and her staff had to fight the Defense Department, which used billboards to advertise federal programs. Mostly, however, it inspired more political First Lady cartoons. One showed a wife complaining to her husband about his junked cars: "Mrs. Johnson says they have to go and I say they have to go!" Lady Bird was drawn as "a woman driver," hitting billboards along the road and another cartoon showed two weary congressman, one sighing, "What's so tough about a twisted arm? Wait until you're hit with a full powder puff!"[26]

Beautification helped make Lady Bird Johnson a vivid personality of the era, but the international media kept the focus on Jackie Kennedy. Once again, bus tours included a drive past her home. One magazine actually published a map illustrating where she went about her normal private life. Evenings she was pestered at the theater or the ballet after ushers called the press. She was most distressed by the threat to her children when photographers ventured too close. Printed details on their schedules became a security concern.[27]

When Robert Kennedy ran for the U.S. Senate, Jackie campaigned for him. She remained interested in politics because of him, but primarily kept working on the JFK Library and the arts center. The late president's memory remained her focus. When a portion of land at Runnymede, England, was dedicated in his honor, Jacqueline attended the ceremony, and released a statement to the press, quoting Churchill and John Buchan, and spoke of it also being an honor to her own "countrymen who have lived and died in the spirit of Runnymede"—a reference to American soldiers killed in wars, including Vietnam. In thanking President Johnson for providing a government plane to take the family to England, Jacqueline painfully confided, "It was such an emotional and difficult day for me—so many thoughts at all my loss[es] surged in me again."[28]

Meanwhile, books on the late president began appearing, and one would thrust Mrs. Kennedy back into headlines. Sanctioned by the family, William Manchester had written *The Death of A President*, partially based on Jackie's taped memories. Since so many others were suddenly writing books on the assassination, she believed it would be best to have one authorized version. As she later recalled, "Now in hindsight, it seems wrong to have ever done that book at that time." Disagreements with Manchester were publicly divulged. From Washington, however, came reassurance from two old friends. LBJ wrote to her, "Lady Bird and I have been distressed to read the press accounts of your unhappiness about the Manchester book. Some of these accounts attribute your concern to passages in the book which are critical or defamatory of us. If this is so, I want you to know while we deeply appreciate your characteristic kindness and sensitivity, we hope you will not subject yourself to any discomfort or distress on our account . . . your own tranquility is important to both of us, and . . . We are both grateful to you for your constant and unfailing thoughtfulness and friendship."

At the time, Jacqueline Kennedy also saw a personal goal of federal legislation realized. LBJ forwarded to Congress the Historic Preservation Act, and it passed. He had added in his message to Congress about the Bill that "Lady Bird wants it."[29]

The most criticized "Great Society" initiative, the "War on Poverty," eventually assisted about 13 million needy people in some manner and was also of interest to the First Lady. Mrs. Johnson asked about each individual program, "Will it work?" She said, "I could make a lifelong work doing something, anything about poverty children." In formal remarks to the Presidential Task Force on Poverty, she emphasized that poverty was "the common enemy of all mankind." She traveled to meet the "people behind the statistics. It makes Lyndon's memos and working papers come to life for me." From urban slums to rural Appalachia, she confronted poverty as Eleanor had.

One such typical trip began at the airport, at the cold winter hour of 7:00 A.M. On the plane, she met with her staff, reviewed her speech, and greeted the press. Upon landing, it was the now classic scene: perfectly coiffed First Lady, smiling and waving, local officials and the ubiquitous bouquet of red American Beauty roses. Then, she delivered a VISTA commencement speech, handed out diplomas, visited a remedial reading lesson, ate lunch in a cafeteria with students, inspected a slum, posed for ten minutes for one child who couldn't manage his camera, went to another classroom, changed clothes, attended a museum reception, and flew back to Washington—in thirteen hours. Lady Bird Johnson's trips would become the prototype for First Ladies.[30]

Whenever she could, Lady Bird promoted the "Great Society" objectives. She told a YWCA convention that "women want . . . a world at peace, a security based on mutual trust . . . fair play for all, not because it is political or expedient, but because it is morally right." She explained, "People don't want handouts . . . They want to learn the skills they can exchange for a paycheck." She told another women's convention that "if this nation is wise enough to pursue peace in the world, we must be strong enough to fight poverty here at home. . . ."

Increasingly, there were the allusions to Vietnam. By early 1966, she acknowledged that "erosions and frustrations" plagued the West Wing. "I couldn't handle the war in Vietnam," she later admitted, "I wasn't big enough." An increasingly frustrated LBJ told her, "This thing is assuming dangerous proportions, dividing the country and giving our enemies the wrong idea of the will of this country to fight." She said the war now consumed their talks, and she privately questioned the real results of frequent bombing.[31] She was now always aware of it. One midnight during a snowstorm, after an enjoyable trip to New York, Lady Bird arrived by train in deserted Union Station and caught a glimpse of floral arrangements. Instinctively, she knew they were headed for Arlington Cemetery, to be laid on the graves of soldiers. After that, she said, "It was hard to think of anything else."

Mrs. Johnson supported LBJ, so she supported the war. When he began reading a progress report claiming that America was achieving its goals in Vietnam to a group of gathered reporters, the First Lady, who'd sat quietly listening to the findings, blurted, "That's not what I've been reading in the papers." Two *Washington Post* reporters thought she said so "with evident bitterness" toward the press.[32]

With her midterm public works, and increasing stress, Lady Bird guarded moments alone for her White House diary. Lynda said ". . . I think she viewed it as important for history . . . and she encouraged me to keep one and said, 'It's good therapy' . . . maybe in saying that she meant it was therapy for her . . . She never used it as a means of venting her anger . . . She's a very judicious woman. She doesn't get emotional. Unlike my father . . . she was never one to scream, shout, curse. I'm sure she was frustrated at times, but she never displayed it. She never raised her voice."[33]

As busy as she was, the First Lady never forgot she was mother of two very different daughters. She strove to keep them close, and whenever she was away, she'd call at night to say, "Remember, you are loved." After the Inaugural, Lynda emerged glamorously on the arm of perpetually tanned movie-star George Hamilton. Luci was pure teenager, once lecturing her parents that they were "unduly controlled and unemotional," and sadly telling the press that her father wouldn't permit her to go to Union Station to meet the Beatles. Reporters made much of her changing "Lucy" to "Luci," buying a convertible, and becoming a Catholic. At nineteen, against some parental reservations, she married Patrick Nugent in one of the most colossal weddings of the sixties.[34]

There was so much interest in the bridegroom that Liz temporarily "requisitioned" one Tom Johnson from the West Wing office to handle Nugent's press—the first time a man worked on the professional East Wing staff.[35]

In the autumn, Mrs. Johnson resumed work. On preservation matters, she kept in frequent contact with Mrs. Kennedy, writing, "I certainly understand your feelings about coming back to the White House." Jackie also knew there could only be one First Lady in charge. Though she didn't write this, she implied it by acting as consultant, saying it was "so hard from far away" to keep abreast of the work. In one long letter, asking Lady Bird to "forgive the paper" of legal-size yellow sheets, business was mixed with the personal:—"I saw the prettiest picture of you by a campfire—I hope you have some carefree times like that—with all you have to do and a wedding . . . I bet poor Luci will still be writing thank you letters from wedding presents when her first baby arrives!" Jackie asked if a particular donor, "who was a temperamental creature," had taken back some important paintings he had loaned. "If so, the Fine Arts Committee should threaten, persuade, seduce, coerce him to leave them permanently to the White House! even in his will—"

Mrs. Kennedy continued that "The State China service could be so beautiful . . . Just a word of warning—DON'T let the American china companies do it . . . The results always looked more like hotel china than the Truman & Eisenhower plates do . . . Jansen is the one to do it . . . & luckily they have a N.Y. office—so one avoids the buying it abroad problem!" Jackie also wrote of "trying to keep the . . . ground and 1st floor as 18th & 19th century as possible—so no one in the future will ever change it—& it will remain always & glimpse for Americans back into the days of our country's beginning—I was just wondering if Mrs. Roosevelt's [portrait] outside the East Room didn't bring the 20th century in so much—that it really jars the unity of that whole floor. . . . The problem one runs into is . . . one admires and reveres Mrs. Roosevelt—so she should have a place of honor—Why

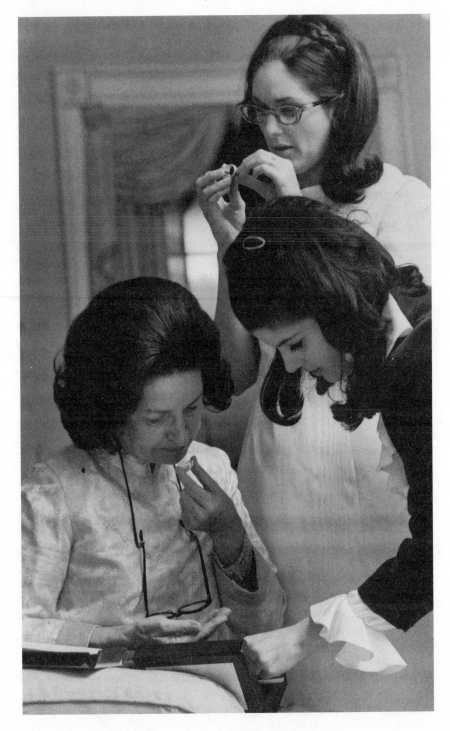

not there? But then later people of different administrations will start according places of honor to their heroes, and the whole harmony of the early years of the White House will be lost. I think it would be wonderful if you could establish the precedent that that floor would never change—Couldn't Mrs. Roosevelt have a place of honor in the Queen's Room . . . or [as] the first thing visitors see as they enter the East Wing—the feminine wing of the White House—"

At the painting's unveiling, Lady Bird said she had chosen "a place in the Great Hall of the State floor where all the people who come through will see it, because all the people were her concern . . . little people and big people, most of whom had never met her—feel that she was their friend." Eleanor was Lady Bird's admired role model, not Jackie's—who admitted as much—but in accordance with the suggestion, Mrs. Roosevelt was moved to the East Wing entrance hall. Furthermore, Lady Bird would begin the custom of having the two most recent First Ladies' portraits flank the doors to the Diplomatic Reception Room. On the china question, she wanted to leave her own mark and had native wildflowers woven into the design, by an American firm. Mrs. Kennedy emphasized that "whatever you do will be perfect." She closed her letter with "much love—and my love to the President in these always trying days for him."[36]

When she resumed globe-trotting, Mrs. Kennedy now played the "unintentional role" of "ambassador-at-large." After a visit to Spain, one Spanish diplomat said, "The ties between our nations are better for her visit." Her excursions remained oriented to history and art. When she went to Mexico, she was prompted by her intense interest in the Mayan civilization. Internationally, however, she had unwittingly become classified as one of "the Beautiful People" and star of the era that Diana Vreeland dubbed "youthquake." When the youthful Jackie began appearing in miniskirts, her influence on fashion once again had a tremendous impact.[37]

Ironically enough, just several blocks away from Jackie Kennedy lived a woman she'd once "run" against, Pat Nixon. Lady Bird was often with Lyndon at his evening meetings with foreign advisers, and occasionally at his morning political conferences. When Dick Nixon came to confer with LBJ at the White House one morning, he was received by both Johnsons, in bed. Nixon told LBJ that he believed a stronger defense was needed against the North Vietnamese, and he'd been defending the administration in his foreign speeches. Lady Bird broke in to ask about Pat, whom she invited annually to the White House Senate Wives Luncheon, but Pat always sent regrets.

Mrs. Nixon had said that she was relieved to be out of politics, but by 1966 she admitted to being "restless." Still, while Dick increasingly made political appearances, Julie thought that he "tended to gloss over

Mother's reluctance to go with him," and Pat asked her whether she thought she'd been "a failure to Daddy." Meanwhile, Julie had begun her freshman year at Smith College, and at nearby Amherst College David Eisenhower was in school. They began dating, and Mamie encouraged it.[38]

That fall Mamie turned seventy years old. She was enjoying retirement with Ike, who the year before had suffered two heart attacks in two days, and had been moved to Walter Reed. Again, she had ensconced herself there, and Lady Bird extended any help she could, even sending a "Mamie Pink" carnation. The Johnsons made several calls, sent a telegram and flowers for Ike, and had their doctor keep in touch with his. Mamie was extremely appreciative of the "many kindnesses," and did a little lobbying of her own. She suggested to the president that he appoint the DAR's president-general to the American Revolution Bicentennial Commission, because "I have heard only the finest reports on her and feel that she would make a responsible and energetic member. . . ." When Ike recuperated, Mamie took him for their annual respite to Palm Springs. Though the Eisenhowers were the Republican celebrities of the golf community, both cautiously avoided the growing party split between moderates and conservatives, marked by the election of their old acquaintance, the new governor Ronald Reagan.[39]

In 1965 "Friends of Ronald Reagan" had been formed by a circle of California businessmen who financed him, including the public-relations fees of Stuart Spencer. Mrs. Reagan had continued to consult astrologers, and one told her that she saw Ronnie in an official state job. Michael Reagan thought that his father didn't have "really strong ambitions" to run for office, but that Nancy "prodded him," and told Ronnie that her father would contribute $200,000. At his formal announcement for governor, a friend recalled that Nancy Reagan was nervous, but believed that "we" had to accept the run. Though she resisted making speeches, she began making solo campaign appearances, taking questions. At colleges, while admitting that alcohol was a crutch for her generation, she opposed marijuana use because she believed it had lasting effects. But when she remarked, "Why not a generation that didn't need any crutch?," she was applauded. She believed that most Americans didn't want to be "liberated" from morals. A loyal staff and advisers became as important to her as family, especially after Ronnie won.[40]

When Reagan was inaugurated at one minute after midnight, only Nancy and a few friends knew that astrological charts had dictated that decision. At the Inaugural, Nancy was stunningly beautiful. With her modified brunette bouffant, and looking tanned and thin in a white beaded, off-the-shoulder Galanos gown, her copying of Mrs. Kennedy was visible. Nancy emulated Jackie in yet another role. Just days after

Ronnie won the election, she sent an aide into Hollywood to fetch her a copy of *The Making of the President*.[41]

The '66 election had also given Gerald R. Ford his second term as House minority leader. For Betty Ford, it meant an almost always absent husband. In election years, during Congressional recess, he'd be away traveling and speaking for six-week stints, except for one weekend in between, and effectively she became a single parent raising four sometimes-difficult children.

Betty attended Lady Bird's frequent entertainments for Congressional wives, which included a tour of the family quarters. That year, with the election of her Houston oilman husband to the House, Barbara Bush became a Republican colleague of Mrs. Ford's. When she first entered the White House as a guest of Lady Bird's, Mrs. Bush felt "awe-struck and excited." She recalled being "charmed by Mrs. LBJ," and found her to be "much prettier in person than pictures." Mrs. Johnson took to her as well, invited Barbara to one of her "Women Do-ers" lunches, and, with George, to the LBJ Ranch. Mrs. Bush became a "particular favorite" of the First Lady's. Meanwhile, as wife of a Congressional leader, Betty Ford purposefully instigated more volunteer activism among Republican wives. She continued to suffer physical pain, partially alleviated by the prescribed painkillers. It was a lonely and depressing time in which she admitted to being "resentful" of her husband's absence and feeling "neglected." One day, she took her daughter and drove off to the beach without telling anyone. She said she had just "snapped." Jerry would later admit that his absences had temporarily "put a strain on the marriage."[42]

Barbara Bush went to Washington, and Nancy Reagan to the state house, but Rosalynn Carter went to neither. Jimmy Carter had initially begun running for Congress against archconservative Lester Maddox, but when he suddenly switched to the race for governor, so did Carter. Rosalynn found this larger campaign "discouraging" but "exciting." At one stop, she handed a tobacco-chewing citizen a flyer for Carter. He spat on her. Jimmy lost by twenty-thousand votes, but was already laying plans to run for governor in 1970. And Rosalynn was pregnant with her daughter Amy, born the next fall.[43]

Meanwhile, the Reagans came to the White House for the annual Governors' Conference Dinner in 1967, and Lady Bird found him "sleekly handsome." When asked if she'd like to be First Lady, Mrs. Reagan acted surprised. "I've never thought about it." Still, Nancy Reagan's first glimpse of the White House left her "awed." Because Nancy had a cold, Lady Bird made sure she was standing out of the draft when dinner guests gathered on the lawn to watch LBJ take off in his copter.

The governor's wife hired a former MGM publicity agent as her

secretary and proved to be an activist. Publicly, she expressed the opinion that pulling out of Vietnam would be "immoral," but privately she
became genuinely concerned about the returning soldiers. She made
frequent trips to hospital wards and—and as Mrs. Hardy had done—
spoke with one wounded vet after another, listening carefully to their
war stories. Mrs. Reagan accepted an offer to write a syndicated newspaper column and—as Mrs. Roosevelt had done—Nancy turned all
proceeds over to the National League of Families of American POW-
MIA. She also became seriously committed to "Foster Grandparents,"
which linked the lonely elderly with handicapped children. In fact, so
quickly dedicated to the cause did she become that when Nancy made
an official trip to Australia, she helped establish a Foster Grandparents
program there before she left.[44]

California was ablaze with student uproars, and Nancy was bewildered by the drug use, demonstrations, long hair, and miniskirts of
what she called "the age of permissiveness." She feared violence, and as
a "deterrent to murder," defended the death penalty. She demanded
that her driver lock all car doors when she journeyed through Berkeley
because some radical "might recognize me." She nonetheless publicly
agreed that student complaints that the state colleges were too large
were "justified."[45]

Some thought that fear was the reason behind her decision to move
out of the rickety but beautiful governor's mansion and rent a private
home. When the leased house was about to be sold, wealthy friends
bought it, and kept the rent at the same price. Sensitive to charges that
her decision not to live in the governor's mansion stemmed from racial
considerations, Nancy said it was only the fear that the house was a
firetrap, and she fretted over her son's welfare. Ron was the only child
then living with her. Patti was away in school, and Michael and
Maureen only visited. She also openly disliked Sacramento because nobody "can do hair," and was happy to often "escape to Beverly Hills."

She was familiar with several of the governor's aides, like William
P. Clark, Cabinet secretary, but feeling "intimidated" by her, he asked
his assistant, Michael K. Deaver, to answer her needs. So began a close
alliance. Deaver astutely observed the Reagan relationship, concluding
that although Nancy's full-time "career" was protecting Ronnie as his
"closest adviser," she used her "persuasions with care, knowing when
and how hard to apply the pressure." Like Deaver she was a moderate,
and though she mouthed right-wing views, Nancy in fact proved to be
calm amid strident reactionaries.[46]

Ronnie's secretary Helene von Damm claimed that the staff tensed
with fear when she came to the office. Politically, Nancy was less concerned with policy, but was "quite vocal" with "strong opinions" on
both personnel and Ronnie's schedule. Helene felt that Nancy's "ambi-

tion was stronger than his," and that she viewed all people—whether employee or friend—"as a means to an end." Her interest in personnel actually was policy, for it meant keeping or releasing those whose views might help or hinder Reagan's image. Conservative Von Damm resented Nancy's influence.[47]

When conservative press aide Lyn Nofziger discovered that a large number of homosexuals were working for Reagan, he asked aide Ed Meese to break the news to the governor. They requested resignations, but kept it secret. Eventually, the press caught wind of this and began reporting it. Nofziger, without the Reagans' permission, leaked the names of the individuals involved, infuriating Mrs. Reagan because it breached the privacy of the men and their families. She refused to acknowledge Nofziger, then pressed for his dismissal. Reagan later joked that he should have Truman Capote "crawl . . . through the halls to see if there are any of them left." Through her best friend, Betsy Bloomingdale, Nancy had befriended Jerry Zipkin, and through him she came to know Capote. When he was arrested and imprisoned for disorderly conduct in California, Nancy called Deaver to order, "[Y]ou must get him out. It will kill him." He called Meese, and Capote was released. Though Deaver admitted that Mrs. Reagan could be "intense" and "brittle" in public, he marveled at how in private she was also gentle and fair. As for her own image, Nancy maintained firm control. In her official biography, which stated that she was born "in Chicago, the only daughter of Dr. and Mrs. Loyal Davis," she fibbed. She was in fact born in New York, daughter of Kenneth Robbins.[48]

Like Nancy Reagan and Jacqueline Kennedy, Lady Bird Johnson was fascinated by Truman Capote as she conversed with him at a private dinner, astutely observing that the "alchemy of image" had transformed him into a sixties celebrity. Rarely had a First Lady been so conscious of her era's pop culture. "What a decade, what a remarkable generation I live in!" she observed. Whether listening to Herb Alpert and the Tijuana Brass play in the White House, or joining "pop" artist Andy Warhol and his model Edie Sedgwick at a New York museum opening, amused by it all.[49]

Lady Bird used the lingo, asking one southern university official if they had trouble with "way-out" students. She felt the press was focusing too much on "beards, pot, LSD, and draft-card burners." She was amused by the "high hairdos," at Luci's wedding, and Lynda's mesh stockings in "the very spirit of 1967," but she chastised television coverage of violence as a factor in stirring the "strange sickness that besets us in this age." Mrs. Johnson found comfort in a saying: "Have confidence. There is nothing terrible that lasts forever, or even for long."

She had even wanted to order china "in the spirit of the sixties," but feared it "would take a daring First Lady."[50]

Mamie Eisenhower took enthusiastic interest in Mrs. Johnson's ponderings about china. In turn, Lady Bird sent her a photograph of plates painted with the images of First Ladies. She complimented Mamie's first solo writing piece, in McCall's magazine, about her fifty years of marriage, and made her the guest of honor at the '66 and '67 Senate Wives Luncheons. On her birthday, the Johnsons sent an antique compote plate, for which Mamie effusively thanked them.

While friendly with the LBJs, and supportive of his Vietnam policy, Mamie remained loyal to the Republican party and supported Richard Nixon for president in 1968. Milton believed that the "influence attempt" to get Ike to give Nixon an early endorsement was Mamie's. In 1967, when Ike listed Republicans he considered possible candidates in 1968, he named Reagan but not Nixon. Before the microphones, Mamie piped up to Ike, "You forgot Dick!" He added him.[51]

Although Lady Bird's invitations to Bess Truman to join Mamie and her at the Senate Wives Luncheons were declined, there was mutual admiration. She sent a bottle of perfume to Bess, who sent her a complimentary editorial on beautification. Remaining at the top of the Gallup Poll as most-admired woman, however, was still Jackie.[52]

With obvious political benefit for the administration, Mrs. Kennedy made another trip as unofficial ambassador, this time to Cambodia. There, she fulfilled a lifelong dream by inspecting the ancient, endangered ruins of Angkor Wat. In French she delivered a dedication speech naming a boulevard for JFK. The personal guest of Prince Sihanouk, she was greeted by girls throwing jasmine petals in her path. Bathed in the complimentary publicity, her prominent political envoys, Michael Forrestal and Lord Harlech, had a discreet mission. They respectively served as personal diplomats for the American and British governments and tried to influence Sihanouk to exercise his power in urging the repatriation of prisoners then being held by the National Liberation Front.[53]

It was Lady Bird who became the first incumbent First Lady to travel to Southeast Asia, joining LBJ for the Manila Conference on Vietnam, and visiting New Zealand, Australia, Thailand, Malaysia, and South Korea. In Pago Pago, the First Lady gulped the ceremonial beverage of a narcotic juice wrung from a tree root by the natives' bare hands. Drinking from an open gourd, she became the first woman to consume the concoction, and the gathered Samoans broke into wild cheering. But there was a striking, sober note during the trip. Lady Bird noticed a sign with a message that was becoming all too familiar:

HEY, HEY, LBJ, HOW MANY KIDS HAVE YOU KILLED TODAY?[54]

The international situation had seriously worsened. In June 1967, the First Lady learned from a 4:30 A.M. call to Lyndon that war had broken out in the Middle East. Some weeks later, as she enjoyed a relaxed cruise with Lynda and her fiancé, marine Chuck Robb, Lady Bird thought about Vietnam, the increase in rioting, and Democrats abandoning LBJ. She felt "a miasma spreading across the country . . ."[55]

Amid the turmoil came a moment of joy. When Luci gave birth to "Lyn" on June 21, the new grandmother remarked, "He's the only non-controversial thing around here." Jacqueline Kennedy wrote her, "It is sad that he arrived at such a troublesome time for the President . . . with Mr. Kosygin keeping all of you from just being together . . ." A week and a half earlier, Jackie had written LBJ, "I hope all the joy of his arrival can, for a little while, make you forget all the burdens of your office. A baby really is a miracle."[56]

LBJ was in fact growing increasingly closer to and dependent upon his daughters and wife. When he'd once complained about how Lady Bird had committed him to an event he didn't want to attend, a friend snapped back at him, "Yes . . . but she also got you where you are today." He seemed increasingly to appreciate that. There'd been an earlier time when LBJ's fondness for women seemed blatant, but Lady Bird philosophically explained that he loved all people and "half the people are women." As Lynda said, "She knew his feelings and loved him anyway." During her tenure, when the first published accounts of FDR's love affair with Lucy Mercer appeared, Lady Bird surprised Nancy Dickerson by saying she thought Eleanor's reaction had been unfortunate, because it was only "a fly on the wedding cake." Lady Bird had no expressed jealousy. At one state dinner, she observed that LBJ had sat next to and danced with "the prettiest woman in the room." It was that sort of understanding with which Mrs. Johnson could state that she knew that she was the most important woman in his life.[57]

It was he who increasingly sought her. When they once went swimming together, LBJ discussed everything from the budget, to—as she wrote, "the dreadful decision that if nothing, nothing, nothing, comes of the peace offensive—when to resume the bombing." The next morning he grimly confided to her that they might lose the war.

She recognized what LBJ perceived as a liberal bias, and delicately wrote that in retrospect he probably should have made more of his own appointments right away rather than carry on many of JFK's. She noticed when Bobby Kennedy didn't applaud the president's State of the Union speech more than three times.

Eric Goldman wrote that Mrs. Johnson was "even less ideological than her husband, and had an uninflatable modesty about the value of her policy opinions, especially in foreign affairs. . . ." But if uninformed of secret military maneuvers, Lady Bird was apprised of imminent or breaking events by LBJ. After weeks of intense discussions, she surmised that bombing of North Vietnamese fuel reserves would begin. She admitted to being partially frightened when she viewed a simulated attack, captured North Vietnamese weaponry, and a vast camouflage parachute at a military center, and sensed "awed silence" when she came to speak with wounded men.[58]

Liz believed that since LBJ had "all the wise men [military advisers] meeting around his bed early in the morning or at lunch . . . she was part of it. And so she was hearing it, constantly . . . she did not offer great opinions unless asked. And often he would ask. As she said, 'He did me the honor of valuing my opinion.'" As LBJ committed more men to Vietnam, Lady Bird remarked ominously, "I just hope that foreign problems do not keep mounting. They do not represent Lyndon's kind of Presidency." After Nancy Dickerson told West Wing adviser Jack Valenti that she believed Defense Secretary McNamara was beginning to differ with LBJ on Vietnam, she was summoned and cross-examined by the First Lady in her private office.[59]

In October 1967, Lady Bird Johnson went to Williams College, to speak to the graduating class at their new Center for Environmental Studies, and to Yale University to speak on environmental protection. There, Vietnam hit home.

As she headed into the hall to speak at Williams, the First Lady caught glimpses of signs, one reading CONFRONT THE WAR MAKERS IN WASHINGTON ON OCTOBER 21. She noticed that some graduates wore white armbands, mourning for those killed in Vietnam. When Mrs. Johnson was introduced, a group of protesters walked out. A fast pulse of emotion caught in her throat, but she made her speech. She was livid, but concentrated on controlling her temper. Mrs. Johnson was cheered, but on leaving, she was followed with a low buzz of "Shame, Shame!" She felt she'd been the "bait" for the "hate and anger."

At Yale it was worse. As she arrived, met by president Kingman Brewster, Lady Bird was greeted by pickets. After changing in a guest room, she emerged and was met by more picketers, who raced alongside her car. When Brewster introduced her, he compared her to Mrs. Roosevelt, but recalled how he'd spoken against World War II in his youth. To Lady Bird, the message was that Brewster was being polite, but supported the protests. Liz recalled the trip as the "roughest time," and in retrospect felt "we should have junked the speech and faced it. We had to walk through a really crowded area outside the room of catcalls and boos and hisses . . . but she didn't stop going, even to the places where we'd find the pickets . . . they'd show up everywhere . . ." While she believed that the students were isolated, for herself Lady Bird Johnson determined to "not live only in the White House, insulated against life. I want to know what's going on—even if to know is to suffer."[60]

Mrs. Johnson didn't agree with the protesters, but she never spoke out against their right to protest. She later reflected that the Vietnam war was "long" and "undeclared," and if ever another such situation arose, Lady Bird said, "it had sure better be preceded by an Alamo or a

Pearl Harbor so that there is a clear-cut declaration and coalescing of the American people."[61]

Her October experience, however, was not an isolated incident. As she recalled, for about six weeks leading up to her speeches, the flame of bitter divisiveness over Vietnam had thoroughly engulfed the nation. The night before the great October 21 antiwar march on Washington she felt "under siege," but chose not to leave town. Two weeks later, she was sitting in an old Anglican church, in the traditional Tidewater region of Virginia, when the minister suddenly lectured her and LBJ. "We are mystified by news accounts suggesting that our brave fighting units are inhibited by directives and inadequate equipment from using their capacities to terminate the conflict successfully. While pledging our loyalty, we ask humbly: Why?" Lady Bird said she turned to stone, but was internally boiling.[62]

The past spring, she'd been thinking about retirement. The ranch offered her peace, and she increasingly relished driving her own car in the early evening, awash with Southwest colors. Lady Bird thought that if the war was ending, or if LBJ lacked support, he'd step down, and believing she could "have some effect" on his decision, she consulted his doctor for a briefing on Lyndon's health. He ominously recommended that she stay closer to home. Mrs. Johnson was quoted as confiding to an unnamed political figure, "If I can prevent it, Lyndon will not run again. It will kill him."[63]

December would see her meeting with the interior secretary, reviewing environmental accomplishments, and attending Lynda's White House wedding to Chuck Robb. Across the street in Lafayette Park, as they had done at Luci's wedding, antiwar demonstrators staged a large protest.

After Christmas, Mrs. Johnson received a heartening letter from an old friend to whom she'd sent a gift: "I was thinking . . . you should have some Christmas prize for your sensitivity in every year finding the most treasured things.

"I hope that someone gave you something you love as much on Christmas Day—and I hope for you that the New Year will bring you all you hope for yourself—as I have had here—when one can put all one's cares and obligations aside—

"If you are ever in New York and have any free time—you know how I would always love to see you—I never know when you are coming—and I know when one gets to New York for a stolen day from Washington—every second is full—but perhaps we can grab a cup of tea together some time—

"Thank you again dear Lady Bird—and all my love to you and the President. As ever Affectionately, Jackie."[64]

Then, 1968 began.

9

1968

IT WAS A BLEAKLY cold day as the three women sat on the beach, facing the Florida ocean. Pat Nixon opened up to her daughters about the inevitable, and Julie recalled that her mother said "flatly, almost tonelessly, that she could not face another presidential race. She spoke of the 'humiliation' of defeat. It was apparent to us that she simply no longer had the heart to fight the battle. . . ." Polls showed that Nixon was the leading Republican favorite for the '68 election. Julie recorded that "Mother is opposed to running but at least she is reconciled to it now. . . ." Meanwhile, Julie became engaged to David Eisenhower, a fact that sent Mamie into "uncomplicated excitement."[1]

The East Wing, still stinging from the Williams and Yale incidents, had become cautious. The First Lady was asked to meet fund-raisers for the starving Biafran children. The request went first to the State Department, which recommended that the First Lady should "decline," using "too busy a schedule" and that she "made it a general practice" to support American causes only as her excuses. They further recommended that she "use the same line" in response to a request that Mrs. Johnson lend support for Iranian earthquake victims. But even the most carefully controlled events could now explode without warning.

At about two-thirty in the afternoon on January 18, Lady Bird Johnson's first "Women-Doers" Luncheon of the year was going as planned. Instead of the usual eighteen guests, there were fifty invited women, including Eartha Kitt, a black chanteuse currently famous for playing Catwoman on the *Batman* television series. The luncheon program's title was "What Citizens Can Do to Help Insure Safe Streets," a "grim subject for a pleasant meeting like this," the First Lady admitted, as she introduced the issue. When the scheduled speakers finished, Eartha Kitt rose and unwound her anger, aimed directly at Lady Bird: ". . . I have lived in the gutters . . . I know . . . The youth of America today . . . are not rebelling [and] . . . are not hippies for no reason at all . . . I am sorry, Mrs. Johnson, if I am going to offend the President or you, but I am here to say . . . the youth . . . do not want to go to school because . . . when they come out, they will be snatched away from the mother and sent off to Vietnam . . . the boys of this country are doing everything they possibly can to avoid being drafted . . . They feel that 'if I have any kind of life at all, I am going to enjoy it as best I can because I may not be here tomorrow.' . . . 'If I . . . get thrown in jail . . . I don't stand a chance of going off and being shot in Vietnam.' . . . They will smoke a joint and get high . . . in order to avoid whatever it is to get shot at."

No public comments had ever so confronted a First Lady, but they echoed the nation's seething frustrations over Vietnam and racial tensions. Gathering her thoughts, Lady Bird stared back at Kitt: "Because there is a war on—and I pray that there will be a just and honorable peace—that still does not give us a free ticket not to try and work on bettering the things in this country that we can better . . . I am sorry I cannot understand as much as I should because I have not lived in the background as you have. Nor can I speak as passionately or as well as you can. But I think we must keep our eyes and our hearts and our energies fixed on constructive aims. Violence will not help it."

The press flurry was astounding, and Lady Bird expressed regret that the meeting's positive recommendations were eclipsed by "the shrill voice of anger and discord." Betty Ford, for one, thought Lady Bird "proved herself the perfect First Lady," and hundreds of telegrams and phone calls supported her. LBJ's pastor praised "all the work you have been doing to urge more justice and opportunity especially for Negroes," and apologized for all people "including Negroes who are ill-mannered, stupid and arrogant . . ." An Oklahoma radio station banned Kitt's recordings. The New Jersey governor's wife, a luncheon guest, said as the voice of the "average American," that "[T]he young American boy doesn't want to go to war and his mother doesn't want him to go. But if he has to, I believe America is worth it." Not everybody agreed.

New York radio station WBAI, identified by *Variety* as "a favorite with New York liberals and hippies," praised Kitt and said listeners supported her. Besides playing her music as a tribute, they did a radio parody of Lady Bird chiding LBJ for inviting "peaceniks to the manse." Dr. Martin Luther King said Kitt made "a very proper gesture," which "described the feelings of many persons." Democratic congressman Kastenmeier said Kitt spoke at "the right time in the right place . . ." Outside the White House, members of the Women's Strike for Peace picketed with signs, one reading EARTHA KITT SPEAKS FOR THE WOMEN OF AMERICA.

In a private memo to the First Lady, Liz reported that Eartha Kitt had not only been cleared by the FBI, but she was involved in crime and juvenile-delinquency programs, and had even testified on behalf of LBJ's bill on the issue. Though she reported that Kitt "was not well thought of by her people. She had married a white man," neither was she "a peace marcher," or involved in "peacenik activity."

Responding to the flood of mail, Mrs. Johnson mentioned the war directly: "Every American is deeply concerned over our problems in Viet Nam. However, we cannot ignore this critical situation at home." Meanwhile, Kitt defended her actions at a press conference with no apology to the First Lady. "I listened to all the ladies . . . They talked about flowers down the streets of America and making bigger and heavier street lights . . . I'm not against that—but I'm quite sure it does not squelch juvenile delinquency in any ways . . . Mrs. Johnson and Mr. Johnson did not start this particular Vietnamese war. . . . But they are in the position like the father and mother of our country . . . we expect them to be responsible for us as a nation . . . we have been split . . . If Mrs. Johnson was embarrassed, that's her problem."

Lady Bird Johnson would continue to be picketed by antiwar protestors.[2]

Three weeks later, the First Lady again willingly confronted Vietnam by entertaining some of the maimed soldiers. Most responded to her questions with monosyllabic responses. Others were just silent. One man in particular struck her. He'd lost the full lower half of his body, amputated at the waist.

On March 31, she greeted a "detached" Lynda, who'd just gone through the ordeal of saying good-bye to Chuck as he left for combat in Vietnam. Tired, she flatly asked her father, "Dad, why do they have to go to Vietnam?" Lynda was to have a child the next fall. She later

recalled, "I was a big pregnant reminder that it was his policy that was separating husbands from wives, children from parents." Afterward, Lady Bird read through a speech LBJ was making that night. To herself, she recalled what he'd been increasingly saying since the tumultuous autumn, "I do not believe I can unite this country."[3]

That night on TV, President Johnson caught most of the nation by surprise. He paused just for a moment, looked at Lady Bird in the room with him, and then announced, "I shall not seek, and I will not accept, the nomination of my party for another term as your President." Lynda later poignantly recalled the war's effect:

> The family discussed the pressures. We were all very aware . . . With friends in the war, and family—it was one more way that personalized the war . . . Chuck volunteered to go . . . He didn't have to. There were a lot of fancy people whose sons didn't go, but needless to say it would have been very awkward not to have his . . . sons-in-law go . . . When Chuck began to send me letters, my father would want to read them. I would get angry—"They're my letters!" . . . he sent recorded tapes and my father found them more revealing of the real situation than all his Generals' briefings. When Father suffered, she suffered. He was as much a casualty of the war as anyone else, and in that way mother was too. When there were people protesting "Hey, Hey L.B.J. how many kids did you kill today," it hurt and made her angry . . . . he was her husband, not the President. . . . At the end, I think she had a great sigh of relief . . . She didn't want to stay in that role . . . She would stop and say in amazement, "How in the world did this happen to me?"[4]

Four days after the announcement, while Lady Bird was having her hair done, Lynda burst in, crying. Dr. Martin Luther King had been murdered. The First Lady felt "poised on the edge of an abyss," fearing riots. They came immediately, angry and frightening. Just four blocks from the White House, stores were burned. The emerging "Black Power" movement took on a sense of urgency. The term "Negro" would vanish, from the press and the mainstream. The term was now officially "black."

Both Nixon and Humphrey attended the King funeral, and so did Jacqueline Kennedy. The day before the funeral, she arrived in Atlanta, and calling on Coretta King, explained, "I came because I know what is going through your heart and mind now." She told the King children that their father was "a very brave and very great man," and before the funeral at the local black church, returned to sign the guest book, and tell Coretta that her husband's death "will help to free us from the violence and tragedy which hate often produces. He will always be remembered as one of our nation's martyred greats . . ." During the primaries, she told Arthur Schlesinger she would campaign for RFK's presidency, but added, "Do you know what I think will happen to Bobby? The same thing that happened to Jack . . . There is so much hatred in this country . . . I've told Bobby this, but he isn't fatalistic, like me." After Atlanta, she went to Palm Beach, where she saw Aristotle Onassis. A month later, she would join him and his daughter for a cruise.[5]

Meanwhile, Lady Bird kept a commitment of a five-day tour of Texas's natural environment, with forty-four European editors. Before the tour, she was scheduled to open HemisFair '68 in San Antonio with a speech, which she rewrote in light of the King murder and ensuing riots. It was gentle, it was healing, it was typically Lady Bird: "So let us not set the fires of hatred but quench them . . . we are living in a great age of variety . . . What we have become, we owe to dozens of different peoples . . . ancient barriers between black and white have been falling. They are falling despite a cruelly tragic setback—sometimes swiftly, sometimes slowly . . . And in these troubled tragic hours, we need to remember that we are moving forward. This land is our land . . . to rend apart—or to work for . . ." As she dedicated the American Pavilion, a soft breeze snapped a flag, at half-staff for King.

Congressman George Bush attended the fair, as did protesters, and a solid line of police in helmets guarded the First Lady's every move. There was no violence, but Mrs. Johnson made note of the fact that when she dropped her compact, all the glass shattered, and it sent an "involuntary chill" through her. In Washington, fires kept burning and hoses were slashed. Just on the edge of it all sat a concerned Nancy Reagan in a nearby hotel suite. She instinctively knew it was not a good year to run for president.[6]

The city had only just recently won home rule, and Walter Washington was appointed mayor. Lady Bird had advocated that a black be chosen, and lobbied for Washington. After she was approached by friends who wanted to help pay for rebuilding the burned city, she dispatched Liz to the mayor. He sorrowfully reported, "Right now, the militants want no help from anyone . . ."[7]

Three weeks later, former president Eisenhower suffered another major heart attack, and was moved to Walter Reed. Mamie wrote the Johnsons that "he is doing as well as can be expected at this time." Nixon's campaign lifted her spirits, and in her sparse hospital room next to Ike's, she kept a bowl of Nixon campaign buttons, wearing a large one herself.

Mrs. Eisenhower was concerned about Vietnam, feeling "sadly" about "these wonderful youngsters that were being killed," but she also felt that civil unrest was partly due to an "element that they publicize too much. . . ." As her daughter-in-law remembered, Mamie "viewed everything that happened in the Sixties from afar. All that confusion, the permissiveness, it seemed like the world was coming apart. For years she read West Point literature . . . duty, honor, country. People in the old army were very patriotic . . . but even patriotism was up for scrutiny." Even Mamie would admit "times have changed—*very much* . . ."

For a brief few hours, she gratefully accepted Mrs. LBJ's annual invitation to receive with her at the Senate Wives Luncheon. Lady Bird and Mamie had become close, the First Lady frequently inviting her elder to the White House because "[s]he just always enjoyed that." Lady Bird was impressed by how Mamie "called people by their first names, including—delightfully enough—the staff." After, Mamie wrote her, "I felt sad that it was your farewell . . . you made a marvelous and thoughtful gesture in including each state flower [on the new china]."[8]

Two weeks after the lunch, a phone call awoke the First Lady at 4:20 in the morning. In New York, Jackie Kennedy was startled in the wee hours to take a call from Stas Radziwill. The news was the same for both women. Bobby Kennedy had been shot.

Mamie heard the news at Walter Reed in the morning and sobbed, "Oh, my Lord, what's happening?" In New York, Dick and Pat Nixon had gone to bed after watching some California primary returns. David Eisenhower and Julie were still watching when the news flashed. David quietly told the Nixons. The next day Pat slipped into her husband's study, weeping. "Dick, that poor boy just died. It's on the radio."

The Johnsons immediately wrote to Jackie, "We grieve with you today & know your help must be of great comfort to Ethel at this time of anguish." Pat Nixon attended the St. Patrick's Cathedral funeral, her privacy now elusive. Not only was she publicly campaigning for something about which she had personal misgivings, but her every move was shadowed. LBJ had assigned Secret Service agents to even candidates' families. At the end of the mass, Lady Bird found herself suddenly before Jackie Kennedy. "I called out her name and put out my hand," she recalled. "She looked at me as if from a great distance, as though I were an apparition." Later Jackie wrote the Johnsons, "I do thank you so much for your wire about Bobby—and for all you did, in those sad days—to make it possible for him to be laid to rest with all the love and care and nobility that meant so much to those who loved him. Sometimes there are no words to say things—only this—I am deeply grateful." Her horrible premonition of just nine weeks before had come true. She now feared for her children's safety.[9]

Days after RFK's funeral, Ike had his fifth heart attack. Mamie fiercely guarded his fragile condition, making sure all visits were limited, including that of President and Mrs. Johnson. LBJ went in directly to see Ike, but Mamie asked, "You'll leave your girl out here to talk to me, won't you?" They spent an hour together and chatted about mundane matters. More important, they managed to get some legislation initiated. Mamie revealed that she was staying at Walter Reed because Ike would worry about her being at Gettysburg; she confided that she feared the idea of living there alone. The First Lady went to the president, and LBJ immediately proposed legislation to provide presidential widows with Secret Service protection (Mrs. Kennedy's was a special provision, not law). On the second day of the Miami Republican Convention, Ike had another heart attack.[10]

Once again, Betty Ford went with Jerry to the convention, having to step over antiwar demonstrators who lay on the street outside the hall. For Barbara Bush, it was her first convention, and among those suggested as running mate to Nixon was her husband. At the last minute, another presidential candidate arose. Ronald and Nancy Reagan were thrust momentarily into the limelight when Ronnie declared himself a presidential candidate on opening day. Nancy had resisted attempts to draft Ronnie. Only when she was momentarily absent was he talked into letting his name be considered for nomination; ill-advised, it died a-borning. Never again would he make a decision of such magnitude without first consulting with Nancy.[11]

For Pat Nixon, there was the thrill of nomination, but in the flood of media scrutiny she drew back a bit, admittedly stiffening on television, preferring print interviews as the lesser of two evils. She disliked questions prying into her privacy and turned to focus on Nixon's political agenda as well as the volunteers working diligently in the campaign. Publicly, she elaborated her "issue" by urging women to work in politics: "Instead of complaining, go to work . . . for a candidate whom you believe to be qualified."

On personal questions, she developed standard responses, though she felt "artificial" about doing so. She diligently guarded the details of her difficult early years. As she told Gloria Steinem, she "never had time to think about . . . who I wanted to be, or who I admire or who I identify with . . . I had to work."

H. R. Haldeman, Nixon campaign chief of staff, oversaw every detail. At two rallies, though Mrs. Nixon was on the stand, she was completely ignored, with no introduction. Haldeman and his aide John Erlichman thought she served no purpose, but Nixon himself demanded that such an oversight never again occur.

Erlichman claimed that Mrs. Nixon was "strong and very definite in her opinions . . . with an ability to sense what voters might be thinking." On the brusque Haldeman, Erlichman gingerly hinted that "Pat Nixon was not slow to read others' feelings toward her. . . ."

Pat Nixon sought out women of all parties to learn what issue was most important to them, telling reporters, "I fill him [Nixon] in on what women think. They are thinking peace at home and peace abroad."

Nixon said that while Pat had once given "quite persistent critiques," she'd grown to "hate politics." With her mixed emotions, the '68 campaign was inordinately difficult for her. [12]

Watching on TV, Mrs. Johnson thought the Chicago Democratic Convention a "seething cauldron of emotions . . . hippies and yippies and police standing by . . . one of the spectacles of our times!" Also watching on television were Bess and Harry Truman, disappointed that LBJ didn't run again but warmly supporting Humphrey, as did Lady Bird, in a rare openly partisan speech:

> . . . I have never thought of myself as a political person . . . But . . . I have come to respect and love our party . . . of the people . . . we are in danger of forgetting the *real* issue . . . Will America, having forged so far ahead under President Kennedy and President Johnson toward a more just and compassionate society, now turn back? . . . The past five years, I know, have been years of turmoil and movement and controversy. And too often, in the heat of controversy, we have forgotten . . . the accomplishments . . . None of them is yet perfect. But if they survive and grow and improve, they will mean a fuller life for many, many people who were born with the odds stacked against them. . . . If the opposition wins in November, will they see their victory as a mandate to turn back: to end all these beginnings . . . I *know* who offers the best chance . . . [13]

A month later, on September 7, the traditional Miss America Pageant, viewed by mainstream America on TV, became the setting for what the press termed "bra burners." Suddenly, during the crowning, from the back of the theater a banner reading WOMEN'S LIBERATION floated over the crowd. Earlier, one woman had tossed her "sexist" bra into the trash. For most women, as politically disparate as Jackie Kennedy and Nancy Reagan, such action seemed radical. Time would unfold their own degrees of support for equal rights of women.

And then, two weeks before election day, Jacqueline Kennedy married Aristotle Onassis. America and Europe reacted harshly, as if, as Norman Mailer later wrote, "She did not belong to herself. . . ." There were jokes, a comedy album, even a "Goodness gracious, great balls of fire!" remark from Mamie Eisenhower, when asked about it. When a friend told her that by remarrying she would "fall off your pedestal," Jacqueline didn't hesitate with her response: "That's better than freezing there."

It would have been understandable if she had ignored the hundreds of reporters and photographers who converged on Onassis's Greek island Skorpios, yet she graciously obliged: "We know that you understand that even though people may be well known, they still hold in their hearts the emotions of a simple person for the moments that are the most important of those we know on earth—birth, marriage and death. We wish our wedding to be a private moment in the little chapel among the cypresses of Skorpios with only members of the family present—five of them little children. If you will give us those moments, we will gladly give you all the cooperation possible for you to take the pictures you need."

One reflective old friend was understanding. Recalling Jackie's eyes at RFK's funeral, Lady Bird thought that "this complete break with the past might be good for her." Mrs. Johnson went to sleep feeling that "as a result of the wedding . . . I feel strangely freer. No shadow walks beside me down the halls of the White House . . . I wonder what it would have all been like if we had entered this life unaccompanied by that shadow?" The new Mrs. Onassis lost her Secret Service protection, pension, and franking privilege (though Frances Cleveland hadn't lost the latter two when she remarried). But after the trauma of RFK's death, her new life was tonic. At Skorpios, one could escape to rejuvenate. The gregarious Onassis was famous for cheering spirits and making people laugh. He was a doting stepfather. And Jacqueline found something spiritually compelling in him, unrecognized by most, and revealed in a letter she had written to Schlesinger several years previously, illustrating how she found Onassis to be a companion not unlike Jack had been: ". . . I disputed your idea . . . please don't say that Jack was not Greek but Roman—I found something . . . that Melina Mercouri says—It almost expresses what I feel about being Greek . . . there is a desperate defiance of fate—which Romans never had—Lyndon Johnson is really the Roman—a classic Emperor—McNamara—maybe even George Washington are Roman—but not Jack."

Then Jackie attached a clipping, underlining certain telling lines: "This conflict of man with the gods is the essence of the Greek tragedy and a key to the Greek character . . . The Greeks are mystics. This mysticism can be traced to the influence of the sea—the boundlessness and the mystery of the sea. . . . The Greeks are curious and it is this curiosity that inspired a search and a thirst for knowledge. . . ."

With Jack Kennedy, she'd been drawn inexplicably to the sea and shared a curiosity for knowledge. Now, with Aristotle Onassis, she was drawn to and shared the same.[14]

On election night, Pat Nixon's emotions were turbulent. When Mayor Daley held back Cook County returns, she had a sickening memory of the 1960 campaign, when he'd done the same, and she literally became ill. When it was clear that Dick had won, she burst into tears of relief and joy. In complete privacy, her husband embraced and held her. At Walter Reed, Mamie stayed up all night, waiting for the news that Nixon had won.

En route to a respite in Key Biscayne, the Nixons stopped in Washington to see Ike, and Mamie met them at the door with a tray of champagne. Then they were welcomed by Lady Bird Johnson and her husband at the White House. There was a political conference, lunch, and then the two women, political friends for three decades, conferred. Pat confronted her new role. In Florida, a friend observed her "quiet, philosophical mood," as if she was "storing up her energy for what lay ahead."[15]

When Pat made a second visit, Lady Bird wondered what aspect of the new administration programs she would adopt as a project, but reflected that each First Lady should make her own mark.

In tribute to Mrs. Johnson, her committee was going to plant a million daffodils and twenty-five hundred dogwood trees on and near Columbia Island, which thousands of travelers pass going to and from the airport; a bicycle and footpath would also be installed. Then Interior Secretary Udall made a surprise "special announcement." It would be called Lady Bird Johnson Park.

For herself, Lady Bird had one regret: "I wish I could have worked harder and been more aggressive . . . It fitted my life to do all the things I did. I just wish I could have done more of them. There wasn't any more time or vigor."[16]

She remained ever conscious of her era, even at the end of it. Her diary entries proved how aware she remained of Vietnam. Through beautification, she'd become aware of the blight of cheap, fast advertising, and its larger context in the national consciousness: ". . . our civilization grows more complex . . . as things get easier they get harder . . . to understand. . . ." Indeed, it was a legacy of many faces. Lady Bird had helped make the environment a political issue. At every level, LBJ advocated it, reminding his Cabinet that their department buildings should be landscaped, and signing nearly three hundred laws that in some way related to environmental protection.

She'd spurred something else. Liz first noticed it when small towns formed beautification committees: "And always on that letterhead something new had been added—a woman, or two, who probably had been the garden club lady knocking on the door, getting no answer, until Lady Bird put it on the agenda . . . a lot of women mayors would come up from the environmental route. . . ." Her most enduring legacy was the most intangible. It was no exaggeration to say that this First Lady was a pioneer for environmental protection. When one reflected upon that, it was a simple but astounding accomplishment.[17]

After attending an Inaugural prayer service, the Nixons proceeded to the White House, where Pat, in rose coat and fur hat, was hugged and kissed by Lady Bird. They laughed about who should go through the doors first. There was the traditional coffee, and then they rode together in the motorcade to the swearing-in. Lady Bird Johnson, Mamie Eisenhower, Betty Ford, and Nancy Reagan watched Pat Nixon hold the Bible as her husband took the oath. Before leaving, Mrs. Johnson sought out Mamie to thank her for always coming to the Senate Wives Luncheons. Mamie recalled how Edith Wilson had done the same for her. Once again, the sorority transcended politics.

Back at the White House, Mamie compared the East Room, with all the conferences held there, to an office, and Mr. West joked that that she do something about it. Mamie chirped, "Well, don't think I won't!" She joined Pat to review part of the parade, both watching Nancy Reagan ride by as an official with Ronnie. Afterward, Nancy visited maimed servicemen at a nearby VA hospital.

In his campaign, Nixon had pledged to end the war. During the ride back to the White House, the Nixons, standing and waving, had suddenly been ordered to sit by the Secret Service.

Protesters were throwing rocks at Pat Nixon and her husband.[18]

PART II

The Me Decade
1969–1981

. . . not a bullying power, not the power to make people afraid. The power to make them see new things as possible.
Barbara Deming
We Cannot Live Without Our Lives, 1974

10

"Blessed Aloneness"

AT A WHITE HOUSE reception for one thousand campaign volunteers, the thin, smiling woman with the tall blond bouffant took the podium in the East Room and spontaneously exclaimed, "We're going to invite our *friends* here and *not* all the big shots." The president interrupted to joke, "Of course, *all* our friends are big shots."

It illustrated Pat Nixon's style. On her own, she was exuberant with a common touch, but if there was one public voice to be heard, she believed that it should always be his.

The difference since her departure as the most acclaimed Second Lady in history and her assumption of the First Ladyship was marked. She was less idealistic about politics and more wary of the press. She cared little about devising a spectacular image. In a time of high national emotions, Pat Nixon was "by fate a public person, a woman of private thoughts, a human being at peace with herself." Amid the louder clamor of bitter war and scandal, few took the time to notice her inbred power of perceptive observation.[1]

Nixon highly praised her "genius for personal understanding" and believed it was unmatched "in the history of American politics." In fact, Pat Nixon's ability to detect a person's feelings derived not alone from an intense spirit, but also from her years as a teacher.[2] Self-sufficient, even from her family, Pat had forged her own path, developing a strong sense of herself, without any of the pettiness that insecurity often bred. She stayed nonjudgmental even of enemies.

Pat Nixon resembled Grace Coolidge. As teachers, they focused on children requiring special attention. For Grace, it had been the deaf, for Pat it had been poor Mexican-Americans, often outcasts and victims of scorn. Children seemed to respond to Pat Nixon as openly as she did to them. Without pretense, she dived into crowds of them, embracing, kissing, and leading them by the hand, because she felt like it. There was something in her that seemed to mesmerize and draw children.

She believed that publicly the First Lady must always be an unquestionable decorous example of high virtue, a symbol of dignity, yet refused to fall prey to the trappings. Like Eleanor, she insisted on traveling throughout the world, immune to weather and accommodation hardships, refusing to be impeded by staff, security, press, and even the president, often impervious to protocol. Pat Nixon washed her own nightgowns and personal laundry. Rooms were redecorated for the president and Tricia, but the First Lady kept hers as Lady Bird had left it. When an embarrassed new congressman mistakenly showed up for a White House affair to which he had not been invited, Pat Nixon simply asked him to stay. Maureen Dean, wife of White House counsel John Dean, recorded the surprising sight of the First Lady as she squatted on the floor of Air Force One, playing with the dogs; at Christmas, after working with engineers, hammering and setting up decorations, she asked them to join her for an eggnog. After holiday dinner was served, she let the staff go to their families.[3]

"By blocking out the negatives, the positives focus more prominently in my mind," she revealed to writer Lester David, "A long time ago, I learned that if I worry about what might happen, my energies are sapped." That salubriousness toward life's turmoil helped Pat Nixon endure. It came from deep spirituality, not necessarily conventional religion. Mr. West thought her "composed," with "serenity," a positive energy force, surrounded by her favorite color, yellow. This determined focus of positive affirmations pyschologically empowered her. Pat affirmed, "I'm never tired. I am never afraid . . . I don't get ill." When she *did* get ill once with a severe cold and cough, she refused to break a scheduled interview and photo shoot. "I never cancel."[4]

At 110 pounds and five feet six inches, her physical prowess belied litheness. She swam with fervor, and bowled, determined to improve her skill. Her husband confessed that her endurance outlasted his. She proved her skill at archery and javelin throwing, and once, surrounded by women in seventies miniskirts, suede "midis," Afro hairstyles, and caftans, joined them in yoga exercises. Pat Nixon loved the freedom of the outdoors, whether running alone on the California beach or hiking in a nearby Washington forest. Once slipping out for a lone walk down the beach without informing anyone, the First Lady relished the fact that she'd eluded the Secret Service. As she returned, she noticed them beyond the bluff. She'd been trailed all along. Pat said the "most difficult task" of her role was "to be so guarded . . . you don't have enough . . . blessed aloneness."[5]

She didn't like being called "shy," because she wasn't, but Pat, like Jackie, didn't mind spending hours alone, reading. Except for her daughters, who maintained their own schedules, and lifelong confidant Helene Drown, who lived in California, the First Lady had no intimates. The president's communications chief Herb Klein thought that Pat Nixon "is not one to confide her innermost thoughts—even to family." She herself admitted, ". . . When I get into my own room, I feel at home, and that's where I really live." What some called

aloofness was instead, as one observer noted, "a relapse into private reflection, an effort at retaining at least some of the privacy that she had forfeited to her husband's ambition."[6]

Nixon staff writer William Safire said the words "saccharine," "square," "Itsy-poo," and "plastic" had been incorrectly used to portray her. He said she was "revered by tens of millions for the wrong reasons, and treated with condescension by millions of others for different and equally wrong reasons. She is not the way she tries to appear and she is not the way others have tried to make her appear."[7]

In every aspect, this First Lady would emphasize the human being. She found her greatest satisfaction in the symbolic role, "because I enjoy people so much." Some cynics blanched at the seemingly bland notion, but the spare words summarized her "theme." One of her staff members said Pat "was aware of what contact with 'the First Lady' meant to the average American who might have a chance to be around her."[8]

It was the objective view of Helen Thomas of UPI that Mrs. Nixon "was the warmest First Lady I covered and the one who loved people the most. I think newspeople who covered her saw a woman who was sharp, responsive, sensitive . . ." She continued, in an interview, that Pat "is concerned about people's feelings . . . a very strong woman, and sometimes a very stubborn woman . . . she never forgets her days of poverty . . ."[9]

Pat Nixon steadfastly refused to do and be something simply to emulate her immediate predecessor. She took Lady Bird's advice to establish her own office in the tiny blue dressing room connected to the bedroom, and installed a utilitarian typing chair, in which she spent thousands of hours. Throughout the day she remained accessible to her staff, responding promptly to their phone calls and notes. Patti Matson, press assistant and advance woman, was impressed by the First Lady's memory and attention for detail: "We'd get material back with her PN note saying, 'I believe we wrote an answer to this several weeks ago. . . .'" She did not keep a journal, but made shorthand notes on her schedule to "reconstruct a conversation or an event," revealing that Dick "always asked if I could do that because he said that it isn't easy to recall later the exact wording of a conversation."[10]

Her first press secretary, reporter Gerry van der Heuvel, had been chosen by Mrs. Nixon, but within nine months, the president's chief of staff, H. R. Haldeman, ousted her. The First Lady acquiesced only after arranging another job for her at the State Department. Connie Stuart, an industrial film producer, was chosen as replacement not only by the First Lady but also by Haldeman. Connie said there'd been some talk about hiring a male staff director for the First Lady, but "the women press in the Seventies wouldn't stand for that. Neither would Mrs. Nixon. She wanted a woman and she knew a man wouldn't wash. She made that choice. . . . During the campaign, men had run all of the family's schedules. Not *anymore* could they!"

In time, however, Haldeman became displeased with Mrs. Nixon's press and blamed Connie Stuart. She, too, would leave, and press assistant Helen Smith would become press secretary. After a trip went particularly well, or some crisis was averted, the First Lady always remembered that it was her staff's work more than any other's that had made the difference, and she frequently showed her appreciation of them by giving gifts. After a Latin American tour, she sent candy to "*El Presso*" from "*El Jefe*" (the boss). She was personally close to them, they confided personal problems to her, she even swatted flies for one staffer's daughter's pet frog.[11]

Mrs. Nixon received an average of fifteen hundred letters a month. It was obvious that she couldn't handle every single one, but she insisted that she be kept honestly informed of issues being addressed to her, and receive a weekly percentage of unfavorable mail. She wanted all mail answered within three days, and congressional mail the day it was received. She felt correspondence was a vital part of her role, worked four hours a day on it, and found it helped keep her informed of the public's views on many a "major national issue under discussion." She gave outgoing mail her pointed attention, because "[w]hen a letter from the White House arrives in a small town, it's shown to all the neighbors, and often published in the local paper. It's very important to the people."

Like Eleanor Roosevelt, she involved herself in the most desperate pleas. When a suicidal drug addict wrote, Pat personally arranged for immediate psychiatric care, resulting in a rescued life and broken addiction. An aged illiterate Italian immigrant wrote of her long desire to become a citizen. The First Lady ordered her staff to help, and they learned that with twenty-five years of residency the literacy rule could be waived. When a noncommittal staff letter was attached to a response to someone who had shoplifted and was now unable to get a job, Mrs. Nixon wrote across it, ". . . doesn't really help her, does it?" Because of Pat, the person was referred to a Civil Service rehabilitation program, and soon got a job. Mrs. Nixon refused to use the expedient "autopen." For those who'd taken time to write her, she personally signed every piece of outgoing mail, as had Bess Truman and Mamie Eisenhower.[12]

Mamie was going through a private turmoil, spending the last eight months of her marriage in Walter Reed Hospital. On March 28, Ike's heart failed. When the Nixons called on her, she told the president Ike's last words, which he quoted at the Capitol eulogy. They began, "I've always loved my wife . . ."

The Nixons became Mamie's second family, and she was a frequent overnight guest, ensconced in the pink Queen's Suite. After state dinners, the unique in-law sorority duo indulged in Mamie's "girl talk," and Pat would include her in day events if she was visiting. Mamie even got along well with the outrageous Martha Mitchell. One electrician said it "seemed like old times to have Mamie there," and Mr. West thought that "the influence of Mamie Eisenhower was to be felt" in Pat's style of formal entertaining. She received the annual presidential widow's twenty-thousand-dollar pension, but Mamie, like other elderly widows, worried about money, shopped at the Gettysburg A & P, used coupons, and fretted about buying London broil before it went on sale. As she explained, "I can't get raises since I live on a fixed income." Recalling Edith Wilson's belief in presidential widows' rights to a pension, Mamie believed it was only fair, "after all we do."[13]

Two months after Ike's death, Pat Nixon invited Lady Bird Johnson and Lynda Robb for tea. Lady Bird was enjoying an active "retirement," establishing awards for Texas beautification, spearheading the installation of Austin "hike and bike" trails, benches and flowering trees, accepting membership on the National Park Service Advisory Board, and becoming the first woman to serve on the National Geographic's Board of Trustees. At the dedication of "Lady Bird Johnson Grove" in the Redwood National Park, President Nixon drew a series of parallels between his and LBJ's careers—the House, Senate, vice presidency, presi-

dency—but saved the most astute comparison for his conclusion. "Both of us were very fortunate that we married above ourselves." Helen Thomas reported that before he left office, LBJ had hoped that the Nixon family "will not have to endure what he feels were unfair attacks and ugly things said about him and his loved ones."[14]

Vietnam would affect Pat as it had her predecessor. Mrs. Nixon would see the war-torn nation herself when she joined the president in her first foreign trip, to Guam, India, the Philippines, Indonesia, Thailand, Pakistan, Romania, England. And a previously unannounced excursion into South Vietnam.

On such trips, Pat Nixon refused to be serviced by an entourage. She considered staff a barrier and unfair expense to the taxpayer. She did her own hair, packed her own suitcases, dressed, and clocked herself to schedule. In Guam, on a tour of a training center for the mentally retarded, the first person to whom she extended her hand was an amputee. As Nancy Dickerson wrote, "Mrs. Nixon never flinched; she shook the stump of his elbow, and if she was surprised, she never showed it, displaying good human instincts despite the chaos of a scrambling entourage of reporters and television crew around her." In Pakistan, sweltering on a lawn, she endured unbearable humidity for an interview on a velvet sofa as two air conditioners were brought out and blown on her. In Bucharest, she revealed that whenever she arrived in her room in a foreign nation, she turned to "say hello to the four corners," suspecting that bugging devices had been placed there by the host government.

In preparation for her journey into South Vietnam, the head of Pat's Secret Service detail strictly warned her that "this is one day you're not going to get away from me!" As Nixon met with President Thieu, the First Lady entered the combat zone, taking tea with Mrs. Thieu in a palace fortressed with armed guards. From there it was to an orphanage, above which army helicopters circled. Then Pat Nixon took off in an open-door copter, flying just eighteen miles from Saigon, catching sight of U.S. troops scattered in the jungle below on her way to a military hospital. By her side were military guards with machine guns and bandoliers, cartridges of bullets over their shoulders.

Pat would later admit to having "a moment of fear going into a battle zone," especially not knowing "the movements of the enemy." Everywhere around her were jeeps full of soldiers carrying loaded rifles and bombs. Dolley Madison had missed being kidnapped by British soldiers, Eleanor Roosevelt had walked through Guadalcanal just hours before and after attack, but Pat Nixon was literally in a line of fire. No First Lady had ever so wittingly risked her own life in her role.

At the hospital, one reporter thought that she might have risked "good relations with some diplomats, brass and bureaucrats" when she "made it clear she had little time for high-level formalities and wanted to see more of the men who were hurt. . . ." When hospital officials tried to explain how their institution worked, the First Lady "brushed them aside" by saying, "I came to see the boys." For two hours, she walked through the wards, speaking with each wounded man, taking names so she could write to their families, squatting to whisper privately with them. She recalled the experience by making a subtle statement on behalf of the administration Vietnam policy. "I feel that they know a great deal more about the conflict there than many of us do at home . . . our servicemen [are] . . . proud to be helping to defend freedom there." South Vietnam's First Lady said Pat Nixon's five-hour trip "intensified our morale . . ."

In Vietnam, the president unfolded what would be called "the Nixon Doctrine," keeping previous U.S. commitments in Southeast Asia, but making no new ones, and "Vietnamization," withdrawing Americans while training natives to defend themselves. But LBJ's war quickly became Nixon's. Weeks later, when Mrs. Nixon held a tea for Korea's First Lady in California, six thousand antiwar protesters convened outside with bullhorns and microphones, chanting, cursing, and playing rock music.[15]

After Vietnam, the Nixons made the first of many trips to their San Clemente, California, home, down the beach from where she'd accepted his wedding proposal.

The most pronounced irony in their marriage was the difference between perception and reality. In public, they were very formal. On one occasion, Pat, her daughters, and Rose Mary Woods took off in the presidential helicopter, laughing and chatting, but the president communicated with none of them—not even with his wife, who sat directly facing him, inches away. Helen Thomas even quoted Nixon as saying that he wasn't comfortable being open with most people, "not even with his own wife." She thought they publicly "moved through life ritualistically," but privately they were "very close." Behind closed doors, Nixon was "unabashedly sentimental," often telephoning Pat during the day to praise her work, remembering anniversaries other than weddings and birthdays, and surprising her with frequent gifts. He was fiercely protective of her in public. Though both Eleanor Roosevelt and Jacqueline Kennedy had been photographed in their bathing suits, Nixon strictly forbade such pictures of Pat. In the beginning of his presidency, the couple spent much time alone together. One New Year's Eve they spent alone together, watching Guy Lombardo on television. A candid photograph taken with a telephoto lens showed them walking down the beach, arms around each other, where he proposed marriage.

The First Lady said she'd "be hurt" if he sent her one of his famous memos, but five days after the Inaugural, he did send a formal note regarding the "most desirable" table to hold two dictaphones and a telephone. He ordered the protocol changed that had the president served first. Whenever Pat was present for dinner, he wanted her served first, even before the ranking guest. If the guest's wife was there, Pat and she were to be served together, before the men.

According to Julie, because Pat sensed that Nixon was "very vulnerable," she sought to "protect" him. She had no reservations about strongly defending his single-mindedness, and pointed out that when he cracked jokes, the press often failed to report them, because "it makes him seem more human and likable." Of his critics, she stated that "Lincoln had worse critics. He was big enough not to let it bother him. That's the way my husband is." She rarely wore black because he hated the color on women, an emotion stemming from his Quaker background. When she laughingly joked that they were destined to meet because their parents had coincidentally bought adjoining burial plots, several reporters noticed that she had tears in her eyes.

Safire believed that as the president's "partner," she shared his "prejudices and scar tissue." Nixon said that criticism of him bothered her more than him, but he became extremely angry when she was criticized, and excitedly pleased when she was praised. Connie Stuart thought that the president put Pat "high on a pedestal. He once called me into his office and just spoke about her. He cherished her. He idolized her . . . He admired her as his wife but also as the symbol, the First Lady. . . . He never wanted her hurt . . . because of . . . his work. He wanted her protected and insulated." Nixon remained sensitive to her dislike of celebrity because it "interferes with her ability to live her life . . ."

"I'll have to have a room of my own," Mrs. Nixon told the chief usher. "He wakes up during the night, switches on the light, speaks into his tape recorder or takes notes—it's impossible." As Julie recalled, Pat Nixon had long "been intimately involved in negotiations and decisions" but now "would never play that kind of role . . . my father tried increasingly to separate his political and personal life."[16]

11

"Mrs. RN"

"ANY WOMAN WHO IS FIRST LADY likes being First Lady," affirmed Richard Nixon, "I don't care what they say. They like it." Not since Truman had a president taken such interest in the role and understood its traditional province and political impact. When asked by political candidates "how to win," Nixon always told them, "first pick the right wife. [She] has an enormous impact in bringing the man to people that the candidate is unable to reach."

Nixon was sensitive to his First Lady's position. After Pat voiced her disapproval of the procedure of receiving state visitors because it blocked most guests' view of the official party, Nixon sent a detailed note to Haldeman that "Mrs. RN" would be the one to make such changes, and he must follow them. Another time, he scolded Haldeman's failure to inform Pat of a reception for men and women college students, writing that "Mrs. RN would have liked to have been there to receive them, and I think should have been . . . whenever both men and women are present at any kind of a reception. . . . I would like for her to be included unless she has something else scheduled at that time."[1]

When the president ordered something related to the First Lady's role, Haldeman responded, but if the order came from Mrs. Nixon herself, it was usually ignored. She didn't want to bother the president with every single incident, and only when she felt strongly about something did she raise it with her husband.

Though interested in her role, the president never attempted to push his wife into any chore. One aide told reporter Donnie Radcliffe of *The Washington Post* of the First Lady, "She's one person Nixon would never tackle." Mrs. Nixon once frankly said that politics was a "life I would not have chosen," and when another suggested that at least she'd enjoyed a good political life, Pat replied, "I just don't tell all." The president told his cousin writer Jessamyn West, ". . . She's very good *onstage*, so to speak, even though she prefers not to be onstage." As Herb Klein summarized, "The White House was not her idea of happiness ever after."

The closeness of her daughters was of vital importance to Mrs.

Nixon. Several evenings a week, Pat scheduled special dinners of candlelight and music with her family, providing solidarity. To her, Julie and Tricia were personal friends, and each served as occasional "assistant First Lady" at different social events. As mother, she'd been disciplinarian; as First Lady, she exercised parental prerogative. When Mrs. Nixon mentioned that she'd agreed to talk about her daughter in a scheduled interview, Tricia protested. Pat retorted that "twenty-four-year-olds don't rule the world."

When asked if she'd want Tricia to marry a politician, Mrs. Nixon quickly responded, "I would feel sorry for her if she did." Of David's interest in politics, the First Lady said, "It scares me!" Curiously enough, though she didn't want her daughters to be political wives, Pat Nixon offered that "Julie might run for something some day," and suggested that if she were young again, she might pursue a political career herself.

The Nixons showed the normal inevitable tensions of a relationship. Pat had "a fetish about neatness," and refused to permit their dogs into the family rooms, although Dick would. The president hated unpunctuality in anyone. On one occasion, when they were scheduled to depart in the helicopter, Mrs. Nixon was delayed. A Secret Service radio crisply announced, "The President is waiting for Mrs. Nixon, he is not boarding, he is waiting at the ramp and looking at his watch!" Pat calmly listened to the message, and continued what she was doing, finally joining him about ten minutes later. She was no docile wife. At San Clemente in the summer of '69, during which the Nixons hosted a dinner in honor of the *Apollo* 11 astronauts, who'd just become the first to land on the moon, they also entertained the press. As reporters gathered around the pool to present the president with a gift, Pat was on the far side standing near Donnie Radcliffe. Playfully, Nixon shook the box. "It feels light, it must be expensive!" Radcliffe watched Pat smile and heard her murmur, "How grateful!" Radcliffe laughed. "It was exactly the kind of thing any wife says to her husband. Not anger, exasperation."[2]

Before she returned to Washington, Pat Nixon presided over a ceremony turning over her childhood home to the community as a children's center. At the dedication, she remarked about her past, "The sad things that happened were character building . . . we felt we had a good education and we made progress, and I know those who live here now will continue that spirit." Area residents were now largely poor Mexican-Americans, and Mrs. Nixon spoke to specifically inspire them, but picket signs conveyed the present reality: AMERICAN PARADOX: CHILDREN'S PARKS IN THE USA—CHILDREN'S GRAVES IN VIETNAM, and CHILDREN PLAY IN THE USA, BABIES BURN IN VIETNAM. The First Lady became an easy target for antiwar demonstrators. At one public appearance, as seemingly festive confetti showered upon her, protesters calmly told her, "If this were napalm, you would now be dead." At a community center, she was greeted by the sight of women dressed as witches, chanting an antiwar verse.

The protests came as Mrs. Nixon foraged publicly into her project. Nixon thought that she "bridled at the idea that . . . her interests had to be compartmentalized," but on February 18 Mrs. Nixon had held a press lunch and announced that she'd initiate "a national recruitment program" formally enlisting thousands of volunteers. Her staff would dub it "volunteerism," a term as cumbersome as "beautification."

The First Lady genuinely believed in the power of mass voluntary efforts as a force with substantial results: "Our success as a Nation depends upon our willingness to give generously of ourselves for the welfare and enrichment of the lives of others." She herself had volunteered for political and community causes, and witnessed the cumulative effect of such organized groups. Its strength became tangibly evident when she focused on community services.

Her first "Vest Pockets of Volunteerism" trip had her inspecting and encouraging ten different programs, including a ghetto garden development, a day-care center for migrant workers' children, and a Braille-reading group at a Jewish temple. Pat Nixon toured the Wesley Social Service Center in the inner-city Watts section of Los Angeles, visiting volunteers who taught local underprivileged children everything from music to weight lifting. She explained that matching volunteers with pressing social problems "can often accomplish things that legislation alone cannot. This is where I think I can help, encouraging what my husband has called those 'small, splendid efforts' of people trying to make life better for others. . . ."

Susan Porter, in charge of the First Lady's scheduling and appointments, also assumed the role of special-projects coordinator, and recalled that Mrs. Nixon "saw the volunteers as unsung heroes who hadn't been encouraged or given credit for their sacrifices and who needed to be." In three distinct ways, the First Lady advocated voluntarism. Besides national and local tours of volunteer-run facilities, she and her staff scanned the press and public correspondence for volunteer efforts and sent unsolicited personal letters of commendation to the groups.

Finally, she used the White House to meet with volunteer organizations, local groups that had evolved in response to community problems, and outstanding individual volunteers. She herself belonged to several volunteer groups, including the women's Voluntary Action Panel for the White House Conference on Food, Nutrition and Health, Women in Community Services, and the Urban Services League. Locally, Mrs. Nixon became closely associated with the quasi-government–sponsored National Center for Voluntary Action, attending its awards ceremonies, conferring with its leaders at local headquarters, hosting its meetings, and participating in a briefing on the center's objectives, held at the State Department. The center helped to formulate the Domestic Services Volunteer Act, an official declaration by Congress. By her example, Pat Nixon helped advocate its purpose of recognizing volunteers.

Using her first White House Thanksgiving to practice her belief in community outreach, the First Lady organized a public meal for 225 senior citizens who had no families. They were transported in buses from a dozen area nursing homes. The Eisenhowers and Nixons presided at different tables. Mrs. Nixon described her plan to the General Federation of Women's Clubs and had them foster similar dinners nationwide for "forgotten citizens." She would repeat her tradition, next inviting wounded servicemen. Though presidents since George Washington had been issuing Thanksgiving proclamations, Pat Nixon became the only First Lady to issue one. Alluding to the civil unrest over Vietnam, she recalled that the Pilgrims "experienced their own times of hardship yet were able to find hope amidst their fears. Thanksgiving gives all of us the opportunity to reflect upon the positive aspects of our lives."[3]

The country remained divided on the war. The October '69 "Vietnam Moratorium" saw 250,000 converge on Washington in antiwar protest. That day, the First Lady was tense, but went ahead with her in-house schedule. Meanwhile, in reaction to media coverage of the protest, Nixon spoke on television, appealing to "the great silent majority" to support him, after which, the networks launched editorial rebuttals.

The First Lady was keenly aware of Nixon's media critics, and she advised him to hold more television press conferences, rather than speeches, so he could directly respond with his views rather than have them interpreted, but he felt that preparation for them took too much valuable time. When Vice President Agnew attacked the press for their "narrow and distorted picture of America," Pat Nixon "privately questioned the wisdom of speaking out so bluntly through Agnew," and "it worried her that the networks were so clearly stung," according to Julie.

Though she guarded her public remarks, parried controversial questions, and thought carefully before answering a loaded one, Pat Nixon privately remained sensitive to the times. She read *The Washington Post* and *The New York Times,* and carefully combed the daily "Presidential News Summary," which contained both praiseful and critical media reports on the administration, frequently marking sections of particular importance to her. She also perused administration studies and issue papers. Pat attended the first Cabinet meeting, and a "domestic briefing" along with the secretaries' wives. By no means was she involved in the details of specific problems, but she sought to understand general issues. She believed it was important for the wives to be informed on policy and also wanted "to make women a part of the Administration."

If Mrs. Nixon felt strongly about an issue, she might attempt to influence the president. He told reporters that the First Lady had strong political opinions but wouldn't voice them to the press because she believed a president and his wife should "not publicly disagree on policy issues." He privately recorded that, "her criticisms from time to time are not intended to hurt, and she usually does understand the problems that we have."

Herb Klein stated that the First Lady "was never hesitant to discuss issues with her husband . . ." and had often "critique[d] the efforts of the [campaign] day, ranging from small details to the effect of the candidate's view on the issues. When she spoke out everyone from the President down listened." Connie Stuart concurred that "Pat Nixon had strong opinions. Not policy, but perceptions. . . . She could advise him on the atmosphere . . . a strategic, stylistic approach . . . She was probably more direct with him than he with her." As First Lady, she continued to gauge public sentiment. "I often say I'm his eyes and ears," she said. "He's very interested to have me report . . . We've always been a team. I've helped him in many ways."

When she traveled with the president, Mrs. Nixon avoided luncheons to go into "the field" and inspect public-works projects, then "report to him just as I do when I am going by myself." She visited sites related directly to administration programs, specifically to illustrate issues on which the president was simultaneously conferring. When Nixon was in Chicago meeting on environmental issues, the First Lady was out inspecting land reclamation, thermal pollution, and conservation projects, and dedicating a small strip of undeveloped park. As he dealt with law-enforcement leaders in Denver, she toured a rehabilitation home for juvenile delinquents.[4]

While Nixon was prominently identified with the war, many of his domestic achievements were being realized, from 100 percent increases in National Endowment of the Arts funding to astounding environmental protection legislation—the founding of the Environmental Protection Agency, the Clean Air Act, and Water Quality Improvement Act being just the most prominent. The First Lady publicly highlighted some of the programs, the most visible being the administration's "Legacy of the Parks" program, for which she made an extensive three-day trip through Virginia, Michigan, Minnesota, Oregon, and California. Public lands that had been developed, protected, and maintained by the federal government were turned over for community recreation, and in a series of colorful ceremonies Pat officially transferred nearly fifty thousand such federal acres—at an estimated real estate value of $11 million—to state and local control.

At the presentation of Border Field on the Mexico–U.S. line, the

First Lady was "disturbed" that a barbed-wire fence kept hundreds of Mexicans from watching. The mayor of Tijuana sat next to her, and said someday he'd like her to visit. She turned and asked, "How about today?" After her speech, he pulled down the fence for her to enter Mexico. "I do hope this will be a common beach. We're such good friends with Mexico. We don't need a border," she remarked. She walked into Mexico, carrying several of the tiny barefoot children, and on the beach embraced and kissed bearded surfers, asking, "Is this a good surfing beach? Come up to San Clemente, it's better. . . . Yeh, I'll see ya' there!"

Mrs. Nixon matched her role to other administration programs. She was a member of the President's Committee on Employment of the Handicapped, and honorary chair of HEW's "Right to Read Project," filming the introduction for the literacy program's promotional film. In dedicating a senior center, she boasted that "Under the Nixon Administration['s] . . . Older Americans Act, federal funding has increased eightfold." After the president first addressed the "energy crisis" in a speech, Mrs. Nixon led the press on a tour of a model home to conserve energy at the Bureau of Standards. She would attend the White House Conference on Children, participate in a Conference on Food, Nutrition and Health session, and sit in on the Governors' Conference on Drugs.[5]

Pat resisted the pressures of both the media and women's movement to go public with the degree of her political knowledge. She claimed that "I don't speak on political issues because I don't have all the necessary background. . . ." Her decades in politics, however, had clearly honed considerable skill. "I have my own ideas," she told the press, "I've been in this field so long I don't think anyone could brief me." One aide said she "kept international secrets and confidences," and another called her "a quietly effective ambassador at high levels." Patti Matson said the "discreet" Pat, with "background papers and Administration information," might discuss issues while entertaining legislators "on her own turf, [but] didn't lobby on the Hill. . . ." While few knew the details of Mrs. Nixon's degree of power, her knowledge of internal agendas was perceived. West wing aide Diane Sawyer thought that Pat was "intelligent, eloquent and observant," and Safire called her "politically hip." Only once did the First Lady suggest that she knew more than it appeared: "I know a lot, but you have to keep it to yourself when you're in this position."[6]

Like Lady Bird, Pat obviously had no power over decisions involving Vietnam, but Nixon often informed her of movements before they were announced. Publicly, she continued to keep on a positive mask. When the press sought to get her reaction to antiwar demonstrators on the north side of the White House, she ducked the question and spoke instead of the peaceful South Lawn: "The view inspires me." Privately, however, she was shaken by the casualties of war. When she met a large group of disabled and maimed servicemen, Pat Nixon was "haunted" by the sight. Sometimes Mrs. Nixon was also the victim of protests. When she attended the kickoff concert of her "Summer in the Park" program, near the Washington Monument, some protesters booed her and raised clenched fists when the national anthem was played. The First Lady thanked performer Stevie Wonder for helping to calm the antiwar crowd.

The president tried to downplay the more strident elements of the antiwar movement and instead emphasized the patriotic "great silent majority" who supported his policy that the United States had to fight until "peace with honor" was achieved, and that visible opposition weakened negotiations. The White House identified what it believed to be a "liberal bias" in the press, and in a startling memo, Nixon ordered that under no circumstances was his staff to speak with the *The New York Times* or *The Washington Post*, or return phone calls, and to treat the latter "absolutely coldly." The relationship remained antagonistic, but Nixon made one exception to his anti-*Times* and *Post* policy. His wife. He wanted the First Lady's publicity to get out to all the press.

On May 9, 1970, the massive National Day of Protest in the capital, Pat Nixon decided to leave the safety of Camp David, and return to the White House, which was surrounded by hundreds of thousands of protesters. Though she worked on correspondence, the First Lady also watched the demonstrations on television and from a window. Several weeks later, Julie and David's college graduations had to be celebrated in private with the family, including Mamie, because of threatened massive student protests at their campuses. At the family gathering, Mrs. Nixon remained unusually somber and detached, later confiding to Julie that she was "finding it difficult" that national tensions hadn't dissipated at all since 1968. At Kent State in Ohio, an ROTC headquarters was burned, and the next day national guardsmen fired on protesters throwing concrete chunks. Eleven people were wounded. Four were killed. When Pat Nixon heard about Kent State, she was in "disbelief," and "appalled by the tragic deaths."[7]

Part of the First Lady's motivation for her 4,130-mile second national voluntarism tour, was to prove that not all students were protesting. Pat Nixon went into the heart of the antiwar movement by touring colleges with campus volunteer efforts, and though it was reported that her schedulers had tried to avoid those that were "demonstration-prone," she did encounter demonstrators. While many students verbally expressed antiwar sentiment, they personally warmed up to her. At her four press conferences along the way, Mrs. Nixon shared a microphone with many students who prominently wore peace buttons.

In Cincinnati, she spoke to students just after William Kunstler, antiwar lawyer for the Chicago Seven protesters, and received as hearty an applause as he had. One student told the press, "She wanted to listen. I felt like this is a woman who really cares about what we are doing. I was surprised. I didn't expect her to be like that." A bearded student with peace button kissed her because, as he said, "She reminds me of my mother." Though under a death threat, she continued her tour. Because she didn't want federal money spent on her travel, Pat had hoped to use commercial or chartered flights, but security during Vietnam prevented it.

The First Lady continued her voluntarism efforts on other fronts, following the progress of the Domestic Volunteer Services Act through the *Congressional Record*, which she read daily, and touring national utility and food "co-ops." For some in the press, however, because "volunteerism" touched many areas of concern, it lacked definition. The "project," though a practice dating back to Martha Washington's concern for Revolutionary veterans, had become institutionalized into the modern Ladyship. The women's press corps wanted a more specific story to sell their editors, and a First Lady as involved in an issue as Lady Bird had been in beautification.

Mrs. Nixon consciously resisted the formula, but though the press balked, it was an important decision, reinforcing the fact that, though

based upon past precedent, the Ladyship was interpreted by the incumbent. Pat Nixon may have sacrificed visibility rather than risk criticism, but other factors contributed to her low press profile.

Most important was what one of her aides called "the tempo of the times." Vietnam and the antiwar movement so dominated the press consciousness that *any* First Lady who didn't address them as her primary concerns would likely be eclipsed by them. That became apparent in Lady Bird's last sixteen months as First Lady. Though Pat Nixon had nothing to do with war and unrest, nor had she ever misled the press, her image became a victim of the crossfire. The work of her staff, caught between the overbearing West Wing and the demanding press, was often overlooked by both. Others perceived another problem. Patti Matson thought that Mrs. Nixon "suffered a lot of fallout from Nixon haters." Even broadcast journalist Judy Woodruff would admit that Pat was "much maligned and misunderstood . . ." Safire believed Pat's caution with reporters was partially to avoid being any more hurt than she had been by them. If she was jaded in any aspect of her role, it was her feeling that the press was out to get the Nixons. When a certain reporter approached her, she kept smiling but audibly whispered to Safire, "Watch out for this one—I've read her stuff and she doesn't like us."[8]

Her press policy was almost verbatim Jackie Kennedy's: "Treat them with kid gloves and butter them up." Like Lady Bird, she cautiously avoided controversy at every turn. Even her official biography stated that she was "staunchly behind" Nixon's '62 run for governor, glossing over the fact that she had in fact protested it. In print interviews, Pat never permitted the use of tape recorders. Even friendly reporters, like Allen Drury, Helen Thomas, and Lenore Hershey noted that she always maintained her guard. When asked about Tricia's "avoidance of the press," the First Lady admitted, "We're all like that."

While television proved a medium that failed to fully convey her personality, Nancy Dickerson among others said the First Lady's mellow voice was good for television narration. Pat didn't draft out formal speeches but spoke from her shorthand notes. She photographed extremely well, and with high cheekbones, strong jaw and chin, wavy blond hair, spare figure, and expressive eyes, resembled a professional model. Like every First Lady since Eleanor, she was approached to write a syndicated column and hold weekly press conferences, and turned down both offers. But Pat didn't want the press ignored, and consequently instituted two briefings a week for reporters with Connie Stuart.

The darling of the press proved to be the attorney general's wife, Martha Mitchell.

Few Cabinet wives had ever been as famous with the press and public as Martha, but her paranoiac outbursts were sometimes an embarrassment to the First Lady. When Martha hosted a luncheon for Pat and Cabinet wives, Connie Stuart hurriedly told the press by innocent error that Mrs. Agnew and the wives were hostesses. After the lunch, Martha dashed out to a pay phone to call reporters and emotionally blurt out that "Connie Stuart is trying to kill me. . . . How can anyone take over my party? It's just unbelievable. I cried my eyes out today. Somebody should get down and bleed for me. I try so hard."

Martha said she spoke for herself, and she was often quite funny. After John Connally was praised by the administration upon becoming a Republican Cabinet member, Martha Mitchell harrumphed, "If he's so great, why don't they make him Pope?" It was Pat Nixon who warned her that in Washington, "best friends will become your worst enemies."

Pat Nixon maintained her respect for a free press. As late as 11:00 P.M. she made herself accessible to reporters' questions relayed through her press secretary. Mrs. Nixon told reporters, "I admire the press. It isn't easy to go out day after day and get news." When Haldeman ordered that reporters covering social events stay behind velvet ropes, Pat Nixon refused to permit it. When he attempted to limit the number of reporters covering events, Pat had his order rescinded.[9]

Pat had to be constantly vigilant to counterbalance Haldeman. As Helen Thomas said, "She was so much more sophisticated than the Palace Guard I wondered why her husband did not listen to her more often." With the circuitous structure of West Wing management, however, Haldeman increasingly controlled direct access to Nixon, and the president was never aware of the extent of the attempts to limit his wife's schedule and appearances. As Pat told a staffer, "I like to fight my own battles."

The West Wingers constantly meddled. Haldeman even chastised the Social Office for a "barren" menu of "hard" cheese and "unfancy" apple strudel, and sent Erlichman up to Mrs. Nixon to ask her to turn over her correspondence to staff. Chuck Colson wanted the East Wing to cultivate Frank Sinatra as a lead entertainer to bring in "younger lights." The West Wing rarely gave the First Lady's staff notice of a presidental trip. Connie Stuart sent a terse "High Priority" memo to Haldeman that "[t]he spirit of detente and cooperation between the President's staff and Mrs. Nixon's staff seems to be sagging." Operating under what she called "a directive from Mrs. Nixon," she outlined the reasons why the First Lady must be included on all trips, among which was that she received excellent local press, "a subject that is very much on her mind these days." Nothing changed.

Helen Smith "couldn't believe that Haldeman could be that stupid." When she couldn't endure certain decisions, Pat judiciously raised her objections in the presence of both her husband and Haldeman. If she felt strongly that she'd be an asset on a trip, she went to Nixon alone, telling him flatly, "Dick, I want to go too." He would always comply. Under orders, Haldeman would respect Mrs. Nixon. When, for example, Nixon asked for a list of outstanding films for the First Lady's choice, Haldeman followed though, and Pat Nixon picked *Dr. Zhivago.* Another time, the president ordered him to check with her before replacing a clock in the Oval Office. Pat could often fight him on her own. Haldeman ordered tiered "bleacher" seats for the East Room entertainments without consulting her, but she rarely permitted their use. He gave permission to country-western singer Johnny Cash to have his planned White House concert recorded and sold as a commercial album. Mrs. Nixon stopped it cold.

West Wing operations were more out of her control. To Mrs. Nixon, there were increasingly unsettling signals of Haldeman's growing power and bad judgment. He misrepresented the president on a number of occasions, even lying to the dogkeeper that Nixon ordered him to stop "overexposing" the dogs to press photographers. When Haldeman masterminded the elimination of Herb Klein's job as communications chief, the First Lady expressed bewilderment as to why the loyal Klein would leave. Nixon looked into it, enraged to discover that Haldeman had misrepresented Klein as wanting to leave.

The First Lady didn't permit her own judgments on the personalities of the president's men to interfere with her view of their capabilities. Henry Kissinger sensed Mrs. Nixon did not approve of his appointment as secretary of state when, after his swearing-in, she departed without standing in the receiving line. But Pat pragmatically viewed him as beneficial to the administration's goals in foreign affairs, and highly respected his expertise. With Haldeman, however, she questioned not only his personal motives but his effectiveness to the president.[10]

When she decided something was important as a public symbol of the administration, the First Lady took immediate action. Such was the case on Memorial Day weekend, 1970, when she heard that an earthquake started an avalanche in the twenty-two-thousand-foot Huascarán Mountain area of Peru. Three weekends later, as Pat heard worse reports of the devastation, she voiced her concern. "I felt that national and international attention should be focused on the problem of helping these people trying to rebuild their homes after the earthquake." She pointed out that though eighty thousand were killed in the quake, there were eight hundred thousand left homeless, and told her husband, "I just wish there were something I could do to help." After he made a few calls, within hours Pat arranged with voluntary organizations to gather food, clothing, and medical supplies, and then, to officially launch "a volunteer American relief drive," decided to go to the devastated regions herself.

A week later, she was headed to Lima on a plane, with another behind her carrying nine tons of donated necessities. Despite Peru's political conflicts with the U.S. government, at a speech at the airport Mrs. Nixon took to the podium: "The United States would like you to know . . . that we will continue to assist you as you complete your reconstruction . . ."

After attending the official requiem mass in the Cathedral of Lima honoring the victims, Pat Nixon then traveled on a small cargo plane 170 miles to Callejón in the treacherous Andes mountain range to inspect the worst-hit areas of the "indescribable catastrophe." After landing in a valley on a narrow and short, dirt soccer field the First Lady alighted from an open helicopter over the Andes. In a tiny mountain village, she tightly embraced homeless townspeople who trailed her as she went up hills of rubble and under beams of destroyed structures. The sight of still, twisted land was shocking, but when Red Cross workers tried to coax her into resting, the First Lady said, "I didn't come here to sit."

Pat Nixon's presence had a direct political power. In the two years since President Velasco had been in office, he'd leaned toward an anti-American policy, courting Soviet ties and seizing American-owned properties. Now, he used the lavish presidential palace for the first time, to entertain Mrs. Nixon. One Peruvian official stated, "Her coming here meant more than anything else President Nixon could have done."

An editorial in Lima's *La Prensa* said Peruvians could never forget Pat Nixon. The "profound significance" was that she served as "messenger of material aid and moral support," and showed "the spirit of the North American people . . . Certainly an act like Mrs. Nixon's is not common in an age in which at times the rules of international protocol are limited to a formal and conventional response such as a telegram . . . In her human warmth and identification with the suffering of the Peruvian people, she has gone beyond the norms of international courtesy and has endured fatigue in an example of solidarity and self-denial." A newspaper cartoon appeared showing a group of Peruvians waving American flags around a blond woman in business suit with briefcase. Only Jackie Kennedy had been so honored as First Lady with an international cartoon.

Upon return, Mrs. Nixon remained vigilant about maintaining humanitarian aid through the Taft Commission for Peruvian Relief, and the Peru Earthquake Voluntary Assistance Group, and was the official sponsor of a supper-dance Peruvian fund-raiser for "Oxfam-America." President Velasco awarded Pat the Grand Cross of the Sun, the oldest decoration in the Western Hemisphere. In her speech, Mrs. Nixon emphasized that "the people of . . . all the Americas," were "one family."

A month later, Velasco's Peruvian Independence Day speech spoke of "U.S. solidarity with Peru as signified by the special visit of Mrs. Nixon." The Associated Press's Fran Lewine wrote that no First Lady had ever undertaken a "mercy mission" resulting in such "diplomatic side effects."[11]

Pat's "personal diplomacy" was not tangible in print or on television, but the individuals who met her repeatedly spoke of it. She often lost her role's inhibitions, resulting in a natural ease with all races and classes. It was an adjunct use of the Ladyship for the presidency, a last vestige of its human aspects amid growing security constraints, a combination of the hostess and symbolic roles. Helen Thomas said, "That is where she shines, more so than any other President's wife in recent history." Even a male reporter offered that "she does an excellent job of making people feel warm . . . that doesn't seem to me such a bad thing for a First Lady to do. . . ."

Pat often repeated her belief that the White House belonged "to all the people. . . . Everybody in America loves it." The head of the tourist office recalled, "She knew exactly what she wanted for the mansion: a warm house which was more accessible to the public." She said she herself couldn't drive up to the mansion without being impressed. "I never take it for granted."

Not since Florence Harding had a First Lady come down from the family quarters to see tourists, sign autographs, shake hands, and pose for pictures. Whether he came to present her with the "4-H Report to the Nation," or for her to present an award to the Truck Driver of the Year, the common man responded to Pat. When a group of hill people came to give her a quilt, many were overcome with nervousness. When she heard their weeping, Pat Nixon wordlessly went around the room and hugged each individual tightly. Tension dissipated. When a little boy doubted it was her house because he couldn't see her washing machine, the First Lady gently led him by the hand down halls, through doors, up an elevator, and into the laundry rooms. Her personal contact was with small groups, but its cumulative result was staggering: In her first term, Pat Nixon shook hands and spoke with nearly a quarter of a million citizens, in the White House alone. Because it wasn't hard news, it went unreported.

Mrs. Nixon frequently left Washington to attend national conferences—an Iowa meeting on nutritional education, a Miami retired teachers' convention, a Houston assembly of the Future Business Leaders of America. Free of the formality of the White House, she was more physically at ease. On one trip, she picked up children so their parents could snap pictures, punched a soccer ball onto a field, played golf, and danced a comical jig as she walked across the green. When she was given a polo mallet, she jokingly swung it toward reporters, and bantered, ". . . if they'd just lend me a horse . . . Can you see the Secret Service on polo horses? . . ." The press broke into laughter. If she made little people big, she democratized the "big shots" as well. For once the nimble Alice Longworth was confounded, complaining in a magazine that her friend Pat Nixon kept calling her "kiddo." For Alice's next birthday, Pat ordered a White House cake inscribed "Happy Birthday, Kiddo."[12]

She'd long been irritated by the perception that the White House was the exclusive preserve of the rich and famous. Her most visible effort was to counteract the "Student Prince" guard uniforms initially ordered by the president. For the police who served as tour guides Pat ordered a less menacing uniform of gray trousers and blue blazers, guns hidden underneath, and sent them to Winterthur to learn how tours were guided "in a real museum." She conceived of pamphlets describing the rooms so tourists could absorb everything as they saw it, then had them translated into Spanish, Italian, French, and Russian for foreigners. She had a short history of the house and grounds recorded and placed in boxes around the mansion's fence posts, and ordered the south fountain turned on in winter.

When tourists finally inched into the house, they often had to wait for long periods in the East Wing colonnade. To keep them interested, Pat enlarged display cases there to include new and changing exhibits of historical items. She worked with engineers on developing a lighting system to make the house literally glow soft white, focusing on the fine architectural details. She now had the flag flown, day and night, even when the president was not in residence. The grounds became more publicly accessible when she began fall and spring garden tours, even writing the introduction for the first history of the White House gardens. For groups unable to visit, she recorded an introduction to a film history of the White House.

During Pat Nixon's tenure, ramps were installed for the physically disabled. She instructed the guides to face deaf groups and talk slowly so their words could be understood by those who lip-read. For the blind, she ordered that they be permitted to feel the textures and shapes of the antiques. She started "Candlelight Tours" at Christmas because most workers were unable to see the decorations during morning tour hours. Because of security restraints, she initiated interdenominational worship services in the mansion, and insisted that, besides the Congressional and Supreme Court families, White House maids, butlers, and telephone operators and their families be invited. When the public began writing for invitations, she had the dates of their Washington visits filed and if a service was scheduled, invited ordinary citizens.[13]

She'd quietly been conducting a refurbishment, creating the Map Room, renovating the China Room, and refurnishing nine others. Under her direction, the collection went from one third authentic antiques to two thirds, with the addition of nearly three hundred newly acquired objects.

There were other alterations. On a routine February day in 1971, Pat Nixon had no knowledge of the subtle changes taking place in some of the White House rooms. The president had ordered the installation of a secret taping system for his phone calls in the Oval Office, Lincoln Sitting Room, and his EOB office. His daughter Julie would write, "He routinely drew out others, encouraging them to expound views different from his own by indicating that he might share their ideas. Thus, at times he appeared indecisive and vacillating, as the tapes would demonstrate to his detriment. . . ."

Meanwhile, Pat continued refurbishing. She approved the fund-raising effort to have silver medals made of every First Lady, and personally posed for the likeness done of her. Her predecessors Bess, Mamie, Jackie, and Lady Bird approved their likenesses and were sent the first sets of medals.

Mrs. Nixon's professional forte in decorating emerged in the overall scheme of the rooms, and she sought to obtain specific items of excellent quality. Her enthusiasm was high, but she avoided publicity, because, as one journalist noted, "She had tremendous respect for other people and for their places in history and their accomplishments."

Much was made in the press of the fact that Pat Nixon had removed a mantelpiece on which Jacqueline Kennedy had had inscribed that she and JFK had lived in that room. In fact, the new mantelpiece had been ordered by Mrs. Johnson. But the new curator, Clement Conger, himself worsened the misperception. A staunch Republican, he repeatedly made cutting remarks to the press about Jacqueline Kennedy's restoration, dismissing it as mere publicity. He called her Blue Room "Boudin's boudoir," and said the rooms should always be American, not French, ignoring the fact that he brought in English pieces, and that the furniture of the Monroe era—which the room emulated—was all French. He announced that the White House should be like the homes of all those who had "all the money and all the taste in the world," although many presidents and First Ladies had neither. Conger overlooked the fact that had it not been for Mrs. Kennedy, he'd never have had the job as curator, nor the opportunity to purchase his priceless antiques through the Historical Association's book. She had created both entities.

For her part, Pat Nixon never once made even a slightly disparaging remark in public or private about Jackie's work, and in fact praised her for creating the mechanics that permitted others to build upon it.[14]

And it was Pat Nixon's invitation to the White House that Jacqueline Onassis accepted.

When the John F. Kennedy Center for the Performing Arts opened in 1971, Mrs. Onassis did not appear. With all the expected publicity, it might have proved too emotional for her. Since 1964, she'd attended JFK Center board meetings and consulted with architects and designers. Recording meeting notes, Edward Platt recalled that she "asked detailed questions with great intelligence on every subject under discussion. She obviously prepared herself well."

The former First Lady did, however, return to Washington that year, with her children, prompted by the completion of her and President Kennedy's official White House portraits. Pat wrote to Jackie asking what arrangements she wanted made for the traditional presentation ceremony. Mrs. Onassis responded, "As you know, the thought of returning to the White House is difficult for me. I really do not have the courage to go through an official ceremony . . ." Jackie suggested a private evening. Pat agreed, and except for four staff members who arranged logistics, nobody else was told.

After the portraits were viewed and Jackie thanked Pat for choosing a prominent display area for JFK's painting, they toured the recently redecorated rooms. Jackie told Pat, "I never intended for Boudin's work to remain in the White House forever. Every family *should* put its own imprint there . . . Don't be afraid to change, always upgrade." She later said to Mr. West, "I think it looks lovely." When the families were served dinner, the butler put ice in Jackie's white wine as they'd always done when she was First Lady. Mrs. Onassis and the Nixons reminisced about how their lives had crossed through the fifties, and Nixon called her "bright and talkative," but avoided any subject that might distress her. She wrote Pat that it was "a moving experience . . . The day I always dreaded turned out to be one of the most precious ones I have spent with my children."[15]

When Mrs. Nixon next saw Helen Thomas, she expressed her disappointment that the story of Jackie's visit had been publicized. "I don't know how it leaked . . ." With that, Thomas gave the First Lady "a brief lecture," stating that "there is no such thing as a leak. There is legitimate news which governments or people want to suppress. But news, fortunately, does not always break at what you think is the proper time, and it cannot be managed or programmed." Thomas said that after listening wordlessly, Mrs. Nixon thoughtfully understood.

Pat Nixon brought other great women home. One object of pride that she helped obtain for the mansion was a life portrait of Louisa Adams, relinquished by descendants. Pat got Dolley back to the White House, so to speak. The Philadelphia Academy of Art wouldn't donate its portrait of Mrs. Madison to Conger, but in response to Mrs. Nixon's persuasive letter, they gave it on permanent loan.

Mrs. Nixon was interested in her predecessors, avidly reading

Joseph Lash's *Eleanor and Franklin*, but carefully avoided being drawn
into a reporter's discussion of the book's detail on the Lucy Mercer
affair. "Queen Mother" Mamie spent part of three consecutive Christmas seasons with Pat, who continued to be solicitous of her, presenting
an award to her, taking her to a Kennedy Center performance, joining
her in the dedication of the Palm Springs Eisenhower Hospital, along
with Nancy Reagan. As a former First Lady, even Mamie became the
target of antiwar student protests. Just prior to receiving an honorary
degree at Wilson College, she learned that protesters had gathered and
piled skulls and shrouds in front of the speaker's platform. She refused
to get out of her limousine. Providence alone soothed the nerves of
frantic officials. It began to rain, and the ceremony was moved indoors.

To fund a scholarship in her name, for Eisenhower College in Sen-
eca Falls, New York, a hundred-dollar-a-plate seventy-fifth birthday
party celebration was held for her at the Washington Hilton, with a
mammoth pink-peppermint birthday cake, entertainment by Lawrence
Welk and Ethel Merman, and both Dick and Pat Nixon in attendance.
If she always appeared bubbly, in private Mamie was often reflective.
The night before Tricia Nixon's 1971 wedding to Edward Cox, she
stayed at the mansion, and admitted to Pat, "I've regretted all my life—
and I regret it even more now that I'm alone—that I didn't go with Ike
more often."[16]

Other guests at the wedding ranged from Ralph Nader to Martha
Mitchell. When asked if it sparked thoughts of her wedding, Alice
Longworth snapped, "It doesn't bring back one goddamn memory."
The next day, Tricia's wedding shared the front page with information
from a classified document on Vietnam, obtained through Daniel
Ellsberg, former Defense contractor, a leak that many feared weakened
the U.S. position with the Soviets and North Vietnamese. Two months
later, Erlichman directed "plumbers" to illegally break into Ellsberg's
psychiatrist's office to discover, among other things, if he was part of a
larger conspiracy.

On the "Mayday" antiwar demonstration that year, the White
House again seemed besieged, but the First Lady determined to continue with her schedule as planned, saying, "We are not going to
buckle to these people." But there was no ignoring tear gas. As Pat,
Julie, Tricia, and Mamie Eisenhower lunched, a guard outside accidently dropped a tear-gas canister, and it wafted through an open window, sending them from the room.

Mrs. Nixon directly responded to questions about the war, agreeing
with Julie that if women were permitted in combat she'd be willing to
die in Vietnam "to save freedom for 17 million people." On amnesty
for draft deserters, the First Lady stated, "I think that those who ran
should not be accepted back at the moment. I do feel that if they

decide to serve, maybe in a volunteer capacity or something like that, and earn their way back into the country, that would be another thing."[17]

Another woman played a symbolic role for the patriotic prowar stance. Pat Nixon and Nancy Reagan shared more than the billing of "co-patronesses" of the American National Theater and Academy. Mrs. Reagan began a second term as California's First Lady in 1971, increasing efforts on behalf of Vietnam veterans, and hosting a series of dinners for returned POWs. When the Reagans toured Vietnam, Nancy made a point of visiting each hospital where there were wounded Americans. She and Ronnie globe-trotted, as representatives of the Nixons. At Versailles, Nancy was particularly fascinated to see the steps where soldiers marched as they stormed into Marie Antoinette's bedroom and took her into custody.

During the '70 election Nancy held her first press conference to clarify the accusations of Jesse Unruh, who was running against Ronnie, that she solicited antiques for her own personal use: She was collecting donated pieces that would be given to the director of finance, owned in perpetuity by the state, for use by future governors. Others opposed Reagan for more personal reasons. Patti Reagan even wore a pro-Pat Brown T-shirt when her father ran against him, resenting her parents' public lives and conservative politics.[18] The late sixties had radicalized many Americans, and the early seventies were a transition begrudgingly incorporating such changes, a time of tremendous adjustments.

Julie reflected that "on top of the powder keg," of "this time of unprecedented domestic violence in the country," her parents "were trying to go on as if everything was fine in America. And it wasn't." When invited to a school reunion at the White House, rock singer Grace Slick, a Smith classmate of Julie's, and her escort, Abbie Hoffman, attempted to put LSD in the punch. Although "wholesome" pop singers like "New Christie Minstrels" and "The Carpenters" were invited to entertain in the White House, the social secretary admitted that they had to "check with people who know the entertainers, to find out how they will behave," and avoid "another Eartha Kitt." But the antiwar message slipped in even with the Ray Coniff Singers when singer Carol Feraci pulled a banner out of her dress, "Stop the killing." Neither the president nor First Lady knew that pornographic movies were shown in the mansion by an employee who obtained them from a White House policeman. It never leaked to the press.

Pat Nixon didn't sport the outrageous fashions of the seventies, but liked American designers because "they are now using so many [synthetic] materials which are great for travelling because they're non-crushable." One family photo showed the Nixons' battle of the hemline in the seventies: Julie in a "mini," Tricia in a knitted "maxi," and Pat in a dress that stopped in the middle of the knee. Still, when the First Lady posed in full-page color photos for a woman's magazine, dressed in pants, "pop art" black-white checks, culotte "jumper" pantsuit, and even the new "menswear" suit, it illustrated how social changes brought on by the women's movement were melding into the mainstream.[19]

Nixon respected the professional abilities of women. He had the Equal Employment Opportunity Commission defend women in discrimination suits, appointed the first two women generals, and hired Barbara Hackman Franklin as his assistant, with the task of compiling lists of qualified women for government positions. In a year, the number of high-level appointee jobs for women had tripled, and over one thousand women were employed as middle managers. Pat Nixon was on the record as saying, "My husband has always felt that women can do anything a man can do, and as well," and she became the first First Lady to publicly call for the appointment of a woman to the Supreme Court vacancies, catching the press corps by surprise.

With the First Lady pushing him, the president asked the attorney general to compile a list of women lawyers and judges who might be qualified. To a magazine editor, Mrs. Nixon defended her belief. "Our population is more than fifty percent women, so why not? A woman will help to balance the Court." A month later, on October 18, she raised the issue again by telling reporters that she would personally lobby for it. Two days later, however, Nixon, feeling that the women recommended to him were unqualified, appointed Lewis Powell and William Rehnquist. The First Lady was "annoyed" that her rare public advice had "gone unheeded." At dinner, before other guests, she made her argument again, until he wearily cut her off: "We tried to do the best we could, Pat."

Though she thought the newly formed Women's National Political Caucus "sounds pretty wild," Pat made a point of specifically saying she supported their goal of getting more women elected "even if they were not Republicans. I've always believed in supporting the person, not the party." Mrs. Nixon remained acutely aware of inequities. She christened the USS *California*, but thought it hypocritical that navy law forbade women to come onto such vessels. She told a journalist, "Mothers . . . hold up *the young men* who may be President, but *not* the daughters." Pat endorsed the equal-opportunity move that permitted women to become military social aides at the White House, and in Yugoslavia offered the opinion that both their Parliament and the U.S. Congress had too few women members. King Faisal of Saudi Arabia— who never permitted women to mix publicly with men in his nation— allowed Mrs. Nixon in his presence, Kissinger believing he did so "to pay respects to the mores of our country and the personality of the First Lady."

Pat Nixon became the first incumbent First Lady to publicly support the Equal Rights Amendment: "I am for women. I am for equal rights and equal pay for equal work. . . ." The ERA had been part of the Republican platform in 1968, and Pat urged that it be adopted again in 1972. The First Lady argued that "it was time to formally recognize that women in employment and other areas deserved equal treatment with men." For a woman who had supported herself, her father, her brothers, put herself through school, and held down several jobs at any given time, Pat Nixon's support of the ERA was neither gratuitous nor politically motivated. It was personal.

Pat Nixon also met with the Status of Women committees, National Association of Women Lawyers, Women's Forum on National Security, National Federation of Business and Professional Women's Legislative Conference, National Association of Bank-Women, the Labor Department's Women's Bureau, Congress of Career Women Leaders, the International Conference on the Role of Women in the Economy, and Forum on Women in Population and Development, among many others. Women's groups that represented her own background in farming, radiology, and education were of particular interest to her; and among several dozen organizations she belonged to were the American Business Women's Association, Business and Professional Women's Club and the Day Care and Child Development Council of America. Nixon had said abortion was "an unacceptable method of population control," but the First Lady was a pro-choice advocate, stating, "I think abortion should be a personal decision." Although the first First Lady to voice such an opinion, let alone mention the word "abortion," Pat was no strident feminist. Instead of "parades" or "loud techniques" to further women's rights, she suggested women concentrate on lobbying Congress directly and above all "be qualified." She recalled that when she worked as an economist, "I competed against and worked with men . . . I was the head of a section, and I never felt discriminated against. . . ."[20]

Like Lady Bird, Pat encouraged camaraderie with fellow political wives. In December 1969, Betty Ford had been invited with her husband to a preparatory briefing on Republican prospects for the '70 election. With her children maturing, and her time increasingly free, Betty helped develop a television series on the three branches of government and successfully worked on getting corporate funding, resulting in forty half-hour programs. She also supported the ERA's passage from a personal perspective. After her father had died, during the Depression, her mother had been the sole family supporter, studying real estate and becoming an agent, and Betty had worked to supplement the income. During her first marriage, her husband fell seriously ill, and she momentarily envisioned that her life would be spent supporting him as an invalid, receiving less pay as a woman for the same work done by a man. ERA was an issue on which certain Republicans agreed with certain Democrats.

In 1971, when she traveled with the president to Georgia for the funeral of a senator, Pat Nixon first met Rosalynn Carter, nine days after Jimmy had been inaugurated governor.

From the beginning, Rosalynn was a political adviser, an integral part of not only the campaign—during which she worked chicken-processing plants, tobacco auctions, dog shows, shrimp boats, and livestock sales—but also the governorship. Initially, she was "terrified" of making speeches, and even became sick from nerves. Gradually, beginning with short talks, Mrs. Carter became an articulate public speaker. It was during the campaign that she'd become deeply troubled about one particular problem. After Rosalynn met an exhausted factory worker who toiled on a night shift just to make ends meet to care for her mentally retarded child, Mrs. Carter asked Jimmy what he'd do about the problem. "We're going to have the best mental health system in the country," he told her, "and I'm going to put you in charge."

At the 1971 Governor's Conference reception in the White House, and again when the First Lady came to Georgia on behalf of a voluntarism project, Rosalynn observed Pat Nixon. "As First Lady of Georgia I began to see what a great influence a First Lady has, even on the state level. At that time Jimmy was thinking about running for President . . . That could be a great opportunity. I found that a First Lady could work on almost anything . . . When I started thinking of the First Ladies—Jackie Kennedy, Mrs. Eisenhower, Pat Nixon—I began to think about what they had done in the White House and realized that a First Lady could pick and choose, make her own way."[21]

Pat Nixon, as she neared the end of her first term, was indeed making her own way.

– 12 –

The Blithe Ambassador

NINETEEN SEVENTY-TWO was the year of Pat Nixon's liberation. It commenced immediately, on January 3, when she became the only First Lady to travel to Africa.

The trip began when the president was invited by William R. Tolbert, Jr., to his inauguration as the president of Liberia. The nation had been founded a century and a half before with the colonization of freed American slaves. Tolbert was a friend of both Nixons, and her husband asked Pat to go as his personal ambassador. Right after it was announced, Ghana and the Ivory Coast invited her to tour, and she promptly accepted. For eight days and ten thousand miles, Pat Nixon explored the African west coast.

It was not mere ceremony, for the First Lady met privately with the leaders of all three nations. The State Department prepared talking points for her on issues including Rhodesian and South African policy and future economic aid. Upon arrival in Liberia, Mrs. Nixon was honored with a nineteen-gun salute, a tribute reserved only for the heads of governments, following which she reviewed the nation's honor guard. Tolbert praised Pat as "testimony" of the permanent "solidarity" between the United States and Liberia, and after the Inaugural they privately conferred, the upcoming Nixon trip to China being one subject among their "substantive talks."

The next day she watched a vivid entertainment of native music and dancing. When presented with a native costume, she jumped up, and into it. The women, seeing she was game, spontaneously wrapped a lappa cloth turban around her head, and the press went wild. She viewed the costume as a "symbol . . . making me one of them . . . The people in Liberia are proud of their heritage and their culture. They don't wear western dress . . . they wear tribal dresses." Awarded Liberia's highest honor, the Grand Cordon of the Most Venerable Order of Knighthood, Pat said it represented the nations' "mutual respect" and "love of liberty."

In Ghana, the First Lady joined a native dance to tribal music. When introduced by the president of Ghana, as she prepared to formally address the National Assembly, he whispered to her to take an unscheduled bow. She got up, bowed, and said into the mike, "I'm taking orders from headquarters. He says to bow!" The assembly broke into laughing applause. One tribal chief said her trip bonded U.S.-Ghana relations in a way "not even a lion could destroy."

At the Ivory Coast, she was met by a quarter of a million people, many in tribal masks and feathers and shaking rattle gourds, and cheered along the route to the capital with *"Vive Madame Nixon!"* Besides political leaders, she conferred with "people of all walks of life" in the three African nations, remarking that U.S. relations with them were "built on equality . . . I hope that it will always remain that way." On the trip home, she mentioned to the press that Nixon would be running for reelection.

Pat had indeed played a political role, privately, reporting to the president, among other things, that the Ivory Coast president "did not believe in using force against South Africa." Nixon himself "realized

the substitute was doing a much better job than the principal would have done," but also noted in his diary, "She was very put out that in her talk with Erlichman today, and also she said in any conversations she had had with Haldeman, that neither had mentioned the African trip. . . ." When he said Haldeman had praised it as the single event of the administration to receive "universal approval," Pat said, "[W]ell, at least, they should tell me."

Chuck Colson sent a seven-page memo about her trip to the president: ". . . Mrs. Nixon has now broken through where we have failed. . . . People, men and women—identify with her—and in return with you." The First Lady accepted Colson's "discovery" of her power "with a grain of salt," sending a copy of it a friend marked, "Copy—for your eyes only. Thought you'd be amused at late recognition!"

As she mixed naturally with both blacks and whites in Africa, it was apparent that Pat never consciously courted anyone. Like Mrs. Kennedy, she didn't acknowledge bigotry, choosing to illustrate her civil-rights support in public deeds. Photographs showed that when she embraced and kissed people, she made no racial distinction. At one event, when the black Central African Republic ambassador's wife came upon Pat, the two women slid their hands into a clasp. When a photographer snapped a picture of them, they slightly raised their inter-twined black and white hands, the symbol of solidarity. Reporter Nancy Dickerson, no particular friend of the administration, wrote that more blacks were entertained as guests at the First Lady's tribute for Duke Ellington than at any other previous time in White House history. On the controversial busing issue, Pat preferred the concept of working through a formal interracial committee to bring about school desegrega-tion. Under Nixon, segregation dropped to 8 percent.

The seventies saw heightened awareness of ethnicity, and particu-larly marked was the movement for the rights of American Indians, now termed Native Americans. During Nixon's term, Native Amer-icans stormed the Bureau of Indian Affairs to protest its policies, and two hundred members of the American Indian Movement secured Wounded Knee on South Dakota's Oglala Sioux reservation. The First Lady was momentarily caught in the fray. While dedicating a Min-nesota park, she was interrupted by shouting Native American pro-testers. She paused in her speech to remark, "Well we have a few friends here! Thank you for coming." She continued speaking, and they continued shouting.

Pat Nixon was the only twentieth-century first-generation American First Lady. Her mother had been born in Germany, and her father was a proud Irish-American, but though she was honored by the American Irish Historical Society, and participated in the "National All German-American Heritage Group Conference," she wanted to be identified as thoroughly American. It was precedent: First Ladies had always under-stated their ethnicity. When the West Wing, while planning a trip to Ireland, arranged a gathering of her Irish cousins without her previous permission, Pat initially feared the "artificiality of a public family re-union." Nevertheless, in Ireland, she presided comfortably over a lun-cheon of thirty Ryan relatives.[1]

It was in a land more mysterious to Americans that Pat Nixon scored her most visible "personal diplomacy." Long before it was an-nounced, Pat Nixon knew the president was going to the People's Re-public of China. As Chou En-lai conferred with Henry Kissinger in planning the details of the historic visit, he told him, "Bring Mrs. Nixon."

In preparation, Mrs. Nixon studied China's Communist party struc-ture, learned several key Chinese phrases, and familiarized herself with Mao's "little red book." "Oh yes," the First Lady retorted when escorts fed her the party rhetoric, "I am acquainted with his philosophy." Re-fusing to be drawn into potentially explosive political debates, she did suggest that communism seemed to afford "a well-rounded education." Only subtly did she suggest her preference for the ancient buildings to the monolithic structures of the Cultural Revolution. Only once, at the ballet, did she meet the infamous Chiang Ching, Mao's powerful wife.

Her relaxed pace through Peking, in red coat and blond bouffant, permitted the network television cameras to cover her at close range. With the president in closed meeting, wherever Pat went and whatever she said made news: surprising Revolutionary Committee members but delighting peasants at the Evergreen People's Commune, where she spoke of being raised and working on a farm; petting a pig's ear, and telling how she'd raised a prizewinner as part of the 4-H Club; visiting a school where it was recalled that she'd been a teacher. She toured a glass factory to talk with workers, a free clinic to watch acupuncture, and a kitchen to sample goldfish.

Chou En-lai became so smitten with her that he gave two rare giant pandas to the blithe ambassador as China's personal gift. As Paris had been for Jacqueline Kennedy, China proved to be Pat Nixon's "moment," her turning point as an acclaimed First Lady back in America.

The president issued a joint pact with the Chinese to not dominate any nation in the Asian Pacific and to oppose those that did so, likening the alliance to a bridge linking the two nations, but one newspaper said that another bridge was needed "to span the gulf between people," and credited Pat for the latter. ". . . the American people, much mis-

understood and denounced by enemy countries as being war-minded imperialists, could use some goodwill." Another trip to an old enemy was planned. Pat Nixon was now going to the Soviet Union, the first incumbent First Lady to do so.[2]

Two months before the Soviet trip, North Vietnam invaded the neutral Demilitarized Zone, armed by Soviets and threatening the still-present American troops. It was a sensitive situation, placing the Soviet trip in jeopardy. The president could not demand that the Soviets reduce their support. But, in a subtle way, the First Lady could convey the discontent of the U.S. government. When the president came across Soviet ambassador Dobrynin, he told him that Pat was appreciative of Mrs. Dobrynin's invitation to talk over the upcoming trip. It was only a suggestion, but within hours a meeting between the women was scheduled, the night before which Nixon briefed the First Lady. When the women met, they talked of sites Pat saw on her first Russian trip, and then the First Lady added that "we do not want anything like Vietnam to interfere with the summit." As Pat recalled, she "went right home and told her husband about our meeting, and he immediately called Kissinger and assured him that the Soviets were in favor of the visit."

In the Soviet Union, tight security prevented the First Lady from walking the streets as freely as she had in China, and she privately complained to officials. But tighter security didn't prevent her from shaking hands with a Russian bear, tossing a basketball out to students, and leading Soviet "First Lady" Victoria Brezhnev by the hand through a crowded Moscow subway, and into schools. With Pat and Victoria arm-in-arm came a visualization of the intangible notion of détente that their husbands were hammering out. Mrs. Nixon was the first First Lady to insist on *always* maintaining her own separate itinerary while traveling with the president, and in several instances, as in the Soviet Union, she brought the First Ladies of the host nations into places they'd never been in their own countries. Privately, she directed the purchase and shipment of needed equipment to foreign hospitals.

Even behind the Iron Curtain, people were aware of Pat's humanitarianism, and sent appeals on behalf of Soviet Jewry. Although limited in how she could respond to the pleas, Mrs. Nixon could strongly defend the capabilities of American women. Premier Aleksei Kosygin, seated next to Pat, asked how many women were in Congress. Mrs. Nixon responded, One senator, five congresswomen. He interrupted her to say that professional women in America were "arrogant," and launched into a disparaging monologue on how American women reporters were "rock bags." Pat defended the press with equanimity: "American reporters do their job as they see fit; they present diversified points of view."

Immediately upon their return, the Nixons helicoptered to the U.S. Capitol, where Congress assembled for the president's report, but it was when First Lady Nixon walked in that the entire body spontaneously delivered a standing ovation. A few weeks later, as she was flying back from California, Mrs. Nixon, hearing that a flash flood had killed over two hundred people in South Dakota, altered her schedule to fly into Rapid City and attend the memorial service. A local paper observed that "she has brought to the ordinary citizen proof that the presidency of the United States is close to its people in times of tragedy and trouble, not just at ribbon-cutting events."[3]

The same day, June 18, Mrs. Nixon "barely noticed" the small reports of a "third-rate" break-in at the Democratic National Committee headquarters, located in the Watergate hotel-office-residence complex. Five days later, though her schedule showed no public activity, she was preparing for a *Life* magazine interview. She knew nothing of the president's phone call with aides about Watergate that day. But it had been recorded, on his secret taping system.

At that very moment, Pat Nixon was belatedly being praised for her diplomacy in newspapers throughout the country and on all three television networks—including administration critics. The *Los Angeles Herald Examiner* had a cartoon of Pat Nixon with a globe behind her, bouquet in hand, captioned "Our Best Foot Forward." When AFL-CIO president George Meany noticed a picture of her in Treasury Secretary George Shultz's office, he gesticulated toward it with his cigar. "There's a great gal. Terrific. She comes through nicely."

To many, the image of Pat Nixon had become the realization of the American Dream, product of the "work ethic," an authentic Middle American of the "great silent majority" her husband extolled, and her popularity was greatest there. For a woman who'd lived only in New York, Washington, and California, that seemed paradoxical, but as one small paper wrote, "Mrs. Nixon imparts no particular region or class image. She is just plain American. . . ." Columnist Robert Thompson thought Pat was the ideal balance for the seventies, "proving that women can play a vital role in world affairs" and retain a "feminine manner." At least one West Wing adviser, Doug Hallett, finally recognized her power as a symbol, writing to Chuck Colson, "If we can't improve the President's public image in the next 120 days, what do you say we drop him and run Mrs. Nixon instead???"

In her first term, Pat had visited thirty-nine of the fifty states, and logged more international mileage than Eleanor Roosevelt. She'd become a public figure apart from Nixon, but took the praise in stride, and typically deflected it toward the administration agenda: "These were journeys for peace, and I believe we will eventually achieve the peace my husband has been seeking for so long." Later, Pat Nixon would offer that her greatest degree of power was in her ambassadorial role. "It was crucial at that stage in history to establish personal friendships in third world and communist countries for the United States."[4]

While Pat publicly supported Nixon's '72 bid, Julie would later reveal that her mother "opposed my father running for a second term" and would have "been relieved" if he had bowed out. Yet, ironically, she had an even larger role in this campaign. One West Winger said Pat "understood the name of the game, but she was never used against her will. She was politically astute in the broadest sense of how it related to power and people and she had good, strong gut reactions about what she thought was right." In campaigning, she was exceptionally perceptive, and when asked which family member was the best at it, she gave herself a rare plug: "I hate to brag." Pat explained, "I always look the person in the eye . . . when you meet the eye, a friendship is started." Her draw had spawned a unique "Pat Nixon Club," of political supporters in Virginia. A century before, the "Frances Cleveland Club" had vigorously angered the president, but Mrs. Nixon's recognition only brought pride to her husband.

In planning campaign appearances for the First Lady, Nixon suggested to Haldeman that he "always have a Cabinet officer or other good speaker on the program" with her. "In Pat's case the big receptions are probably a good idea in the country because they really mean a great deal to people who are not in Washington. I again urge, however, the necessity for beefing up the staff work in getting better scheduled events . . . I consider this top priority." Two months later, her appearances were still on his mind: ". . . they must really be worthwhile and should be only in key states . . . As I have said on several other occasions, I want the appearances . . . to receive the same considered appraisal that appearances I make receive. In many instances they can be more effective than I can be, particularly in the time before the convention." In his diary, he recorded, "I am going to hit Haldeman hard . . . and see to it that . . . Prince [speechwriter] . . . does a better job in preparing material for Pat . . . It just seems that they [West Wing] won't really buckle down and get something done unless they think they are doing it for me . . . a grievous error."

In the weeks preceding the convention, Pat avoided raising "unpleasant subjects" with the president, since, as Julie recorded, "frequently they nettled, because often by the time she was aware of what was being planned, it was too late to make changes." She wanted to review his convention film biography because she heard it was poor, and Nixon himself recorded, "I'm going to see that some way we avoid her seeing it . . ." Other suggestions she made could be taken. Noticing that the convention platform backdrop was blue, she told him to not wear a suit in the same color, and he noted, "Reagan had picked a white coat for that reason."

Sitting behind Pat Nixon in her box was Nancy Reagan, but Barbara Bush was not at the Miami Convention that again nominated Nixon. After George's Congressional term ended in 1970, Nixon appointed him ambassador to the UN, and Barbara was living in New York. Just after the election, they returned to Washington when George was named chairman of the National Republican Committee. Mamie narrated a short film, *Tribute to My Beloved Ike*, but it was Pat Nixon who became the first First Lady to have a film devoted to her role shown at a national convention. Following it, she made a simple speech, the first by an incumbent First Lady since Eleanor Roosevelt in 1940: "I don't come out much from the wings, so this is quite unusual for me . . . I shall remember it always." The convention was a pinnacle for this private person who'd struggled with public life for thirty years.

When reporters asked her about the Watergate break-in, she replied curtly, "I only know what I read in the newspapers."[5]

Privately, the First Lady was alarmed, later admitting that she was unsettled that increasing power was vested in a small crew headed by Haldeman, around the president, himself having little direct role in the campaign strategy, and becoming more removed from his staff. Pat later told Julie, "I think I made a mistake protecting Daddy too much and in giving in too much, but I knew he was busy, the war was hanging over us . . ." She confessed to being "disturbed about Watergate stories," but when she asked Nixon about them, he told her that "there is nothing to it." Democrats nominated Senator George McGovern as their candidate, and Pat found him "unthinkable," with "radical and half formed" ideas. She didn't dislike him personally, however, and thought his "best assets" to be "apparent sincerity" and "dignified bearing."

In the fall, Watergate questions began to dominate those presented to the First Lady. Asked if the scandal would hurt the campaign, she tersely responded, "The polls haven't indicated that. They know he [Nixon] has no part in it." Pat added that she and the president didn't discuss Watergate, and she felt "it has been blown all out of proportion." One person whom Pat, and many others, believed was overreacting to it was Martha Mitchell. Nixon believed that as chairman of his campaign, John Mitchell's involvement in Watergate was partly due to the distractions of his wife. "Without Martha," Nixon wrote, "I am sure that the Watergate thing would never have happened."

In the election, however, Vietnam remained the most important issue. At one Boston fund-raiser where she was speaking, the First Lady's appearance attracted thousands of protesters who burned a car, smashed windows, and fought with police. When actress Jane Fonda charged over Hanoi radio that the United States had bombed dikes on purpose, the First Lady, "barely controlling her anger," dismissed the claim, adding, "I think she should have been in Hanoi asking them to stop their aggression. Then there wouldn't be any conflict."

Nixon policy had some unexpected Missouri supporters. Though remaining loyal Democrats, the Harry Trumans sported more conservative views. Truman remained anti-Nixon, though he was polite
when the president and First Lady visited him in 1969, and Bess gave
Pat a rare tour of their house. Mrs. Truman wholeheartedly agreed with
Nixon's mining of Haiphong Harbor. Expressing disapproval that her
Democratic party had become liberal, it was hard to discern whom she
supported in '72. Mrs. Onassis's views on Nixon and Vietnam were not
publicly divulged, but reporters Marvin and Bernard Kalb released a
story that her trip to Cambodia had actually been "a subtle probing
mission . . . to pave the way for further diplomatic exchanges between
the two countries [Cambodia and the United States]." The idea had
been then-Defense Secretary McNamara's and was arranged by Averell
Harriman.

Jackie avoided politics, but public interest in her hadn't abated, and
the paparazzi doggedly tracked her, even using telephoto lenses. One
Ron Galella several times threatened her safety, obstructed the Secret
Service from protecting her children, and "relentlessly invaded" her
every single routine move. She had no alternative but to bring him to

court. The judge ordered him to stay one hundred yards from her home and fifty yards from her.

Mrs. Onassis's public support of RFK had obviously aligned her with the "doves" on Vietnam, and in '72 she made campaign contributions to McGovern. Betty Ford, on the other hand, called herself a "hawk" and agreed with the bombing of Haiphong Harbor, but was nevertheless relieved when her two eldest sons had high draft numbers and missed being sent to Vietnam. Congressman Ford was still away most of the time, and Betty admitted that alcohol provided "pleasure and escape." At the same time, she continued taking prescription painkillers, and the pills often quadrupled the alcohol's effect. When she'd begun suffering from pancreatitis, she stopped drinking, but resumed after two years. She remained medicated, having come to depend upon pills.

Emotionally, she was still depressed. "I was convinced," she wrote, "that the more important Jerry became, the less important I became. . . . I couldn't accept that people liked me for myself." She felt inferior about not having a college degree, and saw herself as less accomplished than both her mother and Martha Graham. Alcohol helped relieve her "feelings of inadequacy," though Betty never drank heavily or uncontrollably. But neither did she mention drinking to the psychiatrist she twice consulted.

On Labor Day weekend, Pat Nixon left on a several-thousand-mile solo campaign trip. After going to Hawaii with the president, she took off on her own to Hilo. Then it was New Jersey, New York, Chicago; Montana, where she shouted a speech into forty miles-per-hour winds at an airport; Wyoming, then to Idaho. At a Yellowstone Park ceremony she sat for an hour through a sleet storm. Back in California she took a ride in a NASA-simulated space rocket, and dedicated a community center in 102-degree heat, then to Oklahoma, Texas, back to New York, where she met up with Nixon, and then clear across to California again. A week later, she was solo again, in Pennsylvania and New York. She reviewed the Columbus Day parade in Chicago, shaking hands with four thousand women in two hours, headed to Buffalo and reviewed the Pulaski Day parade. She joined the president in a blitz of one-day stops. Four days before the election, she was in Chicago, Oklahoma, Rhode Island. The next day she was in North Carolina, New Mexico, and back in California.

Nixon was acutely aware of how burdensome another four years in politics would be for her, writing that "the road had been hardest of all for Pat . . . My deepest hope was that she felt that it had all been worth it." Nixon won reelection in a landslide. The House, however, remained Democratic, and Jerry Ford's dream of becoming speaker seemed dimmer. He promised Betty that he'd retire in four years. To Betty, the growing Watergate scandal just seemed "like such an inept effort."[6]

A month after the election, Nixon ordered new mining of Haiphong Harbor and renewed bombing on military targets. This time North Vietnam relented. As Pat Nixon overheard her husband talking with Kissinger on the phone about Vietnam, she realized that through so much of his work he alone knew the complex intricacies. She remained "reluctant to probe" as Watergate continued to unravel.

The day after Christmas came news of Harry Truman's death. The Nixons and the Johnsons attended the funeral and paid respects to Mrs. Truman. The widow buried her emotions in privacy. In time, Bess resumed her quiet routine of getting her hair done at Doris Miller's local salon, doing her own grocery shopping, and playing bridge. She appreciated the assistance of her retained Secret Service agents, but with typical independence refused to have them stay with her in the house.

Two weeks later, the bombing and mining of North Vietnam ceased. Nixon asked Kissinger to break the news to the First Lady and give her "a rundown on affairs." Kissinger said he'd never heard Pat "so elated . . . [and] enormously pleased." She told him, "It took stout hearts to see it through . . ." Kissinger was amazed at how "with pain and stoicism" she endured the "calumny and hatred that seemed to follow her husband." A peace accord was accepted by North and South Vietnam and the United States. Just hours before, alone in his room, LBJ had suffered a heart attack.

The irony, thought Haynes Johnson, was that Lady Bird "who had stood by him in every crisis and on whom he relied so much, was away." Nixon, long an admirer of Lady Bird's, sought to find her a role, dictating in an action memo, "We should consider Lady Bird for an Ambassadorial appointment or replacement on the UN Delegation if that's open . . ."

The day after LBJ's death, the president told the nation on television of the end of America's role in the Vietnam War. Afterward, Pat silently embraced him. Again, Kissinger drew an observation: ". . . she was not capable of the fantasy life in which romantic imaginings embellished the often self-inflicted daily disappointments . . . Her dignity never wavered. . . . She made no claims on anyone; her fortitude had been awesome and not a little inspiring because one sensed that it had been wrested from an essential gentleness."[7]

Several days before, Pat Nixon had once again held a Bible upon which her husband took the presidential oath. Unseen by all except those sitting behind the podium, the Nixons grasped for each other's hands. On the stand, besides Barbara Bush, Betty Ford and Nancy Reagan, Mamie was visibly prominent. At the Inaugural Youth Concert, author and Vietnam veteran Armistead Maupin recalled sitting next to her in a VIP box as the rock band "The Mob" played its loud heavymetal sound, the former First Lady smiling with white-gloved fingertips in her ears. Her daughter-in-law wryly remarked that "Mamie didn't care much for Janis Joplin. . . ."

After the ceremony, while Nancy Reagan made a quiet side trip to visit wounded vets, Mamie, in the motorcade, rode down Pennsylvania Avenue, but was shocked when it suddenly speeded up. Protesters were throwing rocks and debris. Within days, antiwar signs would be gone. New protests and signs would soon appear calling for Nixon's resignation.[8]

One reason Mrs. Nixon had supported a second term was that she "wanted to see congressional action on the crucially important welfare reform, health care, and environmental proposals . . ." When she read through *The Weekly Compilation of Presidential Documents* in early '73, the First Lady underlined the passage of the president's Congressional message on human resources. Other issues left her less optimistic.

The First Lady had taken an increasingly dim view of Haldeman's abrupt manner toward his underlings, his attempt to replace an aide particularly close to her, and his approving a redesigned interior configuration of Air Force One, which separated her from the president in a tiny compartment. Mrs. Nixon took the matter into her own hands, and vetoed Haldeman's notion.

In February a Senate "Watergate" Committee began work. In March, presidential counsel John Dean informed Nixon that "plumbers" Howard Hunt and Gordon Liddy had not only directed Ellsberg's psychiatrist's office break-in, but Watergate, working directly for Erlichman, who, along with Mitchell, Haldeman, and Dean, was part of the decision to use campaign funds for the attorneys' fees of the burglars. Pat sensed the tension around her husband as he withdrew "into his own world" and became "closed off" to her. She was "troubled" by his mood, acquiescing in his wish for her to remain uninvolved in his decisions. Their relationship remained "a delicate, polite one that did not allow for much second-guessing." Julie told him he wasn't giving Pat enough recognition for her confidence in him. "Mother's trying so hard to make things right, and you don't realize it. It's hard for her too." He tersely responded, "I guess so," then reflected, "You're right, it's hard for her too. I'll try." As it became apparent that Haldeman and Erlichman were involved in the scandal, Pat conferred with her family, and they encouraged Nixon to get the resignations of the two aides. He did so.

With the return of POWs, the Nixons hosted a dinner in their honor on the South Lawn. There were thirteen hundred guests, the largest White House dinner ever. Around 1:00 A.M., about a half hour after kissing Pat good night, Nixon asked his daughters if he should resign. They gave him reasons not to. In retrospect, Julie thought he hadn't asked the First Lady her opinion because he knew that she was urging that he see it through.

Seven weeks and four days later, the First Lady was rocked when she heard that Haldeman's aide Alexander Butterfield had testified before the Watergate Committee and revealed Nixon's secret taping system. Mrs. Nixon knew her husband recorded oral memos on Dictaphones, but not that he recorded his calls. She thought the tapes should have been destroyed, and "saw immediately," as Julie recounted, that "unlimited access to the President's private, candid conversations spelled disaster." The president undoubtedly learned her view from quotes in the press, but she never offered the advice directly. The First Lady's "gut feeling" was that even making the tapes had been "crazy." And that the president could "never survive" them.[9]

The tapes were immediately sought by both the committee and special prosecutor Archibald Cox; the president refused to release them. Cox publicly demanded them, and was quickly fired. The president's relationship with the press rapidly deteriorated. And yet, while the West Wing became openly hostile to the press, the First Lady managed to retain her unbiased view of their rights. The West Wing had kept a "Freeze List," including East Wing reporters Judith Martin and Candy Shroud. Mrs. Nixon had never been consulted on that decision, nor on the one to ban Dorothy McCardle of The Washington Post. After McCardle was reinstated, it was Pat Nixon who wrote a personal letter to her, expressing regret over the West Wing's treatment.[10] Furthermore, Pat thought John Dean's "enemies list" absurd. Days after the list was released, the First Lady was meeting with "enemy" Dr. Michael DeBakey, who later wrote her a warm, encouraging letter.

Watergate snowballed to include questions besides the break-in and cover-up, some aspects directly affecting the First Lady. The impression was given that the Nixons had used federal funds to improve San Clemente, while in fact the Secret Service and GSA had ordered the spending of about $10 million on security and communications equipment, the installations and transportation to carry out their work. The First Lady thought too much was being done, but each time she protested, she was told it was necessary. Pat's deep sense of privacy was most irritated by the plethora of stories about their taxes, which she'd initially opposed releasing. No other political wife had divulged so much personal financial history, and when she had to co-sign the statement of their tax audit, Dick sensed "her tightly controlled anger."[11]

Rumors of financial misconduct aimed at the vice president, however, were true. Though he claimed innocence, evidence emerged that Agnew had accepted large kickbacks as governor of Maryland. Betty Ford for one believed him, "I thought you'd have to be off your rocker to accept bribes in that position." She also felt that photographer David Kennerly was wasting his time snapping Jerry as a potential replacement for Agnew, feeling that Ford was "much too valuable [to the President] in the House. . . ."

Agnew resigned under fire, and Betty Ford was besieged by reporters. On October 12, while the family was eating, the telephone rang
again. It was Nixon. "I've got good news, but I want Betty to hear it
too." When he told them that he'd chosen Ford, Betty thought, "I
didn't know whether to say thank you or not." In a scant hour, the
Fords rushed to the White House, and just before Nixon announced the
nomination on television from the East Room, Betty Ford dashed to her
old friend in the front row, Pat Nixon, and squeezing together, they
shared a chair, since none had been provided for Betty.

On her first public trip, the Second Lady traveled through Georgia
with the six-car "Artain," as the administration's host of the ongoing
tour. The governor's wife, Rosalynn Carter, was "anxious" to meet
Betty because of similarities she'd sensed between them. They paraded
together in the back of a car, waving to crowds. When reporters asked
Mrs. Ford if she was "on something," Betty frankly responded yes, she
took a Valium a day. A clarification pointed out that it was for her
pinched nerve.

A fetching photograph showed a beaming Betty Ford as she descended a gracefully curved staircase on the arm of Jimmy Carter. After
Mrs. Ford left, the governor told reporters, "The longer he [Nixon]
stays in office, the better it is for the Democrats. . . ." Regarding his
own "political future," Jimmy said he was "going back to his peanut
farm."

At the 1972 Democratic Convention, Carter had placed Henry
Jackson's name in nomination, and there was some serious talk of making Carter a vice presidential candidate. He wasn't chosen, but he'd
earned national recognition. Shortly after, he informed Rosalynn that
he'd be running for president in 1976.

Besides traditional chores, and her collecting antiques for the Governor's Mansion, Rosalynn Carter was a working member of Jimmy's
Commission to Improve Services to the Mentally and Emotionally
Handicapped, volunteered once a week at Georgia Regional Hospital,
and toured every other hospital in the state, determined to "do everything I could . . ." for the mentally ill. The upshot of Rosalynn and the
committee's work was an increase in personalized care—community
health centers multiplied, new centers opened, and nearly 60 percent of
Georgia's mentally ill were being helped. Mrs. Carter worked with the
Commission on the Status of Women's Prison Committee, established a
Work Release Center home for women prisoners making the transition
to freedom, and hired rehabilitating prisoners to work in the mansion,
one black woman, Mary Fitzpatrick, serving as Amy's nanny. After a
trip to the LBJ Ranch to meet with Lady Bird Johnson, with whom she
became friends, Rosalynn created the Georgia Highway Wildflower Program. Although Mrs. Carter was a faithful Baptist, after attending a
Bible class where the preacher emphasized a woman's subservient role,

she rose and left. As Mrs. Carter evolved into a feminist, another woman began publicly supporting feminist issues.

After the vice president's wife stated in a television interview that she agreed with the 1973 Supreme Court ruling on *Roe* v. *Wade*, legalizing abortion, she got a small flurry of protest mail, but it was immediately established that Betty Ford was not without public opinions. If she couldn't answer honestly, she remained silent. One evening, the Second Lady was chatting about her refurbishment of Admiralty House, slated as the first official vice presidential residence, when Clifton Daniel interrupted to ask, "Do you really think you are ever going to move into that house?" Betty Ford "paused, shrugged slightly, and said nothing."[12]

– 13 –

1974

As HERB KLEIN left his job as communications director, he said he "thought of Pat Nixon often, knowing she must be puzzled by the growing scandal around her husband. . . . Inwardly she might be ruffled or angry, but outwardly I have never seen her lose her calm or get emotional in public." Nineteen seventy-four would test that calm. In January, a reporter yelled out to the First Lady as she departed from a concluding reception, "Is the press the cause of the President's problems?"

"What problems?" she shot back, over her shoulder.[1]

Refusing to relinquish her positive outlook, Pat managed to keep going one day at a time, often anonymously strolling the avenues. John Fitzgerald, real estate tycoon, remembered one afternoon, two blocks from the White House, when he noticed her wearing a scarf and dark glasses. He advanced toward her, and she smiled, silently putting her finger to her lips. "Just out for a little window-shopping," she said, breaking into a smile, and thanking him for keeping "our secret."

Many of the reporters who'd been covering her felt conflicted. They remained personally fond of her, but had the competitive pressures to get a Watergate story out of her public events. "In other words," Pat realized, "it doesn't matter what we're doing—the press is just looking for cracks." At one point, she conceived a series of TV ads calling for support of the president, but it never materialized.

The West Wing certainly didn't help matters. Haldeman's antagonism was now assumed by West Wing press secretary Ron Ziegler, but East Wing press secretary Helen Smith let him have it: "I would like to request that when the President makes an important announcement such as he did yesterday that Mrs. Nixon's press office be notified immediately and directly. It is a serious lack of consideration for Mrs. Nixon . . . not to be given the opportunity to watch such an announcement and later report . . . reactions to the President . . . Another case in point is that neither I nor . . . Susan Porter were notified about Mrs. Nixon's appointment to the National Voluntary Service Advisory Council . . . I cannot stress too emphatically that closer cooperation between the President's and Mrs. Nixon's press offices will benefit all. . . ." Alexander Haig, the President's new chief of staff, was sent a copy. Nothing changed. Pat kept reassuring her staff, "We'll have better days."[2]

In the midst of widening speculation about Nixon's direct involvement in Watergate, the First Lady undertook another solo "personal diplomacy" mission, a 9,195 mile journey to the Inaugurations of the presidents of Brazil and Venezuela. Reporter Donnie Radcliffe said Pat's trip was "heroic." The only reason the press covered it so heavily was "to monitor her, to see if she'd break down and talk about Watergate. It wasn't a hard news story, except for the fact that the President sent her out as his emissary . . . she did a superb job in a very difficult time." In Brasília, she was the only foreign representative to get a standing ovation. Two decades before, in Caracas, anti-American crowds had thrown stones and rocked her car, spitting at, and threatening to kill her. Now, as a sign of respect for her returning so triumphantly, people ran along trying to touch Pat or the car.

On her return, a reporter asked Pat whether the president had covered up the FBI investigation of Watergate through the CIA. Smilingly but firmly, she cut the question off. "No. I really don't wish to speak of it. . . ." Because it was her birthday, her staff and the press surprised her with cake and champagne. When the press again raised Watergate, Pat deflected it: "You all drink some champagne." After that trip, recalled journalist Myra MacPherson, even the cynical reporters held Pat in esteem. She'd stuck to her schedule and dealt with rough questions, even though she had the flu.[3]

Meanwhile, the president was scheduled to appear at the reopening of Nashville's Grand Old Opry, and word was sent to Mrs. Nixon to join him there. The Nixons, sitting together, were called down to the stage, and he rose and walked down to center stage to play "Happy Birthday" on the piano to her. Upon conclusion, the First Lady impulsively walked downstage from behind the president, toward him with open arms. East Winger Terry Ivey said Nixon "turned his back," and

Helen Smith said that he "ignored her outstretched arms" and made some of the staff wince. As Donnie Radcliffe recalled, "[E]veryone in the press was so devastated that he didn't focus on her. . . ." His piano tribute to her, however, had been unplanned and interrupted the scheduled program. As Pat was approaching him, Nixon had already begun to turn around to gesture for the show to continue without further delay. The ill-timed move gave witnesses a perception that increased public speculation about their separated private lives.[4]

Like many of her predecessors, Mrs. Nixon was satirized. In the *Watergate Coloring Book*, for example, she was posed, after a series of official aides had done so, coming into the Oval Office with a slip of paper, offering her resignation as First Lady to the president. Although satire was an acceptable form of political humor, limits on questionable "reporting" were now pushed further than they'd been for any incumbent First Lady.

There had been hushed speculation on presidential marriages before, but Watergate made Pat Nixon the first First Lady to have hers scrutinized while she was in the White House. There was a fable that Pat had had a first "secret marriage," and an attempt to link the president to a "Communist spy." The truth was that in 1966 cocktail waitress Marianna Lui, born on mainland China, served Nixon in Hong

Kong, and with a fellow waitress joined him and Bebe Rebozo in their hotel suite for fruit and drinks to ask legal advice on Lui's desire to immigrate to America. The women had to catch a ferry home. The meeting was brief. Months later, when she was hospitalized, and Nixon was again in Hong Kong, she received a bouquet from him and a card with his New York home address. When one magazine affirmed that the Nixons were about to divorce, the First Lady joked about co-respondents, "I've had more time, so let's think up someone we could name . . . Peter Rodino?"

Meanwhile, syndicated columnist Maxine Cheshire was hoping to brew a mini-Watergate, claiming that Mrs. Nixon had stolen jewelry presented to her as a state gift by Saudi Arabia. The Foreign Gifts and Decorations Act, which previously prohibited the president and government officials from accepting gifts from foreign leaders, was amended in 1966 to extent to the ruling to include "a member of the family and household" of officials, but Mrs. Nixon broke no law. There was no stipulation or even suggestion that a First Lady must turn in a gift prior the end of her term. Before there were any such laws, other First Ladies had followed their own rules. Eleanor Roosevelt immediately gave an aquamarine ring given her by Brazil to the FDR Library—the only such institution in existence when the president it honored was in office. Mamie Eisenhower kept diamond earrings given her by the Saudis, and Jackie Kennedy kept a jeweled belt given her by the king of Morocco, both items given as personal gifts. When the reporter approached Liz Holtzman and Sam Ervin, of the House and Senate Watergate committees respectively, to go after Pat Nixon with the "scandal," both refused.

The strangest canard, later printed by investigative reporters Carl Bernstein and Bob Woodward, was that Pat Nixon turned to heavy drinking during Watergate. It was not simply exaggeration but completely untrue. As Kissinger said of the entire context in which the rumor was printed, *some* facts were correct, but "the inferences are *all* wrong." Mrs. Nixon, like all of her immediate predecessors except Eleanor Roosevelt, might take a cocktail before dinner, unless it was "a working night." In China, for example, she never drank the toasts, but merely raised her glass to her lips. Helen Thomas once noticed—and was disappointed—that Mrs. Nixon wouldn't take an aperitif with guests, but as reporters stared at Pat, Thomas was conscious of the First Lady's belief that she must always be an exemplar. Only in '74, for example, would it be acknowledged that she smoked. As late as '72, Pat publicly claimed that she *never* drank, telling a reporter she didn't like the taste.

The reporters claimed several sources for the charge, but people who came in frequent and close contact with Mrs. Nixon never saw evidence of any drinking. She met with large groups every day, and if she were consuming alcohol, it would've been apparent to at least some of those several thousand people. There was not so much as an off-the-record report. Julie admitted that the president seemed to be drinking more heavily, but never suggested her mother had. Commentator Victor Lasky stated, "One thing is to be anti-Nixon, everybody has that right, but the stuff on Mrs. Nixon was really below-the-belt. . . ." Even to nonloyalist observers, and at least one cynical journalist, it seemed out of character that, at this late date in her political career, Pat Nixon would need a crutch. One of the quoted sources, her doctor, never released any such information and contemplated legal action, but one anonymous source, a storytelling servant, propagated it for some time later, while retailing White House yarns.[5]

Meanwhile, by order, Nixon's tapes and other materials had been turned over to the House Judiciary Committee, and transcripts were made public. Pat spent twelve hours reading the 1,254 pages, and was surprised by what she learned. As Julie said, "The Richard Nixon on tapes was not the Richard Nixon the family saw every day." For one thing, his use of profanity was unfamiliar. Pat tried to be upbeat, joking about what "deleted expletives," would have sounded like on the tapes in LBJ's drawl to JFK's dropping of "r's." In retrospect, her greatest regret as First Lady would be that the president hadn't confided in her about the tapes. She revealed to Helene Drown her vigorous opposition to the president's *release* of the tapes, comparing them to "private love letters—for one person alone," but by now Nixon realized that had he refused to turn them over, he'd be held in contempt of court and impeachment would be likely.[6]

In May, when she was asked if she'd "let" the president resign, Pat shrugged back: "Why should he? There's no reason to. . . . I have great faith in my husband." To complaints that she was "hiding" and that she was a "recluse from Watergate," Pat cracked, "What in the world do they expect me to do, go streaking along the Tidal Basin?" The more reporters pursued her, the more she stonewalled, the more they admired her. Helen Thomas recalled, "Everyone in the press knew that she was completely apart from Watergate and had nothing to do with any of the scandals, but she was swept up in it."

Privately, Pat acknowledged that the situation had bitterly deteriorated. "It's right out of the *Merchant of Venice*. They're after the last pound of flesh." During the First Lady's annual Senate Wives Luncheon in May, Second Lady Betty Ford presided as the group's president. Outside were picketers, one carrying a sign: PICK OUT YOUR CURTAINS, BETTY. Mrs. Ford was embarrassed, and mentioned the placard to Mrs. Nixon. "Oh, I never watch the news," she said, dispelling Betty's discomfort. The increasing oppressiveness of the Washington summer seemed oddly apropos.[7]

In June, the Nixons then headed for their trip to Austria, Egypt, Saudi Arabia, Syria, Israel, and Jordan. In sixty-five months, Pat had visited thirty-one nations, an average of one every 120 days. Her record as goodwill ambassador would remain unmatched.

Meanwhile, the shocking news came from Atlanta that Martin Luther King's mother had been shot. Rosalynn Carter and Betty Ford reacted similarly. Both went to comfort the widower. The Second Lady was surprised that no administration representative was going to the funeral, and took it upon herself to attend. At his home, Martin Luther King, Sr., asking to see her, cried in Betty's arms. Mrs. Ford calmed him and escorted him to the car.

Upon the Nixons' return, the House Judiciary Committee voted 27 to 11 in approving the first article of impeachment, charging that Nixon had obstructed the Watergate investigation. Article II charged abuse of presidential power, and Article III addressed his refusal to comply with the committee's subpoenas.

Personal and political friends sought to rally Pat from the sidelines. One of the sorority wrote her, "This is not an engraved invitation but I would love to have you come up here when the President goes away—you could rest, walk, read, and gossip with me—now please everything would be on the QT. What fun we would have . . . come a running." It was signed "Mamie E." As wife of the NRC chairman, Barbara Bush sat between Pat Nixon and Julie at a luncheon of loyal Republican supporters at the Capitol Hill Club. Mrs. Nixon would later recall Mrs. Bush as "a highly likeable personality," and Barbara found the First Lady to be "one of the most courageous, loyal women I've ever known."

So, through July, Pat Nixon kept working—correspondence, meeting groups, overseeing a restoration of the Queen's Bedroom. It was she who held the family together—including the president. Though his decisions sometimes made her "angry," she still believed in him. Nixon was taken aback by her strength, recording, "But, God, how she could have gone through what she does, I simply don't know." David told a reporter, "I . . . worry about her. . . . She is a shoulder to everyone—but whose shoulder does she lean on?" Only to Helene Drown did Pat express real despondency. "Dick has done so much for the country. Why is this happening?"

In retrospect, Mrs. Nixon would question the circumstances of Watergate, believing it was "partly an international scheme, or, at the very least, that double-agents were involved." To her, the burglary itself was so bungled that it seemed almost purposeful, as if a setup. Questions remained unanswered, but as the heat continued, she told a staff member, "They're out to get us. . . . They want us out of here. But it's all politics and will go away."[8]

On August 2, it was Julie, not Pat, that the president told with finality that he must resign. Julie went to the First Lady.

She was in her bedroom and came into the doorway as Julie approached and told her the decision. Pat Nixon's usually placid face filled with alarm. "But why?" Julie said he had to, or he'd be impeached. The First Lady's mouth began to quiver. They held each other gently, knowing they'd break down if they hugged. Pat had tears in her eyes. Julie left. And then, once again, Pat Nixon silently began doing what had to be done. The servants were off at lunch. Pat Nixon began gathering packing boxes.

Earlier, however, before being told the news, the First Lady had sensed the end, telling the curator to cancel the china being ordered. When a reporter innocently asked whether she'd be joining Nixon on a possible trip to Europe, Mrs. Nixon admitted, "You never know what's going to happen. You live for each day."

The president's decision had been prompted by the Supreme Court's order to turn over a group of tape transcripts that included one for June 23, 1972. On it Nixon and Haldeman had discussed getting the CIA to limit the FBI investigation of Watergate for political purposes, not national security as the president had maintained. With this evidence, the charge of obstruction of justice seemed certain; at the least impeachment was nearly certain when Congress reconvened on August 19. Over the weekend, the First Lady and her family had each reviewed the incriminating transcript.

When it was released on Monday the fifth, the support of most loyalists eroded. As Barbara Bush reflected, "This was very naive, I realize, but Nixon really fooled us." Even the First Lady's press aide Terry Ivey told Woodward and Bernstein that she resented the president permitting Julie publicly to defend him in a May press conference. Mrs. Nixon still believed he shouldn't resign, but not out of blind loyalty. Rather, she looked at the options with keen political perception, believing he should face impeachment hearings if even to "narrow the charges," rather than accept the "blanket indictment" that resignation represented.[9]

Betty Ford hadn't permitted herself even to consider the possibility that she'd become First Lady, but now felt it would be "terrible" if Nixon was impeached. She considered calling Pat Nixon "to try to talk to her," but hesitated because "it seemed wrong to want to invade her privacy." Betty had scheduled a trip to New York that week. On Monday the fifth, Jerry told her she better not go. The reality of it began to hit her, as it did Mamie, who wrote Mrs. Nixon, "I only want to say I'm thinking of you today—always you will have my warm affection as will your husband President Nixon." The former First Lady had kept abreast of the growing scandal; Barbara Eisenhower recalled, "She just couldn't imagine Dick being involved in this." When she heard of the imminent resignation, however, her grandson thought Mamie "was pained but not shocked. She was surprised by very little. She didn't have many illusions. . . ."[10]

Nixon drafted his resignation speech. The night of August 7, the family gathered for their last White House dinner. Mrs. Nixon sat on the edge of a couch, holding her chin high, a familiar sign of tension to her husband. When he walked in, Pat kissed and threw her arms around him: "We're all very proud of you, Daddy." When the photographer came in, however, she became upset, and gently told him it was no time for pictures. Nixon insisted, "for history." He first asked Pat to walk with him one last time in the Rose Garden and have their picture taken together, but, as he wrote, "that was simply expecting too much." Upstairs, the family linked arms for a group picture Pat would "hate" because "[O]ur hearts were breaking and there we are smiling."

The next night Nixon announced his resignation to the nation. Through his secretary, Pat and the family asked to be with him in the Oval Office when he delivered it, or at least to be in the next room. Nixon told her to tell them "it was simply out of the question, because I would not be able to get through the speech without breaking up if they were even nearby." He asked them to watch on TV. By the time he returned to the family quarters, the muffled sounds of chanting crowds outside could be heard. Pat assumed they were supporters, and tried to steer the president to the window. The crowd was singing "Jail to the Chief."[11]

Meanwhile, in suburban Virginia, Betty Ford felt "numb," like "an actor on a set, being told where to go and what to do. . . . There was no time to think about what impact this was going to make on our lives. . . ." There wasn't time for her sons to get haircuts, and one, Jack, had to be helicoptered from his job at Yellowstone.

Pat Nixon stayed up all night and continued packing. The next morning, in a pink-white dress, with tired eyes and plainly dressed hair, she and her husband shook hands with the household staff. Then the family descended in the elevator to the East Room, where the president would give his farewell. When she heard the word "television," Pat's voice was anguished: "Oh, Dick, you can't have it televised." He replied that "it has to be. We owe it to our supporters. We owe it to the people." Pat breathed deeply.

The Fords were being spirited to the White House in a limousine. For Betty, it still seemed "impossible." She and Jerry were rushed into the ground-floor Diplomatic Reception Room, where they'd watch on television. The Nixons entered the East Room, stood on a platform, and the president began his speech.

Alice Roosevelt Longworth watched on television as Nixon quoted her father's diary, hearing for the first time the devastating effect her mother's death had had on Teddy. Helen Gahagan Douglas, who'd run for the Senate against Nixon in the bitter 1950 election, "expressed compassion" for the family. Jacqueline Onassis was traveling with her children in Greece, and with no television nearby, she didn't see it live. Neither did Lady Bird Johnson, in Florence, Italy. Mamie Eisenhower in Gettysburg, Rosalynn Carter in Georgia, and Nancy Reagan in the Governor's office in Sacramento watched on television. Barbara Bush, however, in the East Room, witnessed it all. Mrs. Nixon couldn't look directly at the faces of staff and friends weeping in the audience. She closed, then opened her eyes to the unreal scene.

Kissinger called the scene "horrifying and heartbreaking," and was outraged that the president praised his parents but "omitted his wife, Pat, who without his capacity for make-believe must have suffered the most grievously of all." Reporter Wauhilla La Hay was "infuriated" by the omission. But Nixon felt he couldn't now trust his emotions to mention Pat. In retrospect he wrote, "I knew how much courage she had needed to carry her through the day and night of preparations for this abrupt departure. . . . She had been a dignified, compassionate First Lady. She had given so much to the nation and so much to the world. Now she would have to share my exile. She deserved so much more."

They descended the stairs, met with the Fords, and all four headed out of the house, the expansive lawn before them, the Washington Monument looming in the August haze, a helicopter down the path. All eyes followed Pat out. "I just want to go down in history as the wife of the President," she had said in 1970.

The women linked arms, Pat whispering to Betty, "My heavens, they've even rolled out the red carpet for us, isn't that something? . . . Well, Betty, you'll see many of these red carpets, and you'll get so that you hate 'em." Betty, like Lady Bird, extended herself under trying circumstances to comfort her predecessor; Pat, like Jackie, departed stoically.

As she made her way to the helicopter, Pat Nixon, as one observer reported, kept her "chin up, head unbowed, and no apologies. . . . She has done nothing to be ashamed of." She kept one arm around Nixon's waist and the other around Betty. Helen Smith ran to catch up with her, and squeezed her hand. Pat returned the impulse, but looked on-ward.

Mrs. Richard Nixon had never stopped being Thelma Ryan. She'd recall that the most "haunting" memory of her life was not these moments of August 9, but the sight of terminally ill children whose spirits she buoyed by sneaking them out of the hospital for night sledding. The press accounts of August 9 still viewed her as the long-suffering political

wife. None recounted a young woman who'd long ago taken to the California sky in a one-seater plane, learning how to fly.

After embracing Betty, Pat climbed into the helicopter. From inside, she turned back, one last time. The muggy air was stifled with sobbing, muting the chalk sticks of the mansion's columns, the red carpet jutting above the manicured greensward, beneath her. She turned to enter and slipped from sight.

The helicopter took them to the airplane. Inside Air Force One, Pat Nixon removed herself into "blessed aloneness" in her tiny compartment. Inches away, on the other side of the partition, sat her husband. He ceased being president at high noon, as they sailed over the plains, heading for the blue Pacific. Julie said they were in "suspended reality," and "exchanged no words." But when the copter had lifted them off the lawn, Nixon overheard the voice of the woman he once told, "You have the finest ideals of anyone I have ever known." Speaking to no one in particular, it was Pat Ryan Nixon. "It's so sad. It's so sad."

Upstairs, in the East Room, a wanly smiling Betty Ford in powder-blue suit held a Bible upon which Gerald Ford placed his hand, and the sensation made her feel as if "I were taking the oath with him, promising to dedicate my own life to the service of my country." As the "most disciplined, composed first lady in history," Pat Nixon, thought one reporter, would "be a tough act to follow." Betty Ford followed the advice given for this day in her *Living Bible*, "I will keep a muzzle on my mouth." The oath of office "cut" through her. Instantly, it hit her.

"I was the wife of the President of the United States . . . But I wasn't sure what kind of First Lady I would be."[12]

– 14 –

The Dancer

SECONDS AFTER REPEATING the oath of office, President Gerald Ford, in front of those gathered in the East Room, including Barbara Bush, turned to kiss the new First Lady, whispering, "I love you." In his speech immediately following, he told the world, ". . . I am indebted to no man and to only one woman, my dear wife, Betty. . . ." For the first time in history, a new president in his first address credited, let alone referred to his First Lady.[1]

The Fords returned to their suburban home, feasting on lasagna with friends. For ten days, they remained there, while Julie Eisenhower packed her parents' remaining possessions. That night, Betty Ford lay awake, thinking, "My God, what a job I have." The next morning a staffer called about a scheduled event to take place in six days. "What state dinner?" asked a shocked new First Lady. She'd assumed the role "overnight" with no transition. "I had to move carefully . . ."

While she didn't formally consult with any of the sorority, she felt "a lot of support" from "friends" Lady Bird and Pat, and the former wrote the new president, "Please tell Betty I think of her often in her new life." Betty said that as a "satellite" around First Ladies since Bess Truman, and an assistant hostess for First Ladies at large Congressional receptions, she'd received "a lot of training that was invaluable." But she remembered one woman in particular.

Ever since she was a child, Betty Ford had been impressed by Eleanor Roosevelt: "[S]he eventually became a role model for me because I liked her independence . . . I really liked the idea that a woman was finally speaking out and expressing herself rather than just expressing the views of her husband. That seemed healthy . . ."[2]

Others were quick to note a similarity. As they gathered in the State Dining Room for Betty Ford's first press conference, reporters were curious about this relatively unknown woman who'd already stated that she was pro-ERA, pro-choice on abortion, had consulted a psychiatrist, been divorced, and used tranquilizers for physical pain. Several publications, Newsweek among them, compared Betty's willingness to offer bold opinions with Mrs. Roosevelt's.

On whether Ford would run for president in '76, the new First Lady said that "two years is quite a long ways away and I wouldn't want to commit myself one way or another."[3] She announced that she'd focus on the advocacy of using the arts for underprivileged children, and ERA passage. "I think that almost every First Lady realizes that she needs a project," Mrs. Ford would reflect, "before their husband is even the nominee, they're [the press] asking them to present a program. I don't think you can be effective if you spread yourself too thin. . . ."

Initially, she didn't see the Ladyship as "a meaningful position," but once accepting the reality of the situation, rather than let the role change her, she changed it. "I wanted to be a good First Lady . . . but I didn't believe I had to do every single thing some previous President's wife had done." She decided, "I'm just going to be Betty Bloomer Ford," and "might as well have a good time doing it."

She called it "a demanding privilege," and "a great opportunity," but also a "salvation" that gave her a "career." Her son Jack thought that the Ladyship gave her "a national forum she never had. . . . She'd always had an impact on my father when he was Minority Leader, but few knew it or sought her to get to him. But she also became more conscious of her impact. That awareness changed how she viewed herself."

The longer she was in the Ladyship, the deeper her perceptions became about it. She considered the role "a twenty-four-hour-a-day volunteer job." It was Betty Ford who first suggested that First Ladies of the future might be salaried as official hostesses—goodwill ambassadors. She believed that in the long run, the First Lady not only had more power over the president than a vice president did, but was more important as a political symbol, describing the Ladyship as "the heart of the nation"—while the presidency was "the mind"—and thought it only fair that it be better staffed than the vice presidency. If a woman vice president was chosen, she didn't think it would change the balance of power between a First Lady and president.[4]

Gamely, Betty loved being First Lady. When singer Tony Orlando was asked spontaneously to perform at an outdoor dinner, the First Lady was coaxed onstage to entertain with him. As tourists streamed through for weekend tours, she routinely came out onto the balcony, waving and posing for their pictures. She unabashedly admitted, "Yes, I'm a ham. I think all theatrical people are. We absolutely love an audience." She said her work as dancer and model was "beneficial" because she was comfortable onstage, before spotlights. At a hotel, showered with seven thousand rose petals, serenaded by violins, Betty danced up the red carpet.

There were some adjustments about which she joked, "You have to compartmentalize and file things in your head. And I have not operated that way, particularly since I stopped working in 1948!" Inspired by Lady Bird, she had hoped to keep a diary, but admitted, "By the time I get through the day, I couldn't possibly tape it. I don't even want to remember it!"[5]

Her creative imagination as hostess rivaled Jackie's. "This house has been like a grave," Betty declared. "I want it to sing." For table centerpieces, she employed American crafts, from Steuben glass to Native American reed baskets. She used different-colored taffeta and antique tablecloths, candle-holders made from old wooden spools used at a historic New England textile mill, and mixed the colorful state chinas from past administrations. There was also a subtle political purpose to her return to round dining tables. More women could be seated at the president's table than protocol pecking order permitted along the E-shaped configurations. At his table, Betty Ford placed political women "who needed a leg up."[6]

She believed that the Ladyship hadn't "altered me in any essential way," but rather she "found the resources with which to respond to a series of challenges. You never know what you can do until you have to do it." She simply "flowered." Almost exactly as Grace Coolidge had expressed it, Betty said, "For some people in a public situation . . . an inner strength takes over. . . ."

Except for those who married incumbent presidents, Betty Ford was the only "unelected" First Lady, and admitted that had she had to participate in a presidential campaign, her candor would almost certainly have been a political liability. However, by 1974, the role of women in American society was shifting, and she perfectly mirrored it. Mrs. Ford believed that she *had to* become visible and active. "I suppose a First Lady could possibly be like a Bess Truman, but it's unlikely." Finally, Betty would open the creaky gates of propriety, not by contrivance, but by following the simple rules of Grace Coolidge and Frances Cleveland: being her natural self. "I've spent too many years as me," she affirmed, "I can't suddenly turn into a princess." That self was spontaneous, spirited, honest, and downright jazzy.[7] The refreshing hiatus of Betty Ford was ripe for the times, and the times ripe for her.

Under the veneer of the gracefully slim figure, of brilliant green-blue eyes and glossy streaked auburn hair, was a woman of rigorous principles. Betty had never refrained from frankly speaking out against social injustice, even if it went against mainstream or conservative thought.

There was still a free-spirit bohemian in Betty Ford, the single woman who'd overcome restrictive conformity by studying not only the movement but the theory of modern dance, who went to New York as a self-supporting teenager, introduced modern dance into the Grand Rapids black ghetto and organized that conservative city's first exposure to the form. Her fresh sense of humor poked fun at the staid notion of the First Lady. She spoke deliberately, articulating every thought. She manifested little fear about exploring new ideas and listening to different views. "I think it's silly to live a fictional life."

Betty Ford's public persona and private person merged.

In a heartfelt high school commencement speech, Mrs. Ford illuminated her own creed: ". . . trust and believe in yourself . . . each individual makes his own dreams . . . What is important in our lives is not so much what we have in the way of intelligence and talent, but what we do with these gifts . . ." Jack said his mother had a "stubbornness" with her "positions of principles" and a 'born-with-it' insight which she imparted."[8]

With her uncanny penchant for tardiness, she was unique for a First Lady, and the president had to rein his temper, finally warning her that she must be ready by six-thirty for one particularly important event. Betty sailed out of her room, at seven, to a grinning Jerry. "For once we'll be on time." The event actually started at seven-thirty. The First Lady had the last word: "He is a male chauvinist. He was late for our wedding. He was out campaigning."

She had a sense of mischievous fun, whether rolling back a slip of skirt to prove to a doubter that it was real denim or joining Pearl Bailey on stage to sing the Michigan fight song.

Occasionally, private person collided with public persona.

Moments before she appeared on national television, wearing a tight Chinese red gown with a high slit, Betty quickly panicked that "a First Lady should not come onstage showing her thighs." She was introduced, came before the cameras, and attempted to glide out demurely while walking with her legs crossed.[9]

As far as security permitted, "Pinafore"—her Secret Service code name—slipped out of the White House for a hamburger at McDonald's, picked up hand lotion at a discount drugstore, or shopped for shoes at a department store. Whether wearing a hat made of beer cans, a foil crown as she crossed the dateline, or popping her head up from behind a giant urn, she broke into a laughing smile easily. On occasion, when the president took off early for a trip, the First Lady waved to him from the balcony, while the press snapped pictures. They didn't know she was often wearing a nightgown under her coat. Her cheerfulness was infectious; in white slacks and baseball cap, Betty applauded Secret Service agents playing football and brought a case of Gatorade. She sang to lift her husband's spirits, or even, as her daughter Susan recalled, did "a little tap dance." Betty Ford had remained always, the dancer.[10]

Mrs. Ford said that "98 percent" of the time she was in good spirits, but the other 2 percent she was "miserable . . . cool and distant." Those moments were usually marked by the tremendous physical torture of her arthritis and pinched nerve, which sometimes led to depression.

When she declared, "I have to be honest," most didn't realize part of that need stemmed from a deeply rooted faith. Daily, she read her *Living Bible* and a Saint Francis prayer that hung in her bathroom. Her intensely private faith most publicly emerged in short flashes during interviews, like her definition of success: ". . . being flexible and willing to give, understand, love and still keep your own identity." In her candidness, she mentioned, but did not make an issue out of, her physical ills and how she dealt with them. "Life is made up of problems," she said in 1974, "I can't imagine anyone not having problems."

Occasionally, there were curious remarks about her drug and alcohol use. Just two months into her Ladyship, Jerald F. terHorst recalled in print how "tranquilizers and alcohol failed to relax her [pain] sufficiently. . . ." In a *Newsweek* cover story, one friend was quoted as saying she'd seen her "so doped up." Myra MacPherson, in her book *The Power Lovers*, which was published during the administration, mentioned that the First Lady admitted to "taking tranquilizers, [and] drinking." Nobody, including the press, questioned or sought to investigate the degree of her medication, as First Lady Betty Ford kept any alcohol consumption to a minimum. She might have one nightcap with the president, or a cocktail on Camp David weekends. She didn't drink heavily because "there was too much at stake, too much responsibility." When keeping a full schedule while in pain, Mrs. Ford did depend upon tranquilizers, but otherwise steeled herself into working and attempting to ignore her discomfort, as Ida McKinley had. And, too, there was a psychological boost in her "moment in the sun," because, as she wrote of herself, "People with low self-esteem crave reassurance from the outside world." That self-view was her single public deception as First Lady. There would be no press or public inference that she lacked confidence.[11]

Betty's ease pervaded. She redecorated the Oval Office using "earth tones" and live plants. She dribbled a basketball with one of the Harlem Globetrotters until the president complained of the noise. The casualness even extended to the Secret Service. Once when she was in Air Force One's powder room, her agent, waiting outside for her, commanded the First Lady to sit down because of a rough landing. "I am . . ." she yelled back from the other side of the door. In the stiffly regal Yellow Oval Room, she frequently put one of her cigarettes in the hands of a statue, as whimsical "evidence of my disrespect." She turned the annual Senate Wives Lunch into a paper-bag lawn picnic, the women delighted to be seated by picking numbers, instead of protocol.[12]

Nothing marked the dramatic change in the Ladyship more than Betty Ford's eagerness to cooperate with the press, a relationship illustrated when she once did away with speech cards and remarked, "I'd rather say what I want." She determined immediately to establish an open dialogue, and hoped she'd be remembered for "being able to communicate with people." Though she turned down the offer to write a column as had every First Lady since Eleanor, unlike them all, Betty was comfortable on television, though her press secretary clarified, "She's not the type to face the nation. She *is* the type to chat with it. . . ." When 60 Minutes approached the East Wing about taping Mrs. Ford, she was responsive, and tentatively agreed to a future interview.

"When somebody asks you how you stand on an issue," explained Betty Ford of her "policy" of candor, "you're very foolish if you try to beat around the bush—you just meet yourself going around the bush the other way." She considered criticism to be the media's "privilege," and thought it difficult only if one didn't "firmly believe in yourself and what you want to accomplish."[13] She was unhesitant to elaborate on earlier revelations, even freely mentioning her previous marriage, adding that she and Jerry ran into her first husband in an airport. Mrs. Ford continued to discuss how she'd benefited from psychiatry and used it further to speak at mental-health meetings, adding that such care also improved physical health. Another one of her early revelations as First Lady, however, hit a Puritanical national nerve.

The remark came about when, in her first weeks, Mrs. Ford offered to Myra MacPherson, "They've asked me everything but how often I sleep with my husband and if they'd asked me that, I would have told them." MacPherson asked. Betty quipped, "[A]s often as possible!" Sleeping in a separate room, she said, was "just too far to go" as a concession to tradition. She was surprised as letters poured in calling her cohabitation "immoral," but cracked, "I guess if you're President that part of your life is—I guess you're supposed to be a eunuch." By making the "President's Bedroom" into a family room, and the "First Lady's Bedroom" into their own, the Fords did become the first presidential couple to share the same bedroom since the Coolidges, but the press exaggerated the fact. Couples after the Coolidges had maintained separate rooms, but often shared one—except for the FDRs. The difference was the Fords' open affection. TV cameras even caught the sight of the president giving the First Lady's bottom a pat.[14]

As a "night person," she awoke later than the president, didn't "talk before 10 o'clock," and usually breakfasted alone in her sitting room. Her schedule was similar to her recent predecessors', but her responsibilities were different in that she initially operated as her own "administrator," even redrafting standard First Lady correspondence replies to directly address a writer's question in the first paragraph. The First Lady presided over Monday afternoon staff meetings, in the family quarters, and worked from both the Treaty Room and a desk in her bedroom. Mrs. Ford assured her division heads they could call her anytime, and joked easily with them, once placing an enlarged photo of herself dancing with Cary Grant in the East Wing, signed, "Eat your heart out, girls."

She voiced the opinion that federal allocations for East Wing staffing and operation were grossly inadequate because "growth comes with change and as issues and responsibilities grow, more money should be funded." Mrs. Ford retained Patti Matson in press advance, and Susan Porter in scheduling, but replaced Mrs. Nixon's press secretary and social secretary, after first securing diplomatic posts for both of them. As social secretary, she first appointed Nancy Ruwe, soon replaced her with Maria Downs, and made TV producer Sheila Weidenfeld the press secretary. For the first time in the Ladyship, an official speechwriter, Kaye Frances Pullen, was hired to prepare drafts. Betty Ford would be making frequent speeches on a variety of topics, and they would become her eloquent, bold hallmark.[15]

Weidenfeld sought the advice of Liz Carpenter and was the first East Winger to attend the president's press secretary's daily staff briefings. She was remarkably eager, even challenging the president's press secre-

tary to a swimming race to win one of his staff members for the East
Wing. Jack thought Sheila "did a heck of a job, and got the points
across, but you can't make someone something they're not. You can
highlight certain aspects."

Mrs. Ford's friend Nancy Howe remained as personal assistant. A
dramatic friction developed between Howe and Weidenfeld, who believed, with some justification, that the personal assistant was attempting to limit the First Lady's activist commitments. There was jealousy,
Howe once screaming at Weidenfeld in front of the First Lady, who
remained above the squabble. Ford's first press secretary recalled Howe
interrupting the First Lady's comments in an interview. When she
broke in to remind Mrs. Ford that she had background reading to do,
Betty, "calm but firm," replied, "I know dear." At one juncture, Jerry
advised Betty, "Tell your staff they work for you. You don't work for
them."

As always, the West Wing Press Office battled The East Wing's,
even taking charge of releasing the news about Mrs. Ford's illness. But
it was someone in the East Wing who'd actually helped save her life.[16]

On Thursday, September 26, Nancy Howe went for an annual
checkup and suggested Mrs. Ford do the same. A doctor routinely examined Betty. He left, then returned with another doctor. That evening at the White House, the president's doctor asked to see her.
When Betty arrived, a specialist was also there. She was "getting sus-
picious," and as she emerged from the room, the president waited for
her. A lump had been discovered in her right breast that the doctors
wanted to biopsy immediately. There was a chance of cancer. For
twenty-four hours, the Fords told no one.

On Friday, Betty maintained her full schedule, hosting a Salvation
Army luncheon, then joining Jerry and Lady Bird Johnson at the dedication of the LBJ Memorial Grove of five hundred white pine trees,
planted along the Potomac near Lady Bird Johnson Park. Mrs. Ford
went smilingly through the event, then gave Mrs. Johnson, Lynda
Robb, and Luci Nugent a tea and a tour of the private rooms. Lady Bird
said Betty "never said a word about her problem. She's terribly brave
and should have canceled. I salute her courage and her character." At
5:55, Mrs. Ford arrived at Bethesda Naval Hospital "in good spirits,"
and the news was broken in time for the six o'clock news reports, presidential press secretary Ron Nessen telling the press frankly that if the
nodule proved malignant, "surgery would be performed to remove the
right breast." From her hospital-room window, the First Lady looked
down and saw all the television lights focused up at her.

At nine that night the president, son Michael, and daughter-in-law
Gayle joined Betty in the presidential suite as she dined with Susan and
Nancy Howe. Ford observed that she was "tense but very strong," and

displayed "no apprehension." Back at the White House that night, it all hit Ford with tremendous impact. "The thought that the woman I loved might be taken away from me was almost too much to endure." Before retiring, he sent her three dozen red roses—her favorite.

At six the next morning, the First Lady tried to make light of her hospital gown and toeless socks as "one for *Women's Wear Daily.*" The president kissed her, and as she was put under anesthesia, Mrs. Ford recalled, "I had a pretty good premonition it was going to turn out to be a malignancy and that my breast would have to be removed."

When the president received confirmation from the doctors, it was "the lowest and loneliest moment" of his presidency. He sat at his desk in the Oval Office and cried. Then he helicoptered to the hospital to see his wife in the recovery room.

Though groggy, Mrs. Ford quipped to her family, "If you can't look happy, please go away. I can't bear to look at you." She felt positive about life and the fact that suddenly, all across America, women were having breast examinations and mammograms. She thought it ironic that had she not become First Lady by a stroke of fate, the press wouldn't have focused on her cancer, provoking this positive effect.

During her hospital convalescence, the president visited his wife daily. The separation affected his presidency, and he wrote, "That whole period of her absence was difficult. . . . Although I tried to concentrate all my energies on the job of being President, I was feeling pretty low, and I guess it showed." It echoed the sentiments of Woodrow Wilson over his wife Ellen's illness. Meanwhile, Betty Ford was making a discovery. "Lying in the hospital," she wrote, "thinking of all those women going for cancer checkups because of me, I'd come to realize more clearly the power of the woman in the White House. Not my power, but the power of the position, a power which could be used to help."

By the time Mrs. Ford was back in the White House two weeks later, the ensuing media coverage of her honest revelation was credited with saving the lives of thousands of women who discovered breast tumors. Thousands of dollars came in, which the First Lady donated to the American Cancer Society. The East Wing was flooded with about sixty thousand cards, letters, and telegrams, 10 percent from women who'd had mastectomies. They were moving, and extremely personal: Mrs. Ford referred to them as "a wonderful story . . . of appreciation of life. . . ."

The First Lady later told the American Cancer Society, ". . . I just cannot stress enough how necessary it is for women to take an active interest in their own health and body. Too many women are so afraid . . . they endanger their lives. These fears of being 'less' of a woman are very real, and it is very important to talk about the emotional side

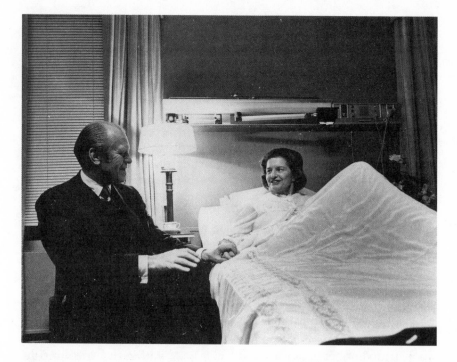

effects honestly. It was easier for me . . . I had been married for 26 years and we had four children . . . But some women don't have these same emotional resources, and it is very necessary to deal realistically with the fears. . . . It isn't vanity to worry about disfigurement. It is an *honest concern*.

"When I asked myself whether I would rather lose a right arm or a breast, I decided I would rather have lost a breast. The most important thing in life is good health, and that I have. That is the medical side. Cancer also produces fear—and much of that fear comes from ignorance about the progress already made and ignorance of the need for preventive medicine for men and women alike. Cancer . . . also strikes the spirit. And the best doctors in the world cannot cure the spirit. . . . All of us can . . . open our hearts and our minds to dealing with the fears that the victims have . . . I believe we are all here to help each other and that our individual lives have patterns and purposes. My illness turned out to have a very special purpose—helping save other lives, and I am grateful for what I was able to do."

As *The New York Times Magazine* stated, if she "achieved nothing else during her husband's Administration, the light her trouble has shed on a dark subject would be contribution enough."

Mrs. Ford proudly reflected, "No one had talked about mastectomy publicly before. . . . Since then, it's never gone underground again, which is great. I've never regretted it." For some months after the surgery, there was speculation that Mrs. Ford was not in good health. She underwent chemotherapy for a year after the surgery and was fine. Although she momentarily lost her "self-esteem" the fact that the cancer came so soon after she became First Lady, Betty said, "was probably one of the most fortunate times for me, having to recover from cancer. It helped me get my mind off that and get on with the job that I was trying to accomplish and apply myself to. . . ."

Jack Ford believed that the positive public reaction to her honesty was "when she truly realized she had her own identity. . . ."[17]

In a great sense, part of Betty Ford's popularity was due to the man behind the woman behind the man. Theirs was a relationship of mutual respect. Betty may have assumed the traditional roles, but Jerry never asked her to conform for political expediency. He'd married an independent woman, not a docile lady. Like other presidents, he could have disregarded her views. He did not. The First Lady was bothered that "while I was getting so much praise Jerry was getting criticism. He was a good sport. He was proud of me and even in cases where he didn't agree with my views, he was all for my spouting them." The best metaphor of the relationship was Betty's edict to have the wall separating the rooms for the First Lady and president on Air Force One torn down.

Betty felt "a great sense of security just knowing we were in the same territory," but it took getting used to. She frequently woke up, turned to the president next to her, and asked, "What are you doing here?" Their playfulness often unfolded in public. When Hispanic singer Vicki Carr, in a gown barely covering her bosom, asked Ford what his favorite Mexican dish was, he quipped, "I like you," but sheepishly recalled, "Betty overheard the exchange, and needless to say, she wasn't wild about it." At a fund-raiser, Betty once grabbed the mike from him as if she were about to begin one of her frank discussions on social issues, much to his momentary horror.

Mrs. Ford was more conscious of the president's sartorial image than he sometimes seemed to be. When she saw his ankle-high formal pants, she "didn't know whether to laugh or cry," and helped arrange an updated wardrobe for his appearances. Ford wasn't bothered by comedian Chevy Chase's characterization of him as a bumbler, but the First Lady thought it "stupid," admitting "it really wasn't funny to me." When he fell down airplane stairs in front of the press, she pointed out that it was raining, and, enthusiastic to get going, he merely slipped on the wet stairs.[18]

The First Lady reviewed the daily news summary, and Jack recalled that she "discussed political issues with him [the president]. If something hit her hot button she would pursue it. She read through the *Congressional Record.* She would look at my father's briefing papers on issues which summarized key points . . . She was an effective conduit of information *to* him, and *from* him, and along the way add[ed] her own opinions . . . not like the budget—but women's, social issues, domestic programs . . . in the course of any day . . . everything is political in nature."

Mrs. Ford admitted that while she disagreed with the president on some matters, she strove to deemphasize them because she "wouldn't want to embarrass him by opposing his position. That I'll do in the privacy of our own sitting room." Ford's reaction to his wife's *public* opinions echoed FDR's to Eleanor's, and Betty said, "He encourages me to do my own thing."

She was a canny judge of his speeches, frequently advising they be tighter and livelier. ". . . men overdo it a little," she offered. "If you leave the audience wanting more rather than trying to keep their eyes open, you're better off." She viewed her influence as "the impact a woman usually has on a marriage, as far as we can provide the sounding board to a man who is so intensely involved in problems of such importance . . . to the world. For them to have someone to bounce ideas off without having them become argumentative is very important. It gives them an opening to examine their feelings and their thoughts. . . ."

In the relaxed atmosphere after dinner, Mrs. Ford used her "pillow talk" most. "It was those times when you had the opportunity to . . . lobby for the things which interested you. . . . You have to take the President's time when you can get it. . . . We often used the bedroom as a meeting place." Feminist Ford was not above using a bit of subtle coquetry either: "[I]f you bring up a subject long enough with a man, why finally he gets so tired of it he agrees to anything." She wielded power best "when I figured he was most tired and vulnerable." Jack said his mother "put 'women in government' high on her agenda, and consequently his." Betty Ford's first coup was getting Republican Anne Armstrong appointed as the first woman ambassador to England.[19]

FDR had been the first to appoint a woman to his Cabinet, but the last time it had occurred was under Eisenhower. From the start, the First Lady had lobbied for a woman Cabinet member, so when Carla Hills appeared on a list of HUD candidates proposed by his chief of staff, Ford gave her credentials particular attention. And appointed her.

Mrs. Ford soon after remarked, "If I can get a woman on the Supreme Court, I'll be batting 1,000." The day after the Hills appointment was announced, a cartoon appeared picturing Betty whispering into Jerry's ear, "Now, about the Court, dear . . ." As soon as the resignation of Justice Douglas was official, the First Lady rushed to the president. While they danced at a judiciary reception, the First Lady mentioned the name of a woman she thought qualified. The president stopped her cold by saying, "Well, the top man on the list is here

tonight." A shocked Betty said she "had to accept his judgment," and though disappointed, would continue to "research" for qualified women candidates for the bench.[20]

As they related to women, Betty Ford also involved herself in the president's programs. While Ford was in Japan, the First Lady addressed an economic briefing for representatives of national women's groups on behalf of his WIN (Whip Inflation Now) program, established to counteract the national recession that had set in. "It's important that we, *as women*, take a lead in this fight because we *are* the consumers," she told them. "We *are* the people who decide how our families spend their money. We feel the pinch . . . more acutely . . . and we need to be as knowledgeable on every aspect of the economy as possible."

Besides supporting WIN by signing a "consumer's pledge" to buy "only those products and services priced at or below present levels . . . [and] conserve energy . . . ," Betty had her pumps redyed several times, bought makeup in economy-sized bottles, and changed her appearance in solid-colored dresses with the use of different accessories, particularly her trademark scarves that draped over her shoulders. She ordered that weekly menus be planned around supermarket specials, substituting soup for the costly fish course, favoring inexpensive fowl, and serving smaller portions. As far as the president and WIN were concerned, however, Jack recalled, "there was a lot of ribbing" from him and his mother." Mrs. Ford would later admit that WIN "sort of flopped."[21]

Betty Ford's influence was more dramatically felt that autumn when she urged the president to make his most controversial decision, the pardon of Richard Nixon.

"She was one of several persons who did," chronicled Helen Thomas, "but I was told that the First Lady's opinion was a crucial factor in the President's final decision." Mrs. Ford simply stated, "I think it had to be done." Jack said she felt "[i]t was healing . . . not only for the country . . . For their family as well, especially Mrs. Nixon . . ."

When Betty showed the family quarters to her press secretary, they came across a photo of the Fords and Nixons together, and Mrs. Ford pointedly stated, "Pat is a wonderful woman, a good friend of mine . . . A strong woman. Luckily." Mrs. Ford sent Mrs. Nixon birthday cards, notes, and spoke often and glowingly of her. She refused to speak, even off the record, to Carl Bernstein, then co-writing *The Final Days*, about the end of the Nixon administration.

Ironically, the pardon actually caused renewed suffering for Pat Nixon. She said the day the news reached San Clemente was the "saddest" of her life, believing it to be acknowledgment of "surrender to his enemies." That night Nixon, suffering from phlebitis, which caused a dangerous blood clot, was hospitalized at Long Beach Memorial Hospital. Several days later, the condition became life-threatening. When Ford, in Los Angeles, telephoned and asked if he should visit, Pat unhesitantly responded, "I can't think of anything that would help Dick more." Upon arrival, he immediately embraced her.

Each day, the former First Lady drove with two Secret Service agents in a pale blue Lincoln Continental the fifty miles from San Clemente, spending about three hours at her husband's side, returning home alone at dark. Sometimes she helped volunteers in sorting and answering get-well messages. Her therapy was gardening, and while the former president sank into quietness, she determined to remain upbeat and look ahead, "concentrating on surviving each day, not on living."

Out of the ashes, new life was emerging, and many noticed that as Pat psychologically pulled her husband from near death, a "camaraderie" was developing. She was also now determined to live as a private citizen. When a former staff member came to visit, Pat herself drove to pick her up at the San Diego airport. She relished the realization that she'd never have to grant another interview. She read five books a week, avoiding any on the Nixon era but rediscovering works of Hemingway, Maugham, Thomas Wolfe, and Jane Austen. She even drove down to Tijuana with a friend, browsing through discount stores and posing for a tourist photo in a donkey cart wearing a sombrero. Popular myth pictured her as a recluse; for once, the veil between image and reality served well. She went completely unrecognized. To the surprise of many, she accepted an invitation to the dedication of a California school named in her honor. While there, she told a reporter, "If I had a choice, I'd rather be admired less and have my husband tormented less."

Unknown to the press, Betty Ford would pay a private visit to Pat Nixon at San Clemente, visiting the compound with a retinue of Secret Service agents. Lady Bird kept in touch with Pat as well, corresponding and sending her annual Christmas gifts, one year pralines, another year a collection of Anne Morrow Lindbergh's published diaries. Pat was never again to see her closest friend in the sorority. Mamie was only occasionally making her winter trek to Palm Springs now, and though scheduled to spend some time with the Nixons one year, she became ill and was rushed East. The two would keep in contact by mail and telephone only. Nancy and Ronald Reagan came to dine with Pat and Dick Nixon at San Clemente not long after the resignation, and the Reagans invited the Nixons to dine with them at their home.[22]

In the last days of Reagan's governorship, prominent national journalists were already making note of what some perceived as Nancy's power. When one of her phone calls to the governor interrupted a meeting, one Republican asked reporter Lou Cannon, "Jesus Christ, who's running the state?" To Girl Talk magazine, she said her sole "joy."

was "being Mrs. Ronald Reagan." Asked if she ever viewed herself independently, she answered, "No, I never do. Always as Nancy Reagan.
My life began with Ronnie." Asked if she'd like to be First Lady, she
circumvented by replying, "I just want to be Ronald Reagan's wife.
Whatever." Finally, asked what she would do if she weren't married to
him, Mrs. Reagan fell silent, then gasped, "Oh heavens! I don't know,
I've never thought of it. I don't know what I'd do . . . Kill myself!"

Meanwhile, in the new year, Betty Ford declared, "I think men
realize women are coming into their own."[23]

- 15 -

Ms. President

IN THE INTERNATIONAL Year of the Woman, Betty Ford would prove
to be Woman of the Year, the first "Ms. President."

Though it had no legislative power, Mrs. Ford considered her husband's executive order establishing 1975 as International Women's Year
to be moral support for the ERA battle. Surrounded by leading feminists, the president signed the order establishing a National Commission on the Observance of IWY. As the ink dried, First Lady Ford
razzed her husband, "[Y]ou've come a long, long way," paraphrasing a
popular cigarette ad of the seventies, referring to women's equality. The
power, the rights, the issues, and the visibility of women were becoming the theme of Betty Ford's Ladyship.

In the White House, she hosted the first meeting of the four commissions in the federal government on the status of women, and met
with the "Ten Outstanding Young Women of America." She popped up
at the opening of a National Archives exhibit, "Her Infinite Variety: A
200 Year Record of America's Women," which was an Interior Department recognition of IWY, and there sought out the members of its
Mexico Conference delegation. With liberal congresswomen Bella
Abzug and Pat Schroeder, among others, Mrs. Ford joined the feminist
group, pausing for a special recognition of Amelia Bloomer, the woman
who popularized the first woman's pants, "bloomers," and one of her
collateral ancestors.

When she met with the Womens' Stockbrokers Association, the
First Lady asked about women's increasing interest, knowledge, and
professional roles in stock brokerage and investment. Two days later,

she met with members of the Future Homemakers of America, then holding a conference on homemaker problems, subjects of the sessions running the gamut—from single parenthood to living up to expectations raised by advertising, and "Depression, Alcohol and other Drugs," and the isolation of the housewife.

The First Lady addressed them, stating that though she once chose to be a dancer, she had a second *"profession"* as homemaker, and illustrated how being a housewife was a logical reason for supporting the ERA: "Whether . . . a career in the home or outside, what is important is that she make that decision herself—without any pressures to restrict her choice. . . . So what's all this about liberated women being career women? Anyone who feels good about what she's doing in the home should have the same sense of liberation. . . . And I hope that with the new emphasis on freedom of choice, the respect and stature homemakers deserve will be recognized."

Mrs. Ford shifted her focus when addressing the Cleveland IWY's Congress, in what was a most remarkable speech for a First Lady and certainly the most progressive made by any president's wife since Eleanor Roosevelt: "While many opportunities are open to women today, too many are available only to the lucky few. Many barriers continue to block the paths of most women. . . . This year is . . . the time to . . . work for the invisible many, whose lives are still restricted by custom and code. . . . These definitions of behavior and ability inhibit men and women alike, but the limits on women have been formalized into law and structured into social custom . . . the first important steps have been to undo these laws that hem women in and lock them out of the mainstream of opportunities. . . .

". . . my own support of the ERA has shown what happens when a definition of proper behavior collides with the right of an individual to personal opinions. I do not believe that being First Lady should prevent me from expressing my views. . . . Being ladylike does not require silence. The ERA . . . will not be an instant solution . . . It will help knock down those restrictions that have locked women into old stereotypes of behavior and . . . open up more options . . .

"The debate over ERA has become too emotional because of the fears of some—both men and women—about the changes already taking place in America . . . part of the job of those who support ERA is to help remove this cloud of fear . . . the fight of women to become . . . accepted human beings is important to all people of either sex and whatever nationality. I hope 1976 will be the year the remaining four states ratify the 27th Amendment . . . to show that the great American experiment in *human freedom* continues to expand. But changing laws, more job opportunities, less financial discrimination and more possibilities for the use of our minds and bodies will only partially change the place of women.

"By themselves they will never be enough, because we must value our own talents before we can expect acceptance from others. The heart of the battle is within. . . . We have to take that 'just' out of 'just a housewife' . . . Downgrading this work has been part of the pattern in our society that has undervalued women's talents in all areas . . . we have a long way to go—part of that distance is in our own mind. . . . The long road to equality rests on achievements of women and men in altering how women are treated in every area of everyday life . . . patterns of discrimination . . . must be ended before women are truly free . . . As the barriers against freedom . . . because of race or religion have fallen, the freedom of *all* has expanded. . . . On the eve of the nation's third century, let us work to end the laws and remove the labels that limit the imaginations and the options of men and women alike. Success will open hearts and minds to new possibilities for all people . . . but we must keep *moving on.*"[1]

Betty Ford became the first recipient of the National Women's Party's Alice Paul Award. The party had been formed by Paul in 1913, and after the Eighteenth Amendment had been passed giving women the right to vote, the party had convened on August 23, 1923, to pass a resolution to fight for additional rights. Alice Paul wrote the first ERA, introduced to the House in 1923, by Susan B. Anthony's nephew, a Kansas Republican congressman, and to the Senate by Kansas Republican senator Charles Curtis. For over fifty years, the National Women's Party had the ERA introduced in each succeeding Congress.

Mrs. Ford worked everywhere for ERA. She had an East Room slide presentation on ERA shown to White House staff, and her invitation circulated to even the male West Wing: ". . . bring co-workers . . . I think it's vital to both the men and the women who work here to have a clear understanding of the legislation." And just three weeks into the "Year of the Woman," Betty Ford burned the wires and rocked the conservatives.

She began by writing to William Kretschmar of the North Dakota legislature and leading foe of ERA ratification. Then it was a phone call to Illinois's ranking minority Republican senator, William Harris, respecting his right to be anti-ERA, but imploring him to vote it out of committee. "I do think the Senate should have a chance to consider it as a whole, don't you? . . ." When busloads of conservative sects lobbied the Missouri legislature, declaring that ERA would make abortion, homosexual relationships, and unisex rest rooms, hospital rooms, and dormitories permissible, the First Lady called to bolster the wavering votes of two legislators, telling one, "Now, don't be bowled over . . . I realize you're under a lot of pressure . . . I know the agitators . . . I am not a wild-eyed Liberal on this . . . That's not the point . . . women should have . . . opportunities." The First Lady persuaded the Illinois legislature to vote ERA out of committee, and the two Missouri representatives not only voted for ERA, but it passed. Betty Ford was having a genuine impact, and Sheila Weidenfeld thought the First Lady was particularly persuasive because she listened carefully to opposing views.

Unknown to most, Mrs. Ford continued to suffer the excruciation of her oesteoarthritis and pinched neck nerve, unable to move about easily. On at least one occasion, an expert in rheumatology from a local medical center had to be called in. But she kept lobbying for ERA over the phone even wearing a neck brace.

Before the Georgia, Nevada, and Arizona state legislatures were to vote on ERA, the First Lady lobbied individual members within different contexts: For men, ERA also "frees," because a husband shouldn't pay alimony when a woman was able to work; to conservatives, she spoke of preserving a daughter's education since ERA guaranteed equal education, job opportunities, and compensation; to loyal Republicans she said, "We want to think of the . . . party as being a leader in supporting the cause of basic human rights." At the end of a tough week of battling, she helped win an ERA victory in Nevada, and the League of Women Voters offered to assist with informational background to small towns where interest was perking. Vacationing in Florida, Betty made her point by always wearing an oversized ERA button, and urging the governor to get ERA onto the Senate floor for a vote. When picketers appeared outside the White House, in black mourning, one sign read, BETTY FORD IS TRYING TO PRESS A SECOND-RATE MANHOOD ON AMERICAN WOMEN! She was proud to be the first First Lady to be picketed for her own political stance. By February, the First Lady had received 3,246 letters supporting her on ERA, 2,119 opposing.[2]

Besides the challenge and fulfillment of "lobbying right from my office in the White House," Betty's pride increased. The more speeches she made, the more professional she became. And though it was her early personal life that implicitly forged her convictions, she thought the "ERA helped my role of First Lady as far as identifying me. . . ." She relished "setting an example of the 'typical housewife,'" making her point that housewives earned the right to not only legal equality but social security and establishing credit, and by asking how many husbands would be able to pay the salaries of a cook, chauffeur, nurse, and baby-sitter.

As word of First Lady Ford's convictions spread, the extremist reactionary Phyllis Schlafly "managed to rally battalions of housewives" in her "Stop ERA" crusade. Coming from the far-right fringe, Schlafly also co-authored a book accusing the president of making secret deals with the Soviets. Now she fired off a telegram to his wife demanding "an accounting of how much federal money has been spent by you and other White House personnel in making long distance calls to legis-

lators," for the ERA. One Schlaflyite wrote the First Lady that her "intervention" on ERA was "an atrocity," and another accused her of attempting "to dictate to State Legislatures . . ." One legislator from Schlafly's state called Betty's efforts "demeaning to the stature of the First Lady," which provoked a St. Louis radio station to editorialize that "we heartily approve of Mrs. Ford's working . . . politics would be strengthened by increased activity by women as office seekers, party leaders and political activists at all levels . . . [help] shake off its political apathy, and reverse the disgracefully low voter turnout. When we start regarding political activity by a first lady, or any citizen, as 'demeaning,' our democracy is in big trouble . . ."

As the public learned that the first wave of reaction had been critical, a second, larger wave of support flooded in. One woman wrote Betty, "After so many First Ladies who wouldn't go near anything but furniture and gardens, it is truly gratifying to find a woman who is interested in doing a little more for her country." Another championed her by bestowing the mighty comparison, "This is the first time since Eleanor Roosevelt that a President's wife is coming across as her own person, and a worthwhile person at that."[3]

Mrs. Ford was terse in reference to Schlafly, avoiding the moralist's rhetoric in a formal debate, but wryly wondering how she could espouse a woman's place as a housewife while touring the country, leaving her husband alone at home. Schlafly, unlike those women who'd benefit most from ERA, had household help to assume the traditional chores, and when she barked that ERA would destroy motherhood, Mrs. Ford retorted that "I wasn't so sure mothers shouldn't have *rights.*" Betty was incredulous at the charge that by not making breakfast for their husbands, pro-ERA women were promoting unisex lavatories and the demise of Bible readings. She "never heard a good Phyllis Schlafly argument." To those curious about her ERA support, Betty responded, "Like many women, my husband and children are my first priority, although I recognize that's not true for everyone. But my specific lifestyle or yours is not the issue; the issue is having the option to choose."

To conservatives, she sent a conciliatory response that "the public is not used to First Ladies speaking out on controversial issues," but hoped she could "help make people realize that the ERA is not a symbol of radical feminism. . . ." Her "Family-Oriented" response calmly explained: . . . the ERA will not force women to abandon [homes] . . . Millions of American women either by choice or necessity work outside the home. These women are often stuck in low-paying jobs with limited opportunities for advancement. I want for my children and yours the opportunity to use their talents to the fullest. I want an America where we live up to the ideal of each citizen having the right to life, liberty and the pursuit of happiness. . . . America has been unique in its faith in freedom for the individual, and that faith must be reaffirmed. . . ."[4]

For hundreds of thousands, the ERA of the seventies represented both legal and symbolic change, as the Civil Rights Bill had to blacks in the sixties.

Betty Ford's intolerance of racial prejudice was exemplified by her private life. One of her closest and oldest friends was Clara Powell, "second mother" to the Ford children, who happened to be black. As Betty said, "She and I brought up the children together." When she had joined the Fords at their local church, another family stopped going. It only strengthened Betty's bond to Clara. When they cleaned together, Betty blasted a Fred Waring song, "Get Out on Your Knees and Pray," as they went on all fours to scrub the floor, side by side. Clara, a frequent White House guest, would be among the few intimates invited to watch election returns with the Fords. "She had a wonderful influence on my life and theirs," recalled the First Lady.

Although she felt busing didn't necessarily lessen educational disadvantage, in public Betty further illustrated her sensitivity to equality. She went to services in Chicago's black community's Shiloh Baptist Church and then attended a large reception in honor of all the city's black preachers. She praised the National Council of Negro Women for "emphasizing the idea of Unity of Women," was "grateful for what you are doing," declared her support, and thanked them "for giving me the privilege and honor to meet with you." The following year, she would again ask them to the White House, as well as the new "National Black Women's Agenda."

Reactionary letters to Mrs. Ford's ERA support often asked how she could be "promoting a bunch of lesbians." To this charge, the First Lady pointed out that she wasn't sure that she was "in step with the lesbian faction," and defended Americans with alternative lifestyles, writing, "I do think lesbians are entitled to free speech, the same as anybody else. God put us all here for His own purposes; it's not my business to try and second-guess Him, and I think Anita Bryant's taking action against the gay population was ill-considered. I don't believe people should lose their jobs because of their sexual preference . . ." Whether people agreed or disagreed with her view, it was astounding that she voiced it. Eleanor Roosevelt had assured her friend Lorena Hickok, who was a lesbian, that she was unembarrassed to be publicly seen with her, and Lady Bird Johnson had been publicly nonjudgmental in the Walter Jenkins scandal, but no First Lady had ever willingly expressed her opinion on the sensitive issue as freely as Mrs. Ford.[5]

If she brought attention to issues untraditional for a First Lady, she also kept her vowed commitment to help children with special needs. Betty not only raised funds for the lesser-known Hospital for Sick Children (as opposed to Washington Children's Hospital) where abused, abandoned, and retarded children were the wards, but brought its needs to the attention of a businessman, who donated two new rooms. When she dedicated a Florida school, the local board was so impressed that it awarded a large grant to build a special wing there for handicapped students. She supported No Greater Love, which benefited MIA and POW children.

Mrs. Ford, who at fourteen years old had volunteered to teach dance therapy to retarded children, advocated that "early training can make a tremendous difference in their later capabilities." Dedicating New York's Arts for Living Center, she focused on the "use" of the arts as a social service for the underprivileged and as a means of breaking down racial prejudice, recalling when she had defied disapproval by teaching dance in the black ghetto, "I found that appreciation of any type of art form is certainly a good common denominator. It bridges gaps created by differences in heritage or background or economics. It develops talent which can be very important to the direction of a person's entire life, and . . . provides a sense of accomplishment . . ."

At the dedication of Bennington College's Arts Center, the First Lady recalled Martha Graham having "touched our hearts with fire and infused us with spirit. Isn't that what the arts are about? Nourishment for the soul? The arts, especially for me the dance, draw out our emotions and make us more alive. Very often the arts help me to see life in a new way . . ."[6]

Betty Ford was more closely associated with dance than any First Lady since Julia Tyler of the 1840's. At her first state dinner, the band played "Betty Coed," and the First Lady danced until one in the morning. On other nights, journalist Eric Sevareid and Senator Mark Hatfield frolicked to the Mexican hat dance, and after Betty twirled satirist Art Buchwald, he sent a framed poster from his book *I Never Danced At the White House* with "Never" crossed out. She endured the two left feet of the president of Finland, and at a state dinner for the Israeli prime minister, Betty even joined in the lively Jewish hora as it snaked into the marble hallway. During her Ladyship, there was great press focus on dance as Soviet defector Mikhail Baryshnikov premiered with the American Ballet Theater, and she had New York City Ballet dancers Edward Villella and Violette Verdy perform at the White House. With Mrs. Onassis, Betty Ford served as honorary co-chair of a tribute to Martha Graham in New York, presenting her with a bouquet on stage, later telling reporters, "More than anyone else, she shaped my life."[7]

Even though a local newspaper headline screamed that President Ford had said "Drop Dead!" to New York Mayor Abe Beame's request for federal aid as "the Big Apple" verged on bankruptcy, they loved Betty most in New York. On her first public trip there, she was nearly crushed by an overenthusiastic citizenry and over one hundred journalists. Her WIN remarks on low-cost clothing brought predictable moans from Seventh Avenue, but after spotting designs of Albert Capraro—and liking the price of two-hundred-dollar evening gowns—she chose him as her primary designer. Betty turned over rare silks the president bought for her in the Far East for Capraro to design into her favored Nehru collar gowns.

Mrs. Ford went to New York to accept the Parsons School of Design Award for fashion leadership, chosen by critics who didn't bestow it gratuitously because she was First Lady. A "flattered" Betty reminisced about her own career in the industry, and praised "versatile, practical and expressive" American design. When she awarded a special scholarship fund for fashion students, Betty expressed the belief that the exercise of imagination through fashion illustrated "our individuality, energy and optimism." On her speech card, she scribbled herself a message, "More about Am. fashion just as imp. as European." It wasn't innocuous chat. In the seventies, American designers were reaching higher global prominence, particularly visible with the increase in status "designer labels," on blue jeans, polo shirts, and accessories. This First Lady even made note of the gold jockstrap Halston designed for "Rudi" Nureyev as he danced Graham's new work, Lucifer. It was hard to envision any other First Lady making note of such an item, or even saying she noticed.[8] And yet, curiously enough, dean of the sorority, ninety-year-old Bess Truman, according to her daughter, "liked Betty Ford's forthright style . . . even though it differed from hers."

The elderly woman, equally thrilled about a rock and roll song, "America Needs You, Harry Truman," visited Washington in the Ford years, touring the White House without notice to see Christmas decorations and, at a lunch with old friends, impressed Katie Louchheim with her "unforgettable" old "terse way of putting things." Louchheim kept Bess up to date on the women's movement and sent her an article from Ms. magazine, but publicly there was no word on whether Bess Truman supported the ERA.

As Edith Wilson had felt about Eleanor Roosevelt, Mamie Eisenhower was bewildered by feminism in the Ladyship but personally liked Betty. She received a White House photo inscribed: "To Mamie—A Great First Lady—with great affection to a very dear friend with whom I share many happy memories, Fondly Betty Ford," and the First Lady extended a White House invitation for her birthday, but Mamie was physically unable to make the trip.

Her daughter-in-law said that as Mamie "got older she got much more outspoken." When assigned a woman Secret Service agent, she was heard to tell her, "You should be home taking care of your husband." She was shocked to be the only woman in church with a hat and gloves on anymore. Barbara was "certain Mamie was against ERA," and those who marched for equal rights "were alien people to her." As the former First Lady told a reporter, "I never knew what a woman would want to be liberated from." To writer Nick Thimmesch, Mamie cracked, "I don't know about this Ms. business. . . ." She clearly stated that she felt women should bear children, there was a right "time" to do so, and she felt "sorry" for those who didn't. Yet in an ironic way, by the very definition of what she was doing—publicly speaking her own opinions—Mamie was becoming liberated.

She grew to accept the desires of other women to pursue their own lives. Barbara affectionately recalled that Mamie initially "didn't approve of my going back to school and working, and yet she said, 'Well, I don't know what else you're going to do. . . . I guess it's better than just sitting around . . . all day.'" Tentatively at first, always with the understanding that she was doing so for Ike's memory, Mamie also began to make public speeches at the age of seventy-nine. After a year of reclusive illness, she emerged to speak at an Eisenhower College commencement. In graduation robes and cap, she looked fantastically youthful. Her remarks were witty and sentimental, and the new role of public speaker seemed to suit her well. She playfully winked at photographers, and when presented with the first alumni rocker, sat with her legs crossed in a Dietrich pose, her eyebrows raised in mock surprise.

Barbara was delighted that Mamie was emerging on her own. "She got involved in a lot of organizations—that she'd never done. . . . She seemed to sort of come into her own . . ." Mamie began to speak freely about her early life to Barbara. "She wanted me to know. . . . That she had also once been independent . . . That she too had been her own woman at one time."

In New York, Jacqueline Onassis was an activist for historic preservation. The city's landmark Grand Central Station was being threatened with demolition, and with several other prominent New Yorkers, she made public appearances to halt the wrecker's ball. She told gathered press, "We've heard that it's too late to save this station, but that's not true. Even at the 11th hour you can succeed and I think that's exactly what we'll do." She posed for photographers in front of Grand Central, and led the press conference in its famous Oyster Bar restaurant, where she went around to shake all the hands of eager waiters and cooks.

Shortly after, there was an urgent message from Greece. Onassis had collapsed, and Jackie rushed to his side with a heart specialist. Against the protests of those who wanted him to be kept at home, she insisted that he receive expert medical attention, at the American Hospital in Paris. There, she spent long stretches of time at his bedside, and doctors told her that he appeared to be improving. In the previous months, Caroline had helped film a documentary for television, which was to be aired in several days. Ari felt it was important for Jackie to return to the United States and see the program. Back in New York, she stayed in daily touch with his doctors, assured that his condition remained stable. At week's end, he suddenly contracted pneumonia, and died before she could get back to him.

After his funeral, she personally delivered a statement to the press: "Aristotle Onassis rescued me at a moment when my life was engulfed with shadows. He meant a lot to me. He brought me into a world where one could find both happiness and love. We lived through many beautiful experiences together which cannot be forgotten, and for which I will be eternally grateful." A month later, she returned to Greece to help found a memorial foundation in his name and again spoke with the press, telling them, "My main purpose for coming to Greece, apart from loving the country, is to put into practice the last instructions of my late husband in order to preserve his name."

Jacqueline Onassis had been wanting to return to work for some time, even considering anchoring an NBC special on endangered artifacts of Venice and Angkor Wat. In her first months as a single woman again, she attended the opening of the new International Center for Photography and wrote an unsigned piece about it for *The New Yorker*. That year she joined Viking Press, a publishing house, as an editor. Her employment was symbolic of her evolving consciousness of the women's movement. At a fund-raiser that she co-hosted for Harvard's Schlesinger Library on the History of Women, Kennedy administration ambassador John Kenneth Galbraith spoke of how "women are being treated as people" at the school.

The former First Lady retorted, "When Harvard men say they have graduated from Radcliffe, then we've made it."

For the first time since she was a reporter, Jackie wrote a signed piece. For *Ms.* magazine, she revealed her personal development as a feminist, and she agreed to appear on the issue's cover. With "a sense of adventure," she'd pursued journalism as a means of "having a job and experiencing the world," and if she "hadn't married," she might be somewhat like a friend who began writing about fashion and ended up covering Vietnam. "What has been sad for many women of my generation is that they weren't supposed to work if they had families."

Privately, Mrs. Onassis gave large donations to the *Ms.* Foundation, becoming a lifetime subscriber, and also, according to its founder, Gloria Steinem, donating to "many projects . . . that help women to help themselves." Steinem thought that Jackie's choice to "choose personal work over derived influence . . . may be more helpful to women than the conventional kind of power she has declined." Though she didn't march, Jacqueline Onassis supported the ERA. She was not the only one.[9]

When Betty Ford and her husband went to China later in the year, they were welcomed by a contingent including Barbara Bush and her husband, who'd been made the new representative to the republic. Moderate Republicans who loyally supported the president, both George and Barbara Bush supported the ERA. Barbara admired Betty, saying it "was easy" hosting her about Peking "because Betty Ford and I are friends, and because she is an undemanding and nice lady." For herself, China was liberating. With children grown, she had time for herself, and flourished. Precisely as Lou Hoover had done, Barbara bicycled about Peking, recording historical and artistic wonders with her camera.[10]

That year, Mrs. Ford made several international trips with the president, one to Belgium, Spain, Austria, and Italy, another to Romania, Poland, and Yugoslavia. On the China trip, she also went to the Philippines, proving a powerful match for its tenacious "First Lady," Imelda Marcos. Imelda insisted on taking her counterpart by copter to a far-off mountaintop to see monuments. Betty had neither the time nor energy to go. Mrs. Marcos insisted. Finally, Betty suggested they walk. They didn't go to the mountaintop.[11]

If she could keep up with Imelda, she could also disarm mighty egos. Pragmatic and often cynical Henry Kissinger had continued in his visible role as secretary of state, but he fell under Betty Ford's spell. As he conferred with the president one night in the family quarters, the First Lady, in slippers and robe, prepared coffee and tea for them in the kitchen but felt "electricity in the air." The *Mayagüez*, an American container ship, with thirty-nine crew members, had been seized by a gunboat crew from the new Communist government in Cambodia while sailing to Thailand. The president determined to prove that the United States wouldn't tolerate such "piracy," but after diplomacy went unanswered, he ordered the marines to take back the vessel.

Mrs. Ford believed that the Ladyship had changed drastically in the previous decade, and a First Lady now had to "study and remain aware of the world situation." Betty complemented Ford's policies with her own grace, and by the spring of 1975, that touched new Americans. Tens of thousands of them.[12]

As the news broke of South Vietnam's surrender to the Communist North, and the taking of Saigon, the First Lady was with the president in the family quarters discussing the unfolding events with others. It was a poignant moment, and when Ford mentioned the two young marine guards who were killed during the last of the airlifts, the First Lady gently but persistently suggested, "You should write notes to their parents." On April 24, the evacuation of thousands of South Vietnamese had begun, and White House photographer David Kennerly, who'd been given permission to travel there to record the airlift, reported the scenes of horror to the First Lady. She was "furious" at the mistreatment and "worried about getting people out." As she read an account of an American journalist's rescue of his Vietnamese family at the time, she phoned him to say she found his story moving, but also of political importance.

Betty became increasingly worried about the planeloads of orphans en route to the United States and thousands of adoptive American parents. The first plane had crashed, killing two hundred. With the president, she flew to San Francisco to welcome the arriving, confused Vietnamese orphans. For Betty, who even seriously considered adopting one of the refugees, it was particularly heart-wrenching since her chemotherapy treatments reduced immunity to any disease the children might be carrying, and she was prohibited from holding them. Mrs. Ford was ordered to remain behind a glass viewing area. [13]

In the midst of this, the first East Wing scandal in the First Ladyship's history rocked Washington.

Columnist Maxine Cheshire learned that Nancy Howe and her husband, Jimmy, had illegally accepted a free vacation from Korean lobbyist Tongsun Park. When Jimmy Howe discovered that Cheshire was about to publish the story, he shot himself in the head. Mrs. Howe was asked to leave the East Wing due to mental distress. [14]

Meanwhile, by mid-May, about 20,000 of the 127,000 Indochinese refugees who had managed to escape to U.S. safe havens were processed through immigration, free to seek housing and employment where they could. It was Betty Ford who eloquently assured them:

". . . many of you are troubled, and you wonder what lies ahead for you . . . America offers you the same opportunities that it has offered countless generations of immigrants—our welcome is genuine, and our intentions are sincere. I know that you have experienced great hardship, and that your situation here is not ideal. But this is only a temporary situation which, when resolved, will allow you to realize a new life . . . and a promising future for your children and your children's children." She reassured them that many Americans retained cultural traditions, quoted "a lovely Vietnamese proverb," and concluded, "I know you have the industry, the strength and the courage to seize that opportunity. I want to extend to you, on behalf of all American immigrants, as we are all immigrants, a warm, heartfelt welcome." [15]

The articulate voice of Betty Ford was again about to resound through the nation. If the First Lady sparked laughter with a cameo appearance on the television comedy *The Mary Tyler Moore Show*, she would drop jaws on *60 Minutes*. CBS promised it would be "an unusual interview with an unusual woman . . . completely frank as she discusses her attitudes toward her role . . ."

Mrs. Ford said interviewer Morley Safer's questions caught her "off

balance," but since they were taping, she felt she had to answer them. She responded with personal views, emphasizing that they weren't necessarily the administration's, and that she "wasn't forcing my opinions on anybody. . . ."

She expounded on past revelations, speaking of seeing a psychiatrist, and on the Supreme Court *Roe* v. *Wade* judgment, the First Lady said it was "the best thing in the world . . . a great, great decision," helping to take abortion "out of the backwoods and put it in the hospitals where it belongs." She thought smoking marijuana had become as routine for youth as the "first beer" had been for her generation. The one answer of Mrs. Ford's that would spin the nation's TV antennae, however, was not a view she'd previously expressed. When asked about whether it was immoral for young people to live together before marriage, she retorted, "Well, they are, aren't they?" She thought it might even limit the high divorce rate. Then Safer followed up with "the question."

"What if Susan Ford came to you and said, 'Mother, I'm having an affair?'"

For a brief second, Betty was silent, then calmly replied, "Well, I wouldn't be surprised . . . she's a perfectly normal human being . . . if she wanted to continue . . . I would certainly counsel and advise her on the subject. . . ."

The Sunday night it aired, August 21, was during vacation season for most of Middle America. In journalism it was the deadly season of slow news. The majority of Americans were *not* watching 60 *Minutes*. Consequently, they learned of it the next day in newspapers' headlines, with sensational implications. The phones in the East Wing began ringing and didn't stop. The Fords *had* tuned in. At one point, Jerry jokingly threw a pillow at her.

Ford said he had "no illusions as to what the reaction to her remarks would be," and was "proud" of Betty's honesty, but 60 *Minutes* had blurred the line between private person and public persona. Betty responded in the context of the former when she was in the context of the latter. It hit another Puritanical nerve.

The Los Angeles Police Department took issue with her views, a Texas minister called it "gutter type mentality," and Betty Ford became the first First Lady since Frances Cleveland to be censured by the Women's Christian Temperance Union. Billy Graham said if his daughter were having an affair, he'd cry. The chairman of the Quakers telegraphed Ford: "We . . . deplore the views . . . contrary to . . . chastity outside the marriage. . . ." The right wing was most scalding. William Loeb, editor of the *Manchester Union-Leader*, wrote that "The immorality of Mrs. Ford's remarks is almost exceeded by their stupidity . . . a disgusting spectacle. Coming from the First Lady in the White House, it disgraces the nation itself. . . . As President of the United States, he [President Ford] should be the moral leader of the nation. He is not in a position of any ordinary husband making the best of his wife's foolish and stupid remarks. . . . He should repudiate what Mrs. Ford said." One citizen wrote Betty was "no lady—first, second or last," another suggested she "resign" as First Lady.

When Rosalynn Carter was asked the same question as Betty had been, she piped up, "I would be shocked. But, of course, my daughter is only eight years old." Journalist Jules Witcover believed that ". . . conservatives tend to be moralists, so there is no telling what Betty Ford's frankness had cost her husband in his continuing effort to appease them, and for that matter to court the electorate at large as the nation's first unelected President." Ford initially cracked that he lost 10 million votes because of 60 *Minutes*. As the negative mail continued, he wanly joshed that it was 20 million.

When the White House released figures on the unfavorable reaction, however, an avalanche of Betty's supporters responded. One wrote that Betty kept "abreast of these changing times . . . [was] flexible & . . . aware that what was once considered right and proper changes from generation to generation." One thought it "refreshing to hear some frank, positive answers instead of wishy-washy dodging of issues . . . the negative response is disgusting. . . ." The "Last of the Puritans" said she wasn't sure she agreed with Betty, but she was "deeply grateful that we have someone in the White House who thinks integrity is more important than political advantage."

When a Dallas housewife wrote to Mrs. Ford about how the press had twisted the 60 *Minutes* comments, the First Lady wrote back to her. The woman sent a copy of Mrs. Ford's letter to the AP: ". . . I consider myself a responsible parent . . . in a home that believes in and practices the enduring values of morality and personal integrity . . . these are not easy times to be a parent. Our convictions are continually being questioned and tested by fads and fancies of the moment. I want my children to know that their concerns . . . whatever they may be, can be discussed. . . . I do not believe in premarital relations, but I realize that many in today's generation do not share my views . . . It is difficult to adequately express one's personal convictions in a fifteen-minute interview." From the AP, the letter proliferated across local newspapers, and the tide swelled for Betty Ford.[16]

Within months after 60 *Minutes*, Betty's 50 percent Harris poll approval rating jumped to 75 percent, noting that older, southern, and rural Americans disapproved most. After the poll, a cartoon hung in the East Wing which jested that the president could win an election if he didn't have to run against the First Lady.

Mrs. Ford believed that "being able to relate to the public—whether it's male or female—as just an ordinary person," was the reason for her surging popularity. She thought the public saw her as an "open woman who had a lot of concern for other women in her particular era, whether it was with women's rights, or cancer . . . arthritis . . . Different people know me for different reasons." Jack Ford assessed that "[s]ince the things she touched on affected people's lives directly, she had more impact in some areas than my father. . . . She was a strong modern role model for women her age and of similar backgrounds throughout the country." Betty related to both professional and traditional women. One woman's magazine editor thought Mrs. Ford "couldn't be a better example for American women," and Nancy Dickerson wrote that year, "It is not too much to say that Betty Ford single-handedly triggered a national dialogue on the changing morals of the emerging generation."[17]

As Mamie had been in the fifties, Betty had become a symbol of the seventies, also attuned to pop culture. From her new wardrobe, she wore "avocado," "lilac," and "rust," popular colors of the era. She relaxed in slack suits, and had her own "mood ring," which changed colors according to emotions. Though skipping the hit film *Jaws*, because "sharks eating people never appealed to me," she most enjoyed the dance craze of disco. Before rehearsing a soft-shoe number for her performance at the annual Gridiron Dinner, the First Lady had one request of her dance teacher. "Could you show me how to hustle?" And then, in jumpsuit, the First Lady did the hustle.[18]

When events affected her with dramatic personal impact, Betty Ford addressed the larger picture. After two assassination attempts on the president's life that September, the First Lady reaffirmed her belief that "there should be gun control. I never thought guns were something people should casually have around."

Mrs. Ford said she was a "fatalist," but it was her health that became a factor in Ford's greatest decision that fall of 1975. Even as vice president, he'd told reporters that he'd taken a "blood oath" to Betty that he would retire in 1977. Only after her one-year tests had proven that she was clear of cancer did the president decide to run for election in '76. The First Lady affirmed to Helen Thomas, "I want him to run. He couldn't be running unless I wanted him to."[19]

Rosalynn Carter, however, had been "running" for a full eighteen months, planting and cultivating grass-roots support. She lost her wig in Boston, danced in a Maine Knights of Columbus hall, attempted to slice a hard peanut cake in Texas, and washed her own clothes in Hollywood. When local reporters didn't know what to ask, she discussed Carter's stand on the issues. Rosalynn developed rules: Insist on news-section coverage, not the "women's page"; head toward radio station antennae; stop at courthouses to learn local political information; stay in the homes of private-citizen supporters, and learn the issues that most bother them.

To reach more people, Rosalynn kept a schedule apart from Jimmy. In one town, she made twelve speeches. After a late night New Hampshire reception, she slept for two hours, drove to Massachusetts, then flew to both Carolinas for press conferences. She covered twenty-three cities in three-and-a-half days. She focused on the black vote, speaking at black churches, dining at restaurants, and staying in hotels run by blacks in black areas. She went into ghettos, "a living refutation of the myth that Southern white ladies don't dare venture into black neighborhoods," wrote reporter Howard Norton, who covered her. He also noted the "rednecks" who hooted "nigger-lover" at her.

Besides discussing issues important to her—mental health, the elderly, prison reform—she also learned about those likely to confront Jimmy. If someone questioned what Carter would do as president on any number of issues, she'd call him to get the facts. She learned to make a patent "stump speech," "twist the questions to make the points I wanted to," and intelligently discuss the economy, Congress, trade, and global issues. When in Georgia, Rosalynn was on the phone raising funds from individuals in local communities. As she spoke of how "we" can win "our" campaign, Rosalynn Carter was doing something no campaign wife had done so strenuously and blatantly since Florence Harding. She was unabashedly running for First Lady, unequivocally, unembarrassedly viewing it as a full-time job. "It wouldn't devastate me to lose. . . . But we are in this to win."

Also emulating Florence Harding, Nancy Reagan consulted her astrologer, Carroll Righter, at his Hollywood mansion. When Righter told her that '76 wasn't her husband's moment for the presidency, his aide claimed that Nancy "didn't like what she was hearing. . . ." As Jules Witcover chronicled, Mrs. Reagan, "painted in some quarters as a kind of West Coast Dragon Lady," was protective of Ronnie and "didn't want him to make a fool of himself, but she was quickly convinced he had a serious chance and was generally supportive thereafter." In April '75, during their Easter stay in Palm Springs, Betty Ford and her husband had met with the Reagans. Though the meeting was polite, it was clear to the Fords that the Reagans were running in '76. Sheila Weidenfeld claimed that Mrs. Ford found Nancy to be a "queen bee," and "cold fish."

After an introduction by Merv Griffin, Nancy Reagan had hooked up with astrologer Joan Quigley, who told her she hadn't seen "so superior a stellium" since examining Jacqueline Kennedy's charts. By 1976, Joan had determined that Nancy's charts showed "she was destined to be world famous." About once a year, Nancy called Joan for her reading.

Nancy called a family conference to confirm that Reagan was going to run. Michael said her "goal" was "orchestrating the appearance of a solid family unit . . ." Several months later, when he was married, both of Reagan's wives attended, and there was a momentary uncertainty when the groom's "parents" were summoned for a group picture. Jane Wyman said to Nancy, "Don't worry about a thing. Ron and I have had our pictures taken together before. If you'd like to join us, fine." Nancy gamely joined Jane.

Mrs. Reagan was careful to maintain a proper image. She'd attracted vicarious but unwanted publicity when her best friend, Betsy Bloomingdale, had pleaded guilty to the felony of altering importation invoices for two Dior gowns from France. Mrs. Reagan remained staunchly loyal to Mrs. Bloomingdale, and in return Betsy would keep a low profile at the convention. Mrs. Reagan felt that the impression created by her husband's single secretary, Helene von Damm, traveling with him alone could easily be misinterpreted. Von Damm stopped doing so. She admitted to being "the tough guy" on limiting Ronnie's campaign schedule. Campaigning reminded Nancy "of being on location for a movie," but she expressed jealousy of Betty Ford's campaign traveling perks as the incumbent First Lady.

Nancy Reagan claimed, "I don't think in terms of being First Lady," but admitted, "Nobody believes me." Weeks after Betty Ford's 60 Minutes appearance, she told the Grosse Point, Michigan, Republican Women's Club that she deplored "the new morality," and without mentioning Betty by name, made it clear that she thought First Ladies shouldn't answer "unseemly questions." She was "appalled" at the 60

Minutes interview, even though her own unmarried daughter was now, in fact, living with a man. On the need of one to consult a psychiatrist, Nancy said it "means that you yourself are not really trying to get hold of yourself. . . . It's sloughing off your own responsibilities." On abortion, she carefully differentiated her personal feelings from her political ones, saying, "I can't get past the point where I realize that you're taking a life," but came short of being anti-abortion, instead terming the *Roe* v. *Wade* decision "government interference." Once, quickly, Nancy did qualify that she might find abortion acceptable when "the mother's life is in danger." She opposed Mrs. Ford on ERA, stating it wasn't "the best way" to attain equal rights, and called it "ridiculous." She disliked the term "Ms." and women wearing pants because "a woman should look like a woman," admitting that her anti-ERA stance "just maybe" had influenced Ronnie to change his view and agree with her. Nancy's perspective was clear. "I will never understand why people feel a need to go on television talk shows to confess private problems."

Time magazine quoted Mrs. Ford as saying that she thought it paradoxical that Nancy Reagan had herself enjoyed a professional career, and yet was so vehemently anti-ERA.[20]

There was speculation another woman would reenter politics, on her own. In early 1976, rumors spread that Jacqueline Onassis would run for the U.S. Senate from New York, a fable of which she disposed drolly, "I'd win, of course." Jackie was fulfilled in the profession of *her* choice. She left Viking Press and joined Doubleday, where she bought a novel, *Call the Darkness Light*, which focused on the hardships of women working in nineteenth-century textile mills. While still at Viking, she had edited a book on the Russian culture—for which she herself did research at the New York Public Library and traveled to the Soviet Union. Even there, she was instantly recognized.

She flew to Los Angeles to help Rosey Grier in his efforts on behalf of ghetto youths. "I'll do what I can to help you," she told him. Jackie drove and walked through Watts, visited several black families in their homes, dropped in unannounced on a community center, and stood on a street corner talking with teenagers. Her appearances in Washington were rare, but in January 1976 Jacqueline Onassis joined Betty Ford and her husband in the presidential box for a Bicentennial gala at the Kennedy Center. They hadn't seen each other since 1963. When the former First Lady came into view, the audience broke into spontaneous applause. One newspaper headlined the story: STILL VERY MUCH A FIRST LADY. The Bushes were there, and Barbara, enchanted to glimpse Jackie, elbowed a friend next to her. "Let's not be stuffed shirts, this is exciting! Isn't she beautiful?"

After the White House had announced the firing of some high-level staff and Cabinet members, George Bush had been called back from

China to replace William Colby as director of the CIA. Democrats successfully pressured Ford into promising that if they confirmed Bush at the CIA, he wouldn't later be made a vice presidential running mate. Ford acquiesced. For Barbara, the changes were hard. Because of the classified nature of George's work, he no could longer share it with her. Mrs. Bush would "confess" that in the mid-seventies, "I went through a difficult time, really, because suddenly women's lib had made me feel my life had been wasted." She felt "inadequate," and later admitted to suffering from depression, thinking, "Here's George working with all these wonderful women, and they're doing all these exciting things." She admitted to being "jealous" of the "young women" of the era who had both career and family. She would not sit home for long.

Described as a "tough" tennis player who "loves to win," Barbara developed an additional skill. This woman had shaken with fear two decades before when asked to speak before the Houston Garden Club. Now, she organized her slides of China, developed a lecture, and began touring the nation, raising money for her local Houston church, where she'd once taught.

At the White House, when Betty Ford addressed the Republican Women's Federal Forum, which she'd helped form in late 1973, she named Barbara Bush as one of her co-founders. The forum, Betty said, "can and should become a permanent fixture" giving ". . . Republican wives and career women in every phase of government and politics . . . a chance to get together, to exchange ideas and to keep informed in a pleasant, social setting. . . ." She believed the group vital to organizing women "from the legislature, the Executive Branch, and the national party structure," adding that "the percentage of registered voters is 53% women as to 47% men—so you realize how important we are as a group—fortunately men are beginning to . . ."

As 1976 opened, Betty Ford carried this message to all spheres. With more educational and employment opportunities, she said, women were making "more interesting wives" as well as "more interesting businesspersons."[21] She thanked administration "spouses" gathered for a political briefing for their "patience and understanding of the demands of your spouses' jobs [which] keep this Administration going," welcomed them at a briefing on the '77 budget and the president's State of the Union Address, briefings which were organized so that wives— and several husbands—could answer authoritively when asked. She attended an ERAmerica concert of the "minstrel of the women's movement," Helen Reddy, performing her ERA rallying theme song, "I Am Woman." Reddy said Betty was her inspirational "booking agent" for holding two local concerts. To the bipartisan National Association of Commissions for Women, Betty commented, "By now I guess no one wonders where I stand on women's issues. At least, no one's complained lately about my being shy on the subject. . . ."

In every aspect of her role, Betty Ford emphasized women. She used her "job" of mother to begin conversations with women of all walks of life. In the goodwill role, she accepted honorary presidency of the National Lupus Foundation because it is a disease that strikes women. On national television, she was honored at the annual "Women of the Year" awards, recipient of the Inspirational Leadership trophy. And though she turned down the offer because of her fear of flying, even feminist octogenarian Mae West was invited to the Ford White House for a state dinner.

By 1976, the ERA had been endorsed by over one hundred national political organizations, supported by all presidents since Eisenhower, and ratified by thirty-four of the thirty-eight states necessary for it to become the Twenty-seventh Amendment to the Constitution. The deadline for legislative action was March 22, 1979. Betty Ford, regardless of the expediency of avoiding agitation of the right wing during the primaries, remained Betty Ford, spanning the progressive to the traditional. One of her briefing papers well illustrated that span. An East Wing staff member drew a cartoon of the First Lady waving an "ERA Today" flag. And suggested that she "read under the hair dryer."[22]

16

"Remember the Ladies!"

WHEN CHIEF OF STAFF Donald Rumsfeld compiled a list of expendable staff that could reduce salaried positions by 10 percent, he came to tell the president that some of the East Wing staff could be cut, and asked him to broach it with the First Lady. "Oh no," said Ford, "I'm not going to do that. You are chief of staff. This is *your* plan. You go up and settle it with her." Ford observed that "the East Wing staff hardly changed at all."

Sheila Weidenfeld felt that Rumsfeld and nearly all of the male West Wing staff viewed a potent Ladyship as only a noxious liability to the presidency, and a First Lady was only "a follower" to be treated with "kindness and condescension" as the "quintessential political wife." The war between the wings was calmer than it had been under the Nixons, but according to several women, there was a surprising degree of sexism from the men who worked for Betty Ford's husband. Darlene Schmalzried, one of those who prepared the daily news summary, resigned because she was paid less than her male counterpart.

Weidenfeld had trouble getting wire-service machines for her press office and claimed that a plan to have Mrs. Ford testify before Senate committee hearings on cancer was stopped by one of the president's domestic council members. Nancy Dickerson said that many in the "male-chauvinist stronghold" considered Betty a dangerous "albatross." When a presidential adviser heard that an aide had routed an issue briefing paper to the First Lady for a speech she was to deliver, he quickly retrieved it, "on the theory that the less she knew, the better."

Mrs. Ford, in an interview, stated that she didn't "always jibe" with her husband's longtime aide, now chief assistant, Robert Hartmann. Her "resentment" likely stemmed "from his trying to run my husband's life . . . I feel he oversteps his boundaries." For one staffer, she bought a joke "male chauvinist pig" necktie. When she felt the West Wing infringed on her role, the First Lady intervened. During the planning stage of Queen Elizabeth's visit, as the State Department and West Wing mapped out a schedule, Mrs. Ford telephoned the president's National Security Council chief, Brent Scowcroft. "General, I want this visit to be completely handled by my staff." It was.

Regardless of how some in the West Wing might view the issue, none attempted to stop Mrs. Ford's ERA lobbying, and only one had casually asked if it might be an intrusion on state's rights. Grudgingly or not, they realized that she was a campaign asset.[1]

Initially, she taped radio spots for New Hampshire, but hadn't planned to campaign solo. As Ford's campaigning was confined to weekends, however, she recalled that "I had to go." Delivering "a major policy speech" was not her "long suit," and she feared that she'd not be "a good politician" because she usually ended up saying "what was on my mind, and that could cost my husband votes." She would swing with dancing senior citizens and fish fry with fifteen thousand, but during the primaries Betty Ford avoided the Bible Belt.

Quickly, she overcame her hesitancy in discussing issues. After speaking in New York, she flew to Iowa to take the president's place—he had to deal with the crisis in Lebanon—in courting delegates, making handwritten changes on her speech cards to emphasize her partnership: "And we are a team. So when he couldn't come, I asked to come." That same day, she spoke at a tribute to Mary Louise Smith, chairman of the Republican National Committee, appealing to conservatives: "Our differences—which are part of the political process—will not divide us, because of the strength of our common political faith." At an earlier fried-chicken picnic, sitting across the platform from Betty Ford was Nancy Reagan.

Betty wasn't worried about Reagan's jump in the polls, attributing it to media coverage because of his sudden announcement that he had decided to run. When a fight with Reagan became apparent, however, the First Lady began telephoning all the women delegates and alternates of the crucial Mississippi delegation, making detailed notes on each individual, how they were committing, what issues concerned them, and if they'd support Ford.[2]

In New Hampshire, Nancy Reagan trooped alongside Ronnie, listening to speeches and shaking hands. During the primaries, she noted that besides "big government and individual freedom, high taxes, inflation, recession," an issue most often raised with her was "the breakdown in family and morals. . . ." In taped memoirs she made some time later, Nancy said she couldn't "accept as admirable a modern morality that makes permissible almost any act" that threatened her list of the most important elements of life, including "selflessness," honesty," "sincerity," and "the concept that it is better to give than to receive." To her these were "ideals" that "have endured because they are right. . . ." Without "the marriage contract," she thought cohabitating was "playing house." She compared America's "new morality" to Babylon and the decline of the Roman Empire. Her most genuine concern, begun in the sixties, continued to occupy her thoughts, and she worried about "drug pushers in the school playgrounds." Nancy wasn't judgmental in her view of young users, recognizing them as victims of older pushers. She also acknowledged the abuse of alcohol by her generation, but hesitated to equate it with marijuana because she believed the medical reports that said the drug had a cumulative and more permanent effect. She did not come by such opinions casually, but studied briefings and weighed the findings. Mrs. Reagan practiced what she preached, never drinking much, and she abruptly quit cigarette smoking when her friend Robert Taylor died of lung cancer.

Mrs. Reagan also worried about contemporary film themes, believing that "pointless violence" in films encouraged "unbalanced people" to imitate what they saw, but named *Patton* as a film that put violence "into perspective." She complained that most seventies films were "wrong," "trash," and "unhealthy," and that "explicit sex . . . and crude language appeal only to our lowest instincts," were "not a pretty sight," and "degraded" the American family. And finally, she declared that going to the movies cost too much.[3]

Meanwhile, Carter was emerging as Democratic front-runner, winning New Hampshire, Florida, Illinois, Pennsylvania, and North Carolina; and it had been Rosalynn who'd urged him "to enter *all* the primaries." Illustrative of her influence, she convinced her husband to make an unscheduled flight to appear in Rhode Island and South Dakota. They limited the loss in the former and won the latter. The Carters headed to the New York convention as winners.[4]

If Nancy and Rosalynn echoed their husbands' stands on the issues, Betty was combining her husband's with her own.

To the National Federation of Republican Women, she pointed out that the number of women delegates had increased from '72. In her prepared speech before a grass-roots Republican group, a past male president was acknowledged, but Mrs. Ford scribbled in the name of its newly elected leader, a woman. In another speech, she emphasized unity "despite our different backgrounds and ages." At the GOP Women's Federation, the First Lady mentioned that she was seated between the national party chairperson and the HUD secretary, "and both of them women!" At the New York Republican State Committee Convention's "Salute to Women," Betty emphasized: "The spirited and talented women I've met during my travels have truly been an inspiration. My own commitment to equal rights has been reinforced. . . . Increased visibility and attention to the accomplishments of women are so important for young people, who often pattern their lives after a person of achievement . . . it's wonderful to see women succeeding at many different jobs from policewoman to diplomat."[5]

On the trail, she was on a roll, but Mrs. Ford admitted to being "on a shorter string" because she frequently became tired. Constant travel exacerbated her arthritis and pinched nerve, but her staff and the press didn't realize the extent of her pain. She suffered in silence, even with her family. While her doctors continued to medicate her, however, Betty Ford consciously avoided any alcohol for fear of falling asleep, particularly on exhausting trips. She was sensitive to alcohol's effects, telling her daughter that "when you drink, you lose control."[6]

As she barnstormed America, Betty Ford visited two of her Democratic predecessors. The Fords made a special effort to see Bess Truman in Independence, where the president dedicated a statue. Betty recalled, "Imagine, she apologized for not answering the door personally. What a stoic woman. I've always been a Harry-and-Bess fan. . . . When Jerry got the Vice-Presidential nomination, she told me she let out a shriek of joy." In April, in Austin, Texas, at the LBJ Library, Betty Ford was literally greeted with open arms by an old friend, Lady Bird Johnson.

Mamie "liked Ford and supported him," recalled her grandson. "It went far back . . . But when she was out in California she would avoid getting involved in any of that feud between the Ford people and the Reagan people."[7] She didn't publicly campaign, but she did make a public appearance in 1976. Along with Nick Thimmesch, on her sixtieth wedding anniversary, as the Bicentennial Freedom Train headed toward Gettysburg from York, the former First Lady boarded the traveling museum. She looked thin in her pink fifties dress, the only one in gloves and hat that steamy day. Besides her white earrings and red-white-and-blue neck scarf, she wore a large jeweled American flag pin. "Patriotism isn't dead," she said, smiling. Along the train's route, people waited to see her, and she was delightedly caught off guard. Mamie mused on how airplanes had replaced trains for distance travel, believed Americans overemphasized money, and proudly revealed, "I'm still wearing the same clothes I had . . . in the White House" because of high cost and unappealing fashions. She hesitated to give advice to the "new generation," because it "might not work today." As the train slowed into the station, she reflected on her relationship with Ike— "you never really know a person; you only understand them. Nobody knows anybody's inner thoughts."[8]

Betty Ford had developed an eager interest in her predecessors. She had a collection of Julia Grant's and Frances Cleveland's menus, hoping to "duplicate [them] completely," on historic anniversaries. When she was presented with a book of First Lady biographical sketches, published as part of the series begun by Mrs. Kennedy for the White House Historical Association, Betty called it "the day equal opportunity came to our guide books," and offered "I suspect we have had a good deal more in common than not." In the State Dining Room, she was surrounded by portraits of Dolley, Eleanor, Bess, Mamie, Jackie, and Lady Bird, and a table with Jane Pierce's book, a letter written by Mary

Lincoln, a watercolor painted by Carrie Harrison, and Margaret Taylor's pin.

In a unique Bicentennial event, First Ladies were linked again. In Plymouth, on June 29, First Lady Ford opened the exhibit, "Remember the Ladies: Women in America, 1750–1815," the title of which was taken from Abigail Adams's famous letter to her husband. The book accompanying the exhibit had been acquired for Viking Press by Jacqueline Onassis, who also served as an individual sponsor of the show. In white knit dress, the First Lady told the crowds, "I look forward to the day when the wish of Abigail Adams is answered . . . this exhibit is dedicated to those neglected Americans . . . those forgotten ladies . . . who should give us the strength and courage . . . to seek equal rights . . . for women today. . . ." The "Woman's Coalition for a Third Century" presented her with their "Declaration of Interdependence," while a small group of anti-ERA hecklers tried to shout her down. However, about one thousand supporters cheered her with "ERA all the way," and drowned out the protesters. The exhibit had a section focusing on First Ladies Washington, Adams, and Madison, featuring Dolley's red velvet gown, but Mount Vernon wouldn't lend Martha's bathing suit.

Betty Ford made references to her own place in history when presenting her Frankie Welch gown to the Smithsonian: "When I brought visitors to this hall, never in my wildest dreams did I expect to ever be here myself. . . . But let's face it, I can't help but be thrilled . . . to become part of an Institution." The director pointed out, "As bicentennial visitors pour into the Museum . . . the exhibit to which they most often ask to be directed is the First Ladies."[9]

Others of the sorority were celebrating the national birthday. On July 3, Pat Nixon attended a Bicentennial party held in honor of her and Dick, signing autographs and greeting old friends until one in the morning. During the primaries, the Nixons made a return tour of China on the anniversary of their first trip. When pro-Nixon articles and essays began to appear, the former First Lady remained unimpressed: "What's the use? It isn't going to change anything." Then *The Final Days* came out, portraying Mrs. Nixon as an alcoholic. She managed to get hold of a copy of the book from one of Nixon's secretaries, and overriding her husband's admonishings, began reading it.

The Bicentennial saw Lady Bird Johnson making her stage debut in North Dakota and Canada, reading historical passages to the music of Copeland and Schuman. She continued fund-raising for the LBJ Memorial Grove, and with Betty Ford attended the Broadway opening of *1600 Pennsylvania Avenue*, which focused on characters as forgotten as Elizabeth Monroe and Eliza Johnson, among others. On July 6, Mrs. Johnson came to Washington, one of the select guests invited to the state dinner for Queen Elizabeth.

That afternoon, Pat Nixon was so exhausted she could barely stand.

She stumbled a bit, changing into her bathing suit, but sat on the pool's shallow steps. At dinner she was quiet, and ate little, retiring early.

As the sun set in Washington, the guests, including Alice Longworth, began arriving at the White House, for the white-tie dinner. In California, Julie Eisenhower wanted her mother to join her in watching it on television, but in her darkened bedroom the former First Lady was asleep in her clothes. Julie assumed she was just tired. The next morning, Pat had trouble opening a coffee can. Her husband noticed that the left side of her mouth was drooping and her speech was slurred. Without alarm, he awoke his daughter. "I think your mommy's had a stroke." Pat agreed to go to a hospital, but insisted on packing her own suitcase.

At Long Beach Memorial Hospital, doctors confirmed her stroke and reported that Pat was "in the life-threatening phase"; they admitted that if it didn't "get any worse, she's not going to die," but one doctor was in awe of her grit. "Mrs. Nixon is amazing. . . . Some people in this condition become very despondent. They feel life is all over, they give up the fight. There is none of that here." He also revealed, "Everything is related to stress," and that she'd never had hypertension or blood-pressure problems. Nixon told reporters that "she's going to see this through. She's a fighter. . . ." They'd weathered much together, and when one sank dangerously, the other fought to lift the weaker. When asked if her reading *The Final Days* precipitated the stroke, the former president stated, "All I say is Mrs. Nixon read it and her stroke came three days later . . . the doctors don't know what caused the stroke, but it sure didn't help. . . . I will never forgive them. Never."

Meanwhile, at the New York Democratic Convention, the "nominee" for First Lady, Rosalynn Carter, met a former First Lady. Jacqueline Onassis sat enthralled at her first convention since 1956, saying she not only approved of, but supported, Carter as the Democratic nominee. With Mrs. Carter were her longtime friend and personal assistant Madeline MacBean, and press secretary Mary Hoyt, a journalist who'd served Eleanor McGovern in the same capacity. Asked what she thought of Betty Ford, the nominee's wife said, "She's going to be a hard act to follow." When debate had ensued over Carter's possible running mate, Mrs. Carter focused on what sort of wife that man should have; "I want someone I can call on to help me with the things I'm planning to do if *I* get in for president." If she noticed her misstatement, she didn't say so. Walter Mondale was chosen, but not before Mrs. Carter inquired about his wife.

Meanwhile, as Betty and Nancy prepared for the Kansas City Republican Convention, Pat Nixon was making what doctors called "nothing short of an amazing fight to recover." From New York taxi drivers to young Illinois Democrats, six thousand letters and telegrams poured in each day for her, eventually totaling a quarter of a million. She began physical therapy, and wouldn't permit even her daughters to see her struggle until she realized how much they needed to know that she was progressing. Nixon told reporters, "The determination and fire in her eyes I've seen so often in difficult times in the past is coming back . . ." When she left the hospital, pushed in a wheelchair by her husband, about fifty members of the staff were out front to cheer her on. The press was there, too, and she smiled broadly at them. "I feel fine but I'm a little frightened about the driver." As she was wheeled near the car, Pat Nixon got up and walked a few steps.[10]

Absent from her first convention since 1952, Pat Nixon was not mentioned by Republicans at Kansas City. Focus remained on Betty and Nancy. On the trail, when they'd frequently run into each other, they were polite. Jack Ford pointed out that his mother never had "personal differences" with Mrs. Reagan, it was "just political tension." Mrs. Ford thought the media focused on them "as though she and I . . . were the contestants." Betty was already on the convention floor when the band struck up Tony Orlando's theme song and Susan urged her and Orlando to dance as they headed into their box. She had no idea that at the same moment Nancy Reagan was making her entrance across the vast hall, timed carefully for press coverage. When Betty was accused of stealing Nancy's "play," the former said, "My feeling was that Nancy didn't want to play. She sat in a glassed-in box, separate from the hurly-burly of the whole convention, except for the time she went upstairs to the television booth to be interviewed."

Nancy felt that the "self-conscious" "friction" between her and Betty was a "contest of the queens," spurred by their individual staffs repeating things "that weren't necessarily true" about one to the other. She said their relationship had never extended "very far," and that they were two "different people" from "different worlds."

Nancy was troubled by the "inconsistency" of the national party's "limited" support of Reagan's campaign, and "regretted" that she'd been assigned an enclosed viewing box, but felt that the press had treated them fairly. Regardless of staff attempts to isolate Maureen and Michael, Nancy invited them along with her two children to a family dinner the night Ford won the nomination. She poured champagne for them all, and with her voice cracking, toasted Reagan. Michael was particularly touched that after all the turmoil they'd been through, Nancy would invite Jane Wyman's children and warmly open up to them. She then emboldened them to enter the convention hall "with our heads up." Her husband hugged and kissed her: "I love you, too, Mommy."

It was a joyous week for the First Lady. Earlier in the week, Betty

Ford had danced the disco number "the bump" with Tony Orlando on stage.

When ninety-one-year-old Bess Truman heard the news of Ford's nomination the next morning, she told Betty Ford, "I let out such a whoop and holler that my maid came running in to find out what was wrong with me." As the president rehearsed his acceptance speech, Betty offered that it was "much too long," and influenced him to edit it. She judged his delivery and, as he recalled, "criticized my tendency not to smile when I was on TV. . . . As usual, she was right." Betty also wanted him to choose a woman as vice presidential candidate, admitting, "Everyone knew I was working on him in that direction." Mrs. Ford strongly advocated ambassador Anne Armstrong. She was on the president's short list, and he "came close. Very close" to choosing her, indicating, in retrospect, that he should have. If Ford had had his first choice, Barbara Bush and Betty Ford would be sharing the "ticket." Several times on the night he chose his running mate, Ford "wished George Bush had been available." Though Vice President Nelson Rockefeller had removed himself, Betty preferred him and was "surprised" by Ford's choice of Senator Bob Dole.

The Doles, Fords, and Reagans smiled together on the platform the final night. As Reagan later thanked his delegates, Nancy turned away quickly. She was crying. But through her tears, she made note of their grass-roots support. "Nancy and I," Ronnie told the faithful, "aren't going to . . . say, 'Well, that's all for us.'"

During the convention, Mrs. Ford had trounced Democrats in a speech, declaring, "We all know elephants eat peanuts, and that is exactly what will happen in November." While she had no illusions about the tradition of a campaign wife's public visibility being limited largely to goodwill and photo opportunities, she continued to infuse it with espousal of her beliefs.[11]

When asked, along with Mamie and Lady Bird, to name the "most meaningful American" to her, Betty chose Susan B. Anthony for her "personal convictions, a strong conscience and the moral courage to pursue those convictions actively," but on the forty-sixth anniversary of the Nineteenth Amendment, the First Lady wrote directly to the ninety-one-year-old Dr. Alice Paul that all "owe a great debt to you and the other fearless women who won the right to vote. Your foresight in proposing ERA after securing the vote has paved the way for today's hopes for ratification. Remarkable women like you give courage to all who work to expand the rights . . . my hope is that another year will find us with an ERA . . ."

On the anniversary, as women held an ERA vigil in Lafayette Square, the First Lady sent a telegram declaring she was "shoulder to shoulder with you in spirit. . . . As your vigil outside the White House ends, I assure you mine inside the White House continues . . ." She had in fact exerted influence that day on the "inside," when Jerry proclaimed "Women's Equality Day," urging ERA ratification by those states that hadn't yet given it.

That same day, the president delightfully shocked arts advocates when he unveiled his Arts, Humanities and Cultural Affairs Act of 1976, seeking $50 million in supplemental Congressional funds for National Endowment for the Arts and Humanities' grants. In his announcement, Ford credited the power that moved the funding. "Over the years my wife Betty has been an influence on me in many areas, including the arts. She has shown me not only the need for creativity in the arts, but also how the arts can . . . fulfill the humane values . . . extending the vision, enriching the minds, and raising the spirits of all Americans and all peoples everywhere."

That night, Betty Ford's influence was again illustrated as the president bestowed a special Medal of Freedom. He'd presented three others, but now it was to Betty's beloved mentor of yore, Martha Graham. The First Lady had "stuck to my guns" to insist not only upon a separate award presentation but a dinner for Graham. She personally arranged the entire evening, down to the placement of sculptures of dancers as table centerpieces. Ford thanked Graham for "counselling and inspiring so many young people, including Miss Betty Bloomer . . ." Graham's company then gave their second White House performance, the first having been given for Mrs. Roosevelt.

Not to be overlooked, Rosalynn Carter was also being visibly linked with the arts that night, attending a Washington concert by Leonard Bernstein, raising funds for the Carter campaign.[12]

Rosalynn "professed not to be concerned at all" by Jimmy's controversial *Playboy* interview in which he said he had "lusted" in his heart for others. She shrugged that he "talks too much, but at least people know he's honest. . . ." When asked if she'd ever committed adultery, Mrs. Carter cracked, "If I had, I wouldn't tell you!" But it was Carter's comment that he'd never do what Nixon and LBJ did, "lying, cheating," which made Texas Democrats livid. Jimmy quickly called Lady Bird to say he was "truly sorry" if he caused her "any discomfort or embarrassment." Mrs. Ford thought Lady Bird was "not going to be happy" about the interview, and when she dedicated a Texas medical institute in October, she was again joined by her old Congressional friend. Mrs. Johnson was "distressed, hurt and perplexed" by Carter's comments, but when pressed to say whom she'd vote for, quietly remarked, "I'm a Democrat."

Although Mrs. Carter discussed presidential issues and continued to advise Jimmy long distance, she also spoke of her own goals, and the campaign even published a little booklet, *Rosalynn Carter*, outlining her background, experience, and beliefs on what a First Lady should do. She confidently told the National Conference on Aging that she'd focus on problems of the elderly and promised the electorate at large, "When my husband is elected President I want him to establish a President's Commission on Mental Health. . . ." It was a historic precedent. No "candidate" for the Ladyship had ever discussed what she would do if "elected." After she had given an emotional introduction for Jimmy, he kissed her and asked the crowd, "How many of you would like to have this woman as First Lady?"[13]

Nineteen seventy-six also marked a rediscovery of ethnicity, prompted by Alex Haley's *Roots*, about an African slave family in America, and Irving Howe's *World of Our Fathers*, about Jewish immigrants. Mrs. Ford was particularly sensitive in ethnic communities. At a Lithuanian Folk Dance Festival, she was not only presented with a native costume, but joined their dancing. Of their "concern about your first homeland," she told them, "The President has . . . long supported 'the aspirations for freedom and National independence of the people of Eastern Europe by every proper and peaceful means.'" She was a grand marshal in Buffalo's Polish community's Pulaski Day parade, marching down the avenue, and pinning a "Vote for Betty's Husband" pin on Walter Mondale. In Los Angeles, she told "Chinese-Americans for Ford" that the president had "turned the economy around and restored trust in our government." When she wore a babushka, strolled through a Polish Pittsburgh neighborhood, and danced the polka at a street festival, people hung out windows to cheer. She told Milwaukee Germans, "I love pig's knuckles," joined in folk songs, and even raised an empty beer stein for the crowd.

Another ethnic event best illuminated the character of Betty Ford. She attended a National Jewish Fund Dinner to present a key to the grounds of a Bicentennial forest being planted in Israel. Rabbi Sage was speaking, when suddenly he had a heart attack. In the confusion of the moment, she calmly took the podium, saying, "Can we all bow our heads for a moment for Rabbi Sage? He is going to the hospital and needs our prayers. Would you rise and bow your heads." She spoke "in my own words," a prayer, ". . . Dear Father in Heaven . . . you can take care of him . . . you are our leader. You are our strength. You are what life is all about. Love and love of fellowman is what we all need and depend on. . . ." It was a public flash of her private faith. The situation replicated one two decades before, when a speaker at a dinner had a stroke and Mrs. Roosevelt had quietly soothed the audience.[14]

Betty also appealed to a segment of the population not usually associated with First Ladies. In a fad of the era, Betty had applied for and received a citizens-band radio license, with the "handle" of "First Momma." While traveling through Wisconsin, her voice crackled over the radio with a plug: "Please 'keep on talkin' for President Ford. We appreciate your help in keeping the Fords '10-20' at 1600 Pennsylvania Avenue. 'Happy Trip' . . ." Country-western radio stations reported it as lead news and claimed her as one of them.[15]

Gerald Ford had first mentioned his idea of reviving televised debates to Betty, and she strongly supported it. When Carter dined and remained alone only with Rosalynn for a full three hours before the first debate, some aides thought it a mistake. The candidate, as reported by Jules Witcover, said that on the contrary, "nothing was healthier for him psychologically than to be with her." Rosalynn and Betty gave their husbands the same advice: Discuss issues in human terms. Mrs. Ford had been on the hustings during the first debates, but attended the final one, and was "surprised that Carter was as good and as well informed as he was." He gained a major point as Ford was asked about the Iron Curtain. When the president said that there was "no Soviet domination of Eastern Europe," Mrs. Ford understood and explained that she, too, felt, after traveling to Romania and Poland, that the spirits of the peoples of those nations were not "dominated." Many later acknowledged that Ford's comment was a miscommunication, and it hurt him.

In the last days of campaigning, Betty feared that the president was overextending himself, and she worried that his aides were assuring him that the campaign was running smoothly when, she said, "in fact it wasn't." Near election day, Betty said she wouldn't be "downcast or broken-hearted" if her husband lost. In one sense, Betty Ford had already "won." A First Lady's willingness to express her views had not been a detriment to the campaign.[16]

On election night, they were in the White House, watching the close returns. Mrs. Ford was frustrated that they lost by only 2 percent, and believed that if they'd had another week, Ford would have won. Among other factors, she considered Reagan's opposition a reason for their loss. Meanwhile, in Atlanta, Jimmy Carter thanked and congratulated Rosalynn: "We've done it . . . I couldn't have done it without you . . ."

With his family, before two hundred reporters in the press auditorium, a hoarse Gerald Ford whispered that "the real spokesman for the family," the First Lady, would read his concession telegram to Carter. Mrs. Ford also thanked campaign workers and asked all to join in support of the president-elect. Because of her arthritis, the Fords decided to retire to the dry, warm climate of Palm Springs. What her work would be as former First Lady remained uncertain, though it was proposed that she establish a Betty Ford Cancer Institute in Los Angeles.[17]

The weeks before the Inaugural marked the smoothest transition from one party to the other. Betty Ford and Rosalynn Carter held a "joint conference" with their husbands, and the former was "very cooperative" in helping the latter review domestic details. At their first scheduled meeting, Betty had been in pain, but steeled herself instead of canceling. Their staffs also worked in tandem. Sheila Weidenfeld held in-depth transition meetings with Mrs. Carter's press secretary, Mary Hoyt, discussing the need for a larger East Wing staff, and the inevitable struggles with the West Wing. Mary Hoyt also sought a professional management consultant on restructuring the East Wing to Mrs. Carter's goals. The East Wing had become a permanent, important, and visible part of the working presidency. Now, it would almost integrate. As Jimmy Carter revealed, "Rosalynn is my secret weapon."

Meanwhile, the departing First Lady finished up business. She personally guided the loyal telephone operators through the family rooms; many of them had worked there for decades, but had never seen the third floor. Just days before she left, however, Mrs. Ford was still advocating ERA, meeting with the National Women's party and National Women's Political Caucus members. Serving in the sweet spot of the breezy "Me Decade," her First Ladyship had been an exception to the rule. Her power had impacted quickly. In just twenty-nine months, Betty Ford had widened the political and symbolic First Lady role and paved it for all possibilities, just by being Betty Ford. She reflected, "I would hope that I left the impression that it's all right to be independent, and have your own opinions as well as be a typical wife in a very happy marriage. . . . You can be both . . . I've had the fulfillment and still have my husband admire me, even though I disagreed with him."

It was undeniably a frustrating situation for her to be denied a full term, having not only adjusted well to the role suddenly thrust upon her, but also beginning to exercise power for women's issues when, just as suddenly, she was out of the job. Mrs. Ford would reflect, "I think I would have been a lot more active. I would have accomplished a lot more. I think I was hesitant to become too aggressive for fear it would be offensive to some people. I was aggressive but—I see even wives of governors today who are active, and young women who are very capable. I look at them and I think what wonderful First Ladies they would make because . . . they have learned to use the power of the office . . . there's a lot of power there. You can ask for just about anything and you'll get a support system . . . in some part of the United States. I don't think I took advantage of that to any great extent." Betty Ford stated that had she had a full term, she was certain she'd have been able to influence the appointment of the first woman on the Supreme Court, and help get the ERA passed. She joked that maybe she'd return to the White House as social secretary someday.[18]

On Inauguration Day, Mrs. Ford was "anxious" to leave. As she rushed to put on makeup, boots, and mink, she saw the "blessing" that it "might be the last time I would have to conform . . ."

Across the street, at Blair House, Rosalynn Carter was also up early, at five-thirty, and through the window glimpsed the building that would be her home in just a few hours. As she dressed in her turquoise suit, capelike coat, and knee-length thermal underwear, she fretted about her coiffure being too short.

Mrs. Ford thanked the house staff in the East Room. The Carters came for the traditional coffee, and the group departed. The two First Ladies rode in the car together to the Capitol, Betty saying it was tense as she made "inane conversation" about how Rosalynn would enjoy herself. Under the circumstances, they got along well. Not since Mrs. Hoover had ridden down the avenue with Mrs. Roosevelt had an outgoing First Lady sat beside a woman who "defeated" her for the Ladyship. Rosalynn recalled, "I'm sure her thoughts are as deep and varied as mine, but like most people, we do not express them."

The Carter Inaugural festivities were inclusive of all socioeconomic

classes, a "people's" event, best symbolized when, suddenly, during the motorcade back to the White House, the new First Family got out of the cars to walk. That night, the new First Lady appeared in the gown she wore to Jimmy's gubernatorial inaugural. At one of the twenty-five-dollar-a-ticket balls, the new president asked crowds, "How many of you like my wife's old blue dress?" Rosalynn was overwhelmed by "the obligations and responsibilities we have just assumed," and her occupying "the same rooms where Dolley Madison, Mary Todd Lincoln and Eleanor Roosevelt lived."

If Rosalynn was sensing the ghosts, Betty was shaking them off. After the ceremony, the smiling Fords left by a side entrance to a waiting helicopter, she not wanting the public or press "to know how it really hurt." The helicopter skimmed over the city, filled with decades of memories for her. Here she'd become wife and mother, and a legend in her own right. It was also where she'd lived for weeks without her Congressional husband and where she'd suffered physically and psychologically. She'd later consider what life would have been like had she remained in the White House. Betty suffered from an undiagnosed "addiction," but "there was no way to project what might have happened. It was the kind of thing people can control for years and then lose control. I did sense that I was already getting into trouble with pills." As she left the copter and boarded the plane, that past was shed at the tarmac. Or so she thought.[19]

17

The Partnership

"A FIRST LADY," explained Rosalynn Smith Carter, "is in a position to know the needs of the country and do something about them. She can have real influence . . . I think that the wives of Presidents need to be informed and to speak out on matters that are important to them." The world would soon discover how much influence she had. What made Rosalynn so different from her predecessors was her admission of the fact. "It would be a shame," the so-called "Iron Magnolia" stated calmly, "not to take full advantage of that power."

Rosalynn was interested in the specifics of complicated political, economic, international, even scientific issues. By definition of her role, those issues that the new president faced also confronted Rosalynn Carter. It was when she entered the Oval Office that she caught her breath to absorb "the reality" that "I was First Lady."[1]

The first public sign of her power was the president's decision to send the First Lady as his official envoy to Latin American countries just six months after her Ladyship began. Before the trip, with assistance from National Security Council (NSC) adviser Zbigniew Brzezinski, she had hundreds of hours of briefings by the State and Treasury departments, NSC, and Organization of American States experts and, in addition to her regular Spanish language classes, she devoured everything from Latin literature to poetry. Officially termed as *"portavoz"* (spokesperson), Mrs. Carter was *"determined* to be taken seriously." Along with State Department officials, she left for Jamaica, Costa Rica, Ecuador, Peru, Brazil, Colombia, and Venezuela. A *New York Post* cartoon had her as a Carmen Miranda in *South American Way* sailing a ship of state.

In each country, she first delivered a brief statement on America's policy toward the respective nation, then addressed the Carter issues of human rights and nuclear weaponry, and urged that the host country sign the American Convention on Human Rights, approved by the president while she was traveling. In Jamaica, she was considered "a kind of queen," but Rosalynn raised the touchy issue of that country's courtship by Fidel Castro among other subjects during her seven-hour talks. In Costa Rica, she discussed demilitarization and arms reduction, and promised to bring up the issue of its beef exports with the president. For three hours in Ecuador, she met with military leaders and considered American assistance in radar, antitank missiles, and pilot training. There, as a woman, she noticed, "I could get away with a lot of things another representative of our government could never do." In Peru, she mediated a disagreement with Ecuador over arms buildup. In Brazil, she discussed nuclear energy, and stirred a minor controversy when she met with American missionaries whose human rights had been violated. In Colombia, she asked sensitive questions about drug trafficking and Americans being held as prisoners—one of whom she later helped free—and in Venezuela inquired about the kidnapping of a U.S. citizen. It was an astounding role for a First Lady.

When an American reporter remarked that she was neither confirmed by the Senate nor elected to office, she shot back, "I am the person closest to the President of the United States and if I can explain his policies and let the people of Latin America know of his great interest and friendship, I intend to do so!" She took notes throughout, and kept a card of "talking points" ready in her purse. After each meeting, she drafted a long memo, which was wired back to the president and State Department. What was interesting in these macho nations was that Mrs. Carter had to serve in the role of surrogate president as well as hostess. It was an interesting insight into what role a woman U.S. president might someday play.

A week after her return, in San Jose, the First Lady delivered a policy report, assessing the facts, findings, and results of her undertaking. The Senate sent a unanimous congratulatory message, and a national poll gave her a 74 percent approval rating as "ambassador," 72 percent considering the Ladyship a better source of diplomatic information for the president than the State Department. White House pollster Pat Caddell sent a memo to Carter stating that "she clearly helps the President across the board." Before he sent the note on to her, Jimmy scribbled, "Rosalynn—don't run against your husband!"[2]

Few presidential couples had blended so splendidly as equal halves of the whole, intellectually and spiritually. "When a husband and wife are interested in each other, you affect each other. We just happened to be in the White House," she explained. A West Wing staffer thought the relationship was "unabashedly affectionate in public but not cloying." Jimmy Carter was not uncomfortable expressing emotion, whether kissing Rosalynn—and Betty Ford, Lady Bird Johnson, Jacqueline Onassis, Mamie Eisenhower—or even exchanging affectionate letters with Mae West. Sometimes the Carters almost appeared to be fraternal twins, having in some way merged into one persona. On Air Force One they passed time reading the Bible together in Spanish. At the Gridiron dinner, they entertained together, by jitterbugging. One often completed the other's sentences. Of his relationship with the woman he sometimes called "Rosie," Jimmy wrote, "We communicated easily, and often we had the same thoughts without speaking. We had been ridiculed at times for allowing our love to be apparent to others. It was not an affectation, but was as natural as breathing." To see the First Lady looking over papers on the president's desk in the Oval Office was not an unusual sight.

Unquestionably, Mrs. Carter had a degree of political power not seen since Eleanor Roosevelt, but as a couple, the Carters seemed almost replicas of fellow southerners James and Sarah Polk of the 1840's—pious, hardworking, and political.[3]

The president's press secretary, Jody Powell, explained that "everything they've done has not been a case of Jimmy Carter doing it with a *supportive* wife. It had been Jimmy Carter and Rosalynn Carter doing it together as a *team.*" It was the partnership that had enabled Rosalynn to promise on the California campaign trail that Carter would appoint a Presidential Commission on Mental Health. "And then," as she recalled, "I went home, and told Jimmy." The partnership spawned not only hard news but satire. On *Saturday Night Live*'s "news" segment, a photograph was shown of them affectionately pressing each other's

cheeks, comedian Chevy Chase narrating, "In an effort to show their solidarity, President and Mrs. Carter have epoxied themselves to each other."

Nobody attempted to usurp the partnership. "If you want something said to Jimmy, say it to Rosalynn," advised one insider. "Miss Lillian" called Rosalynn "very ambitious," and admitted, "Even if I, his mother, want Jimmy to do something, I ask Rosalynn first." Only the president affectionately teased the First Lady about her assertiveness. As they once discussed current movies, Rosalynn remarked that she disliked "all that violence and bloodshed" in films. Jimmy drolly quipped, "But you like Democratic Party politics."

Because she sought to prevent the president from becoming "isolated" and wanted common citizens "to feel that they are part of the government process," Rosalynn undertook the "eyes and ears" role. Keeping "current with what was going on in the Administration," Rosalynn said, "when I went out in the countryside and people asked me about what was happening in the White House, I tried to tell them in general terms. . . ." She felt that role was vital: "I could go out and visit a home for the elderly or go into a house and talk to people whose heating bill was so high they couldn't buy groceries. . . . When I would come home, Jimmy and I would talk about it and I could tell him what I found and how people felt. . . . Maybe something I said would help him as he made a decision. . . . I never *liked* to travel with Jimmy. . . . I just sat. I'd sit for the press conference. I'd sit for his speech. I had too much else to do."

The partnership had obvious benefits for her Ladyship.

Rosalynn recalled a typical scenario: "We would sit on rocking chairs on the Truman Balcony . . . and we would talk about what he had done during the day and what I had done . . . I'd say, 'I just want to get my [project] legislation out of the HHS.' . . . I'd have Jimmy call the staff and say, 'What's the status of Rosalynn's legislation?' Or I'd just say I want my legislation out of HHS—Monday, 9 a.m.!'" And the president would call. On the partnership's benefits to *his* job, Carter said, "There's very seldom a decision that I make that I don't first discuss with her . . . very frequently, to tell her my options and seek her advice. She's got superb political judgment. She probably knows the human aspects of the American people and their relationship to the government better than I do. We have an absolutely unconstrained relationship, an ability to express our doubts and concerns to each other." He was acutely aware of her advantage, even threatening to withdraw her scheduled appearance at a congressman's campaign fundraiser when the legislator voted against the administration. "Sharing" the presidency actually helped him function: "If I had to bear the responsibilities of a President without her it would be much more difficult for me."[4]

The president also acknowledged the need for her Ladyship to flourish solo, because "she can also exert her own individual personality in areas where I couldn't possibly address the issues with adequate attention." He realized, "It is, in fact, an unwarranted constraint on her ability, and talent, to make her just be a mirror of me, or subservient to me, or always working in lockstep with me. . . ." While more alike than dissimilar, both maintained separate, often opposing views, with different strengths and preferences. He took criticism more philosophically, but "reading the morning newspaper" was her most trying task. When Jimmy played continuous Willie Nelson country music, Rosalynn authoritively turned the volume down. He'd turn it up again. She thought that jogging made him underweight. He asked her to stop harping on it. Riding in the presidential limousine, Jimmy looked back at the follow-up security cars, his sense of government economy shocked. Rosalynn cooled him down: "Just don't look back, Jimmy. Don't look back!"

As Rosalynn stated, "Jimmy has always felt I have capabilities and should do those things important to me. Back in those days I would advise him about the business and we became good friends and partners and developed this respect we have for each other. He always listens to me, but he doesn't always react. I sometimes have very different opinions." To some outsiders, her criticisms seemed harsh, but a family member pointed out that it was merely the blunt process of banter in which they thrashed out public issues. Jimmy said he encouraged her criticism: "We don't let barriers arise between us personally. I think she sees that if she and I ever disagree publicly, even on an issue of relative insignificance, then the disagreement would be magnified out of proportion. So she tries, I think, on her own initiative to let our disagreements be resolved and discussed more privately."

Her frequent bone of contention was the timing of announcements of his major decisions, from the Panama Canal treaties to Mideast crisis decisions to New York budget cuts. She argued that unpopular decisions could be made in a second term. He retorted that he did things for the good of the country, even if they were not politically expedient. She'd respond, "The thing you can do to hurt your country most is not get reelected." Rosalynn was acutely aware that the problems Carter had to address were unpopular and controversial, and she feared the outcome of approaching them head-on. He rarely relented.[5]

Producer Peggy Whedon, though recognizing the First Lady as a feminist with a "vein of iron," described her as "a delicately beautiful lady." She could be stubborn and demure, approachable but formidable. Hazel-eyed, brunette, slender, the First Lady appeared pert, yet had the patina of a professional woman. Part of the paradox was in her distinctive voice. In a cultured Georgian accent, her words had a gracefully rounded lilt, even though she might be discussing nuclear disarmament. The girlish quality belied a maturity of mind. Rosalynn possessed a penetrating intelligence that bordered on being scholarly. With rigorous expectations of excellence from all, she strove to improve and challenge herself. Jimmy took particular pride in her "strong mind." Education, said the First Lady, "is something that comes in installments to the end of your life. When you stop learning, I think you start dying."

Rosalynn needed little adjustment to become First Lady. With gusto she dove with relish into the role. Unlike other First Ladies, she immediately cooperated with and accepted the constraints of security, even wearing a heavy and hot bulletproof vest and raincoat. She had no doubts about her capabilities, no fears that she couldn't accomplish everything she wanted to.

Rosalynn's humor emerged like Eleanor's, in recounting the ironies of public life. Mrs. Carter recalled one trip when Jimmy left ahead of her, not realizing the bottom of her pantsuit had been packed off with him. She took the train to join him, dressed in the suit top and a "tightly buttoned raincoat." She had two different pairs of contact lenses, one for reading, the other for distance, but revealed that she often wore one from each set when delivering a speech, to "read with one eye, and look at the audience with the other."[6]

Mrs. Carter was deeply religious. "I do and I say what I think is right, and if I have prayed about it first, I can be sure it *will* be right." The First Lady prayed several times a day, sometimes with the president, sometimes alone. They read their Bibles daily, often together.

Rosalynn was hip to elements of the era. She enjoyed the sexy comedy movie 10, and questioned only the appropriateness of showing it to guests who'd come to meet Pope John Paul II in the White House—the first pontiff to visit.

The First Lady was particularly attuned to the growing health movement of the late seventies. She jogged almost daily and avoided having her family served foods that might contain any preservatives. She felt that manufacturers should remove any of their products even suspected of containing harmful ingredients "and not wait for the long series of tests and investigations." As with Betty Ford, three months after she became First Lady, a lump was discovered in her breast, but it was benign, and the day after the biopsy she attended a lecture.

Family remained essential to her. It was Rosalynn who'd persuaded Jimmy to include a passage about the family in his Inaugural Address. Amy was the only one of their four children in permanent residence, and Rosalynn had a tree house built for her to give constancy to the little girl's life. Like her mother, Amy took Spanish lessons, and the two had snowball fights on the lawn. "Amy attends some state dinners because we like her to be with us," explained Rosalynn.

The First Lady wanted to keep Amy in a public school, and chose one near the White House. Sixty percent of its students were black, 30 percent foreign born, and most were the children of embassy workers. Amy's best friend was the daughter of a Chilean embassy cook. The school had an "extended day" program that permitted "working mothers" to bring the children as early as 7:30 A.M. and pick them up as late as 6:00 P.M., during which times they participated in extracurricular programs. The First Lady, who often brought Amy to morning class, qualified as a "working mother."

Joel Odum, a friend and staffer, said Rosalynn "never lost that small-town quality of genuine concern for family, friends, and friends of friends. . . . She never thought she was better than any other human being. . . . I remember her saying 'Can you believe we met Burt Reynolds and Lee Majors?'" Mrs. Carter showered particular kindness on the household help, and took an interest in their well-being. When the son of a Plains friend was in an accident, lingered in a coma, and then died, it was the First Lady whom the mother credited as being the most comforting, with frequent calls from the White House.

She was deeply compassionate when it came to making decisions to assist the disadvantaged, and acutely sensitive about injustice toward the underclass. She had a personal empathy. "My father was a mechanic and my mother was a seamstress," she candidly admitted. "We were very, very poor, and we worked very hard . . . I have always worked. I understand people who work for a living."[7]

Her background had ingrained a strict adherence to the work ethic, and it shaped her view of the public: "People are the same everywhere you go . . . basically people are good, honest, they work hard, they want to be self-sufficient to support their families." Thrift was part of her, and as First Lady she still kept the books. In her weekly meetings with the housekeeper, she frequently suggested changes "to take advantage of leftovers," had chicken served at least weekly, and fish when it was on sale. Rosalynn cringed when, after she requested some routine information, a load of government statistics was delivered over a weekend, having been compiled by employees working overtime. She'd just called to get background for Amy's book report.

Like Martha Washington, Rosalynn had made her own clothes, and like Edith Wilson, she brought her sewing machine to the White House, but there was no time to use it. On the campaign trail, she'd worn drip-dry dresses that packed easily. As First Lady, she wore colorfully printed bell-sleeved tops and wide long skirts; her evening gowns reflected the "Gypsy Look" of the seventies. Her favorite designer, Dominic Rompollo, created a turquoisish "Rosalynn Green" for her. Her tastes resembled Pat Nixon's, with high neck, long sleeves, simple cuts. Rosalynn didn't duck from photographers when she was in casual

clothes, even blue jeans and a "Jimmy Buffet & the Coral Reefer Band"
T-shirt. But it was she who had argued against a lax code at the Inaugural as some had urged to the president-elect. She felt people enjoyed
dressing up for such events, and at her suggestion it was "black tie
optional."[8]

Rosalynn assumed the hostess role in an admittedly detached manner: "My social secretary would bring me menus and suggestions for
entertainment. I would choose one. I was through." She made some
changes. Like the McKinleys, the Carters defied protocol to sit by each
other's side at some occasions. They gave single guests permission to
bring dinner partners of their own choice. But it was her decision to
serve *only* wine at state dinners that caused a press furor. Not since the
nineteenth century had a First Lady initiated a "dry" policy. Along
with "Sahara Sarah" Polk and "Lemonade Lucy" Hayes, there was
now—as dubbed by Washington satirist Byron Kennard—"Rosé
Rosalynn." Just as "Lemonade Lucy" had done as the Ohio governor's
wife, "Rosé Rosalynn," as Georgia's governor's wife, never served hard
liquor and wasn't going to start now.

The coverage of her liquor ban irritated Mrs. Carter. "They make
me sound like a real prude. I'm not a prude!" Unlike the Polk and
Hayes edicts, Rosalynn stopped serving hard liquor not for moral or
political reasons, but simply because "[i]t's not necessary, and I'm saving money." Liquor and beer were available in the private quarters to
family and guests, on their anniversaries the Carters had champagne,
and at Christmas the First Lady's mother made Lane Cake, which
called for wine, though "Miss Allie" admitted that "it's better with
bourbon."

When housewives asked for her favorite recipes, Rosalynn Carter
sent her "Plains Special" Cheese Ring—which included peanuts—and
Strawberry Cake—which included Jell-O. Mary King of the campaign
staff said Rosalynn wanted to be certain not to alienate "poor or mid-
dle-class" citizens. The Carters did host "Old-Fashioned Gospel Sing-
in'" and square dancing on the South Lawn, but the First Lady was also
a student of the Latin culture, with worldly tastes in music and literature, and she sought to bring the best of the arts to the White House.

Rosalynn hosted the first poetry festival, with simultaneous readings
in the state rooms, and the first jazz festival, broadcast live by National
Public Radio. She opened herself to varied artistic perspectives,
whether it was attending a Kennedy Center lecture on Gustav Mahler,
a performance of *Annie*, or having Andy Warhol in for tea. Under her
enthusiastic patronage, a series of classical-music concerts held in the
East Room were aired for public television, *In Performance at the White
House.* Rudolf Serkin, Vladimir Horowitz, Andres Segovia, Isaac Stern,
Leontyne Price, and Pinchas Zukerman were just a few of the distin-

guished roster Mrs. Carter invited to perform. The Carters did cut the pomp of trumpeters that preceded a presidential entrance at state affairs, but "Hail to the Chief" remained at her insistence.

Mrs. Carter carried through a third phase of Mrs. Kennedy's restoration and Mrs. Nixon's acquisitions, by helping establish the White House Trust Fund, the goal of which was a $25 million endowment to permanently provide funds for necessary furnishings, and replacing others on loan. Rosalynn sought commitments from foundations and individuals, so that "recurring and special fund drives will not be necessary in the future to insure that the White House stands as a symbol of the collective cultural heritage of its citizens." Pat Nixon and Jacqueline Onassis, as well as the other living members of the sorority, agreed to serve as her honarary chairpersons.[9]

Mrs. Carter was aware of her White House predecessors, but not overwhelmed, explaining that "each one of us has dealt with this challenge in her own way." Though she "vigorously" denied that she consciously modeled her role after anyone, she did admit that she played the same "eyes and ears" role that Eleanor Roosevelt had, and that Lady Bird Johnson had "advised" her "to enjoy, enjoy, enjoy! Be very confident in what you'll do and decide what you'd like to do and *just do it!* Don't worry about what others say!" Like Lady Bird, Rosalynn had the same sense of urgency: "[T]hese are precious years during which I can contribute," and like Mrs. Roosevelt's, her energy stemmed largely from altruistic motivations. While she admitted, "I can help change things," she emphasized, "I'm not doing all this just for Jimmy. I feel I'm doing it for the country." With "opportunities," she felt "responsibility," often asking herself, "Am I taking advantage of them as I should?" She wanted to use her power "wisely and honestly and to good purpose" and "determined that the White House will be a place that people can turn to for help." Only then would she feel her Ladyship was "worthwhile."[10]

Her schedule reflected her work ethic. She arose in time for the seven o'clock morning news shows, and breakfasted with Amy at seven-thirty. Initially, every Tuesday, Wednesday, and Friday, from 9:00 A.M. to noon, Rosalynn had Spanish lessons. At the age of fifty, she determined to learn the violin, and mornings and some late afternoons she practiced with Amy. She took her Spanish textbooks when she traveled, but there was rarely a spare moment for Rosalynn Carter. Though she had some trouble with the air pressure in airplanes, like Pat, Lady Bird, and Eleanor, she was an inveterate day-tripper around America. She talked issues on Phil Donahue's show, toured a snowblower's manufacturing plant, headlined a tribute to Marian Anderson, wore a solar-energy T-shirt for Sun Day, and even welded her initials into a Trident submarine. She was game for even the zany, once posing with Congressional wives dressed as past First Ladies. Through the smiling and hand-shaking, the photo opportunities and citizen kissing, she was observing, listening, and reporting back to Jimmy.

On Wednesday afternoons, she had a permanent fixture in her schedule. The First Lady and the president had a working lunch in the Oval Office, or just outside on a flagstone terrace. The weekly lunches began, as Jimmy chronicled, because of the many domestic decisions requiring their joint input, but rapidly developed into substantial political meetings. Rosalynn recalled that after each put in their working hours, "Jimmy always called at 4:30 for tennis, or jogging, or bowl-ing. . . . I always tried to get exercise every day. It was important for me to be with him." It was her "favorite hour."

After dinner, Mrs. Carter's time was often occupied studying gov-ernment reports and issue papers. To help her get through them quicker, the First Lady, along with the president, took a speed-reading class on Tuesday nights in the Cabinet Room. Within a year, she dou-bled her capability. Rosalynn often worked into the wee hours on speeches. "I feel I have to be doing something every minute. I wish I could relax like Jimmy."

During the week, at about 9:00 A.M., that briefcase went with First Lady Carter, and was opened, emptied, and refilled with work by four-thirty. Rosalynn Carter quipped that the First Ladyship was "one of the most demanding jobs of the federal government excepting maybe, per-haps, the job of the First Lady's husband."[11]

– 18 –

Office of the First Lady

DURING THE BUSINESS HOURS of her first days as First Lady, Rosalynn Carter showed up in the East Wing dressed in a suit, and was ensconced in her own yellow-and-apricot office overlooking the North Lawn. She worked behind a kneehole mahogany desk, on which were stacked piles of memos and issues reports. Mrs. Carter took the office because she wanted the private quarters to remain just that; no First Lady had ever made her own office in the East Wing. To avoid tourists, who passed through the wing into the mansion, she walked across the lawn in the warm weather, and through the basement in the winter. Her only com-plaint was that the president's energy conservation made the East Wing particularly cold, and she had to wear long underwear.

As soon as she reached her office, the First Lady consulted with her press secretary, Mary Hoyt. It was important that Hoyt keep abreast of East Wing work because it was integrated into the entire administration, particularly decisions and reports that dovetailed with the president's. She quickly realized that "the public and the press had little understanding of the pressures of scope and dimension of the First Lady's job."

The First Lady's longtime personal assistant, Madeline MacBean, and Hoyt had "frank talks on who would be in charge," and both realized they had their hands full. The sheer volume of work turned out by the Carter East Wing, however, demanded the structuring, definition, and hiring of the first East Wing chief of staff as a separate, official, paid position. Kit Dobelle was named director of the East Wing, at an annual salary of fifty-six thousand dollars, the same amount paid to presidential West Wing chief of staff Hamilton Jordan. The president publicly defended the First Lady's need for "somebody competent" to run her offices. Dobelle was present at the daily briefings of the senior West Wing staff.

When in town, Mrs. Carter was in her office every day, presiding at weekly staff meetings. Mary Hoyt recalled Rosalynn as a boss: "We knew when the door to her office was closed it had to be important. We didn't bother her. She was well organized, but when we tried to draft a daily schedule for her it almost became impossible. She and the staff simply didn't know what was going to happen. . . . Initially, her speeches were prepared . . . but in time we learned . . . she wanted them to be very current and she wanted to do it by herself. . . . Rosalynn was always well briefed . . . if she were going to the Midwest she knew that she needed to know farm policy, and would want to be briefed on it far enough ahead of time by the President's staff. Within a short time she got to be such a pro and demanded far less in advance . . ." At Tish Baldrige's suggestion, Mrs. Carter had her urgent messages "red-tagged" on a table outside the elevator. Every time Rosalynn walked by the table, she grabbed the red tags.

Now officially called the "Office of the First Lady," the East Wing expanded its press office to include research, and its projects divisions to include community liaison. Rosalynn's department heads became close to her, and Mary Hoyt said that Mrs. Carter was "a tough boss in the sense of a perfectionist, no nonsense in the sense of purpose, flexible in the sense of looking for alternatives." She was "adamant" that staffers call her "Rosalynn," and Mary Hoyt was initially uncomfortable with "informality," but soon agreed, "You cannot be stiff when you work together day and night."[1]

Rosalynn streamlined her administration. To deal with time-consuming autograph requests, she ordered cards printed with her signature. In response to questions about various aspects of White House life, she had a free, illustrated color pamphlet written and sent out. She utilized fully the tradition of volunteer staffing of administrative chores, and at a time when more professional women worked for the president, Rosalynn had men working for her, from temporary and gratis advisers on short-term projects to Paul Costello, her assistant press secretary.

Through the East Wing, Mrs. Carter had the "resources of government agencies," and would hold her own meetings with HUD secretary Patricia Harris and HEW secretary Joseph Califano "as it related to my projects." She did not relent in her strong lobbying of the president for more salaried staff slots, and when he balked that everyone in government felt that need, she retorted, "But I'm not anybody you talk to in government. I'm your wife!" He would not budge. When Rosalynn suggested "borrowing" staff from federal departments and agencies, it was Jimmy who retorted, "They shouldn't have anybody they can spare." She continued to struggle with the situation. "With more staff, I could've done so much more."

Asked if a First Lady should be salaried, Rosalynn was hesitant to answer. "I like to help the women's movement, so it always made me a little bit nervous to say no, but if the First Lady is salaried, there would have to be a structured position for her. . . . I would be tied down to those duties defined by the institution of First Lady. The President's salary was $200,000 a year. You have a place to live, you have people to drive you where you want to go. I always felt that was sufficient."

Rosalynn Carter strongly believed that "project work" was the greatest way a First Lady could have an impact on the general American public. Her project files, organized by state and subject, were the best proof of her wide network and vast diversity of work. Her initial step was fulfilling her campaign promise to enact a President's Commission on Mental Health.[2]

On the day she hoped to begin work as commission chairman, only twenty-eight days after the Inaugural, the Justice Department's Office of Legal Counsel informed the First Lady, "The law prohibits the President from appointing a close relative, such as a wife, to a civilian position." The president himself telephoned to see if there weren't some "loophole," but was informed that only "honorary chair" was permissible. "So," the First Lady told reporters, "I am going to be a very active honorary chairperson."

A commission office was established in the adjacent old Executive Office Building. From the beginning, Rosalynn Carter had determined to make a difference in the field of national mental-health services, but realized that there was limited press interest when, on the day after Carter officially signed the executive order establishing the commission, *The Washington Post* opted instead to write about her "dry" policy. She acknowledged that mental health was not "sexy" compared to "no booze in the White House," but was understandably frustrated.

She knew the statistics, the most startling of which was that mental illness in some degree affected one in four American families. Public awareness of it had emerged only since the Second World War, and there hadn't been a full study of national scope since 1961. The First Lady understood that those suffering from mental illness carried a stigma and, in some instances, ostracism. "If only we could consider mental illnesses as straightforwardly as we do physical illnesses, those affected could seek help and be treated in an open and effective way," she declared. "Politically, the issue had always been shuffled to the back burner, but fortunately, we were now in a position to make mental health a top national priority." With Dr. Tom Bryant as chairman and executive director, and Peter Bourne, the president's special assistant for health issues, as primary coordinator, the First Lady and a board of twenty commissioners of social workers, medical experts, lobbyists, and psychiatrists began barnstorming the nation, holding public hearings, consulting hundreds of local community professionals, doctors, legislators, and former mental patients, while simultaneously developing thirty task forces, staffed by over 450 volunteers, concentrating on specialized issues, and holding their White House conferences in the State Dining Room.

Among other things, the First Lady discovered that national and

state bureaucracies had "fragmented and fraught" programs, some services overlapped, and many people in need were being completely overlooked. Just nine months after becoming First Lady, she reported to the Washington Press Club, "We have worked hard. And now we have thousands of pages of data that add up to what I can only describe as a compelling mandate for change. . . . I urge you to study the evidence."

The First Lady and her commission prepared recommendations, and the final report was turned over to the president. Mrs. Carter said the most shocking fact was that many mental-health centers served patients poorly or not at all, and the commission suggested that a 1963 act overseeing the centers be amended to strengthen the community-center services, as well as making changes in housing, health insurance, Medicare and Medicaid aid, and offering assistance to states in helping the most chronically mentally ill. There was also an advocacy recommendation for a bill of rights protecting the mentally ill from discrimination. Her direct impact was quite real: after Rosalynn toured the National Institute of Mental Health, and learned that new research was often left incomplete because of short-term, low federal grants, funding increased.

In speech after speech on mental health, Mrs. Carter turned her project into a serious government initiative with grass-roots support in all directions. At a Los Angeles dinner attended by film and society notables, actress Jennifer Jones announced her establishment of a foundation for mental health and education, and the ecstatic First Lady table-hopped, and eloquently told this audience they could assist in changing stereotypes of the mentally retarded by treating the subject in more sensitive and realistic films. Meanwhile, the president ordered every department and bureau to submit timetables in which the commission recommendations that didn't need Congressional approval would be initiated. Rosalynn found the slow progress on the Hill and at the Department of Health and Human Services frustrating. As she put it, "I knew [Secretary] Califano had his priorities, but I also had mine—and I saw the President more often than he did!"

Though the press failed to cover her mental-health work extensively, the public most affected by it cherished Rosalynn. Among the thousands of letters she received on the subject, one mother of a mentally retarded daughter, struggling financially to provide her with proper medical care, and supporting "national health insurance," wrote her that "you are an outstanding First Lady and one that American females can emulate."[3]

Rosalynn Carter promoted voluntarism as Pat Nixon had, and recalled how she'd greeted her at the airport when Mrs. Nixon came to Georgia on a project. She realized voluntarism "reaches into so many areas," but "was always trying to get people to take care of the problems in their communities, because government can't do it all. . . ." When one problem was investigated, she sought to learn if there was a similar situation "nationwide."

Rosalynn wanted to get to know the "real" Washington, and seemed to be everywhere in the "metro area," painting a hospital wall, trying out the new subway system, shopping for her family groceries in a local supermarket, jogging in her sweatpants and cap on the canal tow-path. Even when she gave her Inaugural gown to the Smithsonian, Rosalynn insisted it be a populist presentation, outside, open to local residents and tourists.

She combined her interests in community self-help and the men-tally retarded by lending strong and visible support to the Green Door, a home established by two volunteers who sought to give purpose and self-esteem to some of the mentally retarded at Washington's St. Eliz-abeth's Hospital. She prompted civic groups and local businesses to make a variety of donations for the improvement and maintenance of D.C. General Hospital, and interceded with philanthropic organiza-tions to strengthen the fledgling Community Foundation of Greater Washington.

Akin to Ellen Wilson, Eleanor Roosevelt and Lady Bird Johnson, she took an interest in the condition of neighborhoods and made an unannounced tour of slum areas. She contacted Arthur F. Burns, who'd recently been replaced by the president as Federal Reserve Board chair-man, as well as top officials at HUD and Congressman Henry Reuss, chairman of the House Committee on Banking, Finance and Urban Affairs, to enlist their help in investigating how the neighborhoods could be aided.

Rosalynn actively promoted a national childhood immunization plan and helped reach the goal of immunizing 90 percent of the na-tion's children against measles, which, in turn, dramatically curtailed a multitude of other children's illnesses. She was convinced that the fed-erally funded Cities in Schools program, which offered welfare and health services through the public-school system, could be expanded with only minor funding, and was willing to testify in Congress to that effect.

The First Lady encouraged Christian youth worker Bill Milliken to further develop his pilot programs of Project Propinquity, which tried to instill confidence and discipline in ghetto youngsters through educa-tion, trade skills, and counselor support. Through Mrs. Carter, Milli-ken was given an EOB office from which to work. A committee of department representatives was established, along with $2.7 million in federal funding, to be matched by states and localities. Rosalynn hosted a breakfast for over two hundred business leaders to enlist them as pro-spective donors and be briefed by Milliken. One reporter quipped that the infant program advanced rapidly because of "the three F's—Faith, Fundraising and the First Lady."[4]

Rosalynn became an equally fervent advocate for senior citizens, assembling "a task force to inventory federal programs for the elderly . . ." She toured and inspected dozens of senior and convalescence homes, conferred frequently with the president's counselor on aging, and held a roundtable conference with advocates like Maggie Kuhn of the Gray Panthers, and Congressman Claude Pepper, chair of the House Select Committee on Aging. They devised a brochure containing recommendations on how best to serve the elderly, which was distributed to national and state organizations. Meanwhile, the First Lady lobbied Congress on behalf of the Age Discrimination Act, to do away with mandatory age retirement in government, and to raise the limit to seventy in the private sector. She lobbied for the Older Americans Act, a funding increase in elderly services, as well as the Rural Clinics Act and Social Security reform.

Rosalynn presided over the White House Conference on Aging, and at a National Council on Aging session, she was introduced as "the most socially active First Lady since Eleanor Roosevelt." In a speech before the National Conference on the Aging, she said she wanted to develop an educational system to make seniors aware of what and where federal, state, and private programs were available. Having campaigned heavily among the elderly, she felt herself "developing a responsibility for them."

The issue was also personal. Only the mothers of First Ladies Kennedy, Eisenhower, Truman, Coolidge, Cleveland, Edith Wilson, and Julia Tyler had lived to see their daughters assume the role. Few had as much impact on their daughters' lives as did Allie Smith on Rosalynn Carter. Widowed at a young age, Mrs. Smith solely supported her four children, and Rosalynn said it had a "permanent influence" on her. Mrs. Smith was the Plains postmistress, but retired at the mandatory age of seventy. When her daughter became First Lady, Mrs. Smith found part-time work in a local flower shop; she and Rosalynn's mother-in-law who, as a sixty-eight-year-old retired nurse became a Peace Corps volunteer in India, were inspirations, prompting Rosalynn's resolve.

Before a senior citizens' lobbying group, the First Lady went to Capitol Hill to pitch the administration's hospital cost-containment bill: "I get furious how cost containment . . . has been bogged down in Congress. We're going to beat the special interest groups and have decent and affordable hospital costs in America." In May, the president first "cleared with Rosalynn" his Congressional proposal to limit annual individual hospital increases by 9 percent and, with her, further tooled out a "fixed fee schedule" for physicians, more stringent bylaws for nursing homes, and expanded outpatient services.[5]

A friend recalled how the First Lady discussed the 1978 Civil Service Reform Act with her family and the president. When it was suggested that discrimination based on "sexual preference" be included, Rosalynn supported the idea. In Plains, "Rosalynn saw one person who was discriminated against and it touched her, and taught her, and she made example of it . . . she completely lacked . . . judgmentalism on people's personal lives and choices."

In both private and public, Rosalynn had a thorough abhorrence of racial intolerance. When she'd learned that local white ministers refused to preside at a funeral for a young white boy because his family lived in a racially integrated community, the First Lady privately shamed a Baptist minister into performing the service. She addressed the women of the Congressional Black Caucus, and held a special lawn reception for one thousand members of a Blacks in Government conference. She was awarded a Doctor of Humane Letters degree from Morehouse College, a black institution, and hosted the first musical festival honoring black Americans, including performances by rock-and-roll's Chuck Berry and disco singer Evelyn "Champagne" King. Even Eartha Kitt was invited back to the White House.

Rosalynn opposed federal funding for abortion, stating, "I think we should pursue the alternatives." Still, while she said, "I personally don't like abortion," Mrs. Carter added, "I am not for an amendment to the Constitution to make it illegal, because I've seen what happens when abortion was made illegal in some states. . . . We should try to prevent the need for abortion, by pushing for organized family planning, better sex education and less red tape in the adoption procedures." As governor's wife, she had persuaded Jimmy to establish family-planning centers in each of Georgia's 159 counties.

While she did not specifically focus on women's issues as Betty Ford had, she successfully lobbied the Pentagon to hire more women as honor guards in the mansion and pushed to have more minority women involved in the president's reelection campaign. She told Attorney General Griffin Bell that she'd like to see a woman on the Supreme Court, and she phoned him to suggest qualified woman judge Stephanie Seymour for an Oklahoma court. The First Lady's Office assembled a roster of women qualified for presidential appointments. Carter also appointed three Cabinet members and undersecretaries who were women—more than any other president—among many other lesser posts.

The First Lady thought women should work, even suggesting it might lower the divorce rate because work would raise their self-esteem. She assessed her job as a result of the women's movement: "The role of First Lady has changed as the role of women has changed . . . Women take . . . professions. I don't think that any man who would be President of the United States would have a wife with no ambition, who'd just sit and do nothing."

Rosalynn did stump for ERA. She was able to convince a crucial member of the Indiana legislature to vote for it, and at an ERA fund-raiser, a dance with the First Lady was auctioned. She would, however, regret not lobbying more publicly in states that eventually defeated it. "I can look back and see . . . it would have made a difference if we had started a little earlier."

Carter appointed Lynda Robb, along with Bella Abzug and Carmen Delgado Votaw, as chairs of his Women's Advisory Committee. One night, several hundred women activists and appointees gathered in the East Room, among them three generations—Lady Bird Johnson, Lynda Robb, and her daughters.[6]

Lady Bird was frequently in Washington for long visits, and the traditional mantle of Queen Mother seemed to devolve upon her. In September 1977, she spent her first night in the White House since leaving, in preparation for the next day's Panama Canal Treaty signing. Lady Bird sat at Rosalynn Carter's table for one of the annual Senate Wives Luncheons at the White House. A nervous Kitty Hart, who thought "Texas" when Lady Bird asked what current Broadway plays she should see, hastily blurted out, "The Best Little Whorehouse in Texas." Lady Bird thought not. Lynda Robb recalled another after-noon, when the president presented her mother with a Congressional Medal of Honor. "Afterwards she said, 'Why don't we go over to Woody's! The January sale is on' . . . Someone recognized her and shouted, 'Look, it's Mrs. Carter!' They knew it was some First Lady. . . ."

It was Lynda Robb who persuaded her mother to attend the Houston Women's Conference. There, Lady Bird Johnson made the historic gathering a sorority trio, joining Rosalynn Carter and Betty Ford. All three First Ladies became associated with ERA as a solid front.

While Jacqueline Kennedy Onassis continued to support the women's movement privately, she led a trainload of legislators and lob-byists to Washington in a successful attempt to save Grand Central Station, even conducting an impromptu press conference. Her public statements and appearances continued to reflect interests from her Ladyship, and historic preservation remained her focus. Flanked by New York's mayor and controller and carrying a hard hat, she shoveled cement in a ceremony marking the conversion of several unused build-ings into off-Broadway theaters, run by the Forty-second Street Re-development Corporation, of which she was a director. As the Municipal Arts Society's representative, Jackie signed their tenancy lease for offices in the historic landmark Villard Houses. Riding the Staten Island ferry to inspect a Snug Harbor restoration project, she took the helm, hair blowing in the wind.

At the annual RFK Memorial Tennis Tournament, when asked about her White House restoration project, her response reflected that she remembered the most minute details. When a person mentioned that he had the autographs of every Twentieth-century First Lady except Ida McKinley and herself, she quipped, "You're going to have a rough time getting in touch with Ida," and signed "Jacqueline Kennedy" on the back of her engraved envelope.

In Israel she toured Roman ruins, and attended the ceremony dedicating a new Museum of the Jewish Diaspora at Tel Aviv University, visited a kibbutz classroom, and planted a pine tree in the John F. Kennedy Memorial Forest, near Jerusalem.[7]

Florence Harding and Eleanor Roosevelt had been spared the public revelations of their husbands' outside relationships. Mary Lincoln had endured the printed gossip of her husband's "love" for another. In the seventies, Mrs. Onassis, Mrs. Johnson, and Mrs. Eisenhower would share similarly unfortunate distinctions. It was Rose Kennedy who helped deflate speculation. She said that President Kennedy and Jacqueline "had one of the most loving, understanding and devoted relationships that I can imagine. . . . He loved her and was proud of her and appreciated her. And it would be hard to imagine a better wife for him . . . She developed his interests in art, music, and poetry—he learned to delight in poetry—because she took such pleasure from it."

About stories of LBJ, Lady Bird said with equanimity, "He had very many women friends with whom he shared varying degrees of companionship—you just can't keep any strong person on a leash." She never doubted who was the most important and loved person in his life, "and that's me." It was, however, the elderly conservative Mamie Eisenhower who not only frankly addressed infidelity rumors, but did so on national television.

The story of Ike and Kay Summersby had become one of public notice with Merle Miller's oral history of Harry Truman, *Plain Speaking*, in which he claimed that Ike had written to General Marshall at the end of the war requesting permission to divorce Mamie and marry Kay. It appeared that Ike might have written a letter requesting permission not for himself but for aide Harry Butcher, who did divorce his wife and marry a Red Cross worker he'd met overseas. Summersby's posthumous memoirs built upon the story, and ABC began preparing a miniseries based on it.

At that point, Mamie Eisenhower gave her son John permission to release four hundred love letters Ike had written her during the war, some of which were published as *Letters to Mamie*. They showed a couple separated by war, and a concerned wife, but they gave no indication of divorce, and revealed a publicly unemotional general as a vulnerable and attentive husband who longed for his wife. Differences hadn't interfered with an old loyalty. When she stopped in Kansas City on her annual drive to Kansas, Mamie Eisenhower telephoned Bess Truman, whom she still admired.

Mamie evidently watched the miniseries, and afterward reassured friends, "[D]on't you bother your pretty little heads about it for one minute. We both know it just isn't true." During a television interview with Barbara Walters, Mamie remarked, of the Summersby story, "There were many things that I had heard and I would hear, and he had told me long before they said anything about it. They were afraid to say it to my face. I knew most of these things that went on. So why would it bother me . . . I wouldn't have stayed with him five minutes if I hadn't had the greatest respect for him." The former First Lady felt that "all marriage is in jeopardy," and required compromise. When Walters commented with amazement on Ike's letters to her, Mamie piped up, "Yeah, and he wrote 'em longhand too."[8]

At the end of her first year, Rosalynn Carter's political pragmatism was already more evident than Jimmy's. On national television, the First Lady, not the president, stated that he had erred in not consulting Congress earlier and more often, and that the "toughest" decision was "to follow through and pursue his programs despite criticism and declining ratings in the polls."

To much criticism, Jimmy had eliminated the playing of "Hail to the Chief" at South Lawn ceremonies welcoming heads of state. At one such event, in late 1977, however, there was another distraction. Outside the White House gates was the largest protest gathering since Vietnam, with two groups shouting down the president. Police had to break the mob up with tear gas. It drifted to the welcoming stand and momentarily caused Carter to choke up and stop his speech. Then he turned the rostrum over to the visiting head of state. It was the shah of Iran.

The First Lady stood listening, with tears in her eyes.[9]

- 19 -

"Most Special Adviser to the President"

AT THE PRESIDENT'S February 28, 1978, Cabinet meeting a new presence was felt, sitting on the side with departmental aides, listening silently, scribbling notes. Though she was an administration "nonofficial," her daily printed schedule would now always note when the Cabinet was meeting.

Only once did the First Lady unconsciously slip into the absent vice president's chair.

Rosalynn said that to her knowledge, Cabinet secretaries hadn't "minded a bit," and felt that those criticizing her attendance were "opponents trying to portray Jimmy as weak." She did not ask questions, but she'd come to get answers. As she later emphasized, "I was always calling and asking questions about why things were being done. . . . he [Jimmy] finally said 'Come to the Cabinet meetings and you'll know why we're doing things' . . . it was helpful to people in the country because I could go out there and let people know in an intelligent way what was happening with the Administration. I think that's important."[1]

What she did in the private quarters was just as important. In the room they shared, the day before Carter delivered his 1978 State of the Union Address, she went over the draft, suggesting changes and additions, some of which he incorporated. In the Oval Office, their weekly lunches had become political meetings. The partnership had rapidly evolved to a high level.

Her son Jack said Rosalynn was "almost like another Cabinet member," and senior adviser to the president Hedley Donovan characterized the First Lady's power as that of a "true senior adviser," and "intimate political counselor," equating it with the vice president's as an "ultimate example of the 'organic adviser . . .'" Like all other advisers, she gave her opinions on issues the president asked her to consider and brought to him those of which she believed he should be made aware, armed with answers or evidence of personal accounts, statistics, projected results, and views of experts she might have consulted in the process. She did not make his decisions, and was not so much "deputy," "surrogate," or "co-president" as she was a sort of "Most Special Adviser to the President."[2]

The president insisted that all his aides address their issues and questions to him by memo. The rule was broken only for his press secretary and First Lady. She did send memos to West Wing staff, one simply marked "R," stating that "Jimmy has too much to do already," and "instructed" against overscheduling. The president frequently sent her not only his memos, but those sent him by his staff and Cabinet, often with a scribbled, "Ros, what think?" It wasn't gratuitous solicitation. At some private meetings, he would interject, "Well, Rosalynn thinks that . . ."

She frequently scanned the president's speeches for dramatic impact and clarity, and helped redraft them. On one she scribbled, "Less detail here?," another time, "So what?" on an energy speech. Carter said that because she was better than he at seeing issues "from the viewpoint of the average American, I don't mind her criticizing my speeches." When he delivered his first energy policy speech in 1977, it was the First Lady who made the final edit. She even helped enlist a new speechwriter for him, Robert Maddox.

Carter finally addressed a pressing rumor that he might retain Arthur Burns as chairman of the Federal Reserve Board by saying that he hadn't yet discussed it with Bert Lance, Charlie Schultze, Mike Blumenthal, and "I haven't even talked to Rosalynn!" At one point during the investigation hearings into the financial affairs of his OMB chief, Bert Lance, the president and his wife "both decided that it might be better for Bert to stay and fight it out." Only Rosalynn did he tell of further developments, and both were "certain he would resign."

It was not, however, just a matter of her offering occasional remarks on speeches or personnel. She consciously studied the minutiae of details on even complex issues, immersing herself in the thick of policy. When the president had questions relating to health and welfare, he consulted Rosalynn first, and while she didn't presume to offer definitive advice to him on issues outside her realm, she easily delivered speeches on strategic arms limitations and civil rights and, with her interest in alternative energy resources, participated in a discussion of home heating oils. The president admitted that "aside from a few highly secret and sensitive security matters, she knew all that was going on. When necessary, she received detailed briefings from members of my domestic and national security staff. . . . Rosalynn had strong opinions of her own and never gave up one of her ideas as long as there was any hope of it being accepted." However, as with all advisers, he felt no particular obligation to give her advice special consideration, and often rejected it. Several sources claimed that she was vehemently opposed to some proposed business tax breaks and advised him to veto them. He did not. She sometimes wanted the president "to be a little demagogic" on the Soviet Union, "But he won't."

"She was more political," thought Joel Odum, "She had a . . . different point of view. . . . People told her things they wouldn't tell him." The First Lady worked in tandem with the West Wing. When a critical *New York Times* op-ed appeared, it was she who fired off a memo to Jody Powell: ". . . we should demand equal time . . . I don't see how they can refuse. We could get Sol Linowitz or someone supportive . . ."

In fact, the president's two closest aides highly respected the First Lady. Jordan admitted, "If Jody Powell and I strike out, the best thing to do is get Rosalynn on our side. . . ." Powell said that in decisions affecting the administration's overall direction, she was "always in the middle."

If the First Lady had no trouble with the West Wing, the East Wing occasionally did. As Mary Hoyt recalled, "East Wing–West Wing tension will always have a life of its own. The mere physical location— that lack of proximity . . . does make for a separateness. The male chauvinism . . . was long there. But with Mrs. Carter, the First Lady could not be overlooked. . . . The West Wing depended on Rosalynn and Rosalynn depended upon the West Wing." When Mrs. Hoyt attempted to get decent salaries for the overworked East Wing, she thought it odd that "at the same time reporters were writing about the lack of equal pay for equal work they never had anything but criticism for the size of Rosalynn Carter's staff." The press provoked public mail, and "that only caused tensions on the part of the West Wing."

More than any other West Wing adviser, however, the First Lady could be harsher in her appraisal of any given situation simply because she had no ground to gain, and no job to lose. "I have very strong opinions about almost everything," she offered. "I always let Jimmy know how I feel, even though he disagrees and doesn't react well to my viewpoint." Because Rosalynn's power rarely slipped, when it did, it seemed overmagnified in the press. As the president held a press briefing that ran overtime, the First Lady's audible whisper of "Jimmy, let's go!" and his departure within a minute were reported. To imaginative observers—and political critics—it smacked of a First Lady overpowering a president. By 1978, speculation about her power mounted, with unnamed "insiders" feeding the media. One official anonymously told *Newsweek* that of the "few people . . . I fear," the First Lady was "at the top of the list."

Rosalynn had her defenders. At the peak of her advisory role, she would earn a 59 percent approval rating. An LBJ speechwriter said she played a legitimate role because, "The President can run the Presidency any way he wants to run it." Conjecture about her power was so well disseminated that Andrei Gromyko stopped to tell her that she was "famous" in the Soviet Union for her "background and accomplishments."[3]

Inevitably, a First Lady who exerted *any* power would be harshly criticized by those who resented women in politics. Even in a favorable review she would be called a "cold-blooded politician" and "ruthless strategist," with a "thirst for victory." She felt the press overstated her power, but was unhesitantly defensive of her role: "They say nobody elected me. So what! I'm here!" Most bewildered by criticism of her attending Cabinet meetings, and believing there was a degree of sexism in it, she "never considered not attending them because of the criticism. . . ." I'm not doing what I'm doing for people who write about it. I'm doing it for the people I can help."

Some reporters considered Rosalynn to be disappointing copy. By the late seventies, many newspapers' "women's pages" were being turned into "lifestyle" sections. Since Mrs. Carter's activities were so divergent, many editors didn't know whether she should be covered by a style, metropolitan, or national news section. Inevitably, her project work suffered from lack of coverage and she had a "fuzzy" press image.

It was odd. Reporters finally got what they'd sought since Eleanor Roosevelt—a powerful and accessible political activist. Still, the press could be not only apathetic toward her, but harsh. When it was discovered that mass murderer John Gacy had been one of thousands of individuals who happened to have his picture taken with the First Lady, the photograph was widely published, as if to link her personally with him. In response to journalist Desmond Wilcox's inquiry to reporters about the pressures on a First Lady, CBS's Lee Thornton said she had little sympathy because Rosalynn was a "tough cookie" who "wanted the job, ran for office," and "knew what it was all about," further observing that "the women who get into the White House actually want it . . . more than almost anything . . . in fact both of them [Betty Ford and Rosalynn Carter] wanted the job . . . all this talk about loss of privacy is just so much hooey."[4]

At the moment, Betty Ford's life was attracting renewed press attention, but for quite unexpected reasons.

Betty thought that with retirement, Jerry would be home more often. Instead, his life remained full, with travel, lecturing, teaching, and serving on boards. Mrs. Ford was trying to organize her new home as well as write her autobiography. Still taking painkillers, she also drank, thinking it might alleviate some of the stress. She also turned petty when provoked over small incidents, withdrew from people, and became "totally passive." She would admit, "Inside, I was empty." Her family realized something had to be done.

Along with medical experts, they conducted an "intervention," confronting her condition, during which Susan recalled how she'd recently had to carry her up some stairs, at a concert. Gradually, Betty Ford faced the situation and began the arduous process of detoxification. She couldn't sleep, and she became physically ill. On the last day of a full week, she turned sixty, and was taken to Long Beach Naval Hospital.

When she got there, the former First Lady faced a huge sign, ALCOHOL REHABILITATION CENTER, and was appalled at the notion that they had brought her here. When she'd had cancer, Betty had the presidential suite. Now, she initially defied her assignment to a room with three other women.

Meanwhile, at the urging of doctors and family, she issued a public statement about her addiction to painkillers: "It's an insidious thing, and I mean to rid myself of its damaging effects. There have been too many other things I have overcome to be forever burdened with this." Among the thousands of supportive messages was a statement from the National Institute on Drug Abuse's director: "Her courage in calling the problem what it is will lead to more candor in the way we discuss prescription drugs. By dealing with the problem as it is, she will make it easier for hundreds of thousands, or millions . . . to face [it]."

Alcoholism had plagued the families of many First Ladies. Sons of Dolley Madison, Abigail Adams, Eliza Johnson, and brothers of Bess Truman, Eleanor Roosevelt, and Ida McKinley, to name but several, had all suffered from it. Still, a First Lady had never been known to be an alcoholic. Betty Ford then issued a second public statement: ". . . I have found I am not only addicted to the medication I have been taking for my arthritis, but also to alcohol. . . ." After two weeks, she recorded in her diary, "What in the hell am I doing here?"

At Alcoholics Anonymous meetings, Betty was forcing herself to reveal all her emotions and personal problems to a roomful of sailors and other strangers. She heard prostitutes using four-letter words. Only gradually would she acknowledge that she had something in common with these people. The former First Lady finally admitted to herself that she was an alcoholic. As Steve Ford glimpsed her laughing at the "off-color" jokes of sailors, he suddenly realized that "she needed to be in a real world where people didn't care who she was." The Ladyship's power had ironically worked against her. Steve said, "Her doctors would prescribe whatever she wanted, because they didn't want to make a First Lady mad." While hailed for "heroism," Mrs. Ford felt she was undeserving, but it strengthened her growing acceptance of herself. When, at one meeting, someone called on "Betty" she stood up and began talking, only to realize there were other Bettys in the room. Gradually, she stripped her First Lady self-identity "amidst a sea of Styrofoam coffee cups and a fog of cigarette smoke," and realized that the problems had their own particular effect on her, not as a celebrity, but as a woman. Betty felt her previous honesty about breast cancer "made it easier" to address her dependencies, "because the mastectomy had proven to be beneficial for so many women. . . . If we were as open as we were about the cancer perhaps it would help women. . . ."

That summer of 1978, when Rosalynn Carter and her husband visited Mrs. Eisenhower, the former First Lady asked her junior animated questions about the changed role. At Gettysburg College, Mamie spoke longingly of Washington to a reporter. "I guess I lived in the center of everything for so long, I miss it." In the fall, she took a suite at Washington's old Wardman-Park Hotel, from which she commuted to Gettysburg on weekends. It brought her back in touch with friends, lunches, and the theater. On her eighty-second birthday, her son reported that she was "in excellent spirits."

She wrote at the time that she admired all First Ladies because "each one had difficulty before the role was well established," and said of it, in light of the media's glare, "Everybody is an actor or an actress. Nobody is completely himself. It isn't possible especially in public life." In reference to her successors, she said, "I don't want to say anything that can be interpreted as being critical of other people or the way they do things. I have my own ways, but I don't much like the overly casual way." She didn't refer to anyone specifically, but her doctor claimed that Mamie felt Rosalynn shouldn't make decisions she wasn't "chosen by the people to do."

However, as she spent the hot August afternoon together with the Carters sipping lemonade on the back porch where she played solitaire, Mamie took to Rosalynn. Despite their thirty-year age difference, they began to discuss how each how each viewed the First Lady role, and Rosalynn thought it "was a good idea of how times had changed . . . she was doing totally different things like entertaining. . . . She told me about hanging skeletons and black cats at Halloween. . . ." Rosalynn recalled that as she spoke "about my projects," Mamie gasped with mock horror. "I can't believe you're doing that!" she told Rosalynn. "I was busy *all* the time, but I never did all *those* things! But—my *daughter-in-law* does those kind of things!"[5]

The Carters' proximity to Gettysburg that summer would prove historic for another meeting of peers, and Rosalynn's role was dramatically illustrated during the twelve days of peace accord conferences mediated by the president between Israeli prime minister Menachem Begin and Egyptian president Anwar Sadat. In preparation for the meeting, Carter wrote, "I discussed the situation with Rosalynn, who was thoroughly familiar with the issues involved in the Middle East dispute and understood what was at stake." When he briefed Kissinger, she joined in. He "wanted Rosalynn with me . . . for personal support and advice, and to help me with the routine duties between negotiating sessions."

Though she wouldn't be sitting in on all the negotiations, Jimmy told her that both the Israeli and Egyptian "First Ladies" would be joining their husbands: "There are going to be a lot of hard feelings and tough fights. The atmosphere will be more congenial if all of you are there." Jihan Sadat of Egypt, one of the few visible women to call for equal rights in the traditional nation, and who worked on welfare projects, seemed a Middle Eastern counterpart to Rosalynn, and named "sensitive feelings for other people," and "simplicity and modesty" as traits she emulated in Mrs. Carter. Aliza Begin of Israel said she had "a relaxed, informal relationship" with Rosalynn. The president kept Rosalynn completely informed of each development, and she maintained a diary during the nearly two weeks that would total almost two hundred pages. Several times she flew back to the White House, keeping her own as well as the president's previous commitments, knowing "It was essential not to show any emotions, good or bad, about the progress of the peace talks, which could only create speculation, but with things so positive it was hard." At the last minute, she orchestrated the arrangements for the historic signing of the Camp David Accords by the men, on the White House North Lawn.[6]

Mrs. Carter's comprehension of, and interest in, foreign affairs was substantial. She lobbied Senate wives in attempts to influence their husbands' support of Carter's Panama Canal treaties. Scheduled to dedicate a nuclear submarine along with Senator John Glenn—who planned to criticize the president's SALT II treaty—she worked with Jimmy in composing a rebuttal speech, defending the treaty. She sat in on many of the daily foreign-affairs briefings given for the president and some of his staff by NSC chief Brzezinski. She helped initiate a professional adult international-exchange program, the Friendship Force, and served as honorary chair. On her trip to Puerto Rico, the First Lady deftly handled the question of its statehood as she met with editors at a conference, as well as government leaders. Before a trip to Florida, she was briefed by Brzezinski on Cuban policy.

Rosalynn attended the inaugurations of Bolivia's and Ecuador's presidents, and the funeral of Pope Paul VI—the first time a First Lady was ever granted such a privilege. When Pope John Paul II made his first trip to America, neither the president nor vice president was able to welcome him at the Boston airport. Brzezinksi sent the president a memo: "The unanimous choice at the working-group level was—and is—the First Lady." She went.

While she sat in a January 1979 Cabinet meeting, Rosalynn heard Jimmy reveal that Iran was in "a state of revolution." Anti-shah rioting had broken out, and Carter had quietly ordered that Americans there begin to evacuate. Days later, he agreed to have the U.S. support the shah and his military, maintaining a loyalty that dated back to Truman. The crisis in Iran, however, only grew, and Rosalynn noted that on television reports the anti-shah protestors called for the return of an exiled Moslem fundamentalist, the elderly mullah Ayatollah Khomeini.

Rosalynn wasn't the only woman cautiously following developments in the Middle East.

With her husband, nearly a year after she had begun her detoxification, Betty Ford would visit the Middle and Far East, kissing a camel and accepting Saudi prince Fahd's personal invitation because it was a rare recognition of a woman's status. Not long after the shah had left

Iran, Betty Ford met him and the empress in Egypt, but when the couple's conversation turned to the lavish skiing resorts of the nation, Mrs. Ford began to sense how the poor factions could resent modernization. From Egypt, the shah would go to Morocco, and was then granted temporary asylum in Mexico. That April, Rosalynn noted in her diary how Jimmy was being pressured to give the shah asylum in America. He resisted, and told her, as she recorded, that "the Iranians might kidnap our Americans who are still there. . . ."

Letters praising Mrs. Ford and asking for help for addictions continued to arrive. After guiding a close friend onto the road to recovery from his severe alcoholism, she realized she was capable of helping. Together they began raising funds for an alcoholic rehabilitation center at Eisenhower Hospital, as yet unnamed. As the full year of her sobriety approached, she had a stronger sense of self. She remained committed to ERA, striving to enlist more conservative, older women. When she had a facelift, there were both admirers and critics, but she noted that in California "people have their faces lifted as casually as they drink iced tea." It had been after attending the unveiling of her White House portrait in a ceremony with Rosalynn and their husbands—during which Jimmy kissed Betty—that Mrs. Ford looked at the painting and mused that perhaps she "really *can* look that good." The unveiling was Mrs. Ford's first visit back to the White House, but she had mixed feelings about living there again as speculation arose as to whether her husband would run in 1980. She thought Carter was "trying very hard," but didn't believe he was succeeding.

Mrs. Ford was greatly agitated by the administration support for cutting Medicaid for abortions. "What happens to a poor woman who's on welfare, or a married woman who already has four or five children who just can't afford to take care of any more?" she wrote. She was concerned that over a third of the women seeking abortions were teenagers, and feared they'd have "back-alley abortions." She saw far-reaching social problems resulting with the perpetuation of unmarried girls becoming mothers unable to raise children without assistance. The longer Betty Ford was out of the White House—like Eleanor Roosevelt, and to a degree, Grace Coolidge—the more liberal she became.[7]

On May 15, the White House formally submitted Mrs. Carter's Mental Health Systems Act to Congress, and the First Lady went to Capitol Hill to tell the Senate Subcommittee on Health that it was a desperately needed overhaul of national policy.

Meanwhile, her advisory role was to take on even greater proportions. That spring, when the disastrous Three Mile Island nuclear-power plant accident occurred, the First Lady personally reviewed the president's crucial speech to reassure the nation, and even proved to be an effective debater against an anti-nuclear protester at one New England speech. On June 12, she was in the closed session with only the president's top advisers when he told them his intention to run for a second term. Rosalynn already knew that Senator Edward Kennedy might oppose him for the nomination. Through a network of loyal supporters in small towns across the country, she first detected the threat and so warned other advisers in a Treaty Room strategy meeting. Long conscious of reelection, and with an eye to improving relations with the Fourth Estate, Rosalynn initiated a series of social events for journalists and supported the hiring of public relations specialist Gerald Rafshoon. Rafshoon recognized the value of the First Lady for the campaign beforehand. She could boast of accomplishments in a way that Jimmy couldn't.

Rosalynn was a visible power that spring when the president ruminated at Camp David for two weeks about his direction of the seemingly apathetic mood of the nation. After reviewing his scheduled speech on energy, she had decided opinions. "Nobody wants to hear it. . . . They just want to be told that . . . somebody understands the situation and has it under control." Jimmy had already begun to decide not to deliver it, but Rosalynn's advice only bolstered his decision. It proved wise.

The next day she and the president held two meetings with five top advisers, including Powell, Jordan, and the vice president, to discuss the focus of his speech to the nation. Rosalynn was keenly sensitive to the irritated national mood—the "malaise" as Carter later dubbed it—and believed most of it was pinned on the president, first by the press, then by the public. She listed inflation, a drought hurting southern and midwestern farmers, and escalating oil prices. She had earlier received a memo from Pat Caddell and conferred with him on the subject. At Camp David, she helped the president concentrate on the larger issues that he needed to address, as opposed to the details he seemed to be emphasizing. Constructing various drafts of his planned speech, Jimmy aired them first with Rosalynn, and she advised him to accent the positive and emphasize the hope for national improvement. It was also the First Lady who urged that they together read through philosophical histories of the American people and culture, and meet with a sociologist in preparation for the famous "crisis of confidence" speech.

The speech was largely received with support by the public, and many of the president's advisers felt the time was ripe to purge the Cabinet of those who'd become contrary to the administration. The First Lady agreed, on the condition that it be swift, as a sign of control. She was particularly eager to have HEW secretary Califano replaced, believing his high public profile was "politically and unnecessarily" damaging Carter. The secretary had also given only wan support to her mental-health proposals. She considered that embarrassing not just to

the administration but specifically to her. He'd also chosen a chair for
the Citizens' Advisory Committee on Mental Health and failed to first
consult her. When asked who had decided that the Cabinet purge
should take place as quickly as possible, the First Lady momentarily
confused her pronouns and said she had, then clarified with "we." It
was reported by *Newsweek.* She was more upset, however, by coverage
of the purge with a sensational peg.[8]

While Rosalynn had reflected at Camp David, nearby, Mamie had
done so also, with Barbara Walters, for a taped national interview. She
now lived permanently in Gettysburg. Washington as she'd known it
had changed, and after just a few months she left.

In the spring, at Gettysburg, she fell and broke her wrist. Still, she
retained her wry humor. "I'm 19 in my mind, but I'm 82 in my body.
Somehow they don't go together!" Mamie refused to make any demands
on friends or family, with whom she kept in touch by phone. As she
explained to Barbara Walters, "I like to be independent . . . people will
be sympathetic with you for a while. But after a while they've got their
own little fish to fry. They don't have time to worry about you anymore." Ensconced in her vast pink bed, she piled tins of candies, note-
card boxes, books, correspondence, magazines, cigarettes, and favorite
miniature Coca-Cola lighter on the side where Ike had slept, so she
wouldn't feel lonely. As Barbara Eisenhower explained, "She lived
longer than anybody who had a rheumatic heart problem, and outlived
her life expectancy by fifteen years. She took care of herself. To some it
seemed like she was luxury-loving and inactive. That wasn't it at all."

At one point that summer, she stayed in the house for seven weeks,
and wouldn't emerge "until I can smile." Still an avid soap-opera fan,
she watched movies and TV shows from or about the fifties. Barbara
recalled that Mamie "liked it and was hurt that anybody thought the
fifties was not a terrific era." She liked reading "racy novels," and
cracked with joking mispronunciation, "To think—at my age—learning all about phonography." She continued responding to public mail,
spending hours handwriting letters, and enjoyed trying new junk foods
or venturing out to a local hamburger joint.

Among the gifts she received was *Spring of Devotion,* a book of poetry sent by Nancy Reagan's mother. Through all of her winters in
California, Mamie had enjoyed sassy Edie Davis, and David Eisenhower
recalled that "For quite a while, they talked every Sunday." Though
the connection with the Reagans was obvious, Mamie resisted being
drawn into supporting him. David believed that she "might have
thought that Ronald Reagan was not electable. She wasn't anti-Rea-
gan, [but I think] she didn't expect him to win." To her doctor, Mrs.
Eisenhower did offer one opinion. "Ike said a long time ago that that
fellow George Bush was Presidential material . . . when he was a Re-

publican Congressman from Texas . . . I hope I can do something to help him. . . ."

In September, however, Mrs. Eisenhower suffered a stroke, and on November 1 she died of cardiac arrest. President Carter eulogized her as "a warm and gracious First Lady [who] carried out her public and private duties in a way that won her a special place in the heart of Americans and of people all over the world. To generations of Americans, in war and peace, she embodied sincerity and traditional values." Scheduled to air for her birthday, the Barbara Walters television interview was now shown in memoriam. The last question was how Mamie would like America to remember her. She was caught off guard, even flustered, then, without pause, laughingly quipped, "Just a good friend."

At Mamie Eisenhower's Kansas burial and Norfolk, Virginia, memorial service was a face rarely glimpsed in public. Pat Nixon, looking chic in tweed suit and modified bouffant, with no sign of her stroke, joined Rosalynn Carter at the latter event, the first of the sorority she'd seen since her illness. Pat had no shyness about what she'd been through. When Clare Luce said she seemed not to have suffered from the stroke, the former First Lady intensely replied, "Yes, but I *did* have a stroke. You don't know the struggle I had getting back the use of this hand . . ."

"Watergate is the only crisis that ever got me down, "she reflected to Julie. "And I know I will never live to see the vindication." Meanwhile, she became a grandmother, and wanting to be closer to their family, the Nixons moved to New York City later that winter. Pat longed to leave isolated San Clemente: "We're just dying here slowly."[9]

Other California Republicans were hoping to move East.

In October, Ronald Reagan told some of his '76 senior staff of his plan to run for president. As aides jockeyed for favorable positions, Nancy Reagan assisted pragmatist campaign director John Sears in getting rid of ideologue Lyn Nofziger, who'd managed to return to Reagan's side. Mrs. Reagan explained that since her husband "doesn't understand undercurrents" that existed among their arguing campaign staff, she sought to bring accord. While she trusted the abilities of both Sears and Mike Deaver, by November 13, when Reagan officially announced, the two advisers weren't speaking. At Nancy's prompting, a meeting was finally held between Ronnie, Deaver, Sears, and his aides, Jim Lake and Jim Black. And herself. When the campaign needed an expert finance chairman, the choice, Daniel Terra, said he accepted because of "Mrs. R's charm." Another volunteer provided a special service to the Reagan campaign. Nancy's friend San Francisco astrologer Joan Quigley offered chart readings through the campaign for the Reagans.[10]

On October 20, Jacqueline Onassis was joined by Lady Bird

Johnson and the Carters for the dedication of the John F. Kennedy Library. Later that day, Rosalynn overheard Jimmy remark, "Let him come on in . . ." on the phone. When she asked to whom he was referring, he explained that the shah had cancer, and needed treatment available only in the United States. He also told her that the American embassy in Tehran had been refortified with security, and that Iranian officials had reassured him that personnel in the complex would be safe.

Two weeks later, an international crisis jolted Rosalynn Carter. When she heard about the horrifying conditions—and the rumor of a holocaust—threatening the millions of homeless Cambodian refugees attempting to flee that nation, she gravely conferred with the president, then immediately planned to undertake a mission to the refugee border camps in Thailand.

As the sun rose on the autumn Sunday of November 4, the telephone rang for the president. It was Brzezinksi. Iranian terrorists had stormed the American embassy in Tehran, trapping nearly sixty Americans inside. With no one ruling party in Iran, it was assumed to be a temporary situation. Several days later, militants sent word that if the shah was returned, inevitably to be murdered, the detained would be released. The United States refused. The Americans became hostages. On day three of the "hostage crisis," after her "intensive briefings" by the State Department and a meeting with American relief agencies, the First Lady flew out to Thailand.

She knew that starvation and extermination had already wiped out nearly half the Cambodian population, but when she arrived after the twenty-four-hour flight and saw the camps with her own eyes, she felt that nothing could have "prepared me for the human suffering . . ." There before her lay thousands of emaciated human beings slowly dying of disease; the stench of waste, the blistering heat, the buzz of mosquitoes, all contributing to the shocking unreality. She was "momentarily paralyzed by the magnitude of suffering." Stupefied, she began moving through the camp which stretched as far as the eye could see, human skeletons with bloated stomachs lying on straw mats, listening to the sound of moans and illness. She entered an "eerily silent" tent of children and held a four-month-old baby who weighed four pounds. Before she left, the baby died.

After touring a Laotian camp, and a center in Bangkok where a small percentage were processed for emigration, she tried to convince the king of Thailand to provide further aid to the refugees at his nation's borders, but he balked, citing corruption of those who controlled allocated funds. Upon return to the United States, she immediately urged UN secretary general Kurt Waldheim to appoint one overall coordinator for international relief, asking that he not mention her efforts because other nations would be less cooperative if it was a U.S. initiative. The same day, a relief coordinator was named. Her excursion prompted the formation of the National Cambodian Crisis Committee and Cambodian Crisis Center, which became the clearinghouse for all donated aid. She taped national television appeals, spoke across the country, and held White House events to raise funds for the relief program. The president directed that U.S. quotas of refugees be increased, that efforts be made to bring food directly into Cambodia, and the Peace Corps efforts accelerated. It was an understatement to say that Rosalynn Carter was partially responsible for the alleviation of the crisis stage.

Rejoined with Jimmy, she was fully briefed by him on the Iranian situation, and he said it was she who first "strongly" advised him that the United States should "stop buying Iranian oil and announce this decision as soon as possible," or otherwise Americans "might think you are under pressure from the Iranians. . . ." Several Cabinet members agreed. The president took the First Lady's advice.

As the days passed into weeks, Rosalynn Carter became impatient, pleading with the president, "Do something! Do something!" Christmas came, and went, and the hostages began their second month. Two days later, the Soviets invaded Afghanistan. It effectively killed Carter's SALT II treaty. He ordered that Americans boycott the 1980 Olympics in Moscow and began grain embargoes. And Rosalynn—now campaigning in primary and caucus states as Jimmy remained close to the White House—went right into Iowa, facing angry farmers and Kennedy's now official challenge to the president for the Democratic presidential nomination.

The First Lady admitted to being "fiercely defensive" of Jimmy against critics on the "hostage crisis," but as other crises kept piling up on each other, Rosalynn found herself asking the same question: "Why are all of these things happening to us?"[11]

– 20 –

"A Taste for Power"

ON THE NORTH Lawn, outside the White House, a small tree stood, barely noticed by the preoccupied, tense reporters and tourists. Wrapped about its fragile trunk was a yellow ribbon. It had been tied there by the First Lady, one of many citizens to so honor the hostages throughout the nation.

The situation frustrated Rosalynn. She believed that Khomeini was

reveling in the international press coverage, and she was "infuriated" to see the hostages demeaned with scarves over their eyes. However, she carried on, using a standard stump speech with a flexible lead state-ment, changing it as hostage developments occurred. At one point, negotiations seemed to indicate that the hostages were in fact going to be released—a hope then dashed, as many were, and would continue to be. When she heard that, the woman whom the press had termed "iron" broke down crying. She argued with Jimmy to do *something.* "Like what?" he asked. Her "iron" was back. She suggested mining Iran's harbors.

With the more philosophical Jimmy keeping close to the White House during the hostage crisis, Rosalynn Carter was to assume an un-precedented role. The First Lady was to be the visible "candidate," substituting for the president in the primaries. From June to November, she had already helped raise about $1 million for the campaign. Instead of attending teas, she was in hard hat inspecting a New Hampshire packing plant, Pennsylvania electric works, and Harlem housing-rehab project. In those months of the primaries, as she became better known to the press and public, a rather wonderful thing was happening. While she'd always been confident, she now combined a smooth balance of public panache, political power, egalitarian advocacy, and immunity to barbed press. More than any other First Lady at any other time, in the winter and spring of 1980, Rosalynn Carter seems to have metamorphosed precisely into the modern Eleanor Roosevelt.

While Jimmy considered her his most potent factor in the campaign, he continued to rely on "the partnership." Before she headed out on the April campaign trail, he told her of a secret hostage-rescue mission about to begin. She was in Detroit when he obliquely told her only, "The news is bad." Late that night, in Austin, he finally told her that the aircraft to be used in the rescue mission had crashed in the Iranian desert and killed eight men. Upon her return, the First Lady rushed to the Cabinet Room, where the president was briefing his senior staff on the tragedy. As she packed her bags to face yet another hostile audience on the exhausting campaign trail, Rosalynn tried to shore up. She told an Indiana crowd that the failed rescue mission "has made a dramatic change, because now the Iranians realize we can do something about it."

Privately, she advised Jimmy with equal strength, even successfully suggesting that he not debate contenders Kennedy and California governor Jerry Brown. After Iowa, the First Lady reported to the president how the discontent of farmers was being "substantially alleviated by the improving prices of grain." And, after one particularly bad showing in a primary, a Carter aide told senior adviser Hedley Donovan that "the Leader of the Free World took quite a chewing-out from his wife last night."

Rosalynn had already begun working New England in October. When it came to the Kennedy threat, she was particularly tough, warning that "I relish a fight." When reporters asked why she bothered working Kennedy country, she replied crisply, "My husband is the President of Massachusetts too."

When Senator Kennedy had announced his candidacy in Boston, the press focused primarily on one woman. Not his wife, not his daughter, not his mother, but his sister-in-law, Mrs. Onassis.

In the time since she'd left the White House, Jackie had scrupulously avoided all attempts to gain her endorsement, save for those issues and people of genuine personal interest. She had done radio and television narration for the National Trust for Historic Preservation, as well as the first Senate campaign for John Glenn. Now, political commentators wondered if she'd be seen after the announcement ceremony. She ended speculation at a reception for the International Center of Photography, when a reporter asked. "Sure." Jackie smiled. "I'll campaign."

Soon after, she was on the telephones as a volunteer, and sold sev-

eral tables at a thousand-dollar-a-plate fund-raising dinner. She worked
the Boston campus of Regis College and a largely Republican St. Louis
suburb. In Puerto Rico just before its primary, as she chatted with the
vendors and gawkers in the streets, she was hailed as a "near-goddess."
For Kennedy to keep going, it was crucial he win New York, and she
campaigned there vigorously. Headlining a Greek-American fund-
raiser, Mrs. Onassis shook hands and signed autographs for fifteen hundred attendees who paid twenty-five dollars each to attend. She spoke
Spanish with El Salvadorans, and stretched across street-corner fruit
stands to shake hands with Korean store owners. New York proved to
be one of the few key primaries that Kennedy won. Privately, however,
Mrs. Onassis was realistic about the chances of taking the nomination
from an incumbent president. As Teddy White recorded, she "called
together in her apartment a group of older friends to explore some
graceful way of getting her brother-in-law out of the hopeless campaign."[1]

Political coverage was also being focused on the purported power of
Nancy Reagan on the hustings. Lally Weymouth, in a New York Times
story, offered detailed investigation into an incident that illustrated the
extent of Nancy's power. Several weeks before the New Hampshire primary, Reagan adviser John Sears overheard another adviser, Ed Meese,
saying that Sears, along with Lake and Black, would be fired from the
campaign. Sears suggested to Nancy that former Reagan aide William
Clark be invited to head the campaign, because of the rivalries. She
called Clark, who couldn't join. Nancy admitted to doing so without
consulting her husband, but pointed out that she was only being "helpful," which she thought quite different from wielding influence. Mrs.
Reagan emphasized that she wasn't attempting "to pull strings" on firing
personnel. On the heels of this, a loud argument ensued with the three
men telling Reagan that they wanted Meese to go. Lake and Black
traveled with Nancy to Chicago the following day, trying to persuade
her to help get Meese out. In the meantime, she personally called
friend William Casey to head the campaign. He accepted.

Nancy kept an even keel, and considered Meese's perspective. As
adviser Peter Hannaford said, she attempted "to ameliorate the tensions." Her presence, however, was strong. The day of the primary,
sitting next to Ronnie as he told the troika they were fired, she
prompted Sears into responding.

As Sears himself said after the debacle, Nancy was closer to Reagan
than any other human being, but outside observers jumped to assume
that she forged Reagan's political positions. Nancy would only say she
and Reagan often discussed "how to approach an issue," though after
nearly three decades of their partnership she admitted, "I influence
him." She didn't order him. Her influence, however, was substantial,

and in reality, it conflicted with the supposition that she was conservative.

Mrs. Reagan was shrewd in political interviews, listening carefully
to the question. If she could not answer honestly, she skillfully replied
with vague incomplete sentences, feigned ignorance, or simply repeated
Ronnie's public stand. When asked if she agreed with his view that
Vietnam was "a noble cause," Nancy responded by explaining why *he*
felt that way. She did not reveal what she thought. Sears, for one, said
that particularly on women's issues she was a counterbalance to the
reactionary conservatives. Nancy had considerably softened her harsh
stances of 1976. While she still supported abortion only in cases of rape
or incest, or when the mother's life was endangered, she'd become more
moderate on equal rights, supporting equal pay for equal work and
stating that after eight unsuccessful years of struggle for the ERA, the
women's movement should now concentrate on "the statute route."
Some felt that Ronald Reagan's campaign promise to name the first
woman to the Supreme Court was Nancy's suggestion. On another occasion, when reporters questioned Reagan's view that marijuana was
more cancerous than tobacco, Nancy stage-whispered to him, "You
wouldn't know." Ronnie responded, "I wouldn't know."

On other social issues, she maintained the conservative line, against
gun control and for the death penalty. And sometimes there were slips
of the tongue. During a speech for wealthy Chicago Republicans,
Nancy told her husband in a live broadcasted telephone call that she
wished he could be with her to "see all these beautiful white faces."
Though she later caught herself to add, "beautiful *black* and white
faces," she was severely criticized. She attracted negative press coverage, exemplified by Julie Baumgold's *New York* magazine profile, edito-
rializing that Nancy "always suppresses the little touch of the bitch
inside. . . ." If conservative Republicans had unjustly despised First
Lady Eleanor Roosevelt, liberal Democrats unjustly despised candidate's
wife Nancy Reagan. Never before in history had press perceptions of a
presidential candidate's wife prior to the convention evoked such un-
reasonable odiousness. Her son, who had liberal views, noted that because she was a "strong" woman, it was inevitable that she made
enemies. Mrs. Reagan took valid criticism well, but she said that the
"unfair" remarks hurt her.

If Nancy was *publicly* anti-ERA, anti-abortion, and anti–gun control, another candidate's wife, Barbara Bush, supported all three issues.
In the January Iowa caucus, George Bush won with 33 percent of the
vote, 3 percent more than Reagan. It reflected poorly on Sears, Black,
and Lake. Without Ronnie's knowledge, Nancy had been meeting with
Sears "in corridors and corners," trying to work out campaign staff
problems. To protect her husband from news of the growing infighting,

she said she'd "make up excuses." After Reagan won New Hampshire and—according to Mike Deaver—Nancy "stage-managed" Sears, Black, and Lake out, she called to tell Deaver, "We need help." Deaver returned as a personal aide in public relations but part of a "team" with Nancy, writing that they were "united by our shared belief that her husband needed to be protected, whether he wanted it or not." It paralleled the work of Mrs. Harding and Harry Daugherty, who had recorded, almost precisely as Deaver would, how he and the candidate's wife could "team" together and "push . . . our candidate."

As a media orchestrator, Deaver was superb, but Nancy held her own in ingratiating the Fourth Estate. When her old friend, now a CBS news reporter, Mike Wallace, asked Ronnie tough questions, Nancy angrily scrutinized him and yelled at Wallace during a break. The air was tense. Then Mrs. Reagan literally jumped into his lap, giggled, and broke the tension.[2]

At the Republican Convention that nominated Reagan in July, all four Reagan children were there, but Patti, well known as a liberal, and Ron, now apprenticed to the Joffrey Ballet, didn't plan to campaign. Maureen would campaign, but felt that Nancy and her father "don't need anybody else but themselves."

Past political rivals were also there. When Reagan's idea of having Ford on the ticket as vice president was proposed, the former president would reflect, "Betty's recovery was never talked about, but subjectively it was a factor." Ford turned down the offer, Betty "grateful" and "relieved," flatly stating, "My new life in recovery was precious to me and I was glad to be done with politics." Nancy Reagan was also "relieved" by the decision, but Betty Ford wasn't quite done with politicking. At the convention, the former First Lady "wanted to be a part" of a scheduled ERA rally and was disturbed at "how many Republicans came to try and talk me out of it." Many told her it "wouldn't reflect well" on Republicans, but she was "mad at the party" for now abandoning its longtime ERA commitment. Only as a favor to Jerry, who asked but didn't *tell* her not to march, did she bow out. Watching the parade from her window, she was "a dutiful wife" but a "disappointed feminist in one quivering package."

The Reagans paid a courtesy call on Betty and her husband, but whether it was her feminist alliance or another factor, Mrs. Ford was not invited to certain events that were a former First Lady's due. The snub did not upset her. With "self-confidence," she had faced "the fact that I wasn't a favorite of everyone's. And that was all right. Not everybody is a favorite of mine."

Meanwhile, in the Bush family suite, a phone call came in for George from Reagan. He listened for a moment, smiled, then upturned a thumb to Barbara. Reagan, however, asked Bush to keep the fact that he'd chosen him as vice-presidential running mate secret for the moment.

When the news was announced, Barbara rejoined a jubilant George in the hotel corridor as reporters crowded around. When a woman reporter asked Mrs. Bush and her husband about their support of ERA and flexible stand on abortion, George Bush replied that to reach political harmony there were often "concessions" that had to be made. Some thought there might be a personal "gulf" between the Californian Reagans and "Eastern Establishment" Bushes, Germond and Witcover writing, "Neither he nor Nancy Reagan was entirely comfortable with George and Barbara Bush," and initially, Mrs. Reagan admitted, "I didn't like George Bush. However, the Bushes were loyal. Barbara looked Reagan in the eye and said, "Governor, let me promise you one thing. We're going to work our tails off for you."[3]

At the New York Democratic Convention, Mrs. Onassis attended a breakfast fund-raiser but didn't attend the sessions as she had in 1976. For Rosalynn Carter, the summer had brought more bad news. Just before leaving for the July 1980 inaugural of the new president of Peru as Jimmy's representative, the First Lady heard alarming speculation in the press about her brother-in-law Billy having acted as an unregistered agent for Libya. She called the president twice in one morning, "saying she needed to be calmed down before leaving for South America." But he would reflect that "Rosalynn and I had a kind of blind faith that we would be successful in overcoming great political odds, as we had done so many times before." At Camp David, just before leaving for the convention, Rosalynn and Jimmy called each delegate, asking them to oppose Kennedy's open-convention proposal, and to retain their loyalty to the president. Her doubts quickly dissipated. Throughout the roll call, she checked her ballot and—as Carter was renominated—jumped and wildly cheered.

Rosalynn personally considered Reagan to be no threat because his "politics were so bad. . . ." When Reagan remarked in a gaffe that Carter had chosen to open his campaign in an Alabama town where the Ku Klux Klan had been founded, a "particularly alarmed" Nancy insisted that more help was needed, and told Reagan pollster Dick Wirthlin to get Stuart Spencer, an expert in political public relations, to join the crew. Spencer was a past foe from the '76 campaign, when he'd vilified Reagan for Ford. Nancy, however, put aside past disputes to get Reagan elected. Mrs. Reagan, meanwhile, felt that although Carter "may have been well informed . . . there was something grim and moralistic about him that made people feel bad."

During a swing through Missouri, Carter called on ninety-five-year-old Bess Truman, and emerged with the message that she "asked me to point out that she has a heart full of love for the people of this country." It was short of a formal endorsement. In 1976, Carter had requested permission to visit her for political support. According to her Secret Service agent, Bess, being a staunch Humphrey supporter, refused. Margaret Truman would state that the Carters "ignored" Bess except for birthday messages. However, for her part, Rosalynn had sent flowers with the birthday messages, and told one writer, "Since Jimmy and I have lived in the White House, I keep hearing things about Bess Truman. Marvelous things. She was without a doubt one of the most beloved occupants here." According to Katie Louchheim, Mrs. Truman thought that Rosalynn Carter "was more like Eleanor Roosevelt than any First Ladies in between," and Bess had always made a point of saying how much she admired Mrs. Roosevelt. Bess remained adamantly independent. At a private luncheon, she balked when it was suggested that she move in with her daughter. Katie Louchheim recalled Mrs. Truman's "caustic" response: "When that time comes I'll go to a home."[4]

Whether Bess supported Carter or Reagan wasn't divulged. Others took sides. Betty Ford, though openly opposing Reagan's views on abortion and ERA, supported her party, and agreed to help rally support among moderates. Just nine days after she joined with Jacqueline Onassis and Rosalynn Carter at the Kennedy Library dedication, Lady Bird Johnson had joined the First Lady at a Carter fund-raiser. The Nixons supported the Reagans.

In the heat of the campaign, Rosalynn took a moment to savor a personal triumph. In September 1980, Congress passed and funded her Mental Health Systems Act. From the primaries to the convention, she and Senator Kennedy had maintained polite relations, and worked together toward the goal. As had been done for Lady Bird's bill, both East and West Wings had lobbied Congress to get Rosalynn's bill passed. On July 24, Carter's chief domestic affairs adviser, Stuart Eizenstat, had been informed that the First Lady was prepared to arm-twist House speaker Tip O'Neill "to request expedited floor action . . . before she leaves for Peru . . ." Even before the bill passed, Carter's proposed budget included the commission's recommendation for a $47 million increase in research funding.[5]

On the trail, Rosalynn, with a soft blond hue to her hair and pastel linens, hit hard on Reagan in regions where Carter support lagged. She was dubbed the party's "most effective platform defender," and William Safire, in his essay "Women and Power," praised Rosalynn's East Wing as more effectively run than Jimmy's West Wing.[6]

Meanwhile, speculation on the power of Rosalynn, Nancy, and Keke Anderson—wife of the Republican congressman who bolted the party and ran on a third ticket—provoked wide media coverage. Safire, for one, believed that Lady Bird was a "forerunner" of the new breed of candidates' wives, but that whichever woman became First Lady she would be "assertive, influential and closely involved with the conduct of the Presidency," believing they all shared "a taste for power."

It was a point illustrated, even in satire. A pack of political playing cards included portrayals of Mrs. Carter as a ventriloquist and Mrs. Reagan as a queen. One cartoon appeared with Nancy screaming her defense of Ronnie while Rosalynn, encouraged by Jimmy, put on boxing gloves. What enraged Nancy most was Carter's charge that Reagan's belief in a strong defense made him a warmonger.

Mrs. Reagan was frequently contrasted with Mrs. Carter, as she had been with Betty Ford in '76. Nancy made a point of saying that while she wouldn't attend Cabinet meetings, "I'd be active in my own way. . . ." An adviser observed that she worked her "powerful influence" subtly by keeping physically close to Ronnie in strategy meetings, and a reporter called her Ronnie's "alter ego." She limited his schedule when she believed it to be too heavy, and vetoed certain media interviews. Sometimes her influence showed publicly. Before Ronnie could respond during a television interview, she cut off the journalist, "That's not a fair judgment or statement." A close aide offered that she was "the single most important influence" in Reagan's retinue. In reference to Nancy, Congressman Barry Goldwater said, "Women control politics. They're always in the background, but I've never known a situation when they weren't pulling the strings."

Eerily, precisely sixty years before, Florence Harding had consulted her astrologer about her husband's fall campaign, and refused to discuss her possible plans as a First Lady because she feared it could provoke an earlier predicted "tragedy." Mrs. Reagan conceded, "I don't like to project into the future. I'm superstitious," and refused to forecast her role. She made a good-luck habit of bowling an orange up the airplane aisle and passing around chocolates to the press.

Pressured by reporters to name some "project," Nancy mentioned drug abuse. As she campaigned in New York, Mrs. Reagan stopped at Daytop Village, a drug-abuse rehabilitation center for youths. She had an in-depth conversation with Carol Burnett, whose teenage daughter was then suffering from drug addiction, and Art Linkletter, whose daughter died while on LSD. As governor's wife, she had attempted to arrange for former addicts to speak with youths and told parents that young people would be more convinced by their peers than they would be by doctors. Among the dozens of reporters who covered her, only Donnie Radcliffe of The Washington Post reported Nancy's interest in drug abuse with in-depth follow-up questions. Most others either ignored the issue or incidentally mentioned it, focusing instead on her power.

"I Love Nancy" campaign buttons with a red heart and picture of her were counteracted by Democrats with "Jane Wyman was Right" buttons. Stevenson had been the first divorced candidate, but Reagan was the first to be remarried. His first wife, still an actress, strictly adhered to her self-imposed rule of not speaking publicly on either Reagan or the campaign. Jane Wyman's taciturnity helped make the divorce a nonissue. When a television talk-show interviewer attempted to stir rumors that as a young actress, Mrs. Reagan had been sexually active, Nancy merely gave him a stare, and said nothing. He reiterated, "Oh, come on, did you fool around?" She tersely responded, "I don't know what you are talking about." No such irrelevant yet personally offensive questions had ever been posed to a candidate's wife before. Under the circumstances, Mrs. Reagan managed superbly. Though speculation about her personality, her power and ambition, her friends, her children, began to snowball, the seemingly fragile woman never cracked.

In October, Mrs. Reagan began a round of independent trips, although one staffer thought Ronnie's "performance always revived when she was around." Separated for just four days, Reagan called her chief aide and cracked, "[G]ive me back my wife."

In a speech to Baltimore Republican women, Nancy resounded a theme of "back to normalcy," which Florence Harding had hawked to the same type of audience in 1920. "We *must*, we just *must* win, so that we can make this country the way it always has been. People want a feeling of respect and pride in their country again, and with your help and God's, we'll bring it about." Earlier that day, she made a sentimental trip to the Bethesda, Maryland, childhood home she had been raised in by her aunt, and recalled Fourth of Julys when she put a red-white-and-blue collar on a dog. "We'd have a big parade—do they do that anymore? In those days, we did that kind of thing. Oh, I wish they would come back." A reporter covering the event said her "philosophy of nostalgia" was a "paean to the past glories of the nation and the simple pleasures of an earlier time, though part and parcel of the Reagan ideology." Joining Mrs. Reagan in Baltimore was Barbara Bush, fresh from delivering a speech at the nearby all-women's Goucher College. Just after the convention, Mrs. Bush and her husband had invited the Reagan family to their Houston home, and toward the end of the campaign the two women came to understand each other's styles, Nancy declaring, "[N]ow we've gotten to be good friends and really like each other very much." They discovered that they'd both gone to Smith College, though Nancy had graduated the June before Barbara had begun.[7]

Initially, some claimed that Mrs. Reagan was "totally against" Ronnie debating Carter. After consulting her astrologer, however, Nancy felt strongly in favor of Ronnie debating Carter. Many argued that it was too risky, but, as Joan Quigley recalled, "Nancy finally persuaded everyone that her gut feelings were sound." It was Joan who consulted the charts to choose the time, date, and setting. With Reagan's ease, many declared him the victor. Rosalynn would reflect that Jimmy made several mistakes in the debates, and while she thought Reagan "gave relatively superficial answers," she admitted that his "general demeanor" had helped him greatly in press and public perceptions.

Election day fell on the first anniversary of the taking of the hostages. On Rosalynn's last day of campaigning, she blitzkrieged Wisconsin, Illinois, Missouri, and Alabama. "Damn, damn Khomeini," she wrote with sad frustration. "All the understandable disillusionment of the American people fell on us." Hours before the polls opened, she realized the inevitable. In Georgia, Carter told reporters, "Well, I've just made my mind up. I just talked to my wife and I'm going to vote the same way she does." Before the polls closed, however, Rosalynn cried as she rested her head on her husband's shoulder. "I'm bitter enough for both of us," she would say. "I don't like to lose."

Meanwhile, across the country, the Reagans heard the election returns on the television. The phone rang. It was the president, who was conceding.

Nancy Reagan slipped into a "perfect size six" green dress. Her "honey"-colored modified bouffant with "Moonglow" touches looked impeccable. As her husband told supporters in his victory speech, "She's going to have a new title in a couple of months."

She was dressed and she was ready.[8]

– 21 –

Retro Romanticism

A TRADITION CONTINUED. As Rosalynn Carter conducted Nancy Reagan on a tour of the family quarters, she mentioned her work for the White House Trust Fund, and some of the historic objects she'd obtained for the house. As they walked through the rooms, Rosalynn had no bitterness of any kind toward her successor, and recalled how Betty Ford had shown none toward her four years before. Nancy, however, felt a "chill in her manner," but although "disappointed" at Rosalynn's hesitancy to personally take her through all the private rooms, she "also understood." After they were through, Nancy went to join Ronnie, who was meeting with Jimmy in the Oval Office. Carter invited them to make a return tour while he and Rosalynn were away.

However, the national press printed rumors that Nancy had told the Carter transition chief, Jack Watson, that she'd like the Carters to move out early, and that she'd ordered a Lincoln Bedroom wall to be knocked down. And although both stories were untrue, they became chapters of a growing legend.

Contrary to all implications, Nancy Reagan and Rosalynn Carter had no personal animosities. Their differences were strictly political. To the house staff, who had grown to love the Carters, Rosalynn was philosophical. "You'll like the Reagans. They will be different from us, there's no doubt about that. But you'll like them." Nancy viewed the Ladyship as a "hard job," and felt each First Lady had "found a way that is right for her, and just because it's not right for another doesn't mean it's wrong." When she heard that Rosalynn was hurt about the two rumors, Nancy called her to commiserate that she had "reason to be upset too, that anyone would think I was that insensitive."[1]

New, often daily, episodes followed. Just two weeks after the election, the Reagans' son Ron married a fellow dancer in a civil ceremony.

Reports stated that the Reagans weren't previously informed. (In fact, Ron had called them the night before.) Their actress daughter Patti said hypothetically that she'd smoke pot and live with a boyfriend if she chose to, even while Reagan was president. The Reagan children were all independent—often of their father's political views—but it provoked press speculations that personal relationships were strained.

Meanwhile, the *Los Angeles Herald Examiner*'s Wanda McDaniel created a censorious two-part profile of the new First Lady, reprinted in *The Washington Post* among other papers, and encouraging devastating preconceptions. McDaniel compared the Reagan ascendance to a royal restoration of coaches and trumpets, and "Nancy Reagan will be the queen of it all." A string of accusations was posed: that Nancy craved the "limelight," argued with Mrs. Bush, and ignored an NAACP speech at the convention. It quoted a "respectable" writer's recollections of her rather captious remarks about Betty Ford and her recovery. One intimate predicted that Nancy "will be the most prominent First Lady since Jackie," but another pointedly blurted out that Mrs. Reagan had "been playing" Mrs. Kennedy "forever."

To *The Washington Post*'s Donnie Radcliffe, Nancy did admit that she wanted the guidance of Jacqueline Kennedy's White House social secretary, Tish Baldrige, because she "knows how to do the sort of things I'm talking about." In an interview with McDaniel, Nancy pointed out, "You couldn't ask for two more adverse people than Eleanor Roosevelt and Bess Truman . . . My way certainly wouldn't be Rosalynn Carter's way. . . ."[2]

Speculation, however, continued to mount about Mrs. Reagan's power. Her friend Republican lawyer Roy Cohn recalled one incident, when William Simon visited the president-elect and stated in no uncertain terms his conditions for accepting the job of Treasury secretary, instead of becoming defense secretary as he wished. "Mrs. Reagan was sitting there . . . while Bill Simon was listing his requirements," Cohn chronicled. ". . . She was drinking it all in . . . And let me tell you, Bill Simon walked out of the president's life that day. I mean, he couldn't get a phone call through after that. . . . She pointed out to the president that you don't hire people who make demands before they have the job."

Conducting an efficient East Wing transition was longtime friend, lobbyist, and Democrat Nancy Reynolds, who also arranged a dinner introducing the Reagans to Washington leaders. Reynolds had an objective balance in considering her friend's power: The new First Lady wouldn't concern herself with B-1 bomber production, but Mrs. Reagan might defeat advisers "out for personal gain," and knew "what will play in Peoria." She said Nancy "doesn't mind being the heavy with the staff, she's very protective of the Governor's schedule because he's a

man who can't say 'no,' and Nancy is the one who often has to do it."
Mrs. Reagan avowed that she'd make Ronnie take afternoon naps, by
pointing out that "President Kennedy said that it makes good sense."
Her influence on Ronnie was humorously illustrated when both were
uncertain how to receive Holy Eucharist in the Episcopal service.
Nancy accidentally dropped it in the chalice of wine. Ronnie followed,
and dropped his in also, on purpose. It was also now circulated in print
that the president-elect of the United States called his wife "Mommy."
Nancy conceded that one personnel appointment she had a direct hand
in was replacing the White House physician with "an old family friend"
who'd been recommended by her stepfather, though she had been "cautioned" by some unnamed "aide" not to mention him yet by name.

There was a curious aspect to the Reagans that the press naively
mentioned but never explored. On election day, when someone spoke
of imminent victory, Ronnie knocked on wood. When Deaver began to
mention the transition before the polls closed, Reagan wouldn't "jinx"
the outcome, and was reluctant to talk about it. On election day,
Nancy's designer, Adolfo, was nervous about discussing her future:
"Let's only discuss the present, not the future. It's bad luck." About her
beliefs, Nancy continued to concede only to being "superstitious."[3]

If she fretted about Ronnie, she also strove to handle herself with
care. In the last days of the campaign, with limited sleep, she'd always
appeared perfect and fresh, doing her own makeup, giving minute attention to the appearance of her wardrobe. By her side had been aide
Peter McCoy, now to be her chief of staff. Her first press secretary,
Robin Orr, was replaced with public-relations executive Sheila Patton,
later Tate, and longtime aide Elaine Crispen was made personal assistant. Drawn from public relations and loyalty, Nancy Reagan's East
Wing was shaping up.

Most of Mrs. Reagan's press continued to focus on her "style."
She'd already stated that state dinners would be "gloves with white tie,"
with no disco dancing following. Nancy Reynolds was collecting quan-
tities of information on youth drug abuse, but it wasn't paid much heed
by the press. Nancy did state at the time that she was considering several approaches to some antidrug program as First Lady, possibly a drug
advisory committee, and though uncertain which direction she would
take, felt that while it was easier for parents to say yes, they should
more often "say no." Press coverage of the issue was virtually nonexis-
tent. In a long profile in People, for example, one single line mentioned
that among her projects would be the "noncontroversial" one of "rehabilitation of drug users."

As Reynolds worked in personnel, Tish Baldrige helped establish
East Wing administration, and would live in the White House for the
first two weeks. There was another connection to Nancy's predecessor.

When the campaign staff searched for an eastern base for the Reagans during the debates, the Virginia country home that Jacqueline Kennedy had designed was rented for them.[4]

As Washington prepared for the Inaugural, the press had stories afresh with the arrival of "the Group," a wealthy coterie of Mrs. Reagan's friends, including Jerry Zipkin, Betsy Bloomingdale, Mary Jane Wick, Jean Smith, Lee Annenberg—the latter appointed as chief of protocol, while Mrs. Wick's and Mrs. Smith's husbands were made chief of USIA and attorney general, respectively. There would be eight Inaugural balls, but at $250 a ticket they were among the more moderately priced events. The best hotel suites brimmed with moguls arriving by private jets and railroad cars, reveling at brunches, lunches, "the Candelight Dinners," breakfasts, and cocktail receptions. The Reagans were invited to many private events, but unable to attend most. When, however, Nancy Dickerson held a dinner dance at her Virginia mansion, Merrywood, Nancy Reagan and her husband attended. It had been the home of a teenage Jacqueline Bouvier.

As the Reagans sat on a raised platform in high-backed velvet chairs, the aura of the Gala was compared to a royal court coronation. Frank Sinatra—"Frances Albert" as Mrs. Reagan called him—sang "Nancy with the Radiant Face," to her, and Johnny Carson cracked that it was the first administration to have its own Hollywood premier. Sinatra had also managed the gala for Jack and Jackie Kennedy.

The new First Lady was attended by her Inaugural gown designer James Galanos and hairstylist "Mr. Julius" Bengtsson. Her Inaugural trousseau included a donated Inaugural gown, valued at $10,000, a $10,000 Maximillian mink coat—a gift from Ronnie—and a fur-lined raincoat at $1,000, with other evening gowns and day suits in velvet and silk, custom-made shoes, some sparkling with rhinestones—one pair running $200—and matching handbags—a white satin one was estimated at a lower price of $350. The cumulative worth was approximated at $25,000. Mrs. Reagan's personal appearance was a focal point for both the press and herself as a forecast of things to come. At a De la Renta fashion show at the time, an I. Magnin buyer declared that "Nancy Reagan will be good for business just like Jackie Kennedy was—it will help everyone." She said her Inaugural clothes were made by a variety of her favorite American designers—Bill Blass, Adolfo, Galanos—because "I like to give everyone a chance." What she didn't say was that most of the couture was often an outright "gift" from them to her.[5]

On Inaugural morning, in her last fifteen minutes as First Lady, Rosalynn Carter was positively euphoric. From Iran, there was good news, and as usual, to the end, this First Lady was informed. In snow-white coat she rushed down the elevator just before noon to greet the

Reagans at the North Portico, bubbly and cordial toward Nancy, who was dressed in electric "Reagan red." Barbara Bush in blue joined Joan Mondale.

Mrs. Carter tried to put her successor "at ease," recalling how Betty Ford had done so for her, yet all the while Rosalynn was "feeling very smug." Nancy perceived it as "uncomfortable and unhappy," and her version had Rosalynn being quiet. Perhaps as the most fitting final tribute to her power, Rosalynn knew a secret shared by only a handful of international officials.

Rosalynn, Nancy, and Barbara took their places among others at the Capitol's Inaugural stand—on the west front for the first time in history. Ironically, just as Reagan became president, Rosalynn Carter became most joyous. She knew that across the globe the hostages were being freed at precisely that moment. But public eyes were not on her. They were on the new First Lady. Her red coat covered a seventeen-hundred-dollar dress, although her fifteen-hundred-dollar alligator purse was visible. So was her bright red oval hat. In his Inaugural coverage, Roger Mudd of NBC pointed out to television audiences that it was "reminiscent of Jackie Kennedy's pillbox from twenty years ago."

Almost exactly as Nellie Taft had described her anxiety upon becoming First Lady in 1909, Nancy Reagan said it all "felt unreal . . . like a dream. . . . *My Lord, here I am standing here, doing what I've seen other women do in photographs and on television. And it's me.*" And like Mrs. Taft, Nancy fretted that her Inaugural ensemble had been misplaced.

After the ceremony, luncheon, and parade, as Barbara Bush returned to Admiralty House, and Rosalynn Carter to Georgia, Nancy Reagan stepped into the White House as First Lady for the first time. In her "novel" *First Family*, Patti Davis would record that when the family went upstairs, the "mother" sighed, "There's just so much history here! Imagine all the people who have just been within these walls. But, good grief, I just can't wait to redecorate." Although Nancy wouldn't confirm her plans, she confessed her belief that "houses always have to be refurbished." Ted Graber, her decorator, was staying in town after the Inaugural. To work. But if a 1981 *redecoration* was not exactly a 1961 *restoration*, the stunning appearance that night at the Inaugural Balls of the new First Lady was the heaviest hint as to whose image she cast herself in.[6]

At the last of the balls, held in the Smithsonian's National Museum of American History, the Reagans danced to an updated sound of "You'll Never Know How Much I Love You," a big-band song of the past. With her hair uncharacteristically swept back into a chignon, Mrs. Reagan's diamond earrings were prominent, and she was dressed in a dramatic flowing sheened white cape, with long white gloves, white

jeweled satin shoes, and glistening one-shoulder beaded white gown. Several yards away, on display in the First Ladies Hall, was the white-caped, white-gloved, white-shoed and white-shoulderless-beaded-bodiced Inaugural ensemble of Jacqueline Kennedy. The past seemed to merge with the present.

The era of Retro Romanticism was being ushered in.

Particularly, predictably, Democrats were the most appalled. Maryon Allen, former Democratic Senate wife and *Washington Post* columnist, was one of the first to declare she was "sick" of "the absolutely appalling overconsumerism." None criticized the deserved right to a sweet victory, but rather the scale of it, considering current statistics. The entire three-day festivity would cost $16 million. National unemployment was up to 7.4 percent. For those Inaugural guests who'd bought one thousand dollars or more worth of tickets, there was a "Taste of America" at Union Station, with samples from the nation's more exquisite restaurants. Some of the city's residents who lived on the surrounding streets entered the cordoned-off area, but not to provoke. Rich and poor mingled with each other. Everyone was simply hungry.

Days after the Inaugural, socioeconomic statistics affixed themselves to the First Lady. In fact, Nancy Reagan had not been responsible for pricing tickets, choosing menus, or planning the events. That was done by the Inaugural Committee.

Her only direct personal decisions had been what to wear.

After the extensive press detail on her Inaugural trousseau, *Time* stated that the fashion industry was flourishing "despite the recession." *The New York Times* quoted a dowager at the Inaugural as saying that Nancy Reagan gave rich mature women a "lift" because they were "tired of having to apologize for ourselves . . . we're not afraid to show it." Historian Deborah Silverman, for one, found disturbing symbolism in the Inaugural's "full-fledged cult of visible luxury and unrestrained flaunting of wealth." She blamed Nancy Reagan for epitomizing it, as she "unleashed a new era of style that melded the nouveau-riche values of the de la Rentas and Blasses with the rugged individualism of western entrepreneurs and their wives."

The entire Inaugural coverage of Mrs. Reagan had preoccupied itself with what she represented, not who she was or what "substance" she would bring to the role. In just the campaign and transition period, she'd unwittingly earned more nicknames than most women who served as First Lady—"The Iron Orange," "The Evita of Santa Barbara," and even "Little Gun," a double-entendre reference to her "firing" of staff and the "little gun" she once said she kept at her bedside. Such negative press prior to an Inaugural was unprecedented. Not since Mary Lincoln had a woman been so accused of being ravenous for power and display of it before even having a chance to prove herself as First Lady.

And Act One had only just begun.

A friend since childhood, actress Colleen Moore, reassured Mrs. Reagan that she wasn't just "a movie star," but "the star of the world."[7] Dancing, singing, or dramatizing, playing matinees and evenings, it was

Nancy Davis Reagan starring in the role of the First Lady. What she would do backstage, however, would prove equally entertaining, and even more enduring.

"They ought to elect the First Lady," Nancy Reagan had once said onstage in her lead role in *First Lady*, "and, *then*, let her husband be President."

PART III

The Avaricious Eighties
1981–1989

There is an expectation today that a woman can be and should be all the person she is capable of being. She wants and values the choices to have children. She will be her husband's wife if she chooses to marry. But she will be a person, seriously committed to her own voice in society. We are not finished yet in this great massive revolution to full personhood and full equality. . . . American women have a great hunger for more power. They have been too powerless, and they'll get it whatever way they can.

Betty Friedan,
quoted in *First Lady*, 1986

"Queen Nancy"

FIRST LADY AND FOURTH ESTATE faced off. In maroon pumps and Adolfo red suit, she nervously introduced her chief of staff as "our token male," and spoke about the Foster Grandparents Program. Reporters were told not to ask questions, but one did. "You're not going to let your husband cut [partial Foster Grandparents funding] are you?" Nancy gently chastised her for asking, but replied, "No, I'm not." She suggested they "[g]et your Kleenex ready," as the program's promotional film began and the lights dimmed. Reporters prepared questions, but under the cover of darkness, Nancy Reagan made her getaway.

A self-described "nester," she was redecorating with Ted Graber, who designed for, as he wrote, "the merchant princes who are today's royalty." They created a dramatic setting with hand-painted Chinese wallpaper in the presidential bedroom and Nancy's collection of lacquered boxes and porcelain birds scattered about. Whether the press liked the "California look" of the Reagans' private quarters was moot. Who paid for it was another matter. Nancy returned the perfunctory $50,000 decorating fund to the government, seeking instead $200,000 in private money. Those initially solicited were selectively chosen, nearly 75 percent of the "call for public assistance" provided by wealthy Reagan friends. Reagan financier Holmes Tuttle solicited nearly twenty individuals "with oil interests" in Oklahoma City and Houston. They alone gave $270,000—just weeks after Reagan decontrolled oil prices— "anxious to show their appreciation for Reagan policies. . . ." When that news broke, the "call" was stopped. At $822,641. Overlooking the fact that the large contributors received substantial tax breaks, Nancy said, "Since no money came from the taxpayers, nothing seemed wrong to me about redoing the White House."

After the redecoration job was done, Nancy most adored her "romantic" dressing room, which made her feel "that I was born in the wrong century." The new First Lady loved the splendor of the mansion, though she admitted it was "nothing like that of Buckingham Palace or Windsor Castle." Nancy frankly admitted, "I want more pomp."

It had been for her first state dinner, for British prime minister Margaret Thatcher, that Mrs. Reagan began her habit of directing flower arrangements and pretesting the entire meal, often recommending changes in sauces, vegetables, and even their names. Her viand was veal, her favorite desserts used fresh raspberries. In early 1981, Washington caterers were selling veal at about eight dollars a pound, and raspberries at six dollars for half a pint. When a working mother wrote the First Lady and asked just how she was supposed to feed her family on the new reduction of food stamps, she was sent a copy of Nancy's recipe for crabmeat and artichokes, which cost about twenty dollars to prepare. As the press reported, the reality of life outside the black iron gates on many bitter cold and stifling hot nights was less amusing. Experts disagreed on the reasons for the growing number of "bums" and "bag ladies," but nobody denied that they were "homeless." Nowhere else did the situation seem more devastatingly ironic than along the rows of park benches in Lafayette Square, across from the White House.

In March, when Nancy saw son Ron dance at the ballet and made an exploratory visit to New York's drug-abuse center Daytop Village, her dining in an expensive restaurant with Zipkin and Mrs. Bloomingdale attracted more negative press. Her crush on Frank Sinatra hadn't abated, even amid press speculation about his ties to organized crime. Many other friends had high profiles emphasizing their conspicuous consumption. Those California friends who lived or entertained in Washington, according to caterer Eric Michael, "spent tons of money on lavish layouts." Still, Nancy felt it was "important that a First Lady not let her old friendships wither. . . ." To her credit, she was loyal to her friends. To her detriment, their sybaritism further devastated her image. The aspect of her role that most bothered Nancy was the lack of privacy. But by pulling back, she even guarded what was clearly part of her public life. When she held several meetings with experts on drug abuse, including briefings by Dr. Carleton Turner, the administration's drug-abuse expert, the East Wing refused elaboration on it. That proved damaging.[1]

Like Mary Lincoln and Edith Wilson, Nancy Reagan was moved by the metaphysical. She remained skeptical of her husband's belief that Lincoln's ghost haunted the Lincoln Bedroom, until she noticed that his slanting portrait, which she kept straightening, continued to shift. When her hairdresser began to hand her a gold letter opener, she said it was bad luck to pass any knife object from one hand directly to someone else's. She wouldn't permit shoes to be stored above head level. At the Reagan Ranch, she kept a large carved pagoda "to keep evil spirits away." If she accidently put something on inside out, she dared not take it off. Mrs. Reagan wore her trademark red because it was a color she "finds lucky." And like Florence Harding, she followed the zodiac.[2]

On March 30, Nancy Reagan joined Barbara Bush for a lunch preceded by a tour of an art gallery, just blocks away from the Washington Hilton where Ronnie was speaking. During lunch, the First Lady had a queer sensation.

Sometime between the Inaugural and the ides of March, the woman who had "volunteered" her services to the Reagan campaign, clairvoyant Joan Quigley, had sensed "[s]omething bad" about the third month, and informed the First Lady. For "some reason," Nancy Reagan suddenly told fellow lunchers, "I think I'd better get back to the White House." She just "got up and left."

At the White House, a Secret Service agent informed her of "a shooting at the hotel . . ." Nancy raced to George Washington University Hospital and bolted in, yelling to the press, "[H]e's alright, he's alright!" It was Mike Deaver who met and calmed her, but kept her from seeing Ronnie. She was shunted into a stifling cell-like cubicle. Finally, demanding to see Ronnie, she was escorted into a room filled with doctors, nurses, and Secret Service agents surrounding her husband, who smiled at her from underneath an oxygen mask. He had been shot by one John Hinckley. Nancy granted the necessary permission to operate.

An hour later, the First Lady beelined into the recovery room, held the president's hand, saying she loved him, and then started to cry. One witness called it "a genuine and absolutely pure display of love, amazing, incredibly touching, overpowering." The president recorded in his diary, "I pray I'll never face a day when she isn't there . . . of all the ways God has blessed me, giving her to me was the greatest—beyond anything I can ever hope to deserve." Doctors termed Nancy "persistent" in questioning, "savvy" in medical knowledge, and "tough" in dealing with Reagan's precarious condition, and she "wanted a progress report every afternoon . . . She wanted to know everything and would let nothing slip unexplained. She'd ask why incessantly . . . She wanted exact answers . . . she'd double-check . . ."

Reagan's secretary Helene von Damm said that Deaver and the First Lady "put out the word within days that the President was hale and hearty," and requested that Vice President Bush keep a low profile. Doing so helped lift national morale over the shock, and shift focus from the larger picture of violence that it represented. The official photo of her holding Ronnie's right arm had first had airbrushed out the nurse holding his left side. As early as 6:00 A.M. Nancy would phone her press secretary to provide human-interest news from the night before. Mrs. Reagan publicly continued to repress her emotions. She lost ten pounds, making her gaunt and provoking speculation that she was secretly ill. Since she felt she "couldn't tell" the press how acutely she was actually suffering from anxiety, the conjecture continued.

She worried each time Ronnie left the complex. As they emerged

from their car at outside events, she was struck with fear. She successfully helped stop the publishing of the president's schedule in newspapers. When strangers inquired of her friends about her, she panicked: On the East Wing's suggestion, a journalism student had phoned Zipkin at his listed number for a story on her project interests. Zipkin called Nancy, and the bewildered student was intensely grilled by security. Roy Cohn watched Nancy during a play when an actor onstage fired a cap gun. He said she "jumped halfway out of her chair." There was a marked capriciousness to her, swinging from mercurial snaps to a warm gentleness. The event that she would only refer to as "March 30" shook her more deeply than anything in her life and forced her to accept the harsh reality that there were aspects of the presidency from which even she could not protect her husband.

Her reaction to "March 30" was stoic in public, frightened in private. The First Lady publicly stated that she opposed gun control because it was "putting one law on top of another," and crisply declared, "I think people would be alive today if there was a death penalty." Privately, however, she called San Francisco and hired Joan Quigley to chart the president's daily horoscope in great detail. Initially, only Deaver was fully aware of the First Lady's "special assistant."

Support also came from the sorority. Exactly one century before, when Republican Lucretia Garfield's husband had been wounded by a gunshot, Democrats Julia Tyler and Sarah Polk had written to comfort her. Now, Republican Nancy Reagan received similar letters from Democrats Jacqueline Onassis and Lady Bird Johnson, the latter telling her that LBJ had needed several weeks to fully recover from his gallbladder surgery. Nancy heeded LBJ's example, insisting that Ronnie's schedule be light. It was he who urged her to attend England's Prince Charles's wedding to Diana Spencer, because "it would be good for me."[3]

For the wedding, Nancy took her hairdresser, maid, nurse, four staff members, a photographer, and ten Secret Service agents. It was learned that a $75,000 Steuben glass bowl had been discounted to $8,000 dollars as Nancy's gift to the couple. Unknown even to her press secretary was the origin of a $250,000 diamond-ruby jewelry set that Mrs. Reagan wore overseas. It was from Bulgari. She also wore the diamond necklace she'd worn to the Inaugural. It was from Harry Winston.

It was Joan Quigley's opinion that Mrs. Reagan used her position to court New York high society, and then having done so, used that to impress the British royal family. "I think it meant a lot to her to be an accepted member of a group that was privileged, exclusive and snobbish, and she valued all her superficial status symbols and having the means to spend extravagantly. . . . Nancy felt that as First Lady she had achieved the ultimate in social position. . . . She was always very impressed by British royalty. Whenever she had Charles in tow or Princess Di, she would name-drop." The First Lady was shocked when, staying at Balmoral Castle, she was served a breakfast of American cornflakes.

During her visit to England for the wedding, Mrs. Reagan dined with a princess, lunched with a lord, supped with the royal family, took tea with the Queen Mother, and hopped to a private ball for European royalty. The queen's arrival at a polo match driving her own station wagon had been preceded by the First Lady's arrival in a six-car entourage, herself ensconced in a black limousine. In England, the First Lady told reporters that she felt the monarchy was "wonderful. I would hate to see it ever disappear." She bragged to her husband, "Nobody can give a royal wedding like the British." Not since Angelica Van Buren had a First Family member so cavorted with a royal family. It didn't help matters when the assistant manager of the Beverly Wilshire Hotel admitted publicly, "We don't do anything more for [Mrs. Reagan] than we usually do for visiting royalty." A caricature begun in the English press became an American postcard, designed by Alfred Gescheidt, showing a smiling First Lady—superimposed in ermine robes and crown. "Queen Nancy" took to the throne.

Through the spring, Nancy had conducted a "series" of "unpublicized" meetings with government and private-sector drug experts, including the American Council on Marijuana president Robert DuPont, a former Drug Abuse Prevention chief. She visited Second Genesis to investigate the methods of that rehab center. At a private lunch, she debated priorities in fighting drug abuse, asserting that it shouldn't be portrayed in films: "I want to get everybody's advice before I decide what I will do." Meanwhile, the "Queen Nancy" postcard thrived, selling out in stores. Copies were pinned on the House Rules Committee office bulletin board. *The New York Times* reported "Democratic strategists on Capitol Hill are already planning to use Mrs. Reagan's 'Queen Nancy' image to woo blue-collar voters in next year's elections."[4]

By now, Ronald Reagan had become a legend, melding reality with a heroic image by both surviving a bullet and dispelling maladorousness over it. Political critics, however, weren't daunted by personal admiration. If it was politically unwise to criticize him because of potential public reaction, "Queen Nancy" would serve the purpose.

When the Reagans returned to the White House after their summer vacation, pictures of her redecorated rooms appeared in *Architectural Digest*, which retailed for $4.95.

At ninety-five cents each, "Queen Nancy" postcards sold out faster.

The president attempted to counteract the fresh spate of criticism by comparing Nancy's *redecoration* with Jackie's *restoration*. After touring the Maryland warehouse of old White House furnishings, Mrs. Rea-

gan and her decorator saw items they wanted to use—which happened to be historical—and restored them. Mrs. Kennedy had gone wearing jeans, searching for specific historical pieces from certain rooms, examining craftsman markings and carrying them out herself. The curator even stated publicly of Nancy's redecoration, "They didn't feel any need to consult me on the upstairs though they did use the antiques I collected." He further expressed "disappointment" over her "lack of support" for the White House Preservation Fund. Every First Lady since Mrs. Kennedy had named members to her White House Preservation Committee to seek historical items. Mrs. Reagan did not. Nancy defended herself by ignoring these facts and stating that the Lincoln and Queen's bedroom suites were "hardly in the private quarters." They were in fact not only on the private floor but inaccessible to the public.

The excess of the private funds was spent on necessary house repairs, but later, when the mansion received official museum status, the East Wing claimed that it was thanks to Mrs. Reagan. In fact, the curator's staff had followed specific criteria to earn the status. It was merely granted during the Reagan tenure. There was no denying the important fact that Nancy Reagan made the mansion's general appearance appropriate and beautiful—restored floors, windows, doors, marble, new and necessary plumbing. However, contrary to Reagan press releases, it was not a "historic restoration" of presidential history as Mrs. Kennedy's had been.[5]

Just as *Architectural Digest* appeared, it was announced that a private foundation had offered to purchase a nineteen-piece "Nancy Red" china set for $209,000, about $1,000 per setting. It wasn't overpriced, but its being billed as a *necessity* during a widespread recession appeared insensitive. When an East Winger remarked that Mrs. Kennedy had bought new crystal, she was reminded that Jackie had done so as a means of aiding the poverty-stricken workers at the West Virginia glassware company. It was also not a matter of a delightfully surprising and sudden donation, as Mrs. Reagan later implied. In a May 1981 interview, the First Lady stated on the record that she wanted to "get some new china." The first day the new china was shown, the Reagan administration proposed a $41 billion cut in welfare programs, and announced that catsup qualified as a vegetable for the subsidized school lunches of underprivileged children, a statement retracted after considerable ridicule.[6]

More than any other incident, the china purchase symbolized "Queen Nancy," and it prompted the first time a president was publicly asked to defend his First Lady's judgment. At an October press conference, he harrumphed that "Nancy's taken a bum rap . . . we can't set the tables with dishes that match," and the set was bought with private funds. It did little to reduce the temperature of queen fever, but it did give satirists and artists an entire new industry. Greeting cards had her selling off Rosalynn's calico gowns and in a Blackglama mink eating government cheese. Even Ronnie's personal aide had a Nancy Reagan Halloween mask. Political cartoonists had a heyday not seen since Eleanor Roosevelt. *Rolling Stone* magazine's "Mrs. Gipper" lampooned her monthly, and *Saturday Night Live* made Nancy Reagan a regular feature, played by a man in drag, Terry Sweeney. Joan Rivers cracked that when a flying saucer landed on the lawn, Nancy came out screaming, "It's mine! It's mine!" Comedian David Letterman announced that Nancy was approached to "attack the number one crisis facing young people today," to which she asked, "Bad grooming?"

Mrs. Reagan tried to appear thick-skinned about it. When the First Lady heard about the *third* cutout-doll book of *Nancy*, partying in "tiara," and "scepter," she ordered copies and let the press know she had. At a New York dinner that fall, Mrs. Reagan began her speech in deadpanned seriousness, addressing the "Queen Nancy" issue. "Now that's silly," she snapped with mock sharpness. "Everyone knows that a crown would mess my hair." A new card appeared. The crown was gone—but her hair was messed.[7]

Barbara Bush, for one, joked that Nancy should have bought the china "one piece at a time," but the Second Lady was sensitive to the First. When she read a complimentary quote about Mrs. Reagan, Mrs. Bush telephoned the woman to thank her. Barbara didn't think that First and Second Ladies had to be close friends, but that "mutual respect for each other" was necessary. Barbara, however, was already involved in a project.

It had been in preparation for the 1980 campaign that she gave literacy serious study. "I once spent the summer thinking of all the things that bothered me—teen pregnancy, drugs, everything—and I realized everything would be better if more people could read and write." As she explained in a speech as Second Lady, quoting Lady Bird on using the "bully pulpit," she wanted a project that "would not be controversial, help the most people possible and maybe not cost more government money." Among many related projects, she joined the board of Reading Is Fundamental, coaxed a publishing CEO into forming a private sector Business Council for Effective Literacy, worked with Laubach Literary International Program, a local center for reading disabilities, and served as honorary chair of the National Advisory Council of Literacy Volunteers. Approached to take a high profile, she retorted, "I'm not going to overshadow Nancy Reagan. I'm the second wife. My time will come."

Of the china purchase, Rosalynn Carter said, "I didn't think I had to rush." Upon "retirement" to Plains, she and Jimmy plunged into work—beginning with installation of a tongue-in-groove attic. As she wrote her memoirs, Rosalynn learned the technology of a word processor. Both Carters donned blue jeans and did carpentry work for Habitat for Humanity, which provided housing for the underprivileged. Rosalynn continued mental-health projects with Emory University, and there was speculation that she'd run for the national or state legislature. Like Eleanor Roosevelt, she resisted a political candidacy, but not commentary. She criticized Reagan policy, particularly his dismissal of her mental-health act and funding reductions via block grants, because "it's going to cost the country untold human lives."

Mrs. Carter refrained from politics when she met Mrs. Reagan again, in the White House that fall. Both were somber. President Sadat had been killed, and Nancy, among others, successfully argued against Ronnie attending the funeral. Instead, the former presidents Carter, Ford, and Nixon . . . and Rosalynn—because she was a close friend of Jihan Sadat—were going. In Egypt, Rosalynn joined Middle Eastern "First Ladies"—the new president's wife, Susan Mubarak, Mrs. Nimeiri of Sudan, and the former empress of Iran.

On the trip, Nixon broke the ice by warmly complimenting Rosalynn's appearance. Then Mrs. Carter asked about Mrs. Nixon. Pat might also have attended, but was just then in the process of moving into their new home in Saddle River, New Jersey. There, they'd relinquish their Secret Service protection because of its cost to taxpayers, but Pat still forayed into New York weekly.

At the time of the Sadat funeral, Betty Ford had a previous commitment. On an earlier trip to Washington, she had met briefly with Nancy Reagan over tea, but in the fall, she steered clear of her former residence. Betty was stumping for the ERA, one issue on which she felt the administration was disappointing. She named unemployed black women and single working mothers as those most hurt by budget cuts, saying that "we have to have people in the Administration who are more open-minded in dealing with these problems." On Columbus Day, Betty Ford spoke on the steps of the Lincoln Memorial. "As a woman and as a Republican, I don't see how we can continue to stand up and be proud if we have not guaranteed the rights of half our population. We've gotten past the point of asking. We are . . . demanding recognition of our right to equality." Then Mrs. Ford stepped aside. The once-hesitant feminist Lady Bird Johnson said civil-rights legislation was "won because it was the right thing to do and was long overdue. The Equal Rights Amendment is the right thing to do and is long overdue. . . ." The amendment, nonetheless, would die.

Lady Bird Johnson had strong words for Reaganomics, and gently chastised Reagan's lack of support for civil rights. She feared nuclear-weaponry buildup, and said Reagan's education cuts "put our future in peril." Lady Bird taped TV spots for, and devoted time and money to,

Meals on Wheels, providing food to the elderly, but strongly disagreed with Reagan's contention that the private sector would fully compensate for the void of government aid. Chairperson of her communications company, estimated to be worth as much as $20 million, she nevertheless felt that the wealthy benefited too much from Reagan's tax plans, and could afford to pay more taxes. She too was affected by new Reagan policy. The administration decided that discount military stores could no longer service former presidents and First Ladies. Lady Bird stopped shopping at the nearby PX.

The senior of the sorority made no public remarks about the Reagans, but then Bess Truman remained unmoved by her inclusion in a Gallup Poll of most-admired women. "I don't know why," she responded when told. Before her $3.95 seafood-combo platter arrived, the ninety-six-year-old former First Lady shocked a restaurateur by imbibing a highball. "I didn't think a little lady in a wheelchair would have such a high-powered drink before lunch."

Mrs. Onassis refrained from public comment on the Reagans. When her longtime friend former chief usher J. B. West died, however, Jacqueline Onassis helped arrange for his burial at Arlington Cemetery by calling "First Lady to First Lady." Only a president could order burial there of nonmilitary persons, and Reagan immediately granted Jackie's request. Nancy claimed that "we called each other Jackie and Nancy, even though we've never met. We feel like we know each other." Mrs. Reagan said that in speaking with Mrs. Onassis, Mrs. Ford, and Mrs. Nixon, they advised she "do the things that you're interested in . . ."[8] She was trying. On a New York trip, Mrs. Reagan studied the approach of yet a third drug-rehab center, Phoenix House, remarking that drugs made "brains turn to mush." She told the National Federation of Parents for Drug-Free Youth and the American Council on Marijuana that drug abuse endangered "our whole next generation," and she'd been "trying to learn its causes and consequences." There was no explanation of how the administration's budget cuts of drug programs by 25 percent would work in tandem with its First Lady's project. Her chief of staff, Peter McCoy, said that since the West Wing hadn't "appointed people in the drug area," her activities "might be in conflict with White House policy." McCoy left, his role temporarily filled by White House public-relations chief Michael Deaver's aide Joe Canzeri.[9]

The First Lady's connection to the first Reagan scandal, however, eclipsed any drug work. The media learned that one thousand dollars had been given to NSC adviser Richard Allen from a Japanese magazine, *Shufo no Tomo*, which he kept in a White House safe. The magazine purported to have been given "an interview" only because it had offered payment to Mrs. Reagan. The truth was that she'd posed for one picture, and knew nothing of the "thank-you fee." As the "serious judgment errors" unraveled, she supported Deaver and West Wing chief of staff James Baker in dumping Allen for public-relations damage control. In the midst of the Allen scandal, her social secretary had announced that there was a tablecloth shortage at the White House. Angry Muskegon residents, suffering one of the highest unemployment rates in Michigan, sent Nancy a Band-Aid, thread, a Christmas seal, a turkey wishbone, a peso, and an empty book of food stamps. The East Wing had no comment, but a cartoon "Queen Nancy" was asked how she felt about the Allen money. "Really steamed!" came the answer, "I could've used that extra grand for new tablecloths!"

It was more than "Queen Nancy" that made it, as Nancy said, "a very rough period." Libyan terrorist threats not only prevented her from Christmas shopping but caused the cancellation of her traveling to drug-abuse events, a fact kept from the media at the time. Extending the first peace pipe, she invited reporters to partake in holiday fare. They prodded repeatedly as to whether she could forget March 30. "From time to time," Nancy whispered tearfully. She confessed that nobody "sets out to be a bad First Lady." Of "Queen Nancy" she said, "I wouldn't have wanted to know that person . . . maybe part of it was my fault . . . when I'm hurt or troubled—my tendency is to pull back . . . on the other hand, I think perhaps the press jumped a little too quickly without knowing me." She had a valid complaint about her position. "Anybody can say anything they want, and you have no recourse . . ." If Nancy personally had denied every innuendo, she would appear defensive. Her press secretary was. When a reporter asked about public criticism, she snapped, "How do you know? Did you take a poll?"

In fact, an early December *Washington Post–ABC News* poll gave the First Lady a 23 percent disapproval rating, which had risen since June from 18 percent, the "sharpest" critics being "blacks, lower income people and Democrats . . ." A December 22 *Newsweek* poll had 66 percent of the population saying Nancy's conspicuous consumption was wrong "during a time of Federal budget cuts and economic hardships," and compared to Jackie, Lady Bird, Pat, Betty, and Rosalynn, 61 percent said she wasn't sympathetic with "the problems of the poor and underprivileged." Nearly half disapproved of her, and of the sorority, she was rated most unpopular.

The Democratic national chairman, who would later become a confidant of the First Lady's, commented, "Their life style obviously presents some political problems. . . ." Mrs. Reagan's longtime friend CBS correspondent Mike Wallace gently forced her to face the music. "Don't believe it's all malice, because where there's smoke, there's some fire." Betsy Bloomingdale defended Nancy: "Let's face it, Lady Bird Johnson was a very rich lady, nobody questioned what *she* spent on her clothes." It was true that, on her gowns, Nancy wasn't spending much—of her own money.

A *Washington Post/ABC News* poll in February, 1981 had shown that 23 percent felt that Reagan cared more about helping the rich than he did the poor. A year later, that figure had jumped to 54 percent. The year 1981 had marked the deepest recession in several decades. It ended with an 8.9 percent unemployment high. The president was weekly battling for deeper budget cuts in federal programs that assisted the underprivileged. On January 20, the first anniversary of the Inaugural, the Reagans danced to a Lester Lanin tango. The president, in white tie and tails, joked that it was like being "on the set of *High Society,*" but all eyes popped at the sight of Nancy. Her gown was covered entirely in glimmering black sequins on which was planted a huge beaded white star. And she hadn't paid for the gown.[10]

It was after the Allen situation, as the Reagan tax forms were being prepared, that the First Lady asked some of the president's staff if she could continue her arrangement with designers, predominantly her three favorites—Galanos, Blass, and Adolfo—to accept and wear publicly their new evening gowns, daysuits, and accessories. How many items and how much they were worth was never disclosed, but at least one lender, Jean Louis, had sent twenty-two thousand dollars' worth. Described as "loans," they remained in the First Lady's clothing storage hall. Some in the West Wing suggested that the gowns be immediately reported, returned, and that the First Lady promise to stop the practice. Instead, on January 14, the East Wing contacted the Parsons School of Design with the news that Nancy would be sending about a dozen gowns to them to distribute to permanent collections of fashion schools and museums for display and study. The story leaked to the press, and, unfortunately, was hyped to give the wild misperception that she was almost unloading hot items. Four days later, as a means of PR damage control, a letter under the signature of the First Lady's personal assistant was sent to the designers, explaining, "Although Mrs. Reagan has decided that she will no longer accept designer-loaned clothing, she . . . intends to continue her practice of donating . . ." The letter was printed in the press.

Mrs. Reagan promised to divulge specifically on a requisite report which "loaned" items she would retain. Her office offered the fact that the alternative to divulging on the report was "to pay for them." Unlike most other women who made such donations to museums, the First Lady didn't take a tax deduction—since she hadn't paid for them—and neither did the designers.

Most political critics didn't understand that the fashion "industry" wasn't dominated by the handful of famous designers but—by some accounts—was the third-largest industry in America, the leading one in

New York, providing more tax revenue and employing more workers there than any other single business. Fashion editor Nina Hyde felt that "with the American fashion business downturn at the moment and the industry's push for gains in the international market, Mrs. Reagan as a showcase for American clothes has an enhanced role. . . ." Executive Judith Kroll believed Nancy had a "trickle down" effect because, in the working job of First Lady, she affirmed that "working women don't have to wear pantsuits and ties to be taken seriously." The First Lady's style, while not leading a "look," like Mrs. Kennedy's, did have some effect; one Fifth Avenue clothier even ran ads suggesting, "Do as Nancy Does: Store Your Old Furs in a New Silk Raincoat."

At five feet four inches, a perfect size 6, there was no denying that Nancy Reagan had panache, and usually looked ravishing. She was genuinely interested in haute couture. Dressed primarily in red, black, or white, she chose with a discerning skill her Bill Blass fashions, for example, by videos sent her by the designer. When she heard that her gown on display at the Smithsonian may have been stretching, she was "so alarmed" that its designer came to work with a conservationist in preserving it. At its presentation ceremony, Nancy had announced the creation of a "First Ladies Fellowship," which annually funded scholars studying the technological and socioeconomic aspects of the American clothing industry throughout history. "We have a grand tradition of clothing design in America and a dedication to fine craftsmanship that is unparalleled," she remarked. At the ceremony, her eyes also caught the bright "Nancy Red" tie of a young man. "I see I've got influence everywhere," she giggled.

Long before she became First Lady, Nancy—like many socialites—had been offered, and accepted, free gowns. For designers it was both gratitude and advertisement. In Mrs. Reagan's case, she did not keep all the gifts, but made a habit of donating items to costume collections. As First Lady, she'd merely continued doing so. But it raised several serious issues that were neither willingly answered by Mrs. Reagan nor pursued by the media. Her apparent breach as First Lady was that "loans" meant she should have returned the dresses to their lenders, and not pass them on as "gifts" to third parties. In addition, several designers, among them Geoffrey Beene, questioned whether the gowns' construction was necessarily worthy of display and study. Prior to 1981, had she taken tax deductions for her donation of gifts? The serious question, however, was whether her temporary use of the gowns constituted a "gift," and most damaging of all, if Mrs. Reagan had violated the 1977 Ethics in Government Act. According to that, the Reagans were not only re-quired to report all "gifts" valued at over thirty-five-dollars, but "finan-cial liabilities exceeding $10,000" on the public disclosure form.

Whether Nancy Reagan broke the ethics law was never resolved, but in one sense the damage was done, and the ripple effect was increasingly political. Most devastating was that the same week Nancy's gown donations were announced came news that the poor waited in long lines to get surplus government cheese. *The Wall Street Journal* blamed the First Lady for the growing departure of women from the GOP. Political analyst William Schneider said she compromised the young presidency by proving an administration "bias towards the rich." CBS showed a woman being evicted because of impoverishment at the hand of Reaganomics, and followed with a "New Clothes Scandal" segment. One of her handbags cost more than the annual allotment of food stamps for a family of four. And that fact was widely reported across America.

In her designer gowns, dining off her red china, Nancy Reagan became a monster, hated by advocates of the poor, dismissed by the politically astute, a cause of embarrassment to subdued Republicans.

Commentator Barbara Grizzuti Harrison stated that other First Ladies had also enjoyed the good life, but none would "flaunt a personal style so at odds with the national moods as had Nancy Reagan, who seems not to have grasped the principle that, in order for national morale not to plummet, there must be a sense of shared circumstance between the rulers and the ruled . . . Thirty million Americans are living under the poverty line, and Nancy shows few signs of being sensitive to their plight." Suzy Robson, a Washington actress who briefly came to be known for her Nancy Reagan parody, also played Queen Marie Antoinette in front of the White House at a "Let Them Eat Cake" sketch, kicking off a nationwide fund-raiser rally for the nation's hungry. It was a metaphor of how the two images—America's greedy, imperious, out-of-touch First Lady and the greedy, imperious, out-of-touch French queen—became intertwined as one caricature.

Of the entire debacle, the First Lady merely stated, "I'm sorry that what I've been trying to do has been misinterpreted." Privately, Nancy frantically sought help from her special "consultant." She telephoned Joan Quigley about her image problem. "I'm getting a terrible press. It's so unfair. I'm really a very nice person. Can you tell me what to do? I'm willing to pay you. . . . I want everyone to love me."

Quigley felt that Nancy herself had a power that was "almost psychic," but that "part of Nancy's problem" was that she "expected to be treated like Jackie. . . . The state of the union and the mood of the country were as unlike as Nancy and Jackie, who despite certain superficial similarities, were very different women." Joan accepted the fact that Nancy "had not written so much as a perfunctory thank-you note. I knew I could expect nothing from Nancy other than the token sum I would ask and she would agree to pay." Still, for payment, Joan would advise her on which publications she should grant interviews to, among those requesting one, as well as the astrologically correct times to talk to reporters. Joan tried not to call through the switchboard, but used the codename Nancy gave her, "Joan Frisco," when she had to. She was utterly discreet.

Publicly, West Wing pollster Dick Wirthlin carefully offered to a reporter that Nancy began to realize that her actions made her not "as helpful as she might have been. . . ." Behind closed doors there was alarm.[11]

A Camp David meeting with Wirthlin, Deaver, Canzeri, and Stu Spencer convened to deal frankly with the liability of the First Lady. "They worked out a scenario of how to turn her image around," a source told journalist Fred Barnes. Some suggested that Nancy assume an almost nineteenth-century hostess role. Deaver and Wirthlin disagreed, feeling that she could become an administration asset. She would not have to change dresses or friends, but thoroughly closet them to her private life, as well as attempting to be more comfortable with the press. Finally, they scrutinized her "project." There were only two Foster Grandparent divisions in the area. A bona fide "project" like beautification was needed.

The results of the brainstorm were presented to an initially "somber" First Lady. When she realized, however, that her image posed potential danger to her president's political life, she had the greatest motivation to help destroy "Queen Nancy." But she steadfastly avowed that drug abuse was what genuinely concerned her. The cynical image makers called it "too depressing." Nancy remained adamant. Her press secretary suggested "can-do" projects. Another said it was a "First Lady issue" already tied to Betty Ford. Nancy held her ground. "If you try to do something that really isn't you, then you're going to get in trouble."

James Rosebush became her chief of staff, hired by and reporting to Deaver. Rosebush not only had a sense of balance in dealing with the reality of the "Queen Nancy" problem, but had also been operating the administration's private-sector initiative. He brought direction. Since the administration was cutting federal funding of drug-abuse programs, and Mrs. Reagan approached the issue as a parent hoping to help youths, the focus became clear.

Nancy Reagan would emphasize the grass-roots efforts of nonprofit groups, and elementary and high school children who'd either confronted, overcome, or were rehabilitating from drug addiction. Nothing more. Nothing less.

In the first weeks of Rosebush's tenure, the First Lady and a planeload of reporters took off for a two-day drug-abuse trip, to Florida and Texas. In Florida, in contrast to a grammar-school stop to see ALPHA—a motivation program to steer third to fifth graders from drug use—she spent an emotionally exhausting three-hour session in a STRAIGHT program, which had parents interact with their drug-addicted teenagers in often brutally honest sessions. She was stupefied by stories of "how they had prostituted themselves . . . burned crosses in their arms, taken insecticides, turned their younger siblings and pets on to drugs. . . ." With spontaneous eloquence, she began telling the parents that the greatest pain humans experienced was usually between parent and children, and she respected them "for acknowledging their family problems." Even the Secret Service agents cried.

In Texas the First Lady met with Governor Clements and a citizens' action group, part of an umbrella Texas War on Drugs Program headed by industrialist Ross Perot. Successful in initiating legislation to close drug-paraphernalia shops and revoke licenses of doctors who overmedicated, the program was funded by Perot, one estimate being $1.2 million. It suited the private-sector emphasis of the Reagan view of fighting drug abuse, and the First Lady hoped to have replicated programs. "Which," her press secretary admitted, "really means finding one major leader in each state to fund much of it." Meanwhile, anti-Reagan picketers marched during her meeting. One sign read: NANCY REAGAN: IS SAVING CHILDREN IN FASHION? Reporters carefully watched for her reactions, and asked if she'd got a "bum rap" in the press the last year. Mrs. Reagan merely responded, "I just want to talk about children and drugs."

A week later she told governors' wives in the White House, "There is a secret war in this country . . . The enemy is drugs and it is taking captive millions of our children, and even killing them." Nancy approached them with assuredness. "I have decided to seek the help of those with the real influence—the governors' wives. . . . Our role as women . . . must extend beyond worrying about our children . . . we must organize . . ." She promised them a report from her forthcoming White House briefing on drug use and the family. A month later, she addressed the morning session of an East Room meeting of medical, corporate, and civic leaders, kicking off the new Drug Use Prevention Program. Down the hall were vitrines of drugs: cocaine, marijuana, pills, heroin, and the paraphernalia used to hide them in. Weeks later, Reagan announced formation of a drug task force, and boosted his drug policy adviser Carleton Turner to director of the White House Drug Abuse Policy Office.

In March, behind the scenes, Nancy's press secretary sounded out Helen Thomas about having the First Lady perform at the annual Gridiron Dinner. A satirical number was written by Sheila Tate and presidential speechwriter Landon Parvin, the First Lady agreeing only on the condition that she spoof herself. She memorized her lyrics, and secretly rehearsed on the dinner stage.

After a short break at the Gridiron Dinner, a clothes rack full of dresses was wheeled onto the stage, and a woman in feather boa, yellow boots, flowered dress with safety pins, cartwheel hat, and butterfly bloomers peeked through and began singing. It was the First Lady. In comic voice, she bemoaned that the china was the "only thing new," her couture was all "second-hand," and pouted, "Even though they tell me that I'm no longer Queen, Did Ronnie have to buy me that new sewing machine?" The media leaders rose with shouts of "bravo," and "encore," but Maine governor Joseph Brennan pointed out, "There are still ten million unemployed." The First Lady was relieved, and the East Wing announced it as the turning point for the "new" Nancy, but both she and her staff would have to vigilantly maintain it.[12]

When she joined the president in Europe for a June economic summit, her attendance at a scheduled dinner hosted by Vicomtesse Jacqueline de Ribes with a society guest list was canceled. In Germany and Italy, she visited drug centers. Her press secretary announced that Mrs.

Reagan had returned the Bulgari jewels given her in 1981 just after she'd worn them to the royal wedding. The only criticism came from the French fashion press when she wore a daring outfit of rhinestone-hemmed black knickers.

Upon return, she traveled to the heartlands, declaring that "no area is safe from the [drug] threat." She answered questions on a live radio call-in program, raised funds to send recovering addicts to a New York conference, and told them, "I'm so proud . . . I could just pop." When a radio caller asked about the government's role, Nancy said, "I don't think financing is the real problem," and illustrated her point by mentioning the success of Alcoholics Anonymous, "and it's not federally funded." She still encountered hostilities, trailed by large protest contingencies. MARIE ANTOINETTE HAD IT COMING, read one sign. When Nancy spoke at the University of Iowa, marchers shouted "Nice dress, Nancy—ten thousand bucks?" and "Your husband's policies are driving us to substance abuse."[13]

The deep Reagan cut of 26 percent of federal funding via block state grants deeply shook some drug-abuse programs. In Los Angeles, for example, cuts would reduce $9.6 million to $7.6 million, jeopardizing the existence of some of its eighty-five programs. It remained a potential problem for the First Lady's project, casting doubt on her effectiveness. Columnist Charles McCabe snapped, "It is the cynical use of all the public relations apparatus of the White House to get the First Lady off the hook . . . that frosts me, and I daresay a lot of other Americans."

However, the truth was that Nancy Reagan's interest in drug abuse went back to 1967. Only the attempt to publicize it was public relations. In the face of criticism of her husband's cuts, she unswervingly kept to her focus, and her determination helped keep criticism at a simmer. Meanwhile, she was enduring a trauma exceeded only by March 30.

Mrs. Reagan was only the second twentieth-century First Lady whose father saw her assume the role, a distinction shared solely by Nellie Taft, Caroline Harrison, and Julia Grant. Every night she phoned Loyal Davis, all the while knowing that he was dying. When he took a turn for the worse, she flew to her parents' Phoenix home and accompanied him to the hospital. There, Nancy moved into an adjoining suite for ten days, her senior staff operating from a nearby motel, the first "temporary" East Wing established without a West Wing staff. On August 19, with Nancy at the side of her beloved "Bopa," he died. For some time, she held his hand. Then, fearing that her ailing mother would learn of his death on the news, she rushed back to tell her. The next day, Alfred Bloomingdale died of cancer, after several weeks of salacious details about his relations with a young mistress. Although she risked a backlash of criticism, the First Lady remained steadfastly loyal to Mrs. Bloomingdale. "Not only did she hold my hand all the way through the illness, but she even went to see him in the hospital," said Betsy. "And she was *most* supportive through the other problem." A third funeral, weeks later, also posed potential criticism. Princess Grace died, and Nancy headed the U.S. delegation to the politically insignificant but notoriously hedonistic principality of Monaco. It was stressed that she went out of "friendship," having known Kelly in Hollywood. No censure ensued.[14]

It was a fourth funeral, the next month, that proved the most historic, attended not only by Nancy Reagan, but by Betty Ford and Rosalynn Carter. Living longer than any other First Lady in history, Bess Wallace Truman had died at age ninety-seven.

Her decline had begun with a series of illnesses, the most serious being a broken hip she suffered when refusing to stay bedridden. Though housebound, Bess remained lively, cracking jokes, aware of everything, even asking that yellow roses from her trellis be brought in so she could smell them. When her doctor joked that she was made of leather, she nodded. "That's right." He said she died because "[t]he old engine just ran out." To the end, she'd seen herself as a private citizen, not public personage, telling Katie Louchheim she hadn't written an autobiography because "[t]wo hams in the family are enough."

Lady Bird Johnson, Betty Ford, the Carters, and the Reagans all issued statements in memoriam. Of the trio who attended her Missouri funeral, Mrs. Ford had known Mrs. Truman. "The others," said Tish Baldrige, who helped facilitate some of the arrangements, "came to give honor to the office." Bess Truman's death marked another historic first. Carved on her gravestone was recognition of the role, "First Lady, 1945–1953."

Lady Bird Johnson had planned on attending, but while with Luci, who was suffering an ulcer in the Mayo Clinic, the former First Lady developed a fever, and was also confined. On her seventieth birthday weeks later, she created the National Wildflower Research Center, to conserve and propagate regionally indigenous wildflowers, and kicked it off with a gift of sixty acres of land and $125,000. In Washington, she attended a fund-raiser event for the National Women's Education Fund, selling "Go Wild (Flowering) With Lady Bird" seed packets from a booth. Pat Nixon, with small reserves of energy for travel, sent a basket of flowers to Mrs. Truman's funeral. In Saddle River, she now had an extensive garden that she often cleared and landscaped, and she hosted there a reunion of her East Wing staff. On day trips to New York, she took her grandchildren to the set of the television program *Sesame Street*, and even posed for a rare photograph, with the Big Bird character. When Pat lunched, others in the New York restaurant gave her a standing ovation.

Mrs. Onassis didn't learn of Bess Truman's death until the day of the funeral, upon returning from her first trip to China—for the opening of a Peking hotel, designed by her friend I. M. Pei. On the long flight, she delighted stewardesses by chatting and asking about their jobs and backgrounds. Upon learning of Mrs. Truman's passing, she composed a hand-delivered letter to the family and sent flowers. Circumstances prevented Nancy Reagan from finally meeting the woman she'd long emulated, but Barbara Bush saw Mrs. Onassis several times, including a "Literary Lions" fund-raiser for the New York Public Library, which was also attended by Lady Bird Johnson. When Mrs. Bush came to the offices of Doubleday publishers to discuss her book, C. Fred's Story, "written" by her dog to help raise funds for literacy, her editor brought the two women together in private conversation. When Mrs. Onassis returned to her office, where Mrs. Bush's Secret Service agents waited, the former First Lady jested, "Can't I get rid of you guys?" Barbara was particularly proud of her book since its earnings marked "the first time I can write a check to a charity on my own funds. . . ."

That year, during one of her many international trips, to several African countries, Barbara Bush and her husband were accompanied by an observant doctor, who happened to be black. Louis Sullivan, president of the black institution Morehouse Medical School, had formed a friendship with the vice president when he came to dedicate a building there. Bush invited Sullivan to come to Africa with them. At the University of Harare in Zimbabwe, the Second Lady delivered a particularly stirring speech to adult women in a literacy program. Sullivan was impressed, and during the trip he spent time with her discussing his belief that a child's learning capability was formed in its early years, a reason for superior prenatal and postnatal attention, and furthermore, "the need for a medical school that would train doctors to work in underserved communities." Mrs. Bush accepted his invitation to join Morehouse's board, and began traveling "to proselytize," helping raise $15 million.

Barbara Bush continued to see much of the former First Ladies. She sat by Lady Bird at Averell Harriman's memorial service and conversed with Rosalynn Carter for a second time at the Kentucky Derby, having briefly met her at the White House prior to departing for Sadat's funeral. And in October, she stood with Betty Ford, in the emotional dedication of the Betty Ford Center. The naming of the center caused the former First Lady not a small amount of consternation. She cringed when she heard patients say they "went through Betty Ford," but her stamp was evident. As board president, her office was at the center, and she worked closely with patients. She refused to permit it to become a haven for rich VIPs, having them enter from the waiting list as did those who needed Medicaid to meet treatment costs.

In considering the current First Lady's role in also fighting drug addiction, Mrs. Ford offered, "I think Nancy Reagan has made a tremendous impact in an area in which she really had no knowledge at all. . . . Once she got rid of doing the White House and the plates and the clothes, people stopped talking about that because she's come up with this drug program. And that's good." Rosalynn Carter concurred that "in the beginning, she didn't particularly have a project. . . . But then she saw what influence she had, and got very involved with her drug project."[15]

Indeed, fighting drug abuse increasingly became identified with the First Lady. The East Wing stopped releasing information on Mrs. Reagan's gowns because it claimed "nobody is interested any longer."[16]

"Queen Nancy" seemed banished to media Elba.

– 23 –

Picture Perfect

IT WAS RONALD REAGAN himself who explained precisely how he ran his presidency. "Surround yourself with the best people you can find, delegate authority, and don't interfere." That included the First Lady.

And, in her starring role of *First Lady* in 1939, it was observed that "Nancy not only knows his own lines but everyone else's. She picks up the cue her terrified classmates forget to give, improvises speeches for all and sundry. Just part of the game for Nancy." Things hadn't changed.

Clearly, from their own frank admission, Nancy and Ronald Reagan were co-dependent, a traditional perception of the psychology of relationships which came under intense examination in the eighties. Mrs. Reagan later explained to Barbara Walters how Ronnie, as the adult child of an alcoholic, tended to be detached, and that even she—the person closest to him—had communications difficulties with him.

Reagan was blunt about how enmeshed they were in each other's personal issues. "In some ways Nancy and I are like one human being: When one of us has a problem, it automatically becomes a problem for the other; an attack on one of us is an attack on both of us. When one suffers, so does the other." When people criticized Nancy, Reagan felt helpless anger, and was frustrated that his high position gave him no power to help her. "Here I was the president, and I was unable to stop my own wife from being hurt."

Ronnie and Nancy had what some harshly criticized as an unreal perception of marriage, but even the president admitted, "From the start, our marriage was like an adolescent's dream of what a marriage should be." Reagan even felt, "If ever God gave me evidence that He had a plan for me, it was the night He brought Nancy into my life. . . . God must think a lot of me to have given me you [Nancy]." He said he missed her "if she just steps out of the room." Reagan also described her as a person who was "skeptical" of others, and said a "bear rearing up its hind legs" to protect its "mate" described "how Nancy responds to someone who she thinks is trying to hurt or betray one of hers." "My life really began when I met Nancy."

Whenever Ronnie seemed to be lacking, or faltering in something, Nancy rushed to enable him. For example, when the president began to fall asleep in front of the pope, the First Lady made coughing noises and shuffled her feet, and found it an "agonizing" experience.

Reagan's refusal to recognize "anything evil in another human being," said the First Lady, "infuriates me. . . . It can also be difficult to live with somebody so relentlessly upbeat. . . . Frankly, it sometimes made *me* angry that Ronnie didn't get angry more often. . . ." Nancy admitted that she realized in retrospect that she "spent a lot of time

worrying when I really didn't need to. . . . There have been times
when his optimism made me angry, or when I felt Ronnie wasn't being
realistic and I longed for him to show at least a *little* anxiety. And over
the years I think I've come to worry even more than I used to because
Ronnie doesn't worry at all. I seem to be doing the worrying for both of
us." Reagan accepted Nancy's advice as her way to "protect me" and
"keep me out of trouble."

As far as how their view of a realationship translated into the presidency, Reagan wrote, "As in any good marriage, I value her opinion
and we talk over everything, but she'd be the first to tell you I can be a
stubborn fellow when I don't agree with her. . . . I'm not sure a man
could be a good president without a wife who is willing to express her
opinions with frankness that grows out of a solid marriage." He called
her "an extra set of eyes and ears," and praised her "instinct about
people," because she ususally focuses a more skeptical eye on people,
especially those in a position to harm me."

One source "close to the Oval Office" was quoted as saying there
was "a little private session every evening . . . in their living quarters. . . . He goes trooping up there with a briefcase of papers, runs
down key issues with Nancy and gets the word. Next day, everybody
else gets the word—but we all know it's been checked with Mommy."
It seemed to overstate her power, but even Larry Speakes observed of
the Reagans in private that the president was "content to spend most of
his time with his wife and no one else. He almost never reveals his
personal emotions to anyone but Nancy." Nancy Reynolds stated that
the president "trusts her even when he disagrees with her." The president's political adviser Ed Rollins said that when the Reagans disagreed
on a political issue, Ronnie "ponders whether he's going in the right
direction or not . . . he heeds her advice . . . it's easier for her to make
judgments . . . based on performance, where sometimes other factors
enter into the President's judgment."

In time, even the First Lady admitted, "I talk to people. They tell
me things. They pass along ideas. And sure I tell my husband . . . I'm
not above calling a staff person and asking about it . . . I make no
apologies for looking out for his personal and political welfare. We have
a genuine, sharing marriage. I go to his aid. He comes to mine. I have
opinions. He has opinions. We don't always agree. But neither marriage
nor politics denies a spouse the right to hold an opinion or the right to
express it. And if you have anything less, it's not a marriage. . . . It's
silly to suggest my opinion should not carry some weight with a man
I've been married to for [nearly] 35 years."[1]

Interest in her role was partially a media fascination with her previous profession. Garry Wills believed that Nancy Reagan "subtly altered the standards for combining the worlds of politics and

entertainment . . . an important part of the process that merged Hollywood and Washington. . . ." He thought the several theatrical "looks" she'd learned became advantageous in her First Lady role, and that having been typecast in "unremittingly good" character parts of nurses and what she called "a young wife with children," was superbly suited for the idealized image of First Lady. During the live televised services for families of marines killed in a Beirut bombing, Ronnie occasionally hugged people, but as Deaver recalled, Nancy "just naturally reached out and pulled them to her," and did the same with families of those downed on a Korean airliner. It reinforced the good mother image.

Besides her own role, Nancy's lifelong exposure to theater also served well her role as wife of the president. She managed his visual image—crisp suits, no more hair tonics. Before he headed down to televised press conferences, the First Lady instilled confidence in him, held his hand, and admonished that when Helen Thomas, dean of the press corps, signaled its end, "you leave." As the genial Ronnie drew toward the press at a state dinner, reporter Sue Watters recorded that Nancy "grabbed his arm to pull him away. . . ." As a photographer began snapping pictures of him pulling a ball from one of their dogs, she chided, "Don't! . . . it may look like you're being mean to the dog." He stopped. [2]

Nancy Davis had never been a docile wife content to turn over the control of her destiny to her husband. It was untrue that she completely relinquished her acting career for marriage. She merged her career with his. As husband and wife, they'd acted together in a movie, three TV dramas, and a GE TV ad. Both Reagans had learned the stage technique of assisting a co-star for the good of not only their own appearance but the entire performance. One pulled for the other. The Reagans frequently answered questions by quoting each other, and admitted doing so. After thirty years, it was natural, and how this translated into the presidency was fascinating. She rarely wanted staffers fired because she personally disliked them. Her motive was simply to "protect" Ronnie. She sought to avoid criticism of him at all costs— even if at her own expense. In the end, her getting him "up" redounded with benefit to her, as the other half. Nancy Reagan would never alter her deceptively simple definition of the First Lady's role, which said it all: "I want to help my husband." It wasn't the political discussions of the Fords, nor the business partnership of the Carters, but a Hollywood version no less a genuine "team." Nancy and Ronald Reagan were in business, together. She was no meddler; she was half of the team.

Mrs. Reagan did like her share of the spotlight, said Sheila Tate, noting friendly competition with the president when Nancy learned that she was a lead network news story. When NBC came to film her, and Ronnie tried to pull away correspondent Chris Wallace, a temerity emerged. "But the camera crew is ready," she lectured the president. "You're holding everything up." Wallace noticed that "the worshipful gaze she focuses on her husband in public [was] nowhere to be seen." Still, the better each appeared, the better for the team. Both strove to avoid anything that might damage the other's role. Even when Nancy flirted, Deaver noted, it was to "use this power for Ronald Reagan."

The Reagan relationship was a nationally televised romance, and became part of the pop culture, a "Ron & Nancy" persona emerging. Bed slippers appeared, one foot with Nancy tucked in, the other foot with Ronnie. "Ron & Nancy" greeting cards appeared. On the cover of *Vanity Fair* magazine, the president and First Lady of the United States were shown hugging and dancing, and inside was a magnified close-up of their lips kissing. They wrote an article about their joint White House life for *TV Guide*. Not only did she sing "Our Love Is Here to Stay" to Ronnie on national television, during a PBS *In Performance at the White House* program, but both acted for a scripted scene focused on their romance and acting careers that was videotaped for a museum exhibition, "Hollywood Legend and Reality." Whether they were president and First Lady or actor and actress was undiscernible. Part of it ran:

NANCY: . . . the Hollywood of our day was certainly different from the Hollywood of George Lucas.

RONNIE: Oh, I don't know. We had some great special effects. . . . When we kissed I saw stars. . . . I'm still seeing stars. You free for a movie tonight?

NANCY: Sure am. But isn't there something you're forgetting?

With that, the First Lady pointed to the camera to remind him that it was his exit line.

Not since Woodrow wooed the Widow Galt had dewy presidential romance produced such an amount of copy—a result in part due to their innumerable joint public appearances. That also raised public consciousness of the First Lady as a political being.

Part of the optimistic quality that endeared Ronald Reagan to the public and helped dramatically to shift upward the national mood was derived from his utter contentment with Nancy—as subtle as it was consistent. It was another case of a presidential couple's private life empowering itself positively into the public presidency. Looking at a photo of her, Ronnie said, "I can't imagine life without her." When Deaver asked if she'd considered their burial spot, Nancy "sharply" shot back, "Never."[3]

As one former aide to the president explained simply, "[S]he is a very powerful person because they love each other."

Sometimes their love sparked different emotions in others. Helene von Damm, divorced and remarried four times, seemed at times to manifest a jealousy. Around Reagan all day, every day, she needled Nancy about that by combating the First Lady at every turn. If friction arose between his wife and his staff, Reagan always sided with his wife. Michael Reagan said Nancy was his father's one "Achilles' heel."[4]

More than any other person, Mike Deaver understood the Reagan chemistry, and best discerned Nancy's power: "It is not just that she knows or understands her husband as no else does. . . . She has made him her career, and the White House did not change or enlarge her methods or motives . . . she has used her persuasion with care, knowing when and how hard to apply the pressure. If he resists, she will back off and return to that issue at another moment. She has not gotten involved at all . . . unless there is a controversy around him, or he needs to be convinced that an action is unavoidable. She knows that you cannot barge in and tell him . . . that someone he likes has lost his effectiveness or has ill served him. She will wage a quiet campaign, planting a thought, recruiting others of us to push it along, making a case: Foreign affairs will be hurt . . . our allies will be let down . . . Nancy wins most of the time. When she does, it is not by wearing him down but by usually being on the right side of an issue." Nancy admitted that disagreement didn't close the issue. "I'll wait . . . then I'll come back at him again."[5]

The president would admit, "We talk about everything. Sometimes, we disagree on someone . . . or something, but never very seriously. It's good to talk about it and have other input." As Nancy said, "We disagree. We don't fight." If he went against her advice, however, Ronnie said, "She just I-told-you-sos me." Helene von Damm snipingly recalled only one time when the president adamantly refused Nancy's wisdom, after she had been "relentlessly pursuing the ouster of a person and badgering the President mercilessly."

Occasionally, Mrs. Reagan's sagacity emerged publicly. When questioned about whether he would fire those aides who had stolen Carter's briefing book to prep him for the 1980 debates, Ronnie—who admitted to hating firing people—dodged the issue. Nancy, standing behind him, nodded her head several times, affirmatively. Family friend C. Z. Wick gave a political interpretation: "She's micro and he's macro. He's the big picture in terms of the whole country, while she's very good with the people who are close to him." Ron Reagan noted her media savvy, saying his mother knew "how he plays best, how he comes off best, under what circumstances, and in what surroundings."

"There aren't any secrets between us," the president casually admitted. "I just assume she's cleared for top secret."[6]

Nancy often awoke at six-thirty, breakfasted lightly with Ronnie, flipping television channels to catch segments on the news shows. Before he left for the office, Ronnie always kissed Nancy. Evening news shows were a fixture as they ate together off TV trays, fifties-style, and if there were no functions, both were in bed by eleven. Frequently, when she couldn't sleep and was hungry, she ate bananas, so as to not awaken the blissful Ronnie.

Mrs. Reagan made about three dozen speeches a year. She was particular about whom she quoted. When a speech to the Girl Scouts was prepared for her, incorporating a quote from her predecessor and the organization's former president, Lou Hoover, the quote was removed, but to an entertainment-industry audience she quoted Mae West on Hollywood drug use in the thirties. As Ronnie did, she often repeated from movies, like *Dark at the Top of the Stairs* and *The Wizard of Oz*. To deflect questions she didn't want to answer, she quoted Scarlett O'Hara from *Gone With the Wind*: "I'll think about that tomorrow." Once she literally sang instead of speaking. During a Broadway tribute to Mary Martin, having performed in *Lute Song* with her, Mrs. Reagan resang her part, making her the only First Lady to perform on Broadway.[7]

Mrs. Reagan would go through three speechwriters, three social secretaries, three projects directors, three press secretaries, and five chiefs of staff. Her choosing a longtime public Democrat as her first social secretary shocked conservatives like Helene von Damm who believed it was part of Nancy's attempt to court Eastern society, but it was early evidence of the First Lady's ability to rise above partisanship for the ultimate good of the presidency. There were other particularly expert East Wingers. Her first project director so progressed in her grasp of the drug issue that she left the East Wing to serve as the State Department's assistant secretary for international narcotic matters. Her successor came not only as director of the nation's largest rehab center, Cennikor, but as a former drug addict himself. Sheila Tate, who had worked in the same PR firm as Liz Carpenter, gave columnists homey Nancy anecdotes, "all designed" to present a positive image. Donnie Radcliffe, in her profile of Tate, described her as "hardheaded and intense," throwing mean stares to keep reporters in line, making a point with "The Select Use of Sarcasm," and butting heads with Rosebush. When animal rights groups questioned the First Lady's wearing of fur, Tate retorted it was just "a dead animal."

Tate was a loyal workaholic who never upstaged her boss. In one memo, she instructed an aide to combat criticism of the drug program: "Don't get defensive—be hurt. She [Mrs. Reagan] was hurt. She was trying to do something helpful and constructive and she's sorry they don't see it that way." When her successor, Jennefer Hirshberg, bragged, in an exclusive to Donnie Radcliffe, that she looked like Farrah Fawcett, Tate warned, "There isn't room for but one female lead in this White House, and it ain't Farrah Fawcett." Within months, Hirshberg was replaced with Nancy's longtime friend Elaine Crispen, then serving as personal assistant.

Since Edith Roosevelt, a First Lady's staff funding had been at the whim of the "general budget" for White House operations. Mrs. Reagan's East Wing became the first to fully benefit from a 1978 Congressional enactment, Public Law 95-570, stating, "Assistance and services . . . are authorized to be provided to the spouse of the president in connection with assistance provided by such spouse to the president in discharge of the president's duties and responsibilities." There were sixteen salaried staff members, with a annual budget of $650,000. The senior staff met three times a week, scheduling events often a half-year in advance, dealing daily with issues as they arose. If the First Lady attended a staff meeting and didn't get the details she wanted, she phoned Deaver then and there. Tate noted that whenever Nancy began swinging her foot, she was displeased about something under discussion. Rosebush attended daily briefings held by the President's chief of staff, and he said the Wings worked in tandem, in part because of "Mrs. Reagan's interest in politics and her husband's schedule," with "substantive issues," usually drug policy, being the subject of discussion.

Inevitable East-West tensions arose. All East Wing *women* were excluded from a senior staff Christmas party—although West Wing women were invited—and denied tennis privileges unless invited by a West Winger. When budget restraints required staffers to double up in hotel rooms during a trip, East Wing women were assigned shared quarters, while the men—including the luggage handler—were given their own rooms. Only after Tate threatened not to go at all was there equality. One former East Winger told reporter Lois Romano that since Mrs. Reagan called Deaver "for whatever she wanted . . . that diminished our value within the entire operation." Joanne Bistany, of the West Wing, pointed out that even there sexism against women existed because "Nancy Reagan prefers to deal with men, and that certainly has the effect of setting a pace."8

Joan Quigley sharply described the First Lady as having perceptions that seemed "preternaturally acute," adding, "Her insights into the desires and motives of others were equally sharp. They enabled her to use and manipulate people for her own purposes. However, she avoided doing favors for others even when it would have been very easy for her. She did the minimum necessary to persuade people to do what she wanted done. When Nancy talked about people, even people very close to her, she always got a little dig in. . . . She was clever about manipulating people and situations and was never restrained by sentiment or consideration of the feelings and needs of others." Quigley was chilled after Nancy kissed her. "This woman could chew someone up and swallow and spit out the bones and never feel a thing."

Depending on who was being quoted, Nancy Reagan had a myriad of attractions and deficiencies, but as Sheila Tate put it perfectly, the First Lady was "complicated, and that makes her very interesting." Patti Davis felt that her mother had a "rigidity." Donnie Radcliffe found an "unapproachable" detachment, noting that while she knew the reporters who traveled with her, Nancy could sometimes look at them without "a glimmer of recognition." Some termed her caution to be paranoia, spoke of a vulnerability that seemed like abandonment, and found themselves wanting to protect her. She admitted to being a perfectionist and expecting the same of staff, making her, as Deaver said, "very demanding." Don Regan said she didn't thank staffers but depended on the "praise of others." Son Ron said she was "a handful . . . I don't think I'd want her to be my boss." When the First Lady disagreed, she confronted, and arguments were resolved because she frankly aired them. She had specific idiosyncrasies, yet not only heard out other ideas, but sought a devil's advocate view. As was said of Mary Lincoln, Nancy Reagan could at once exasperate and frustrate, then charm and touch. She herself said, "It does not mean you don't recognize the negatives, but you don't have to dwell on them."

Jim Rosebush believed that Nancy's motives came from "her own drive for success in whatever she did," "a built-in desire to achieve, and a "degree of political competitiveness." In that she challenged herself, she was like Florence Harding. There were other resemblances. Evoking Julia Grant of the Gilded Age, she obviously enjoyed the material luxuries of the Ladyship's lifestyle, but she was no spendthrift. In hotels she ordered modest fare from hotel room service, and consumed the fruit provided in gift baskets. She was also an unabashed pack rat. As her deputy press secretary said, "She saves everything," from notes to Estée Lauder freebies. Like Julia Tyler, she could solicit opinions on political issues with eyelash-batting helpless innocence, but as Rosebush wrote, "When she asked you a question she almost always already knew the answer."[9]

Mrs. Reagan was extremely aware of her and Ronnie's health. They usually drank bottled waters and juices with dinner, wine consumption being confined mostly to formal dinners and celebrations, and partook of and served only decaffeinated coffee. After developing lip cancer, Nancy became even more careful about being in the sun. She kept *The Davis-Christopher Textbook of Surgery*, written by her father, on hand. On Air Force One and Marine One, cigarette packs with the presidential seal were provided as souvenirs, but none dared to light up in her presence. At least two of her staff learned to go for hours without nicotine, and everyone who traveled with her learned to swelter since air-conditioning made her too cold.

Mrs. Reagan took valid criticism well. As Nancy Reynolds stated, she "never equated disagreement with disloyalty." To those loyal to her, she was loyal in return. When her maid Anita Castelo, a native Paraguayan, was charged in an attempt to purchase and smuggle small-arms ammunition to Paraguay, the First Lady offered a character affidavit, being "familiar" with Castelo's "truthfulness and honesty." Castelo was found to be innocent, and Nancy warmly welcomed her back to work. Nancy had a wide sense of humor, her laughter frequently at her own expense. Far from being offended, when Mrs. Reagan saw her son appear in a skit with the actor who played her in drag on *Saturday Night Live*, she found it "funny." She was no prude. After she told reporters that Ronnie kissed her under the mistletoe, one blurted out, "What happened after that?" She coyly cracked, "If you can't figure it out, I'll never tell." Nancy timed her waltz into the East Room just as Sinatra, rehearsing for a dinner that night, broke into "The Lady Is a Tramp."

She was at her best when relaxed, in private. Even LBJ Democrat Ann Hand found that Nancy "laughs so easily," with a "cozy manner," and said if people met her personally, "they'd love her." Engaging herself directly with the person with whom she was speaking, the First Lady was a warm talker, and, a voracious reader, she remained well-read on current topics from film to politics. Deaver said she had a "stronger curiosity" than the president, was sensitive to the subtleties of human nature, comfortable with "free spirits and intellectuals," and "enjoys reaching out to new people of whatever political coloring."

Mrs. Reagan cried easily when moved, and she was moved easily, but Deaver noted that it was family discord that most made her "uptight and emotional." Her children often good-naturedly teased her. On Christmas Eve, when she'd put on carols, they'd change it to rock music. In her dressing room, she kept framed letters from Ron and Patti and a painting of her and Patti together. Mrs. Reagan never interfered with their choices in adult life, and although both voiced political opinions often in conflict with the president's, she sought always to keep an open line of communication with them. "It's always been difficult for me to understand how children could turn against their mothers. . . ." In discussing *Mommie Dearest*, the ugly portrayal of Joan Crawford by her daughter, Mrs. Reagan emphasized, "I just don't think you write a book like that about your mother."[10]

As the months passed, she came to see her role in context. She read Edith Roosevelt's biography, and found one on Ellen Wilson to be a "fascinating study," and interesting "to compare the duties and obligations of First Lady Wilson with those of recent First Ladies. . . ." On a memo about Eleanor Roosevelt, this Mrs. R. wrote, "I note with a tinge of envy how Mrs. R was able to go horseback riding in Rock Creek Park." In one conversation, she discussed the criticism of Mary

Lincoln's clothes purchases, Jackie Kennedy and civil rights, and her own recollections of Mamie Eisenhower's strong personality. When she learned that most revelations emerged from the women's papers, her press secretary cracked, "You better watch where your papers go!" Because her father had chastised her for not writing a diary while she was governor's wife, Nancy now assiduously kept a handwritten one in a large ledger. "There isn't any clearly defined role for the First Lady," she offered. "You make of it what you want . . . I didn't realize that you had such a tremendous platform. . . . That's the way it's been all through history . . . Everybody who's been here knows the job's tough. I would never criticize another First Lady . . . [but] Criticism comes with the job." By 1983, she'd come to accept her full public role. On her tax returns, Nancy Reagan listed her occupation as "First Lady."[11]

Particularly in her hostess role—for example, planning menus—Nancy Reagan reflected her era. "With expensive tastes and the money to indulge them, Americans went food crazy during the 80's," chronicled Bill Barol in *Newsweek*. "The food craze most representative of the decade was West Coast nouvelle—tiny portions of exquisitely arranged foodstuffs. . . ." Nancy Reagan's dinners usually offered her favorite fruit sorbets, small soufflés, light meat entrées, delicate meat sauces, and attractive baby vegetables. She even tried the "new" Coca-Cola.

In an age when one could walk on the street and hear only what one wanted to via the Walkman radio, get instant cash with a bankcard, heat take-out gourmet dinners in several dozen seconds in the microwave, and retrieve phone messages and TV shows with the push of a button, Nancy Reagan suited her era. Glitzy glamour, conspicuous consumption, instant gratification, extravagant comfort—Nancy's image was all eighties. Entertainment was used to raise funds for sociopolitical ills—from Ethiopian starvation to American farmers. Besides her professional skills, and the fact that she would be First Lady longer than any other in the twentieth century except Eleanor and Mamie, the sophistication of media technology cast her indelibly. East Wingers videotaped her TV clips, and Nancy Reagan had her own VCR.

Initially, Nancy charged Sinatra to plan entertainment, emphasizing her preference for the retro romanticism of café-society songs. Often, the only way to see a retired legend—Jimmy Stewart, Ginger Rogers, Esther Williams, Bette Davis, Pat O'Brien, Cary Grant—or a "hot newcomer"—Sigourney Weaver, Tom Selleck, Joe Piscopo and Arnold Schwarzenegger—was at Nancy's place. Company dressed and played the part. As one guest, comedienne Joan Rivers, cracked, "No scum here tonight."[12]

Not since Eleanor Roosevelt had there been such an episodic quality to the Ladyship—Nancy's shifting status with various Reagan children, her trio of hairdressers, the White House Santa Clauses, from Mr. T to Dom DeLuise. Sometimes, at high points of drama, Nancy appeared on the networks nightly. She herself said she'd "lived many lives" as First Lady.[13]

The Washington Post's Donnie Radcliffe, who followed Nancy Reagan more closely than any other journalist, became as thorough a chronicler of her as Bess Furman had been of Mrs. Roosevelt. Radcliffe initially developed a column, "Washington Ways," to handle the influx of Nancy Reagania. It helped turn the East Wing into a desirable beat. More printed stories—from U.S. News and World Report to Women's Wear Daily—appeared about Mrs. Reagan than even Mrs. Roosevelt. On television, more broadcast clips—from Issues and Answers to Entertainment Tonight—mentioned the First Lady than Jacqueline Kennedy. Mrs. Reagan stirred comment, provoking the closest media and scholarly study of the Ladyship ever. Not since Mrs. Kennedy had there been an incumbent who so interested the public that books were written about her.

She admitted that her being "naive" about the "intense scrutiny" of the Ladyship was "strange for someone who had been in public life as long as I had." She told Andy Warhol that "I don't think of image at all," and didn't miss the acting profession, but Deaver said that Nancy Reagan had "a far keener sense of fame" and a "better public-relations antenna" than anyone he knew. Initially, her choice of words created faux pas, as when she remarked that the pope was "so, so virile," and her reference to drug abuse as a "democratic" illness was misunderstood as partisanship. But Nancy rapidly became confident before the microphones. She wanted to know every detail possible before making an appearance—who'd be flanking her, what their backgrounds and interests were, at what point in the event did she arrive and depart, were other speakers' remarks available so she could avoid repeating themes? When a columnist praised her for bringing "a lot of romanticism" to the eighties, Nancy marked the passage. "Good introduction for someone [to deliver for me]?"

Nancy Reagan not only read Women's Wear Daily, Vanity Fair, Town & Country, and Interview, but the Los Angeles Times, The New York Times, The Washington Post, USA Today, and The Wall Street Journal. She relished the weekend political-policy commentary shows, and befriended a startlingly wide cross-section of print and broadcast journalists, most prominently George Will, and counted William F. Buckley, Frank Reynolds, and Washington Post and Newsweek owner Katherine Graham as confidants. The First Lady watched network news each night not only because she found it "interesting," but "to see how it's interpreted."

Rosebush noted, "Nancy Reagan has never been one to blurt out a response without considering its consequences." She balanced self-protection with caution about alienating the media. Delivering a speech to the Advertising Council, chastising the glamorous image of drugs, the First Lady deleted references to the "news media." Tate clarified that Nancy wanted to focus on the "popular entertainment" media. Earlier that week, Ronnie had lashed out at the "news" media "for focusing on individuals affected by the economy." As much as careful words and video images, however, pictures forged the "new" Nancy Reagan.

The "photo op" reached new heights under Mike Deaver. Not only was he deputy chief of staff and Nancy's political confidant, but manager of the administration's staged settings and photo angles. Largely taken by an official photographer who became close to the First Lady, the perfect-color shots dramatized every public moment and emotion, and quite frequently the private ones as well. Mrs. Reagan was adept at striking the right pose and angle under the best light, opening her mouth as if talking to the guest who stood beside her for a souvenir picture, advised and guided by media experts. The camera rarely turned out a bad Nancy photo—in the Statue of Liberty's crown, break dancing in New York, flamenco dancing in Spain, avoiding nudes at an art exhibit, placing a miniature flag at a grave in the Normandy Beach cemetery. Whether on a Broadway stage or in a German castle, her advance staff checked the color scheme of sites at which Mrs. Reagan would be appearing. The shade of her clothes would be chosen accordingly. Even when she was to be "spontaneously" photographed before a Venetian landmark, a masking-tape marker was placed on the cobblestone for her to stand on to make it picture perfect. With public-relations, film, and photo experts behind the scenes, Nancy was impeccable before the camera.

By 1983, all signs of "Queen Nancy" were largely gone. Although, for example, she hosted a state dinner at a movie studio for Queen Elizabeth, at which most guests were Hollywood stars, attended Prince Andrew's royal wedding, and told Barbara Walters on national television that she thought of Charles "as family," there was no longer press criticism. There were minor resurgences of rebuke, as with the astronomical costs of her advance and accompanying staff and logistics for her foreign trips, but because of escalated protests and terrorism, strict measures were necessary, and out of her control. As Eleanor Roosevelt had done, Nancy Reagan passed out candies to her press entourage, but, equally, she had her own enemies and allies in the Fourth Estate. Still, as Richard Nixon said, "She has done an outstanding job in overcoming some of the negative media treatment she received earlier in the Administration and now rates as one of history's most successful and popular First Ladies."

Besides the traditional East Wing press, West Wing correspondents watched Nancy. And she watched them. Sam Donaldson told of reporters sunning themselves on the greensward near the press room. The First Lady spied them and, soon after, there was an ivy bed and chain-link fence there. The toughest veteran reporters knew they weren't dealing with a patsy. Consequently, there would be no attempt to spare her the sort of harsh assessment usually confined to the president. Sometimes rightly, often wrongly, she was inevitably accused by the ubiquitous "insider" for nearly everything that smacked of intrigue. If Ronnie was "Teflon-coated," the egg always stuck to Nancy.[14]

Initial coverage of First Ladies' projects inevitably waned. Realizing this, the East Wing consciously targeted the media in 1983 for the drug program. And Mrs. Reagan got steady work. In the MTV generation, Nancy sang with a chorus in the video *Stop the Madness* and honored antidrug pop singer Michael Jackson at the White House. The First Lady went to Hollywood to film a cameo appearance on the national sitcom *Different Strokes*. Viewed by 32 million—the vast majority being children—it was the most popular television program for those aged six to eleven years old. With Joan Rivers, she chatted about drug abuse, becoming the first First Lady to do a late-night television talk show. Reporting at 6:00 A.M. she co-hosted a full week of the morning show *Good Morning America.* Within two hours after one of her weeklong appearances on the afternoon show *Hour Magazine,* the National Federation of Parents for Drug-Free Youth received twenty six calls for help from parents. The First Lady narrated parts of two one-hour public television programs, *The Chemical People,* aired on nearly two thousand PBS stations, as well as a later sequel.

She knew the power of the media and how the system worked. Mrs. Reagan illustrated her point that modern entertainment glamorized drugs by referring to pot smoking in movies, drinking in the opening scenes of TV dramas, and lyrics of pop music referring to being high, in a speech to one thousand TV writers and, behind closed doors, to two dozen film executives. After the media focused on drug use by sports figures, the First Lady spoke at Super Bowl halftime—the year's largest television audience—and initiated annual White House tennis games with pro-am celebrities playing to raise funds for a Nancy Reagan Foundation that donated money to rehab centers.

In the face of cynics, critics, and apathy, Nancy Reagan in the eighties, as Barol of *Newsweek* said, helped "open a tap in the national consciousness . . ." By May of 1983, Nancy Reagan publicly admitted, "Never in my life have I felt as compelled to do something about an issue." She further observed that by 1981 "the proportions of the problem had grown. Drug abuse had broken over America like a huge wave over a beach, a wave we should have seen coming on the horizon. It hit the nation and our children with a fury." It then struck one out of three U.S. households.

As she jetted from schools to rehab centers, and began to realize drugs' insidiousness at all levels of society, Nancy began to grasp the psychological roots of why small children used drugs, admitting, "When I was in school, peer pressure was that your saddle shoes always be dirty." She also understood its physiological effect, once casually explaining the potency of specific drugs on specific parts of the brain, knowledge she'd gained from her father. But something more personal committed her: "The first time I received a letter saying that I had saved a person's life, I wept. I never dreamed *I* had the ability to do that—to influence people unknown to me. . . ."

The letters, never released publicly, were the greatest gauge of Mrs. Reagan's effect. Poignant, often desperate, they told tens of thousands of gruesome and jolting tales, often scrawled in grade-school handwriting on cartoon stationery or ragged lined yellow pages from all regions and demographics. A fifteen-year-old imprisoned for probation violation and drug possession told of growing up with a drugged father who fed her pills so he could laugh as she stumbled and tried to speak, and later raped her. A grade-schooler poured out personal details and at the bottom asked Mrs. Reagan, "HELP!" Often they pleaded with her to continue. Besides her mail, Nancy kept abreast through the media. Within days of reading about a local drug addict in the black community, she phoned the drug policy adviser to arrange the boy's requested help for entrance into a rehab center.

Mrs. Reagan never showed intolerance toward the drug users in the rough process of breaking their addiction. She approached it with personal empathy, having had friends whose children died from overdoses. She admitted that her children had smoked pot, adding, "I understand it. It's like having the first cigarette." She was shocked but unflinching when an eleven-year-old girl told of how her mother had put drugs and alcohol in her bottle to keep her quiet, or when a Swiss boy revealed he'd become a prostitute to support his habit. She did not judge those in the armed services who used drugs, stating that narcotics "ease the alienation and isolation. It should come as no surprise to you that young people in the military sometimes feel alienated and . . . sometimes turn to drugs."

The East Wing worked with a wide network of franchised drug-abuse programs. There were rehab centers like Phoenix House or Cennikor, which used different methods. There were parent groups like the National Federation of Parents for Drug-Free Youth, which began a "Nancy Reagan Speakers Bureau," managed to help introduce and pass antiparaphernalia legislation, ran a "youth corps" of upper-class students to serve as educators and role models to younger students, maintained a toll-free national hot line, and held annual informational conferences. In 1984, the First Lady and her staff emphasized civic and other traditional organizations' enlistment in her drug fight: The Girl Scouts developed a merit badge for being drug-free, the Kiwanis put up two thousand roadside billboards across America with the First Lady's face, and cause: HELP SAVE A GENERATION OF CHILDREN, FIGHT SCHOOL-AGED DRUG ABUSE. And there was private industry, like the publisher who printed antidrug comic books.

Nancy's positive impact on small children was due in part to the symbolism of her position. Since drug abuse for the very young often stemmed from low self-esteem, the fact that she was coming to focus on them, frequently as individuals, boosted their own self-impressions. It was when a student offered Nancy "really good drugs" in a play session that her eyes widened as she repeated, "No, no, no, no." A whole generation—eventually even comediennes—began repeating the single catchall phrase that became identified with her. Even pop singer Grace Jones worked it into the lyrics of her song "Crack Attack." While attending an Oakland school, she told a student that if approached to try drugs, he should "just say NO! That's all you have to do." In sixteen months, five thousand "Just Say No" clubs emerged in American schools, and in Brazil, Sweden, England, and Jamaica, focused on peer pressuring peer. One teacher in a "Just Say No" school nevertheless told Nancy that extracurricular activity was as crucial as just saying no.

Mrs. Reagan used the same phrases and asked the same questions, and made no bones about it. As Rosebush wrote, "[S]he took a modest, realistic approach. She never pretended that she was a drug expert nor did she ever imply she could solve the problem or wipe out its effects." The First Lady consciously kept her focus on the role of a parent and youths. Nancy so cherished the parental bond that it was an idealized expectation; she told Chris Wallace that it evolved from her own childhood separations from her mother. The positive aspect of this was the genuine depth of compassion she felt for parents who'd become consumed by their children's demise but fought to save them. "When you get right down to it," she said of parents in general but in reference to her own, "they're the ones who are going to put their hands in the fire for you."

Before departing her sessions with students or parents, the First Lady always asked, "What else can I do?" Many wanted her to at least

attempt to get federal funding increased. She always retorted that she increased awareness, not funding. Unlike Jackie, Lady Bird, Betty, and Rosalynn, Nancy refused to become involved in even tangential legislation. To the consternation of even the East Wing, Mrs. R. refused to align her project with a government agency or request further funding for her own staff. Rosebush stated that while she "refused to be a government spokesman," the drug policy adviser was the First Lady's closest liaison on the issue, and the two often conferred, he frequently briefing her on new policy, statistics, or treatments. Publicly, she refused to address even related political issues, patently responding about Ronnie's commitment, "He is doing all he can to step up interdiction and improve on the criminal justice system." When Congressman Michael Barnes phoned Rosebush to have Mrs. Reagan testify to a House Committee—like Rosalynn and Eleanor—on the drugs' effects on youth, he approached Mrs. R. "She would have nothing to do with it."

In other ways, however, the American First Lady's project was having international consequences. During a Bonn economic summit dinner, British prime minister Thatcher turned to Reagan and asked, "Tell us, how's Nancy's drug program going?" At that, the seated chiefs of several nations began discussing their nations' drug problems for a full hour, culminating in their directing foreign ministers quickly to organize for the next day, a "special session . . . to find ways of improving international cooperation in the war on narcotics." As Nancy Reagan began to visit rehab centers worldwide, the often unpublic wives of the host nation's leaders began asking what she'd discovered in their own countries and how she was handling it in America.

Drug abuse was timely and controversial, linked to larger issues like international trafficking, civil liberties of drug-testing, highway fatalities, the AIDS epidemic, and economic dependence—from drug-producing nations to previously impoverished dealers. Some criticism was subjective cynicism. The London Daily Standard blasted that her "endless self-publicity parade on the subject in America has had no discernible effect on that nation's supposed drug problem." Often, the criticism was unfounded. When a National Zoo employee wrote to her that certain animals were drugged, the East Wing thanked the writer, forwarded the letter, and the employee was fired. Without any knowledge of it, she was blamed. There was media controversy when antidrug concert planners claimed that she had requested that particular entertainers with "offensive lyrics" not participate if she was to appear as scheduled. The planners then asked the First Lady not to appear because of her "censorship." In fact, Mrs. Reagan had long been previously scheduled to be overseas, and had only considered making a video statement, not an appearance.

Sometimes the appearances themselves eclipsed the purpose. At a

Beverly Hills dinner in her honor, a Hollywood minister delivered an invocation thanking God that "You have given her to us as one of the great leaders of our time," while marching waiters delivered desserts with mini–American flags stuck in them as Tony Martin sang the theme song from *La Cage aux Folles*, a musical about a drag show.

Other criticisms validly raised other issues not being addressed. While she stated, "I believe that parents are the answer to it all," there was no mention of children without parents, or parents who were themselves addicts. When she supported the use of home drug tests by parents on their children, one editorial called it the most "severe, immediate threat to *all* Americans' civil liberties and ethical sense." Some critics wanted her to focus on certain drugs, and not others. NORML, supporting marijuana legalization, protested her appearances for including pot in her campaign. An open newspaper letter admonished her that "if your campaign against drugs is anything more than don't-offend-anyone-busy-work, you will stand up in front of the convention and tell your generation that OUR DRUG, ALCOHOL, IS BY NUMBER OF ABUSERS, THE MOST DANGEROUS AND TREACHEROUS DRUG. . . ."[15]

To these criticisms and calls for her to use some political power for drugs, Nancy Reagan calmly kept her own counsel. "A woman is like a tea bag," she often said, smiling, to drug groups.

"You don't know her strength until she's in hot water."

— 24 —

On the Line with Mrs. R.

SHE SAT AT THE meridian of it all, East and West Wings, ideologues and pragmatists, security, scheduling, personnel, press, political, household and social staffs, from the central position, overseeing the eighteen-acre White House complex.

And they all called her "Mrs. R."

The suite on the north side symbolized the many facets of Nancy Reagan's role: the gym where she often watched Ronnie maintain his health, the cosmetology room and the twelve double hall closets with items of clothing tagged by dates of when worn and before whom, to avoid appearing in the same dress twice, all meticulously filed by subject: shoes, gowns, suits, bags, hats. But it was the First Lady's headquarters that perfectly illustrated her power base. Her office was quite literally at the very center of the White House. On the middle floor of the residence, her office was situated halfway between the wings, removed yet precisely the vortex of it all. The room was splendidly outfitted, with yellow curtains, built-in bookcases, pale green and white walls, one of which was covered with twenty-five framed antique wildflower prints made into a perfect square, and silver-framed photographs of the Queen Mother, Prince Charles, and Princess Diana on nearby tables.

The single most important item, however, was her white telephone. The First Lady had a special line installed for her use, and on this unlisted number she could maintain private conversations, dial direct, and get incoming calls, without them being tracked and recorded by the government operators. "When I die," said Nancy Reagan, "I'm going to have a phone in one hand and my phone book in the other."[1]

All day, she used the elongated phone, its white cord capable of stretching across the room as she moved about. Whether it was a West Wing aide or East Wing staffer—or the parents of an addicted child—they were on the line with Mrs. R., and could be for upward of twenty minutes, as the first of as many as a dozen such calls that day. And wherever she was in the world, every day Nancy Reagan called her mother.

Even Mike Deaver became exasperated when Nancy once phoned him seven times before noon. Precisely as Louis Howe had taken Eleanor Roosevelt under his wing, so, too, did Deaver do with Nancy Reagan. Begun as a tutelage in PR, it had quickly grown to include political maneuverings to the point where the First Lady could carry on solo with the tactical skills she'd learned. To imply that she was a naive tool for Deaver, however, was a gross misunderstanding. As Stu Spencer admitted, "She doesn't always go with us. Many times, she thinks we're wrong."

She had opinions on the other two of the "troika" closest to the president. Nancy had a good working relationship with chief of staff pragmatist Jim Baker, and had immediately preferred him in that role over the more ideological Ed Meese, being particularly impressed with Baker's expert preparation of Ronnie during the '80 debates. As presidential counselor, Meese addressed the homeless issue by saying that "many who say they have nothing to eat really only want a free meal," and failed to wake the president with the news that navy jets had shot down Libyan fighter planes. The media censure following both incidents galled Mrs. R. and eroded her confidence in Meese. She called Meese "a jump-off-the-cliff-with-the-flag-flying conservative," a person so "rigid" in his beliefs that he preferred losing to winning a compromise. His financial deals, she said, "made me squirm," and "weakened both the Justice Department and the presidency. She considered him highly unorganized. She said that "ambitious" Jim Baker's "main interest was Jim Baker," and she predicted he would someday run for "higher office." The First Lady defended her own consultations with Deaver and Baker by stating that she only had Ronnie's interests at heart when she interceded: "[T]here's not really a conspiracy on their part, plus me, to get messages to Ronnie." She would also "facilitate a situation" by relaying something she picked up from her husband to Deaver.

Nancy Reagan asserted, "A First Lady has the power to make a difference." Others put it more bluntly. "No matter how much she denied it, the role of 'power behind the throne' suited her to perfection," wrote Helen von Damm. "She was a schemer married to someone who was unable to conceive of a Machiavellian thought." Laurence Barrett, senior White House correspondent for *Time*, assessed the First Lady as a "shrewd woman who has influence on her husband . . . good political instincts of her own . . . a very fine nose for staff matters."

Speculation was no longer on whether she had power, but on *how much*. The public seemed no longer to mind a First Lady exercising power in any degree. By 1983, the First Lady's general popularity began inching up, never again to recede. An NBC poll found her to be more liked, eight to one. A Wirthlin poll found her more highly regarded than any single member of her husband's Cabinet. Eventually, a *New York Times* poll gave her a 71 percent approval, while the president lagged at 62 percent, his disapproval at nearly 30 percent, hers only 14 percent.

Deaver quipped that Nancy "wouldn't know a continuing resolution from a New Year's resolution," but she knew a liberal from a conservative. Film director John Huston, an early intimate of hers, said that the notion she was "an archconservative and reactionary" was "absurd, absolute nonsense." The president's conservative secretary Helene von Damm believed that Nancy was "slowly diminishing the influence of all the conservatives of the Administration." Von Damm kept a "Deaver/Mrs. R Index," a list of "nuisance" conservatives whose communications with Reagan, Nancy and Deaver had decreed, must be kept from him. Von Damm still passed the conservatives' messages to Reagan in the Oval Office, but if he planned to read them later, upstairs with Nancy, von Damm remarked, "That's only for reading here."

In her second job, in personnel, von Damm said the First Lady also took eager interest in any federal appointments relating to the arts. When liberal Republican Frank Hodsell—chosen to head the National Endowment for the Arts by Baker—fought von Damm over the ideology of their separate lists of proposed board members, he finally circumvented her by forming a Presidential Advisory Committee on the Arts. Mrs. Reagan not only backed Hodsell's committee but agreed to serve as honorary chair, saying she'd do everything except "dancing the polka like Julia Tyler" for them. When Reagan's legislative liaison met with the Senate Appropriations Subcommittee on Interior Agencies, he let them know that Nancy "urged that endangered funding for the President's Committee on Arts and Humanities be saved." Nancy avoided commenting on the ideology of those she wanted in or out. As time progressed, however, almost all of those officials she thought should leave were conservatives, and indeed her power in "personnel" became extremely political. As von Damm recorded, that was particularly true of Reagan, "who attracts people who believe in certain policies. . . . It wasn't just a matter of patronage, it was a matter of which direction the Administration would move in."

Mrs. Reagan didn't hold differing opinions against people. Although she defended Nancy in an op-ed piece, Lucky Roosevelt, for example, was made chief of protocol, even after she publicly took issue with Nancy's anti-abortion stand. Nor did the First Lady confuse ideology with ability, successfully having a Carter assistant secretary of state, Thomas Tracy, retained. Whatever an individual's ideology, if he or she posed a danger to Ronnie, she reacted forthwith. When a usually loyal senator was otherwise, the First Lady, while chatting with his wife, snapped, "I'm bothered by your husband's unwillingness to support Ron at a time when he needs you." After hanging up, she received a call from the senator. The following day, the president received the senator's support. When her plane rolled off course on the runway, a witness said the First Lady was more "anxious to find out what was going on in Washington" with Reagan's push for Nicaraguan Contra aid with Congress.

"If there's any part that I play," Nancy Reagan admitted, "I'm very aware of people who try to end-run him, have their own agendas, and are maybe less than forthright." Whether or not she came to fully realize it, just her casual suggestions in conversations made workers jump in fear. As Chris Wallace stated in his prime-time political documentary on the First Lady—the first of its kind—"In Washington's corridors of power, she's a respected and feared political operative."

In attempting to learn just how powerful she was, Wallace concluded that Nancy was "even more powerful" than previously believed, and said most people interviewed described her as "relentless." When he asked political figures, "Are you a little scared of her?," one official was reduced to stammering. "Nancy's not nice when she's angry," a West Winger told Donnie Radcliffe. "There's a great fear factor, especially among staff types who don't want to be on her bad side." As for the West Wing, adviser Ed Rollins added, "[W]hen she's concerned about something, we . . . respond to her very quickly," and heed crucial "warning signals." When his secretary told him, "Mrs. Reagan's on the line," Rollins said, "After my heart starts again, I certainly listen very attentively." Director of communications David Gergen understated, "It would concern me a great deal to learn that she was unhappy with me." When told the First Lady was calling, Larry Speakes "always experienced a bit of discomfort." Even Chief of Staff Baker cracked, "I would prefer to be on her good list instead of her bad list."

The First Lady's "perceived power" took on a life of its own. When Deaver told von Damm that she had "too many plants" in her office, she fretted that it was surely a "directive from Mrs. R." White House aides, usually at the lower level, so feared her guillotine that the plethora of news leaks about her became increasingly anonymous. Mrs. Reagan turned this to advantage by managing her own press leaks. Helene von Damm sniped that besides White House invitations and "intramural schemings," the First Lady used the press as one of the "weapons in her arsenal," by talking matters over with a media-savvy Kitchen Cabinet including Mary Jane Wick, Nancy Reynolds, Stu Spencer, and Deaver, and they in turn offered her view to sympathetic reporters. Helene contended that most reporters "played along with her fiction of being uninvolved in substance because they didn't want to lose access to her."

Not all of her power was political. She successfully managed to get a postage stamp to honor Dr. Harvey Cushing, her father's former superior—no small task considering that only about fifty out of fifteen hundred such requests were approved. She was also credited with many altruistic moves—arranging for organ transplants for children, getting a former addict hired by a law-enforcement agency, facilitating the visit of Mstislav Rostropovich's sister from Russia for his birthday. When Soviet pianist Vladimir Feltsman became persona non grata after his expressed wish to emigrate to America, Mrs. R. discreetly became involved in efforts to assist him, through the U.S. ambassador in Moscow. Feltsman was permitted to leave, and within one hour of his arrival in America he was handed a letter from Nancy inviting him to perform at the White House. "If she personally can't do anything," said her press secretary, "Mrs. Reagan passes on all letters asking her for help to various people of assistance in the White House or other agencies." About 50 percent of such requests were sent to outlets outside the East Wing. As always, most who appealed to the First Lady viewed her as "a mother figure who can solve all their problems or will share them with the president."

Mrs. Reagan would allow that her "certain political role" could "render a service" to the president, and admitted, "We speak of politics all the time. . . ." Nancy had estimable ability to judge the motivations of those around the president. With the Cabinet, her judgment was not so much on their specific capabilities in commerce or defense, but how their performance and media response to them might hinder the president. Though von Damm said the First Lady had particular interest in ambassadorial appointments, Mrs. R.'s savvy seemed best directed toward the West Wing, specifically those involved in media and political relations. With those whom she felt strongly should leave, presidential spokesman Larry Speakes said the First Lady "won't give up until he or she is gone." Von Damm was among them.

When the president appointed von Damm as ambassador to her native Austria, she accepted. Then she was beckoned to the private quarters, for a meeting with Mrs. R. "I expect that you'll turn down the President," she told Helene. "You can't go. At least not now." A shocked von Damm felt Mrs. Reagan "didn't consider anyone indispensable. Far from it." She later tried to phone Mrs. R., but the First Lady wouldn't take any of her calls. Von Damm accepted the position.

Mrs. Reagan was glaringly absent from her induction ceremony. Eventually, Helene would be forced to resign. Others met with similar fates. After ambassador to the Vatican Bill Wilson contacted Libyans without authorization, the "uproar," said *The New York Times*, "led Mrs. Reagan to prevail on her husband to dismiss Mr. Wilson. . . ." Nancy felt the negative press surrounding the investigation of labor secretary Ray Donovan meant he must resign even if he were found innocent. He did. When she heard that HHS secretary Margaret Heckler had compromised administration programs, she was bounced to Ireland as ambassador. One Republican senator said the First Lady felt that the EPA's Rita Lavelle "was way out of line and more loyal to big business than Reagan," and "nagged" the president until he "insisted on the resignation." The same senator pinpointed Nancy as being the one who urged the president to appoint Henry Kissinger to a blue-ribbon commission on Central America.

It was Deaver who had inspired the removal of secretary of state Al Haig, but it was she who broached it successfully with the president. She considered Haig's appointment to be "the biggest mistake." Nancy vigorously denied "firing" Haig, but the line was fine when it came to the degree of her influence. It was never a case of the First Lady personally crafting ousters, for there were usually others—quite often Deaver and Spencer—who'd first called for the same dismissals. And increasingly, it was the conservatives who were fired.

Speakes said the First Lady found conservative Lyn Nofziger, political liaison chief, to be "rambunctious" and "profane," and von Damm said Mrs. R. "snubbed him by failing to include his name on invitation lists, and allowed talk to simmer in the press that she disapproved of his rumpled appearance and bearing." Nofziger had barely lasted a year.

The often embarrassing interior secretary James Watt became a liability in the First Lady's view when he made a puerile remark about the "evils of rock music," and banned a public Beach Boys concert. Speakes observed that the First Lady "registered her disdain" for Watt by immediately inviting the Beach Boys to play on the White House lawn. His public remark about a commission consisting of "a black, a woman, two Jews and a cripple" not only offended the First Lady, but once again reflected poorly on Ronnie. Shortly, Watt was gone. His replacement by Bill Clark of the NSC was believed by many, including Speakes, to be the "behind-the-scenes" handiwork of the First Lady. Nancy supported the notion of having Baker become NSC adviser and Deaver take his place as chief of staff, but conservatives Meese and CIA director Casey managed to block the moderate influence. Bud McFarlane was chosen for NSC, but Nancy continued to find Clark "abrasive," particularly toward Deaver and Baker, and von Damm would accuse Mrs. R. of "poisoning the water" against him even with Reagan. When

Clark left Interior, Nancy made it clear that she didn't want to find him back on the White House staff. He did not reappear. She thought Clark ill qualified, especially when "he couldn't name the prime minister of Zimbabwe" before the Senate Foreign Relations Committee.

The moderate second secretary of state, George Shultz, was one of those with whom the First Lady evidently shared similar goals. In early 1983, according to von Damm, "behind the scenes," the First Lady and secretary of state were "plotting" to lay the groundwork for an eventual U.S.-Soviet summit by managing to "smuggle" in Soviet ambassador Anatoly Dobrynin without West Wing or press knowledge, to confer with Reagan. His way of entry was metaphoric. Von Damm said the Soviet ambassador had come in through "the East Wing. The venue of entry was later said to be apocryphal, but not the implication. By 1983, the First Lady was said to have "decided that her husband's tough stand against Communism . . . was simply costing him too much politically," and that she prompted the notion of him as a "peace president." Reagan admitted that Nancy was "persuading me to lower the temperature of my rhetoric." Political columnists Evans and Novak corroborated this by reporting that Clark had been "in the bad graces of Mrs. Reagan because of his anti-detente stance toward the Soviet Union. . . ." But someone other than Deaver had also advised the First Lady.

Paid and sometimes contacted through Mrs. Bloomingdale, astrologer Joan Quigley had continued advising the First Lady over dates and times for events, as well as "very detailed hour-to-hour reports" for her and the president's schedules. On more specific crises, they would sometimes talk several times a day. Nancy had State of the Union addresses, short trips, overseas trips, all public appearances, speeches, press conferences, one-on-one meetings—even the exact timing of when Air Force One was to leave the ground—all scheduled in accord with astrological readings. As far as the president's arms-control policy, Quigley claimed to have been on the line with Mrs. R. for three hours, convincing her that Reagan's and Soviet premier Mikhail Gorbachev's charts showed that "with the proper attitude [they] could cause an entirely different situation to exist between the two superpowers. So she convinced the President." Quigley contended that consulting the stars to guide his presidency was no secret to Reagan. Before making a decision, he'd ask the First Lady, "What does Joan think?"[2]

Whether the stars were consulted for the prospects of '84 was not revealed, but as Nancy Reagan neared the end of her first term, there were signs of ambivalence. Just after the assassination attempt, she'd told friends, "Let's get through this four years and all go back to California." She not only feared another attempt, but political defeats that would bruise Ronnie's pride and might affect his health. She'd come to enjoy aspects of her role, but suffered through personal traumas without privacy. "We've got to have a long conversation about this," she told him that fall, "and decide some things in our own minds." Privately, she canvassed political contacts. Eager strategists realized they just had to wait until she decided and consulted with Ronnie. The watch for a sign from Nancy prompted a *Doonesbury* strip of her offering to redecorate again.

The Reagans "sat down, reviewed it together, looked at the pluses and minuses, the challenges that would come . . ." When, however, speculation about her health prompted rumors that Reagan wouldn't run because of her, and the stock market sharply fell, the First Lady was bowled over. "Because of *me!*" she snapped to close friend Senator Paul Laxalt.

The formal announcement that Reagan would run for a second term was scheduled, again, in accordance with Nancy's astrological consultation.

Even before primary season, the First Lady "reviewed" the Democratic candidates with Spencer, giving him "as good and as clear and as helpful an analysis of Mondale and Glenn and Hart as any of the so-called political pros." He called her skills those of a "tactical politician." As early as October, she'd assessed that Glenn wouldn't be nominated, identified the upsurge for Hart before it happened in New Hampshire, and while she thought he'd be formidable against Mondale, pinpointed the latter as the future nominee. She was on the line with Rollins when she believed that Reagan-Bush staff weren't "being as effective," and noticed that "Mondale was making a very heavy effort . . . [in California], and she wanted to make sure we were alert to it." After her call, Rollins "made a few changes." As she suggested, another $1 million was spent there. Spencer recalled that advisers often conveyed their "ideas and concepts" to her, and she was especially astute on "precinct organization, phone banks, coalition buildings . . ." Rosebush said she was "quick to pick up on . . . lack of [support] . . . at the end of every campaign day, she would head for the telephone to share her perceptions about issues and voters' concerns with the top advisers. . . ."[3]

There was a unique change to the distaff of the '84 campaign. The Democratic contenders' wives on the campaign trail announced—without press prompting—their intended special projects if "elected" First Lady: Joan Mondale, arts advocacy, Lee Hart, education, Annie Glenn, speech therapy, Norma Cranston, women's activism in politics. After a quarter of a century of highly visible projects, the Ladyship had evolved to the point where it was politically astute for a campaign wife to name a project.

While others campaigned for candidates, the primary season found Jacqueline Onassis whistle-stopping to Albany to lobby for protection of landmark status for places of worship, to help block proposed construction of a tower over New York's St. Bartholemew's. After meeting with Governor Cuomo, she spoke before a packed legislative assembly and a battery of the media. "The future of New York City is bleak if the landmarks that mean so much to us and our children are stripped of their landmark status. If you cut people off from what nourishes them spiritually and historically, something within them dies." Her efforts weren't confined to the nineteenth century. The former First Lady personally lobbied the city comptroller to grant protective landmark status to Lever House, designed in the fifties.

Retaining both a fascination with India's history and friends there from her tour as First Lady, Mrs. Onassis hosted a reception for the Metropolitan Museum of Art's India Festival, and visited the country several times in conjunction with her job. After working with her as his editor, novelist Louis Auchincloss remarked, "She's a shrewd and imaginative editor of prose and she has impeccable taste in illustrations." That spring, however, Mrs. Onassis, vigilant about living as a private citizen, declined an invitation to join a conference on the role of First Lady, hosted by Betty Ford at the Ford Museum in Michigan. Mrs. Ford believed that study of the Ladyship was "an area [whose] time has come." Guests included daughters, East Wing staffers, and historians of First Ladies. Lady Bird had planned on being there, but a sudden illness prevented her attendance.

Pat Nixon had suffered another, minor stroke in August 1983, and the next summer developed a lung infection. Her energy was reserved. She made day visits to Julie and her growing family in nearby Pennsylvania, and took short trips with them—to Williamsburg and Disney World—but didn't join Dick on his grueling trips to China. In preparation for her own visit to China, Nancy Reagan consulted Pat Nixon by phone on the Chinese culture, and the latter offered that life had changed there drastically since her 1972 visit. (Pat also advised Nancy, "Without Camp David you'll go stir crazy.") Nancy was in China during the First Ladies conference, but Rosalynn Carter was there with Betty Ford as a unified front, jointly appearing on television news programs and doing interviews together with the dozens of journalists covering the event. Many leaders in drug-abuse rehabilitation now credited Betty for the movement of "getting straight." As the director of San Francisco's Community Substance-Abuse Services stated, "Betty Ford made it okay . . . to have a problem and deal with it. She has been a national treasure."

Rosalynn Carter retained her interests—helping dedicate the Woodstock Conference Center for Women, serving on the board of the National Association of Mental Health. In Washington, she attended a Women's Action for Nuclear Disarmament Conference, stating that it was important to elect a president in '84 with "national security policies . . . that reject nuclear weapons." She also admitted, "I loved living here and being so close to the seat of power." A board member of the Gannett News Service, she wrote a piece during the '84 convention for *USA Today.* Mondale won the nomination, but the historic news was his choice of Geraldine Ferraro as the first woman vice presidential candidate. On that nomination and Jesse Jackson's prominence, Rosalynn declared that it proved "there is no height to which women and minorities cannot rise in the political world."[4]

Ferraro's nomination also created the first possibility for another unique role, the first "Second Gentleman." In discussing it, Ferraro's husband, John Zaccaro, sounded not unlike a candidate's wife of the early twentieth century, complaining of the lack of privacy and stating, "I don't tell her what to do, and she doesn't tell me what to do." His Republican counterpart made headlines with her remark that Ferraro was a "four million dollar . . . I can't say it but it rhymes with rich." It was a rare display of public anger from Barbara Bush. Ferraro initially thought it a "terrible class put-down," but after Barbara immediately telephoned her to apologize and then called again, the vice presidential candidate was impressed that she'd be "so nice," and pronounced her "a real person."

Mrs. Bush did emphasize that she liked the fact that a woman had been nominated, but cracked, "Any year but this year . . ." She thought media focus on Ferraro's selection, however, was sexist, and that qualification was the only valid question. She stated that she'd continue to campaign for women candidates, and on the ERA, Mrs. Bush was frank. "Everybody knows that [I support ERA], so I'm not going to change—but I'm not as convinced anymore that the Equal Rights Amendment is half as important as seeing that women get equal pay for equal work, pension plans, deductions for child care and seeing that husbands who are delinquent in child support are made to make the payments." It was the kind of talk not heard from Nancy Reagan, who reportedly had strong opinions on Bush. In discussing a personal complaint about the vice president with her friend Roy Cohn, the First Lady urged Cohn, "Write him a real rough letter. Let him have it." Cohn believed that she "never forgave him for the stunts he pulled on her husband during the primaries in 1980 . . . Nancy *really* remembers." Cohn was one of the first to call her "the most powerful First Lady since Mrs. Wilson."

During their vacation prior to the convention, when the president was asked what he was doing about U.S.-Soviet arms negotiations, he seemed to stumble for a quick answer. Nancy quickly gazed at him, lowered her head, kicked some dirt, and whispered, "Doing everything we can." Her voice was picked up by the microphones and on camera.

The president responded, "Doing everything we can." His voice picked up as well. Later, she said she was talking to herself, and he said he'd remained silent because he refused to answer questions at an officially designated "photo op." As Garry Wills pointed out, that reasoning "would seem to give his wife even more influence—the power to change his stand on a point of principle." Lou Cannon, who covered Reagan closer and longer than any other journalist, also observed at the time that a "shrewd" Nancy proved herself "one helluva smart cookie," by foreseeing that it was "foolish" for Reagan to make appearances before and during the convention. "So," said Cannon, "she neatly got the campaign schedule changed." Director of the convention William Timmons received five phone calls from her by eight in the morning. When an overconfident strategist blustered that Reagan-Bush would easily defeat Mondale-Ferraro, the cautious Mrs. R. tersely responded, "You better be right."

Nancy Reagan became the third First Lady to address a convention. First a film about Nancy, including clips of her movies, was shown. Then the real Nancy appeared onstage, immediately transmitted onto the massive movie screen behind her. As she faced the audience to speak, Ronnie, in their suite, was beamed up on the screen. He was watching her. The audience yelled for Nancy to turn around and see him see her. She turned, waved to Ronnie, and the audience began calling for him to wave back. He waved, and watched her wave, as she watched and waved. Once again, First Lady and president, reality and image, Hollywood and Washington, became one. Privately, image was not reality. Michael Reagan was insulted each time he saw her telling the press "how wonderful it was to be a grandparent," since, "as often as Nancy was in Los Angeles on shopping trips and visiting friends, she never came to see her own grandchildren." Asked about the rumored strain, Mrs. Reagan said, "It's just plain not true."

At a convention women's lunch, the First Lady invited Reagan supporter Joan Rivers to perform because she found it "an odd combination." When some Republican women feigned shock at Rivers's "off-color" quips to submitted questions, Nancy cracked that she read others far more raucous, sent up by the same women who acted offended. Meanwhile, an ERA group, calling themselves "Ladies Against Women," spoofed it all outside, carrying picket signs NANCY FOR QUEEN and saying they were sponsored by the "China Friendship League." Asked if the Reagan-Bush forces were overconfident, Mrs. Reagan said, "[N]o, no, no, no, no, no," adding that not only was she a "worrier," but "superstitious, too."[5]

On October 7, after Ronnie stumbled with statistics in the first debate in Louisville, he told Nancy that his staff's preparation had been "brutalizing." Mrs. R. was livid, even yelling on the line at Deaver,

"What have you done to my husband?" Instead of traveling as scheduled with Ronnie, she flew to Washington with Senator Laxalt, venting her anger. The *Los Angeles Times* reported that Laxalt "promptly relayed the 'brutalized' quote to reporters." Mrs. R. freely admitted, "I was upset because I thought they'd gone about it all wrong. And they had. They overloaded him." She successfully advised Deaver to return to Reagan's "variations on a single speech" routine instead of the divergent texts they'd given him. During rehearsals for the second debate in the comfort of Camp David, she popped in, wearing a "4 More in 84" sweater to get up Ronnie's spirits, staying long enough to ascertain that her prescription was being followed. Asked about it later, she smiled, "Well, the second debate was better, wasn't it?"

At the time, national attention was focused again on the historical role of First Lady with conferences and ceremonies celebrating the centennial of Eleanor Roosevelt's birth. Mrs. Reagan hosted a White House luncheon for friends and family of Mrs. Roosevelt. Val Kill was also dedicated as a museum and national historic site. At the ceremony, "the Roosevelt Special" trailer, filled with memorabilia and voice recordings, was opened before its national tour. "If we had a process of secular canonization," said the governor of New York, "there would be no candidate surer of success than she." The elusiveness of the Ladyship, however, emerged that year in a Siena College poll attempting to "rank" First Ladies, with the confusing inclusion of family hostesses, and comparison of an Eleanor Roosevelt—subject of intense media scrutiny and dozens of biographies including portions of thousands of her letters—to the likes of an Elizabeth Monroe—almost never mentioned in the press of her era and whose letters were burned.

The campaign brought Mrs. Reagan to new levels in her role. For the first time, she publicly defended Reaganomics. "His policies have brought about a drop in unemployment, a drop in interest rates, the creation of new jobs, and the lowest rate of inflation in years. This benefits everybody. The idea that Republicans are only for the rich is simply untrue." When Mondale said Reagan's age was a possible impairment, Nancy used the opportunity to point out it was politically "insulting" to "older Americans." After Reagan won by a landslide, the First Lady admitted to attempting to influence him to "cut the deadwood out of the Cabinet," though he kept it intact.[6]

There were other resolutions. The First Lady admitted to an "estrangement" from Michael Reagan. After an initial meeting, Nancy turned to him: "I made a mistake . . . I'm sorry." He said it was "the first time she had ever apologized, and I knew she meant it." When he next came to see her and his father, Michael choked in trying to reveal the trauma of his molestation dating back to his childhood. It was Nancy who acted as his safety net, comfortingly stroking his neck.

When he uttered the word, Ronnie was shocked, but Nancy repeated, "He was molested, honey." When Ronnie asked questions, she retorted, "Let Mike get it out of his system. . . ." Not only did her patience and compassion help him, but to counteract sensational speculation before his book appeared, it was Nancy who volunteered to issue a statement saying that she and the president believed his story could help other children who'd been molested. Michael also recorded that she called him aside to make certain his forthcoming book would focus on the positive. He smiled, thinking, "Nancy, the consummate protector."

At the Second Inaugural, there were some reported sightings of "Queen Nancy." The First Lady's Inaugural trousseau totaled forty-six thousand dollars, nearly double that of 1981. Deborah Silverman said 1981's "public splendor" had evolved into 1985's "private luxury" of exclusive, closed parties, propagated by Nancy's coterie, which *Time* compared to "the affected ladies" of Louis XIV's court. One thing was certain: Nancy's critics were still around.

As Mrs. R entered her second term, she'd become a consummate "Mrs. President"—so dubbed by reporter Bernard Weinraub. Rollins said she had talks with Chief of Staff Baker and outside advisers about the direction of the second term, her priorities remaining "his image, his staff and his schedule. . . ." After the election, however, Baker and Treasury secretary Don Regan had spoken of switching jobs. Meeting with them and Deaver, Reagan accepted the change easily. To Regan it seemed to have "already been settled by some absent party." He would come to know who she was. It would prove to be the "one decision," Nancy later said, she wished she "could take back."

"As with many jobs," Mrs. Reagan explained, "the more knowledge and experience you gain, the more secure you feel in the position. . . ." Weinraub put it more bluntly. Nancy Reagan had become "the source of ultimate access to her husband, a woman who has discovered that she has power—and likes it."[7]

25

Mommy

THE VAST STONE "open arms of the church," St. Peter's Square, half of it sealed off for security, dwarfed Nancy Reagan, in a black business suit and black roller-brimmed hat. She marched past the Swiss guards wearing red, blue, and orange, through a series of audience halls and finally to the Papal Library. It was unprecedented. For twenty-five minutes, the First Lady met in private with Pope John Paul II, discussing drug abuse. Then she introduced him to Julius, her hairdresser, and Anita, her maid, and gave him a crystal box engraved with her initials. She was so shook up that she forgot her black gloves and black handbag. Her visit to Italy, however, had also been marked with a cartoon bitterly spoofing her as placing a wreath at Mussolini's grave.

In Air Force One, crossing the Atlantic, Deaver noticed that the First Lady seemed "physically ill." One of the Reagans' appearances on this European journey was to be at Bitburg, a Germany cemetery where several Nazi storm troopers were buried. Donnie Radcliffe was interviewing Mrs. R. When she asked about Bitburg, Mrs. R. remarked tersely, "I don't have any comment on that."

And, according to the *Los Angeles Times*, the president's new chief of staff, Don Regan, wasn't too thrilled, either. He grumbled about having been seated with "Julius" and "Anita."

By all indications, Mrs. Reagan was pro-Israel. In Beverly Hills, when she accepted the honor of a large flower garden named for her at Hebrew University in Jerusalem, the First Lady stated her hope that it would "bloom eternally on the campus . . ." The university was in a disputed area of the West Bank, first part of Israel, then captured by Jordan, and regained by Israel in 1967. As columnist Hank Greenspun wrote, although the State Department and president held the line that the West Bank's ownership had to be determined through Mideast negotiation without a U.S. role, "This did not deter the First Lady['s] . . . concern for . . . the justness of the righteous nation's causes . . ." Nancy was genuinely sensitive to Jews who'd suffered through the Holocaust. While the press focused on her famous and wealthy friends, Nancy also had many others; one was a woman who'd survived the concentration camps at Auschwitz and Bergen-Belsen. For over thirty years, the two women had remained in close touch.

The First Lady supported the move begun by Jewish leaders to change the president's stalwart decision to visit the Bitburg cemetery. Deaver opposed Nancy's view, and she wouldn't acquiesce to him, either. Deaver bluntly stated, it was "my first serious conflict with Nancy Reagan," and ended in "a very painful, emotional confrontation . . ." He chronicled, "Almost to the last minute, she insisted the trip should be canceled. She said so to me. She said so to her husband." Reagan's diary recorded that Nancy was "uptight about the situation and nothing I can say can wind her down." She argued how "offensive to Jews" Bitburg was. Finally, Reagan stubbornly told her, "Nancy, I simply don't believe you're right and I'm not going to change my mind." Deaver had long planned to leave the White House and join a PR firm, but the First Lady had successfully convinced him to remain. Now, she did not stand in his way. Five days after Bitburg, Deaver decided to depart.[1]

Meanwhile, Don Regan sensed something unusual. Perplexed at how the schedule could be so "plagued by inexplicable changes," he inquired of it to the scheduler. Finally, Deaver revealed the reason for the uncertainty. When Regan heard it, he assumed Deaver was joking. He was not. Regan didn't know the blond socialite who'd also attended an April 17 state dinner, but their stars were crossed. "Virtually every major move and decision made during my time as White House Chief of Staff," he wrote, "was cleared in advance with a woman in San Francisco who drew up horoscopes . . ." To Regan, Mrs. R. referred to Joan Quigley only as "my friend." Regan devised color codes for the president's schedule according to Quigley's charts, green for positive days, red for negative days, and yellow for uncertain days. Apart from that, he made harsh assessments of Mrs. R.'s power: ". . . [her] intense identification with her husband and his political fortunes was the random factor in the Reagan Presidency. Mrs. Reagan regarded herself as the President's alter ego not only in conjugal but also in the political and official dimensions . . . he permitted it to exist and . . . never reversed any of the situations created by his wife's intervention . . ."

Because he abruptly judged Nancy "out of her proper area of competence," Regan initially thought of ignoring her, and suggested that a deputy be hired as liaison to the First Lady. She got him on the line. "When I need something, I'll call you directly. I don't see any need for an intermediary." That ended that. For Regan, the zodiac remained the most difficult adjustment. Deaver blankly advised him, "Humor her." And so, the gruff Regan accepted what he could not change: ". . . there was no choice *but* to humor her . . ."

Just before he left, Mike Deaver told NBC, "She's very fond of Don

Regan, and thinks he's doing a good job. They have a very good relationship . . ."[2]

Less than two months later, a crisis precipitated the first battle between the First Lady and chief of staff.

On a steamy July morning, in the presidential helicopter, Nancy Reagan sat across from her husband, staring at him with undivided attention. He did not look at her as they headed to the hospital. In 1984, the president had undergone removal of an intestinal polyp. In March 1985, a benign polyp was discovered. Now, another checkup was under way when doctors discovered something else. At Bethesda Naval Hospital, Nancy, although thoroughly alone, sat "unflinching," according to Speakes. "I want you to tell me everything," she instructed the doctor.

The president had cancer.

It was advised that surgery the next day would be easiest on the president. She felt, "my best approach was to play on his feelings," his dislike of a medical formula he would otherwise have to take again. Nancy bluntly told him, "You've got something that needs surgery. What do you want to do?" She did not mention the word "cancer." He agreed without questions, one aide remarking, "He depends on Nancy to get whatever [medical] detail he needs on something personal like that." A statement was issued by Speakes, leaving out the words "cancer" and "malignant," divulging minimal information. The First Lady had requested it. That night, in the White House, she stayed up until 1:00 A.M. to receive the good news that there was no further evidence of cancer. She hadn't stayed with Ronnie to "avoid speculation by the media," which could provoke alarm in Wall Street and the international market. Meanwhile, a carefully worded document was drafted by the White House counsel temporarily transferring the presidency to Bush. Mrs. R. witnessed Ronnie signing it, and he teased the woman he still called "Mommy," cracking, "This doesn't mean you become George's First Lady."

If March 30 had been the day she reaffirmed her priority of Ronald Reagan, July 14 symbolized Nancy's independence, a personal maturing that became adjunct to the priority.

As the president went into surgery, Senator Bob Dole was publicly criticizing Reagan's economic plans, and the First Lady quipped sarcastically to Regan, "When you call Bob Dole, be sure to thank him for his remarks . . ." Throughout the nearly three-hour operation, she stayed nearby, Larry Speakes noticing that she used the "elaborate communications equipment . . . laying down the law" to Don Regan.

A *Newsweek* story, headlined THE DON AND NANCY SHOW, stated that the First Lady "quickly established the guiding principles of the post-operative White House," aides saying she'd have "veto power" over any tentative appointments. She had the president's schedule for the subsequent weeks pared down to only essential duties, including a state dinner, and accelerated their departure for a three-week California vacation. The *Post* reported that Mrs. R. and Regan "worked closely together to control almost all access to the chief executive," and that she carefully chose the photo of the recuperating Reagan that was publicly released. It showed the First Lady leaning over to kiss him, artfully blocking the view of a tube inserted into his breathing passage. Regan even praised her "skills as a manager of the media" when she went to the children's ward, and had "humanizing" photos taken of her there.

Although she stated that only Regan could see Reagan daily, the chief of staff went ahead and scheduled in the vice president and NSC chief McFarlane, less than twenty-four hours after the surgery, without first consulting the First Lady.

Described as "adamant," she refused to permit it. When McFarlane, through Regan, continued to press for a personal meeting to discuss something urgent with the president, word came back from Mrs. R. "Whatever it is, Bud can put it in writing."

Regan "did not ask" McFarlane what was so urgent. At one point, McFarlane promised to put his message in writing, then failed to do so. Later in the week, when the First Lady did permit McFarlane to meet with the president, Regan made notes that about twelve minutes was devoted to a question about "Middle East/Hostage Release/problem." McFarlane made his point that improved relations with Iran could be a positive step, and he asked the president in general terms if he agreed. No other specifics were discussed. The First Lady was not present.

Meanwhile, press speculation about how much power Mrs. R. was exercising was rampant. When the Reagans poked their heads out of the hospital window for photographers who began shouting questions, it was the First Lady who responded from three floors above, repeating Ronnie's response because she told them it was "easier for her to speak than him." A breathing tube had been placed down his throat, making it sore and difficult for him to speak. Nancy told Regan that the president could only "nod and mumble . . . and only she could understand what he was saying."

Don Regan seemed to be playing a role of "prime minister," with higher press visibility than any other chief of staff in history. The First Lady had been making her daily trek to the hospital by car. Regan took the presidential helicopter, justifying that the round-trip drive to the White House wasted a full hour and a half. The First Lady asked Speakes about it, and he informed her that no person uses it unless authorized by the president. Mrs. R. immediately got on the line with Regan at home, and "innocently" questioned him, "You're not going to use a helicopter, are you?" Regan said he was, but after the head of operations warned him, "The buzzards are out," Regan swiftly changed his routine. Two unnamed sources told *The Washington Post* that Mrs. Reagan "was not pleased" about Regan's high profile. It usurped the president's, and weakened his image.

Personally, Nancy Reagan overcame the stress to perform with valor as surrogate president in the ceremonial role. "I'm pinch-hitting for my favorite scout," she told a mammoth Boy Scout jamboree. When she spoke on a battleship, however, an official explained that "Mrs. President doesn't rate honors." There was no salute. Nancy determined to maintain the image of "business as usual," and her decision to illustrate it at a diplomatic event was a wise one. Both First Lady and vice president attended the previously scheduled reception, Bush having already learned that Nancy wished "to stand in for her husband," and deliver the "principal speech" that had been prepared for the president. He acquiesced graciously. Rosebush believed that "to the chiefs of foreign missions, it showed that a President's wife could represent a strong government not weakened by the President's ill health." After the surgery, when Bush's chief of staff called Stu Spencer for advice on how the vice president should proceed, the longtime Reagan consultant suggested that he "consult every day with First Lady Nancy Reagan and do what she says." Bush did. Mrs. Reagan elatedly planned the public return of the president to the White House, suggesting that she and Ronnie be photographed waving from the balcony, because it "would make a great picture."

President Reagan acknowledged his wife's powerful role during the crisis in his weekly radio address. "First Ladies aren't elected, and they don't receive a salary. They have mostly been private persons forced to live public lives, and in my book, they've all been heroes. Abigail Adams helped invent America. Dolley Madison helped protect it. Eleanor Roosevelt was FDR's eyes and ears. Nancy Reagan is my everything." She hugged him during the taping, and he thanked Nancy for her "strength" and "for taking part of the business of this nation," concluding, "Thank you, partner."

Ten days after the surgery, however, the parallel between Nancy Reagan and Edith Wilson emerged in its most dramatic manner yet. A cancerous lesion on the president's nose was a condition common to many who'd had long-term sun exposure. Mrs. R. directed that its detection and removal be handled confidentially. When Speakes and Regan managed to learn that Dr. Burton Smith, who'd operated on the president, and Mrs. Reagan were withholding information from them, the duo had to cajole the First Lady into even admitting that a biopsy of tissue had been taken. According to Speakes, she then demanded that the precise nature of it be withheld from the media, at one point snapping, "Dammit, Larry, the President does not have cancer!" He retorted, "Let me advise you that if you mislead the public, you'll make more trouble for yourself than is necessary." Speakes said, "Mrs. Reagan and Dr. Smith had gone to extraordinary lengths to prevent the press, not to mention the President, from learning the full story." Reagan himself didn't learn it was cancerous until four days later. As part of the scheme, the tissue sample had actually been sent under the name of a White House nurse.

The press noticed the scab on the president's nose. Speakes, "under orders from Nancy Reagan," was barely able to skirt the issue. He then wrote her a strong memo saying he must inform the press; otherwise, he offered to resign. He sent a suggested statement. The First Lady responded by memo: ". . . too medical . . . could make people jump to conclusions . . . [that] I *know* we don't need right now . . . Why can't we just say . . . He had a pimple . . . which he . . . irritated . . . Routine examination was done and nothing further is necessary. It was exactly what they thought—an irritation of the skin." A statement was released, without Speakes's usual signature or the words "cancer" or "biopsy." The cover was blown by none other than the gregarious president, who casually explained the truth to some of the press. Livid reporters grilled Speakes, Helen Thomas asking why he had handled the situation so clandestinely. He hinted by responding that "if you had two grains of salt for sense, you could figure it out."

At his first public appearance after the surgery, a reporter asked the president about his health, and got an idea of how protective Nancy could be.

"Just fine," he responded.

"It's not too much for you?" asked another reporter.

Ronnie put his hand to his ear, "What?"

"No," asserted the First Lady.

As the Reagans retired to their "Ranch in the Sky," for summer vacation, Lou Cannon reported that "the First Lady has had full control of his schedule and effectively isolated the chief executive even from his own staff," ordering that McFarlane's contact with Reagan be limited to phone calls and writing. Mrs. Reagan's diary recorded that she was even "trying to conspire to prevent Ronnie from riding at the ranch." She also recorded that the phone calls from McFarlane and Casey were "on the secure line," but "I don't know what they were about."[3]

Summer was not all stress. Some weeks before the president's surgery, the First Lady finally met the woman she emulated. With her husband, Nancy Reagan attended a June fund-raiser for the Kennedy Library at Teddy Kennedy's home. So did Jacqueline Onassis. Mrs. Reagan focused intently on her, as they engaged in a short conversation. While their previous phone conversations hadn't made the two First

Lady "soul sisters," Deaver said Nancy was "touched" by Jackie's encouragement, admitting that she "was in awe" of her predecessor. Upon their second meeting, at a dinner on Martha's Vineyard that summer, Mrs. Onassis reminded the First Lady of the inevitable criticism: "You're going to be there a long time; you might as well get used to it." Nancy recorded that she invited Jackie back to the White House to see the changes she had made. Mrs. Onassis "prefers not to return to Washington, but if she changes her mind she'll let me know." Deaver noticed that while Nancy's high respect for Jackie remained, "the awe is gone, a reflection more of Nancy Reagan's new public confidence than anything else."[4]

That fall, Nancy met another famous peer for the first time.

After a meeting with the president, Soviet ambassador Andrei Gromyko had chatted with the First Lady in the Red Room, telling her to "[W]hisper the word *peace* to your husband every night." Nancy charmingly shot back, "I will. And I am also going to whisper *peace* to you every night." The First Lady's motivations were two-pronged. Not only did she genuinely support a U.S.-Soviet accord for military peace, but she knew, according to Deaver, that it was "the correct move politically." He said it was she who "pushed everybody on the Geneva summit," and "would buttonhole" the secretary of state and NSC chief,

among others, "to be sure that they were moving towards that goal."
She'd not won fans in the right wing for it. Her successfully advising
the president to limit appearances at navy dedications and army bases
and arguing "that he should soften his language" on the Soviets, had in
fact provoked hard-liner Bill Clark to leave Reagan's side for good.
"With the world so dangerous, I felt it was ridiculous for these two
heavily armed superpowers to be sitting there and not talking to each
other," she admitted. Some speculated that in fact Nancy Reagan was a
"closet liberal." As Deaver revealed, "She lobbied the president to
soften his line on the Soviet Union; to reduce military spending and
not push Star Wars at the expense of the poor and dispossessed. She
favored a diplomatic solution in Nicaragua . . ." Conservatives dubbed
the shift of Reagan policy as "Nancyism."

After Mrs. Reagan announced her plans to accompany Ronnie to
the Geneva summit, so did the wife of General Secretary Mikhail Gorbachev. Not since Lenin's wife, Nadezhda Krupskaya, had a Soviet
leader's wife played a political role. Stalin had his wife, also named
Nadezhda, shot to death. Neither Nina Khrushchev nor Victoria
Brezhnev played more than ceremonial roles. Anna Chernenko had
once been spotted, voting for her husband. Tatyana Andropov was
seen, once and last, at her husband's funeral. On foreign trips, Kosygin,
a longtime widower, had been accompanied by his daughter Ludmilla.
Now a woman unique to the Russias was "First Lady." Not only did she
travel everywhere with her husband, but in London, the former Raisa
Maximovna skipped visiting Marx's tomb to see the crown jewels and
buy Cartier diamonds with an American Express card. Balancing the
style was substance. Raisa had studied and taught Marxist-Leninist theory, remarked that she had "respect" for religious practices, and served
on the government's Culture Fund. The general secretary admitted that
he and Raisa "discuss everything." When she met the First Lady of
France, Raisa asked, "Give me some advice. I'm a beginner at this job."

Just prior to the Geneva summit, Regan had told Donnie Radcliffe
that the First Lady's role would reinforce Reagan's "natural inclinations
in . . . [arms talks] . . . without giving away the shop . . . watching his
moods, his health," but that she and Raisa wouldn't discuss disarmament or human rights. He emphasized that Mrs. R. "doesn't get into
throw-weights or warheads or methods of transporting those warheads."
But when he added that women in general were more interested in the
diamonds of South Africa than its apartheid policy, he raised the ire
not only of women generally, but an already antagonized First Lady.
Nancy called the remark "insensitive and demeaning to women, and I
resented it." He refrained from adding that Joan Quigley had first
cleared the dates for Geneva.

The First Ladies met privately the first day and saw each other at dinners the two subsequent nights. Their first joint appearance before the press sparked a rivalry between them. They were scheduled to deposit "joint messages of peace" in the cornerstone of a Red Cross museum. Raisa arrived first. Then came Nancy, who seemed unaware that Raisa was already there. When Nancy saw her, a network reporter said she gave one of "those old Hollywood double takes." The media-savvy Mrs. R. had met her match. Mrs. Gorbachev's loquacious Marxism prompted Mrs. Reagan to fume behind a closed door, "Who does that dame think she is?"[5]

Mrs. Reagan relished more her White House welcome for Prince Charles and Diana that fall. While the First Lady brought the princess with her to a parents-and-children drug meeting, the Second Lady brought her into the wards of the terminally ill at the Washington Home and Hospice. Friends of the First Lady partied with royals at a Reagan dinner, but Mrs. Bush and her husband were at the theater. They'd not been invited to the White House. In the first term alone, Barbara had traveled 615,000 miles to fifty-seven countries, forty-seven states, and three territories. She continued her literacy project and took on promotion of the administration's private-sector initiatives, or "volunteerism," attending about fifty events related to it. There was little doubt that the vice president would run in '88, but irrespective of the results, Mrs. Bush's growing dedication to a variety of social issues, including the homeless and civil rights, would continue after 1989, whatever role she might then play.[6]

Meanwhile, the roles of women like Diana and Raisa were tangentially affected by one of the most historic occasions of Nancy Reagan's Ladyship. Several weeks before meeting Mrs. Gorbachev, Mrs. Reagan hosted an unprecedented morning session on drug abuse at the United Nations for the "First Ladies" of thirty foreign nations, making her the only incumbent First Lady to speak there. She'd not lost any of the genuine momentum of her antidrug effort, remarking, "I hope I'm right, that we've managed to draw more attention to it. I've seen more on TV now than I ever did before. You like to think you've contributed something." It had become a national crisis, intricately involved in a drastic increase in crime as drug dealers fought for turf. The young remained the greatest victims, and Nancy Reagan's focus. Her reassuring capacity to coax children to open up was increasingly evident, and in 1984 alone she'd made 110 appearances. Over half of her four thousand letters a month were about drug abuse, and twenty hours of her forty-hour work week were spent on the issue. In 1985, she'd gone global. There was precedent for the UN "summit." She'd held a "mother-to-mother" meeting in April at the White House, for seventeen "First Ladies." "I don't get into the other," Nancy said of the political aspects. She did acknowledge that federal money was important in "interdiction and legal penalties," but when the German First

Lady cited unemployment as a reason for drug use, Nancy disagreed. "I suppose unemployment is a factor, but I don't believe it's the main factor. There are lots of well-employed people involved in drugs." Still, several of the First Ladies reported that the conference "had direct bearing on increasing their own public involvement in the fight to curb this epidemic," and sent cables to Nancy about programs they began, a result of her summit.

The UN gathering was colorful. Imelda Marcos, in full-length gown, with two armed guards, followed near Mrs. R. as she greeted others. Imelda engaged in conversation about Nellie Taft's years in Manila, and compared her "power of beauty" to Nancy Reagan's. Nicaragua's Marxist Rosario Murillo emphasized to Nancy the need for a "better relationship between our two countries." Sri Lanka's First Lady suggested that the next such conference be held in a Third World nation where drug production was acute.

Never before in history had so many wives of international leaders gathered together for any purpose. Many were from cultures that permitted women only second-class citizenship, and their participation in Mrs. Reagan's conferences became conspicuous as front-page news in their nations—in some cases their first acknowledgment back home. From Malaysia to Mauritius, the role of First Lady was emerging, and a consciousness about women's changing roles through these visible models was spurred. Many of these women—some of them working professionals—had had no previously defined public role. Following Mrs. R.'s example, they now did. India's Sonia Gandhi became so visible that the native press sought to identify her as a "First Lady," though one report claimed that Indians found it "American sounding." France's Danielle Mitterrand, *"La Présidente,"* admitted that "most people think I have a lot of power." Egypt's Susan Mubarak made literacy her cause and termed herself "First Lady." Even the wives of leaders of anti-American nations, like Rosario Murillo, took on social issues and dressed the part. And there was news that Libya's Safiya Qaddafi was "constantly nagging him [her husband] to look after himself." As the Bicentennial of the presidency neared, the notion had come full circle. America replaced a queen with a First Lady. Europe replaced or augmented their queens with leaders' wives now becoming "First Ladies."[7]

The new year brought changes to the East Wing. Lee Verstandig took over as chief of staff and began rearranging the offices to create a salaried position for his longtime aide that not only didn't exist but was specifically unauthorized and denied. Mrs. R. "hit the ceiling," and "Lee of the Two Dozen Days," was replaced with Jack Courtmanche of the Reagan campaign. She also privately advocated that Sheila Tate be chosen as the first woman press secretary to a president, upon Speakes's retirement.[8]

It was the most loyal aide and friend who commanded the First

Lady's concern that spring. When Mike Deaver was pictured making a telephone call from a limousine on Time's cover, subcaptioned "Influence peddling in Washington," the First Lady soberly warned him that "you made a big mistake. I think you are going to regret posing for that photograph." It was now she who advised him. After his PR firm received large accounts rather rapidly, Deaver had called Mrs. R., who intuitively cautioned, "Mike, be careful. I have a feeling this is all happening too fast." When it appeared that he might have violated an ethics law, the First Lady was advised by the president's counsel to limit her personal contact with Deaver. She publicly declared her belief in his innocence, but refused to discuss the details of the charges: "I'm not going to get into that."[9]

At the same time, Nancy was dealing with a private matter that had become embarrassingly public when her daughter Patti wrote an autobiographical novel with a scalding portrait of her parents. Mrs. Reagan tried to keep private matters private, but Patti became permanently estranged.

Another president's daughter made national headlines some months later. Caroline Kennedy was marrying, and as her brother reflected, "It's been the three of us alone for so long, and now we've got a fourth." At the wedding, Senator Kennedy toasted Jacqueline as "that extraordinary gallant woman. Jack's only love, he would have been so proud of you today." When historian Doris Kearns told Jackie, "You must be very proud," she beamed straight out, "It's the best thing I've ever done." Mrs. Onassis was taking a higher profile in her ongoing historic-preservation fight, but declined an offer to become New York commissioner of cultural affairs. At a Municipal Arts Society event, Charlotte Curtis asked if she would someday write a book. Mrs. Onassis gently deflected by musing that "editing isn't half so hard . . ." She offered that "I'd have liked to study architecture . . . Like Thomas Jefferson. Now there was a man! He could do so many things." When a friend came by, Jackie introduced him as the "the first person to dance the Twist at the White House." Chairing a coalition of community and preservation groups, she told the press that a developer's planned skyscraper at Columbus Circle would permanently "cast a long shadow over Central Park." In the end, it wasn't built.[10]

Nancy Reagan continued her project as well. When the president signed the Anti-Drug Abuse Act of 1986, he turned the pen over to the First Lady; it was an issue of increasing importance to the president because of his wife. Although she still focused on youth, she began to expand her discussion of it as new problems burgeoned. "Crimes committed by young people are often for drug money," she said that year. "You can't reason with a kid who's holding you up for cash—all he knows is he needs his drugs—and he'll do anything to get them . . .

we've come down the road a bit, [but] longer roads and bigger hills lie
before us."

On September 15, 1986, in a unique illustration of their political
partnership, the Reagans appeared together in the first joint address to
the nation by a president and First Lady. Calling for a "national crusade" on the "cancer" of drug abuse, they sat together in the family
quarters, and the president promised to push for antidrug spending of
$3.9 billion—an increase of about $900 million. In the middle of the
appearance, the First Lady spoke, focusing on demand, not supply:
". . . drug criminals are ingenious. They work every day to plot a new
and better way to steal our children's lives—just as they have done by
developing this new drug, crack. For every door we close, they open a
new door to death. . . . It's up to us to change attitudes and just simply
dry up their market . . ."[11]

In an even rarer occurrence, that autumn the First Lady was *not*
going with the president to Reykjavik, Iceland, for his second meeting
with Gorbachev. According to Regan, consultation with Quigley determined the First Lady's absence. Quigley had also forecast "dire events"
for the coming "November-December."

Publicly, the First Lady stated, "The invitation that came from Mr.
Gorbachev was for a business meeting. Therefore, I thought it was improper that I go." After it was learned that Mrs. Gorbachev was going,
the East Wing politely stated that Mrs. Reagan's schedule prevented
her attendance. With the First Lady's absence, however, Speakes believed Reagan to be "deprived of his one indispensable adviser." Nancy
did manage to manage, even from another continent. She kept abreast
of Ronnie's schedule, and spent several hours on the line with his personal assistant, admonishing, "Make certain he doesn't have to have
George [Shultz] and Don [Regan] over every night. They'll keep him up
too late." Interestingly, Nancy's absence marked the one summit that
failed. Still, Reagan's legend remained high. Loyalists began efforts to
repeal the Twenty-second Amendment, which limited presidents to two
terms in office. Even House Speaker Tip O'Neill paid a backhanded
acknowledgment of the Reagans' popularity. "Too bad they can't be
king and queen and didn't [have to] run the government." After Nancy
stated that she believed the number of terms shouldn't be limited, the
East Wing received calls from both men and women suggesting that the
First Lady run as president in name in order to keep her husband as
president in fact, an idea once proposed to Eleanor Roosevelt by Louis
Howe, before FDR *had* run for a third term.[12]

But then, "November-December" arrived.

26

The Invisible Glove

THE FATE OF THE American hostages being held in Iran gravely concerned the president. CIA director Bill Casey informed him that one of those being held, William Buckley, worked for his agency, and was undoubtedly being tortured, although NSC briefings by McFarlane, and then his successor, Admiral John Poindexter, did not dwell on the situation. Released hostage David Jacobsen appeared with the Reagans and begged the press to refrain from discussing the hostages because speculation might endanger those still being held. The day after their meeting, the Lebanese magazine *Al Shiraa* appeared with a story recounting how some Americans, including McFarlane, had gone to Iran to attempt to negotiate for the hostages, and that the United States was supplying arms to that nation. The media called for a press conference, and only after the date was checked against the president's astrological charts, Regan recorded, it was scheduled.

As Congress began investigating the matter, it became clear that with McFarlane's lead, Poindexter had authorized sale of American military parts to Iran for $30 million with the understanding that the hostages would be freed. The United States, however, had received $18 million less than the original amount agreed. Some of that had been diverted by Poindexter aide Lieutenant Colonel Oliver North to Nicaraguan "Contras," fighting the Marxist "Sandinistas" of that nation. Giving authority and guidance was CIA Director Casey. When he learned of this, Reagan appointed former senator John Tower and a bipartisan commission to investigate the scandal, and ordered the resignations of Poindexter and North.

Deaver contended that the greatest irony was that had Regan not tried to get Mrs. R. "out of the loop," she, "getting wind of the affair, could have alerted the president to the facts—and the dangers." Speakes believed that the First Lady was "the one who recognized, often before the President, that an issue like Iran was building up and had to be defused." Asked about the revelation of the secret bank account providing Contra funds, a "brisk" First Lady told reporters, "I don't know how you can be either embarrassed or damaged when you find something has not been done correctly late in the afternoon and you correct it the next day." Asked if Regan would have to be one of those staffers asked to resign, the First Lady just shrugged her shoulders.[1]

Mrs. R. was quickly drawn into it, her drug-abuse appearances repeatedly marred with questions about the scandal. There was even momentary consideration of subpoenaing her before the Senate investigating committee because of notes she may have kept that might indicate the president's involvement in the decision. When the press learned that Senator Durenberger, chair of the Senate Select Intelligence Committee, had surreptitiously briefed Reagan in a private meeting on its discoveries thus far about the scandal, the First Lady defended it by stating, "He [Reagan] just wants more input, which is, I believe, the responsible way to do it. . . ." She was angry that Reagan had been "deceived" by Poindexter's first briefing, and the fact that he and North had taken the Fifth Amendment. Privately, she was "furious" that Regan convinced Reagan to shift his testimony to the Tower Commission. With good reason, she blamed him for the president's poorly prepared press conference of November 19, the first in which he addressed Iran-Contra. Reagan's approval rating was sinking. Once again, through

only her stated role of protecting Ronnie, she sought to "help" him. As she saw it, Regan was damaging Reagan. However unconsciously, Nancy was becoming a pragmatic wedge between Reagan and Regan. At MGM, when Nancy Reagan had been asked her philosophy of life, she wrote, "Do unto others as you would have them do unto you . . . the law of retribution." Don Regan had not been nice. Nancy applied her old philosophy.

Negative media focus on Regan burgeoned. When the First Lady was again asked by the AP if Regan should resign, she "declined to express a view," but when Ronnie briefed her in detail, she called Regan with "many questions, and many suggestions, about the management of the crisis. Her mood was furious, and there was no mistaking her message: Heads would roll. I had the impression that mine might very well be among them." To himself, Regan recalled the negative press that had precipitated the dismissals of Allen, Watt, and Haig. When he asked her whether his being besieged was "paranoia or reality," there was a dead silence.[2]

Nancy Reagan opened the doors of her "Kitchen Cabinet," a diverse collection including PR politicos Deaver and Spencer, journalist George Will, and former National Democratic Committee chairman Bob Strauss. They were described as pragmatic people who told her not what she "wants to hear," but "what she ought to hear." Nancy did not bristle at their critical assessments; rather, she wisely sought and considered them. The notion that she'd be asking advice from a man like Strauss, for example, who had been a political enemy in the '80 campaign, didn't suit the legend of her as oversensitive and unforgiving. It proved her to be the intelligent woman who'd become the real Nancy Reagan. As Donnie Radcliffe reported, "Mrs. Reagan has been operating on two levels. . . . Publicly, she declined comment. Privately, she worked the phone and met [with members of her Kitchen Cabinet] . . ." Radcliffe stated that the inside story was being told largely through the "sources designated by Mrs. Reagan. . . ."

Regan began to sense an organized move to build up enough outside sentiment, through the press, to oust him. Gossip was filtered back to his aides that Deaver and Spencer were calling for his removal. On December 11, *The New York Times* quoted an unnamed adviser to the First Lady, saying she'd put the need for Regan's ouster in "pithy terms," and was "moving cautiously" to avoid the appearance of "pushing Regan over the cliff." It was reported that although Deaver was under investigation, he and the First Lady continued to speak by phone, "at least daily and often several times a day. Two days later the *Los Angeles Times* had a specifically planted but anonymous quote stating that the chief of staff would be gone by Christmas. Days before, in a private meeting held in the family quarters, Strauss, escorted by former secretary of state William P. Rogers, came to a meeting that included the First Lady, to urge Reagan to fire Regan. Mrs. R. made it clear that she agreed, and the group reportedly told the president that the statements in the press proved that the ouster would be popular.

Deaver reported that Nancy bluntly told the president, "I can't deal with that man anymore." The First Lady did admit to admonishing the president: "I was right about Stockman. I was right about Bill Clark. Why won't you listen to me about Don Regan?" The president reportedly retorted, "Get off my goddamn back!" When the press asked her if that was an accurate quote, she replied, "He'll say 'damn,' but he'll never put the two together." Regan was not dismissed.

For her pragmatism, the week before Christmas, ABC News voted the First Lady their "Person of the Week." Asked whether the ouster attempt was over, the First Lady deflected, "Oh, come on, it's Christmas." Though speculation ran high that Regan would find a pink slip in his red boot, the First Lady stood smilingly by his side for a photograph in front of the White House Christmas tree while a cartoon showed Regan stepping up to his office door just as a gargantuan chandelier smashed behind him, cut loose by an invisible glove from the upstairs balcony. It had barely missed him. But her aim was improving.[3]

Between Christmas and January, Regan claimed that in "a series of candid telephone calls," Nancy demanded that he arrange for CIA director Bill Casey's dismissal: "You're more interested in protecting Bill Casey than in protecting Ronnie! . . . Nobody believes what Casey says, his credibility is gone on the Hill." Casey had been diagnosed with brain cancer and undergone surgery. He lay incapacitated in a hospital, but still, by Regan's account, Mrs. R. badgered for his removal. Nancy believed that Casey had been "deeply involved" in Iran-Contra "during a period when he wasn't thinking clearly."

After the president underwent prostate surgery on January 5, a recuperation period of six weeks was strongly urged. Nancy "assured doctors in the recovery room that she would follow their orders." At the same time, she was said to have demanded of Regan in person, at the hospital, that the conservative director of communications, Pat Buchanan, whom she never liked, be fired. When told that he planned to resign by the first of February, she said she hoped it would be sooner.

According to Regan, the First Lady not only suggested changes, but offered alternatives, giving him the name of attorney Edward Bennett Williams as a good CIA replacement. Soon after, Williams's name turned up on a list of suggested candidates, though he ultimately turned it down. As the president's State of the Union Address was being prepared, Regan said the First Lady insisted that she wanted Buchanan to have nothing to do with it, asserting, "The parts about abortion have got to come out. I don't give a damn about those right-to-lifers. I'm cutting back on the Iran stuff too. It's too long and it's not appropriate. Ronald Reagan's got to be shown to be in charge." Nancy's staunch public anti-abortion view had changed. Speechwriter Peggy Noonan claimed that Nancy muttered "no more coat hangers."

Mrs. R. steadfastly refused scheduling of any press conferences in the near future because of Ronnie's health, but Regan "assumed" her desire to have the president give speeches only on specific days and the changing of dates for his meetings with political appointees and freshmen congressmen were ruled by the zodiac. Regan feared that limitation of Reagan's public appearances at that moment would only worsen the perceptions of a weakened presidency. Nancy retorted, "You're not a doctor." He dismissed her with "coarse" words. While the East Wing stated the First Lady had "made sure" that the president "is following the doctors' orders," the West Wing announced that Regan "has the confidence of the President until he's been told otherwise." After Quigley told her, "The malevolence of both Saturn and Uranus turning against him could cost him his life," Nancy became resolute in defying Regan's push for the president to speak and travel so soon after the operation. The second battle was on. At a lunch for governors' spouses, an event usually covered only by the regular East Wing reporters, two of the three network White House correspondents showed up with full camera crews, eager for even a minor Mrs. R. morsel about Regan. The fight became so heated that it competed for headlines with Iran-Contra. That was no mistake.

Regan contended that Mrs. R., having failed to privately convince the president to fire him, now reapplied intense pressure from the outside, through the media. The First Lady slipped away with George Will for a long private lunch. Four days later, on a news show, Will blasted that Regan's "deplorable conduct . . . has been as contemptible as his clinging to it when his usefulness to the president, whose service he was supposed to be rendering, ended, many, many months ago." It succinctly summarized Mrs. R.'s view. Regan retaliated. His defenders told the press that she was "overprotective," which contributed to the view of an "out-of-touch, aging president who can't even referee a quarrel between his wife and his chief of staff."

When Regan said the impression of "shielding" the president was being sent out, she snapped that it was not. Regan tersely insisted that a press conference would go ahead as scheduled. "Okay! Have your damn press conference!" he said she said. Whoever slammed down the receiver first, the result was a final break. Now, the media, which never had direct leaks from the First Lady, began reporting that she had "purposely leaked" the telephone story. It was a standoff. Mrs. R. and Regan dealt "through intermediaries," stonewalling on their positions, leaving Reagan to choose between wife and friend. As one source stated, "it was unimaginable" that Regan could stay "if the tension persisted. . . ." Mrs. Reagan even asked Vice President Bush to tell Ronnie that Regan had to go. "Nancy, that's not my role," he responded. "That's exactly your role," she snapped at him. [4]

Regan said that it was Mrs. R. who "favored" one John O. Koehler to fill Buchanan's position. While meeting with Regan, Ronnie pulled out a "note," stating that he had considered the Koehler appointment "overnight" and liked it. The perfunctory background investigation into Koehler was rushed through. Days later, when it was disclosed that Koehler had once been a Nazi youth, Regan was quoted as blaming "the East Wing" for pushing for his quick nomination.

The president called Regan into the Oval Office, discussing the latter's plan to retire from the post. Now, Reagan urged it, but not before Regan shouted, "I thought I was Chief of Staff to the President, not to his wife." He agreed to depart on Monday, March 1. On Friday, the twenty-seventh of February, the Tower Commission report came out, only strengthening the First Lady's claim against Regan. In the morning, it was decided that Senator Howard Baker would replace Regan. That afternoon, as Regan returned from having his hair cut, the new NSC chief Frank Carlucci was waiting for him. CNN (Cable News Network) had broken the news that Elaine Crispen of the East Wing had "announced" Regan's departure. With that, Regan had an abrupt farewell call with Reagan and left.

Elaine had merely been called for a premature statement on the Monday departure of Regan. The press interpreted it as if the First Lady were usurping the prerogative of the West Wing. As Mrs. R. wrote to the bitter Regan: "I . . . did not issue a statement 'gleefully'—as they put it—before Ronnie did when you left . . . C&N [sic] called Elaine's office for a comment. I told her to say I wished you good luck and we were happy to welcome Howard. . . ."[5]

A new onslaught began. On Monday, March 2, the day Regan had originally planned to depart, The New York Times carried a William Safire essay setting off the wildest speculation about a First Lady's political power since 1919. Titled "The First Lady Stages a Coup," he compared "power-hungry" Nancy Reagan to "an incipient Edith Wilson, unelected and unaccountable, presuming to control the actions and appointments of the executive branch." He took a swipe at a "bloated" East Wing, calling Mrs. R. the government's "costliest 'volunteer'". He publicly called for the First Lady to hold a press conference, asked when she learned of the attempts to free the hostages, whether she knew of the arms swap, and called for her to relinquish diary notes. He furthermore made the claim that she had a say in USIA personnel and travel allocations and was hoping to have Charles Wick replace the retiring Roger Stevens as the Kennedy Center's director. The issue of Mrs. R.'s power proliferated, prompting lead stories in the media, including a debate on *Nightline*.

Perhaps the most devastating vilification of a First Lady's power in the nearly two-hundred-year history of the Ladyship, the Safire piece was followed the next day by a lead *New York Times* story by Bernard Weinraub, "Nancy Reagan's Power Is Considered at Peak," stating that she was "now far more powerful, more confident and more politically involved than at any point in the Reagan presidency, and she intends to remain so for the rest of her husband's term." Although supporters Senator Laxalt and Nancy Reynolds, quoted in the story, softened some of the edge to the debate, they didn't deny the First Lady's power.

Meanwhile, a *Miami Herald* reporter caught up with the new chief of staff and asked if the Mrs. R.–Regan feud was as bad as reported. Howard Baker quipped, "You can believe it. When she gets her hackles up she can be a dragon." Later questioned about his comment in front of the president, Baker clarified, "The First Lady is a distinguished citizen of this nation. She's a great lady of strong convictions. That's what I meant." Asked whether he'd yet been on the line with Mrs. R., Baker remarked, "I haven't talked to Mrs. Reagan today. I intend to do that later today." He and the First Lady planned "a close working relationship." Asked what her "agenda" would be, he cracked, "Whatever she wants to talk about."

Just then, the phone rang in the background.[6]

It was reported that the First Lady "vetoed" proposals for a Reagan press conference, but "recruited" the speechwriter to craft his address to the nation about the Tower findings on Iran-Contra. Asked whether the First Lady planned to "edit" it, the East Wing reworded the inquiry by saying she'd "share" it. Because of the "increasing vacuum of power" caused by the departure of longtime Reagan aides, in conjunction with his "advancing age and illnesses," Helene von Damm was one of many who felt that Nancy's role had become "more imperative." *Newsweek* claimed the president was "oblivious" to many of her moves, a point illustrated by her gesturing to a friend to compliment Ronnie's appearance and her guidelines to her "Kitchen Cabinet" indicating what information should be leaked. Reagan often read information in the morning paper funneled to it from the First Lady through her sources. Furthermore, the *Los Angeles Times* reported that before she left on a solo trip, Nancy left "instruction cards" outlining his personal schedule. One friend called her "keeper of the legend."[7] Behind the scenes, she was also participating in the same sort of issue-oriented politics as Rosalynn Carter had. After the defeat of the president's Contra Aid package, on February 3, 1988, the First Lady, according to Quigley, worked with Howard Baker and "engineered the compromise with Speaker of the House Jim Wright regarding Nicaragua."

But it was the comparison to Edith Wilson that dominated the press. *Time, The New York Times, The Washington Post,* the *Los Angeles Times*—most leading publications referred to Mrs. Wilson's distancing of Colonel House from her husband. And yet, the American people supported her—two to one in a *Newsweek* poll.

In the Regan aftermath, Mrs. Reagan was largely admired, which would be, as one reporter said "flattering to anyone's ego," and she astutely realized that she shouldn't distance herself from good press—even if she did not agree with the facts for which she was being praised. The line between her "perceived" power and "real" power seemed secondary. Whichever, she had more of it than at any other time in her Ladyship.

For her part, Joan Quigley thought Regan had been as "autocratic" as Nancy, but thought the First Lady "behaved very ill-advisedly . . ." She observed, "As Nancy grew stronger, Ronnie weakened. Nancy started out as a partner who complemented and helped her husband by being aware of the people surrounding him, their motives and loyalty. Then she became an equal partner, and after that, the dominant force . . . further ambition took over. She realized that she was a power in her own right. She devoted herself tirelessly to promoting her own interests. . . . She wished to be a political power openly. . . . When she began to reap the honors that for a time were showered on her, her strongest motivating factor was her place in history right alongside her husband, as a dominant and powerful political force in her own right."

In a speech to news editors, Nancy Reagan defended her role: ". . . If the President has a bully pulpit, then the First Lady has a white glove pulpit . . . more restricted . . . but it's a pulpit all the same . . . one thing on which I'm inflexible. The First Lady is first of all a wife . . . that's the reason she's there. A President has advisors . . . But no one among all those experts is there to look after him as an individual with human needs . . . Yes, there are demands of government, but there are also basic personal rights . . . it's . . . legitimate . . . for a First Lady to look after a President's health and well-being. And if that interferes with other plans, then so be it. . . ." She paraphrased *The New York Times* to make a point, saying a First Lady should talk about farm subsidies not hairdressers, and "any man who married a woman that vapid shouldn't be President anyway . . . President Hayes explained . . . 'Mrs. Hayes may not have much influence on Congress, but she has great influence with me.' . . . don't kid yourselves, it's been that way ever since we've had Presidential wives."[8]

Besides the fact that she had every right to serve as an adviser, Nancy Reagan was vindicated by the Tower Commission report, which partially blamed Regan. She'd judiciously made decisions only after consulting a wide variety of opinions from divergent political perspectives. It was never a case of petty animosity that prompted her to urge Regan out. She'd personally liked him as Treasury secretary, and professionally respected his work. As chief of staff, he'd not performed well. Only when he became personally belligerent did she repay in kind. The case for Mrs. R.'s role was made even stronger by the blatant sexism of Regan and his defenders, they all charging that because she was "just a wife," she was somehow incapable of intelligence. Throughout the entire five-month press blitz of the Mrs. R.–Regan affair, none of those who harshly criticized Nancy were women.

Three days after the Safire piece, The New York Times backpedaled with a complimentary editorial on the First Lady. Gossip columnist Liz Smith devoted an entire column to defending the First Lady, declaring, "You've come a long way, Nancy!" since her antifeminist days. And, astonishingly, on the cover of Ms. magazine would appear the woman its editor, Gloria Steinem, had once called "the marzipan wife." Still, as Liz Carpenter pondered at a debate, "I wonder how much more Nancy Reagan's popularity polls would have gone up if she had saved Jill Ruckelshaus and Mary Louise Smith from being fired from the Civil Rights Commission." After much consideration, Smith College decided against granting her—an alumna—an honorary degree because it would be based on "reflected glory." Ultimately, Nancy Reagan became a symbol of a segment of women, independent and involved, but privileged. Though Edie Davis had been a single working mother, the First Lady did not particularly relate her personal experience to the larger picture and lend any especial support to single working mothers. She did say she now supported abortion in cases of endangered mothers or rape, but the crisis of teen pregnancy had specifically been avoided when she addressed "drug-related" issues. She used the old-fashioned term "girl" in reference to herself, even as late as her last interview as First Lady.

And yet, there were defenders of and other signals from Mrs. R. The former president of NOW not only defended Nancy Reagan's role, but suggested First Ladies be salaried. "If the president were the kind of man who prefers to deal with token women," said Ambassador Jeane Kirkpatrick, "he never would have married Nancy Reagan." In one speech, Nancy quoted Mrs. Roosevelt, saying, "I have never wanted to be a man. I have often wanted to be effective as a woman but I never thought that trousers would do the trick." During a 1981 interview, she came prepared with statistics on women in high-level administration posts, emphasizing that they be chosen based on qualifications, and only wanted "an equal shot" at getting such posts.

As Betty Friedan, a fellow Smith alum, good-naturedly told Nancy early on, "Be a good role model now for women and use your power to keep the door open, or open it wide for women." Friedan later, disappointedly, told Chris Wallace that "we expect in America that our First

Lady somehow embody the values of where women are at this time . . . as First Lady, she is an anachronism . . . not only denying her earlier reality but the reality of American women today . . . She can be as fashionable as she pleases. But there's got to be something more than that . . ." Occasionally, however, even Nancy acknowledged her past life. "Now all the women's groups are saying I live vicariously through Ronnie. They forget I had a successful career as an actress before I ever got married. And it wasn't as ordinary then for a woman to have a career."

Nancy Reynolds, Patti Davis, and Maureen Reagan were visible, vocal advocates of equal rights. Maureen believed—and told Nancy— that had she been married to someone other than Ronnie, she'd probably be supporting ERA because her freedom would have been more limited. Nancy Reynolds thought that while Mrs. Reagan was "no feminist," she'd developed "a consciousness" of women who had to work, support a family, and were out on their own." Although Nancy Reagan felt no blossomed kinship with feminists, ironically, in one of her last televised interviews, she matter-of-factly referred to herself in the present tense as "Nancy Davis."[9]

Amid the Regan affair, Mrs. R.'s project efforts had been eclipsed, yet she not only remained committed but began publicly addressing related, often controversial issues. When it was learned that a Reagan Supreme Court nominee, Douglas Ginsburg, had tried pot twenty years before, the First Lady stated, "Unfortunately, the Sixties and Seventies was a time when a lot of people experimented with pot. Apparently he did, and I'm sorry about that." She offered, "I've always said there should be testing of people in high-risk positions." Her speeches became tougher. "Each of us has a responsibility," she stated, "to be intolerant of drug use anywhere, anytime by anybody . . . force the drug issue to the point it may make others uncomfortable and ourselves unpopular. . . . Be unyielding, and inflexible, and outspoken in your opposition to drugs." For what he perceived as her lack of understanding of the situation, *Washington Post* reporter Henry Allen dubbed her a "Maoist commissar advocating the extermination of flies. . . ." As for Ginsburg, and previously turned-down Supreme Court nominee Robert Bork, the First Lady had failed to consult her astrologer. Ironically, she did have a consultation on Anthony Kennedy, who was approved.[10]

At the time of the Ginsburg controversy, Nancy was overcoming another sudden health obstacle—this time, her own. On October 5, she had a routine checkup, including a mammogram. She was alone in the White House when she learned by phone that the test indicated a possible malignancy. Immediately, she consulted a medical book written by her father to see what her options were, and chose radical mastectomy. She had not consulted the president because she felt it was "my choice," explaining, "I couldn't possibly lead the kind of life I lead and keep the schedule I do having radiation or chemotherapy." She consulted Joan Quigley for the right date and time of surgery. For a full ten days, she maintained her packed schedule, including a state dinner, a private party, and a projects trip. In that interim, she revealed her illness to only Ronnie, her brother, and a few discreet East Wingers. Like Ford, Harding, and Wilson, Reagan cried when he learned of his wife's illness. When the news was released, among the deluge came flowers from Raisa Gorbachev, a card from the Portuguese First Lady, and telegrams from Betty Ford, the Nixons, even Rosario Murillo of Nicaragua. After the surgery, Ronnie waited, with two dozen pink roses, and joked, "I know you don't feel like dancing, so let's just hold hands." Though groggy, she cracked back, "Please don't let Bob Woodward in my hospital room," wryly referring to that reporter's startling revelations based on interviews he conducted in the late CIA Director Casey's hospital room.

A former chief of staff, Joe Canzeri, speculated that the First Lady was concerned "about how all this was going to affect the President," and in fact it was reported that the "concern over the operation had diverted much of Reagan's energy and attention from his official duties in recent days." It was also reported at the time that Nancy's mother, in failing health, would not be told the news. Three weeks later, as the First Lady recuperated in the White House, came news of her spirited mother's death.[11] Just weeks after that, Deaver was convicted of perjury, the First Lady sadly noting that he couldn't be invited for their traditional Christmas get-together "while the [appeal] case is pending," but adding it wasn't for her "to decide" if he should receive a presidential pardon. Neither Reagan denied his book's revelations that Nancy was more liberal than Ronnie, though at one party, when she pushed him along, he cracked to the press, "See, she was trying to push me to the left."

She said 1987 was the "lowest" time of her tenure since 1981.[12]

When Gary Hart reentered the presidential campaign in December 1987, the First Lady agreed with his assertion that political figures had a right to some privacy, and believed that if the "press intrusion" into private lives continued, it would "make it awfully hard for good people to go into politics." There'd been minor speculation that she favored the candidacy of Laxalt—who'd not yet made any announcement—over the vice president. The First Lady had sharp comments on George Bush. "He's a nice man and very capable. But he's no Ronnie. He comes across as a 'wimp.' I don't think he can make it. He's a nice man, but his image is against him. It isn't macho enough." Three days after she'd lunched privately with George Will, he lambasted Bush as a "lapdog," and highly praised Laxalt.[13]

As candidates began lining up, there was a unique row of potential First Ladies. For the first time in history, most of the wives had careers: teacher Jill Biden, Cabinet member and attorney Liddy Dole, and lawyers Jeanne Simon, Hattie Babbitt, and Elise Dupont—the latter having run for Congress herself. Everyone announced what their project issues would be as First Lady: Jackie Jackson, civil rights; Joanne Kemp, international human-rights issues, Dede Robertson, single parents' problems; Tipper Gore, lurid rock lyrics; Jane Gephardt, family poverty; Kitty Dukakis, the homeless, among several other issues. Jeanne Simon said she'd be an "ombudswoman," in the style of Eleanor Roosevelt. "There are a lot of working couples, who know that the Presidency, like marriage," said Mrs. Simon, "is a partnership."

A planned television panel of all the wives failed to win all their participation, Mrs. Bush declining because she wasn't "running for office," but in Des Moines that summer the Democratic wives participated in a "First Ladies Forum," discussing their partnerships, their professions, their views on political and social issues.[14] One woman who'd been there made an interesting prediction at the time that media-savvy entrepreneur Donald Trump would be successful in politics. It would be the only public report that election year from Pat Nixon, who remained, in her husband's words, "an expert on politics. . . ." Pat was remembered rather uniquely that year when an operatic adaption of the 1972 trip to China toured America. *Nixon in China* featured the First Lady as a main character carrying its positive message, and the lyrics captured some of her poetic qualities, the staging dramatically recalling the familiar sight of her in red coat, touring through Peking. The real Mrs. Nixon did not come to Washington. In 1986, when Betty Ford visited with the HHS secretary to discuss treatment at the Betty Ford Center for those on Medicare, she did not come to the White House. Save for the perfunctory Senate Wives Lunch, Mrs. Johnson would be the only former First Lady invited.

At the dedication of the Ford Library, Betty had been joined by Barbara Bush, Nancy, and Lady Bird. When the Reagans attended the Atlanta dedication of the Carter Library, Larry Speakes noted, "There's no room for doubt about Mrs. Reagan's feelings for Rosalynn Carter." On the return home, Nancy remarked, "I'm glad that's over." Rosalynn, suffering from a thyroid deficiency, also learned that her severe muscle aches were due to a form of arthritis. Besides taking medication, she began vigorous exercising—even to a Jane Fonda video. There was no greater proof of her partnership than the Carters' co-authorship of a book, *Everything to Gain: Making the Most of the Rest of Your Life*. They addressed a variety of contemporary issues, from gun control to cigarette addiction to global politics. It was the first book ever produced by a presidential team.

In Washington, Rosalynn had a briefing on the mentally ill, which led to a discussion of the "homeless." What shocked her most were statistics of homeless families; she recalled one church that fed "fifty homeless children, from the ages of eight to fifteen. I can't believe things like that are happening. . . ." Although Barbara Bush had once paid a backhanded compliment to Rosalynn as "the bravest woman in the world" for defending Carter's record as she campaigned in Detroit where unemployment for blacks was at 40 percent, homelessness was a concern both women shared. Mrs. R. did not.

As the media reported, a great segment of the homeless population consisted of former mental patients in the early eighties. Long after March 30, Nancy Reagan remained—as a friend called her—a "frightened rabbit" in exposed areas because of the risk of assassination. She was never to shake her fear of mentally ill or unusual-looking people because John Hinckley—who'd shot the president—had been one. Her only exposure to the people who slept on grates around the White House was through a bulletproof tinted window of a rushing limousine. Only later, when the media shifted attention to families who'd lost their homes because of poverty, did she grow aware of their plight. Yet her only reference to the homeless was of a "bag lady" who gave all *her* money to buy *Nancy* two red carnations.

Susan Baker, wife of the chief of staff, brought the homeless to Barbara Bush's attention. Mrs. Bush privately visited Washington and other urban homeless shelters, and with Mrs. Baker—who formed a permanent Committee for Food and Shelter—began to put it on the political agenda of her husband. Barbara also continued a three-decade custom, an annual yuletide visit to a children's cancer ward as a living memorial to her late daughter, a victim of leukemia. Weekly, for several years, she'd continued to visit a woman in a hospice she'd met on an initial tour. It was after walking through an AIDS ward in Harlem that the Second Lady began to privately focus on it as a public issue.

Raisa Gorbachev had met and warmly taken to Barbara Bush, and it was she with whom the Soviet First Lady wanted to visit the National Gallery during her December visit for the historic signing of the Intermediate-Range Nuclear Forces Treaty. Word from the White House strongly suggested that was "not to be encouraged." Mrs. R. didn't go to the gallery. Neither did Mrs. B. [15]

While discussing Soviet alcoholism with Nancy, Raisa raised the issue of the homeless and the poverty of American blacks. Nancy "was not entirely pleased." There were other moments of tension. When Raisa cracked, "I missed you in Reykjavik," Nancy retorted, "I was told women weren't invited." The press gleefully chronicled the "feud." The only political grumbling came from the chairman of the Conservative Caucus—"Ronald Reagan is a very weak man with a very strong wife"—but if the INF treaty was lauded even by liberals, it was positively celebratory for the First Lady, the *Los Angeles Times* calling it "an accomplishment that she feels would end the Reagan presidency on a grand note and help dull the damaging effects of the Iran-Contra scandal."

The West Wing was "puzzled" when its scheduling of the treaty signing at prime time—when most Americans watched the news—was changed. "But," wrote Johanna Neumann, "the East Wing was insistent: First Lady Nancy Reagan wanted the ceremony in early afternoon." Joan Quigley had played a part in history, too.

Nancy Reagan reportedly asserted that 1988 would not be lame duck. Aides told NBC News that she was a "driving force in this final push, determined to secure her husband's place in history." But she was doing quite well with her own place.[16]

The Anti-Drug Abuse Act mandated a weeklong conference, and it was to the experts there that Nancy Reagan delivered her strongest but most heartfelt speech, denouncing all drug users, telling brutal stories of the drug trade. She offered compassionate understanding for addicts, but was tough in condemning dealers. "The casual user may think when he takes a line of cocaine or smokes a joint in the privacy of his nice condo, listening to his expensive stereo, that he's somehow not bothering anyone. But there is a trail of death and destruction that leads directly to his door. . . . I'm saying that if you're a casual drug user, you are an accomplice to murder." She discussed Colombia's omnipotent cocaine-cartel operations and the murder of that nation's attorney general and two of his assistants, among other crimes: "The people who casually use cocaine are responsible because their money bought those bullets. They provided the high stakes that murdered those men plus hundreds of others in Colombia, including supreme court justices, 21 judges handling drug cases and scores of policemen and soldiers." She raised several more grisly examples: deaths of sixteen people in an Amtrak train crash caused by an engineer and brakeman who smoked a joint, the wounding of a mother and killing of her four sons, and the rape, shooting, and burning of a Maryland student—all by drug users. This was not some wide-eyed lady in red telling grade-schoolers to tell drug dealers "get lost" anymore.

In the eleventh hour of her Ladyship, Nancy Reagan was branching out with her antidrug agenda. A few months later, in reddish-orange suit and trademark gold chain necklace, she became the first incumbent First Lady to address a full official body of representatives at the UN. Until America's "forces of law" were completely mobilized against the demand side of drugs, she told the capacity audience, the international supply side would continue to flourish. "We will not get anywhere if we place a greater burden of action on foreign governments . . . it is far easier to focus on the coca fields grown by 300,000 campesinos in Peru than to . . . arrest a pair of Wall Street investment bankers buying cocaine on their lunch break. . . . I do not believe the American people will ever allow the legalization of drugs in our country."[17] On a *Nightline* interview with her, some sobering realities were contrasted with her view, but she felt that giving way to the pessimism was defeating, that if even just a few drug users were helped, "It's better than not saving any." Through the Ted Koppel interview, she addressed the question of drug addicts contracting AIDS, and methods of prevention. Mrs. Reagan adamantly opposed the allocation of clean hypodermic needles or bleach bags to clean needles for addicts, saying, "[T]hat sends the wrong message."

AIDS had begun to strike the world during the Reagan first term. Though it was a drug-related issue, and while Betty Ford and Rosalynn Carter's names headlined at a nationally advertised AIDS fund-raiser, Nancy Reagan's did not. Surgeon General Everett Koop recalled that he'd approached the First Lady about helping to promote AIDS education as an adjunct to her project, but was turned down. Like Koop, Elizabeth Glaser, a museum director who contracted the virus from a transfusion and whose little daughter was born with and died of it, had a private and "intensely" moving hearing on AIDS with the Reagans. "The Reagans were wonderful," recalled Glaser, "but in reality, his administration wasn't going to do more for AIDS. It was a letdown." If publicly mute, however, Nancy developed empathy because some of her friends died.

Longtime Reagan friend Roy Cohn, who suffered from the illness, was a guest at the White House with his male partner, and the Reagans' names had appeared as co-hosts of Cohn's 1985 birthday party. When Elizabeth Taylor came to a White House state dinner just after the news that Rock Hudson had contracted the deadly virus, the First Lady told reporters, "Isn't that a shame?," recalling that she'd seen him just a few months before. "He looked very thin then. He said he'd picked up some bug in Israel." Privately, she made calls to see if French medical experts could get him further help. After Hudson died and Taylor founded the American Foundation for AIDS Research, the First Lady quickly offered her support, and "sent a personal message" to Taylor, hoping it would prove "a very important step" in combating the disease. When makeup artist Way Bandy died of the illness weeks after making her up for photographs, Nancy, through her press secretary, took the opportunity to lend help in the effort to allay drastic fears, pointing out that she'd shaken hands with Bandy, "And we've all been told by the medical community that you can't contract the disease that way."

When the president appointed a commission on AIDS, the First

Lady assisted in getting a gay doctor, a colleague of her Philadelphia surgeon brother, appointed to the panel. NBC's Chris Wallace reported that privately the First Lady was "known to be protective of AIDS patients' rights." It was the Reagans' son Ron who became a public voice on the issue when he helped host a frank AIDS-education television special. He admitted to first discussing his participation with his mother, stating that she did not believe in mass testing by law or quarantining, a suggestion forwarded by Phyllis Schlafly. As Ron, Jr., stated, his parents "lived most of their lives in the entertainment community. Their attitude towards people's sexuality is it's everyone's private business." When the *Post* reported that she invited an old friend and his gentleman cohabitant to spend the night together at the White House in July 1981, the First Lady made no attempt to deny it.[18]

How she felt on other matters was unspoken but evident. *Time* reported that while in her Los Angeles hotel room, Nancy Reagan refused to attend a Bush rally downstairs, and the White House went so far as to suggest that Mrs. Bush not attend—as if not to make Nancy's absence glaringly obvious. Mrs. Bush attended. As Barbara told her husband's campaign media adviser, "I'll do anything you want, but I won't dye my hair, change my wardrobe or lose weight." According to reporters Germond and Witcover, after Bush lost dismally in the Iowa caucus, Barbara pointedly told one aide that he was to make certain it didn't occur again, but when despondency broke out, she cracked, "Enough of this. You know, it's over. Everybody go take out a dirty book and start reading." As the Bush campaign press secretary told Donnie Radcliffe, Mrs. Bush "questioned the need for tough personal attacks," but when the attack was valid, she supported it. The vice president was uncertain about a proposed commercial accusing Dole of double-talking on taxes. Barbara believed the ads were fine. They ran, and Bush won New Hampshire.

Mrs. Bush sat in on strategy planning sessions on the larger "themes and issues," and campaign director Craig Fuller recalled that she'd "ask questions, offer her advice and counsel, never missing a thing. . . . Her position was to let George Bush be himself, don't . . . overcontrol him, let him take questions as often as possible. . . ." Her "constructive" criticisms were made in private, not in meetings, a point he illustrated in recalling a talk between the Bushes following a debate. "I thought one of the weaker moments was when you were talking about homelessness," she told her husband. Referring to his general comment on education, she added, "You ought to be able to elaborate more."[19]

Mrs. Bush was not present for the special celebration of an old friend that April. Washington paid tribute to Lady Bird Johnson in a two-day "Jubilee Celebration," honoring her seventy-fifth birthday and benefiting her Wildflower Research Center. All the living First Ladies agreed to serve as honorary chairpersons for their beloved sorority sister, who, over the years, had made a point of keeping in touch with all of them. The high point was the White House ceremony when the Reagans presented Lady Bird with a Congressional Gold Medal. There were also Capitol Hill tributes.

Spring, however, also brought a book. Helene von Damm and Larry Speakes both published what Mrs. Reagan termed "kiss-and-tell" memoirs painting mercurial and capricious portraits of her. But Don Regan's *For the Record* devastatingly compared Nancy to the "ruthless" Livia who dosed out small measured amounts of poison as she "ruled the Roman Empire from behind the scenes through the manipulation of her much older husband, Augustus Caesar." Mrs. Reagan was "taken aback by the vengefulness of the attack. . . . It comes through to me that Don Regan really doesn't like me." But the bombshell was his revelation of her use of astrology in managing the presidency. For some, it explained some long-perplexing scheduling mysteries. It was bandied about in Congress and spoofed in a television ad posing a security agent telling a clerk, "The very important lady says it's not the right day to pay a lot for this muffler." The only real harm that came was a claim by Jack Anderson that, because Mrs. R.'s calls to Quigley were regularly scheduled and occurred on her outside line, unprotected by security, Soviet embassy officials were able to tap the conversations about Reagan's schedule. Anderson claimed NSC and CIA sources.

When the news first broke, the First Lady had called Quigley and told her not to talk to the press as they tracked her down. Earlier she had told Quigley, "It must never come out!" Quigley was shocked by what she claimed were Nancy's last words to her. "If you have to, lie." Quigley did not. After several years of "friendship," she never heard from Nancy again.

Meanwhile, Mrs. R.'s press secretary admitted that the First Lady had consulted Quigley "for the sake of comfort," explaining that after March 30, few had fully comprehended "how frightened she was." The West Wing stated that it was "unfortunate" that the news leaked, but admitted "astrology has been a part of her concern in terms of his activities." Nancy apologized to her husband for bringing "all this down on his head," to which he apologized to her, "No, honey, I brought all this down on you by taking on this job." Even after the revelations, Nancy knocked on wood for good luck during a *Los Angeles Times* interview.[20]

In June, the Reagans made a visit to the Soviet Union, and the Gorbachevs. In preparation, Mrs. Reagan spent time discussing Moscow with her son, who'd recently been working there for ABC-TV, was briefed by an NSC official, pored through studies from the *National Geographic*, consulted with the librarian of Congress and a Soviet scholar, who'd be part of her entourage. Once again, the Red lady and the lady in red made news. In the Cathedral of the Annunciation, Nancy remarked that a Madonna icon was "very maternal," interjecting, "I'm not finished yet," to ask if religious services were held there. "Nyet," replied Raisa. "Oh, yes, nyet." Nancy smiled. "That I understand." At an art gallery, instead of meeting Nancy downstairs as planned, Raisa waited with the press upstairs and since "the guests are late," began telling them she didn't use astrology, just "practical things." When Nancy arrived, Raisa told the press there would be no interviews. A reporter whispered to Mrs. R. that Mrs. G. had already spoken with them. "Uh-huh!" Nancy murmured. Upon another icon, Nancy remarked to Raisa, "I don't know how you can neglect the religious implications that are there for everyone to see." Nancy termed it all "[a] Mexican standoff." Upon a final stopover in London, she sighed with relief, "I'm happy to see the queen at all times."[21]

Focus shifted to Atlanta, the Democratic Convention, and the nominee's wife, Kitty Dukakis. Rosalynn Carter was a friend to Mrs. Dukakis, and in Austin, Kitty met with an "enthusiastic and supportive" Lady Bird Johnson at a Dukakis fund-raiser, calling the former First Lady "my mentor," and adding, "I know she's there if I need to talk to her." Jacqueline Onassis didn't campaign, but her son introduced Senator Kennedy at the convention, and her daughter appeared with Dukakis at a New York campaign rally. At a luncheon for Mrs. Dukakis, attended by Rosalynn Carter and Lynda Robb, Hattie Babbitt compared Kitty to First Ladies Roosevelt, Kennedy, and Carter," and reporter Lois Romano thought the candidate's wife already "first ladyish." There was one swipe at Mrs. Reagan, by Jesse Jackson, who told crowds, "You can't just say no. You can't just go out and consult an astrologer."[22]

As they flew down to the Republican Convention, George Bush told Barbara of his choice for running mate, but the Second Lady said she'd guessed it would be Senator Dan Quayle, while focusing on the decision the night before by using the "same process of elimination" that George had. "It's a sign of living together for 43 years. You think alike." At the convention, Mrs. Bush asked that her friend Louis Sullivan of Morehouse College introduce her. Nancy Reagan chose actor Tom Selleck, and she matched Eleanor Roosevelt's record to become the only other First Lady to address a convention more than once. "The last eight years," she told the crowd from the podium, "have been the most fulfilling in my life. You gave me a chance to be more than I thought I could be. . . . One era is ending and another is beginning." Earlier, she wistfully admitted that "the time has come for the Bushes to step into the limelight and the Reagans to step into the wings."

That summer the First Lady began readying the Bel Air home bought and rented to the Reagans by their friends, as well as beginning plans for the Nancy Reagan Center, a teenage drug-rehab school and boarding center slated for the L.A. area. She had the street number of the new house changed from "666," which superstition claimed to be evil. Fresh political speculation had the First Lady trying to force the resignation of Attorney General Ed Meese, whose top aides resigned from Justice because of him, all of which damaged the president's reputation. It prompted another card. "Scared of Nancy Reagan? Don't Be. After November, She'll Just Be Another Woman Shopping at Bloomingdales."

Meanwhile, on the Fourth of July, Barbara Bush had appeared on an ABC-TV special for the Bicentennial of the Constitution, before a live audience of 800,000. Earlier that day, a sixty-two-year-old retired construction worker who had only recently learned to read fretted about his appearance before the cameras, as he was scheduled to read the Constitution's Preamble. He panicked, and decided to cancel. In an informal meeting just hours before the scheduled show, Barbara drew his fears out of him. When he explained there were words he didn't understand, Mrs. Bush said she ran into words like that as well, and suggested they read it together before the cameras. On stage that night, the duo began, but as the man's confidence grew, the Second Lady lowered and subsided her voice.

Superficially, most of Mrs. Bush's campaign appearances seemed nonpolitical as she steered clear of campaign rhetoric, but subtly they all focused specifically on her interest in social issues that were political: a South Carolina meal program for the indigent, a Connecticut day-care center, an Illinois mental health and drug-abuse rehab center, a Missouri parent-teacher public-school program focusing on learning disabilities, a Florida employee day-care, school, and after-school center, which she praised as helping eradicate "latchkey children." When she visited a school for the deaf, Barbara "decided that I want to learn sign language." After exploring a museum exhibit about Jewish Holocaust victims, she used the opportunity to reflect her own civil-rights advocacy, writing that "we must always be alert to discrimination and prejudice of any kind." On a commercial flight, which she often took on solo campaign appearances, she told another passenger that she concurred with harsher sentencing for drug kingpins. "I didn't think I'd ever feel that way about the death penalty, but I do."[23]

Before the whispered gossip that Bush had a mistress was about to be printed, advisers Lee Atwater, Craig Fuller, and pollster Bob Teeter held a conference with the vice president on whether to issue an official denial of the rumors. Mrs. Bush came across the conferees, and when told what they were discussing, retorted, "That's ridiculous, the answer's no. Forget about it. What are you even talking about it for? Why are you guys even here?" There was no formal statement, but Mrs. Bush didn't shy away from directly confronting the stories. She "scolded" Donnie Radcliffe when she asked about them. "That's asinine and you know that." When a broadcast interviewer began to raise it, by preceding with, "I hate to ask. . . ." she cut him short. "Then don't." There were other, less serious moments as well. In a New York hotel, when room service came up earlier than expected, she answered the door after wrapping herself in a bedsheet.

Both candidates' wives had high media visibility, each writing a daily, then weekly column during the campaign. Mrs. Dukakis addressed controversial political issues as well as her concerns—from Indochinese refugees to AIDS to the homeless. Again, however, media focus shifted—back to Nancy Reagan.[24]

In the years since January 1982, when she promised to never again accept "gifts" of clothes, the First Lady had done just that and, unlike in 1982, when her acceptance of the "loans" was reported, the gowns and jewelry were neither sent to museums nor all returned to their designers. Designer David Hayes admitted that of the nearly eighty "loaned" suits he'd sent her, only half had been returned to him. Galanos assistant Chris Blazakis said the First Lady only returned that designer's gown "when she wanted it repaired." On top of this was the fact that, in the ensuing five years, the gifts were unreported on both the Reagans' tax returns, and the requisite federal disclosure form listing all accepted "donations" over thirty-five dollars. The total worth of the "loans" was estimated at over $1.3 million. A revelation followed from Harry Winston that Nancy had continued to borrow jewelry, including a $480,000 necklace-earring set and $800,000 ten-carat teardrop diamond earrings. Hayes, trying to lessen the blow, said Nancy was "never greedy. She only takes what she can use." Some tried to soften the point by claiming that the revelation about Mrs. Reagan had been timed to work against the Republicans, since the election was only two weeks away. Still, it was painfully obvious that the First Lady had not told the truth.

Through her press secretary, Mrs. R. stated that she purchased her clothing. Later, an "unapologetic" Nancy backpedaled a bit. "I don't know that I did anything wrong." Teetering on the brink of reemergence for years, "Queen Nancy" now permanently ensconced herself in the pop culture of the Acquisitive Eighties. The postcard, dormant for seven years, reappeared with a caption: "I don't care who wins. I'm not leaving!"[25]

Two weeks before the election, Bush considered that he might lose. "But," he told aides, "If I win, America will fall in love with Barbara Bush." In Houston, he was eagerly chatting with reporters after voting, when Barbara, behind him, boomed, "Hey fella, I've been waiting on this line for a long time. Move along!" During the campaign, as the media pressed Bush on the deficit, he repeated, "Read my lips, no new taxes." Now, the press yelled questions to her as returns came in. And leaving them startled, Barbara yelled back, "I don't read lips."[26]

With the Bush victory, Washington bubbled with plans for the Bicentennial Presidential Inaugural. And tradition resumed.

– 27 –

Tradition

FOLLOWING A TRADITION begun by Edith Roosevelt for Nellie Taft in 1909, Nancy Reagan conducted a personal tour of the White House for Barbara Bush. And, as it had with Grace Coolidge to Lou Hoover—to name just two—the media continued its tradition of contrasting the outgoing and incoming of the same party. Stories emphasized how the independent Reagan children rarely visited and how Bush offspring were always about. Radcliffe observed that the two women had "vastly different values. . . . At its best, their relationship was courteous, at its worst, remote." But Barbara had also striven to reduce any differences by employing her increasingly trademark self-deprecatory humor. "As you know, we have a lot in common. She adores her husband; I adore mine. She fights drugs; I fight illiteracy. She wears a size three . . . so's my leg."

Another tradition followed. Like Julia Grant, Nancy Reagan was forlorn about turning over the Ladyship, according to a news story quoting friends. It further claimed that it was she who'd decided against Reagan publicly endorsing Bush on May 3, the night he'd earned enough delegates for the nomination, as opposed to a large May 11 Republican fund-raiser—a claim denied by both East and West Wings. Mrs. R., upset that the Bushes might be hurt about the story, phoned them, and the president-elect wrote her, "I just want you to know both Barbara and I feel you have been very generous to us over the last eight years . . . I'll be damned if I'll let anything nasty come between us."

The Gorbachevs came to New York in December, Raisa seeing Nancy as First Lady one last time and meeting Barbara for the second time. At a reception for national leaders, former president Nixon met the Soviet couple, but Pat Nixon did not attend. Jacqueline Onassis was scheduled to meet Raisa and her husband, but a devastating earthquake in Armenia cut the Gorbachev trip short.

Though she'd been a public figure for eight years, Mrs. Bush was now confronted with sudden adjustments. As she browsed through Tiffany's, waiting for her watch to be repaired, she sensed all eyes upon her. "My gosh, they think I'm going to buy those diamonds," she told a companion. "We gotta get out of here. . . ." The tradition of pre-Inaugural commercialization that had affected women like Mrs. Kennedy commenced. The Forgotten Woman, a woman's store selling fashions in larger sizes, advertised with a Barbara Bush lookalike. A Washington comedy group now sang "Silver Bells" with the lyrics of "Silver Hair" at a Christmas party. Mrs. Bush wagged her finger at them, then began "singing along . . ."[1]

Meanwhile, in media tradition, early assessments began on the outgoing president and First Lady. Ronald Reagan had stated early in his term, "What I'd really like to do is go down in history as the president who made Americans believe in themselves." In many senses, both Reagans had done so, the First Lady largely by instilling confidence in both parents and children affected by drug abuse. But there were also strident critics, among them Don Regan, who blasted, "[W]e still have our problems—the homeless, AIDS, poor education of our children. The drug war failed on the supply and the demand side. 'Just say no' didn't work." One Reagan aide had told journalist Laurence Leamer back in 1983 that the Reagans "have this terrific personal discipline, but they have no questions. It's an administration without questions. They ignore things that are in the 1980s."

The Reagans also avoided public comment on both the increasingly violent struggle for equality of black South Africans and racial tensions in America, although in small ways Mrs. Reagan displayed some support for the black community. She privately donated money to a summer-camp program for underprivileged inner-city youths. After participating in a meeting of the Comprehensive Auxiliary for the Southwest Community Alcohol and Drug Education, she made a point of telling the largely black audience that she was particularly "encouraged that young blacks are organizing to fight drugs." A black representative of the 1984 Reagan-Bush campaign told the press that he believed Nancy was especially helpful when she visited black community grammar schools as an illustration of her interest in often-neglected areas. When she heard about a black folk-art exhibit near the White House, the First Lady slipped off to view it and asked to meet some of the artists, but when a reporter questioned the administration's policy of support for tax-exempt status for private schools that practiced racial discrimination, she "firmly" shot back, "I am here to look at art." Both Reagans "adopted" a local, largely black elementary school, sometimes visiting there, inviting students to the White House on several occasions, and going to one student's home for a family dinner.[2]

Among those Reagan officials the First Lady named as the most loyal was the single black Cabinet member, HUD's Sam Pierce. As for the Iran-Contra scandal, Mrs. Reagan said that "it will be seen in the context it should be seen in—that he was badly served by people on his staff." She'd indicated that she didn't favor pardons for North and Poindexter. Speakes recalled her watching TV when North cracked a joke about his innocence, and the First Lady responded back, "Not funny, sonny." Sam Donaldson asked what she thought about North being offered $1 million for his memoirs. Nancy joshed back, "I should get $2 million then." As she showed the reporters her last Christmas decorations, Mrs. R. accidently derailed a press car on the miniature train under the tree. "Nothing personal," she cracked.[3]

In addition to the telephone operators and Air Force One, Mrs. R. said she'd even miss the press. She noted that security had become so tight that it made her uncomfortable. During her eight years, a minimum of $44.6 million in improvements throughout the White House complex took place—more repair, construction, and change than had occurred since the Truman administration. The most visible change was the closing of the street next to the East Wing, blocked by large black gates for "security and safety reasons." The mansion, exterior and interior, was shined to a high polish, and gleamed with new white paint, as it never had before.

During Mrs. Reagan's tenure, the Smithsonian display of First Ladies' gowns closed. It would be "reinterpreted." The collection had begun under Nellie Taft in a time when First Ladies were largely judged by the traditional roles—hostess and wife. Paradoxically, the woman who'd become First Lady identified solely through her hostess and wife roles was now in large measure a reason for this "new tradition" of identifying First Ladies first through their degree of political power.

Exercising power was not new to the Ladyship, but the view of the role had changed. Nancy Reagan was excellent testimony that a First Lady could be perfect hostess and devoted spouse, yet unapologetically yield a scepter of consequential power. Mrs. R. advised future generations of First Ladies that "you'll never again be in this unique position to make such a contribution . . . Don't be afraid to . . . voice your opinions, either to him or his staff. In spite of a White House full of people taking care of various aspects of a President's life, you're the one who knows him best. You don't give up your right to an opinion just because you're married to the President . . . everything is magnified, so just keep your perspective and your patience. . . . A First Lady genuinely has the power to make a difference." In the twentieth century, only Eleanor Roosevelt served longer than Nancy Reagan, the latter becoming perhaps the most powerful and controversial of any since the former. For twenty-eight years, each of Mrs. Reagan's predecessors had departed the Ladyship earlier than expected or wished, plans and goals abruptly cut short. In the end, she hoped to be remembered as one "who tried to use her position to the best of her ability to help the young people of our country." It "provided me with the most fulfilling years of my life." And the role had matured her immeasurably. "I don't know how you could be in this position," she admitted, "and not grow."[4]

In the second term, many believed Mrs. Reagan's focus was Ronnie's place in history. Joan Quigley called it "an obsession," but added that "Nancy was almost totally ignorant of history. I was often surprised by how little she knew about it. Highly intelligent, superbly motivated, purposefully organized, she was in no way an intellectual or deeply reflective." Quigley made a biting assessment of her friend Nancy Reagan as First Lady. "My pupil was a consummate actress, but I couldn't help feeling that while she had worked hard and studied diligently, she had never really understood the reason for taking the course."

While Bush Republicans were reveling, Nancy Reagan dined quietly on her last night in the White House with her husband, his daughter, and her husband. Mrs. R. was tearful throughout the next morning, her last. And still a frantic worrier, she was rummaging through the drawers until her press secretary gently stopped her: "If you leave something behind, they'll send it to you. They have your address." Before descending to the state floor, she returned to the First Lady's bedroom. In an empty drawer, she tucked a note for Barbara Bush, along with an orchid bouquet.[5]

Following a tradition set by Edith Wilson and Florence Harding, Mrs. Reagan and Mrs. Bush drove to the Capitol together.

Barbara Bush stood proudly in an Atlantic-blue coat, Nancy Reagan in a Nancy-red coat. After the ceremony, the Reagans left the Capitol by helicopter, viewing the city sights from above. Meanwhile, during the Bush parade down Pennsylvania Avenue, the new First Lady joined her husband, walking down Pennsylvania Avenue. When Barbara saw NBC weatherman Willard Scott standing behind barricades with the public, she broke from the Secret Service, dashed over, kissed him, then trotted back to her place. Meanwhile, the Reagans arrived at Andrews Air Force Base. Just before boarding their plane, Mrs. Reagan caught the eye of George Opfer, and bolted to hug him. He was the Secret Service agent who had told her the sudden news that Ronnie had been shot, and calmed her fears.

Earlier in the day, following a tradition dating to the day Mamie's staff turned the East Wing over to Jackie's staff, the offices were cleared for Barbara Bush's staff. Mrs. R.'s press secretary left a plant given her by her predecessors for Mrs. Bush's press secretary. The deputy press secretary Wendy Weber-Toller recalled the scenes: "It was an unusually quiet day in the East Wing. Most of the staff didn't come in. There were a few calls, everything already boxed up." She thought the State Floor almost eerie. The Social Office was quietly arranging the morning coffee hosted by the Reagans for the Bush party in the Blue Room. Following a tradition set by Mrs. Cleveland, Mrs. Reagan bade farewell to the staff with her husband. The deputy press secretary watched the Reagans make their way to the center of the bare marble foyer, under a chandelier, waiting for the Bushes. "You felt that moment of history in the air. The end of an Administration, end of an era, end of show biz." All was silent. "Eight years were flashing by." Ronald and Nancy Reagan exchanged a "deep glance" one last time, then looked straight ahead. It was just the two of them standing there all alone.

And a photographer from *Time*, to capture it on color film.[6]

PART IV

New Age
1989

. . . While men and women have trouble divvying up the power in a
relationship . . . women are going to
continue to work to support themselves
or the lifestyle of two-income families.
And they will continue to hold good
jobs and make good salaries. But it will
probably be a long while before the
world responds to these changes in a significant way. . . .

Linda Lehrer
Ms. magazine, February 1989

28

The Houston Yankee

IT WAS A GRAY TUESDAY afternoon, a week after the Inaugural. Along the shabby rows of hardware shops, closed storefronts, and liquor stores, a sedan passed the corners where prostitutes walked at night. It pulled up to an oasis, "Martha's Table," a center providing food for the indigent, as well as daytime and after-school activities for homeless children, and also running a mobile soup-and-sandwich kitchen through the city.

"I believe life is right now," said the five-foot-eight woman with warm brown eyes and fluffy snow-white hair who emerged from the car. She looked a handsome picture of First Lady.

The national press was invited in full force while the motherly Mrs. Bush donned an apron, made sandwiches, and, children gathering

about, began reading them a story. "You can forget the government cutbacks." She winked. The chairman of the center felt that her deciding to do this as her first event as First Lady "focuses great attention on the needs of the people in the streets." Weeks later, the First Lady slipped off to donate clothing to a thrift store for low-cost resale to the needy.[1]

In his Inaugural Address, George Bush dramatically departed from Reagan, speaking of "the homeless, lost and roaming," "the children who have nothing," "those who cannot free themselves of . . . welfare, demoralization that rules the slums," "young women to be helped who are about to become mothers of children they can't care for. . . . They need our care, our guidance, and education. . . ." The mark of Barbara Bush was indelible, and while she didn't actually draft it, she did offer to Donnie Radcliffe, "By osmosis things sometimes work. So I felt very good about his speech. He talked about the things, the issues important to me." On the lawn the next morning, the Bushes received several thousand citizens who'd waited through the cold night and took a smaller group of them through the White House for the first such Inaugural open house since Taft in the era of "New Thought." As one woman remarked, "Great stuff. Hey, they got some positive energy going. They seem 'New Age.'"[2]

Comparisons to Eleanor Roosevelt would be many and come fast. But it was Barbara Bush herself who musingly revealed her choice. A television commentator asked whom she'd be like, and began listing: Eleanor, Mamie, Rosalynn, Nancy. Mrs. Bush cut him off. "You forgot Bess Truman." Not only did both operate politically behind the scenes, but Bess Truman was the last First Lady who'd not minded letting her hair go gray and waist "go mature." Both displayed the same wry wit. "My mail tells me a lot of fat, white-haired, wrinkled ladies are tickled pink," joked Mrs. Bush.

In the first hundred days of the Bush term, which many political observers considered a watershed for administrations—stemming from FDR's New Deal—a poll showed the First Lady earning a higher rating than either the president or vice president. In some way, Barbara Bush's immediate popularity in her first weeks was precisely like Mamie's. It was not for anything she'd done, for she hadn't yet begun her work, but for who she *was* and what she seemed to symbolize. Days after a "Barbara Bush Fan Club" had formed in San Francisco, three hundred members enlisted. In her first year, Barbara would receive an average of three thousand letters a week.

She herself explained it best. "I'm everybody's mother."

As Mrs. Kennedy's fashions had influenced young women, Barbara Bush unwittingly became a "formidable symbol of American taste" for middle-aged women. Her primary designer, Arnold Scaasi, said, "She wants to look good and then forget about it." Rather quickly, she unwittingly prompted fashion. As had happened with "Mamie pink," "Barbara blue" became an official and popular color, so titled by the Color Association of the United States. Kenneth Jay Lane, manufacturer of the trademark three-strand artificial pearls Mrs. Bush sported, began a costume jewelry line dubbed the "First Lady Collection," and Majorica Jewelry Limited planned "the White House Collection." Even "Edgar" of The Pleasure Chest boasted a line of Barbara Bush "love-beads." Damon Dresses, specializing in fuller-sized clothes, one suit of which Mrs. Bush had posed in for Life, said the "Bush dress" helped their business. As USA Today summarized, "She isn't inspiring people to imitate her, but to be happy with themselves." Around Washington, buses carried new advertisements for the IKEA furniture store: "Nancy Reagan style at Barbara Bush prices."[3]

It was not the political but the personal philosophy and style that made the Eleanor Roosevelt comparisons valid, a matronly bearing of noblesse oblige. Not since Mrs. Roosevelt had the Yankee "proper casualness" been seen in a First Lady. To the dismay of the Secret Service, as Eleanor Roosevelt had often done with her German shepherd, Meggie, Barbara Bush stepped outside the gates to walk her springer spaniel, Millie, on Pennsylvania Avenue. "Bar" continued to walk her dog in the morning on the drive of the South Lawn, often swathed only in her robe and slippers. Mrs. Bush enjoyed needlework; in the front row of a Congressional hearing, the knitting needles that clacked had been Mrs. Roosevelt's. If family meant grandchildren underfoot in the rambling manse, so, too, had it in 1933.

One factor that made Mrs. Bush instantly popular was her wit. She was an excellent mimic of personalities and regional accents, doing impressions of everyone from her husband and children to Nancy Reagan. When she was followed by cameramen and reporters as she strolled for bargains in Kennebunkport, dressed in blue jeans and sneakers, the First Lady snapped at them, "Haven't you seen an old lady walk a dog before?" And she could still crack a line now and then. When someone sat on an antique table and helped it break, crashing a groaning board full of food, Barbara quipped, "Down in Texas we call people like that 'fat A's.'" For the Gridiron Dinner, she spoofed the press obsession with her white hair by wearing a strawberry-blond wig throughout the long meal and entertainment, remaining straight-faced throughout. After it was learned that she suffered from Graves' disease, and had to have her thyroid destroyed by radiation treatments, she clarified darker speculations by limping along on the arm of her press secretary and telling the women reporters, "I could Indian wrestle any one of you." She offered that because of her radioactive treatment, she was setting off all the White House security alarms. "Without laughter," said Barbara Bush, "you are in deep trouble."[4]

She was old school on observing proper etiquette, a fact spoofed in a post-Inaugural cartoon posing an incredulous Barbara in the Oval Office, asking George as she stared at the piles of notecards, "240 million thank-you notes?" Yet like most of her predecessors when a conflict arose, she minced no words. Friend and journalist Vic Gold observed that Mrs. Bush "*braces* the problem and takes it head-on. . . ." She admitted, "I'm not only outspoken, I'm honest."

Mrs. Bush was adept at both adjusting the plumbing and mowing the lawn, found solitude in her garden, landscaping alone, and swam and played tennis daily. She cooked spaghetti and served it on paper plates, carried her own cash, and went about town without fear—shopping at a local mall, lunching out with friends, catching museum exhibits. She was herself whether throwing out the first baseball of the season for the Texas Rangers or receiving an honorary degree with the president of France from Boston University. Sassy and sedate, Barbara Bush was a Houston Yankee.[5]

Recalling how awestruck and excited she'd first been upon entering the White House, Mrs. Bush admitted, "There's still quite a little of that left." In her new home, she relished eating off the historic presidential china, waving to shocked tourists from an upstairs window, and using the beauty salon for the birth of her dog Millie's puppies. There were adjustments. When she asked to get her husband, "the vice president" on the phone, the operator cracked, "Don't you know Dan Quayle's in Venezuela?" Only when she wanted to tease him did she address George as Mr. President. As for her own identity, she told reporters, "I'm still shocked when I hear those two words together— First and Lady." Like Jackie Kennedy and Edith Wilson, she disliked the term. Barbara most emulated those of her predecessors who "did their own thing."

As for the traditional role, she said she hadn't "necessarily look[ed] forward to being a hostess at the White House," and asked that entertaining follow the style set by Mrs. Reagan, which she called impeccable. In the house, the only redecorating she did was the family sitting room in "classic American taste with a strong strain of New England Colonial," and Mrs. Kennedy's Victorian Treaty Room was converted into the president's private office, in light blue and white, with a portrait of Mrs. Bush's collateral ancestor, Franklin Pierce. Her large family and wide circle of friends helped combat the inevitable isolation, but Barbara also declared that she was determined "to see that George gets out of the White House. . . . It's very good for both of us to get out of the house and be among people who come up and talk to you."

She wanted no more of the exorbitant federal cost of having her foreign trips advanced several times before she arrived. Because her first such journey was to Emperor Hirohito's funeral, she maintained a minimal schedule in Japan and China. In China, as a White House photographer followed her, an overprotective official slammed the young woman into a door and dislocated her jaw. Mrs. Bush reacted immediately and flatly told her guide, "This girl's job is to take my picture, and she got hit. She works for my husband. Ask them to calm down." It was a chilling foreshadowing of the violent massacre of Chinese students that would follow their demonstrations some months later.[6]

Monthly, Mrs. Bush began holding the sort of "round table" press conference that had been conducted by Mrs. Roosevelt weekly, talking about current events. She was comfortable making speeches, but in terms of the intense press scrutiny, she said she had enjoyed being Second Lady and getting away with it. She was quite startled when the news that her dog was pregnant made front-page news. As for her predecessor's relationship with the press, Barbara thought, "Nancy felt besieged at times." Mrs. Bush was not unconscious of how well her easy style played in the media. Her own son George, Jr., said Barbara was "a genius with the media," and "better with the press" than was the president.[7]

Other facets of Mrs. Bush began to emerge. The white-haired motherliness was authentic, but as she explained of herself, "you really shouldn't judge a book by its cover."

When George had taken his first vice-presidential oath, Barbara had chosen the passage on which he placed his hand. "Pray in secret . . . do not your alms before men to be seen of them." Whatever degree of political power for her social causes she might exercise, it would evidently be conducted largely behind leak-proof closed doors. When Donnie Radcliffe asked if she'd have power over policy, the First Lady was coy. "Who knows? . . . even a nice innocent like me might. . . ." They "shared everything" as presidential partners, in the words of Radcliffe, "communicating by simply looking at one another many times. . . ." Iowa Republican Congressman Jim Leach offered that the First Lady was "a key element of this Administration." Bernard Weinraub found her to be "blunt and highly opinionated," and "formidable and powerful." Political columnist David Broder believed that Barbara had not just the "capacity" but the "inclination" to "become a major influence on her husband and the nation." He said that education, AIDS, single working mothers, the homeless, were "personal causes" to Barbara, but "they spill over into consciousness for her husband," and observed that she often diffused political disagreement among advisers by "slipping her arm through the aggravated party's arm and walking and talking until the . . . anger . . . passed."[8]

Mrs. Bush was no newcomer to partisan, Hill, or presidential politics. She was quick to point out that as senator, Quayle had got the Jobs Training Partnership Act through the Republican Senate, and added that Democratic co-sponsor Ted Kennedy could never have done that alone. Behind closed doors, the First Lady joined her husband, the vice president, and his wife in an "unprecedented session" in the Oval Office closely studying and discussing the Twenty-fifth Amendment to the Constitution, outlining presidential disability and the circumstances under which a vice president would take charge of the presidency. The conference, which included the president's doctor and White House counsel, had been urged by political scholars but remained private. Throughout, Mrs. Bush frequently asked questions.

She called the president "Best Friend," or "My George." Of the woman he called "Bar," the president admitted, "She'll go to bat for me, sometimes more than I'm inclined myself. She'll take 'em on head-to-head, dog eat dog. And that's fine. I'm glad to have her defending me. I'd rather have her on my side than not." Mrs. Bush became most heated with those who'd called Bush a wimp, asserting that "nobody could be married to me and be a wimp." But according to one friend, "blind adoration" it was not. "When he gets out of line, she points it out." She had no reservations about jokingly calling him on inconsistencies—publicly. After he complained about packing for the move to the White House, Barbara told an audience, "And where was he last week? That's right, fishing in Florida."

As for her influence over the president, she sent mixed signals. She said that when it comes to running the presidency, her George won't "come to Martha," but admitted that "if I think George is overworked, I am certainly going to complain . . . to him, his scheduler, anybody who'll listen." She refrained from circuitous operating, explaining, "I don't have to talk to his staff, I'll tell George." She was "very candid" with him: "I tell him what I think, and he tells me what he thinks, and then we are united." The First Lady admitted, "It takes two to argue, and he won't." Ever since Bush's entry into politics, she'd decided that "when I disagreed with George Bush it would be in private."

Just after the election, when asked if he'd been discussing his administration agenda with any advisers, George pointed to Barbara. She interrupted, "Just kidding." The new president clarified, "No, she's not." If Rosalynn had voiced her political opinions in weekly Oval Office meetings, and Nancy over the telephone, Barbara did so with her president in the early hours of each morning. The Bushes arose at six, breakfasted, and together pored through national newspapers and watched the morning news on different networks together. Like Sarah Polk, Edith Roosevelt, and a score of others, Barbara brought articles on a full range of issues to her president's attention. Margaret Carlson of *Time* reported that the First Lady "weighs in on everything from policy to personnel," and quoted a close aide as saying that the president "clears his mind" by first discussing issues and speeches with her. Her son offered that she was always "a very outspoken person who vents well—she'll just let it rip if she's got something on her mind." As for her own work as First Lady, Bar stated, "I always tell the President everything I do."[9]

Barbara occasionally blurted out strong opinions on foreign affairs. She was as thrilled that Panama's captured General Manuel Noriega "will stand trial . . . [because] he costs thousands of lives," and sat posing cheek to cheek with Polish Solidarity Leader Lech Walesa. As far as "that dreadful Saddam Hussein" of Iraq, who invaded Kuwait and prompted Bush to send American troops to the Persian Gulf in readiness for possible war, the First Lady suggested to the dictator, "Let your 'guests' [Americans held against their will in Kuwait] go and then let's talk about this." Asked if the president should meet Saddam "face-to-face," the First Lady further advised that Bush would consider "any-

thing to get the Kuwaitis back in their country and get our men out."
The president disagreed, saying he'd meet Saddam only after the Americans were released. When the president visited the troops in the Gulf over Thanksgiving, the First Lady was right there with him, dressed in camouflage army fatigues—and pearls. When Helen Thomas asked the First Lady about her reactions to criticism leveled at the president for sending aides to China after their bloody crackdown on pro-democracy marchers, she got an unusual First Lady response. Barbara Bush rapped her on the head twice.

Mrs. Bush headed the American delegation to the inauguration of Costa Rican president Rafael Calderón, even taking precedence over White House Chief of Staff John Sununu, telling the press, "I will tell my husband that democracy continues to flourish in Costa Rica. I will also tell him that the people of Costa Rica anticipate the future with great optimism." She'd earlier admitted, "Nobody said, 'Don't speak about politics, Bar.' Nobody was right." Barbara did not and was not planning on participating in the heavy, issues-oriented meetings as Rosalynn Carter had. It was goodwill representation more in the tradition of Pat Nixon.

Barbara also presided in the president's place during the annual Kennedy Center honors. She sang "We Are the World," a popular song composed and performed to fight Ethiopian hunger.

That she would publicly withdraw her strong opinions on social issues into the abyss of bland, noncommittal statements seemed unlikely. When Carlson interviewed the "Silver Fox," as the new First Lady's children called her, Mrs. Bush remarked, "I'm now slightly more careful about what I say. Slightly." When those issues became politically heated ones, however, she seemed to withdraw, explaining, "I don't want to diffuse my work for food kitchens for the hungry, for the illiterate, for the sick, by getting involved in controversial things." While she remained mute on what degree of power she had in bringing her social issues to his political agenda, it was evidenced early-on. After Bush had wanly answered a question about the homeless, one of their advocates complained to Mrs. Bush. She raised it with George, who admitted, "So we got into a big argument. She has been telling me I had to do more, and I think she's right." Carlson reported that Mrs. Bush's concern for AIDS had influenced the president's support of increased funding.

Publicly, with the press, she was not hesitant to mention phrases like "homeless," "racist," "gun control," not by dramatically emphasizing them, but merely mentioning them in the course of a natural conversation, naturally raising issues that those in the previous administration hadn't dared to name. Mrs. Reagan had painfully experienced a childhood of being supported by a single working mother who was unable to afford having her daughter live with her. She had friends felled by AIDS. She'd come close to being widowed by a handgun. She avoided using these traumas to personalize the larger public issues being debated. Mrs. Bush would continue her traditional charitable involvement with the Leukemia Society of America and the Children's Oncology Services, but never remain within the confines of safe harbors only.

As for the "project," her chief of staff stated, "She loves life, she loves people . . . Mrs. Bush is calling attention to projects and programs which reflect caring for others; she is continuing to work for a more literate America. . . ." The Houston Yankee had a dual view. She took on literacy as a primary identification—like drug abuse—yet emphasized her wide net of concerns, stemming from responsibility, not publicity. She didn't want to impress anyone. She also assumed the Republican stance of Pat Nixon and Nancy Reagan: Federal funding alone wasn't the cure. As Barbara said, "I feel my job is to encourage the corporate and private sector to help. . . ."

Although Mrs. Bush didn't focus specifically on every single issue that generally concerned her, she raised problems like "affordable housing, catastrophic health and comprehensive health coverage" with reporters. Donnie Radcliffe observed that Barbara "accumulated experts the same way she accumulated friends and didn't hesitate recommending them to George if she thought he could learn something from them." It was precisely the way Eleanor Roosevelt had worked. Even her son Marvin admitted, "I don't know a whole lot about Eleanor Roosevelt, but I do know she was someone who cared about other people a great deal. My mom shares that with her. . . ." The Eleanor comparison was first made by Susan Baker, the secretary of state's wife and a friend of Barbara's: "She sees needs. She involves herself with them, and she gives others the strength and encouragement they need to involve themselves." Senate wife and friend Ann Simpson thought Mrs. Bush had an acute "empathy" for the disadvantaged. "She always has a ready ear for people with stress in their lives."

Although many agreed that she had the potential to be an activist, only time would tell whether she would. If it seemed politically unlikely, it also seemed personally possible. As Barbara Bush explained, "I was a late maturer. I used to tell my children, 'Don't worry if you don't feel a driving need to be somebody or have some aim or goal. It will come. It just comes to some people later.' I tried to learn Chinese when I was 50." As far as her project work, the First Lady would admit after one year, "I doubt I'll take on more. But I'm not guaranteeing I won't." As almost always had happened with First Ladies, it was an unexpected crisis—personal, national, or global in scope—that suddenly forced them to do things they'd never envisioned. Too, the longer First Ladies were in the role, the more they realized how precious time was—a realization that stirred the latent activists. In some ways, her deceptively simple strategy of addressing issues through literacy subtly raised otherwise controversial matters.[10]

The president's new doctor, Burton Lee, was one of the First Lady's allies in the administration. He had served on Reagan's AIDS Commission and he served as her primary informant and private liaison on the issue. Having visited Martha's Table in March, Mrs. Bush came to Grandma's House, a home for babies and children with AIDS. The photographer trailing her into the building with patients, medical experts, and her press secretary recalled a rare political admission. When asked if the federal government was providing ample funding for AIDS, Mrs. Bush hesitated. "There is a deficit, so I leave that to George Bush." But she admitted, "There's not enough money." In a widely seen photograph, she held and hugged an AIDS baby and kissed another child. For a full hour, Barbara discussed with the house's director the fears people had of personal contact. "So what you're talking about is the need for people to care, for friends to come forward . . . for housing?"

Someone mentioned that people should know that personal contact with adults was also safe, so Mrs. Bush turned to an older victim and, before photographers and the full press corps, hugged him. The First Lady told reporters, "You can hug and pick up AIDS babies and people who have the HIV virus. . . . There is a need for compassion." The director of a local clinic beamed to the press, "You can't imagine what one hug from the First Lady is worth. . . . Here, the First Lady isn't afraid—and that's worth more than a thousand public service announcements." The home had not had to plead with the First Lady to make an appearance; she'd initiated it. Her press secretary said Mrs. Bush had wanted the press there in full, to take pictures and write stories as a means of sending her "powerful message that you can help."

Mrs. Bush would go even further in her sensitivity. During an AIDS memorial-night vigil at the Lincoln Memorial, where gatherers held candles, the First Lady would place candles in all the White House windows, visible to everyone. She attended the funeral of heroic teenager Ryan White, who succumbed to AIDS after a long public fight against ignorant reaction to him. Along with the president, she visited several men who had the illness at the National Institutes of Health; photographs of her visit appeared in the press. Some credited Mrs. Bush with being the inside advocate of the president's signing of the Hate Crimes Statistics Act, and inviting the first openly gay and lesbian individuals to a presidential ceremony. And she was moved as she viewed a patch of the national quilt in memoriam for all AIDS victims.

When Paulette Goodman, president of the Federation of Parents

and Friends of Lesbians and Gays wrote the First Lady to "speak kind words to some 24 million gay Americans and their families, to help heal the wounds, and to keep these families in loving relationships," Barbara Bush would respond without dancing around words. "I firmly believe that we cannot tolerate discrimination, against any individuals or groups . . . I appreciate so much your sharing the information about your organization and your encouraging me to help change attitudes . . . [Discrimination] always brings with it pain and perpetuates hate and intolerance."

Mrs. Bush felt that the composition of the traditional American family was changing. "The extended families may not even be related. They may be neighbors, friends." In what would later prove to be her first controversy, her commencement address at Wellesley College, the First Lady emphasized her point that people should be who they are, and be happy with that, no matter how different from conventional society. She illustrated this by talking about a game in which each student had a designated role to play. "At that, a small girl . . . asks, 'But where do the mermaids stand?' And the pastor tells her there are no mermaids. And she says, 'Oh yes there are. I am a mermaid.' . . . Where do the mermaids stand—all those who are different, those who do not fit the boxes and the pigeonholes? . . . Diversity, like anything worth having, requires effort. Effort to learn about and respect difference, to be compassionate with one another, to cherish our own identity, and to accept unconditionally the same in others."

The ripple effect of illiteracy was so prolific as to be nearly untraceable: drug use, careless and promiscuous sex, unwanted pregnancy, poor health habits, unemployment, poverty, voter and civic apathy, crime, economic misconceptions, inability to travel. It was also an emotional and difficult problem to detect and solve. Older illiterates attempted to bluff, fib, or avoid situations involving reading. The stigma had to be overcome, pride swallowed, training sought, begun, and continued. There was no organized visible constituency, victims could not be "turned in" but had to come forward and seek help of their own volition. About 35 million American adults couldn't read above the eighth-grade level. Nearly 23 million were "functionally" illiterate, not beyond a fourth-grade reading and writing level. Many illiterates compared it to imprisonment and blindness.

The First Lady called it "the most important problem we have," explaining, "If we can get people to read, we can get them out of jails and shelters and off the streets and get them back to work." She further explained that "everything I worry about would be better if more people could read, write and comprehend—drugs, teenage runaways, the environment, crime, school dropouts, etc." There was no East Wing publicity blitzkrieg to launch literacy awareness. Instead, Barbara sought to work with programs already in place, continuing with those she'd helped establish and foster as Second Lady. There would be no push for a bill of her own. There was also no promise that she would testify on illiteracy before Congress as Eleanor Roosevelt had done on institutional conditions in Washington and Rosalynn Carter had done on mental health. " I don't get into anything in front of Congress," Barbara Bush said in regard to a proposed National Literacy Act which would have had local libraries be used also as literacy learning centers and the national voluntary organization VISTA recruit a new literacy corps. As one of the bill's fathers, Senator Paul Simon, told Donnie Radcliffe, however, he was certain she'd be a "secret lobbyist" on its behalf with the president. "She is more willing to go on her convictions than her husband. But she will not do anything that will hurt him politically. I can't blame her if the president doesn't go for the bill."

Barbara was already a vocal advocate of Head Start, begun by LBJ, to encourage preschool and early grade-school students to develop reading and other educational skills. She also believed that if such children's parents were also illiterate, they should be strongly encouraged to have simultaneous reading training. To this end, the Barbara Bush Foundation for Family Literacy was formed with an initial $1 million in private funds. "And when I talk about family literacy," she emphasized,

"I'm talking about the big, bouncy kind, the single parent, extended families, divorced, homeless and migrant."

Gradually, the media came to associate literacy with "Bar." On the sitcom *Mama's Family*, as a group of middle-aged "church ladies" praised Barbara Bush's white hair, they dealt with the revelation of their club president's illiteracy with reference to an article in a woman's magazine written by the First Lady on Operation Literacy, which taught adults to read. In time, this incumbent First Lady—like Eleanor Roosevelt—would do a limited series Sunday radio show and write a book to promote her cause.

Undoubtedly through her Mexican daughter-in-law and her grandchildren, who spoke Spanish at home, Barbara Bush was acutely aware of the literacy problems in the vast and growing Hispanic population in America. Immediately, she taped a public-service announcement aimed at the minority group, emphasizing that their native language need not be relinquished by learning English as a means of having "the same advantages." While she wanted "every child in America to speak English," Barbara emphasized that "I'm against legislation that would make English the official language," because "that has racial overtones."[11]

Illiteracy triggered into her particular concern for young mothers who had no choice but to work. As she explained, "Many of them have babies without husbands, which makes it a tough row to hoe for them. And many of them are young, teen-aged women who never had a chance to learn . . . an occupation." Her private trips to homeless shelters as Second Lady had been to meet with families and discuss how they'd fallen into the position. "We've got to acknowledge the fact—and do something about—thirty percent of our homeless who are women with children," she'd said in a speech during the campaign. She came also to recognize a recurring aspect of homeless families. "Men [who] are not being made accountable for the children . . . it is absolutely outrageous. We've collected enormous amounts of money and it's just a drop in the hat for what's being owed to those children. . . . They go on and have new families and don't help the women."

In the late Eighties, a new conflict began emerging as the women "yuppies" began to assume the traditional chores of motherhood. It became a national balancing act, subject of films and television series. Although in every respect the traditional wife and mother who'd never had a professional career—save unsalaried political wife—Barbara Bush, through her daughters-in-law and the women on her staff, became increasingly enlightened. Of such women, the First Lady said, "I don't question it. I just say it's . . . harder. . . . You've got to bite the bullet and pretend you're not [tired], at least until you go to bed. You've got to be loving. Men *and* women." She expressed concern for the problems of adequate day care for children that might emerge in the Nineties as a result of the Eighties phenomenon of working mothers, which she supported. She did state, "Men are going to have to take a lot more responsibility," but emphasized that she was focusing on women who *had* to work and couldn't afford day care.[12]

At Smith College she was to receive an honorary degree from the same institution she had dropped out from to marry George Bush. "I'm saying to young women," she remarked about women getting higher educations, "wait, you've got years to have a family." She also thought that with more opportunity came more difficulties. "In a way, it seems so wonderfully liberated to have a whole world of opportunities so open to you. But it must present immense challenges. You have so many options that it must make it difficult to make choices and set priorities and establish limits. Because today it seems that women are often expected—especially by themselves—to be all things to all people and to be perfect in every role." A T-shirt was being sold at the college with the face of Nancy Reagan, a Smith graduate, on one side, and Barbara Bush on the other. In just nine months, Barbara Bush earned four honorary degrees—Smith, Bennett, Boston University, and Morehouse School of Medicine. When it was initially announced that she'd deliver the Wellesley college commencement speech, some of the student groups protested because Barbara had recognition only "through the achievements of her husband." The First Lady quipped, "Much ado about nothing. I understand it. Even I was twenty once." Then came word that not only would she speak, but she would bring Raisa Gorbachev with her to do so as well. "Barbara Bush's traditional approach is not harmful," the vice president of NOW told Donnie Radcliffe. "It is a reality that many women are burning out now in the workplace. . . . Her idea that it is a physically impossible task to do it all, is the reality." The president of the Women's National Political Caucus believed that Mrs. Bush's message to the women's movement was "You have the power to decide who you are and want to be."

Mrs. Bush was particularly progressive in her belief that women were equal to all political roles. "I think many women, certainly of my generation, can run the world." She spoke often of women in elected government, especially proud that Texas, "the most macho state," had three women mayors. The Bush campaign had a woman press secretary, a situation that wouldn't have arisen had Barbara been uncomfortable with it. As late as '84, she'd admitted to still supporting ERA. As First Lady, she was more cryptic—"I am for equal rights for *all* Americans." She even favored women being in the armed forces. I'm not opposed to women in combat—*if* they are capable of doing exactly the same thing the average man can do, like throw a hand grenade."

The First Lady flew to Illinois to campaign for Congresswoman

Lynn Martin in her campaign for the Senate, even though Martin was one of several women Republicans who publicly met with the president to try to convince him to change his views to pro-choice on abortion. On whether she was "pro-choice," Barbara carefully sidestepped public disagreement with the president, who now no longer was. She simply repeated to insistent reporters that "I'm not going to tell you my opinion." She didn't deny it. When asked her opinion of a vast "pro-choice" rally in Washington at which a "Barbara Bush is Pro-Choice" sign appeared, the First Lady said, "That's what America is all about and it's great," though the East Wing said she meant that people voicing their opinions was "great." Mrs. Bush evidently saw it as a problem of many shades. She did say she was "grateful" when a court order permitted an abortion performed on a comatose woman when there was hope that it might abet her recovery. Mrs. Bush said she supported abortion when "the life of the mother was at risk." She'd stated that her children were "planned," but avoided being drawn into an attempt to stop the anti-abortionists who were bombing clinics when Houston's Planned Parenthood solicited her. Its executive director explained, "She said the abortion issue was vexing to her from a personal point of view and that the number of abortions especially pained her knowing that her son was struggling to adopt a baby. She was taking a very thoughtful but neutral position. . . ." The executive director of the National Abortion Rights Action League felt that the First Lady's views showed her to be "thoughtful, caring, concerned and compassionate not only about children's lives and the quality of the family but about the role of women in the society and the world at large."[13]

Just two weeks into her Ladyship, she startled the press by breaking her rule not to respond to political questions. While she wouldn't get into the "politics and policies" of gun control, when asked if she thought military assault rifles should be outlawed, Mrs. Bush quickly responded, "[A]bsolutely . . . I myself do not own a gun. . . . I am afraid of them." Her conviction stemmed from an earlier hunting incident, when George suddenly moved into the rifle scope. Weeks later, although it was denied that the First Lady's influence had played a part in it, President Bush called for a temporary ban on the weapon's importation. It prompted Senator Paul Simon to suggest that George "listen to Barbara," and the Washington chief of police to declare, "Thank God for Barbara Bush." At the Gridiron Dinner, one reporter, garbed in white wig and blue dress, sang "Pistol-Packin' Mama."[14]

The First Lady's response to the patrol by Black Muslims of an inner-city neighborhood development plagued by drugs was, "Right on." She was particularly supportive of newly appointed drug czar William Bennett's decision to concentrate on Washington, and telephoned to encourage it. *Ebony* magazine boldly declared that Mrs. Bush was "politically and personally committed to equal rights for Black Americans and she will not hesitate to use her highly visible role . . . to prove it." The magazine was the first to draw a civil-rights comparison between her and Eleanor Roosevelt. In reference to a case in Boston where an African-American assailant was falsely charged with murdering a pregnant woman and shooting her husband, the First Lady said that racism "isn't just Boston," and it "made me sick. . . . We have racism in our country and we've got to do away with it." During the course of the interview she thought of her own positive influence on the issue and said what she could continue to do was "speak out like I am right now."

On "people things," Barbara Bush admitted, "Yes, I'm a liberal. . . . I don't mean that as knocking the Republican party, because I think of the Republican party as liberal on social issues. . . . You may not look at me that way . . . [but] you have to look at the big picture like what will help people most. . . . I don't mean that conservatives don't care . . . what I should say is labels are for cans and let it go. . . . You have to—you pay along the way. . . ."

Mrs. Bush's East Wing staff was chosen to include individual personalities and social consciousness that matched those of their boss. Her chief of staff as Second Lady, Susan Porter Rose, now headed the East Wing, having formerly been there under Pat Nixon and Betty Ford. Jean Becker of *USA Today* was hired as deputy press secretary.

Because George had long instructed his personnel director to seek out qualified minorities for his staff, Barbara consciously sought to do so for the "most visible person on my staff," the press secretary. There was no attempt to mask her firm decision to hire a press secretary who was most qualified and happened to be black. After extensive interviews, one such woman was appointed, Anna Perez, who'd worked on the Hill. A friend of the First Lady, Mrs. Art Fletcher, who'd also worked on the previous East Wing staff, in comparing Mrs. Bush's dedication to civil rights with Mrs. Reagan on the same issue said, "They don't even belong on the same roster."

David Broder revealed that the First Lady's friendship with Louis Sullivan had helped win his nomination as HHS secretary, making him the only black Cabinet member of the administration, and a federal department that often reflected her concern for disadvantaged minorities was headed by a Cabinet member whose appointment reflected her influence. The Bush campaign director believed that her being a "good bridge" between George and Jack Kemp, whom she particularly liked, contributed to his appointment as secretary of housing and urban development. Barbara Bush's consciousness of civil rights stemmed back to the Fifties, when her baby-sitter and housekeeper had been continually denied food and board as they and she drove from Texas to Maine. "I made up my mind that we were a team," Mrs. Bush recalled. "And I discovered I was more stubborn than I thought."

On Martin Luther King's birthday, the First Lady headed to a local school, taking part in a Black History Month celebration, swaying and singing from memory the stanzas of "We Shall Overcome" with students. One seven-year-old told the press it was the first time he "held a white lady's hand." She slipped out privately to see a photography exhibit, "I Dream a World: Portraits of Black Women Who Changed America." She strove to deemphasize racial differences, but admitted that she was "not naive enough" to think others did likewise, telling *Ebony* that she sensed other white people noticing when her press secretary was "the only Black person in the room. . . ."

While she acknowledged that aid to the underprivileged was vital, Mrs. Bush also believed inspirational example to be important, and she worried when those minorities who'd become successful "don't go back to help other people." Although she saw herself as helping fight racism, she didn't believe that as a "white-haired White lady" she could go into black, Hispanic, or Asian housing areas and have as much of a positive influence as a successful minority role model could. For herself, Mrs. Bush named liberal Democratic Texas congresswoman Barbara Jordan, television newscaster Maureen Bunyan, Coretta King, and Dorothy Height, friend to Mrs. Roosevelt, as the black women she highly admired, but when asked whom she found "inspiring," the First Lady named Frederick Douglass, friend of Mary Lincoln's, and listed a variety of his achievements in overcoming racism.

As her first winter blossomed into spring, the First Lady made a third public appearance that drew national attention. From the thousands of invitations to graduation commencements she received, Mrs. Bush chose a relatively obscure small black women's institution, Bennett College, in North Carolina. The event took place on Mother's Day, and because Barbara paid for all her trips even if they were "official," the costs were covered by the president, as his Mother's Day gift to her. A personal friend of forty years, William J. Trent, Jr., was for many years the executive director of the United Negro College Fund. He, a local resident, and Bennett's president, Gloria Randle Scott— who sent the First Lady information about the school's single-mother and youth-literacy programs—had first thought of inviting her. Only one other First Lady had appeared at the school to speak: Eleanor Roosevelt. The setting, Greensboro, was site of a famous sit-in during the civil-rights struggle.

Mrs. Bush spoke of Frederick Douglass and Dorothy Brown, an orphan who fought the odds to study at Bennett and become the Southeast's first black woman surgeon. "There are many types of slavery, and education is the key to freedom . . . I can't tell you all the people I've known who have escaped the bondage of ignorance. . . . And I urge you to help the young out there today . . . enslaved by ignorance . . . help your fellow human beings." One local black Republican, Ron Barbee, thought that if Mrs. Bush continued to work with black educational centers, "the Democrats might have something to worry about." It had been another First Lady who'd helped attract blacks from the Republican to the Democratic party a half-century before, and similarities again were obvious. Nancy Lee, a 1945 Bennett graduate, said, "It's the same excitement I remember with Eleanor Roosevelt."[15]

Two days later, a benchmark was passed, wholly unnoticed.

Two hundred years ago to that day, the white-haired, fat, wrinkled wife of George the President had departed in a coach with wild horses, to join her husband, becoming symbols of the break with English monarchs. Now, a self-described "white-haired, fat, wrinkled" wife of George the President prepared for her departure in a jet plane, joining her husband, symbols of a realliance with Europe. Instead of eschewing the queen of England, the president's lady would now walk side by side with her. At the palace, First Lady Bush's car door would be ignored, and Queen Elizabeth would snap to a footman, "Open it!"

One wonders what Charlotte and Martha would have thought.[16]

29

Bicentennial

MAY 16, 1989, was an ordinary Tuesday. This spring, as in those past, the highways leading to the nation's capital burst with wildflowers. The National Gallery of Art filled with schoolchildren, and the tourists queued up as always, to see the historic furnishings and portraits in the White House, wrapping around the gate, inching toward the East Wing.

Tourists enter through the First Lady's end of the house, the East Wing, shuffling along the colonnade and looking into the private faces of public women, eternally smiling from their frames: Julia Tyler, the Lady Presidentress, Bess Truman, the Boss, Mamie Eisenhower, Mrs. Ike, Frances Cleveland, Frankie. Lurking in a room just inside the entrance, "Sahara Sarah" Polk and Madame Regent, Edith Wilson, among others. Down the hall, forever with white collie, Grace "Mammy" Coolidge hangs in the China Room. In the Vermeil Room, Eleanor Roosevelt, "Rover" of World War II, a series of her expressive hands frozen for posterity in all their busy poses.

Invited guests enter through the Diplomatic Reception Room, passing through doors guarded by changing but still-familiar faces. Here are placed the portraits of the two most recent First Ladies—in May of 1989—Mrs. Carter and Mrs. Ford. Others come, and they are shifted from their place of honor down the hall. Mrs. Johnson and Mrs. Nixon had once been there. Mrs. Kennedy was still so popular that protocol has been broken to permanently enshrine her portrait on a visible spot along the gallery. When Nancy Reagan's portrait was donated, it took over the spot Mrs. Kennedy's had occupied. Nancy's portrait shows her in a pose similar to Jackie Kennedy's and on a canvas of the same size. Both were painted by Aaron Shikler.

The tradition of hanging these women dates to 1902. Before that they were only criticized.

Upstairs, in the shimmering East Room, is "Lady Washington." In the Red Room, the merry smile of legendary Mrs. Madison. If you are lucky enough to be asked to the private floor, you can't miss grand Nellie Taft, seemingly floating against the staircase. In the Lincoln suite, Mary Todd can be seen in private, along with her husband. In the Yellow Oval Room, the first First Lady in residence, Abigail Adams, had held her few formal receptions. "Mrs. G." is nowhere to be seen, but she might have taken comfort in knowing that "Lemonade Lucy" was in storage.

Way down at the end of the hall in the southwest corner is a bedroom. Connected to it is a small office. It looks out right onto the Oval Office. This is where Barbara Bush works. Throughout history there's been the musing, Which is the seat of power? The room being viewed, or the room from which it is viewed?

Barbara Bush is conscious of her predecessors. "I do feel their presence. I am grateful to Edith Roosevelt for kicking the President's and Cabinet's offices off the second floor . . . Bess Truman, for the Truman Balcony, Jackie Kennedy for the beautiful upstairs dining room and for starting to replace reproductions with the real McCoy. Pat Nixon for the beauty parlor. Betty Ford for the swimming pool. Lady Bird Johnson for the adorable children's garden and the Mary Cassatt painting on the second floor, and Nancy Reagan for making all the three floors of the White House sparkle. . . . The more I read about First Ladies, the more I feel their presence. As you read about Eleanor Roosevelt entertaining Churchill or the King and Queen of England—you can wander through the rooms. Yes, I feel their presence!"

Their roles set precedents for her. "They all had something I might try to emulate," admitted Mrs. Bush, "for instance, Eleanor Roosevelt—caring. Bess Truman, took care of Harry, Lady Bird Johnson, grace under pressure. Nancy Reagan—protected the White House. . . ." She did not specifically emulate anyone. "I am trying to say that I think each spouse has to define the job for herself. I have priorities— George and the children and grandchildren—and all else falls into place."[1]

And, too, Mrs. Bush would inevitably have her "style" criticized, her influence over the president questioned, her family's privacy intruded on. Two hundred years after Martha Washington had finally arrived by coach and vessel in New York as the first First Lady, with a "staff" of one, her nephew, and with reporters chronicling the details, Barbara Bush arrived in Rome, with her staff and with reporters chronicling the details. In obvious technological and material ways, the Ladyship had changed, but, curiously, certain elements remained.

Mrs. Washington's trip to New York was "advanced" as a semiroyal procession by Gabriel Van Horne, stage line owner; Mrs. Bush's trip was advanced by two press aides. When the First Lady of 1789 returned to her Mount Vernon home and gardens, she considered herself a private person; the same sentiment was felt by the First Lady of 1989 during the French president's trip to her Kennebunkport home and gardens. There was always that diplomatic consciousness: Martha made observations on the incoming French ambassador; Barbara, on the outgoing Swedish ambassador. In Europe, Mrs. Bush had hoped to "sneak in a trip to Ferragamo" to buy shoes. On her journey to New York, when Martha went to buy shoes, she found herself a "very great some body." As she traipsed through Rome, Brussels, West Germany, and London during the NATO conference, Barbara inspected a center for homeless women and dished out food for a half hour in Italy, visited a state-funded working village for the mentally retarded in Belgium, and an adult education and employment program in England. Lady Washington was known to be the benevolent godmother of the indigent Revolutionary War veterans.[2]

It was in England that the most curious relationship had come full circle. Now, Barbara Bush, upon arrival at the British prime minister's home, had her hand kissed by her English counterpart, Denis Thatcher. The American First Lady displayed a 1989 equal opportunity as she promptly returned the kiss on the hand of the British First Gentleman. During the planning of Nancy Reagan's 1985 international First Ladies Conference, the White House had sent out delicate feelers to see if Denis Thatcher should be invited. Polite word came back that he should not. Subject of national satire, this British "First Gentleman" was attempting to limit his public activities, not unlike some of the early American First Ladies.[3]

Mrs. Bush later considered the role of the husband of America's first woman president, and how that position was played by the two "First Gentlemen" of England. "Both Denis Thatcher and Prince Philip have full and busy lives and interests of their own. I would hope that the husband of the President would have the same. It seems to make for a happier relationship." Lady Bird Johnson said of America's first First Gentleman, "I just hope he'll be as supportive as Mr. Thatcher is. I should think it a terrible sort of walking-on-eggshells job. Conflict of interest would be a very great difficulty. I'm sure there's some things he could do, but I don't know quite what it would be."

Betty Ford predicted that by the turn of the millenium, a woman would be elected president, probably having been a vice president first. Of the First Gent role, she believed, "[I]f he was a rancher, then I think he'd stay in ranching. . . ." Of the traditional hostess role, she believes "it would be allocated" to another woman. "I think he probably would be handy at entertaining, perhaps with businessmen at lunch, but I think you'd lose that whole role . . . there'd be the support, but it would be an entirely different kind of support. I think traditionally he'd be there just as Prince Philip is with Queen Elizabeth. But Prince Philip has maintained his individuality very ably. He has his own interests and his own projects. That's the way I would see it operate."

Rosalynn Carter thought that "if he even wanted to have a job and work he could do that. Whether or not the American people would deal with that or accept that, I'm not sure. I know that if he had an interest like mental health or drug abuse or anything that he wanted to work on, he could have all the resources at his fingertips. I don't think there'd be any problem with a first First Gentleman. The only problem that I could see would come if a husband didn't like playing second fiddle . . . I think he can do anything he wants to do as I think a First Lady can do anything she wants to do . . . He could pursue whatever he wanted to pursue . . . When foreign heads of state come, one of the [First Lady's] duties is to entertain the spouse. Now that might be a little difficult to perform if it was always a wife . . . He wouldn't have to pour tea . . . because the wife of the Secretary of State would always entertain the wife of a head of state . . . Maybe he'd appear with her occasionally but keep on with his job."[4]

With regard to future presidents' wives, as women make professional and legal strides, so, too, will the role enlarge. Increasingly, the presidency seems a shared entity. Increasingly, the once-harmless charitable projects have developed controversial aspects or evolved into legislation. Because of its uniqueness, it seems doubtful that a president's wife would relinquish the role to instead continue working in a profession. As the dean of the First Ladies, Lady Bird Johnson said, "I hardly think it would be possible to pursue an occupation for those four years, or eight years as it may be. Because that's job enough in itself." It might be possible that she would assume only a special issue, and leave the hostess role to a surrogate—a woman relative or Cabinet wife—as happened not only with the widower presidents but Mrs. Roosevelt at periods during World War II, and Mrs. Kennedy during her pregnancy. The issue of paying an official White House hostess may arise, though it's unlikely, on the theory that someone would happily volunteer in that capacity.

What in fact may evolve is a semi-official transition team for wives of presidents-elect, perhaps to help get their projects started immediately, to explain in detail conflicts of interest, government ethics, procedures during presidential disability, and funding for the East Wing—the only federal law that in some way pertains to First Ladies. As for projects relating to policy, Mrs. Johnson offered that "they'll do what life has shaped them to do. Since the programs [of a President have] many facets . . . they will find those among them that they can align themselves to with the most enthusiasm and understanding. . . ."

Upon her return from Europe, Barbara Bush continued another unique institution, during the annual Senate Wives Luncheon.

Receiving a Harlem boys' choir, by her side were two old friends, fellow members of the world's most exclusive sorority, Lady Bird Johnson and Betty Ford. Lady Bird had done this for Mamie, Mamie for

Edith Wilson. Mrs. Wilson had known Mrs. Cleveland. At the height of her popularity, Frankie Cleveland had visited elderly Sarah Polk. As First Lady, Sarah Polk always proffered a place of honor to the aged Dolley Madison. Upon arrival in Washington as wife of the secretary of state, Mrs. Madison had paid a call on Martha Washington. There are several such "genealogical" lines: Abigail Adams–Louisa Adams–Julia Tyler–Lucy Hayes–Nellie Taft–Grace Coolidge–Eleanor Roosevelt–Barbara Bush is just one.

If there is any influence of one former First Lady on an incumbent who meets her, it is so subtle and exclusive as to be more mythical than real, yet recent First Ladies are on record as saying they did discuss the role and the problems unique to it with their predecessors. How far this scepter passing goes back through the First Lady generations is not fully chronicled, but Abigail Adams did record a conversation with Martha on their shared fates during an 1800 Mount Vernon visit. And, too, coincidentally, many who'd someday become First Ladies crossed the paths of their predecessors. Lady Bird, for example, first learned of the capital's urban blight from following Eleanor, who first learned of it following Ellen Wilson.

For former First Ladies, there seems to be a bond of shared experience. While differences are obvious, they seem to understand the tremendous difficulties they've all had better than others do. "Members" come and go, and though sometimes they've been rivals, there seems an unwritten rule. Never, in two hundred years, has one criticized another—in public. The understanding remains: They performed the role as they saw fit, and everyone else deserves the same right to do so. Unlike former presidents and incumbent presidents, First Ladies have no set rules or responsibilities.

The public activities of former First Ladies continue to grow. Betty Ford said she was "supposedly a private citizen" but "discovered I still had power to do things, to have a voice on issues. . . ." Former First Ladies even retain official recognition. In the pecking order of State Department protocol, a former First Lady is considered "3C," along with a former president, ranked only after the incumbent president and First Lady, vice president and Second Lady, state governor and spouse, speaker of the House, and spouse, and Chief Justice and spouse.[5]

In 1989, Mrs. Johnson, like Mrs. Nixon, was three years short of eighty years old. She continued her advocacy of environmental protection and cultivation of regional wildflowers. Among the guests in the State Dining Room that afternoon was her daughter, Lynda Robb, herself now a Senate wife. Already there was speculation that her husband might someday run for the presidency. As her epitaph, Mrs. Johnson wanted the words "She planted a tree." Betty Ford, then seventy-one years old, maintained an office at the center named for her and lived in

Palm Springs, with long respites in Colorado. Her husband, who admitted that Betty was "more popular than I," was influenced to stop what little drinking he did, because "I saw how much benefit it was for her." Eighty percent of American women alcoholics were also addicted to prescription drugs, as she had been, and Mrs. Ford began special counseling programs for the unique troubles of women alcoholics and still spoke out on women's issues. Her chief aide, Ann Cullen, had become a "second daughter" to her.

In the spring of '89, Rosalynn Carter was approaching her sixty-second birthday. She continued her work in health and welfare issues. In Atlanta, Mrs. Carter continued to share her husband's work. She participated in the diplomatic conferences hosted at the Carter Center by her husband, to resolve international conflicts, attending one he successfully mediated for Ethiopian factions that summer. Later, that autumn, in the capital for a Gannett Board of Directors meeting, Rosalynn Carter heard Barbara Bush address their morning session, and then the incumbent First Lady invited her predecessor for lunch at the White House. Except for the brief moment before departing for Sadat's funeral, it was the first time Mrs. Carter had been back since her own tenure. Mrs. Bush also invited Rosalynn's two East Wing chiefs, Mary Hoyt and Gretchen Poston, as well as her own chief of staff and press secretary. Rosalynn was curious to see if the antique hand-rubbed wood from her grandfather's barn was still on the walls of an upstairs room. Barbara promptly led the march to find out. Nancy had had the wood painted over, but it was still intact.

Rosalynn maintained her office, run by longtime friend Madeline Edwards, in her Georgia home, and had a cabin with Jimmy in the mountains. A unique sort of sorority powwow met in 1987, when Mrs. Johnson invited Mrs. Carter and Mrs. Ford as overnight guests at the LBJ Ranch, so all three could prepare for a seminar being hosted by Rosalynn at the Carter Library. Pat Nixon had also agreed to serve as sponsor for the event, "Women and the Constitution," but her tenuous health prevented attendance. While corrective heart surgery before the seminar prevented Betty from attending, Lady Bird was there.

That year, Mrs. Johnson talked about the "sorority." She felt that she'd come to know Betty Ford even more since she'd left the White House, and particularly admired her for confronting her addictions. She'd hosted a book party for Mrs. Ford's *Glad Awakening,* as well as one for Julie Eisenhower's book on Pat Nixon, expressing the hope that Mrs. Nixon's health would improve. She hoped to have both Carters come to the LBJ Library and host a party for their jointly written work. As Lynda Robb recalled, "Mother gets along with all the First Ladies and keeps in touch. I remember one Christmas when she was sending off poinsettias to them all. Not all of them get along, but Mother

does." Indeed, if there was a First Lady Central, it was Lady Bird's office, still run by longtime aide from her White House years Betty
Tilson.

During the summer of 1986, two former First Ladies met in private.
Lady Bird Johnson was renting a house on Martha's Vineyard, and Jacqueline Onassis invited her—along with Lynda and Chuck Robb—to
her home there. Turning sixty in 1989, nearly thirty years after having
left the White House, Jackie still remained a center of media attention,
her verve and allure intact. She continued to live and work in New
York City, not only mother to two lawyers but a grandmother of two
children as well, and had a close circle of friends, including Nancy
Tuckerman, who continued to help run her office. She had last seen
Mrs. Carter, along with Lady Bird Johnson, when the three Democratic
First Ladies gathered for the 1979 dedication of the Kennedy Library.

Mrs. Onassis made public appearances as Mrs. Eisenhower had—for
those causes most important to her—and, within the realm of those
specific interests, she would talk to the press. The parallel is the same
for Pat Nixon to Bess Truman—living a life of absolute privacy, and no
interviews. Above all, Mrs. Nixon relished long hours with her grandchildren, reading or playing games with them. She resisted posing for a
White House portrait, and only because of her daughters did she finally
sit for a hauntingly beautiful painting. When Julie's biography of her
was published, Mrs. Nixon only read part of it. She did, however, agree
to appear on a segment of a television interview of Julie. Briefly, Pat
Nixon made her first and only public appearance on television since the

resignation. She looked remarkably well, laughing loudly, talking to her husband, but not to the cameras. But Pat Nixon was no recluse, still popping into New York or to Pennsylvania, or a local shopping mall, and kept a lively interest in international events, particularly in China and Iran, through the early summer of 1989, as a visitor recalled. Mrs. Nixon would later emerge quite publicly, however briefly, at the dedication of the Nixon Library, joined by Barbara Bush, Betty Ford, and Nancy Reagan.

Nancy Reagan's new house—complete with orchid greenhouse—was rushed into print in maps of the stars' homes for Hollywood tourists, and buses passed by all day long. After being unable to get an electrician in, she admitted, "after eight years in the White House, I was spoiled."

Exactly like Julia and Ulysses Grant, Nancy and Ronald Reagan made a grand tour of Japan, although the twentieth-century couple collected $2 million in the process for speeches and appearances, including Nancy's "organization" of a "Just Say No" club. ("That's what was offered," said the former First Lady. "If something is offered . . . are you going to say, 'No, no, no'? And, once again exactly as Edith Wilson

had done when her archrivals Colonel House and Joe Tumulty published their accounts, Nancy Reagan wrote her memoirs, counteracting the autobiographies of Don Regan and Larry Speakes. She claimed, "I really tried . . . I really tried not to be vindictive or mean."

As had Mrs. Wilson's, Mrs. Reagan's book stirred a furor of controversy, many critics excoriating her as vengeful. Don Regan said Nancy "has no gratitude for anyone" and "too much pity for herself." Sally Quinn of *The Washington Post* went so far as to suggest that the former First Lady must have in fact resented her easygoing husband for having to always fight his battles against those who would use him. R. W. Apple of *The New York Times* believed that what Nancy did "was not so radically different from . . . Edith Bolling Wilson." Tony Full of *Newsweek* called it "a powerful behind-the-scenes force with an appetite for intrigue and an obsession with protecting her husband." There were also heated denials by Presidents Nixon and Ford to her claim that they encouraged her to get rid of Regan. But if anything, the book proved that Nancy Reagan was far more politically rational and pragmatic than most had ever given her credit for. And much more progressive.

It was while promoting the book on a Barbara Walters interview that Nancy Reagan admitted that she had become pregnant before her wedding to Ronnie, and that she would have considered having an abortion if they hadn't already planned to marry. There were other claims in other books as well. Rock Brynner, writing about his famous actor-father, Yul, said that while Yul was doing *Lute Song* on Broadway, his mother found out that he "made love to every woman in the cast except her friend Mary Martin . . . that included a pretty chorus girl in the show, the Nancy Davis." She joined the board of Revlon Cosmetics but disassociated herself from the Phoenix House rehab center named for her after some controversy with local residents. "I don't believe I deserve all this negative publicity when I have worked so hard. Tell me, where does one working for these good causes draw the line. . . . I am tired of being blamed for not having done enough myself!" Again, she carefully blurred the facts of what she was being criticized for and defended herself from a defensible charge. Nobody had accused her of not working hard. She had pulled support from the Los Angeles Phoenix House project because local residents there protested its being built in their communities and threatened to picket the Reagans' Bel Air home. "I certainly didn't come back . . . to have demonstrations in front of my house," she retorted. In Washington, she participated in a panel discussion on the Ladyship. *People* magazine wrote that "in the end, it seems, America hasn't lost a First Couple; it has gained a pair of eternally popular demiroyals whose exploits are likely to entertain for years to come."[6]

Whether people liked her or not, there was no denying that Nancy

Reagan's legacy was not only helping thousands of young children steer clear of drugs, but also helping guide the world toward a nuclear-free era, an overwhelming accomplishment. Apart from this achievement, she proved to be one of the most fascinating First Ladies in American history and interesting figures in world history.

Time passes, history recedes. One thirteen-year-old thought that "Mrs. Onassis" was somehow the mother of "Jackie Kennedy." A twenty-year-old knew that President Johnson's wife's name was "Bird something," but when pressed thought only that as First Lady "she was the first to plant flowers on the White House lawn." Eleanor Roosevelt is now more legend than person to the majority of the population in 1989. She is quoted by conservative Republicans, has a high school named after her, and remains the standard-bearer for First Ladies.

The modern age remembers First Ladies largely anecdotally. Lady Washington is doomed to be the placid woman in mobcap, staring down from the schoolroom wall, next to George. Abigail Adams, hanging her wash. Once she was America's most famous woman, but Dolley Madison's name now graces only ice-cream containers and cake boxes. Mention of Mary Lincoln inevitably evokes the question, "Was she insane?" Eerily, she herself had predicted that fate. Julia Grant, an army wife, Frances Cleveland, a bride, Edith Wilson, "first woman president." Nellie Taft, if recalled at all, is reduced, as Mrs. Johnson often is, to being a tree planter; Grace Coolidge, the lady in red, Mamie, the matron in pink. There is no Eleanor Roosevelt memorial in Washington, as was long expected. For now, Mrs. Kennedy's project is still remembered— albeit incorrectly, as "redecorating." There is occasional recognition. A 1989 *New Yorker* cartoon of "Ms. Rushmore" had Martha Washington, Martha Jefferson, Edith Roosevelt, and Mary Lincoln carved in stone, in place of their husbands.

"She alone can render his Fame immortal," declared the first president's wife to live in the White House, Abigail Adams.

To get a full view of most administrations, one had to consider the First Lady's influence. Franklin Roosevelt and his "liberal" policies, as well as his political reemergence despite disability, were due in no small measure to Eleanor. Abraham Lincoln's growing sensitivity to the human costs of slavery stemmed in part from Mary's consciousness. Wilson freely admitted that his ability to govern depended upon his need for his wives' partnerships. Where, truly, would William Howard Taft, Lyndon Johnson, John Adams, Jimmy Carter, Warren Harding, Ulysses S. Grant, or Ronald Reagan have been without Nellie, Bird, Dearest Friend, Rosie, the Duchess, Mrs. G., and Mommy, respectively? Dick Nixon signed papers behind the Great Wall, but Pat helped make it a reality, guiding the world on its first look at the mysterious nation. There is a town in Texas named in honor of Tyler. It does not specify—John or Julia. One ponders the twist of fate. Might there have been a secretary of the arts, an Equal Rights Amendment, and a national system to care for all the mentally ill if 1963, 1976, and 1980 had ended differently?

Some presidents openly admitted their wives' power; most others acknowledged it. Oftentimes, when presidents ignored their wives' advice, it spelled disaster—from Abigail Fillmore's advice not to sign the Fugitive Slave Bill to Louisa Adams's strategy to actively campaign. Sometimes, however, the advice had devastating effects—Florence Harding's push for Charlie Forbes at the Veteran's Bureau, for example, resulting in scandal.

During a campaign, the press examines the political but not the personal partnership, focusing intently on the choice of running mates. After Inauguration Day, vice presidents, staffed in the Old Executive Office Building, become shadows over the West Wing. Meanwhile, the White House is balanced with the First Lady's East Wing. The marital partnership, through the Ladyship, posesses more latent power over the presidency than the business partnership of the vice presidency. A First Lady's role dwarfs a vice president's. Politically, this makes her an unknown quantity, truly the wild card of the executive branch, potentially the most powerful "appointed" post in the federal government. Depending on from which side of the looking-glass it is seen, this flaw in the democratic structure is a blessing or a curse. The only person who elects a First Lady is her husband at the altar. Unlike a president, who can be impeached, her elusive power can't be stopped except by presidents—and not always even then.

A First Lady is accountable to no one. Her job is structured only by arbitrary personal interpretation. The press and public can exert pressure on her to do or not do things, but she'll be criticized whatever she does. So, logically, why not do as she chooses? In that respect, it is the most enviable federal "post." Among the advisers around presidents, First Ladies usually have no ulterior motives. They are the least personally ambitious. They have remained loyal longest. They have been trusted and relied upon throughout the president's earlier career.

Certainly, there are larger trends that dictate an era and are uniquely paralleled by the woman in the White House at the moment. That's what permitted Rosalynn Carter to openly discuss her attendance at Cabinet meetings in the "Me Decade," while Nellie Taft had to attend her husband's conferences clandestinely in the "Progressive Era." But personality, political ambition, and interpretation of one's role in marriage account equally if not more. It explains why Abigail Adams could become enmeshed in the question of war with France in the "Federal Era," and Grace Coolidge could first learn about the Kellogg-Briand Pact only through reading of it in the newspapers, in the

"Jazz Age." Or, why a Florence Harding would meet the press, and a quarter of a century later Bess Truman would not. And yet, certain elements stand up to time. Mary Lincoln was as roundly criticized for "meddling" in Cabinet appointments as was Nancy Reagan. Betty Ford could use the persuasion of her personality to lobby for ERA as Julia Tyler could for Texas annexation. A century apart, Jackie Kennedy and Frances Cleveland suffered from invasion of privacy.

The Ladyship intertwines with history. Public crises are part of the First Lady's personal life; her personal life sometimes becomes a public crisis. She's come from Main Street and plantation, been a business manager and "farmeress," with varying degrees of education. Her shortcomings are maligned, her strengths dismissed as privilege. Singularly herself, she is merely a link in a chain. She must contribute but not meddle, be progressive not radical, political but social, loyal, not blind, civically international, but uniquely American. She is a partner but an individual. A lady but a woman. A queen, and a commoner.

This First Lady paradox has endured through radical social change. Was it anachronistic by 1990? Is all the yes-ma'aming mere patronizing ceremony, diminishing the individual's right to prove herself? The answer is posed with another question: Would those who find it offensive rather have a First Lady officially barred from being able to make decisions—and demands? To even those to whom such chivalrous deference might seem sexist—perhaps most apparently Eleanor and Rosalynn—it has proven useful as a tool whether for personal or altruistic ends. As Helen Thomas said of First Ladies, "They've been amazed and pleased to find out how much power they really have."[7]

Some might see the inevitability of an unelected person having potential power in the executive branch as a flaw of the government structure. Short of a Constitutional amendment requiring presidential candidates to be single, however, the First Lady will always remain as powerful as she (and he, but not always he) chooses. There is nothing Machiavellian about it. It is partly the balance of marriage, the desire to right social wrongs, perhaps the need to gratify an ambition and develop an identity.

In many ways, the First Lady's power defies definition. It simply is, and even if the presidency becomes obsolete, it will always be. When America was colonies, there was Queen Charlotte. In the Confederacy, there was Varina—Mrs. Jeff—Davis. Even if there were some other government, some leader would emerge from a tribunal. If such a leader was a woman, she would wield her power, independently, publicly.

And if such a leader was a man, he just might be married.

Chronological Bibliography and Notes

Because of the prohibitive space and time element involved in providing even a selective bibliography, sources are indicated throughout the endnotes, the full notation appearing in the initial note. Several hundred books alone, for example, were used in preparing the initial draft of what became the two manuscripts. All catalogued books at the Library of Congress on the individual presidents, the presidency, First Ladies, presidential families, and the White House, were initially consulted, and many were utilized as background material. Nearly all letter collections in the library's Manuscript Division relating to First Ladies were also consulted. Background material that is not specifically endnoted is general information from presidential or First Lady biographies. Unless a fact or quote is particularly important or controversial, most notes have been grouped by subject.

Below is an author's guide to some individual biographies, covering the women of both the first and second volumes of *First Ladies: The Saga of the Presidents' Wives and Their Power*. It is by no means an exhaustive list.

Elswyth Thane. *Washington's Lady*. New York: Dodd, Mead, 1960.

Lynne Withey. *Dearest Friend: A Life of Abigail Adams*. New York: Free Press, 1981.

Fawn Brodie. *Thomas Jefferson: An Intimate History*. New York: W. W. Norton, 1974.

Allen Clark. *Life and Letters of Dolley Madison*. Washington, D.C.: W. F. Roberts, 1914.

Virginia Moore. *The Madisons*. New York: McGraw-Hill, 1979.

Harry Ammon. *James Monroe*. New York: McGraw-Hill, 1971.

Jack Shepard. *Cannibals of the Heart* (Louisa Adams). New York: McGraw-Hill, 1980.

Mary French Caldwell. *General Jackson's Lady*. Nashville: Ladies Hermitage Association, 1936.

John Niven. *Martin Van Buren: The Romantic Age of American Politics* (Hannah and Angelica Van Buren). New York: Oxford University Press: 1983.

James A. Green. *William Henry Harrison* (Anna Harrison). Richmond: Garrett and Massie, 1941.

Robert Seager. *And Tyler Too* (Julia Tyler). New York: McGraw-Hill, 1962.

Anson and Fanny Nelson. *Memorials of Sarah Childress Polk.* New York: A.D.F. Randolph & Company, 1892.

Holman Hamilton. *Zachary Taylor: Soldier in the White House* (Margaret Taylor). Hamden, Connecticut: Archon Books, 1966.

William Elliot Griffis. *Millard Fillmore* (Abigail Fillmore). Ithaca: Andrews & Church, 1915.

Roy Franklin Nichols. *Franklin Pierce: Young Hickory of the Granite Hills* (Jane Pierce). Philadelphia: University of Pennsylvania Press, 1958.

Philip Shriver Klein. *President James Buchanan* (Harriet Lane). University Park, PA: Pennsylvania State University Press, 1963.

Justin and Linda Turner, eds. *Mary Todd Lincoln: Her Life and Letters.* New York: Alfred A. Knopf, 1972.

Robert W. Winston. *Andrew Johnson: Plebean and Patriot* (Eliza Johnson). New York: Henry Holt, 1928.

John Y. Simon, ed. *The Personal Memoirs of Julia Dent Grant.* New York: Putnam, 1975.

Emily Apt Geer. *First Lady: The Life of Lucy Webb Hayes.* (Kent, Ohio: Kent State University Press & Rutherford B. Hayes Presidential Center, 1984.

Allan Peskin. *Garfield* (Lucretia Garfield). Kent, Ohio: The Kent State University Press, 1978.

Thomas C. Reeves. *Gentleman Boss: The Life of Chester Alan Arthur* (Ellen Arthur). New York: Alfred A. Knopf, 1975.

Allan Nevins. *Grover Cleveland: A Study in Courage* (Frances Cleveland). New York: Dodd, Mead, 1933.

Harry Joseph Sievers. *Benjamin Harrison: Hoosier President* (Caroline Harrison). New York, Indianapolis: Bobbs-Merrill, 1968.

Margaret Leech. *In the Days of McKinley* (Ida McKinley). New York: Harper & Row, 1959.

Sylvia Morris. *Edith Carow Roosevelt: Portrait of a First Lady.* New York: Coward, McCann & Geoghegan, 1980.

Helen Herron Taft. *Recollections of Full Years.* New York: Dodd, Mead, 1914.

Frances Wright Saunders. *First Lady Between Two Worlds: Ellen Axson Wilson.* Chapel Hill: University of North Carolina Press, 1985.

Ishbel Ross. *Power With Grace: The Life Story of Mrs. Woodrow Wilson.* New York: Putnam, 1975.

Edith Bolling Wilson. *My Memoir.* New York: Bobbs-Merrill, 1938.

Francis Russell. *The Shadow of Blooming Grove: Warren G. Harding in His Times* (Florence Harding). New York: McGraw-Hill, 1968.

Ishbel Ross. *Grace Coolidge and Her Era.* New York: Dodd, Mead, 1962.

Helen Brenton Pryor. *Lou Henry Hoover: Gallant First Lady.* New York: Dodd, Mead, 1969.

Joseph P. Lash. *Eleanor and Franklin.* New York: W. W. Norton, 1971.

Eleanor Roosevelt. *Autobiography of Eleanor Roosevelt.* New York: Barnes & Noble Books, 1978.

Margaret Truman Daniel. *Bess Truman.* New York: Macmillan, 1986.

Dorothy Brandon. *Mamie Doud Eisenhower: A Portrait of a First Lady*. New York: Scribner's, 1954.

Mary V. Thayer. *Jacqueline Kennedy: The White House Years*. Boston: Houghton Mifflin, 1968.

Lady Bird Johnson. *A White House Diary*. New York: Holt, Rinehart & Winston, 1970.

Julie Nixon Eisenhower. *Pat Nixon: The Untold Story*. New York: Simon & Schuster, 1986.

Betty Ford. *The Times of My Life*. New York: Harper & Row, 1978.

Rosalynn Carter. *First Lady from Plains*. Boston: Houghton Mifflin, 1984.

Nancy Reagan. *My Turn: The Memoirs of Nancy Reagan*. New York: Random House, 1989.

Donnie Radcliffe. *Simply Barbara Bush*. New York: Warner Books, 1989.

1. CHERCHEZ LA FEMME

1. *Prologue*, Summer 1987, p. 118.
2. Jacqueline Onassis to author, through Nancy Tuckerman, Dec. 3, 1987, Dec. 8, 1989; *Look*, Jan. 2, 1962.
3. Author interview with Letitia Baldrige, Dec. 28, 1982; as quoted in Mary V. Thayer, *Jacqueline Kennedy: The White House Years* (Boston: Little, Brown, 1968), pp. 305–7.
4. Letitia Baldrige, *Diamonds and Diplomats* (Boston: Houghton Mifflin, 1968), p. 269; Bernard Boutin, Oral History Transcript (OHT), John F. Kennedy Library (JFKL); Perry Wolff, *A Tour of the White House with Mrs. John F. Kennedy* (New York: Doubleday, 1962), p. 51; author interview with James R. Ketchum, June 1988.
5. Jacqueline Kennedy remarks and letters as later quoted in Thayer, pp. 324–25, 347; as later quoted in J. B. West, *Upstairs at the White House: My Life with the First Ladies* (New York: Coward, McCann & Geoghegan, 1973), pp. 243, 247, 248; author interview with Letitia Baldrige, Dec. 28, 1982.
6. Benjamin C. Bradlee, *Conversations with Kennedy* (New York: W. W. Norton, 1975), p. 123; *Washington Post*, Dec. 22, 1987.
7. Pierre Salinger Papers, Box 101, Press Releases Jan. 1958–Nov. 1963, Series, Jan. 1961–Oct. 1963, "Press Releases of Mrs. Kennedy's Social Secretary" Folder, June 21, 1962, press release, JFKL; "White House Collection: Preliminary Catalogue Furniture, Furnishings, Fine Arts, Documents, Acquired 1961–Nov. 1964," courtesy of Jim Ketchum to author; Winzola McLendon, *Good Housekeeping*, July 1984.
8. Jacqueline Onassis to author, through Nancy Tuckerman, Dec. 3, 1987, and Dec. 8, 1989; Arthur M. Schlesinger Papers, Box W-7, Jacqueline Kennedy-1961 File, July 24, 1961, Jacqueline Kennedy-1962 File, Jacqueline Kennedy to Arthur Schlesinger, Feb. 21, 1963, April 3, 1963, JBK General file, Jacqueline Kennedy to Arthur Schlesinger, n.d., Box P-6, JFKL.
9. Jacqueline Onassis to author, through Nancy Tuckerman, Aug. 8, 1989;

Baldrige, p. 268; author interview with Letitia Baldrige, Dec. 28, 1982; author interview with James R. Ketchum, June 1988; Thayer, p. 217.

10. West, p. 200; author interview with James R. Ketchum, June 1988.

11. Jacqueline Onassis to author, through Lisa Drew, Aug. 1988; Pierre Salinger Papers, Box 101, Jan. 1958–Nov. 1963 Series, Jan. 1961–Oct. 1963, "Press Releases of Mrs. Kennedy's Social Secretary" Folder, Press Releases, Nov. 3, 1961, press release, JFKL.

12. Jacqueline Onassis to author, through Nancy Tuckerman, Dec. 3, 1987.

13. Baldrige, pp. 268, 270–71; author interview with Letitia Baldrige; Pamela Turnure to Pierre Salinger, Sept. 7, 1962, PP/5 folder, Box 705, White House Central Subject Files, JFKL.

14. Jacqueline Onassis to author through Nancy Tuckerman, Dec. 3, 1987, Dec. 8, 1989.

15. As later quoted in Arthur M. Schlesinger, A Thousand Days: John F. Kennedy In the White House (New York: Fawcett Premier Books, 1965), p. 671; Look, Jan. 2, 1962.

16. Jacqueline Onassis to author, through Nancy Tuckerman, Dec. 3, 1987, and through Lisa Drew, Aug. 1988; Ralph G. Martin, A Hero for Our Time: An Intimate Story of the Kennedy Years (New York: Fawcett Crest Books, 1983), p. 364; Marianne Means, The Woman in the White House (New York: Random House, 1963), p. 274.

17. August Heckscher, OHT, JFKL.

18. Arthur M. Schlesinger Papers, Box P-6, Jacqueline Kennedy-1961 File, Feb. 10, 1961, JFKL.

19. Martin, p. 364.

20. August Heckscher, OHT, JFKL.

21. Look, Jan. 2, 1962; Jacqueline Onassis to author through Nancy Tuckerman, Dec. 3, 1987; author conversation with Alice Longworth, Mar. 1976; author conversation with Mark Crosby, May 10, 1987.

22. Oleg Cassini, In My Own Fashion (New York: Simon & Schuster, 1987), pp. 305, 307, 310, 312–13, 315, 318; Mini Rhea, I Was Jacqueline Kennedy's Dressmaker (New York: Fleet Publishing, 1962), p. 308; Thayer, p. 176; Marilyn Bender, The Beautiful People (New York: Coward, McCann, & Geoghegan, 1967) pp. 44, 50–53, 241.

23. Thayer, pp. 178, 270; as quoted in Look, Jan. 28, 1964; Prologue, Summer 1987, p. 123; Hugh Sidey, John F. Kennedy, President (New York: Atheneum, 1964), pp. 53, 147–48, 152, 155; Gordon Langley Hall and Ann Pinchot, Jacqueline Kennedy: A Biography (New York: Frederick Fell, 1964), p. 241; Schlesinger, pp. 325, 328; Martin, p. 326; Birmingham, p. 103; Kathleen Bouvier, To Jack with Love: A Remembrance (New York: Zebra Books, 1979), pp. 300–304; William Manchester, Remembering Kennedy: One Brief Shining Moment (Boston: Little, Brown, 1983), pp. 185–86.

24. As later quoted in Hall and Pinchot, pp. 242, 255; Schlesinger, p. 342; White House Central Subject Files, Box 705, PP/5 folder, JFKL; Baldridge, p. 237.

25. As later quoted in Look, Jan. 28, 1964; Clifton Daniel, Lords, Ladies and Gentlemen: A Memoir (New York: Arbor House: 1984), p. 133; Thayer,

pp. 231, 236; as later quoted in Hall and Pinchot, p. 191; Means, pp. 267, 270.

26. Manchester, p. 144; West, pp. 208, 211, 214, 235; Joseph Karitas, OHT, JFKL.
27. Author interview with James R. Ketchum, June 1988; West, p. 202.
28. As later quoted in Sidey, pp. 231, 234.
29. *Prologue*, p. 118; Thayer, p. 235; Sidey, p. 39; Majorie Bair, *Jacqueline Kennedy in the White House* (New York: Paperback Library, 1963), pp. 48, 58; Martin, p. 358; Jacqueline Onassis to author, through Nancy Tuckerman, Dec. 8, 1989.
30. Means, pp. 268–269, 272.
31. As later quoted in Martin, p. 352.
32. Wade Nichols to Letitia Baldrige, Feb. 21, 1962, Box 706, PPF/Jacqueline Kennedy (General), White House Central Files, JFKL.
33. Bradlee, pp. 127, 196; *Prologue*, Summer 1987; as later quoted in McLendon, *Good Housekeeping*, July 1984.
34. Helen Thomas, *Dateline: The White House* (New York: Macmillan, 1975), p. 8.

2. "MADAM PRESIDENT"

1. Pam Turnure to John F. Kennedy, Feb. 26, 1962, Box 705, PP/5 folder, WH Central Subject Files, JFKL.
2. Jacqueline Kennedy to Pam Turnure, as later quoted in Thayer, pp. 33–34.
3. West, pp. 191, 256–57.
4. As later quoted in Thayer, p. 320.
5. Thayer, pp. 214–222; Baldrige, pp. 151, 159, 162–63, 166–68, 266; Hall and Pinchot, p. 201; WH Central Subject Files, Box 705, PP/5 folder, JFKL.
6. Manchester, p. 251; West, p. 220; author interview with James R. Ketchum, June 1988; Jacqueline Onassis to author, through Nancy Tuckerman, Dec. 8, 1989; Tazewell Shepard, *Man of the Sea* (New York: William Morrow, 1965), p. 123.
7. As later quoted in Sidey, p. 338; Schlesinger, pp. 616, 670; Bradlee, pp. 49, 158, 161, 186–87, 212.
8. Author interview with Letitia Baldrige, Dec. 28, 1982.
9. Author interview with James R. Ketchum, June 1988; author conversations with Molly Thayer, Nov. 1981, and Jan. 26, 1982.
10. Sidey, pp. 79–80; West, pp. 204–5, 238; author interview with J. B. West, May 4, 1980.
11. Edward Berube, OHT, JFKL; as quoted in *Look*, Jan. 28, 1964.
12. As later quoted in Red Gadney, *Kennedy* (New York: Holt, Rinehart & Winston), p. 54; *Jackie Kennedy: Her Fashions, Her Home, Her Words* (New York: Wykagyl Publications, 1961), no page numbers; *Sunday Boston Globe*, May 27, 1962; Bair, p. 38; *Look*, July 1961; Dean Acheson, OHT, JFKL; Nancy Dickerson, *Among Those Present* (New York: Random House, 1976), p. 65.

13. Martin, p. 313; Red Fay, *The Pleasure of His Company* (New York: Harper & Row: 1966), p. 187.
14. Author interview with Dave Powers, July 30, 1987; Nancy Tuckerman to Arthur Schlesinger July 23, 1963, Box P-6, Jacqueline Kennedy-1963 File, Arthur M. Schlesinger Papers, JFKL.
15. Jacqueline Kennedy notes during steel strike, April 12, 1962, KP44 Notes Folder, Box 42, Doodles 1962 Series, Personal Papers of JFK, JFKL; David McDonald, OHT, JFKL.
16. Martin, p. 360, and as later quoted, p. 298.
17. Schlesinger, p. 611; Bradlee, pp. 193–94, 230; Arthur M. Schlesinger, Jr., to author, March 16, 1984.
18. *Washington Post*, April 7, 1962.
19. As later quoted in Thayer, p. 153.
20. Manchester, pp. 156–57; Betty Ford, *The Times of My Life* (New York: Harper & Row, 1978), pp. 98–100.
21. Bradlee, p. 167; author interview with Letitia Baldrige, Dec. 28, 1982.
22. Bair, pp. 41, 56, 72–75; Baldrige, p. 243; *Prologue*, Summer 1987, p. 123; Martin, p. 476; Helen Thomas, p. 17.
23. Author interview with Letitia Baldrige, Dec. 28, 1982; author interview with Dave Powers, July 30, 1987.
24. Lincoln Gordon, OHT, JFKL; Adamson to USIA, Box 706, PP5/ Kennedy, Mrs. Jacqueline (General) Folder, White House Central Subjects Files, JFKL.
25. Charles Burrows, OHT, JFKL; Jacqueline Onassis to author, through Nancy Tuckerman, Dec. 8, 1989.
26. Photo, author's collection; Joseph P. Lash, *A World of Love; Eleanor Roosevelt and Her Friends, 1943–1962* (New York: McGraw-Hill, 1984), pp. 539–41; Eleanor Roosevelt to Jacqueline Kennedy, Dec. 1, 1960, and "My Day" column, May 29, 1962, as later quoted in Lash, *Eleanor: The Years Alone* (New York: W. W. Norton, 1972), pp. 320–21; as later quoted in Hall and Pinchot, pp. 225–26; Lawrence Fuchs, OHT, JFKL; author interview with Edna Gurewitsch, July 1988; author interview with Joseph Alsop, Mar. 9, 1988; as later quoted in Joseph P. Lash, *Life Was Meant to Be Lived* (New York: W. W. Norton, 1984), pp. 188–89.
27. White House Famous Names Collection, "Rog-Ror" File, Container 7, the Lyndon B. Johnsons to Eleanor Roosevelt, June 15, 1962, Lyndon Baines Johnson Library (LBJL).
28. As later quoted in Hall and Pinchot, p. 232; as later quoted in West, p. 255; *Look*, Jan. 2, 1962; Gadney, p. 126; Senate Wives Tribute to Lady Bird Johnson, 1966, Box C34, Katie Louchheim Papers, LC.
29. Ishbel Ross, *Power With Grace: The Life Story of Mrs. Woodrow Wilson* (New York: G. P. Putnam, 1975), pp. 328, 341–45; confidential source, April 5, 1987; *Washington Post*, Oct. 15, 1961; George McGovern to Margaret Brown, Dec. 6, 1961, and Dean Sayre to John F. Kennedy, Jan. 5, 1962, Box 22, and Edith Wilson correspondence with "your little Filipino boy," Box 65, Edith Bolling Wilson Papers, LC; Thayer, p. 29.
30. Margaret Truman, *Harry Truman* (New York: William Morrow, 1973), p. 627; Jhan Robbins, *Harry and Bess* (New York: G. P. Putnam, 1980), pp.

181–82; as later quoted in Hall and Pinchot, p. 229; David, p. 21; author interview with Barbara Eisenhower (Foltz), Oct. 22, 1983; author's collection; Arthur M. Schlesinger, Jr., *Robert Kennedy and His Times* (Boston: Houghton-Mifflin, 1968), pp.386–87.

3. ". . . GODDESS OF POWER"

1. Means, pp. 276–77; Jacqueline Kennedy to Bernard Boutin, March 6, 1962, courtesy of Mrs. Onassis to author.
2. As later quoted in *Look*, Jan. 28, 1964; Martin, p. 299; Sept. 24, 1962, Box P-6, Jacqueline Kennedy-1962 File, Arthur M. Schlesinger Papers, JFKL.
3. Bernard Boutin, OHT, JFKL; Sept. 26, 1962 & Oct. 17, 1962 press releases, Press Releases Jan. 1958–Nov. 1963 Series, Jan. 1961–Oct. 1963, "Press Releases of Mrs. Kennedy's Social Secretary" Folder, Box 101, Pierre Salinger Papers, JFKL; Martin, p. 299.
4. Bernard Boutin, OHT, JFKL; author notes from OEOB History Study Group, spring 1982; unpublished History of the Executive Office Building, Draft, Nov. 1963; Jacqueline Onassis to author, through Nancy Tuckerman, Dec. 3, 1987.
5. White House Famous Names, Mrs. John F. Kennedy 1962 File, Jacqueline Kennedy to Lyndon B. Johnson, Feb. 4, 1962, LBJL.
6. Jacqueline Onassis to author, through Nancy Tuckerman, Dec. 3, 1987, and Lisa Drew, Aug. 1988.
7. Jacqueline Onassis to author, through Nancy Tuckerman, Dec. 3, 1987; as later quoted in Thayer, p. 198.
8. Wolff, p. 238.
9. Wolff, pp. 106, 228; as later quoted in Thayer, p. 330; WH Central Files, Box 706, PPF/Jacqueline Kennedy (General), JFKL; *Prologue*, Summer 1987, pp. 123–24; Deputy Director of the USIA Donald M. Wilson to Pierre Salinger, June 21, 1962, Box 705, PP5/Kennedy, Jacqueline Folder, White House Central Subject Files, JFKL.
10. Newton Minow to Ken O'Donnell, April 20, 1962, Box 705, PP5/Kennedy, Jacqueline Folder, White House Central Subject Files, JFKL.
11. *Washington Post*, Mar. 17, 1985; Bair, pp. 76–77.
12. *Washington Post Magazine*, Mar. 10, 1985; *Washington Post*, April 7, 1962; Martin, p. 395; Baldridge, p. 260.
13. Martin, p. 367; Schlesinger, pp. 485, 490; Hall and Pinchot, p. 250; Box 706, PPF/Jacqueline Kennedy (General), Jay Gildner to Mrs. Otis Swainson, April 24, 1962, White House Central Files, JFKL.
14. John F. Kennedy to Jacqueline Kennedy, Mar. 16, 1962, Box 123, "Countries" Series, "Pakistan" folder, President's Office Files, JFKL.
15. Bair, pp. 81, 89; as later quoted in Irving Shulman, *Jackie! The Exploitation of the First Lady* (New York, Trident Press, 1970), p. 77; Bradlee, pp. 64, 69.
16. Pierre Salinger to Ken O'Donnell, Feb. 28, 1962, and Lyndon Johnson to Senator Mansfield, April 10, 1962, Box 705, PP5/Kennedy, Jacqueline (Executive) Folder, White House Central Subject Files, JFKL; Alex Drier,

ABC Community Network, Mar. 28, 1962, and JFK to Drier, Mar. 20, 1962, Box 705, PP5/Kennedy, Jacqueline (Executive) Folder, White House Central Subject Files, JFKL.

17. *Prologue*, Summer 1987, p. 123; Deputy Director of the USIA Donald M. Wilson to JFK, Oct. 17, 1962, Box 705, PP5/Kennedy, Jacqueline (Executive) Folder, White House Central Subject Files, JFKL; Shulman, p. 114.

18. Some photographs of Ravello trip appear in Bair, pp. 120–26; Jacqueline Onassis to author, Dec. 8, 1989.

19. Concerned Citizens of America Committee, PP5/JBK (General) Box 706, White House Central Files, JFKL.

20. As later quoted in Shulman, p. 93.

21. Shulman, pp. 15, 80, 82–83.

22. Means, p. 272; Box 706, PPF/Jacqueline Kennedy (General), White House Central Files, JFKL.

23. Mary Tobin to Pierre Salinger, Nov. 15, 1961, Box 706, PPF/Jacqueline Kennedy (General), White House Central Files, JFKL; Martin, p. 355; Bender, p. 83; *Prologue*, Summer 1987, p. 124.

24. Author interview with Letitia Baldridge, Dec. 28, 1982; *Washington Star*, Dec. 23, 1961, and AP wire to John F. Kennedy, through Pierre Salinger, Dec. 25, 1961, Box 10, Subject Files, Jacqueline Bouvier Kennedy Folder, White House Staff Files of Pierre E. G. Salinger, JFKL.

25. Letitia Baldrige to Pierre Salinger, Feb. 14, 1962, Box 705, PP5/Kennedy, Jacqueline (Executive) Folder, Box 706, PPF/Jacqueline Kennedy (General), Mrs. Westfall, Mrs. Jalliffe to Jacqueline Kennedy, Sam Kline comments on Jacqueline Kennedy, Mar. 11, 1962, Box 706, PPF/Jacqueline Kennedy (General), White House Central Subject Files, JFKL.

26. Letter of Feb. 24, 1961, Box 705, PP/5 folder, Pierre Salinger to Garth Cate, Sept. 5, 1962, Pierre Salinger to Duval Marine, Aug. 6, 1962, Pierre Salinger to H. V. Klinger, April 22, 1963, Lee White to Russell Egner, Mar. 11, 1963, Box 706, PPF/Jacqueline Kennedy (General), White House Central Files, JFKL; Ray-Ban advertisement, n.d., n.p., author's collection. Not only the president's wife but his daughter was exploited; in 1963 Rolton House Publishers came out with the *The Caroline Kennedy First Lady Dress-Up Book*.

27. Bradlee, p. 29.

28. Box P-6, Arthur Schlesinger letter draft memo to Hortense Burton, July 25, 1963, Jacqueline Kennedy General File, Arthur Schlesinger Papers, JFKL.

29. Emma Bugbee, "Eleanor Roosevelt: My Most Unforgettable Moment," *Reader's Digest*, Oct. 1963.

30. Peggy Whedon, *Always on Sunday* (New York: W. W. Norton, 1980), pp. 155–57.

31. Lash, *Eleanor: The Years Alone*, p. 328; author telephone interview with Edna Gurewitsch, July 1988; Lyndon B. Johnsons to Eleanor Roosevelt, Oct. 1, 1962, Mrs. Franklin D. Roosevelt Folder, Container 45, White House Famous Names Collection, LBJL.

32. Schlesinger, pp. 739, 744; Martin, p. 434; David F. Powers, Kenneth P.

O'Donnell, Joe McCarthy, *Johnny, We Hardly Knew Ye* (Boston: Little, Brown, 1970), pp. 18, 375–76; West, p. 262.

33. Press Releases Jan. 1958–Nov. 1963 Series, Jan. 1961–Oct. 1963, "Press Releases of Mrs. Kennedy's Social Secretary" Folder, Box 101, Pierre Salinger Papers, JFKL; August Heckscher, OHT, JFKL.

34. Martin, p. 470; Powers, O'Donnell, and McCarthy, pp. 396–97; Arthur M. Schlesinger, Jr., to author, March 16, 1984.

35. Lash, *Life Was Meant to Be Lived*, p. 195; Lash, *Eleanor, The Years Alone*, p. 331.

36. Lash, *Eleanor: The Years Alone*, p. 330; Emma Bugbee, "Eleanor Roosevelt: My Most Unforgettable Moment," *Reader's Digest*, Oct. 1963.

37. Edward P. Morgan, ed., *This I Believe* (New York: 1953), pp. 155–56; author interview with Edna Gurewitsch, July 1988; *St. Louis Post-Dispatch*, Nov. 13, 1962.

38. Eleanor Roosevelt, "My Day" column, May 29, 1962.

39. Means, p. 273.

40. *Look*, Oct. 31, 1967; Laurence Leamer, *Make-Believe: The Story of Nancy and Ronald Reagan* (New York: Harper & Row, 1983), p. 4, and Nancy Reagan as later quoted on p. 192; Julie Nixon Eisenhower, *Pat Nixon: The Untold Story* (New York: Simon & Schuster, 1986), p. 208.

41. Pat Nixon to author, through Julie Eisenhower, Aug. 2, 1988; Nancy Reagan and Pat Nixon first met during the 1960 campaign, Nancy Reagan to author, through Mary Gordon, Sep. 22, 1987; Eisenhower, *Pat Nixon*, pp. 205–14; Lester David, *The Lonely Lady of San Clemente: The Story of Pat Nixon* (New York: Thomas Y. Crowell, 1978), p. 124.

42. Photographs from June 22, 1962 of Jacqueline and Mamie Eisenhower, Audio-Visual Department, JFKL and Washingtonia Collection, Martin Luther King Library, Washington, D.C.; *Washington Post*, June 23, 1962; "The White House Collection: Preliminary Catalogue Furniture, Furnishings, Fine Arts, Documents, Acquired 1961–Nov. 1964" courtesy of Jim Ketchum to author.

43. Reel-to-reel tape, Audio-Visual Department, #85-877, JFKL.

44. Three items, Jacqueline Kennedy to Arthur Schlesinger, n.d. (1962), Arthur M. Schlesinger, Jr., Papers, Box W-7, Jacqueline Kennedy, 1962 Correspondence Folder (1) and (2), JFKL; as quoted in Thayer, pp. 294–300.

4. 1963

1. Author interview with J. B. West, April 5, 1980.

2. Thayer, pp. 169–72.

3. John Macy, OHT, JFKL.

4. April 1, 1962, Box 706, PPF/Jacqueline Kennedy (General), WH Central Files, JFKL; Jacqueline Onassis to author, through Nancy Tuckerman, Dec. 3, 1987.

5. Press release, Sept. 11, 1963, "Press Releases of Mrs. Kennedy's Social Secretary" Folder, Jan. 1961–Oct. 1963, Box 101, Press Releases Jan. 1958–Nov. 1963 Series, Pierre Salinger Papers, JFKL; Martin, p. 364.

6. Jacqueline Kennedy to Arthur Schlesinger, Jan. 17, 1963, Jacqueline Kennedy-1963 File, Box P-6, Arthur M. Schlesinger Papers, JFKL; *Look,* Jan. 28, 1964; Jacqueline Onassis to author, through Lisa Drew, Aug. 1988.

7. Bradlee, p. 192.

8. *Look,* Jan. 28, 1964; Jacqueline Onassis to author, through Nancy Tuckerman, December 8, 1989; Kay Halle, OHT, JFKL; as later quoted in Thayer, p. 185.

9. Belford Lawson, OHT, JFKL, and G. Mennen Williams, OHT, JFKL.

10. Roy Wilkins, OHT, JFKL; Charles Horsky, OHT, JFKL; Peter Lisagor, OHT, JFKL.

11. Rosalynn Carter, *First Lady from Plains* (Boston: Houghton Mifflin, 1984), pp. 49–50.

12. Author interview with J. B. West, April 5, 1980; author interview with Arthur M. Schlesinger, Jr., March 30, 1984; Schlesinger, p. 851; author interview with Dave Powers, July 30, 1987.

13. Bradlee, p. 215; Baldrige, p. 168.

14. Letitia Baldrige to Pierre Salinger, June 15, 1962, Jacqueline Kennedy statement of March 7, 1961, to *Women's Weekly* editor, PPF/Jacqueline Kennedy (General) Folder, Box 706, JFKL; Feb. 21, 1962, memo and March 15, 1963, memo for John F. Kennedy, Box 705, PP/5 Folder, White House Central Subject Files, JFKL; Thayer, pp. 179–81.

15. Powers, O'Donnell, and McCarthy, p. 413.

16. Nancy Tuckerman memo to author, Feb. 1985.

17. Lyndon Baines Johnsons to Jacqueline Kennedy, Aug. 22, 1963, White House Famous Names File, Mrs. John F. Kennedy File, 1963, LBJL; Jacqueline Kennedy to Arthur Schlesinger Aug. 26, 1963, Jacqueline Kennedy-1963 File, Box W-7, Arthur M. Schlesinger Papers, JFKL.

18. John F. Kennedy to doctors, Aug. 23, 1963, White House Central Subject Files, Box 705, PP/5 Folder, JFKL.

19. Fay, pp. 234–35; Martin, p. 493; Power, O'Donnell, and McCarthy, pp. 436–37.

20. Nancy Tuckerman in telephone response to author, Feb. 1988.

21. Bradlee, pp. 206–9.

22. Fay, pp. 162, 181–83.

23. Kenneth Burke, OHT, JFKL.

24. Martin, p. 497; Jacqueline Onassis to author, Dec. 8, 1989; *Philadelphia Bulletin,* Oct. 4, 1963; Nicolas Fraser, Philip Jacobsen, Mark Ottaway, and Lewis Chester, *Aristotle Onassis* (Philadelphia: J. B. Lippincott Company, 1977), pp. 246–47; Manchester, p. 259.

25. Martin, p. 498.

26. Manchester, pp. 227, 259–60.

27. Author interview with James R. Ketchum, June 1988.

28. Thayer, p. 120; Jacqueline Onassis to author, through Lisa Drew, Aug. 1988.

29. Charles Barlett, OHT, JFKL.

5. NOVEMBER 22

1. Martin, pp. 513, 527.
2. Powers, O'Donnell, and McCarthy, p. 23; Schlesinger, p. 935.
3. Goddard Lieberson, ed., *As We Remember Him* (New York: Atheneum, 1965), p. 106.
4. Powers, O'Donnell, and McCarthy, pp. 23, 25.
5. Saul Pett, Sid Moody, Hugh Mulligan, and Tom Henshaw, *The Torch Is Passed . . ."* (New York: Associated Press, 1963), pp. 7, 9; Lieberson, pp. 217, 222.
6. Lady Bird Johnson, *A White House Diary* (New York: Holt, Rhinehart & Winston, 1970), p. 4.
7. Author conversation with Barbara Eisenhower (Foltz), July, 1988; Pat Nixon to author, through Julie Eisenhower, June 1988; Betty Ford to author, through Ann Cullen, Sept. 1, 1988; Nancy Reagan to author, through Mary Gordon, Sept. 22, 1987; Barbara Bush to author, through Sondra Haley, May 30, 1989.
8. Powers, O'Donnell, and McCarthy, p. 31.
9. Lady Bird Johnson, p. 5; Powers, O'Donnell, and McCarthy, p. 35; Pett, Moody, Mulligan, and Henshaw, p. 15.
10. Pett, Moody, Mulligan, and Henshaw, p. 22; Maxine Cheshire, *Maxine Cheshire, Reporter* (Boston: Houghton Mifflin, 1978), p. 54.
11. Powers, O'Donnell, and McCarthy, p. 40.
12. Pett, Moody, Mulligan, and Henshaw, p. 23.

6. SYMBOL

1. Lady Bird Johnson, p. 6.
2. Author interview with Dave Powers, July 30, 1987.
3. Jacqueline Onassis to author, Dec. 3, 1989; Powers, O'Donnell, and McCarthy, pp. 42–44.
4. Nelson Pierce, OHT, JFKL; West, pp. 276–77; Pett, Moody, Mulligan, and Henshaw, p. 31; *Parade*, Dec. 1, 1963.
5. Lady Bird Johnson, pp. 7, 10; Betty Ford, p. 102.
6. John H. Davis, *The Kennedys* (New York: McGraw-Hill, 1984), p. 455; Jacqueline Onassis to author, Dec. 3, 1989.
7. As quoted in *Look*, Jan. 28, 1964.
8. Author interview with Milton Eisenhower, April 4, 1984; Margaret Truman, *Harry Truman*, p. 628.
9. Belford Lawson, OHT, Cordenia Thaxton, OHT, JFKL.
10. Richard M. Nixon, *Memoirs* (New York: Grosset & Dunlap, 1978), pp. 253–55.
11. Margaret Truman, *Harry Truman*, p. 628.
12. Betty Ford, p. 103.
13. Birmingham, p. 130; Jacqueline Onassis to author, through Nancy Tuckerman, Dec. 3, 1989; Betty Ford, p. 104.
14. As quoted in *Look* Jan. 28, 1964; Jacqueline Onassis to author, through Nancy Tuckerman, Dec. 3, 1989; Fraser, Jacobsen, Ottaway and Chester, pp. 247–48.

15. Davis, p. 538.
16. Richard Norton Smith, *An Uncommon Man: The Triumph of Herbert Hoover* (New York: Simon & Schuster, 1984), p. 426.
17. Bradlee, p. 244; *Look,* Jan. 28, 1964.
18. As later quoted in Lady Bird Johnson, p. 11.
19. Jacqueline Kennedy Onassis, Oral History Interview, LBJL.
20. Jacqueline Onassis to author, through Lisa Drew, Aug. 1988.
21. Jacqueline Kennedy to Lyndon B. Johnson, Oct. 22, 1964, October 26, 1964, May 16, 1964, Lyndon B. Johnson to Jacqueline Kennedy, Dec. 15, 1964, White House Famous Names Collection, Box 5, Mrs. John F. Kennedy-1964, LBJL; Jacqueline Kennedy Onassis, Oral History Interview, LBJL; Jacqueline Onassis to author, through Nancy Tuckerman, Dec. 3, 1989.
22. As later quoted in Hall and Pinchot, p. 263.
23. Jacqueline Onassis to author, through Nancy Tuckerman, Dec. 3, 1989; Thayer, p. 354.
24. Jacqueline Kennedy to Nikita Khrushchev, Dec. 1963.
25. Jacqueline Kennedy to Lady Bird Johnson, undated, Mrs. John F. Kennedy, 1963 File, White House Famous Names File, LBJL.

7. A CAN DO-ER

1. Lady Bird Johnson, pp. 152, 272, 315, 426, 691, 770; author interview with Lady Bird Johnson, Oct. 3, 1987.
2. As quoted in Merle Miller, *Lyndon: An Oral Biography* (New York: G. P. Putnam, 1980), pp. 351–52; Lady Bird Johnson, p. 276.
3. Lady Bird Johnson, pp. 178, 280, 273, 484; *USA Today,* April 16, 1984.
4. As later quoted by Eric Goldman, *The Tragedy of Lyndon Johnson* (New York: Dell, 1969), p. 437; author interview with Lady Bird Johnson, Oct. 3, 1987.
5. Assorted press releases of 1964 public-relations kit, "Whistlestop Tour" Folder, Oct. 13–16, 1964, Container 11, "Duties as First Lady" statement, n.d., "Duties as First Lady" Folder, Container 59, Subject File, Liz Carpenter Collection, LBJL.
6. West, p. 285; author interview with Scooter Miller, March 1982; author interview with Lynda Robb, July 30, 1988; Lady Bird Johnson, p. 317.
7. Author interview with Liz Carpenter, Oct. 4, 1987; author interview with Lynda Robb, July 30, 1988.
8. Lady Bird Johnson, pp. 161–62, 291–92, 710.
9. Author interview with Scooter Miller, March 1982; Barbara Howar, *Laughing All the Way,* (New York: Stein & Day, 1973), pp. 129, 118.
10. West, p. 295.
11. Author interview with Liz Carpenter, Oct. 4, 1987; Elizabeth Carpenter, *Ruffles and Flourishes* (New York: Doubleday, 1970), pp. 6, 10, 117; Goldman, p. 29; Whedon, p. 151.
12. Author interview with Liz Carpenter, Oct. 4, 1987; author conversation with Bess Abell, Sept. 9, 1988; Carpenter, pp. 121, 193.
13. Lady Bird Johnson, p. 327; assorted press releases of 1964, public-relations

kit, "Whistlestop Tour" Folder, Oct. 13–16, 1964, Container 11, Subject File, Liz Carpenter Collection, LBJL; author interview with Scooter Miller, March 1982; author interview with Liz Carpenter, Oct. 4, 1987.

14. Carpenter, pp. 303, 305.
15. East Wing press release, "First Lady's Success Formula: Political Instinct and Energy," Aug. 22, 1964; Thomas, p. 91; Lady Bird Johnson, pp. 266, 363.
16. Lady Bird Johnson, pp. 144, 149.
17. Assorted press releases of public-relations kit, "Whistlestop Tour" Folder, Oct. 13–16, 1964, Container 11, Subject File, Liz Carpenter Collection, LBJL; author interview with Liz Carpenter, Oct. 4, 1987.
18. Goldman, pp. 422–24.
19. Lady Bird Johnson, pp. 44–45, 218, 325; author interview with Scooter Miller, March 1982.
20. Thomas, p. 95; Goldman, p. 422.
21. Author interview with Lynda Robb, July 30, 1988; Goldman, p. 424; Lady Bird Johnson, pp. 52, 59; USA Today April 18, 1984; Washington Post, April 28, 1988.
22. Ishbel Ross, Sons of Adams, Daughters of Eve (New York: Harper & Row, 1968), p. 98; Lewis Gould, Lady Bird Johnson and the Environment (Lawrence, Kansas: University Press of Kansas, 1988), p. 32; Lady Bird Johnson, pp. 200, 202, 470, 587; Washington Post April 28, 1988.
23. Miller, pp. 354–55; author interview with Lynda Robb, July 30, 1988.
24. Lady Bird Johnson, p. 44; author interview with Liz Carpenter, Oct. 4, 1987.
25. Goldman, pp. 434–36; author interview with Liz Carpenter, Oct. 4, 1987.
26. Miller, pp. 352–54; Lady Bird Johnson, p. 17.
27. Author interview with Lynda Robb, July 30, 1988.
28. Lady Bird Johnson, pp. 99, 365.
29. East Wing press release, "First Lady's Success Formula: Political Instinct and Energy," Aug. 22, 1964.
30. Marcia Cohen, The Sisterhood: The Inside Story of the Woman's Movement and the Leaders Who Made It Happen (New York: Fawcett Columbine, 1988), pp. 130–31; assorted press releases of public-relations kit, "Whistlestop Tour" Folder, Oct. 13–16, 1964, Container 11, Subject File, Liz Carpenter Collection, LBJL.
31. Author interview with Liz Carpenter, Oct. 4, 1987.
32. Prologue, Summer 1987, Nancy Smith interview with Lady Bird Johnson, p. 138; Lady Bird Johnson, pp. 60–61, 126–27; author interview with James R. Ketchum, June 1988; West, p. 282; Jacqueline Kennedy Onassis, Oral History Interview, LBJL.
33. Lady Bird Johnson, pp. 73, 97–98; Prologue, Summer 1987, p. 117; Jacqueline Kennedy Onassis, Oral History Interview, LBJL.
34. Lady Bird Johnson, pp. 126–27, 170–71; San Francisco Examiner, Dec. 8, 1963. One afternoon, Mrs. Kennedy took her two children for a visit with former president Herbert Hoover, shortly before his death in 1964—see Richard Norton Smith, p. 426.

35. East Wing press release of June 30, 1965; Mrs. Johnson's speech, Oct. 30, 1965, "Project Head Start Ceremony" Folder, Container 16, Liz Carpenter Subject Files, LBJL; Lady Bird Johnson, pp. 35, 39–41, 59, 219.
36. Author interview with Lady Bird Johnson, Oct. 3, 1987; Gould, pp. 44–45; assorted press releases of public-relations kit, "Whistlestop Tour" Folder, Oct. 13–16, 1964, Container 11, Subject Files, Liz Carpenter Collection, LBJL.
37. Lady Bird Johnson, pp. 157, 138–40; as quoted in Richard Harwood and Haynes Johnson, Lyndon (New York: Praeger Press, 1973), p. 145; as quoted in Miller, p. 391.
38. Lady Bird Johnson, pp. 167, 250, 363–64; Goldman, p. 85; author interview with Liz Carpenter, Oct. 4, 1987.
39. Author interview with Liz Carpenter, Oct. 4, 1987; Chicago Defender, March 12, 1964.
40. Harwood and Johnson, p. 107; Lady Bird Johnson, pp. 115–16.
41. Author conversation with Julie Eisenhower, Jan. 30, 1989; Eisenhower, Pat Nixon, pp. 220–222; Betty Ford, pp. 117–18; Robert T. Harding and A. L. Holmes, Jacqueline Kennedy: A Woman for the World (New York: Encyclopedia Enterprises, 1966), pp. 110, 114–15.
42. Lady Bird Johnson, p. 188.
43. Miller, p. 393; Dickerson, p. 123; Goldman, pp. 234, 256; Lady Bird Johnson, p. 103.
44. Draft statement by Mrs. Johnson, Aug. 31, 1964, EX PP5/Lady Bird Johnson, Container 62, White House Central Files, LBJL, as quoted in Prologue, Summer 1987, p. 130.
45. Lady Bird Johnson, p. 197; Carpenter, p. 150; assorted press releases of public-relations kit, "Whistlestop Tour" Folder, Oct. 13–16, 1964, Container 11, Liz Carpenter Subject File, LBJL.
46. Author interview with Liz Carpenter, Oct. 4, 1987; Nancy Smith interview with Lady Bird Johnson, Prologue, Summer 1987, p. 139 and essay, p. 130; Goldman, p. 427; Carpenter, p. 147; Howar, p. 111.
47. Rosalynn Carter, pp. 53–57.
48. J. Evetts Haley, A Texan Looks at Lyndon (Canyon, Texas: Palo Duro Press, 1964), pp. 67–68; Associated Press report from Billingsley, Alabama, May 20, 1964.
49. Miller, p. 400.
50. Howar, p. 144; Goldman, p. 124.
51. Jacqueline Kennedy Onassis, Oral History Interview, LBJL.
52. Jacqueline Kennedy to Lyndon B. Johnson, Nov. 24, 1966, and n.d. (1966), Mrs. John F. Kennedy-1966 File, Box 5, White House Famous Names Collection, LBJL.

8. THE YELLOW ROSE

1. Lady Bird Johnson, pp. 368, 476, 384–85; Ross, pp. 99–100; Thomas, pp. 83, 86; Goldman, p. 285.
2. Lady Bird Johnson, Wildflowers Across America (New York: Abbeville Press and the National Wildflower Research Center, 1988) pp. 15–17; LBJ, p. 424.

3. Lady Bird Johnson, pp. 215, 234, 236–42.
4. Carpenter, pp. 231–32; Ross, p. 100.
5. Gould, pp. 68, 76, 82, 92, 99, 103.
6. Lady Bird Johnson, p. 249; Gould, pp. 107–20.
7. Gould, pp. 120–32, 134–35, 202; assorted press releases of public-relations kit, "Whistlestop Tour" Folder, Oct. 13–16, 1964, Container 11, Subject File, Liz Carpenter Collection, LBJL; Carpenter, p. 240–41.
8. Lady Bird Johnson's May 24, 1965, speech, the White House Conference on Natural Beauty Folder, Container 15, Subject Files, Liz Carpenter Collection, LBJL.
9. Gould, pp. 71, 212–16.
10. Liz Carpenter, pp. 226, 234; Johnson, pp. 479–80; Gould, pp. 217–20.
11. Gould, pp. 212–13.
12. Lady Bird Johnson, *Wildflowers Across America*, pp. 15–17, 264.
13. "Keep America Beautiful" Folder, Oct. 7, 1965, Container 18, Subject Files, Liz Carpenter Collection, LBJL; *Washington Post*, April 24, 1988.
14. Carpenter, pp. 242–43.
15. Author interview with Liz Carpenter, Oct. 4, 1987.
16. Johnson, pp. 323, 248, 264–65.
17. Goldman, pp. 539–44, 555, 567; Lady Bird Johnson, p. 287.
18. Author interview with Liz Carpenter, Oct. 4, 1987; author interview with Lady Bird Johnson, Oct. 3, 1987; Carpenter, p. 89.
19. Lady Bird Johnson, pp. 271, 377–80, 259, 346.
20. Carpenter, pp. 75, 214–15.
21. Carpenter, p. 76; Lady Bird Johnson, p. 15; *Prologue*, Summer 1987, Nancy Smith interview with Lady Bird Johnson, p. 138.
22. Assorted press releases of public-relations kit, "Whistlestop Tour" Folder, Oct. 13–16, 1964, Container 11, Subject File, Liz Carpenter Collection, LBJL; Gould, p. 73.
23. Lady Bird Johnson, pp. 37, 318, 336, 353, 42, 274, 283–84; author interview with Scooter Miller, March 1982; author interview with Liz Carpenter, Oct. 4, 1987.
24. Lady Bird Johnson, *Wildflowers Across America*, p. 17; Gould, p. 142; Gould, pp. 145, 146, 161; author interview with Liz Carpenter, Oct. 4, 1987; Carpenter, p. 244.
25. Author interview with Liz Carpenter, Oct. 4, 1987; Miller, p. 352; Gould, pp. 157, 159, 162–65, 174–75, 184–85, 190–91 (LBJ passed another 278 "significant" pieces of federal conservation beautification enactments.)
26. Gould, pp. 165, 181–83; File of Lady Bird Johnson cartoons, LBJL.
27. Shulman, p. 215.
28. Harding and Holmes, pp. 114–28; Bender, pp. 44, 53, 234; Jacqueline Onassis to author, through Lisa Drew, Aug. 1988; Mrs. Kennedy's Runnymede speech, n.d. (1965), Jacqueline Kennedy 1965 Correspondence File, Box W-7, Arthur Schlesinger Papers, JFKL; Jacqueline Kennedy to Lyndon Johnson, May 16, 1965, Mrs. John F. Kennedy 1965 File, Box 5, White House Famous Names Collection, LBJL.
29. Jacqueline Kennedy to Arthur Schlesinger, Nov. 23, 1965, Jacqueline Kennedy-1965 File, Box W-7, Arthur M. Schlesinger Papers, JFKL; Jac-

queline Kennedy Onassis, Oral History Interview, LBJL; Lyndon Johnson to Jacqueline Kennedy, Dec. 16, 1966, Mrs. John F. Kennedy-1966 File, Box 5, White House Famous Names Collection, LBJL.

30. Carpenter, p. 15; Lynda Robb to author, July 30, 1988; Lady Bird Johnson speech of July 30, 1964, Coffee for Presidential Task Force on Poverty File, Container 9, Liz Carpenter Subject Files, LBJL; Goldman, pp. 438–40.

31. Lady Bird Johnson, pp. 349, 351, 354; Women's Wear Daily, June 4–11, 1982; Lady Bird Johnson, pp. 358, 360, 362.

32. Harwood and Johnson, p. 123.

33. Author interview with Lynda Robb, July 30, 1988.

34. Lady Bird Johnson, pp. 328, 394, 173; Goldman, p. 115; as quoted in Thomas, pp. 98, 106.

35. Carpenter, p. 307; West, p. 349.

36. Lady Bird Johnson to Jacqueline Kennedy, n.d. (1966), and Jacqueline Kennedy to Lady Bird Johnson, n.d. (1966), Mrs. John F. Kennedy-1966 File, Box 5, White House Famous Names Collection, LBJL; Rex Scouten to author, Feb. 22, 1989.

37. Life, May 6, 1966; Bender, pp. 44, 53, 234.

38. Eisenhower, Pat Nixon, p. 225.

39. Letters between Lady Bird and Lyndon Johnson and Mamie Eisenhower through the 1960's and Mamie Doud Eisenhower to Lyndon B. Johnson, Sept. 28, 1966, are from Mamie Eisenhower Files in the White House Famous Names Collection, LBJL.

40. Nancy Reagan, Nancy (New York: William Morrow, 1981), pp. 147, 149–50, 152; Leamer, pp. 197–98, 214, 222; Michael Reagan, On the Outside Looking In (New York: Zebra Books, 1988), p. 96; People, May 23, 1988.

41. Nancy Reagan, Nancy, pp. 147, 149–50, 152; Leamer, pp. 197–98, 214, 222; Michael Reagan, p. 96.

42. Betty Ford, The Times of My Life, pp. 119–27, A Glad Awakening (New York: Doubleday, 1987), p. 36; Barbara Bush to author, through Sondra Haley, May 30, 1989.

43. Rosalynn Carter, pp. 57–65.

44. Nancy Reagan to author, through Mary Gordon, Sept. 22, 1987; Nancy Reagan, My Turn (New York: Simon & Schuster, 1989), p. 223; Lady Bird Johnson, p. 505; Leamer, pp. 214, 198; Ronald Reagan, An American Life (New York: Simon & Schuster, 1990), p. 187.

45. Nancy, pp. 175, 176; Leamer, p. 228.

46. Garry Wills, Reagan's America (New York: Penguin Books, 1980), p. 357; Leamer, pp. 198–202, 211, 232–33; Michael K. Deaver, Behind the Scenes (New York: William Morrow, 1987), pp. 38–39, 42.

47. Helene von Damm, At Reagan's Side (New York: Doubleday, 1989), pp. 69–72.

48. Wills, pp. 218–19, 359–60, 546–47; Deaver, p. 106; official press-release biography of Mrs. Ronald Reagan, wife of California governor, as quoted in Leamer, p. 227.

49. Lady Bird Johnson, pp. 266, 569, 587.

50. Lady Bird Johnson, pp. 189, 301, 321, 330, 364, 406, 470–71, 478.
51. Lady Bird Johnson, p. 456; letters to and from Mamie Eisenhower and the Lyndon Johnsons, 1964–1967, Mamie Eisenhower Files, White House Famous Names Collection, LBJL; author interview with Milton Eisenhower, April 1, 1984; Steve Neal, *The Eisenhowers* (Lawrence, Kansas: University of Kansas Press, 1984), p. 443; Ross, *Daughters of Eve*, p. 90.
52. Lady Bird Johnson, pp. 182, 312–14; correspondence between Bess Truman and Lady Bird Johnson, 1964–1968, Bess Truman File, White House Famous Names Collection, LBJL.
53. *New York Times*, Oct. 11, 1967, Nov. 4, 1967.
54. Carpenter, p. 64; Lady Bird Johnson, pp. 428, 430, 438.
55. Lady Bird Johnson, pp. 521–22, 556.
56. Thomas, p. 102; Jacqueline Kennedy to Lyndon Johnson, July 3, 1967, and Jacqueline Kennedy to Lady Bird Johnson, June 23, 1967, Mrs. John F. Kennedy-1967 File, Box 5, White House Famous Names File, LBJL.
57. Miller, p. 395; author interview with Lynda Robb, July 30, 1988; author interview with Scooter Miller, March 1982; Dickerson, p. 139; Lady Bird Johnson, pp. 70, 161, 347; Harwood and Johnson, p. 158.
58. Lady Bird Johnson, pp. 493, 134–37, 333, 285, 357, 695, 472.
59. Goldman, pp. 422, 391, 397; author interview with Liz Carpenter, Oct. 4, 1987; Dickerson, p. 136.
60. Lady Bird Johnson, pp. 515, 517, 575–82; author interview with Liz Carpenter, Oct. 4, 1987.
61. Nancy Smith interview with Lady Bird Johnson, *Prologue*, Summer 1987, p. 141.
62. Lady Bird Johnson, pp. 583–84, 588.
63. Lady Bird Johnson, pp. 201, 518–19, 573; Ross, p. 97.
64. Lady Bird Johnson, pp. 592–93; Jacqueline Kennedy to Lady Bird Johnson, n.d., circa Dec. 1967, Mrs. John F. Kennedy-1967 File, Box 5, White House Famous Names Collection, LBJL.

9. 1968

1. Lester David, *Lonely Lady*, p. 124; Eisenhower, *Pat Nixon*, pp. 230–33.
2. Simone Polaine memo to Bess Abell, "Biafran Children File," Box 59, Liz Carpenter Subject File, LBJL; "Remarks" transcript, Jan. 18, 1968; Liz Carpenter to Lady Bird Johnson, Jan. 19, 1968; Lady Bird Johnson to Mrs. E. D. Pearce, Jan. 27, 1968; "Women Do-ers," Jan. 18, 1968, Folder, Container 45, Subject Files, Liz Carpenter Collection, LBJL; combined transcribed remarks of White House and Eartha Kitt press conference, Los Angeles, CA, Jan. 20, 1968, and *Variety*, Jan. 24, 1968; *Washington Evening Star*, Jan. 20, 1968; author interview with Betty Ford, Nov. 3, 1983.
3. Lady Bird Johnson, pp. 625–28, 642, 637, 641; author interview with Lynda Robb, July 30, 1988; Thomas, p. 107.
4. Goldman, p. 606; author interview with Lynda Robb, July 30, 1988.
5. *Three Mothers: Their Life Stories* (New York: McFadden Publishers, 1968),

pp. 51–52; Schlesinger, *Robert Kennedy and His Times* (Boston: Houghton Mifflin, 1978), p. 857; Lady Bird Johnson, pp. 647–50.

6. Lady Bird Johnson, pp. 650, 659, 661; Leamer, p. 214.

7. Carpenter, pp. 238–39.

8. Lady Bird Johnson, p. 677; Mamie Eisenhower to Lady Bird Johnson, May 2, 1968, and May 23, 1968, Mamie Eisenhower Files, White House Famous Names Collection, LBJL; *Parade*, June 26, 1966; Barbara Walters interview with Mamie Eisenhower, 1970, DDEL Library; author interview with Barbara Eisenhower (Foltz), Oct. 22, 1983.

9. Lady Bird Johnson, pp. 679, 681, 684; author interview with Milton Eisenhower, April 1, 1984; Richard Nixon, p. 306; Lyndon and Lady Bird Johnson to Jacqueline Kennedy, and Jacqueline Kennedy to Lyndon and Lady Bird Johnson, n.d. (June 1968), Mrs. John F. Kennedy-1968 File, Box 5, White House Famous Names Collection, LBJL.

10. Lady Bird Johnson, pp. 699–700; David, *Ike and Mamie: The Story of the General and His Lady* (New York: G. P. Putnam, 1980) pp. 254–55; Eisenhower, *Special People* (New York: Simon & Schuster, 1977), pp. 190–91.

11. Betty Ford, p. 133; Richard Nixon, p. 312; Bill Boyarsky, *The Rise of Ronald Reagan* (New York: Random House, 1968), pp. 158–59, as later quoted in Wills, p. 347; Leamer, p. 215.

12. Richard Nixon, pp. 36, 108, 319; John D. Erlichman, *Witness to Power* (New York: Simon & Schuster, 1982), as quoted in *People*, n.d., clipping, author's collection; Eisenhower, *Pat Nixon*, pp. 234, 237–38, 243; Lady Bird Johnson, p. 703.

13. Lady Bird Johnson, p. 706; Lady Bird Johnson speech of Oct. 5, 1968, "Democratic Women's Clubs of Kentucky" Folder, Container 87, Liz Carpenter Subject Files, LBJL; Margaret Truman, *Bess W. Truman* (New York: Macmillan, 1986), p. 420.

14. As later quoted in Helen Thomas, p. 36; Norman Mailer, "Jackie, Prisoner of Celebrity," *Esquire* special edition, "Fifty Who Made a Difference"; Lady Bird Johnson, p. 725; author interview with Milton Eisenhower, April 1, 1984; memo to author from Nancy Tuckerman, Feb. 1985; Jacqueline Kennedy to Arthur Schlesinger, May 28, 1965, Jacqueline Kennedy 1965 Correspondence File, Box W-7, Arthur Schlesinger Papers, JFKL.

15. Lady Bird Johnson, pp. 734–35; Eisenhower, *Pat Nixon*, pp. 246–249; Richard Nixon, p. 334.

16. Lady Bird Johnson, pp. 725, 736–37, 741, 748, 753, 756, 767; author interview with Lady Bird Johnson, Oct. 3, 1987.

17. Material from "The Consumer Is You," Feb. 19, 1968, Women Do-ers Folder, Container 46, Subject Files, Liz Carpenter Collection, LBJL; Thomas, pp. 81, 89–90; Gould, pp. 222–24, 234; author interview with Liz Carpenter, Oct. 4, 1987.

18. Lady Bird Johnson, pp. 713–14, 748; Richard Nixon, pp. 366–67; West, p. 355; *The Inaugural Story*, editors of American Heritage Magazine and the 1969 Inaugural Book Committee (New York: American Heritage Publishing Company, 1969), pp. 91, 165; Eisenhower, *Pat Nixon*, pp. 250–52.

10. "BLESSED ALONENESS"

1. David, *Lonely Lady*, p. 136; Eisenhower, *Pat Nixon*, p. 255.
2. Richard Nixon, p. 1023.
3. *Ladies' Home Journal*, Feb. 1972; William Safire, *Before the Fall: An Inside View of the Pre-Watergate White House* (New York: Doubleday, 1975), p. 608; Eisenhower, *Pat Nixon*, pp. 324, 327; *New York Daily News*, April 12, 1973; author interview with Helen Smith, April 25, 1984; Traphes Bryant and Frances Leighton, *Dog Days at the White House: The Outrageous Memoirs of the Presidential Kennel Keeper* (New York: Macmillan, 1975), pp. 269, 277, 288, 321, 329.
4. *Washington Post*, Aug. 10, 1974; Thomas, pp. 156, 160; *Ladies' Home Journal*, Feb. 1972; Lester David, *Family Health Magazine*, Jan. 1973; West, p. 367; 1971 Virginia Sherwood interview with Pat Nixon, Nixon Archives Project; *Good Housekeeping*, Feb. 1971.
5. *Family Health Magazine*, Jan. 1973; Allen Drury, *Courage and Hesitation* (New York: Doubleday, 1971), p. 228; 1971 Virginia Sherwood interview with Pat Nixon, Nixon Archives Project; author interview with Patti Matson, Dec. 27, 1982.
6. Thomas, p. 165; 1971 Virginia Sherwood interview with Pat Nixon, Nixon Archives Project; Herbert G. Klein *Making It Perfectly Clear* (New York: Doubleday, 1980), p. 2; *Life*, Aug. 25, 1972; Paul Schmidt draft essay on Pat Nixon for *Prologue*, 1988.
7. 1971 Virginia Sherwood interview with Pat Nixon, Nixon Archives Project; Eisenhower, *Pat Nixon*, p. 284; Klein, p. 3; Safire, p. 607.
8. Eisenhower, *Pat Nixon*, p. 267; 1971 Virginia Sherwood interview with Pat Nixon, Nixon Archives Project.
9. As later quoted in David, p. 140; Thomas, p. 165.
10. 1971 Virginia Sherwood interview with Pat Nixon, Nixon Archives Project; Eisenhower, *Pat Nixon*, p. 262; author interview with Patti Matson, Dec. 27, 1982.
11. Klein, pp. 385–86; author interview with Connie Stuart, Mar. 22, 1985; Klein, p. 386; Helen Smith to author, Nov. 2, 1984; *Ladies' Home Journal*, Feb. 1972.
12. Drury, pp. 41, 231; as later quoted in David, p. 136; Eisenhower, *Pat Nixon*, p. 323; *Family Health Magazine*, Jan. 1973; 1971 Virginia Sherwood interview with Pat Nixon, Nixon Archives Project.
13. Richard Nixon, pp. 375–76; 1970 and 1979 Barbara Walters interview with Mamie Eisenhower, Dwight D. Eisenhower Library (DDEL); 1971 Virginia Sherwood interview with Pat Nixon, Nixon Archives Project; Teague, p. 194; Eisenhower, *Pat Nixon*, p. 278; Bryant, p. 266; West, pp. 364–65; Neal, p. 463; author interview with Milton Eisenhower, April 1, 1984; David, *Ike and Mamie*, p. 249.
14. As later quoted in *Washington Post*, Aug. 10, 1974; Thomas, p. 120.
15. Eisenhower, *Pat Nixon*, pp. 268–70, 272; Dickerson, pp. 163, 165, 167, 168; 1972 Fay Welles interview with Pat Nixon, Nixon Archives Project; Thomas, p. 134.
16. Drury, pp. 228, 235–36, 240, 244, 246; author interview with Connie Stuart, March 22, 1985; Thomas, pp. 145, 164; Bryant, p. 247, 253, 309;

Safire, p. 606, and Richard Nixon memo quoted, p. 607; 1971 Virginia Sherwood interview with Pat Nixon, Nixon Archives Project; *Ladies' Home Journal*, Feb. 1972; Richard Nixon to Rex Scouten, July 9, 1969, p. 36, Richard Nixon to Pat Nixon, Jan. 25, 1969, p. 11, all as reprinted in *From the President: Richard Nixon's Secret Files*, ed. Bruce Oudes (New York: Harper & Row, 1989); Julie Eisenhower interview with Barbara Walters, October 1986, *20/20*, ABC-TV; as later quoted in *Washington Post*, Aug. 10, 1974; Safire, pp. 607, 611; West, p. 357; Richard Nixon, p. 434; Eisenhower, *Pat Nixon*, pp. 278–79; David, p. 191.

11. "MRS. RN"

1. 1971 Virginia Sherwood interview with Pat Nixon, Nixon Archives Project; 1971 Virginia Sherwood interview with Pat Nixon, Nixon Archives Project; H. R. Haldeman to Lucy Winchester, Aug. 19, 1969, as reprinted in Oudes, p. 40; Richard Nixon to H. R. Haldeman, Sept. 22, 1969, p. 48; David, *Lonely Lady*, as later quoted, p. 128.
2. *Washington Post*, Aug. 10, 1974; as later quoted in Myra MacPherson, *The Power Lovers: An Intimate Look at Politics and Marriage* (New York: G. P. Putnam, 1975), p. 86; as quoted in Safire, p. 609; Aileen Mehle, "Richard Nixon: 'My Wife Pat,'" *Good Housekeeping*, Aug. 1982, p. 156; Klein, p. 3; *Spirit of '76*, official publication of the 1973 Presidential Inaugural Committee (Washington, D.C.: Presidential Inaugural Committee, 1973), p. 84; as later quoted in Thomas, p. 165; Drury, p. 235; *Ladies' Home Journal*, Feb. 1972; Barbara Walters interview with Julie Eisenhower, *20/20*, October 1984, ABC-TV; Thomas, p. 177; Safire, p. 623; Safire, p. 611; author interview with Donnie Radcliffe, April 12, 1989; Eisenhower, *Pat Nixon*, p. 272.
3. Peter Hay, *All the President's Women* (New York: Viking Press, 1988), p. 159; Safire, p. 608; RMN, p. 536; West, p. 365; *Spirit of '76*, p. 89; Eisenhower, *Pat Nixon*, p. 266; Thomas, p. 172; *U.S. News & World Report*, Aug. 2, 1971; author interview with Susan Porter Rose, Oct. 26, 1982; author interview with Connie Stuart, March 22, 1985; Pat Nixon's in-house, area, and domestic travel schedule, 1969–1974, courtesy of Helen Smith to author; Pat Nixon to author through Julie Eisenhower, April 19, 1989; Marie Smith, *Entertaining at the White House* (New York: McFadden, 1970), p. 282.
4. Eisenhower, *Pat Nixon*, pp. 276–77, 312, 345–46; 1971 Virginia Sherwood interview with Pat Nixon, Nixon Archives Project; as later quoted in Thomas, p. 171; Barbara Walters interview with Julie Eisenhower, *20/20*, October 1984, ABC-TV; Pat Nixon to author through Julie Eisenhower, June 1988; Klein, pp. 385, 387; author interview with Connie Stuart, March 22, 1985; Drury, p. 228.
5. Connie Stuart to Bob Haldeman, August 11, 1970, memo; Elise Kirk, *Music in the White House* (Urbana: University of Illinois Press, 1986), p. 319; Eisenhower, *Pat Nixon*, p. 321; 1971 Virginia Sherwood interview with Pat Nixon, Nixon Archives Project; as later quoted in David, p. 155; Pat Nixon's in-house, area, and domestic schedule, 1969–1974, courtesy of Helen Smith to author; *Ladies' Home Journal*, Feb. 1972.

6. Eisenhower, *Pat Nixon*, p. 296; *Washington Post*, Aug. 10, 1974; 1971 Virginia Sherwood interview with Pat Nixon, Nixon Archives Project; author interview with Connie Stuart, March 22, 1985; author interview with Patti Matson, Dec. 27, 1982; author notes from Conference on First Ladies, Gerald Ford Museum, April 1984; Safire, p. 608; Bryant, p. 247; *Ladies' Home Journal*, Feb. 1972; author interview with Helen Smith, April 25, 1984.

7. *Washington Post*, Aug. 10, 1974; Eisenhower, *Pat Nixon*, pp. 287, 290–91, 303; Richard Nixon to H. R. Haldeman, May 11, 1970, as reprinted in Oudes, pp. 125–26.

8. Eisenhower, *Pat Nixon*, pp. 281–82 as later quoted in David, p. 155; Barbara Eisenhower to author, Nov. 16, 1983; author interview with Patti Matson, Dec. 27, 1982; *New York Times*, Nov. 20, 1986; Safire, pp. 608, 611.

9. *Ladies' Home Journal*, Feb. 1972; Klein, p. 385; Thomas, pp. 155, 170, 172, 230; Dickerson, pp. 168, 183; Drury, pp. 29, 235; author interview with Helen Smith, April 25, 1984; author interview with Connie Stuart, March 22, 1985; Charles Ashman and Sheldon Engelmayer, *Martha: The Mouth that Roared* (New York: Berkley Medallion Books, 1973), pp. 99, 110; Eisenhower, *Pat Nixon*, p. 311; *McCall's*, Sept. 1970.

10. Thomas, p. 170; Helen Smith to author Nov. 2, 1984; H. R. Haldeman to Lucy Winchester, Nov. 20, 1970; Charles Colson to Haldeman, Feb. 1, 1971; Fred Fielding to Stephanie Wilson, July 9, 1971; H. R. Haldeman to Colonel Hughes, April 21, 1969, as reprinted in Oudes, pp. 25, 32, 173–74, 211, 291; Connie Stuart to H. R. Haldeman, Aug. 11, 1970 memo; John D. Erlichman, *Witness to Power* (New York: Simon & Schuster, 1982), as quoted in *People*, clipping, n.d., author's collection; David, pp. 164–66; Eisenhower, *Pat Nixon*, pp. 299, 362; Bryant, p. 325; Klein, p. 387; Henry Kissinger, *Years of Upheaval* (Boston: Little, Brown, 1980), p. 432.

11. Eisenhower, *Pat Nixon*, pp. 292–93; Thomas, pp. 172–73; as later quoted in David, p. 156; 1971 Virginia Sherwood interview with Pat Nixon, Nixon Archives Project.

12. *Spirit of '76*, pp. 83, 88; *The President's Trip to China* (New York: Bantam Books, 1972), p. 27; *Washington Post*, Aug. 10, 1974; Thomas, p. 166, and as later quoted in 159; *Life*, Aug. 25, 1972; Eisenhower, *Pat Nixon*, pp. 264, 283–84; author interview with Patti Matson, Dec. 27, 1982; 1971 Virginia Sherwood interview with Pat Nixon, Nixon Archives Project.

13. Author interview with Helen Smith, April 25, 1984; Kirk, pp. 317–18; 1971 Virginia Sherwood interview with Pat Nixon, Nixon Archives Project; David, pp. 128, 150–51; Drury, p. 43; Bryant, p. 305; author conversation with Helen Smith, March 30, 1989; Richard Nixon, pp. 534–35; Eisenhower, *Pat Nixon*, pp. 264–68, 303.

14. Kirk, p. 318; Eisenhower, *Pat Nixon*, pp. 264, 308–9; *Ladies' Home Journal*, Feb. 1972; Drury, p. 24; Jerrold M. Packard, *American Monarchy: A Social Guide to the Presidency* (New York: Delacorte Press, 1983), pp. 24–25; West, p. 359.

15. Author conversation with Edward Grover Platt, secretary of Kennedy

Center meetings, Sept. 12, 1987; *Life* magazines for Oct. and Nov. 1971; Eisenhower, *Pat Nixon*, pp. 309–310; West, pp. 359–60; Richard Nixon, p. 503; Eisenhower, *Pat Nixon*, pp. 309–310; Thomas, pp. 162–63.

16. *Ladies' Home Journal*, Feb. 1972; Eisenhower, *Special People*, pp. 204, 209; Neal, p. 464; Bryant, p. 266; James Edward Schaaf, *Mamie Doud Eisenhower and Her Chicken Farmer Cousin* (no date, photostat copies in author collection, original in LC), pp. 70–72; Eisenhower, *Pat Nixon*, p. 313.

17. Eisenhower, *Pat Nixon*, pp. 317–18; as later quoted in David, p. 155.

18. Nancy Reagan, *Nancy*, pp. 99, 130, 143, 172, 195–202; Leamer, pp. 200, 211, 239.

19. Barbara Walters interview with Julie Eisenhower, *20/20*, October 1984, ABC-TV; as later quoted in David, pp. 140–41; Marie Smith, p. 286; Kirk, pp. 327–28; Drury, pp. 34, 38; Bryant, pp. 299, 326; UPI 1969 photograph, author's collection; 1971 Virginia Sherwood interview with Pat Nixon, Nixon Archives Project; *Ladies' Home Journal*, Feb. 1972.

20. 1972 Fay Welles interview with Pat Nixon, Nixon Archives Project; *Ladies' Home Journal*, Feb. 1972; Eisenhower, *Pat Nixon*, pp. 300–301, 308, 321–22; 1971 Virginia Sherwood interview with Pat Nixon, Nixon Archives Project; as later quoted in David, pp. 153–54; Kissinger, p. 1130; author interview with Connie Stuart, March 22, 1985; author conversation with Helen Smith, April 25, 1984; for some West Wing attitudes on the women's movement, see Charles Colson to Ken Cole, Jan. 2, 1970, Charles Colson to Henry Kissinger, Feb. 1, 1972, as reprinted in Oudes, pp. 85, 363–64; "With Barbara," local Washington, D.C., television program, circa spring 1969, Nixon Archives Project.

21. Betty Ford, *Times of My Life*, p. 140; Betty Ford to author, through Ann Cullen, April 12, 1989; Rosalynn Carter, pp. 66–74; author interview with Rosalynn Carter, Sept. 12, 1984; *Ladies' Home Journal*, Feb. 1972.

12. THE BLITHE AMBASSADOR

1. Eisenhower, *Pat Nixon*, pp. 285, 299, 329–33; author interview with Helen Smith, April 25, 1984; 1972 Fay Welles interview with Pat Nixon, Nixon Archives Project; *Time*, Jan. 10, 1972; *New York Times*, n.d., Jan. 1972 (Helen Smith files); *Spirit of '76*, p. 84; Richard Nixon, p. 538; Dickerson, p. 160; 1971 Virginia Sherwood interview with Pat Nixon, Nixon Archives Project.

2. Author interview with Connie Stuart, March 22, 1985; *Ladies' Home Journal*, Feb. 1972; *Time*, March 6, 1972; Eisenhower, *Pat Nixon*, pp. 335–36; Judith Martin, *The Name on the White House Floor, and Other Anxieties of Our Time* (New York: Coward, McCann & Geoghegan, 1972), as later quoted in Hay, p. 29; as later quoted in essay by Helen Thomas (no single author) in *The President's Trip to China* (New York: Bantam Books, 1973), pp. 27–31; clipping files of Pat Nixon's trip to China, courtesy of Helen Smith.

3. Eisenhower, *Pat Nixon*, pp. 337–39, 341; *Ladies' Home Journal*, Feb. 1972;

Safire, p. 441; as quoted in Safire, p. 610; *Intelligencer-Journal,* June 3, 1972; *Spirit of '76,* pp. 84, 89; *Spokesman-Review,* June 20, 1972.

4. Eisenhower, *Pat Nixon,* p. 343; Dickerson, p. 162; *Spokesman-Review,* June 1, 1972; *Spirit of '76,* p. 88; *Life,* Aug. 25, 1972; Safire, p. 596; Doug Hallett to Charles Colson, Jan. 12, 1972, as reprinted in Oudes, p. 355; n.d., n.p., Helen Smith Files; Pat Nixon to author, through Julie Eisenhower, April 19, 1989.

5. Eisenhower, *Pat Nixon,* pp. 343, 346, 356–57; Pat Nixon to author, through Julie Eisenhower, April 19, 1989; *Washington Post,* April 30, 1989, and August 10, 1974; RMN to Haldeman, Jan. 28, 1972, Mar. 22, 1972, and Mar. 27, 1972, as reprinted in Oudes, pp. 359, 392–93, 398; RMN, p. 678; EL-VT-6 Audio-Visual Department, Video Tapes, DDE Library; David, p. 154; Thomas, p. 202.

6. As later quoted in David, pp. 166–67; Eisenhower, *Pat Nixon,* pp. 343–50, 394; RMN, p. 649, 654, 686–87; Margaret Truman, *Bess Truman,* pp. 426–27; *New York Times,* May 21, 1968, July 7, 1972, and Oct. 7, 1969; Betty Ford, *Times of My Life,* pp. 135–6, 139, 142, and *Glad Awakening,* pp. 34–7.

7. Eisenhower, *Pat Nixon,* pp. 354, 357; *Long Island Sunday Press,* Feb. 16, 1975; Robbins, p. 187; Henry Kissinger, *White House Years,* (Boston: Little, Brown, 1979), p. 1475; Cokie Roberts, "All Things Considered," National Public Radio Broadcast, April 28, 1988; Nixon memo of Jan. 23, 1973, as reprinted in Oudes, p. 578; *Washington Post,* Jan. 24, 1973; Dickerson, p. 156; Richard Nixon, p. 716.

8. Author interview with Barbara Eisenhower (Foltz), Oct. 22, 1983; author conversation with Armistead Maupin, March 16, 1989; Eisenhower, *Special People,* p. 188.

9. Eisenhower, *Pat Nixon,* pp. 344, 360–363, 366–69, 372–73; Richard Nixon, p. 867; Packard, p. 135; Safire, pp. 626–27; David, p. 163; author conversation with Helen Smith, March 30, 1989; Julie Eisenhower interview with Barbara Walters, *20/20,* ABC-TV, Oct. 1986.

10. Eisenhower, *Pat Nixon,* p. 384; Alexander P. Butterfield to H. R. Haldeman, July 8, 1971, as reprinted in Oudes, pp. 288–89; Dickerson, p. 204; Cheshire, p. 97; Thomas, p. 159; Thomas, p. 199; Eisenhower, *Pat Nixon,* pp. 367–77.

11. Eisenhower, *Pat Nixon,* pp. 319, 375–78, 387, 406; Richard Nixon, pp. 963, 385.

12. Betty Ford, pp. 144–48, 150–51; Richard Nixon, p. 927; *People* clipping, n.d., circa winter 1974, author's files; Rosalynn Carter, pp. 82–111; Eisenhower, *Pat Nixon,* pp. 397, 402; Daniel, p. 126.

13. 1974

1. Richard Nixon, p. 927; Eisenhower, *Pat Nixon,* pp. 397, 402; Klein, p. 386; David, pp. 168–69; as quoted in Thomas, p. 204.

2. Helen Smith to Ron Ziegler, Jan. 18, 1974; David, p. 169; author interview with Patti Matson, Dec. 27, 1982; Richard Nixon, p. 963; as later

quoted in *People*, May 27, 1974; author conversation with John Fitzgerald, April 3, 1989.

3. Eisenhower, *Pat Nixon*, pp. 402, 404; author conversation with Donnie Radcliffe, March 19, 1989; *Washington Post*, Aug. 10, 1974; as quoted in Thomas, p. 204; as later quoted in *People*, May 27, 1974; MacPherson, pp. 84–85.

4. David, p. 187; Eisenhower, *Pat Nixon*, p. 404; MacPherson, pp. 84–85; author conversation with Donnie Radcliffe, March 19, 1989.

5. Cheshire, pp. 92, 133; *People* magazine clipping by Barbara Wilkins, author's file, n.d., as later quoted in *People*, May 27, 1974; Ashman and Engelmayer, p. 186; Bryant, p. 256; author collection; Richard Nixon, p. 963; author interviews with Helen Smith, April 25, 1984, Oct. 1983, and March 30, 1989; *Washington Post*, Feb. 20, 1989; *Ladies' Home Journal*, Feb. 1972; Thomas, p. 160; Eisenhower, *Pat Nixon*, pp. 318, 392; author conversation with Julie Eisenhower, Jan. 29, 1989; author interview with Helen Smith, April 25, 1984; Theodore White, *Breach of Faith: The Fall of Richard Nixon* (New York: Atheneum, 1975), p. 95; *The Star* magazine, Dec. 21, 1976; confidential source to author regarding breakfast conversation with former White House servant, Feb. 9, 1988.

6. Eisenhower, *Pat Nixon*, pp. 407–10; David, *Pat Nixon*, p. 169; as later quoted in *People*, May 27, 1974.

7. As later quoted in *People*, May 27, 1974; author conversation with Helen Thomas, March 23, 1989; as later quoted in *Washington Post*, Aug. 10, 1974; author interview with Patti Matson, Dec. 27, 1982; Eisenhower, *Pat Nixon* interview with Barbara Walters, *20/20*, ABC-TV, Oct. 1984; David, pp. 169–70; Thomas, p. 203; Betty Ford, p. 152; MacPherson, p. 86; Woodward and Bernstein, *The Final Days*, p. 162.

8. Eisenhower, *Pat Nixon*, pp. 401, 412, 415–17, 452; Betty Ford, *Times of My Life*, p. 154; Thomas, pp. 217–18; Pat Nixon to author through Julie Eisenhower, April 19, 1989; *Parade* magazine clipping, Oct. 1985, author's collection; as quoted in David, p. 168; Richard Nixon, p. 1023.

9. As later quoted in *People*, May 27, 1974; interview with Patti Matson, Dec. 27, 1982; Woodward and Bernstein, p. 402; David, p. 181; Eisenhower, *Pat Nixon*, pp. 417–23; Donnie Radcliffe, *Simply Barbara Bush: A Portrait of America's Candid First Lady* (New York: Warner Books, 1989), p. 162.

10. Betty Ford, *Times*, p. 2; Eisenhower, *Pat Nixon*, p. 422; author interview with Barbara Eisenhower (Foltz), Oct. 22, 1983; author telephone interview with David Eisenhower, Oct. 18, 1987.

11. Richard Nixon, pp. 1080, 1084–85.

12. *New York Daily News*, Aug. 8, 1974, Aug. 9, 1974; Henry Kissinger, *Years of Upheaval* (Boston: Little, Brown, 1980), p. 1213; David, p. 185; Richard Nixon, pp. 1075, 1079, 1086–1087, 1089, 1090; Betty Ford, *Times*, pp. 2–4, 157; Betty Tilson, office of Lady Bird Johnson, to author, April 1989; Nancy Tuckerman, office of Jacqueline Onassis, to author, April 1989; Barbara Bush to author, May 18, 1989; Barbara Eisenhower (Foltz) to author, March 1989; Wendy Weber Toller, press office of Nancy Reagan, to author, June 1988; Madeline Edwards, office of Rosalynn Carter,

to author, Feb. 1989; Thomas, p. 225; author interview with Helen Smith, April 25, 1984; Pat Nixon to author, through Julie Eisenhower, April 19, 1989; Eisenhower, *Pat Nixon*, pp. 422–29, 461.

14. THE DANCER

1. MacPherson, p. 33; Barbara Bush to author, May 18, 1989; Betty Ford to author, through Anne Cullen, May 26, 1989.
2. Betty Ford, pp. 159–61; author notes from First Ladies Conference, April 1–4, 1984, Grand Rapids, Gerald R. Ford Museum (GRFM); Gerald terHorst, *Ford and the Future of the Presidency* (New York: Thord Press, 1974), pp. 199, 204; author interview with Betty Ford, Nov. 7, 1983.
3. Thomas, p. 274.
4. *Time*, July 28, 1975; Betty Ford, *Times* pp. 157–58, 179; *Newsweek*, Dec. 29, 1975; *Life* 1975 Special Report; Sheila Weidenfeld, *First Lady's Lady* (New York: G. P. Putnam, 1979), p. 146; author interview with Jack Ford, Nov. 11, 1983; author notes from First Ladies Conference, April 1–4, 1984, Grand Rapids, GRFM; author interview with Betty Ford, Nov. 7, 1983; MacPherson, p. 35.
5. Author notes from First Ladies Conference, April 1–4, 1984, Grand Rapids, GRFM; as later quoted in *Newsweek*, Dec. 29, 1975; author interview with Betty Ford, Nov. 7, 1983; Betty Ford, pp. 222, 229, 246; terHorst, p. 203.
6. Arden Davis, *Wives of the Presidents* (Maplewood, New Jersey: Hammond, 1972), p. 87; Sheila Weidenfeld, p. 131; Betty Ford, p. 226; *Vogue* clipping, n.d. (1975), author's files.
7. Betty Ford, *Times of My Life*, pp. 179, 269; Betty Ford, *Glad Awakening*, p. 38; Thomas, p. 279; MacPherson, p. 29; author notes from First Ladies Conference, April 1–4, 1984, Grand Rapids, GRFM; Sheila Weidenfeld, p. 38.
8. terHorst, pp. 193–94; MacPherson, p. 29; Kay Pullen Papers, Box 4, June 7, 1976, Gerald R. Ford Library (GRFL); author interview with Jack Ford, Nov. 8, 1983.
9. *People* magazine clipping, n.d. (1974), author's collection; *Newsweek*, Dec. 29, 1975; AP Wireservice photo and caption, *New York Daily News*, n.d., author's files; Betty Ford, *Times*, p. 241, 245, 260–61; *McCall's*, Sept. 1975.
10. *Newsweek*, Dec. 29, 1975; Dickerson, p. 233; Betty Ford, pp. 196, 228, 244.
11. terHorst, pp. 49, 201, 205–6; Betty Ford, pp. 39, 253, 264; Betty Ford, *Glad Awakening*, p. 39; *Newsweek*, Dec. 29, 1975; *New York Daily News*, Sept. 28, 1974; Thomas, p. 273; MacPherson pp. 28, 33–34.
12. Sheila Weidenfeld, pp. 43, 52, 57; *Time*, July 28, 1975; Betty Ford, *Times of My Life*, pp. 166, 174–77, 198–99; as later quoted in *Newsweek*, Dec. 29, 1975; Daniel, p. 127.
13. As later quoted in *Newsweek* Dec. 29, 1975; Betty Ford, *Times* pp. 164, 244; author interview with Betty Ford, Nov. 7, 1983; Thomas, p. 272;

Sheila Weidenfeld, pp. 92, 102; *Time*, July 28, 1975; as later quoted in *USA Today*, Aug. 18, 1983; author notes from First Ladies Conference, April 1–4, 1984, Grand Rapids, GRFM.

14. MacPherson, pp. 28–29; *Newsweek*, Dec. 29, 1975.

15. Betty Ford, *Times*, pp. 220, 260, 277; Dickerson, p. 233; Sheila Weidenfeld, p. 37; terHorst, p. 200; author notes from First Ladies Conference, April 1–4, 1984, Grand Rapids, GRFM.

16. Sheila Weidenfeld, pp. 29, 67–68, 95, 101, 403; author interview with Jack Ford, Nov. 8, 1983; as later quoted in *McCall's*, Jan. 1977; terHorst, pp. 203, 209.

17. Gerald Ford, *A Time to Heal* (New York: Harper & Row, 1979), pp. 190–93; *People* clipping, n.d. (1974), author's collection; Betty Ford, pp. 165, 182–87, 194; *Washington Post*, April 10, 1989; *Newsweek*, Dec. 29, 1975; MacPherson, pp. 29, 33; as quoted in *McCall's*, Dec. 1974, as later appearing in *Prologue*, pp. 145–46; Kay Pullen Papers, Box 3, Nov. 7, 1975, GRFL; *New York Times Magazine*, Dec. 4, 1974, as quoted in *Prologue*; Betty Ford, *Glad Awakening*, p. 126; author interview with Betty Ford, Nov. 7, 1983; as later quoted in *Good Housekeeping*, Nov. 1975; terHorst, p. 208; author interview with Jack Ford, Nov. 8, 1983.

18. Betty Ford, pp. 172, 197, 211, 264; as later quoted in *Good Housekeeping*, Nov. 1975; First Ladies Conference, April 1–4, 1984, Grand Rapids, GRFM; as later quoted in Hay, p. 98; MacPherson, p. 33; Sheila Weidenfeld, pp. 142, 168; Gerald Ford, pp. 207, 289, 376–77; *Newsweek*, Dec. 29, 1975; *People*, Dec. 1975 year-end issue.

19. terHorst, pp. 201–2; author interview with Jack Ford, Nov. 8, 1983; *USA Today*, Aug. 18, 1983; *People*, Dec. 1975 year-end issue; as later quoted in *Newsweek*, Dec. 29, 1975; *Time*, July 28, 1975; author interview with Betty Ford, Nov. 7, 1983; author notes from First Ladies Conference, April 1–4, 1984, Grand Rapids, GRFM: They spent hours together each night, she signing correspondence; *McCall's*, Jan. 1977; Betty Ford, pp. 201, 211.

20. terHorst, p. 197; Gerald Ford, p. 240; author interview with Jack Ford, Nov. 8, 1983; *Time*, July 28, 1975; *New York Daily News*, Nov. 14, 1975; Sheila Weidenfeld, pp. 216–17; as later quoted in *Newsweek*, Dec. 29, 1975; Betty Ford, p. 202; *People*, Dec. 1975 year-end issue.

21. *Vogue*, clipping, n.d. (1975), author's files; Chirdon/Porempka Papers, Nov. 20, 1975, Box 1, GRFL; 1983 Betty Ford, *Times*, p. 195; author interview with Jack Ford, Nov. 8, 1983.

22. Thomas, p. 276; Betty Ford, p. 181; *USA Today*, Aug. 18, 1983; author interview with Jack Ford, Nov. 8, 1983; Sheila Weidenfeld, pp. 40, 260; *People* magazine clipping, n.d. (1974), author's files; JNE, pp. 433–42; Pat Nixon to author, through Julie Eisenhower, April 19, 1989.

23. As later quoted in Frances Spatz Leighton, *The Search for the Real Nancy Reagan* (New York: Macmillan, 1988), pp. 114, 125; as later quoted in MacPherson, p. 49; *People*, Dec. 1975 year-end issue.

15. MS. PRESIDENT

1. Betty Ford, p. 202; Chidron/Porempka Papers, Boxes 1 and 3, August through November 1975 events, and Pullen Papers, Box 3, Sept. 26, 1975, and Oct. 25, 1975, GRFL.

2. *People* magazine clipping, n.d. (1976), author's collection; as recorded in Sheila Weidenfeld, pp. 81, 83, 85–87, 89–90, 92–93, 95–96, 101; as later quoted in *Newsweek*, Dec. 29, 1975; Betty Ford to all White House Staff memo, Feb. 6, 1975, White House Central Files, PP5-1, GRFL.

3. Author interview with Betty Ford, Nov. 7, 1983; Betty Ford, pp. 202–5; Weidenfeld Papers, Box 7, Women—ERA—Samples and Public Mail, GRFL, all as quoted in *Prologue*, pp. 147–48.

4. Sheila Weidenfeld, pp. 104, 147; Chirdon/Porempka Papers, Family-Oriented Response on ERA, GRFL.

5. Sheila Weidenfeld, pp. 353, 384; Chirdon/Porempka Papers, Box 1, Oct. 31, 1975, GRFL; Betty Ford, pp. 134–38, 205.

6. Betty Ford, pp. 208–9, 259; terHorst, p. 204; Sheila Weidenfeld, p. 50; Pullen Papers, Box 3, Oct. 10, 1975, May 22, 1976, GRFL.

7. Gerald Ford, p. 141; Sheila Weidenfeld, pp. 128, 136; Betty Ford, *Times of My Life*, pp. 228, 264; Kirk, p. 331; Davis, p. 86.

8. *People* magazine clipping, n.d. (1975), author's collection; Pullen Papers, Sept. 8, 1976, Box 4, Mar. 29, 1976, Box 3, GRFL; Betty Ford, pp. 228, 264.

9. Margaret Truman, *Bess Truman*, p. 429; Robbins, p. 189; Katie Louchheim to Bess Truman, Jan. 21, 1974, Katie Louchheim Papers, LC; Additional Memorabilia, 1972–1978, Post-White House materials, Mamie Doud Eisenhower Papers, Dwight D. Eisenhower Library (DDEL); author interview with Barbara Eisenhower (Foltz), Oct. 22, 1983; *Buffalo Evening News* clipping, Mamie Eisenhower obituary, n.d. (Nov. 1979); Wide World photo, *People* clipping, n.d. (1975), author's files; *New York Daily News*, Jan. 31, 1975; *Newsweek*, Sept. 29, 1975; *People*, n.d. (Spring/Summer 1979), author's files; *Ms.*, March 1979, p. 50, "Jacqueline Kennedy Onassis Talks About Working"; *People* magazine clipping, n.d. (1975), author's files.

10. Later quoted from combined sources from Mrs. Bush's Press "Round Table" Conference, Dec. 15, 1988.

11. Sheila Weidenfeld, p. 234; Betty Ford, *Times of My Life*, pp. 252–53.

12. *Time*, July 28, 1975; author notes from First Ladies Conference, April 1–4, 1984, Grand Rapids, GRFM; terHorst, p. 201; Betty Ford to author, through Anne Cullen, May 28, 1989.

13. Sheila Weidenfeld, pp. 110, 113, 129; *McCall's*, Sept. 1975.

14. Cheshire, pp. 177–84; Betty Ford, *Times of My Life*, p. 235.

15. Pullen Papers, May 20, 1975, Box 3, GRFL.

16. *Newsweek*, Dec. 29, 1975; Sheila Weidenfeld, pp. 161–62, 168, 172–74, 188; Betty Ford, pp. 205–07, 210; *People*, Dec. 1975 year-end issue; Gerald Ford, p. 307; Jules Witcover, *Marathon: The Pursuit of the Presidency, 1972–1976* (New York: Viking Press, 1977), p. 58; David Eisenhower interview, Oct. 18, 1988; as later quoted in Howard Norton,

Rosalynn: A Portrait (Plainfield, New Jersey: Logos International, 1977), p. 199; Chirdon/Porempka Papers, Nov. 19, 1975, Box 4, GRFL; "60 *Minutes* Bulk Mail Samples," White House Social Files and 60 *Minutes* interview with Betty Ford, Elizabeth O'Neill Papers, Box 1, GRFL, as quoted in *Prologue,* Summer 1987, pp. 150–52.

17. Dickerson, pp. 233–34; *People,* Dec. 1975 year-end issue; as later quoted in *Newsweek,* Dec. 29, 1975; author interview with Betty Ford, Nov. 7, 1983; author interview with Jack Ford Nov. 8, 1983; Betty Ford, p. 222; *People,* June 16, 1975.

18. Sheila Weidenfeld, pp. 220, 261, 279; Betty Ford, *Times of My Life,* p. 229; *People,* June 16, 1975, p. 9; Kirk, pp. 332–33; Betty Ford to author, through Ann Cullen, May 28, 1989.

19. Sheila Weidenfeld, p. 185; Betty Ford, *Times of My Life,* p. 255; *People,* Dec. 1975 year-end issue; Betty Ford to author, through Ann Cullen, May 28, 1989; as later quoted in *Newsweek,* Dec. 29, 1975; *People,* Dec. 1975 year-end issue; Thomas, p. 279.

20. Rosalynn Carter, pp. 113–28; Norton, pp. 59–61; as later quoted in *People,* n.d. (1976), author's files; *People,* Feb. 23, 1976, and May 23, 1988; Witcover, pp. 71–72; Betty Ford, *Times of My Life,* p. 256; Weidenfeld, p. 345; Nancy Reagan to author, through Mary Gordon, Sept. 22, 1987; Michael Reagan, pp. 143–44, 146–48; Helene von Damm, pp. 89–90; *Newsweek,* Dec. 29, 1975; Leamer, pp. 251–52; Joan Quigley, *"What Does Joan Say?"* (New York: Birch Lane Press, 1990), pp. 43–45; Nancy Reagan, *Nancy,* pp. 92–98; *Sacramento Union,* June 4, 1972, quoted in Leamer; Sheila Weidenfeld, pp. 357–58; Leighton, p. 160; Nancy Reagan, *My Turn,* pp. 184–85.

21. *New York* magazine, Feb. 23, 1976; *Newsweek,* Nov. 24, 1977, and clipping, n.d. (late seventies), author's files; James Elder to author, March 10, 1987; *People,* Dec. 1975 year-end issue; Barbara Bush to author, May 30, 1989; Sheila Weidenfeld, pp. 212–13; as later quoted from combined sources from Mrs. Bush's Press "Round Table" Conference, March 29, 1989; *People,* Nov. 21, 1988; Gerald Ford, pp. 337–38; Pullen Papers, June 23, 1975, Box 3, GRFL; author notes from First Ladies Conference, April 1–4, 1984, Grand Rapids, GRFM.

22. "Spouses Briefing" file, July 29, 1976, Box 4, Sept. 12, 1975, April 8, 1976, Box 3, Pullen Papers, GRFL; Chirdon/Porembka Papers, Box 8, GRFL; Sheila Weidenfeld, pp. 57, 140; George Eells and Stanley Musgrove, *Mae West* (New York: William Morrow, 1982), p. 285; *People,* June 16, 1975.

16. "REMEMBER THE LADIES!"

1. Gerald Ford, p. 187; Sheila Weidenfeld, pp. 42, 48, 49, 71, 417; *People* clipping, n.d. (1976), author's collection; Dickerson, p. 233; Betty Ford, pp. 172, 224, 203; *McCall's,* Sept. 1975; *People,* Dec. 1975 year-end issue; *Newsweek,* Dec. 29, 1975; author interview with Jack Ford, Nov. 8, 1983.

2. Sheila Weidenfeld, pp. 238, 272, 279, 306, 315–16, 329; author inter-

view with Jack Ford, Nov. 8, 1983; Betty Ford, *Times of My Life*, pp. 256–57; Pullen Papers, Feb. 1976, Box 3, June 18, 1976, Box 4, GRFL; *People*, Dec. 1975 year-end issue.

3. Nancy Reagan, *Nancy*, pp. 92–98, 130–34, 206; Leamer, p. 227; Leighton, pp. 115, 126.

4. Rosalynn Carter, pp. 128–134; Norton, p. 93.

5. Pullen Papers, March 11, 1976, March 20, 1976, Box 3, June 17, 1976, Aug. 17, 1976, Box 4, GRFL; fragment, unidentified, author's collection; Chirdon/Porembka Papers, April 1976, Box 7, GRFL.

6. Betty Ford, *Times of My Life*, pp. 213, 253, 264; Sheila Weidenfeld, pp. 235, 371.

7. Robbins, p. 190; Sheila Weidenfeld, p. 288; author interview with David Eisenhower, Oct. 18, 1987.

8. Nick Thimmesch, "Mamie Eisenhower at 80," *McCall's*, Oct. 1976.

9. *New York Times*, June 30, 1976; *Los Angeles Times*, June 30, 1976; UPI, June 30, 1976; "Remember the Ladies" File, June 29, 1976, June 24, 1976, Box 4, and April 14, 1976, Box 3, Pullen Papers, GRFL.

10. *People* clippings, n.d. (1974 and 1976), author's collection; Julie Eisenhower, *Pat Nixon*, pp. 444–51; quoted in *New York Daily News*, July 10, 1976; *New York Daily News*, July 14, 1976; Rosalynn Carter, pp. 136–37; as later quoted in Norton, pp. 101, 207; Lady Bird to Katie Louchheim, Aug. 16, 1976, File G3, Katie Louchheim Papers, Library of Congress.

11. Author interview with Jack Ford, Nov. 8, 1983; Betty Ford, *Times of My Life*, pp. 201, 258, 261–62; Diana McLellan, *Ear on Washington* (New York: Arbor House, 1982), as later quoted in Hay, p. 26; Sheila Weidenfeld, pp. 341–44; *Newsweek*, Aug. 30, 1976; Nancy Reagan, *Nancy*, pp. 205–7; Michael Reagan, p. 152; Gerald Ford, pp. 401, 403, 405; *USA Today*, Aug. 18, 1983; *McCall's*, Jan. 1977; Nancy Reagan, *My Turn*, pp. 194–95.

12. Pullen Papers, Feb. 18, 1976, Box 1, Oct. 14, 1976, Box 2, GRFL; *Ladies' Home Journal*, Jan. 1976; Betty Ford to author, through Ann Cullen, May 26, 1989; Betty Ford, *Times of My Life*, p. 211; *New York Times*, Oct. 15, 1976; *Washington Star*, Oct. 14, 1976; First Lady campaign buttons, author collection.

13. Witcover, pp. 580–81, 567–68; Sheila Weidenfeld, pp. 359, 366; as later quoted in Norton, p. 193; Rosalynn Carter, 138–40; author notes from First Ladies Conference, April 1–4, 1984, Grand Rapids, GRFM; *Ladies' Home Journal*, March 1979.

14. Sheila Weidenfeld, pp. 365–66; *People* magazine clipping, n.d. (1976), author's collection; Pullen Papers, Sept. 5, 1976, Sept. 7, 1976, Sept. 26, 1976, Oct. 10, 1976, Oct. 20, 1976, June 22, 1976, Box 4, GRFL.

15. Pullen Papers, April 4, 1976, May 27–28, 1976, Box 3, GRFL; Sheila Weidenfeld, pp. 284, 299, 306, 314–15; Betty Ford, p. 260.

16. Gerald Ford, p. 405; Betty Ford, pp. 263, 265; Witcover, p. 573; Norton, p. 94; *McCall's*, Jan. 1977; *Washington Post*, April 30, 1989; Sheila Weidenfeld, pp. 367, 369, 375, 380; Betty Ford to author, through Ann Cullen, May 26, 1989.

17. Betty Ford, *Times of My Life*, pp. 266, 270–73; Rosalynn Carter, p. 142; Sheila Weidenfeld, pp. 387, 389, 393; *New York Daily News*, Nov. 5, 1976; *New York Times*, Nov. 4, 1976.

18. Author notes from First Ladies Conference, April 14, 1984, Grand Rapids, GRFM; Sheila Weidenfeld, pp. 398, 400–4, 413; Gerald Ford, p. 439; Betty Ford, *Glad Awakening*, p. 39; author interview with Betty Ford, Nov. 7, 1983; *McCall's*, Jan. 1977.

19. Rosalynn Carter, pp. 1–2, 3, 7; Betty Ford, pp. 277–79; Betty Ford to author, through Ann Cullen, May 26, 1989 as later quoted in Leighton, p. 193; as later quoted in *People*, n.d. (1976), author's collection.

17. THE PARTNERSHIP

1. Quoted in Davis, p. 89; quoted in *Newsweek*, Jan. 24, 1977, and Nov. 5, 1979; Rosalynn Carter campaign booklet; Rosalynn Carter, pp. 147–48.

2. Rosalynn Carter, pp. 189–214; Norton, pp. 90–91; Pat Caddell to Jimmy Carter, July 30, 1977, "Memorandum: First Lady's Staff," Box 42, Jody Powell Files, WH Staff Office Files, Jimmy Carter Presidential Library quoted in Faye Lind Jensen, "'These Are Precious Years': The Papers of Rosalynn Carter," in *Modern First Ladies: Their Documentary Legacy*, compiled and edited by Nancy Kegan Smith and Mary C. Ryan (Washington, D.C.: National Archives and Records Administration, 1989), p. 146.

3. Author notes from First Ladies Conference, April 1–4, 1984, Grand Rapids, GRFM; Norton, p. 42, Norton, pp. 123–26; *New York Times*, Feb. 14, 1978; as later quoted in *People*, n.d. (1976), author's collection; Hedley Donovan, *Roosevelt to Reagan: A Reporter's Encounter with Nine Presidents* (New York: Harper & Row, 1985), pp. 242–43; *Newsweek*, Jan. 24, 1977; author interview with Joel Odum, May 30, 1989; author notes on visit with Mae West, Aug. 20, 1976; Leighton, p. 161; Jimmy Carter, *Keeping Faith* (New York: Bantam Books, 1982), p. 18.

4. Author notes from First Ladies Conference, April 1–4, 1984, Grand Rapids, GRFM; *Ladies' Home Journal*, March 1979; *Newsweek*, Jan. 24, 1977, Nov. 5, 1979; quoted in *Christian Science Monitor*, May 24, 1984; as later quoted in *People*, n.d. (1976), author's collection; quoted in Norton, p. 67; Donovan, p. 243; author interview with Rosalynn Carter, Sept. 12, 1984, quoted in Norton, x; Desmond Wilcox, *Americans* (New York: Delacorte Press, 1978), p. 338.

5. Jimmy Carter, p. 31; Rosalynn Carter campaign booklet; *Ladies' Home Journal*, March 1979; *Newsweek*, Nov. 5, 1979; Wilcox, pp. 335–38; Rosalynn Carter, pp. 164–65, 178; author notes from First Ladies Conference, April 1–4, 1984, Grand Rapids, GRFM.

6. Whedon, p. 153; *McCall's*, Jan. 1977; Wilcox, p. 338; Norton, pp. 68–69, 105–6; Rosalynn Carter, p. 179; as later quoted in *People*, Nov. 15, 1976, and n.d. (1977), author's collection; author interview with Mary Hoyt, Feb. 8, 1987.

7. Quoted in Norton, pp. 7, 67, 79, 103, 202–3, 218–20; Rosalynn Carter, p. 150; *Christian Science Monitor*, May 24, 1984; Wilcox, p. 341; author

interview with Joel Odum, May 30, 1989; Rosalynn Carter campaign booklet; quoted in Arden Davis, p. 88.

8. Rosalynn Carter campaign booklet; Georgia. *People*, n.d. (1976), author's collection; Rosalynn Carter, p. 153; author conversation with Diana McClellan, June 1981; Wilcox, p. 335; *U.S. News & World Report*, July 23, 1979; Norton, p. 130; *Newsweek*, Jan. 24, 1977.

9. Author interview with Rosalynn Carter, Sept. 12, 1984; Leighton, pp. 208–9; quoted in Norton, pp. 48–49, 100, 120; *People*, n.d. (1976), author's collection; Rosalynn Carter, pp. 154, 158, 173, 226, 305; Jimmy Carter, p. 24; as later quoted in *People*, Nov. 15, 1976; author telephone interview with Gretchen Poston, Dec. 24, 1985; Kirk, pp. 336–37; Norton, pp. 112–13.

10. Author interview with Rosalynn Carter, Sept. 12, 1984; Wilcox, pp. 333, 335; as later quoted in *People*, n.d. (1976), author's collection; *McCall's*, Jan. 1977; author notes from First Ladies Conference, April 1–4, 1984, Grand Rapids, GRFM; Rosalynn Carter speech, April 26, 1979, Box 44, Sarah Weddington's Files, White House Staff Office Files, Jimmy Carter Presidential Library, quoted in *Modern First Ladies*; quoted in Norton, pp. 71, 205; *New York Times*, Feb. 14, 1978.

11. Rosalynn Carter, pp. 161–62; Norton, p. 106; *New York Times*, Feb. 14, 1978; *Newsweek*, Nov. 5, 1979; Wilcox, p. 325; combined photos and captions, Rosalynn Carter, Activities File, *Washington Star* morgue, Martin Luther King Library; Jimmy Carter, p. 56; *Time*, Jan. 7, 1977; Norton, pp. 107, 217; Jimmy Carter, p. 57; *New York Times*, Feb. 14, 1978; Rosalynn Carter, p. 162; quoted in Norton, p. 13; quoted in Norton, p. 220; *McCall's*, Jan. 1977; author notes from First Ladies Conference, April 1–4, 1984, Grand Rapids, GRFM.

18. OFFICE OF THE FIRST LADY

1. Rosalynn Carter, p. 151; *New York Times*, Feb. 14, 1978; *Time*, Feb. 7, 1977; author interview with Mary Hoyt, Feb. 8, 1987; *Newsweek*, Nov. 5, 1979; author interview with Rosalynn Carter, Sept. 12, 1984.

2. Rosalynn Carter, pp. 166–68, 170–71; author interview with Rosalynn Carter, Sept. 12, 1984.

3. Quoted in Norton, p. 156; Rosalynn Carter, pp. 172–73, 218, 270–78; Rosalynn Carter speech to Washington Press Club, Sept. 15, 1977, Box 25, Records of President's Commission on Mental Health, RG 220, Jimmy Carter Presidential Library; Jimmy Carter Library and Museum, Atlanta, quoted in *Modern First Ladies*, p. 149; *W* magazine, Dec. 7–14, 1979; Rosalynn Carter, Activities File, *Washington Star* morgue, Martin Luther King Library.

4. Author interview with Rosalynn Carter, Sept. 12, 1984; Rosalynn Carter, pp. 172, 283–85; *New York Times*, Feb. 14, 1978; Norton, pp. 166–69.

5. Rosalynn Carter, pp. 169, 281–83; quoted in Norton, pp. 18, 21–22, 159, 160–64; as quoted in *Newsweek*, Nov. 5, 1979; in exhibit of "Partner to the President," Jimmy Carter Library and Museum, Atlanta, quoted in *Modern First Ladies*, p. 149.

6. Norton, pp. 37, 210, 216; *Newsweek*, Jan. 24, 1977, Nov. 5, 1979; *Modern First Ladies*, p. 151; *Washington Post*, Sept. 4, 1980; Kirk, p. 343; author interview with Joel Odum, May 30, 1989; *People*, Nov. 15, 1976, and as quoted in n.d. (1976), author's files; Rosalynn Carter, pp. 169, 221, 286, 289, 292–93; author interview with Rosalynn Carter, Sept. 12, 1984; Whedon, p. 154.

7. Jimmy Carter, p. 161; author interview with Lynda Robb; Kitty Carlisle Hart, *Kitty* (New York: St. Martin's Press, 1989), pp. 235–36; combined news clippings, n.d., *New York Times*, *New York Daily News*, *Washington Star*, *Washington Post*, 1977–1979, author's files; author diary, Aug. 1977.

8. Rose Kennedy, *Times to Remember* (New York: Doubleday, 1974), as quoted in *New York Times*, Feb. 19, 1974; *W*, June 4–11, 1982; *Washington Post*, Dec. 8, 1983; Barbara Walters *20/20* interview with Mamie Eisenhower, Nov. 1979, DDEL; quoted in *People* clipping, n.d. (late 1977–early 1978), and n.d. (1976), author's files; Merle Miller, *Plain Speaking: An Oral Biography of Harry S Truman* (New York: Berkley Medallion Books, 1974), p. 455; author interview with Milton Eisenhower, April 1, 1984; Julie Eisenhower, *Special People*, p. 213; David, p. 257–58.

9. Nancy Reagan, *Nancy*, pp. 95–97, 113, 212; Leamer, p. 261; Michael Reagan, pp. 162–63; Whedon, p. 153; Rosalynn Carter, pp. 305–6.

19. "MOST SPECIAL ADVISER TO THE PRESIDENT"

1. *Christian Science Monitor*, May 24, 1984; author interview with Rosalynn Carter, Sept. 12, 1984; Jack W. Germond and Jules Witcover, *Blue Smoke & Mirrors* (New York: Viking Press, 1981), p. 26; *Newsweek*, Aug. 6, 1979.

2. *New York Times*, Feb. 14, 1978; Rosalynn Carter, p. 154; *Newsweek*, Aug. 6, 1979; quoted in Norton, pp. 93, 216.

3. Jimmy Carter, pp. 32–34, 56, 134–35; quoted in Norton, pp. 95–96, 98–99, 207, 217–18; *Ladies' Home Journal*, March 1979; Wilcox, p. 49; *Newsweek*, Aug. 6, 1979, and Nov. 5, 1979; *Modern First Ladies*, p. 151; Donovan, p. 243; Rosalynn Carter to Jody Powell, n.d., attached to Madeline MacBean memo to Powell, Aug. 15, 1979, PP/5-1, Ex., Box PP-3, Subject File, White House Central Files, Jimmy Carter Presidential Library, quoted in *Modern First Ladies*, p. 150; author interview with Joel Odum, May 30, 1989; *New York Times*, Feb. 14, 1978; quoted in Arden Davis, p. 88; as later quoted in *People*, Nov. 15, 1976; author interview with Mary Hoyt, Feb. 8, 1987; Jimmy Carter, p. 222; quoted in Norton, p. 67.

4. Rosalynn Carter, pp. 174–76, 181; *New York Times*, Feb. 14, 1978; Jonathan Yardley review of "First Lady from Plains," *Washington Post Book Review*, April 1, 1984; author notes from First Ladies Conference, April 1–4, 1984, Grand Rapids, GRFM; quoted in *People*, Nov. 15, 1976; quoted in Norton, pp. 99–100; Wilcox, pp. 339–40, 345; *Chicago Sun-Times* photo, redistributed on AP, Jan. 21, 1979; author interview with

Mary Hoyt, Feb. 8, 1987; author interview with Rosalynn Carter, Sept. 12, 1984.

5. Betty Ford, *Glad Awakening*, pp. 8, 39–67; author interview with Betty Ford, Nov. 7, 1983; *People*, Mar. 26, 1979; David, pp. 21, 259; *Buffalo Evening News*, Nov. 19, 1978; *New York Daily News*, Nov. 13, 1978; Mamie Eisenhower to author, April 5, 1976; Barbara Walters interview with Mamie Eisenhower, *20/20*, Nov. 1979, DDEL; author interview with Rosalynn Carter, Sept. 12, 1984.

6. Jimmy Carter, pp. 171, 238–39, 302, 305, 316, 322; Rosalynn Carter, pp. 239, 245, 259–261, 308; Norton, p. 98; Wilcox, p. 326; *Newsweek*, Nov. 5, 1979; Dick Gardner to Jimmy Carter, May 11, 1979, PP/5-1 Ex., Box PP-3, Subject File, and Zbigniew Brzezinski to Jimmy Carter, Sept. 17, 1979, PP/5-1, Ex., Box PP-3, Subject File, White House Central Files, Jimmy Carter Presidential Library, as quoted in *Modern First Ladies*, Jimmy Carter Presidential Library; Rosalynn Carter, pp. 307–8.

7. *People* n.d. (March 1979), author's collection; *People*, March 26, 1979; Betty Ford, pp. 209–10, and *Glad Awakening*, pp. 72–76, 79–96.

8. *Newsweek*, Aug. 6, 1979, and Nov. 5, 1979; Jimmy Carter, p. 463; Germond and Witcover, pp. 26, 28, 29, 35, 39; Whedon, p. 154; Rosalynn Carter, pp. 164, 303–4.

9. Mamie Eisenhower to author, April 19, 1978, and June 4, 1977. *Buffalo Evening News*, Nov. 19, 1978; David, p. 260; author interview with Barbara Eisenhower, Oct. 22, 1983; author interview with Mary Jane McCaffree Monroe, May 31, 1988; Barbara Walters interview with Mamie Eisenhower, *20/20*, Nov. 1979, DDEL; Julie Eisenhower, *Special People*, pp. 210–13, 215–16; David Eisenhower, Oct. 18, 1987; David, p. 22; Julie Eisenhower, *Pat Nixon*, pp. 453–58.

10. Leamer, pp. 263–64; *People*, May 23, 1988; von Damm, pp. 99, 112.

11. Rosalynn Carter, pp. 291–300, 309, 311–14; author notes from First Ladies Conference, April 1–4, 1984, Grand Rapids, GRFM; *Modern First Ladies*, p. 149; Jimmy Carter, p. 462.

20. A TASTE FOR POWER

1. Rosalynn Carter, pp. 317–27; *Newsweek*, Nov. 5, 1979; Germond and Witcover, pp. 90, 164; Jimmy Carter, p. 478; Donovan, p. 301; *People*, March 17, 1980; Theodore H. White, *America in Search of Itself* (New York: Harper & Row, 1982), p. 298.

2. Author conversation with Donnie Radcliffe, May 30, 1989; Deaver, pp. 88–90; *New York Times Magazine*, Oct. 26, 1980; Germond and Witcover, pp. 132–38; author conversation with Jim Rosebush, April 10, 1987; quoted in Leamer, 271–73; Nancy Reagan, *Nancy*, pp. 152, 176; Leighton, p. 165; Nancy Reagan, *My Turn*, p. 206.

3. Quoted in Leamer, p. 274; Betty Ford, *Glad Awakening*, pp. 96–97, 99; network news coverage of 1980 Republican convention, author's notes; Leighton, p. 150; Deaver, p. 174; Germond and Witcover, pp. 170, 171; Nancy Reagan, *My Turn*, pp. 211, 212.

4. Jimmy Carter, pp. 533, 544, 551; Germond and Witcover, pp. 204, 221–22; Rosalynn Carter, pp. 330–333; Nancy Reagan, *My Turn*, p. 219; *Miami Herald*, Oct. 19, 1982; Margaret Truman, *Bess Truman*, p. 429; Robbins, p. 190; Katie Louchheim draft of "The Boss," pp. 3, 4, Box B3, Katie Louchheim Papers, LC; author interview with Jane Lingo, Nov. 22, 1982; author conversation with Betty Monkman, April 6, 1987.

5. Rosalynn Carter, p. 279; *Modern First Ladies*, p. 148; *New York Times*, Feb. 14, 1978; *Newsweek*, Nov. 5, 1979; *New York Times*, Feb. 14, 1978; author interview with Rosalynn Carter, Sept. 12, 1984.

6. Author's collection; *U.S. News & World Report*, Oct. 20, 1980; *New York Times*, May 19, 1980.

7. *U.S. News & World Report*, Oct. 20, 1980; *New York Times*, May 19, 1980; quoted in *Washington Post*, Nov. 21, 1980, reprint of the *Los Angeles Herald Examiner*, Wanda McDaniel, "Nancy Reagan"; *Washington Post*, Nov. 21, 1980; author's collection; Leighton, pp. 152, 155; *Washington Star* clipping, n.d. (mid-October, 1980), author's files; Michael Reagan, p. 177; Nancy Reagan, *Nancy*, p. 215; quoted in *People*, Nov. 17, 1980.

8. Quigley, p. 62; Germond and Witcover, pp. 268, 304; Rosalynn Carter, pp. 337–40; quoted in Leighton, p. 171; Rosalynn Carter, pp. 342, 357; *Boston Herald American*, Feb. 15, 1980.

21. RETRO ROMANTICISM

1. Jimmy Carter, p. 574; *Newsweek*, Nov. 5, 1979; Rosalynn Carter, p. 144; Nancy Reagan, *Nancy*, p. 216; quoted in Leighton, p. 183; Leamer, p. 286; *Washington Post*, Nov. 21, 1980; Nancy Reagan, *My Turn*, pp. 224–25.

2. *Washington Post*, Nov. 21, 1980, and Dec. 12, 1980; all quoted in *Washington Post*, Nov. 11, 1980, reprint of the *Los Angeles Herald Examiner*, Wanda McDaniel, "Nancy Reagan," quoted in *People*, Nov. 17, 1980.

3. Sidney Zion, *The Autobiography of Roy Cohn* (Secaucus, New Jersey: Lyle Stuart, 1988), as quoted in *New York*, Feb. 22, 1988; *W*, Jan. 2–9, 1981; Deaver, pp. 82–83; quoted in *Newsweek*, Nov. 17, 1980; *Washington Post*, Nov. 7, 1980; *New York Times* clipping, n.d. (December 1980), author's files; author diary notes while on 1981 Inaugural Committee, Dec. 15–19, 1980.

4. *New York Times* clipping, n.d. (December 1980), author's files; *Washington Post*, Nov. 21, 1980; *People*, Nov. 17, 1980; Leamer, p. 279, Leighton, p. 161.

5. Quoted in Kirk, p. 347; Leamer, pp. 1–18; *A Great New Beginning: The 1981 Presidential Inaugural Book* (Washington, D.C.: 1981 Inaugural Committee, 1981); *W*, Jan. 2–9, 1981; author diary notes while on 1981 Inaugural Committee, Jan. 20–22, 1981.

6. Quoted in Leamer, p. 13; Rosalynn Carter, pp. 347–52; Patti Davis with Maureen Strange Foster, *Homefront* (New York: Crown, 1986), p. 2; *W*, Jan. 2–9, 1981; Nancy Reagan, *My Turn*, pp. 231–36.

7. Quoted in Leamer, pp. 3, 19; Deborah Silverman, *Selling Culture* (New York: Pantheon Books, 1986), pp. 41–43.

22. "QUEEN NANCY"

1. Ted Graber book quoted in Leamer, p. 290; quoted in Chris Wallace, *First Lady: A Portrait of Nancy Reagan* (New York: St. Martin's Press, 1986), pp. 74, 81; Frances Spatz Leighton, *The Search for the Real Nancy Reagan* (New York: Macmillan, 1987), p. 203; Nancy Reagan speech, May 4, 1987; Eric Michael to author, Sept. 2, 1989; Nancy Reagan, *My Turn*, pp. 246, 248.

2. Quoted in Leamer, p. 296; *New Republic*, Sept. 16–23, 1985; Leighton, p. 240; *Star*, Aug. 6, 1985; "Mrs. R.'s R&R" by James A. Miller, *Life* clipping, Summer, 1984, author's collection; *Washington Post*, May 6, 1986, and Feb. 11, 1986.

3. Wallace, pp. 13, 23, 121–25; Deaver, pp. 21, 23, 25; Donald T. Regan, *For the Record: From Wall Street to Washington* (New York: Harcourt, Brace & Jovanovich, 1988), pp. 3–4; Leamer, pp. 318, 322; von Damm, p. 195; Leighton, p. 248; *People*, May 23, 1988; *Washington Post*, Oct. 24, 1983; author notes, Washington, D.C., April 1–April 7 and late September 1981; *U.S. News & World Report*, June 1, 1981; Sidney Zion, *The Autobiography of Roy Cohn* (Secaucus, New Jersey: Lyle Stuart, 1988), as quoted in *New York*, Feb. 22, 1988; Ronald Reagan, p. 261; *People*, "The Eighties," Fall 1989.

4. Leamer, pp. 334, 339–42; Quigley, pp. 32, 33; *New York Times*, Oct. 13, 1981; Leighton, p. 275; *U.S. News & World Report*, June 1, 1981; *People*, "The Eighties," Fall 1989.

5. Larry Speakes, *Speaking Out: Inside the Reagan White House* (New York: Scribner's, 1988), p. 96; Leamer, p. 332; *Washington Post* clipping, n.d., author's collection; *U.S. News & World Report*, June 1, 1981; author conversation with Betty Monkman, Aug. 1, 1989; *Newsweek*, Dec. 21, 1981; Ronald Reagan, p. 388.

6. *U.S. News & World Report*, June 1, 1981; Silverman, pp. 19, 64.

7. Satire material and cartoons, author's collection; Speakes, p. 251.

8. Author conversation with Byron Kennard, July 15, 1989; Leamer, p. 299; *Washington Post*, Nov. 1, 1988, Oct. 1981, n.d., author's collection, and Feb. 17, 1986; *People*, Nov. 21, 1988; quoted in *Life*, Oct. 1988; Radcliffe, pp. 177, 179, 181, 183; Robbins, p. 191; Truman, *Bess Truman*, p. 429; *Miami Herald*, Oct. 19, 1982; Jimmy Carter, pp. 270, 271; Eisenhower, *Pat Nixon*, pp. 458–59; *USA Today*, Aug. 18, 1983; *W* magazine, June 4–11, 1982; Wallace, pp. 71, 76; author conversation with Anne Cullen of Mrs. Ford's office, July 23, 1989.

9. *Washington Star*, Mar. 4, 1981; Leamer, p. 334; *Washington Post*, Nov. 10, 1981; White House press release, Dec. 4, 1981.

10. *Washington Post*, Nov. 27–29, 1981, Dec. 17, 1981, and Dec. 8, 1981; Wallace, pp. 57, 75; as later quoted in *New Republic*, Sept. 16–23, 1985; Leamer, p. 353; *Los Angeles Times*, Mar. 22, 1987, Nov. 13, 1987, Nov. 13, 1988, and *Washington Post* June 13, 1984; *New York Times*, Oct. 13, 1981; *The Private Eye* column, unidentified woman's magazine, 1982 (author's collection); *Newsweek*, Dec. 21, 1981.

11. *Washington Post*, Jan. 22, 1982, Feb. 6, 1982, Jan. 23, 1983, and Nina

Hyde story, Jan. 1981, n.d., author's collection; quoted in *Newsweek*, Dec. 21, 1981; *Los Angeles Times*, March 22, 1987; Leamer, p. 357; Associated Press story by Maureen Santini, n.d., Fall 1981, author's collection; *Newsweek*, Feb. 1, 1982; *Washington Dossier*, March 1981; Smithsonian press release, Nov. 4, 1981; Quigley, pp. 24, 27, 28, 30, 36, 176; author's diary notes, Nov. 6, 1981, and Jan. 25, 1982.

12. As later quoted in *New Republic*, Sept. 16–23, 1985; James S. Rosebush, *First Lady: Public Wife* (Lanham, Md.: Madison Books, 1988), p. 44; *Washington Post*, Feb. 17, 1982, and March 29, 1982.

13. Rosebush, pp. 63, 64; *Washington Post*, June 9, 1982, and Aug. 7, 1982; Speakes, p. 94; Leamer, p. 368.

14. Rosebush, pp. 41, 89; Deaver, pp. 111, 120; Wallace, p. 147; *Washington Post*, Jan. 23, 1983.

15. *Philadelphia Enquirer*, Oct. 19, 1982; draft of "The Boss," p. 2, Box B3, Katie Louchheim Papers; Daniel, p. 134; author interview with Letitia Baldridge, Dec. 28, 1982; *Washington Post*, n.d., author's collection; author interview with Scooter Miller, March 1982; author interview with Liz Carpenter, Oct. 4, 1987; *Parade*, June 3, 1984; *Ebony*, Sept. 1989; *Washington Post Magazine*, May 14, 1989; Betty Ford, *Glad Awakening*, pp. 114, 115; Barbara Bush to author, June 16, 1989; author interview with Betty Ford, Nov. 7, 1983; author interview with Rosalynn Carter, Sept. 12, 1984.

16. *Washington Post*, Fall 1982 clipping from "Washington Ways" column (n.d.), author's collection, and Jan. 23, 1983.

23. PICTURE PERFECT

1. Chicago Girls' Latin School Yearbook, 1939; *Fortune*, Sept. 1986; *Globe*, Aug. 9, 1983; Speakes, p. 92; *Washington Post*, Feb. 27, 1987; *Los Angeles Times*, Nov. 13, 1988; Wallace, pp. 35–36; von Damm, p. 72; Nancy Reagan speech, May 4, 1987; Nancy Reagan, *My Turn*, pp. 107, 108, 110, 117; Ronald Reagan, pp. 123, 124, 167, 184, 380, 389, 536.

2. Wills, pp. 214, 225; Deaver, pp. 33, 98, 108; Speakes, pp. 239, 249; "Mrs. R's R&R" by James A. Miller, *Life* clipping, Summer 1984, author's collection; *W* magazine, June 4–11, 1982.

3. Deaver, pp. 112, 121; Wallace, pp. v., 33.

4. Michael Reagan, p. 228.

5. Deaver, p. 39; Wallace, p. 40; *Washington Post*, Feb. 27, 1987.

6. Wallace, pp. 18, 24–25, 30–31, 40; *Washington Post*, Aug. 22, 1984.

7. Rosebush, pp. 46–47; Nancy Reagan speeches, March 1, 1982, April 15, 1982, and Oct. 1985; *Time*, Jan. 14, 1985.

8. Von Damm, p. 186; *Washington Post*, Jan. 23, 1983, Oct. 24, 1983, and Feb. 4, 1986; copy East Wing Press Office memo, circa April, 1983, author's collection; Speakes, p. 97; quoted in Rosebush, pp. 32, 38.

9. Quigley, pp. 115, 117, 162; Wallace, pp. vi, 21, 151; "Mrs. R's R&R" by James A. Miller, *Life* clipping, author's collection (Summer 1984); quoted in *Washington Post* Feb. 18, 1986; Speakes, p. 96; Rosebush, pp. 33–35, 47, 109; quoted in Leighton, p. 343; Regan, pp. 272, 287; Deaver, p. 109.

10. White House statement, Nov. 1986; *Washington Post*, Mar. 26, 1982, and Oct. 20, 1987; quoted in Leamer, pp. 298, 353; *Interview*, Dec. 1981; Leighton, p. 355; Wallace, pp. vii, 151; quoted in *Washington Post*, Nov. 21, 1980; Rosebush, p. 62; *Time*, Jan. 14, 1985; Deaver, pp. 116, 118, 120.

11. Nancy Reagan to author, Oct. 29, 1985; author conversation with Nancy Reagan, July 16, 1985; *Interview*, Dec. 1981; Wallace, pp. 38–40; "Mrs. R's R&R" by James A. Miller, *Life* clipping, Summer 1984, author's collection.

12. *Newsweek*, Jan. 4, 1988; *Washington Post* (a.c., circa Dec., 1983); Wallace, p. 68.

13. Nancy Reagan speech at Library of Congress, June 1989.

14. Nancy Reagan speech, May 4, 1987; Deaver, pp. 111, 117; Speakes, pp. 219, 222; Silverman, pp. 8–9; *Interview*, Dec. 1981; *Washington Post* April 24, 1982, Jan. 23, 1983, June 13, 1984, and June 12, 1987; Rosebush, pp. 42, 49, 67; Wallace, p. 151; East Wing Press Office items regarding June 20, 1984, article; *New Republic*, Sept. 16–23, 1985; *New York Post*, March 5, 1985; *Late Night with David Letterman* broadcast, Jan. 12, 1989; Richard Nixon to author, Aug. 16, 1985; *People*, May 20, 1985.

15. *Washington Post* Nov. 9, 1981, April 24, 1982, Sept. 23, 1983, May 1, 1984, March 16, 1985, July 18, 1985, Nov. 2–5, 1985, Jan. 18, 1986, Feb. 18, 1986, May 2–6, 1986, June 29, 1986, Oct. 21, 1986, and n.d., early May 1986, author's collection; Rosebush, pp. 96, 98, 99, 112–113; author conversation with Wendy Weber Toller, July 1989; *Newsweek*, May 20, 1985, and Jan. 1988; Nancy Reagan speech, May 1, 1983, May 4, 1983, May 4, 1987; *Washington Times*, Jan. 18, 1985; Wallace, pp. 97, 128, 147; quoted in Leighton, p. 365; *London Daily Standard*, Feb. 24, 1986; *Washington City Paper*, June 14–20, 1985, and April 15, 1988, and n.d. (early May 1986), author's collection.

24. ON THE LINE WITH MRS. R.

1. *Time*, Oct. 24, 1988; *Washington Post*, Jan. 23, 1983, Jan. 16, 1989; Packard, pp. 33–34; Leighton, p. 214; Nancy Reagan, *My Turn*, pp. 240–41.

2. Von Damm, pp. 72, 143, 165, 182, 220, 225, 227–29, 241, 271, 272, 290–91, 294; Wallace, pp. vi, 61–62, 114; *U.S. News & World Report*, June 1, 1981; quoted in *New Republic*, Sept. 16–23, 1985; *Washington Post*, June 29, 1982, Jan. 23, 1983, June 13, 1984, March 1, 1986, Oct. 20, 1986, Feb. 27, 1987, Sept. 2, 1987, Sept. 12, 1989; quoted in *Time*, Jan. 14, 1985; Nancy Reagan speech May 4, 1987; Nancy Reagan Library of Congress speech, June 3, 1989; quoted in *Parade*, Sept. 28, 1983; Deaver, pp. 110–11; *Washingtonian*, Aug. 1983; *Globe*, Aug. 9, 1983; Quigley, pp. 66–68, 74–84; *Los Angeles Times*, March 22, 1987; Speakes, pp. 62, 84–85, 95–96; *New York Times*, Dec. 20, 1986; Regan, pp. 290–91; Evans & Novak column, n.d. (1985), author's collection; Nancy Reagan, *My Turn*, pp. 242–43; Ronald Reagan, p. 570.

3. Wallace, pp. 110–11, 114–15, 117–18; *Newsweek* Special Report Nov. 11–12, 1984; *New Republic*, Sept. 16–23, 1985; Rosebush, p. 113.

4. *Newsweek,* Feb. 20, 1984, and June 4, 1984; *New York Times,* Feb. 23, 1983, and April 12, 1984; *USA Today,* Jan. 31, 1984, and July 16, 1984; *Washington Post,* Oct. 17, 1983, July 7, 1984, Sept. 13, 1984, and Mar. 4, 1987; Quigley, p. 90; Betty Ford to author, July 6, 1984; author notes from First Ladies Conference, April 1–4, 1984, Grand Rapids, GRFM; Ronald Reagan, p. 396.

5. Sidney Zion, *The Autobiography of Roy Cohn,* as quoted in *New York,* Feb. 22, 1988; Wallace, p. 108; Radcliffe, p. 55; *New Republic,* Sept. 16–23, 1985; *Washington Post,* July 19, 1984, Aug. 19, 1984, Aug. 21, 1984, and Aug. 24, 1984; *Parade,* Oct. 21, 1984; Willis, pp. 227, 239; ABC-TV *Nightly News* coverage of 1984 Republican National Convention; Michael Reagan, pp. 228, 237.

6. *McCall's,* Nov. 1984; Wallace, pp. ix, 108–9; *Washington Times,* Jan. 18, 1985; *Time,* Jan. 14, 1985; *Los Angeles Times,* Mar. 22, 1987; *Washington Post,* Oct. 15, 1984.

7. Michael Reagan, pp. 245, 247, 264–68; *Washington Times,* Jan. 18, 1985; *McCalls,* Nov. 1985; Silverman, p. 141; *Los Angeles Times,* Mar. 22, 1987; Regan, p. 229; Nancy Reagan, *My Turn,* p. 312.

25. MOMMY

1. *Washington Post,* May 4, 1985; *Los Angeles Times,* March 22, 1987; *Las Vegas Sun,* June 20, 1984; Deaver, pp. 111–12, 184; *People,* May 20, 1985; Leighton, pp. 311, 335; Regan, pp. 260, 264; Ronald Reagan, p. 380.

2. Regan, pp. 3–4, 73–75, 288–92, 359; White House guest list of state dinner, April 17, 1985; *Los Angeles Times,* Mar. 22, 1987; Wallace, p. 149.

3. *Star,* Aug. 6, 1985; Regan, pp. 3, 4–7, 8–9, 12–15, 18, 20–22; *Time,* July 22, 1985; quoted in *Newsweek,* July 29, 1985; *Washington Post,* July 18, 1985, July 19, 1985, July 21, 1985, July 24, 1985, and Lou Cannon column, n.d. (August 1985), author's collection; Speakes, pp. 75, 186–200; Rosebush, p. 54; Nancy Reagan, *My Turn,* pp. 272, 279, 281.

4. *Washington Post* clipping, n.d. (June 1985), author's collection; Deaver, pp. 118–19; Nancy Reagan, *My Turn,* p. 284.

5. Quoted in Deaver, pp. 39, 111, 115–16, 120; *McCall's,* Nov. 1985; *Washington Post,* Nov. 16–20, 1985; Regan, p. 300; *Time,* June 6, 1988; Nancy Reagan, *My Turn,* pp. 314, 336–37.

6. Radcliffe, pp. 15–16; *We the People: The 1985 Presidential Inaugural Book,* 1985 Presidential Inaugural Committee, Victor Gold essay, p. 34.

7. Rosebush, p. 59; Leighton, p. 311; *Washington Post,* June 13, 1984, April 25, 1985, Oct. 22, 1985; author personal notes, Oct. 20–22, 1985.

8. *Washington Post,* Nov. 14, 1985, and Feb. 20, 1986; *New York Times,* Dec. 27, 1986.

9. Deaver, pp. 216, 219, 251; quoted in Leighton, p. 346.

10. Deaver, p. 116; Speakes, p. 100; *Washington Post,* Nov. 22, 1984; an informal photograph in Michael Reagan's book of the Reagan family

shows Patti Davis with her mother. The picture was taken in July of 1987; *Los Angeles Times,* Nov. 6, 1988; *Washington Post,* July 31, 1987.
11. *WRC-TV,* Washington, D.C., April 20, 1988; Nancy Reagan speech, Jan. 29, 1986.
12. *Washington Post,* Sept. 12, 1989; quoted in Leighton, pp. 348, 351; Regan, pp. 344, 359 (Although Regan identified this as "November-December 1987," he amplified that it occurred during Iran-Contra, which was Nov.–Dec. 1986); Speakes, pp. 144–45.

26. THE INVISIBLE GLOVE

1. Regan, pp. 23–28; Deaver, p. 260; *New York Times,* Nov. 26, 1986; Speakes, p. 95; *Washington Post,* Feb. 27, 1987.
2. *Washington Post,* Dec. 2, 1986, and Dec. 9, 1986; Regan, pp. 40, 53, 55; quoted in Leighton, pp. 392–93; *New York Times,* Feb. 3, 1987; *New York Post,* Dec. 18, 1986; Nancy Davis folder, MGM files, Academy of Motion Picture Arts and Sciences Library, Los Angeles.
3. *Washington Post,* Dec. 2, 1986, Dec. 9, 1986; Feb. 27, 1987; Wallace, p. 114; *New York Times,* Dec. 11, 1986; Deaver, p. 260; *New York Post,* Dec. 18, 1986; Nancy Reagan, *My Turn,* p. 322.
4. *New York Times,* Feb. 21, 1987; Quigley, p. 158; Regan, pp. 56–58, 65–73, 88–96, 359; *Washington Post,* Feb. 25, 1987, Feb. 22, 1987, Feb. 24, 1987; Nancy Reagan, *My Turn,* pp. 315, 323.
5. Regan, pp. 97–98, 372, 378.
6. *New York Times,* Feb. 3, 1987, and March 3, 1987; *New York Post,* March 3, 1987; Deaver, p. 144.
7. *Newsweek,* March 16, 1987; *Washington Post,* March 3, 1987; von Damm, p. 228; *Los Angeles Times,* Mar. 22, 1987; Quigley, p. 164.
8. Quigley, pp. 160–62; *Newsweek,* March 16, 1987; Nancy Reagan speech, May 4, 1987; *Washington Post,* June 13, 1984.
9. Wallace, pp. 83–84, 96; author conversation with Nancy Reynolds, Aug. 4, 1989; *Nightline,* ABC-TV, Feb. 29, 1988; *Washington Post,* Aug. 23, 1984, Sept. 27, 1984; author notes from First Ladies Conference, April 1–4, 1984, Grand Rapids, GRFM; Speakes, p. 248; *Newsweek,* May 28, 1984; *Time,* Jan. 14, 1985; *U.S. News & World Report,* June 1, 1981.
10. *Washington Post,* June 11, 1987, and Nov. 7, 1987; Quigley, pp. 111, 169, 170; East Wing press statement, Nov. 6, 1987; *New York Times,* Jan. 30, 1987.
11. *Star* magazine, Nov. 3, 1987; Quigley, p. 180; *Washington Post,* Oct. 18, 1987, Oct. 17, 1987; *USA Today,* Mar. 3, 1988; *Los Angeles Times,* Nov. 13, 1988.
12. *Washington Post,* Dec. 18, 1987, Oct. 19, 1987, Feb. 7, 1988; *Washington Times,* Dec. 18, 1987.
13. Quigley, p. 112; *Washington Times,* April 22, 1986, and Dec. 18, 1987.
14. *U.S. News & World Report,* Sept. 28, 1987; *Washington Post,* Mar. 1, 1988.
15. Quoted in *New York Post,* Dec. 24, 1987; *Washington Post,* Feb. 11, 1986;

Speakes, p. 104; Jimmy and Rosalynn Carter, *Everything to Gain: Making the Most of the Rest of Your Life*, pp. 26–27; author interview with Rosalynn Carter, Sept. 12, 1984; Radcliffe, pp. 16, 194–95, 204; *Time*, Jan. 23, 1989; author interview with confidential source, Aug. 18, 1989; Nancy Reagan, *My Turn*, p. 299.

16. *Time*, June 6, 1988; *Washington Post*, Dec. 9, 1987, and Dec. 10, 1987; *New York Post*, Dec. 7, 1987, and Wilmington *News-Journal*, Dec. 4, 1987; *USA Today*, Dec. 9, 1987, and May 4, 1988; *L.A. Times*, Nov. 19, 1987; *NBC Nightly News*, Jan. 4, 1988.

17. *Washington Post*, March 1, 1988, and Oct. 26, 1988; author conversation with Donnie Radcliffe, June 29, 1989.

18. *Nightline*, ABC-TV, Feb. 29, 1988; *NBC Nightly News*, June 27, 1988; Ron Reagan quoted in *People*, n.d. (1987), author's collection; *Washington Post*, Jan. 23, 1983, July 24, 1985, Sept. 28, 1985, Aug. 19, 1986, Aug. 29, 1989; *Parade*, Jan. 5, 1986.

19. Radcliffe, pp. 4, 17, 56, 199–202.

20. Speakes, p. 98; Regan, p. 55; *Washington Post*, May 10, 1988, May 30, 1988, and Lou Cannon article, "Astrologers Used by First Lady . . .", a.c., circa May 1988; *New York Post*, May 20, 1988; *USA Today*, May 4, 1988; *Los Angeles Times*, Nov. 13, 1988.

21. *Los Angeles Times*, Nov. 19, 1987; *Washington Post*, May 30, 1988, and June 3, 1988.

22. *USA Today*, July 21, 1988, Oct. 24, 1988; *Washington Post*, July 20, 1988; author notes during combined television broadcasts of Democratic Convention, July 19, 1988.

23. *Saturday Evening Post*, Dec. 1988; *Washington Post*, April 28, 1988, Aug. 16, 1988; *USA Today*, Aug. 16, 17, Sept. 26, Oct. 24, 31, 1988; 1988 West Graphics, John Cuneo, artist; author conversation with Wendy Weber Toller, June 30, 1988.

24. Radcliffe, pp. 52, 208–9.

25. *Time*, Oct. 24, 1988; *Washington Post*, Jan. 16, 1989.

26. Quoted in Knight-Ridder story by Ellen Warren, April 1989; *Washington Post*, Nov. 9, 1988.

27. TRADITION

1. Radcliffe, pp. 4, 14–15, 26; Jan. 1989, Press Round Table with Mrs. Bush; *USA Today*, Oct. 12, 1988; *Washington Post*, Dec. 6, 1988, and Jan. 18, 1989.

2. *Newsweek*, Jan. 8, 1989; quoted in Leamer, pp. 331, 343; *Washington Post*, April 3, 1982, July 29, 1983; *WTTG-TV* broadcast, Washington, D.C., July 14, 1984; White House Press backgrounder, "History of Participation with Martin Luther King, Jr., Elementary, 1983–1985."

3. *Washington Post*, Feb. 27, 1987, Dec. 13, 1988, Jan. 16, 1989; *Los Angeles Times*, Nov. 13, 1988; Speakes, author's notes, at White House Christmas tree presentation, 1988.

4. *Los Angeles Times*, Nov. 13, 1988; *Washington Post*, Sept. 7, 1988, Jan. 16, 1989; *Washington Times*, Jan. 18, 1985; quoted in *New Republic*, Sept. 16–23, 1985; Nancy Reagan speech, May 4, 1987.

5. Quigley, pp. 39, 110; *New York Times*, Jan. 21, 1989; *Washington Post*, Dec. 6, 1988, Jan. 24, 1989.
6. Author conversation with Wendy Weber Toller, July 18, 1989.

28. THE HOUSTON YANKEE

1. *Washington Post*, Feb. 1, 1989; Radcliffe, p. 76.
2. Radcliffe, p. 29; *Washington Post*, Jan. 22, 1989; author notes, Jan. 19–23, 1989.
3. Barbara Bush interview with *Nightwatch*, CBS-TV, Aug. 1988; *USA Today* April 21–23, 1989; *Washington Post*, May 30, 1989; *New York Times*, July 30, 1989; Press Round Table, March 1989.
4. Radcliffe, pp. 56–57; author's notes; *We the People*, 1985 Presidential Inaugural Committee, Victor Gold essay, p. 34; *Washington Post*, Feb. 20, 1990, April 10, 1990.
5. *Washington Post*, Feb. 5, 1989; *200 Years of the American Presidency*, 1989 American Bicentennial Presidential Inaugural Committee, Victor Gold essay, p. 44; Radcliffe, pp. 6, 53, 147, 201; *Good Housekeeping*, Nov. 1989; *People*, Dec. 25, 1989–Jan. 1, 1990.
6. *Boston Herald*, Feb. 4, 1989; Radcliffe, pp. 33–34, 43–44; Press Round Table with Mrs. Bush, March 29, 1989; *Hello* magazine, Dec. 10, 1988; *Washington Post*, Feb. 21, 1989; Mrs. Bush to author, May 30, 1989; quoted from January 1989 Round Table interview of Barbara Bush with reporters, assorted clippings.
7. Press Round Table with Mrs. Bush, December 1989; Radcliffe, pp. 50, 229.
8. Radcliffe, pp. 194, 196–97; quoted in Knight-Ridder story by Ellen Warren, April 1989; *New York Times*, Jan. 15, 1989; David Broder column, *Washington Post*, "What Makes Barbara Bush So Special," Jan. 21, 1989.
9. *Washington Post*, April 28, 1989; *We the People*, 1985 Presidential Inaugural Committee, Victor Gold essay, p. 34; *Nightwatch*, CBS-TV, interview with Mrs. Bush, Aug. 1988; *Life*, Oct. 1988; Radcliffe, pp. 67, 129, 202, 206; January 1989 Press Round Table with Mrs. Bush; *Time*, Jan. 23, 1989; Press Round Table with Mrs. Bush, March 29, 1989; *People*, Dec. 25, 1989–Jan. 1, 1990.
10. Broder column, Jan. 1989; *Time*, Jan. 23, 1989; Radcliffe, pp. 36, 203, 230; *New York Times*, Jan. 15, 1989; quoted in *Washington Post*, David Broder column, "What Makes Barbara Bush So Special," Jan. 21, 1989; author conversation with Susan Rose, Aug. 7, 1989; *We the People*, 1985 Presidential Inaugural Committee, Victor Gold essay, p. 34; *USA Today*, Jan. 17, 1990, May 9, 1990; *Washington Post*, Dec. 12, 1989, Dec. 14, 1989, Jan. 17, 1990, May 8, 1990, Nov. 6, 1990, Nov. 23, 1990.
11. *Washington Post*, Mar. 23, 1989; Jan. 21, 1990, April 12, 1990, May 8, 1990, May 22, 1990; quoted in *People*, Nov. 21, 1988; Barbara Bush to author, June 16, 1989; *Hello* magazine, Dec. 10, 1988; *Mama's Family*, WUSA-TV, Washington, D.C., telecast, April 14, 1989; *Good Housekeeping*, Nov. 1989.
12. Mrs. Bush's Press Round Table, March 29, 1989; Jan. 1989 Round Table

interview of Barbara Bush with reporters, assorted clippings; Radcliffe, pp. 174–75, 184–85.

13. *Hello* magazine, Dec. 10, 1988; Barbara Bush to author, June 2, 1989; *USA Today*, Jan. 17, 1990, Radcliffe, pp. 60–61, 187–88; *Washington Post*, Sept. 7, 1989, Jan. 21, 1990, Jan. 17, 1990, May 8, 1990.

14. *Boston Herald*, Feb. 4, 1989; Radcliffe, pp. 63, 66, 217–18.

15. Mrs. Bush's Press Round Table, March 1989; Radcliffe, pp. 186, 198–99; quoted in Knight-Ridder story by Ellen Warren, April 1989; *Ebony*, Sept. 1989; *Washington Post*, May 15, 1989, Jan. 17, 1990.

16. Mrs. Bush's Press Round Table, March 1989.

29. BICENTENNIAL

1. Barbara Bush to author, June 16, 1989.

2. *Washington Post*, May 17, 23, 25, 29, 30, 1989.

3. *Washington Post*, June 2, 1989; Rosebush, p. 17.

4. Barbara Bush to author, June 16, 1989; author interview with Lady Bird Johnson, Oct. 3, 1987; author interview with Betty Ford, Nov. 7, 1983; author interview with Rosalynn Carter, Sept. 12, 1984.

5. Author notes on First Ladies Conference, April 1–4, 1984, Grand Rapids, GRFM; author conversation with Office of Protocol, May 25, 1989.

6. *Washington Post*, Dec. 8, 1983, Oct. 3, 1989, Dec. 13, 1989, Dec. 19, 1989; Nancy Reagan, *My Turn*, p. 238; *W* magazine, June 4–11, 1982; Betty Ford, *Glad Awakening*, pp. 118, 128, 130–31, 151, 179, 207–8; author interview with Lynda Robb, July 30, 1988; Jacqueline Onassis to author, through Lisa Drew, Aug. 1988; Julie Eisenhower, *Pat Nixon*, p. 460; *People*, Feb. 20, 1989; Nancy Reagan to author, June 21, 1989; *Newsweek*, Oct. 23, 1989; ABC-TV, Barbara Walters *20/20* interview with the Reagans, Oct. 1989; New York *Daily News*, Jan. 31, 1990.

7. *USA Today*, April 24, 1985.

$\mathcal{INDEX}$